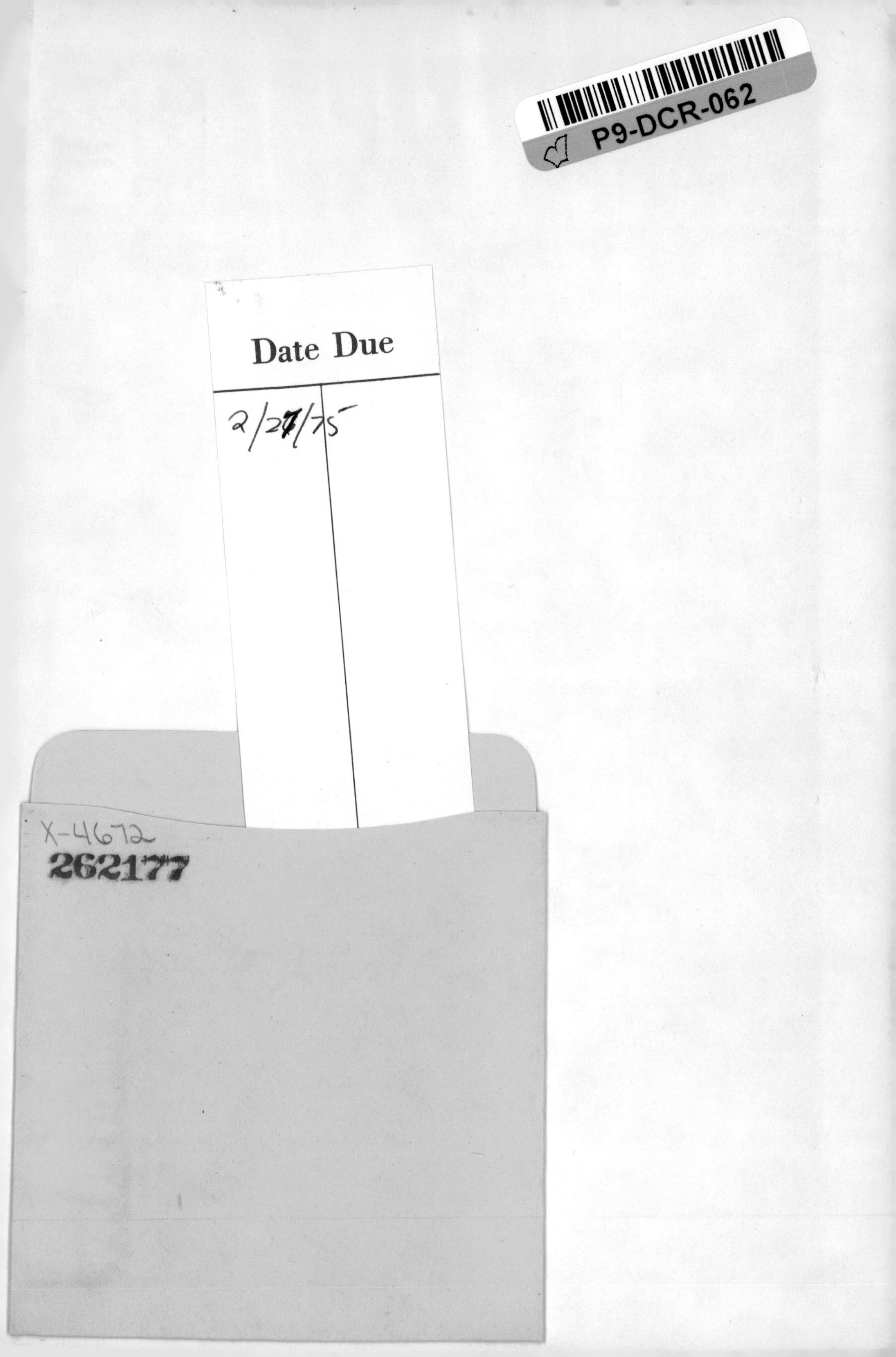
P9-DCR-062
Date Due
2/27/75
X-4672
262177

Metropolis and Region

METROPOLIS

AND

REGION

OTIS DUDLEY DUNCAN
W. RICHARD SCOTT
STANLEY LIEBERSON
BEVERLY DUNCAN
HAL H. WINSBOROUGH

Published for *Resources for the Future, Inc.*
By *The Johns Hopkins Press, Baltimore*

Distributed in Great Britain by Oxford University Press, London

Printed in the United States of America by
the William Byrd Press, Richmond, Va.

Library of Congress Catalog Card Number 60-10656

RESOURCES FOR THE FUTURE, INC., WASHINGTON, D. C.

Resources for the Future is a nonprofit corporation for research and education in the development, conservation, and use of natural resources. It was established in 1952 with the co-operation of The Ford Foundation and its activities since then have been financed by grants from that Foundation. Part of the work of Resources for the Future is carried out by its resident staff, part supported by grants to universities and other nonprofit organizations. Unless otherwise stated, interpretations and conclusions in RFF publications are those of the authors; the organization takes responsibility for the selection of significant subjects for study, the competence of the researchers, and their freedom of inquiry.

This book is one of RFF's regional studies, which are directed by Harvey S. Perloff. The principal author, Otis Dudley Duncan, is associate director of the Population Research and Training Center, University of Chicago; his associates also are connected with the Center. The study was made under a Resources for the Future grant to the University of Chicago.

STAFF EDITORS, Henry Jarrett and Vera W. Dodds

CONTENTS

Part II. Metropolitan Dominance: Hinterland Activities

Part III. Industry Structure and Regional Relationships

Part IV. Fifty Major Cities and Their Regional Relationships

LIST OF TABLES

LIST OF FIGURES

PREFACE

What the metropolis of forty years hence will be like no man can truly foretell. But there is a surfeit of somber prophecies and apocalyptic visions of its future. Prime targets for aerial bombardment, the great cities may be splattered into the hereafter within two-score years—or less. Escaping this fate, they may yet be splattered over the countryside by the rush of their inhabitants to the suburbs. From some descriptions of this movement one might suppose it is as irresistible as the migration of lemmings. Already we have adumbrations of "megapolitan" belts, amorphous and sprawling regions of quasi-urban settlement stretching along coast lines or major transportation routes. Current concepts of the community stand to be challenged. What will remain of "local" government and institutions if locality ceases to have any historically recognizable form? The situations described in this book pertain to the mid-century United States of some 150 million people. What serviceable image of "metropolis and region" can we fashion for a country of 300 million? The prospect for such a population size by the end of the twentieth century is implicit in current growth rates, as is the channeling of much of the growth into areas now called "metropolitan" or in process of transfer to that class.

Facing a future that seems certain to produce novelty and to bring forth drastic transformations, we may be tempted to question the value of meticulous analysis of present structures and arrangements—or, rather, those of the recent past, for the complex information required to describe metropolitan communities only becomes available some years after the dates to which it refers. Indeed, if our curiosity is only about the future, the justification for studying the recent past must be that it contains some seeds of developments to come. To this continuity argument we may perhaps add the thought that to understand the future will require tools for understanding—and these tools can be tested now only against what now exists.

If the prophet becomes impatient when we limit inquiry to the present, the historian may complain that understanding is partial, at best, if analysis of the here and now is not guided by knowledge of antecedents, both recent and remote. We must agree that the investigator lacking a full grasp of trends and directions of change readily falls into the error of mistaking a transient conjecture of circumstances for a basic structural pattern. But before there can be historical explanations of present realities, there must be adequate descriptions of that which is to be explained.

The studies reported in this volume, therefore, provide some "cross-sectional" views of the metropolis in the United States at about the middle of the twentieth century. Numerous earlier monographs on metropolitanism have dealt with the circumstances attending the rise of the metropolitan community and have analyzed the patterns and causes of metropolitan growth. *Metropolis and Region,* by contrast, tries to depict a system of metropolitan communities as it was functioning at a particular point in time. If the former approach can be likened to a cinematic representation of the evolution of the metropolis and the growth of metropolises, our contribution is a "still photograph" of the present metropolises of the nation. Actually, however, the picture is blurred because the subject moved during the period of exposure: our data do not all refer to the same point in time but rather to various dates more or less proximate to the middle of the century. Moreover, each of the several "exposures" was made with a different "filter"—to preserve the analogy.

For further indications of content and approach, the reader is referred to the summary chapter, which is placed at the beginning of the volume. We only wish to add some notes about how the book came to be.

For the past several years the Population Research and Training Center at the University of Chicago has been pursuing a broadly delineated and flexible program of comparative research on American communities. This program is conceived as a contribution to the field of human ecology—the discipline whose task, in Hawley's phrase, includes "the study of the form and the development of the community in human population." The progress of the research program, however, has demonstrated (if proof were needed) the advisability of taking advantage of contributions from a variety of disciplines. An earlier monograph, *Social Characteristics of Urban and Rural Communities, 1950* (Duncan and Reiss, 1956), emphasized demographic analysis. Our more recent studies have entailed closer contact with the work of economists, geographers, and others who are sometimes called "regional scientists," and we have come to share their preoccupations more fully than before.

Some of the work reported in this volume (specifically, in chapter 3) was begun as early as 1955-56 with the aid of a grant from the Social Science Research Committee of the University of Chicago. In 1956-57 a project dealing with regional variation in levels of living and spatial patterns of economic activity was undertaken with the financial support of Resources for the Future, Inc., the Regional Studies Unit of which was carrying out parallel research. Results obtained in the course of our project are partially reported in Part II. The study completed by the RFF group (Harvey S. Perloff, Edgar S. Dunn, Jr., Eric E. Lampard, and Richard F. Muth, *Regional Economic Growth in the United States*, 1960) is complementary in many ways to the present monograph and may be regarded as virtually a companion volume. (While our study is cross-sectional, the RFF book treats of growth and secular trends. Where we look at the economy primarily from the viewpoint of its metropolitan nodes, the companion volume focuses on the region, broadly conceived, and provides much regional description that is omitted here.) In 1957-58, again at the instance of and with the financial support of Resources for the Future, Inc., we carried out the project which produced the materials included in Parts III and IV. In 1958 our program of comparative urban and metropolitan research was placed on a more secure long-run basis with the receipt of a grant from The Ford Foundation providing financial resources for the ensuing five years. One major category of studies envisioned in this extension of our work is addressed to the problem of "strengthening the urban economy and gearing it to the economic development of the nation." The initiation of work under The Ford Foundation grant afforded the opportunity to carry out the research reported in Part I and thus to develop a conceptual framework and to execute some statistical analyses which, together with the investigations already completed, would constitute an integrated and reasonably comprehensive treatment of metropolitan structure in the United States.

Our first indebtedness, therefore, is to the organizations which, while leaving us wholly free to work in the way we judged to be most rewarding, provided the indispensable resources for our work; in particular, we are most grateful to Resources for the Future, Inc., for sponsoring the publication of this volume. A less tangible but no less important contribution was made by our mentor at RFF—Harvey Perloff. The ideas which ultimately crystallized in this study were in large measure initially his. Without seeking in any way to shift responsibility for the research to other shoulders, we must gratefully acknowledge the suggestions and criticisms received from Donald J. Bogue, Donald L. Foley, Leo A. Goodman, Philip M. Hauser, Amos H. Hawley, Richard F. Muth, Albert J. Reiss, Jr., Leo F. Schnore, and Lowdon Wingo, Jr. We also want to acknowledge the indispensable help of our cartographer and draftsman, Karel J. Kansky, our statistical assistants, Nathaniel Hare, Philip M. Marcus, and Erwin Stein, and our competent and faithful typist, Mary Thomas.

In this final paragraph, the director of the research leading to the completion of *Metropolis and Region* exercises the prerogative of speaking for himself alone in order to speak more enthusiastically about the work of his collaborators than would be modest in a collective statement. For at least one participant observer, this research has shown that under favorable circumstances teamwork can be personally gratifying and also—and more important—scientifically productive. The "favorable circumstances" seemingly have to do more with intellectual congeniality and temperamental compatibility than with whether the collaborators are co-equals in academic status. In any event, the parts and the whole of this volume are probably better than, and certainly different from what they would have been, had any one of us borne the entire responsibility. It is symbolic of our success in putting heads together that we can no longer say precisely whose suggestions are embodied in many paragraphs. The general distribution of effort, however, can be indicated. The procedures outlined in Part III were in good part developed by Scott, who then painstakingly applied them in the preparation of four-fifths of the individual city reports in Part IV. The remainder of these reports were prepared by Lieberson, to whose initiative and persistence much of chapters 5 and 6 is also attributable. Part II is largely a contribution by Beverly Duncan, being based on her unpublished dissertation (1957). Chapter 3 draws heavily on the unpublished thesis by Winsborough (1959). Throughout the volume will be found evidence of idiosyncracies which these four companions in a research adventure were good enough to tolerate.

O.D.D.
W.R.S.
S.L.
B.D.
H.H.W.

Metropolis and Region

CHAPTER 1

Metropolis and Region: A Mid-Century Bench Mark

At a time when journalists are making the "exploding metropolis" virtually a household word there is no need to plead the timeliness of an essay on metropolitanism. But though our topic is timely we are not primarily concerned to diagnose a social problem or to suggest remedies for the manifold ills of metropolitan areas. The maladies on this familiar roster—traffic congestion, housing obsolescence, frictions among shifting population groups, financial quandaries, governmental fragmentation, and the like—are most likely not fundamental problems in themselves. Rather, they symptomatically reflect an accumulation of lags in the mutual adjustment of units and functions of the metropolitan community—lags which are perhaps inevitable in a period of sporadic and unco-ordinated, though not unrelated, changes in community structure. Our large cities have grown rapidly. A century ago, on the eve of the Civil War, only New York (the present five boroughs) was passing the million mark; Philadelphia had somewhat more than a half million inhabitants, Baltimore just over 200,000, and five other cities between 100,000 and 200,000. By 1950, when population figures based on corporate boundaries had ceased to be meaningful, the country contained no less than 14 standard metropolitan areas of more than 1,000,000 inhabitants, another 19 with populations over a half million, and, altogether, 151 with populations of 100,000 or more. Such growth reflected the expansion of population and the peopling of the full continental area, the economic development of the country which brought about an astounding rise in productivity and levels of living, and—most important for our study—a concomitant reorganization of the economy. This reorganization entailed a progressively heightening interdependence among territorial units of the economy with the emergence of increasingly prominent focal points at which the patterns of interdependence were administered and mediated: in a word, "metropolises."

The history of metropolitan growth in the United States has been ably analyzed by a succession of investigators; the exposition of metropolitan organization as a late phase of economic development has been provided by pioneer thinkers; and some of the major concepts, including that of the metropolitan community itself, have been applied to demographic and economic data with illuminating results in previous studies. (Our review of this literature appears in chapter 4.) What then is the distinctive task we have set for ourselves? The answer is three-fold.

First, we seek to bring into juxtaposition some of the leading ideas which have been propounded on the nature of the metropolis, its role in the national economy, and its relation to the regional differentiation of the economy. The thesis we hope to establish is that a rich variety of conceptual tools is at hand for the analysis of such problems and that these concepts—oftentimes emanating from diverse and independent sources—have unsuspected ramifications and interconnections. We cannot pretend to have achieved a thoroughgoing articulation of these concepts or the perhaps drastic reformulation that the present profusion of ideas invites. But we may tentatively claim to provide a more comprehensive summary of pertinent theoretical insights than is readily available elsewhere.

Second, to test the cogency of ideas and formulations distilled from the literature, we attempt a comprehensive outline of the major structural characteristics of the United States metropolitan economy as of about 1950. Our work here goes beyond the existing excellent studies of functional types of cities and metropolitan dominance in regard to both detail of analysis and explicit orientation to the problem of the metropolis in relation to the regional differentiation of the economy.

Third, and incidental to the second objective, we provide a systematic survey of the industrial composition and regional relationships of the larger cities of the United States—those most likely to manifest distinctively metropolitan characteristics. The materials of this survey afford an account of where the evolution of the metropolitan economy had arrived by about 1950 and a bench mark for measuring the changes we can anticipate full well in the second half of the century. Although our survey is essentially cross-sectional, it provides the requisite starting point for dynamic investigations. Moreover, we feel that it may serve as an informative context for case studies of particular metropolises and particular regions which may be carried out by investigators working intensively with small segments of the economy.

We identify our approach as "ecological." It embodies what we regard as the soundest elements in the tradition of the discipline which has been most competently expounded in Hawley's *Human Ecology* (1950). Readers who are interested in the perspective taken by human ecology, as compared with alternative approaches to the study of human collective existence, may consult two other recent statements (Duncan, 1959a; Duncan and Schnore, 1959),* for we do not intend to press the issue of disciplinary labels here. Suffice it to say that as far as we are concerned the salient characteristic—if not a unique one—of an ecological approach is its proclivity for analyzing human communities and economic systems in terms of their place in a total ecosystem, the major facets of which are populations adjusting to their environments by means of their technological equipment and patterns of social organization. But if the ecologist's orientation gives him an advantage in "seeing things whole," it also requires that he be willing to exploit the methods and discoveries of related disciplines—demography, economics, geography, and sociology—putting them not always to their original uses but rather to those suggested by his own conceptual framework.

One item remains for prefatory discussion before coming to the main business of this chapter, which is to provide the reader with a convenient summary and guide to the volume as a whole. It will doubtless appear from time to time that what we are up to is the presentation of invidious distinctions between cities that qualify as "metropolises" and those that do not. This is not our intention. Indeed, we have deliberately equivocated at several points on the question of formal criteria of metropolitan status. Such caution is well advised, for cities nowadays vie with one another for recognition as metropolises. One of the unanticipated by-products of the system of "standard metropolitan areas" established by federal statistical agencies a decade or so ago was the scramble of communities for recognition in that system. "There is, unfortunately, a tendency for local areas to view the

* References to the literature are made by author and date of publication; for full citations see the Bibliography at the end of the volume.

establishment of an S.M.A. as a sort of gold star awarded by the federal government," stated one of the responsible officials (Shryock, 1957, p. 170). We can sympathize with anyone whose task is to attach labels and apply standard classifications, for it is the collective variety and individual uniqueness of human communities that impress most investigators.

Of one thing we can be sure: the metropolis is not a creation of the federal (or any other) government, nor is it an artifact of bureaucratic statistical procedures. The scientists of politics, in proof of the contrary, spend much time worrying about how to fit governments to the realities of metropolitan community structure. Actually, the metropolis was not "created" at all. It just grew—or, rather, it evolved over a period of several generations. The mechanisms of its evolution are imperfectly understood, but we have reason to think they are closely connected with the basic conditions of economic development. If this is true, then to understand the structure of a highly developed economy we must investigate the structure of its metropolitan communities; and to understand metropolitan communities we must examine them in the context of a more inclusive system. It also follows that such investigation can never be finished, for the object of study changes its nature and functions continually in response to changes in the conditions that brought it into being.

Moreover, like any complex and polymorphic entity, the metropolis is subject to differing interpretations according to the perspective from which it is viewed. Some of the several ways in which previous investigators have examined metropolitanism are indicated in subsequent chapters. Our own perspective puts heavy emphasis on location and function—where metropolises are and what they do. No great originality is claimed for this approach to metropolitan study, but the particular combination of devices used in portraying the metropolitan organization of the United States economy as of about 1950 is perhaps somewhat distinctive.

Because our account of mid-century metropolitan structure is rather lengthy and involves a heterogeneous collection of analytical approaches, the reader wishing to avail himself of our materials may find use for a synoptic preview of concepts and findings. Accordingly, this chapter presents a summary of the volume as a whole along with comments that may be useful in deciding whether particular parts or chapters of the book warrant special attention for the reader's purposes.

Whatever meaning of "metropolis" is accepted, it is generally agreed that metropolises are a special kind or class of cities. In embarking on a study of metropolitan structure, therefore, we are well advised to take advantage of previous thinking and research on the general problem of urban location and functions (see chapter 2). In what may well be regarded as a classical statement on this problem, Harris and Ullman (1945, pp. 7-9) propose the following categories:

> 1. Cities as central places performing comprehensive services for a surrounding area. . . .
> 2. Transport cities performing break-of-bulk and allied services along transport routes, supported by areas which may be remote in distance but close in connection because of the city's strategic location on transport channels. . . .
> 3. Specialized-function cities performing one service such as mining, manufacturing, or recreation for large areas, including the general tributary areas of hosts of other cities.

Examination of the assumptions underlying this scheme and study of its implications will reveal that analysis of both functions and locations is facilitated by considering relationships between cities and regions—viewing cities as "punctiform agglomerations" (Lösch, 1954, p. 68) of activities and regions as extended areas wherein are carried out activities complementary to those of cities. Some implicit notions of city-region relationships appear to underlie two types of research that have been pursued energetically during the last couple of decades or so: analysis of the urban "economic base" and classification of cities according to type of "functional specialization." It appears to be a workable hypothesis that nearly every city has a more or less standard repertoire of functions performed for its own inhabitants and for its immediate continuous "hinterland"—comprising the area which it serves and upon which it depends most closely, in conformity with the central-place scheme. But many cities have highly distinctive functions that make up important parts of their economic base and that involve them in ramified relationships with a variety of types of "regions," of which those specializing in resource-extracting activities are an important category, though one somewhat neglected in formulations dealing with the economic base and functional specialization. The kind of conceptual flexibility that the actual variety of city-region relationships requires is perhaps most nearly attained in the "interregional input-output" model of Isard (1951). Although, owing to limitations of data and the like, this model is not now directly applicable in its complete mathematical form, it provides a general framework for a "regional interpretation of the functions of the city" (Dickinson, 1947, p. 165). In the present study, we have made more direct use of the "input-output access" approach developed by Perloff *et al.* (1960, Part I).

Before narrowing our focus to the metropolis as a particular kind or class of city, it seems well to explore the implications of some ideas concerning the "urban hierarchy" (see chapter 3). Not a few writers have, implicitly or explicitly, regarded metropolises as the class of cities occupying the uppermost level in some kind of hierarchic arrangement. The hierarchy concept is significant for us in still another respect: it assumes or implies that a collection of cities, if properly delimited, may be regarded as a *system*. The investigator undertaking comparative urban research with the concept of a system of cities in mind will be interested in properties of the system as such, rather than merely the varying traits of individual cities.

The hierarchy notion has been developed deductively by elaborating the implications of the concept of central place, referred to above. On the empirical side, evidence for the heuristic value of the hierarchy concept has been adduced in three different, but convergent, ways. Some writers have attributed much importance to the "rank-size rule" —the finding that many national systems of cities have a distribution of city sizes that can be described rather well by a Pareto curve. Second, geographers in particular have plunged directly into the problem of identifying levels in the urban hierarchy on the basis of data indicating the kinds of services rendered by and facilities found in cities. It is perhaps their cartographic interest that has motivated such attempts to classify cities into a small number of typological groupings on the assumption that a hierarchy exists. Finally, evidence for a hierarchic pattern has been forthcoming in a number of studies designed to reveal empirical correlates of community size. Our own empirical materials in chapter 3 derive from this last approach, being concerned with patterns of variation in industrial composition of cities in relation to their size.

Much of the tendency to hierarchic pattern observed in industry statistics arrayed by city size apparently is due to variation in the proportions employed in certain broad industry categories rather than the proportions in individual industries within these categories. Categories manifesting a tendency to decrease in relative importance with increasing city size include local services (those assumed to have a service area largely circumscribed by the boundaries of the urban center itself), extractive activities, and processing industries (manufacturing industries, a sizable proportion of whose inputs are raw materials). By contrast, non-local services (those with more or less extensive service areas beyond the city boundaries) and fabricating industries (whose inputs are primarily already processed or partially fabricated materials) tend to increase in relative importance with increasing city size. Individual industries within these broad categories exhibit differences in degree of urbanization which, for the most part, are consistent with this summary of the facts.

Intensive study of the industry distributions leads to certain findings which are consistent with the notion that the urban hierarchy in the United States, as far as manufacturing is concerned, is a truly national one. In regard to services, however, it may be meaningful to think of broad regions as having more or less self-contained hierarchies of cities, although some kinds of service industries clearly are organized on a national basis. These conclusions are phrased cautiously, since other interpretations of the evidence are possible.

Although many of the findings are not inconsistent with deductions from the central-place scheme, it would be going too far to claim that they validate central-place theory in any strict sense. Moreover, it is possible to identify certain aspects of the variation of industry composition with city size that call for explanatory principles other than those supplied by the centrality principle. Apparently, large cities generate certain distinctive types of needs or demands, which are then satisfied locally by specialized economic units. The size of the local market in big cities is sufficient to permit both a finer division of labor than is possible in small cities and the realization of numerous "external economies of scale," quite apart from the size of the outlying areas served by those cities (the factor emphasized in central-place formulations). In any case, we may conclude that the evidence supporting the notion of urban hierarchy is strong, and that the factors producing the hierarchic tendency must somehow be closely related to size of community. This evidence justifies the emphasis placed on size as an indicator of metropolitan status in later chapters. At the same time, one must recognize the strong possibility that no single dimension of variation should be overemphasized if a realistic description of a hierarchic system is to be secured.

Further development of the urban hierarchy notion may some day produce a definitive concept of metropolitanism. In the meantime, it is possible to consider the nature of the metropolis without resolving all the issues associated with the hierarchy concept. Chapter 4 reviews some outstanding statements on criteria of metropolitanism and some schemes for delimiting metropolitan community areas. Emphasis is placed on the classic formulation of Gras (1922a, b). Gras thought of the metropolis as an industrially developed city strategically located at a focus of a transportation network—a major city which organizes the hinterland market and mediates inter-regional exchanges and which, finally and quite symptomatically, provides the requisite financial facilities for its own commercial and industrial activities and those of its hinterland. Less relevant here is the complementary idea of the metropolis (developed especially by McKenzie, 1933, and Bogue, 1949) as a type of settlement pattern. Gras recognized that his formulation lacked refinement and specificity, for he urged that detailed statistical investigations be conducted to validate his criteria of metropolitanism. In response to this need, the suggestive study by Vance and Smith (1954) made ingenious use of six indicators—wholesale and retail sales, business services receipts, bank clearings, number of manufacturing branch offices, and value added by manufacture—to identify the metropolitan centers of the South and to indicate how these fit into the national pattern of intermetropolitan relationships.

The problem of delimiting "metropolitan regions" or "metropolitan community areas," unfortunately, has seldom been tackled in connection with a comprehensive study of city-region relationships. For this reason, although several of the published schemes of metropolitan regions reviewed in chapter 4 have considerable value and merit careful study, they often give the appearance of excessive artificiality. Moreover, reasons may be given for supposing that the conventional distinction between "uniform regions" and "nodal regions" (of which metropolitan regions are one species) has defects from a heuristic standpoint. While some types of relative "uniformity" are rather direct reflections of environmental factors, others clearly have a functional basis and thus are by no means unrelated to "nodal" structure. It is often pointed out that "nodal regions" may be heterogeneous owing to inclusion of segments of two or more "uniform regions," but it is also true that some types of metropolis may carve out their hinterlands within an area of relative uniformity. Indeed, this is the assumption behind the whole idea of central-place functions. But apart from this kind of conceptual objection to previous formulations on metropolitan regions, it is important to observe that each kind of metropolitan function may entail a distinctive type of regional relationship. In many instances it is quite clear that some of the more important of these relationships have little connection with the "hinterland" of the metropolis as recognized in schemes of metropolitan regions. In short, we contend that if the problem of metropolis-region relationships is attacked with the aid of the best current theory concerning location and functions of cities, the received image of metropolitan regions will have to be modified considerably.

Some implications of the verbal statement of metropolitan characteristics and functions are put to the test with statistical data in chapter 5. In line with the emphasis of Gras on financial functions, attention is first given to the specialization of cities in lending and the spatial patterns of bank loans—taking such loans as a significant and accessible aspect of the total financial complex. The well-known preeminence of New York City as a financial center shows up strongly in the data, which serve also to identify a group of lesser but nonetheless important centers. These—Chicago, San Francisco, Pittsburgh, Boston, and Philadelphia—together with New York make up what appears to be a "national" credit market. An important fact revealed by the loan data is that there is much inter-city borrowing and lending. In particular, the cities making up the "national market" borrow primarily from each other. Outside the "national market" there is a group of cities depending primarily on that national market, a second group dependent on a "national-regional market," a third borrowing mainly from a "regional-national market," and a fourth largely dependent on "regional" sources of credit. It should be noted, however, that the last category is only encountered some distance down from the top of the city-size scale. Most large cities both borrow and lend over considerable distances—certainly well beyond their "hinterlands" as identified in systems of metropolitan regions. Yet distance does have an important effect, for when allowance is made for volume of credit demanded, loan amounts fall off rather regularly with distance from the lending center.

Commercial functions are represented in our data by per capita volume of wholesale sales and business services receipts. The appropriateness of these indicators of metropolitanism is validated by several findings. The two variables are positively associated with each other. Both increase on the average with increasing city size. Both are higher, typically, in cities serving as Federal Reserve Bank Cities or Branch Cities than in cities lacking such a Bank or Branch in the Federal Reserve System. Both variables are positively correlated with per capita non-local loans and with per capita demand deposits. Thus, financial and commercial functions are closely linked. By contrast, an indicator of manufacturing activity fails to show important correlations with city size, with Federal Reserve System status of cities, and with either the commercial or the financial indicators. What this means is that a "metropolis" identified as such by its commercial-financial complex may or may not have a relatively high level of manufacturing activity —these two possibilities are about equally probable. Significantly, a situational factor which is strongly favorable to manufacturing—i.e., generalized accessibility to the national, particularly the national metropolitan, market—is negligibly or even negatively correlated with the commercial and financial indicators. Thus the accessibility that encourages manufacturing specialization sometimes entails too intense a competition among close neighbors for commercial-financial specialization to develop. The "regional metropolises" and "regional capitals" identified in a later chapter, consequently, are found well outside or at best on the margins of the zone of maximum generalized accessibility.

From a theoretical standpoint a serious deficiency of much of the available data on metropolitan characteristics is that they do not pertain to actual interchanges or flows—whether of goods, money, or people—between the metropolis and other areas. The loan data just described constitute a valuable exception to this generalization. Another significant body of flow data was uncovered in the course of the study, i.e., tabulations of the flow of commercial and financial payments and receipts between each of the 36 zones of the Federal Reserve System. These data, compiled as a by-product of the Federal Reserve accounting system, are believed to reflect the greater proportion of all inter-regional transactions in the United States. In the exploratory analysis of this information reported in chapter 6, the flow of funds is regarded as a global indicator of the metropolitan function of mediating inter-regional exchanges. Emphasis is placed on uncovering salient aspects of the geographical pattern of flows (rather than, say, seasonal or trend movements in the flows) on the assumption that this pattern is indicative of a basic aspect of the economy's spatial structure—its organization around metropolitan centers.

The somewhat formal apparatus used in the analysis is calculated to standardize volume of flows for differences between zones in size of population (assumed to be generally correlated with flow-generating capacity) and to reveal effects of distance on volume of flow between zones. We need not indicate the mathematical and statistical features of the analysis here, and we may ignore some of the details and limitations of the analysis. Suffice it to say that, in accordance with the simple model used, the volume of flows between two zones is found to be directly proportional to the product of their respective populations and inversely proportional to the distance separating them. Together, population and distance afford a reasonably accurate prediction of the relative volume of flow between zones: two-thirds of the variation in flow volume among pairs of zones is accounted for by the model. There is reason to believe that appreciable improvement of the model could be achieved by appropriate refinements. In particular, systematic deviations from the model sometimes appear to represent aspects of spatial orientation of flows not adequately indexed by mere distance. For example, in comparing flows involving the Kansas City zone with those involving the St. Louis zone, it is found that Kansas City has the higher flows with most zones in the western half of the country and St. Louis with those in the eastern half. Kansas City's advantage to the west is considerably greater than would be expected on the basis of the relative population sizes of the two zones and the comparatively small distance advantage that it enjoys over St. Louis with respect to the northwest, west, and southwest. We leave as a legacy to future investigators the problem of working out a picture of hierarchical relationships among metropolitan centers on the basis of flow data such as these.

Altogether, the five chapters in Part I provide a conceptual introduction to the volume by suggesting criteria of metropolitanism and by exploring the problems of analyzing location and functions which these criteria suggest. The statistical materials give a general picture of functional differentiation of large cities, making use of variables assumed to represent important aspects of metropolitanism, and indicate some broad classes of factors that help to explain the observed patterns of functional differentiation.

In Part II (chapters 7 and 8), attention shifts to a generalized category of metropolis-region relationship—metropolitan dominance—that has received a good deal of attention in previous research on metropolitanism. The distinctive feature of our approach, as compared with the tack taken by other students, is that it does not rest on a prior classification of non-metropolitan parts of the country into metropolitan regions. Instead, the entire "hinterland" zone—the territory not included in standard metropolitan areas—is broken up into areal units. These units, the non-metropolitan state economic areas (SEA's) of the Bureau of the Census, are then characterized by certain indicators of type and level of economic activity; and these indicators are studied in relation to certain presumed measures of metropolitan influence. Here, again, is a novel feature of the analysis: metropolitan influence or "dominance" is not conceived as flowing to each hinterland areal unit from a single metropolitan center. Instead, each SEA is considered to occupy a position in a generalized "ecological field" (Pappenfort, 1959), as indexed by a global measure of accessibility, population potential. We study simultaneously the association of hinterland economic activity with this indicator of generalized accessibility and with distance to nearest metropolis (the more conventional indicator of probable metropolitan dominance). An additional variable is taken into consideration, the level of urbanization within the SEA itself; this is assumed to allow for influences of local, "sub-dominant" urban centers.

The framework just described is employed first in a study of hinterland manufacturing activity (chapter 7). While manufacturing activity is concentrated within metropolitan centers themselves, a substantial contribution to the national aggregate is made by hinterland areas. The proportion of the labor force employed in manufacturing in hinterland SEA's is found to increase with rising values of population potential (generalized accessibility) and also with increasing proximity to a metropolitan center. Though the former relationship is somewhat the stronger, both are highly significant and each is somewhat independent of the other. Our first result, then, is in conformity with the observation of Harris (1954) that manufacturing is concentrated toward areas of high "market potential," and with the finding of Bogue (1949) that beyond a certain critical point, intensity of manufacturing activity falls off as distance from the center of the metropolitan region increases. Refinements of these formulations are made possible by considering separately the different kinds of industry making up the manufacturing aggregate. A particularly revealing classification is obtained by grouping industries into two broad categories, processing and fabricating. Processing industries are those a substantial proportion of whose inputs consist of raw materials, and fabricating industries consist of all others—those whose material inputs are predominantly already in processed or semi-fabricated form. The striking finding is that the hinterland localization of fabricating industries is much more highly related to generalized accessibility, proximity to a metropolitan center, and local urbanization than is the locational pattern of processing industries. Examination of individual processing industries reveals some cases of clear orientation toward resource regions rather than toward urban or metropolitan centers. In the case of these industries—to put the matter in overly simple terms—"metropolis" and "region" (markets and resources) exert pulls in contrary directions. The "dominance" of the metropolis, quite evident in the case of hinterland fabricating activity, is strongly attenuated in the instance of processing activity.

In regard to the resource-extracting activities, coal mining and agriculture, treated in chapter 8, one might expect to find little evidence of metropolitan dominance, since these activities are inevitably oriented toward suitable natural resources. Yet careful analysis does reveal significant respects in which extractive activities are influenced by the national system of metropolitan centers. The analysis here proceeds in much the same way as that for hinterland manufacturing, but in each instance attention is given as well to the areal distribution of the resource on which the activity depends. Although coal mining occurs only where coal is known to be in the ground, it does not occur at all such places. Significantly, non-producing areas with known recoverable coal reserves are found disproportionately among areas with low generalized accessibility. Considering the amount of coal produced, with a standardization for the volume of available resources (recoverable reserves), we find a small but quite significant association between coal output in an area and the area's generalized accessibility, as measured by population potential. No similar effect is noted, however, for proximity to a metropolitan center, once allowance has been made for the generalized accessibility factor.

The companion study of agricultural activity (also in chapter 8) proceeds in step-wise fashion. First to be considered is the extent to which potential resources are actually used for agricultural production (indexed by proportion of land in farms, and proportion of farmland in cropland); then attention is given to value indicators (per-acre value of products sold and per-acre value of land and buildings, the latter representing, presumably, a capitalization of long run productive capacity); finally, there is an examination of the adjustment of the farm population (rural-farm population density and proportion of farms operated on a part-time basis or serving primarily as residential units). On the first question, the important factor to be considered is the availability of the basic resource at an acceptable level of quality. Both the proportion of land in farms and the proportion of farmland devoted to crops are most highly associated with an indicator of soil quality. However, generalized accessibility (indexed by population potential) is a factor of substantial though secondary importance, while neither proximity to a metropolis nor local urbanization figures significantly. In marked contrast, the two value indicators manifest substantial associations with only one factor: proximity to a metropolitan center. The evidence suggests that intensive production, leading to high per-acre value of products and enhancing farm land values, becomes more frequent as one approaches a regional market center. Moreover, agricultural land use doubtlessly encounters more severe competition from other uses in the neighborhood of such centers. The picture changes again when density of the farm population is examined. Distance to a metropolis drops out as a significant influence, but both generalized accessibility and quality of soil are associated with density. The latter association, however, is negative, i.e., when allowance is made for other determinants, farm density is higher on the land of low quality than on high quality land. Farm land is more densely settled around the cluster of population nodes in the Northeast—where generalized accessibility is highest—than in the more fertile areas of the Midwest and West. A similar negative relationship is found between soil quality and proportion of part-time and residential farms. No doubt the high generalized accessibility in at least some regions of low soil quality implies accessibility to alternative employment for farm residents, while the poverty of the agricultural resource makes such an alternative an attractive one.

The materials in Part II, then, show that metropolitan influences broadly classified under the heading of "dominance" actually occur in a variety of ways. Most important is the discovery that a somewhat diffused kind of dominance—that reflected in an index of generalized accessibility—must be taken into account in order to interpret any specific influences of a particular metropolis in a given region.

Although the remainder of the volume is divided into two parts, it will be helpful to think of these as a unit. Part III is introductory to Part IV, explaining in detail how the materials in Part IV were compiled; it also includes a summary of the salient conclusions derived from a comparative study of the reports on individual metropolitan centers contained in Part IV. By the same token, Part IV provides the basic information upon which those conclusions (given in chapter 11) rest. Throughout Parts III and IV we are concerned with the following kinds of questions: In what terms should the entire industry structure of a large city be described in order to bring out the relative importance of distinctively "metropolitan" functions and to reveal relationships with "regions"? Where metropolitan characteristics clearly are in evidence and where basic metropolis-region input-output relationships are found, what locational factors can be adduced to explain these characteristics and relationships? Is it possible to construct an outline of major features of metropolitan structure in mid-century America, the headings of which will be both fairly generalized and reasonably realistic?

Procedures for characterizing the industrial structure of standard metropolitan areas (SMA's) in terms that are relevant to the present study are outlined in chapter 9. On the basis of tables derived from an input-output analysis of the national economy in 1947, we establish some broad categories into which the detailed labor force industry statistics of the population census can be fit. First, there is a category of primary resource-extracting industries—not a typical metropolitan specialty but one found in appreciable proportions in some SMA's. Second, manufacturing industries are divided into first stage resource users, second stage resource users, and industries for which resources have quite indirect significance. Within each of these groups industries are classified according to whether the bulk of their output is distributed to non-final markets (for use by other industries) or goes directly to satisfy final demand. The final category, service industries, is broken up on the basis of arbitrary judgements concerning typical metropolis-hinterland relationships. The three categories are local service industries, service industries with substantial non-local markets, and service industries that may be either local or non-local in orientation. With the foregoing categories established and their relative importance in terms of employment ascertained for each SMA from the census statistics, it is possible, first, to carry out some comparative analyses of variation in industry structures among SMA's, and, second, to develop what we shall call the "industrial profile" of each SMA. Presentation of the former—the comparative analyses—completes chapter 9. Attention is given to variation in degree of specialization according to size of SMA and to variation in type of specialization according to the SMA's accessibility to the nearest larger SMA as well as its generalized accessibility (indicated by population potential). The main results may be summarized quickly. The larger the SMA the more likely it is to have a diversified, i.e., less specialized, industrial structure. Activities closely related to resources—including both resource extraction and first stage resource-using industries—are more highly developed in the less accessible SMA's, while second stage resource using industries and manufacturing industries making little direct use of resources are more conspicuous in the more accessible SMA's. All categories of services are inversely related to degree of accessibility; this suggests that in the more accessible locations greater reliance can be placed on non-local centers for certain services and also that competition for the hinterland service trade is enhanced by proximity of competing centers.

Procedures for analyzing "industry profiles" and for relating them to the regional situation of SMA's are outlined in chapter 10. In brief, we look for the particular industries that stand out within the broad categories of industry structure just described. Having identified profile industries, we search for evidence concerning the market and supply areas of each of them. The term "search" is used advisedly, for this kind of information—vital though it is for an understanding of metropolitan economic structure—is not readily available and where available is likely to be scattered and imprecise. The vicissitudes of the search are outlined for one city (Milwaukee); this outline serves to exemplify the methods used in the studies of fifty cities reported in Part IV. Although much extraneous information was brought into view, the key principle of these investigations was kept clearly in mind at all times. We wished to ascertain as clearly as possible what industries in the metropolitan center have direct relationships with outlying regions, to find out roughly what the limits of these regions are, and to interpret these materials in the light of our previously established criteria of metropolitanism. Part IV tells this story as succinctly as possible for each of the SMA's having in 1950 a population between 300,000 and 3,000,000—the obvious candidates (along with the five larger SMA's) for "metropolitan" status. The reader should clearly understand that our purpose was not to compile a handbook or to set out, say, the most up-to-date information that a marketing analyst would like to have. In fact, we deliberately chose to base the work on statistics which were not the most recent in some instances, in order that the quantitative materials would be more nearly comparable in time with the information gleaned from regional geographies, local monographs, fugitive journal literature and like sources. We did, of course, make use of available handbooks, e.g., the *County and City Data Book* and the *Area Manpower Guidebook*. Unfortunately, such collections of standardized items contain little in the way of direct information under our all-important category of regional relationships or market and supply areas. (The compilation of handbooks presenting this kind of information, though a formidable task, would perhaps be a worthwhile endeavor for the United States Department of Commerce.)

The presentation of individual SMA studies in Part IV serves several purposes, of which the most important is that of laying before the reader essentially all the evidence on which our conclusions in chapter 11 are based. The studies, though not completely "up to date," also provide basic information for readers interested in particular SMA's. Not all readers will be equally satisfied from this standpoint, however, inasmuch as there is considerable unavoidable variation in the quality and quantity of information available. Thirdly, the collection of SMA studies provides rich materials for a critique of the concepts of "hinterland" and of "nodal" (including "metropolitan") regions. Considerable effort was made to identify industries whose supply or market areas lie even approximately within the "metropolitan region" of the SMA as identified by previous investigators. The proportion of industries for which any of the "metropolitan regions" delimited by previous investigators was relevant to the actual metropolis-region relationship turned out to be astonishingly low. Finally, recurring themes in the SMA reports provide an inductive basis for identifying general patterns of metropolis-region relationships and for suggesting a heuristic classification of the larger SMA's in the United States.

These threads are brought together in chapter 11, which the reader might do well to study both before and after plunging into the details covered in Part IV. We suggest, first, some salient types of regional relationship. For some industries, although specialization is highly developed, market and supply areas are found primarily within the SMA itself—a situation, incidentally, that is somewhat difficult to interpret in terms of recent theorizing concerning the economic base. A profile industry may be one which dominates an adjacent region from which it draws raw material or other inputs or, more commonly, shares the dominance of that region with competing centers. Other cases illustrate the possibility for the region of supply to be located a considerable distance away rather than to be adjacent to or to surround the SMA. Perhaps the typical case encountered in the "manufacturing belt" is that of a center with both adjacent and distant sources of inputs and both near and far markets, usually shared with other centers. In fact, for many functions, the notion of a "hinterland" in the sense of a continuous adjacent area under the primary dominance of a single center scarcely makes sense in the manufacturing belt. In regard to markets one quite often finds relationships spread over regions considerably broader than those shown on maps of metropolitan regions; some of these are sub-national in scope, others national or even international. On the other hand, where the output is destined for other industries rather than final consumers the market area may be more nearly punctiform than "regional" in character.

Building not only on the materials describing "industrial profiles" and "regional relationships," but also on the empirical regularities set forth in Parts I and II, we attempt finally to condense the entirety of our results into a single classification of SMA's. (Figure 16, p. 271.) In this classification it is the rationale rather than the placement of the individual SMA's in the categories on which we should like to focus attention. The categories and their abbreviations are as follows: (N) national metropolises, (D) diversified manufacturing with metropolitan functions, (R) regional metropolises, (C) regional capitals, (D−) diversified manufacturing with few metropolitan functions, (M) specialized manufacturing, and (S) special cases. This typology harks back to the idea of "hierarchy" treated in chapter 3. However, it does not embody the assumption that categories of cities can be ranked or assigned to levels along a uni-dimensional scale, as do some of the more schematic versions of the urban hierarchy. It would appear that any attempt to bring into juxtaposition ideas about hierarchy and data on functional differentiation must result in a multi-dimensional classification.

The brief characterization of each category which we can give here is no substitute for the detailed specifications set forth in chapter 11 or the supporting evidence in Part IV. However, by citing the most typical instances of each class we can perhaps make the distinctions seem plausible. The obvious instance of a national metropolis (N) is New York, whose "hinterland" in any realistic sense is the whole country and indeed substantial parts of the rest of the world. A regional metropolis (R) like Minneapolis-St. Paul, by contrast, is prominent within a comparatively circumscribed, though possibly large, area. Still more circumscribed is the area of relative dominance of the regional capital (C), of which Oklahoma City is an example. The N-R-C series includes almost all instances where it seems meaningful to think of a continuous "hinterland" in the sense used by writers on the "metropolitan region" or in the sense of the tributary area of a central place. Be it noted, however, that the several "hinterlands" are overlapping and interpenetrating rather than discrete and clearly demarcated.

Among centers with emphasis on manufacturing in their industry profiles, we identify first those whose manufacturing activity is diversified and which have salient metropolitan characteristics; St. Louis is representative of the SMA's in this category (D). Milwaukee exemplifies the next category (D−); the minus sign in this category's symbol calls attention to the relative lack of metropolitan functions on a scale commensurate with the size of these SMA's. The specialized manufacturing (M) cities, of which Youngstown is perhaps typical, in general have quite poorly developed profiles in sectors indicative of metropolitan functions. Their emphasis on manufacturing is great; moreover, this emphasis is often in only one or two leading manufacturing industries. The D, D−, and M categories, therefore, are arranged along a rough scale of decreasing metropolitanism. But even at the top of this scale the regional relationships of the SMA are not very adequately characterized by referring to a particular "hinterland."

The final, miscellaneous category of special cases (S) includes some SMA's with highly specialized and unusual industry profiles—the national capital, a resort and transportation center (Miami), and naval or military centers (e.g., San Diego and San Antonio)—along with some SMA's presenting problems of classification not adequately handled by our procedures. We are inclined to believe that "special cases" of one kind or another would become even more frequent if our inquiry were extended to smaller SMA's and cities, for there is good evidence in earlier chapters that extreme forms of specialization occur with increasing frequency in descending the scale of community size.

We do not presume to assess the importance of the work reported in this volume and summarized in the foregoing paragraphs. However, perhaps one stipulation as to criteria for evaluating it may be offered. This—or any other—treatment of *Metropolis and Region* should be examined against a background of converging but diverse interests and ideas concerning its subject matter. It sometimes happens in the development of science that an important "breakthrough" in understanding is preceded by a period of apparently confused proliferation of varied conceptual approaches and empirical contributions. The breakthrough may take the form of synthesis and reconciliation of seemingly incompatible data and ideas, or it may involve a drastic and clarifying simplification of the hitherto disorderly materials. If we are right in thinking that times are ripening for the appearance of such a signal contribution to the theory of metropolitan structure, then our rather eclectic adaptation of a number of perspectives and analytical techniques may be excused as an effort to temporize with competing claims that we cannot adjudicate satisfactorily. There is some element of security in working in a field in which we can be sure the last word has not yet been said.

PART I

THE METROPOLIS AND ITS FUNCTIONS

It would be worth while to determine statistically what a metropolis really is.
—N. S. B. Gras

CHAPTER 2

Urban Location and Function

What a city does depends so closely on where it is that function and location seem like the two sides of a coin. Deep-water ports are busy with commerce and trade. An urban concentration of chemical industries arises in a valley endowed by nature with bituminous coal deposits, pools of petroleum, pockets of natural gas, sources of brines, and an abundance of water. "Gateway" cities collect the produce of agricultural belts and distribute it over wide regions. The geometry of location, by itself, tells us something about function: the foci of trade and service industries in regions of the interior are likely to occur at approximately central points within those regions. The intimate relation between location and function implied by such examples suggests that an adequate classification of functions could readily be translated into a classification of locations. As yet our categories of both are too broad and too ambiguous for such a translation to read smoothly. But the literature on cities provides valuable beginnings of a joint taxonomy of locations and functions.

CLASSICAL PRINCIPLES OF URBAN LOCATION

"Population and wealth tend to collect wherever there is a break in transportation"—so Cooley (1894) said. At the junction of land with water transportation, of one kind of water transportation with another, or of one kind of land transportation with another, there are needs for storage and transfer facilities, means of servicing vehicles, and a complement of personnel organized to carry out transfers of ownership and distributive functions. In some cases the interruption of a transportation route by a national boundary may have a similar effect. Such a transfer point may be a convenient place for the processing of raw materials or even the fabrication of consumer goods. The "linkage" of industries and the economies of agglomeration (Hoover, 1948, chapter 8) may attract industries to a site where the break in transportation has led to the formation of a commercial nucleus. Hence location at a break in transportation is expected to be associated with the performance of commercial functions and certain types of processing and fabricating functions.

The plausibility of Cooley's hypothesis is enhanced by the data in table 1. This distribution clearly shows that the first cities in the United States to attain what is often regarded as metropolitan size were located at junctions of water with land transportation. Many of the landlocked cities, of course, grew up around breaks created by the building of railroads, but railroads often reinforced the advantages of the port cities too. In 1950, of the 19 metropolitan central cities with populations in excess of a half million, 12 were at coastal locations, 7 were on rivers, and none were at the other locations (Schnore and Varley, 1955, table 1).

Table 1. Distribution of Standard Metropolitan Areas with Central Cities of 100,000 or More by Census Year in which that Size was First Reported, by Type of Location, United States: 1950

Year	All SMA's with central cities of 100,000 or more	Type of location		
		Sea or lake coast	Navigable river	All other locations
1820–1840	3	3	0	0
1850–1880	14	9	5	0
1890–1920	42	10	14	18
1930–1950	35	10	8	17
Total	94	32	27	35

SOURCE: Based on a compilation by Leo F. Schnore.

"Even though the earth had a perfectly uniform surface there would still be towns." This is the upshot of a lengthy analysis by Lösch (1954, p. 68) who ranks with Christaller as co-founder of the "central place" concept of city location. (English summaries of Christaller's work are given by Ullman, 1941; Dickinson, 1947, pp. 30-35; and Vining, 1955. We are indebted to Carlisle W. Baskin for the opportunity to examine his unpublished translation of Christaller's *The Central Places of Southern Germany*.) Lösch visualizes an undifferentiated plain over which raw materials and soil fertility are evenly and adequately distributed. He deduces a "system of town locations" in terms of the "geometry of economic regions" simply as "functions of distance, mass production, and competition." Although the assumptions are artificial and greatly oversimplified, they are capable of generating "logical constructs" or "ideal types" of great variety and complexity. Thus the ideal type of "economic landscape" includes "simple market regions surrounding every center of consumption or production"; for every group of products "a net of these market regions"; and, finally, "a systematic arrangement of these various nets." (Lösch, 1954, p. 137.) A characteristic feature of the scheme is the appearance of a hierarchy of central places at the nodes or focal points of the several nets and systems of nets, with these places exhibiting gradation by size and differentiation in respect to function. (Empirical data relevant to the notion of "urban hierarchy" are presented in chapter 3.)

Application of the central-place scheme for descriptive or classificatory purposes assumes, of course, that the premises of the scheme correspond with reality to some degree. An approximate fit of the model may be expected fairly generally for certain types of commercial functions and small-scale market-oriented manufacturing functions—allowing for topographic distortions and the like. Moreover, still other functions may be fairly evenly spread over a relatively homogeneous "belt" wherein the central-place hierarchy may be expected to emerge, although it may be less evident elsewhere. It is recognized that certain functions, owing to specific site orientation, may be found "clustered" in "districts" or occurring in highly concentrated, "punctiform" locations. Thus, to the complexity generated by the central-place scheme itself must be added the disturbances of that scheme occasioned by topographic irregularity, unevenness of resource distribution, and other factors.

We should note that the break-in-transportation and central-place principles are not wholly separate. Cooley (1894, section X) observed that one type of break in transportation occurs at a collection center where numerous small movements of commodities are grouped into a few large movements. The local movements come together at a common point which, if "conditions are in every respect uniform," tends to occur "at the center of the tributary plain." Therefore, certain central-place functions may well appear as functions associated with a commercial break (as distinguished from a "mechanical" break like a land-water junction) in transportation.

A third basic principle of association between location and function is illustrated by an observation of Heberle (1954, p. 14). In the South, he points out, "The greatest city-building industry, the iron and steel industry, is largely concentrated, except for Chattanooga, in the Birmingham metropolitan area. Here, of course, was an ideal location for this industry because iron, coal, and limestone—the three basic materials in steel production—occur in this same locality." We may refer to this principle as that of location governed by a specific site factor giving rise to the corresponding function. Harris and Ullman (1945), in their valuable exposition of the ideas under discussion here, recognize a category of "specialized-function cities performing one service such as mining, manufacturing, or recreation for large areas," and observe that "the principal localizing factor is often a particular resource." Their presentation, however, tends to broaden the category somewhat by including among the localizing factors those that most geographers would call the "situation." Pittsburgh is given as an example of a manufacturing center "favored by good location for the assembly of coal and iron ore and for the sale of steel to industries on the coal fields." It is not quite clear whether "good location," say, with respect to markets, is to be considered as a factor additional to centrality, break in transportation, or such site factors as resources; the example is not pursued by the authors. In future reformulations of location principles it would be well to determine whether "situational" factors can be defined independently of the factors we have enumerated.

Not all functions of cities, of course, are encompassed by the foregoing concepts, which were originally proposed to deal with what Harris and Ullman (1945) call the "support of a city." Lösch (1954, p. 76) refers to Sombart's "admirable distinction between 'city founders' and mere 'city fillers'; i.e., between occupations that establish cities and those that exist because a city is already there." This remark furnishes a clear anticipation of the "economic base" idea, which is an elaboration of the concept of "support" and to which we shall return presently. One would expect "city filler" functions to be more or less ubiquitous and to exert little if any net locational influence. This no doubt explains why writers on location have discussed only "basic" functions for the most part.

The extraordinary variety of geographic settings of cities and of their apparent responses thereto has led some writers to despair of success in accounting for locational-functional patterns except in terms of specific historical analysis of individual places. Even Lösch, master of abstract analysis, contented himself with a purported demonstration that locational "equilibrium would be possible under certain conditions." His system of "general equations of equilibrium," he conceded, has "no other significance." Furthermore, he considered it "utopian" to assume that such systems "can be gradually improved, and employed to solve practical problems more precisely than with our present coarse methods." (Lösch, 1954, pp. 99-100.) It is, indeed, easy to identify some major difficulties encountered in attempting explanations of urban locations in terms of such principles as those advanced above.

One complication becomes manifest immediately: evidence that a certain locational influence is at work does not preclude the operation of others, nor does the fact that a city has functions of one kind rule out the possibility of its performing another kind of function. For example, a city located near ore deposits may also be close to the center of a relatively homogeneous agricultural region. It would then be likely to perform functions related to the extraction, processing, and shipment of minerals but also to provide central-place services for the surrounding area. Actually, many cities with concentrations of central-place facilities are located somewhat eccentrically with respect to the areas served, seemingly in response to break-in-transportation or site-factor influences. Indeed, one might hypothesize that a prerequisite for the attainment of large size is the diversification of the city's activities over several classes of functions—or, to put it another way, the joint occurrence of several kinds of locational advantage.

The data in table 2 are consistent with this hypothesis. The functional categories here are rather gross and were not defined specifically in terms of the kinds of distinctions among functions we have been considering. Nonetheless, it seems significant that 66 per cent of the "diversified" SMA's (defined in the source study as those specializing in both retail trade and manufacturing) have central-city populations above 100,000, as compared with 58 per cent of the "manufacturing" SMA's, and only 47 per cent of the "retail" SMA's. As for the heterogeneous class of "other" SMA's, perhaps the most significant observation is that there were so few of them. Several of the kinds of functions

Table 2. Distribution of Standard Metropolitan Areas by Size of Central City and Functional Class, United States: 1950

Functional class	All SMA's	Size of central city: 500,000 or more	100,000 to 500,000	50,000 to 100,000
			Number of SMA's	
Manufacturing	59	7	27	25
Diversified	38	6	19	13
Retail	58	4	23	31
Other*	13	2	6	5
All classes	168	19	75	74
			Per cent of SMA's	
Manufacturing	100	12	46	42
Diversified	100	16	50	34
Retail	100	7	40	53
Other*	100	15	46	39
All classes	100	11	45	44

* Includes wholesale, transportation, government, education, resort and retirement centers.

SOURCE: Based on Schnore and Varley (1955), table 7; functional classes taken from V. Jones (1953).

included in this class are relatively common bases for specialization only at sub-metropolitan sizes.

With a more discriminating functional classification, it might be possible to design a better test of the proposition that urban growth to large sizes is more likely to occur on the basis of multi-function diversification than on the basis of intensive specialization in one class of functions. The outcome of any such test, of course, will depend heavily on the way in which the functional classification is designed. A classification standardized for size of place (e.g., Reiss, 1957) would be inappropriate for testing the hypothesis. Morrissett (1958) supplies some statistics compiled by an ingenious technique which are pertinent to our proposition. Apart from details, what he did was to estimate the "*k*-value" for each of 36 industries by city-size groups. The *k*-value is the percentage of the employed labor force engaged in a given industry which occurs at the fifth percentile of the distribution of cities according to percentage engaged in that industry. In effect, it is an estimate of the minimum percentage of employment in the industry—the fifth percentile rather than the lower end of the range was taken as the minimum in order to exclude obviously "abnormal" cities. Summing the *k*-values over the 36 industries indicates in summary fashion how much of a city's labor force is engaged in what might be termed "essential" employment (our term, not Morrissett's). This sum increases with city size not only because *k*-values for many individual industries increase with increasing size, but also because more industries enter the "essential" class. Here are the (interpolated) sums of *k*-values for cities of certain sizes in the United States in 1950, classified into two broad regions ("college towns" are excluded):

Size	*North and East*	*South and West*
10,000	31.5	38.9
25,000	34.1	41.2
50,000	36.8	43.7
100,000	40.7	47.9
250,000	48.6	56.8
500,000	55.6	64.3
1,000,000	58.7	71.0

These and other data in Morrissett's paper indicate clearly that industries which are "sporadic" among smaller cities and towns become "ubiquitous" among large cities. The proportion of "specialized" cities must be relatively high at small sizes; correlatively, the proportion of "diversified" cities is high at large sizes. We may infer as well that economic interdependence takes on an intra-city form much more frequently in large cities than in small. The positive correlation between proportion in "essential" employments and city size is clearly consistent with our main proposition that functional diversification is a prerequisite to the attainment of large size.

The first major problem, therefore, in establishing a clear-cut association between functions and locations is that virtually any city exhibits a mixture of functions (even if we set aside the ubiquitous, "city filling" functions) and its location is some kind of net resultant of several locational influences.

The second major problem is that a strictly cross-sectional analysis of functions and locations is unlikely to bring to light the essentially cumulative interplay of the two as it works out over time. In reading even a sketchy history of a city one is impressed with the complex and contingent character of the events leading to its founding, subsequent growth, and structural elaboration. A trading post is set up in a frontier area. As the land around it is settled and proves to be agriculturally productive, its fortunately central location leads to its growth into a town with a considerable range of commercial and service functions. By what may appear to be completely fortuitous decisions, it is selected as a state capital and a couple of main line railroads are laid down which intersect in the expanding town. Perhaps it is then discovered that the town lies in the midst of a region of oil bearing rock, and it becomes a center of activities oriented to this resource. As the region develops, the town, now become a good sized city, emerges as something of a financial center and is selected as a regional headquarters for a considerable number of firms with national markets. And so on. (For a much longer story about the "evolutionary course of an hypothetical area," see Isard, 1956, chapter 1.) Each major development in such a growth sequence represents a change or elaboration of functions; correlatively, the evaluation of the city's locational advantages must be periodically revised as essentially new locational influences come into play.

It is not too difficult a task to make such a history intelligible in terms of somewhat general principles about locations and functions. But this task almost inevitably entails an *ex post facto* analysis which invites an eclectic if not casual use of concepts, rather than a research design which specifies criteria for acceptance or rejection of explicit hypotheses pertaining to a clearly defined set of cities. If there is to be a *theory* of urban location and function, it must be capable of generating models which account for variation among cities in their functions and for variation among locations in the degree to which they have given rise to cities and complexes of urban functions.

Some hurdles such a theory will have to overcome have been indicated. What they come down to is that the structures we would like to explain are the outcome of an evolutionary process in which new factors come into play at different times and what happens at any given stage depends upon what happened some time earlier: "Growth creates form, but form limits growth" (Boulding, 1956, p. 120, in a discussion of ideas of D'Arcy Thompson). We can imagine that no such theory, at least in its initial form, will be able to treat all relevant variables simultaneously in a deterministic model. Some determinants of location and function will have to be regarded as "exogenous" and at least some will have to be treated as random variables. (A discerning discussion of the problem of testing location theory by empirical evidence is given by Tiebout, 1957b.) Moreover, any respectable goodness of fit will doubtless be attained only by a model that somehow incorporates an account of the complex temporal patterns of dependency between changing functions and changing locational influences. Although the construction of models with these properties can be envisioned, there is little indication that they will be forthcoming soon.

ECONOMIC BASE AND FUNCTIONAL SPECIALIZATION

Although, as we have tried to show, the locations and functions of cities are so closely related that a full explanation of one requires an explanation of the other, still the problem of location and function is one that can be subdivided. One portion of the problem has been tackled with great vigor by the classical and modern location theorists (see Isard, 1956, for summaries and recent developments). These theorists deal with such problems as that of the locational equilibrium of the firm or the possibility of a general equilibrium of all firm locations. If they proceed that far, they seek to account for the location of cities and patterns of urban settlement in terms of such concepts as economies of scale, agglomeration effects, and the like. The chain of reasoning by which the analysis of city patterns is reached is so lengthy that direct empirical examination of where cities are and what they do becomes of limited relevance as a means of testing location theories. It is perhaps significant that virtually all the treatment of actual data in the volume by Isard (1956) is segregated in a single chapter, "Some Empirical Regularities of the Space-Economy"; similarly, Lösch (1954) relegates all his empirical material to a section on "Examples."

Of course, the route taken by the location theorists may, in the long run, prove to be the only way to reach satisfactory explanations of urban structure. But it is more in the spirit of such disciplines as human ecology, regional geography, demography, and sociology to begin with data, the classification of patterns in the data, and the investigation of empirical relationships, seeking all the while to arrive at explanations of observed patterns and regularities by inductive means. The contrast between the abstract, *a priori* approach and the empirical approach is, of course, not absolute, for each draws sustenance and inspiration from the other from time to time. But insofar as there is this genuine distinction between alternative research strategies, it is the latter—the empirical, inductive strategy—that we shall employ in most of this volume. The ultimate goal of both strategies is, of course, the same: to arrive at theories capable of explaining observed patterns and associations of empirical data.

Another part of our general problem has been attacked in highly empirical fashion, i.e., the classification of city functions. Unfortunately, little of this work has involved explicit attention to locational considerations. Nonetheless, these have entered into the interpretation of findings, particularly when cartographic distributions of functional types of cities have been examined. It is even more important to note that the principles upon which empirical taxonomies and typologies have been constructed have locational implications; and it is clear that to explain observed patterns of functional differentiation, as revealed by the empirical classifications, will require reference to location concepts. The two major approaches to classification of urban functions—the economic base approach, and the functional specialization approach—have been rather thoroughly discussed in recent literature; hence we shall not need an exhaustive review of the numerous contributions under each heading. (On the economic base, see Andrews, 1953-56; Alexander, 1954; and Leven, 1956. On functional specialization, see Nelson, 1955; Alexandersson, 1956; and Duncan and Reiss, 1956, Part IV.)

There seems to be a fair consensus in recent writing on the following characterization of the urban economic base:

> The base is that part of an urban economy which is composed of activities whose principal function is that of exporting goods, services, or capital beyond the economic boundaries of the community. The economic complement of the base is made up of service activities. Service activities of the community are primarily engaged in internal trade which involves sales of goods, personal services, and capital to local base enterprises, employees of the base, other service enterprises, employees of service enterprises, and unemployed persons within the community. (Andrews, May, 1954, p. 164.)

This general conception is susceptible to refinement and elaboration, and it lends itself to alternative modes of operational definition. A survey of "base studies" reveals quite a variety of criteria and procedures for specifying the community area whose base is under study, identifying the industry components of the base, and measuring their contribution to the base or to the total urban economy. There is a good deal of controversy and uncertainty as to whether the base is most appropriately defined and delineated in terms of employment structure, income flows, or value added in production. The applications of the base concept are varied too. City planners seek aid from base analysis in forecasting city growth, land use requirements, and the like. Economists work out employment and income multiplier effects (e.g., Hildebrand and Mace, 1950; Tiebout, 1957a). We shall not discuss these applications or the methodological conundrums to which they give rise.

Of greater importance here is the suggestion of Alexander (1954, p. 251) that the base "concept provides a view of economic ties which bind a city to other areas" and "permits the most satisfactory classification of cities in terms of regional function." The author does not elaborate these suggestions greatly; specifically, he does not venture any comprehensive classification of "regional functions." Indeed, few if any of the theorists of the economic base have concerned themselves with the implications of the base concept for analysis of city-region relationships and urban locational tendencies. For the most part, base studies do not attempt to identify the areas to which basic functions export, nor the areas from which inputs to the basic activities are drawn. The base is simply regarded as that sector of the community which trades with the "rest of the world" (one of the well known earlier base studies is entitled "Oskaloosa vs. the United States"). A logical next step in working out the ramifications of the idea of economic base would be to investigate the specific spatial (or "regional") relationships involved in basic functions.

Despite the variations among approaches to economic base analysis, there is one point of fairly general agreement: any reasonably accurate identification of the economic base of a city requires meticulous and time-consuming study. Public sources of mass data—censuses, government economic series and the like—are inadequate for all but the most gross results, because such data are not broken down by export vs. local functions of industries. As a consequence, no one has yet been able to compile a conceptually consistent set of precise statistical descriptions of the economic bases of a sizable number of cities. Comparative study of the economic base has scarcely advanced beyond the point of suggesting a few plausible hypotheses. At best, it is now possible to include only some rudiments of the economic base idea in comparative studies of large numbers of cities. However, it is possible to discern the influence of thinking about the base on recent proposals of methods for functional classification of cities.

Turning to that problem, we take note of Alexandersson's observation that early studies on functional classification rested "their classifications on the total industrial structure without making any distinction between city forming and city serving ratios," whereas in his study the " 'city serving structure' was subtracted from the total structure before the classification was made" (Alexandersson, 1956, p. 22). Similarly, Duncan and Reiss (1956, p. 216) suggested that "the problem of functional classification is best undertaken by considering functional specialization in terms of the kinds of *export activity* of a community which creates an in-flow of money to the community." In both these studies, however, only rough and arbitrary criteria were available for distinguishing between basic and non-basic employment; and both, being largely based on statistics of the employed labor force classified by industries, necessarily begged the question of whether positive deviation from some national norm in respect to industry employment structure is sufficient *prima facie* evidence of the performance of export functions. There is, at any rate, this much in common between the economic base idea and the general rationale for functional classification: both seek to identify what is distinctive in the economic structure of a city in comparison with other cities. Thus Leven (1956, p. 253), discussing the importance of basic activities, writes, "Exports are the distinctive feature of an area's economic structure. They differ markedly from place to place, reflecting the adjustment of an area's production to the natural and acquired advantages of its situation." The approach taken by those attempting functional classifications has been largely to identify what is "distinctive" about an urban economy, either without first determining what is "basic," or using some rough expedient for this determination.

In examining representative studies in functional classification one is impressed by the apparent complexity of the detailed criteria by which cities are grouped into types or categories, the variation of these criteria from one study to another, and the consequent variation in results. Thus in one study (Duncan and Reiss, 1956, table B-17) Boston is described as a wholesale trade center with important educational and military functions; in a second (Alexandersson, 1956, Appendix 1) the only "chief city forming industry" given for Boston is nondurable goods manufacturing; in a third study (Nelson, 1955, Appendix) Boston is identified as a center of finance, insurance and real estate activity and no other; and in yet a fourth study (V. Jones, 1953, p. 29), Boston is classified as a "diversified" city with retail trade predominant in comparison with manufacturing. On the other hand, there is no disagreement among the studies that Detroit is a manufacturing center, although they describe differently its degree of manufacturing specialization. Three of the studies just mentioned (Jones excepted) are alike in recognizing that a city may be classified in terms of several specialties, whereas earlier studies tended to place each city in one and only one functional category. But almost every study has come up with somewhat different functional categories, depending upon the subdivisions and combinations of industries recognized as bases of specialization.

Presumably the choice among alternative procedures of functional classification should be based primarily on the demonstrated greater relevance or predictive power of one classification in comparison to its alternatives, in the context of a well defined problem or class of problems. Considerations of aesthetics, simplicity, convenience, and intuitive appeal should be secondary. In point of fact, however, the purposes for which functional classifications are designed are seldom made explicit, and oftentimes little is done with them after they are finished. Duncan and Reiss (1956) employed functional classes as independent variables in exploring factors related to morphological differences among communities. Schnore (1957) has used a functional classification of suburbs effectively in analysis of differential growth rates. Neither study, however, includes tests of alternative classification schemes.

We must note one other feature of the work on functional classification. As in the case of economic base studies, research on functional differentiation has proceeded with little explicit attention to the problem of the relation of one city to another, or of the city to its hinterland or to the "region" in which it is located. Nor has any systematic effort been made to relate locational principles to patterns of functional differentiation. (Alexandersson, however, does give many useful incidental observations on locational influences.) On the other hand, most of the contributors to the literature on functional specialization have noted broad regional groupings of their functional classes and have offered general interpretations of this form of regional differentiation. It is commonly noted that manufacturing centers cluster in the northeastern United States, whereas cities having trade functions primarily tend to be more characteristic of the Middle West and the Great Plains. Whether the *ad hoc* rationalization of such vague findings greatly advances the understanding of the location-function nexus may be questioned. Interestingly enough, when a geographer, noted for a pioneering study in functional classification, came to study the localization of manufacturing, he abandoned the classification approach for more precise analytical tools (Harris, 1954).

We may state some tentative conclusions from the foregoing cursory survey of work on the urban economic base and functional specialization. These take the form of working assumptions for our own empirical investigations, reported in subsequent chapters. First, the economic base approach still lacks sufficiently definite statement to permit its use in extensive comparative studies and, in any case, the requisite data for its use on such a scale are not available. Nonetheless, in thinking about cities and their settings, the base idea is a valuable concept. Second, if we investigate the ways in which cities differ strikingly one from another, as regards their economic or industrial structure, we will *ipso facto* be getting at "basic" activities in some sense, albeit in a rough-and-ready and possibly incomplete fashion. Third, if a classification of cities according to their modes of functional differentiation is attempted, such a classification should be instrumental to some theoretically relevant problem—there is little need for just another functional classification of cities, however ingenious its methodology. In particular, if the intent of the classification is to shed light on the relationship between a city and its milieu, the categories of the classification should have some bearing on this relationship.

CITY AND REGION: PRELIMINARY CONSIDERATIONS

Although we introduced our discussion with a general consideration of the problem of urban location, it is beyond our means to essay empirical treatment of the manifold ramifications of that problem. Instead, we shall adopt a particular and limited perspective, i.e., we shall examine the relationships between the functions performed by cities and their local and "regional" settings. The specific application of this approach will be made clear as we discuss problems of concept and method in later chapters. Here we wish to indicate some general implications of a viewpoint which focuses attention on the relationship between urban functions and the areas over which activities related thereto extend. Perhaps the discussion can be made more concrete by contrasting two hypothetical examples.

Suppose that city "X" is located with good accessibility to a grain-livestock agricultural region. It serves as a collection, processing, and transshipment point for grain and grain products, and has a well developed meat products industry supplying a market which extends over a substantial part of the nation. It is a wholesaling center serving small towns and agricultural trade centers in the region, and may be a focal point for distribution of agricultural machinery. In addition, it has a complement of business service industries which cater not only to local needs but also serve a wide tributary area.

By contrast, city "Y" is one of a number of manufacturing centers of comparable size in a manufacturing "belt." It is highly specialized in the processing of rubber and the fabrication of rubber products. The raw material inputs for its basic industries do not come from surrounding areas—indeed, they are mostly imported from outside the country and from various points scattered over the nation. The products of the rubber industry flow to other manufacturing centers—some within the "belt" and others located at considerable distances away. Those products which are ready for the final consumer flow through distribution channels which pass through wholesaling centers scattered over the nation, few, if any, of which might be said to be in the same "region" as city "Y." While city "Y" performs certain convenience and ubiquitous services for the immediately adjacent rural territory, it is in sharp competition with other centers for the more specialized service trade of its region. Consequently, for example, its major newspaper may hold circulation dominance only within a radius of 30 or 40 miles. It has no highly developed market facilities for the agriculture carried on in its vicinity, though it may draw on surrounding farms for certain perishable commodities consumed locally.

Now, it may be supposed that both the secular growth patterns and the response to economic fluctuations of these two cities will diverge. The fortunes of city "X" are closely bound up with the regional resource—agricultural land—on which its basic industries ultimately depend. Improving productivity of that resource, other things equal, is a stimulus to "X's" growth; similarly, a rise in regional or national income may be transmitted as an increased demand for "X's" products, and, hence, for the products of its hinterland. The prosperity of "X" is somewhat dependent on such vicissitudes as the weather of its region, changes in national agricultural policy, and fluctuations in foreign demand for national agricultural products. There may be grounds for expecting the secular growth of city "X" and that of the surrounding region to be positively correlated.

Economic conditions in city "Y," on the other hand, may be responsive to labor conditions and the harvest in foreign areas producing crude rubber, to the national demand for durable and nondurable goods incorporating rubber, and to the emergence—perhaps in a quite distant area—of substitutes for rubber products. To only a moderate degree could one perceive a connection between the economic growth and cyclical responses of city "Y" and those of the area that appears to be its natural "hinterland." Should "Y's" industry enjoy rapid growth, it is even possible that it would recruit its labor force not primarily from the surrounding rural areas and smaller towns, but perhaps from a region at some remove.

If we were prepared to follow out details of the relationships sketched here, we would produce a study in what has been called the "regional interpretation of the functions of the city"—an interpretation which, according to Dickinson (1947, pp. 165-166),

> involves a twofold approach: first, an assessment of the effects of the character of the region—its resources, and economic production—on the character of the activities of the city; and, secondly, an examination of the effects of the city, as a seat of human activity and organization, on the character of the region . . . this approach . . . seeks to evaluate both the city and its region, however vaguely defined, in terms of their mutual relations and in the light of their historical development.

In pursuing such an interpretation, we should have to expect quite a variety of patterns in city-region relationships. Our two examples already suggest that the "character of a region" as a site of resource-extracting activities may or may not be closely related to the main functions of a city. The "effects" of the city may be fairly obvious and specific, or they may be attenuated and diffuse. The location of a city in a particular region may, in one case, reflect that region's pull as a market for the city's principal products; in another case, the pull may be that of central or break-in-transportation location within a region of resource extracting activity. An empirical classification of city-region relationships must rest on answers to the questions raised in the following discussion by Alexander (1954, p. 246) of implications of the economic base concept:

> No city lives to itself. It serves other areas which can be said to constitute the city's "market region." In turn, the region serves the city. Such functioning is of immediate interest to geographers because the interconnections between city and region are one type of spatial relationship. Thus, one aspect of urban geography is the analysis of those ties which bind a city to its region. For example, how extensive is the region served by a city? How far and in what directions does that region extend? To what degree is the region dependent on that city for goods and services? Answers to these questions constitute useful criteria by which relationships between city and region are measured.

The three major locational principles stated earlier manifestly embody assumptions about city-region relationships or have implications for those relationships. A break in transportation instigates city growth only if that break lies athwart a trade route linking areas with goods to trade. A city located at a break, therefore, always has relations with at least two "regions"—the one whence shipments come and the one whither they are destined. The central-place principle, of course, is predicated on a city-region relationship in which the "region" comprises the market and supply areas of the city's major functions. Since these areas may not coincide for the several functions, in theory it is possible to have as many "regions" related to a city as it has functions. Finally, the localizing influence of a site factor comes into operation only if exploitation of that factor gives rise to goods or services which the city can exchange for the goods and services offered by some outlying territory. In all likelihood, the relative importance of the three locational principles is one of the determinants of the size and shape of the "region" with which the city is related. The ideal type of central place, as Lösch and Christaller argued so beautifully, is located at the center of regular hexagonal market and supply areas, although Isard (1956, p. 271-273) showed that recognition of factors omitted from Lösch's scheme leads to distortions of the hexagonal pattern, quite apart from topographic variation and uneven resource distribution. By contrast with the geometric regularity of "regions" in the central place scheme, Lösch (1954, p. 11) himself pointed out that in a "district" where a resource is concentrated there may arise a "cluster" of cities, each with a greatly elongated market area. There are reasons for supposing that breaks in transportation occasioned by "natural" interruptions of trade routes will give rise to cities whose tributary areas are asymmetrical and whose locations within their "regions" are eccentric to a greater or lesser degree.

Thus far the term "region" has appeared in the exposition without being defined, and has often appeared in quotation marks so that no close technical interpretation would be placed on it. The concept of "region" is, in fact, a difficult one, owing to the wide variety of meanings given to it, the controversies surrounding some of these meanings, and the excessive claims coupled with methodological weaknesses of certain approaches to regional*ism* (for some of the more salient methodological problems see Duncan, Cuzzort, and Duncan, 1960). Fortunately, we shall be able to offer some simple but useful distinctions without having to adjudicate the various issues which the region concept threatens to suggest.

In the first place, in thinking of city and region, we have in mind a contrast between a dense concentration of population and activities—in areal terms virtually a point, as suggested by Lösch's (1954, p. 68) characterization of a town as a "punctiform agglomeration of non-agricultural locations"—and an extended territory. We therefore think in terms of the manifold nexus between city and region as radiating out from an urban center or as coming into a focus at that center.

Secondly, we conceive of region and city as being differentiated one from the other in terms of their complementary and reciprocally related activities. The relationship is, therefore, a symbiotic (Hawley, 1950, pp. 36-39) one rather than one established by a similarity or identity of the city's attributes to those of the region. This does not gainsay the likelihood that city and region may resemble one another in many respects, and that some such resemblance may be a necessary condition for establishing the symbiotic connection between them. But the resemblance by itself does not constitute a city-region relationship within our meaning of the term.

A third point is that the factors determining the extent and the limits of the region range from those depending primarily on the city-region relationship itself to those that are virtually independent of that relationship. We shall need to refer to the following distinction, which seemingly is widely accepted:

> No matter what criteria are invoked in defining them, geographic regions of all kinds may . . . be grouped under two heads according to whether they are uniform or nodal.
>
> Uniform regions are so throughout. The uniformity is not complete, for there is always a certain range of characteristics permitted by the criteria, and there are irrelevant differences which are disregarded. But within the limits set by the criteria, regions of this kind are uniform. A climatic region is an example. If it is a multiple-feature region its uniformity is defined in terms of the association of features.
>
> Nodal regions are homogeneous with respect to internal structure or organization. This structure includes a focus, or foci, and a surrounding area tied to the focus by lines of circulation. For example, an area of newspaper circulation is a single-feature nodal region, the trade area of a town a multiple-feature nodal region. . . . Internally nodal regions are marked by a diversity of function that goes far beyond the range of minor variation permitted in uniform regions. (James and Jones, 1954, pp. 36-37.)

In what is called a "nodal" region in the foregoing quotation, the "region" is defined by the function which relates the city to the region: it is simply the area over which a city-centered activity extends. It is significant that examples of "nodal regions" usually concern such service functions as wholesale trade or newspaper circulation. The concept has not been used much in connection with activities in which the extraction and processing of resources are prominent. A second significant point is that the exposition of "uniform" regions makes no reference to urban centers. To be sure, a climatic region can hardly be said to owe its "uniformity" to any functions performed by cities. But what about a type-of-farming region or a manufacturing region—broad areas, each characterized by relative uniformity in respect to an economic function?

The existence of a type-of-farming region, of course, presupposes some relative uniformity of conditions suitable for producing certain types of crop: climate, soil fertility, topography, and the like. However, the presence of such conditions alone does not guarantee that a given type of crop will be produced. Another necessary condition is the existence of markets for the crop and some degree of accessibility of the type-of-farming region to those markets. Insofar as the market— which usually comes to focus in urban centers—is a factor influencing the location of resource extracting activities, we may say that even the "uniform" region is partially defined by city-oriented functions. Pertinent illustrations of this point are set forth in chapters 8 and 11 (see figures 13 and 14). Of course, in some cases the city-region relationship is not one-to-one, for there may be several cities serving or dependent on a particular resource region.

To consider another type of "region," take the "manufacturing belt," which is variously defined but generally recognized to extend over a large part of the northeastern and north central portions of the United States. If this is an acceptable example of a "uniform" region, then we must recognize that the uniformity is one generated by similar orientations toward urban centers as mass markets for manufactured goods, as Harris (1954) has pointed out so effectively. Here it is obvious that the "uniform region" (i.e., the manufacturing belt) is not tributary to any single urban center; but the concentration of manufacturing activity which it represents is attributable in large measure to its accessibility to a complex of metropolitan markets. In figure 1 we present, as an illustrative sample, the *non*metropolitan cities of 25,000 to 50,000 inhabitants in 1950 (i.e., those outside metropolitan state economic areas and standard metropolitan areas). The symbol for the location of each is distinguished according to whether the city had less than one-fourth or more than one-fourth of its employed labor force engaged in manufacturing. As a rough but effective measure of accessibility we employ population potential (see Appendix), following the general proposal of Stewart (1947b) and its specific application to manufacturing localization by Harris (1954). The map shows that most of these smaller cities with high proportions in manufacturing are located toward high-potential areas while most of those with little manufacturing are in the less accessible areas. A more precise statistical analysis (see also the results reported in chapter 7) yields the following results:

> Considering the 149 cities of 25,000 to 50,000 inhabitants located outside metropolitan areas . . . one finds a correlation of .62 between per cent of the employed labor force engaged in manufacturing (Y) and the population potential (X) of the State economic area in which the city is located. The observed regression relationship is approximately $Y = 0.8\ X - 1.0$, with X in 10,000's. Outside metropolitan areas and apart from local peaks, potential varies from about 120,000 to about 550,000 [persons per mile]. Consequently, the proportion engaged in manufacturing in these cities varies, on the average, from about 8.5 per cent in areas with the lowest potential to about 43 per cent in the areas with the highest potential. (O. D. Duncan, 1957b, p. 368.)

We conclude that it is dangerous to rely on an absolute distinction between "nodal" and "uniform" regions, or to confine the investigation of city-region relationships to the case of the "nodal" region defined as the service area for a particular city function or functions. Such a limitation is tantamount to accepting the hypothesis that the central-place scheme is a complete and sufficient account of the location-function nexus, whereas we have suggested good reasons why other locational principles have to be acknowledged.

There are two further implications of our discussion of city and region to this point. First, despite references (in the earlier quotations from Dickinson and Alexander) to "the" region served by the city or "the" region on which the city depends, there is no such thing as a single, uniquely defined "region" which manifests a full spectrum of city-region relationships. This is already implied by the central-place scheme, with its hierarchy of market and supply areas associated with different central functions. But it is implicit, as well, in the consideration of relations between cities and "uniform" regions, because there will often be more than one kind of uniform region toward which functions of the city are oriented. A city may depend on a grain-live-

---

Figure 1 (opposite). Manufacturing Specialization and Population Potential, Nonmetropolitan Cities of 25,000–50,000 Inhabitants: 1950

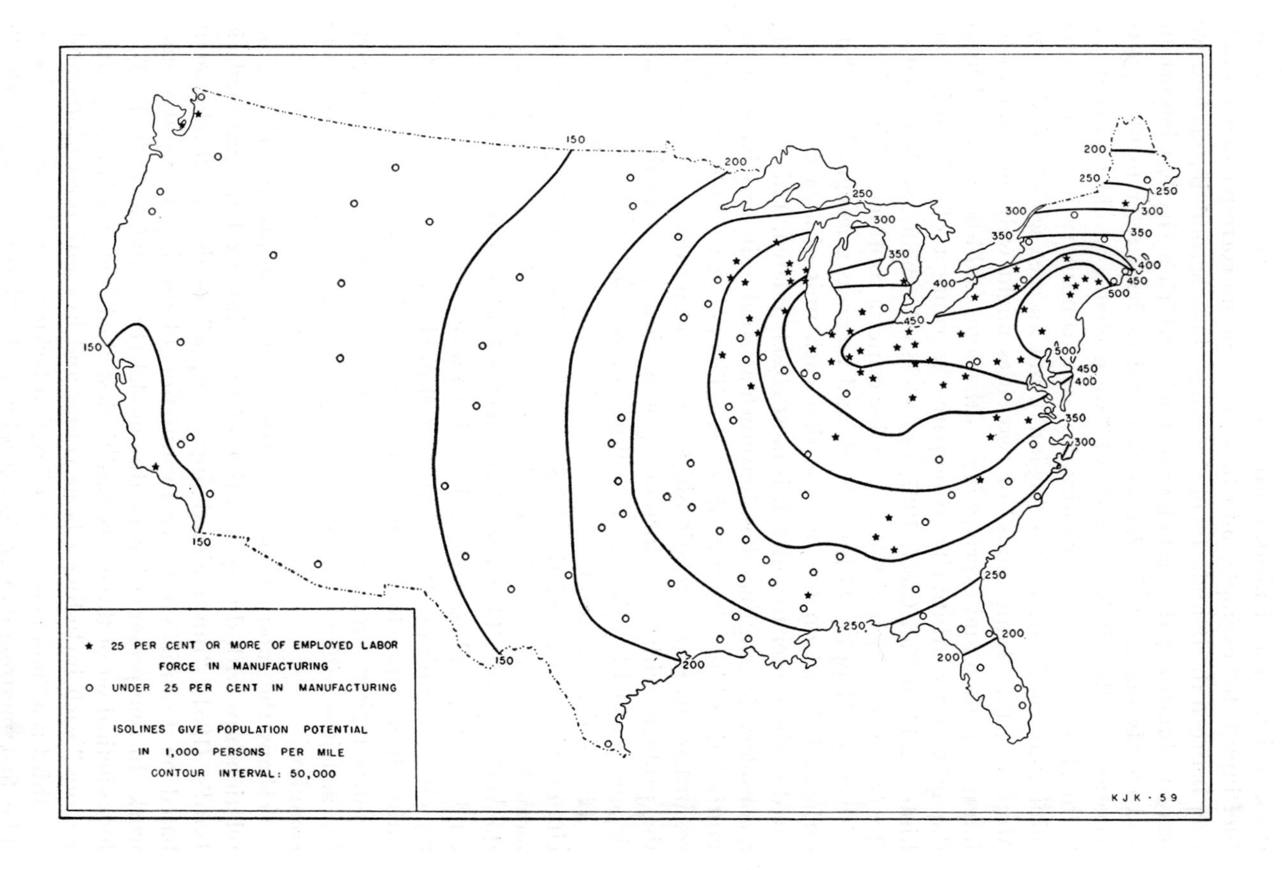
25 PER CENT OR MORE OF EMPLOYED LABOR FORCE IN MANUFACTURING
UNDER 25 PER CENT IN MANUFACTURING
ISOLINES GIVE POPULATION POTENTIAL IN 1,000 PERSONS PER MILE
CONTOUR INTERVAL: 50,000
KJK-59
150
200
250
300
350
400
450
500

stock region for agricultural products and on a coal-mining region for fuel inputs, for example; and there need be no correspondence whatever between the boundaries of the two regions. Second, if somehow we were to lump together all the areas with which a city has important and clearly manifested relationships and perhaps refer to this aggregate area as the city's "hinterland," we probably would find that the "hinterland" was not a continuous area (continuity is one common minimum specification of a "region"), but an area with "holes" in it. Moreover, the "hinterlands" of two cities might well turn out to be interpenetrating and overlapping, so that one could be separated from the other only arbitrarily. (Compare the concept of "discontinuous hinterland" in Van Cleef, 1937, pp. 34-36.) A scheme, such as that of Bogue (1949), which gives every major center a continuous hinterland, with no overlapping of hinterlands and no areas unassigned to a hinterland, is based on the premise that each unit of area can be allocated to the center to which it is most closely related. This is evidently a considerable simplification, inasmuch as areal units may have important relationships with several centers. The points we have emphasized regarding city-region relationships represent an attempt to formulate the problem with some increment of realism over techniques which depend on highly arbitrary techniques of regional delimitation.

The need for conceptual flexibility is apparent if one reflects that a city may have close relationships to a "region" without being centrally located within that region or, indeed, without being located within the region at all. That this circumstance is often ignored reflects the tendency to emphasize central service functions in the study of city-region relationships. If attention is shifted to processing and fabricating functions wherein there is direct or indirect dependence on resource regions—regions characterized by distinctive resource-extracting activities—the geometry of city-region relationships becomes more complex.

Perhaps the most noteworthy attempt to conceptualize city-region relationships with due recognition of the points we have just made is Isard's (1951) "interregional input-output" model, a development based on Leontief's pioneer formulation of the input-output framework. In one presentation of this model (Isard and Kavesh, 1954), a hypothetical set of three "regions" is described. Two are "metropolitan regions," each including a large center and its continuous hinterland; the third is a "nonmetropolitan" region lacking a single clear-cut focus. The first metropolitan region specializes in "heavy manufacturing"; outputs of this industry are not only sold within the metropolitan region but also are exported to the other two regions. Inputs for the heavy manufacturing industry come both from within the region itself and from the other two regions. Similarly, the second metropolitan region's basic industry is "light manufacturing," with both intra- and interregional inputs and outputs. The nonmetropolitan region's basic industry is agriculture and extraction; some of its output is consumed intraregionally, but the remainder is exported to the two metropolitan regions.

Even this highly simplified hypothetical case illustrates how an industrial city may depend not only on its surrounding area—what would usually be called its immediate or continuous "hinterland"—but also upon one or more other "regions" which supply certain requisite inputs for its industries and afford markets for a portion of those industries' outputs. To be sure, if one attempted to trace spatially the origin of every input and the destination of every output, the resulting information (if it could be obtained) would be so complex as to defy analysis. Yet, if any well-rounded "regional interpretation of the functions of the city" is to be had, it will be necessary to acknowledge the actual complexity of city-oriented economic flows. At the present time, the interregional input-output model, even though it involves a number of drastic simplifications of reality, is much too complex to be employed in studies of large numbers of cities. The data required by the model are simply not at hand. Moreover, we may withhold judgment as to the model's theoretical adequacy for such problems as projection of the interregional impact of a major locational shift or of a shift in demand. From our standpoint, it is a sufficient contribution of the model to have called attention to the advisability of describing city-region relationships in input-output terms. This feature of the model is captured in the "input-output access" approach of Perloff *et al.* (1960), which has directly influenced our own empirical work, as reported in later chapters.

CHAPTER 3

The Urban Hierarchy

Comparative studies of cities characteristically have accepted one of two general frames of reference. For convenience, we may label these the "differential" and the "system" frames of reference. The former appears to be modeled on the psychology of individual differences. Members of a population of cities (individuals) are measured on various dimensions or characterized in terms of certain attributes; these traits are then compared and correlated without regard to any relationships that may obtain among the cities (individuals). A classic study of this kind was made by Thorndike (1939), a noted psychologist who computed scores of correlations among traits of cities in trying to determine what characteristics make a city a good place to live. (It helps if the average income is high.) Similarly, Angell (1947) sought to discover factors internal to cities accounting for their variation in degree of "moral integration."

By contrast, the system frame of reference assumes that what cities are like depends at least in part on what cities do (their functions), and that the functions of cities are in some measure a reflection of intercommunity relationships. This viewpoint is implicit in much of the writing on location, for as we saw in the preceding chapter the advantages of a location can be understood only in terms of how that location leads to relations between a city and other places. Indeed, the system framework is implied whenever any characteristic of a city is introduced which refers to its connections with other communities—for example, even such a gross variable as distance from a larger city.

But explicit recognition of the concept of a "system of cities" has come about only within the last quarter century or so. It represents the convergence of a number of ostensibly different approaches to the analysis of urban structure.

Notions about a system of cities almost always include reference to some hierarchic aspect of the system—if, indeed, the system is not conceived entirely in hierarchic terms. It is true here, as in many areas of research, that exploratory investigations are guided by concepts that have not yet achieved precise and definitive statement and not all of whose implications are immediately perceived. No one quite knows yet what a "system of cities" is—i.e., it is not yet possible to state acceptable criteria for rejecting the proposition that a given collection of cities constitutes a system (see Hoover, 1955). Similarly, there are no doubt unanalyzed postulates lying behind the idea of a "hierarchic" system. In common parlance a hierarchy implies ranking or ordering of the elements said to be hierarchically arranged. If we speak of a hierarchy of cities, then, do we mean to imply that each city, or each class of cities, can be given an unambiguous rank along a single dimension? This would be a pretty "strong" requirement. Perhaps it would be well to keep in mind the possibility of "weak" or "partial" orders. For example, given four cities (or classes of cities) we might be able to establish only that a H b (a is higher in the hierarchy than b), a H c, b H d, and c H d. From this it would follow that a H d (H being a transitive relation), but not that b H c nor that c H b. A picture of the "hierarchic" pattern would then look like this:

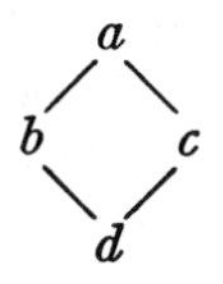

We would not be required to say that "b and c have the same rank," but only that "b and c are not comparable." As might be expected, it is possible to exhibit a hierarchy with perfect ordering if the investigator contents himself with constructing a deductive system, or if he is satisfied with a single-variable criterion of position in the hierarchy. However, in empirical investigations employing multiple criteria it is not likely that all cities will fall readily into such a neat pattern. We return to this question at the end of chapter 11.

ALTERNATIVE APPROACHES

Most deductive analysis of the urban hierarchy takes the central-place scheme (mentioned in the previous chapter) as its point of departure. Three kinds of empirical approach have been prominent: the investigation of the size distribution of cities, under the heading of the Pareto or "rank-size" rule; classification of centers according to levels in the hierarchy; and research on the functional correlates of city size. These four lines of investigation are not mutually exclusive, of course; in particular, there has recently been considerable interest in reconciling the deductive with the empirical approaches. The significant point is, perhaps, that the several types of inquiry are manifesting some convergence although they were opened up more or less independently of each other. It is equally significant, however, that little of the literature on urban hierarchies makes reference to the parallel studies of urban location, economic base, and functional specialization which have been conducted without particular reference to the hierarchy concept. Yet it seems unlikely that these various bodies of literature are without implications one for the other.

We shall be somewhat selective in our summary of the first three of the alternative approaches just mentioned, since each of them has been discussed rather fully in recent literature.

The concept of central place was introduced in chapter 2, where it was noted that elaboration of the assumptions underlying this concept is capable of producing an abstract hierarchic scheme of great complexity. The abstract argument is most fully developed by Lösch (1954); for our purpose here it is sufficient to recall the somewhat more concrete, though still highly schematic, analysis of Christaller. According to Vining (1955, pp. 160, 166-67),

> Christaller conceives of goods and services as being divided into two classes. On the one hand there are dispersed goods, the productions of which are directly connected with the locations of natural resources. The extractive industries—farming, mining, et cetera—yield such goods. On the other hand, there are central goods and services the productions of which involve an assemblage of goods whose productions are geographically dispersed. The central goods and services are then sub-classified. It is supposed that a necessary condition for the existence of an economic activity yielding a particular central product or service is the existence of some minimum number of consuming units within some given range of the site of

> that activity. Central goods and services are regarded as characterized by this minimum number and range and as classifiable in these terms. In such a classification, the lower orders of central goods are those having small ranges and small minimum numbers of consuming units, and the order of a central good increases with an increase of these numbers. . . . In Christaller's conception, the notion of *type* of city or central place refers to the *kinds* of activities pursued at the site of the central place. The clustering of persons into a city or town is a clustering of complementing activities, and distinctions among *types* of places are distinctions among collections of activities.

The types or ranks of central places identified by Christaller are translated by Ullman (1941) as follows: market hamlet, township center, county seat, district city, small state capital, provincial head city, and regional capital city. The norms of population size, spacing of centers, and extent of tributary area provided for these levels of the hierarchy appear to have been derived by Christaller partly from empirical and partly from *a priori* considerations.

Two distinct types of limitation on the applicability of the central-place hierarchical system ought to be recognized. The first is the failure of actual conditions to conform with the assumptions of the system. The second—a limitation of almost all classifications—is that the number and boundaries of categories in the system are necessarily arbitrary to greater or lesser degree.

With reference to the first limitation, it is easy to point out that there is no extensive region of urban settlement wherein resources are evenly distributed and topographic variations are absent. The "reality," therefore, is inevitably more or less "distorted" as compared with the hypothesis. Two opposed methodological precepts are based on this brute fact. On the one hand, one may take the position of Lösch (1954, p. 389): "The ordering forces of the economy operate everywhere, but only when they work relatively alone is it possible to see whether reality corresponds in some measure to our theoretical results." On this view, one would search out regions of relative uniformity in relevant conditions and inquire whether the central-place hierarchy is approximately realized within them. The contrary view is expressed by Bogue (1959, p. 395): "Instead of working with 'ideal types' or trying to visualize metropolitan relations from the data for rare territories where absolute uniformity is approached, nodal relationships should be observed in real-life situations." The critical problem arising in connection with both these positions is how to specify criteria for the acceptance or rejection of the hypothesis that the central-place principle is operating, obscured as it may be by the operation of other factors and principles. It seems that at many junctures in research it is not possible to test a theory directly by the goodness of fit of an abstract model to available data or by an experiment validating or invalidating the theory's basic postulates. Instead, it is necessary to derive consequences from the theory which are open to more or less direct examination. Among the interesting consequences of the central-place principle are these: In any extensive region, the number of large cities is expected to be smaller than the number of small cities. In the absence of marked topographic variation, the spacing of cities is expected to depart from the pattern of a random distribution in the direction of evenness. The economic structure of cities is expected to manifest systematic variation according to their size. The question of size distribution of cities is discussed below. The problem of spacing has been studied in only a cursory fashion (Lösch, 1954, chapter 22; O. D. Duncan, 1957a); we do not pursue the problem here, but commend it to the attention of research workers. Variation in economic structure by size of city is the main topic of subsequent sections in this chapter.

It should be noted that empirical realization of the expectations based on a theory does not conclusively validate that theory; alternative explanations of empirical results may well be possible. Thus, in a recent study of various types of service industry, Duncan (1959b) noted some patterns of variation by size of city which seemingly require reference to principles outside the central-place theory for adequate explanation. Still, it is necessary to admit the relevance of the "centrality" factor in accounting for some of the findings. Findings reported later in this chapter provide partial support for the central-place theory but call attention to the need for supplementary principles to explain observed patterns.

The second limitation noted above—the arbitrary character of categories in the scheme—poses the greatest difficulties for those research workers who are disposed to attach more importance to the categories than to the principle by which they are generated. There is really little scientific reason to argue about whether the number of levels in a hierarchic scheme should be four, five, or seven. True enough, it is possible to devise statistical criteria for generating categories with certain optimum properties (Berry and Garrison, 1958b). But the decision to accept a particular set of such criteria is itself an arbitrary one. The geographers who seek a magic number of "town classes" (e.g., C. T. Stewart, 1958) might find instruction in the fact that sociologists have engaged in a lengthy, controversial, and fruitless search for the "real" number of "social classes." In short, levels, ranks, or classes in a hierarchic scheme should be regarded either as conceptual fictions suitable for manipulation in abstract discourse or as categories of convenience for handling empirical data. On this point we stand squarely with Vining (1955, p. 169): "Like pool, pond, and lake, the terms hamlet, village, and town are convenient modes of expression; but they do not refer to structurally distinct natural entities."

There is another classification problem in connection with the central-place scheme that is somewhat more fundamental. This is the classification of the "goods" exchanged between central place and tributary area. Whereas the formal theory is stated in terms of a "good" (including "services" among "goods") and its "range" (Berry and Garrison, 1958c), virtually all relevant empirical data pertain not to individual "goods"—assuming that such discrete items of exchange can be identified—but to types of industry, occupation, or establishment. Thus the calculations of Berry and Garrison (1958c) purporting to estimate the range of various "goods" actually pertain to such functions as those performed by filling stations, physicians, and photographers, each of which is capable of supplying rather varied sorts of "goods." Evidently we have here another version of the aggregation problem, i.e., that every industry category (for example) is necessarily more or less heterogeneous in its content, with the broader and more readily manipulated categories generally being the more heterogeneous. Like the "town classes" in the central-place hierarchy, the "kinds of goods" in the underlying postulates must be taken either as useful fictions or as instrumental categories, rather than as ultimate realities. We shall have occasion later on to grapple with the aggregation problem in its pragmatic form.

The immediately preceding paragraphs actually have carried us into a second approach to the urban hierarchy: the attempt to characterize it inductively rather than on the basis of reasoning from postulates. The literature here is so voluminous and is growing so rapidly (see Brush, 1953b, and Spelt, 1958, for reviews) that we can do no more than cite a few significant examples. We should note first that many empirical investigations make an initial simplification of the problem by limiting their attention to one or the other end of the hierarchy. Thus J. E. Brush (1953a), studying "The Hierarchy of Central Places in Southwestern Wisconsin," investigates no communities having more than 8,000 inhabitants. By contrast, F. H. W. Green (1958) emphasizes distinctions at the top of the scale, setting forth empirical characterizations of "metropolises," "provincial capitals," "third order centers," and so forth. While it is the latter range of inquiry that is most pertinent to our later work, it seems well to illustrate problems of delineating the urban hierarchy by summarizing a study which treated the entire spectrum of urban places.

Smailes (1944) has set forth a scheme of considerable complexity which purports to describe conditions in pre-World War II England and Wales. The study is notable not only as a pioneering effort but also for its appreciation of nuances and indeterminacies of the classification problem that often are overlooked. The categories identified by Smailes may be summarized as follows:

A. London
B. Major cities
   (1) Regional capitals
   (2) "Provincial cities of . . . great regional importance" and "others cities" meriting "high ranking, not so much because of importance as centres of regional integration, as because of their own size and special eminence in the commercial and industrial life of the country"

C. Cities
D. Other centers—minor cities or major towns (includes three headings: industrial, "county," and resort towns)
E. Towns
F. Sub-towns
G. Urban villages

H. Villages (mentioned but not described)
I. Isolated homesteads (mentioned but not described)

In making distinctions among categories B, C, and D, some reliance is placed on a battery of statistical indicators and the presence or absence of certain types of facilities; this list of items includes bank clearings, employment in insurance, employment in wholesale trade (food trades and textile and clothing trades being shown separately), volume of livestock receipts, and presence or absence of civil defense region headquarters, G.P.O. regional or telephone area headquarters, Bank of England branch, stock exchange, daily newspaper, university or college, medical school, and general hospital with more than 500 beds. These data are handled somewhat informally, since no single item or particular combination of items is regarded as a necessary or sufficient criterion. The distinction between major cities and cities turns on the fact that the latter—although they are important market centers and may have facilities "of first importance in the regional organization of the country for certain *ad hoc* purposes"—lack the "*general* regional importance" of the greatest cities.

The other segment of the hierarchy which is treated in detail is category E (towns). To attain this level a center is supposed to have three or four banks and the shopping facilities expected to be associated therewith, a secondary school and/or a hospital, two or more cinemas, and a local (weekly) newspaper. It should be noted that these criteria are applied with some latitude for those exceptions which appear to have ready explanations. Sub-towns (category F) have some but not all the foregoing features, and urban villages (G) have a bare minimum of urban features. Each of these three categories can be subclassified according to the particular type of profile of facilities which it exhibits.

We omit further qualifications and elaborations of this hierarchic system, emphasizing that we have given it in rather more schematic form than the author does (the symbols identifying the categories are ours). Two general comments are offered. First, several if not all the levels in the hierarchy may be subclassified on a "horizontal" basis: note the distinctions shown within categories B(2) and D. This recalls our proposition that any empirical hierarchic classification is likely to exhibit the properties of a "weak" or "partial" ordering. Second, the divisions between levels are seldom distinct. The author's remark is quite appropriate: "Any grading . . . must in some measure be arbitrary, since the urban scale is as continuous as the social scale. Yet the indefiniteness of boundaries in neither case warrants denial of the reality of a stratification" (Smailes, 1944, p. 41).

Turning to a second type of empirical approach to the urban hierarchy, we recall the formula for the Pareto curve, $y = Ax^{-\alpha}$, where the symbols have the following meanings for our problem: x is the size (number of inhabitants) of a community, y is the number of communities of size x or larger, and A and α are empirical parameters estimated from the size distribution. For example, for the 119 urbanized areas of 100,000 or more inhabitants identified in the *1950 United States Census of Population,* we find that a rather good fit is obtained with the formula, $y = 10^6 \times 9.8528\, x^{-.98356}$. The tabulation below indicates the number of urbanized areas in selected size intervals deduced from this formula, as compared with the actual number:

Size	*Calculated*	*Actual*
1,000,000+	12.5	12
500,000–	12.1	13
300,000–	15.3	17
200,000–	20.8	18
150,000–	19.8	22
125,000–	15.9	16
100,000–	23.6	21

It will be noted that the exponent in the foregoing formula approximates unity, although the departure from unity is big enough to make a difference in the goodness of fit. If we take α as unity, the Pareto formula reduces to $x = A/y$, the so-called "rank-size rule," which expresses the size of a given community as the quotient of the size of the largest community divided by the rank of the given community. The "rank-size" formulation has had the unfortunate consequence of directing investigators' attention disproportionately to the fit of the curve at the very upper end of the size scale (e.g., C. T. Stewart, 1958). Despite some spectacular deviations at this end, it is true that data for a number of different periods and countries show a quite acceptable fit of the Pareto formula over a considerable range of sizes (see, e.g., Allen, 1954; Madden, 1956), given appropriate adjustments of the exponent of x, which is sometimes fairly different from unity. It is obvious both mathematically and empirically that the Pareto or "rank-size" formula cannot hold for the smallest sizes of settlements, although the magnitude of the critical lower limit seems to vary greatly from one country to another. It has been conjectured that the lower limit is related to the phenomenon of nucleation (Duncan, 1959a, p. 687). One would expect the limit to differ, for example, as between a country where agricultural village settlement is the rule and a country where farmers live on isolated homesteads. However, it is difficult to secure the data that would be required for an adequate comparative test of this hypothesis.

The significance of the Pareto distribution of city sizes for our topic, the urban hierarchy, is perhaps not immediately obvious. Early students seemed to regard it as simply a mathematical curiosity; Lotka (1925, p. 307), for example, stated "It may be left an open question how much significance is to be attached to this empirical formula." There are still investigators who seemingly have more interest in the mathematics of the problem than in relating features of city-size distributions to considerations of urban location, structure, and function (e.g., Simon, 1957, chapter 9). A more fruitful interpretation was opened up by Lösch (1954, p. 433-36) and Hoover (1955), who suggested that the size distribution of cities in a central-place scheme should follow the Pareto distribution approximately. An elegant development of this point is provided by Beckmann (1958), whose mathematical model shows that "the empirical rank-size rule . . . is compatible with the ideas on hierarchies of market areas and their central cities as developed by Lösch and other location theorists." There is, however, a troublesome problem not treated by any of these writers.

As was demonstrated above for the United States, the Pareto curve may provide an excellent fit to the size distribution of the largest cities. But the largest cities of a country almost invariably have locational and functional characteristics that cannot be accounted for at all well by a strict central-place scheme (O. D. Duncan, 1957b, p. 365; Schnore and Varley, 1955). Although the Pareto distribution is compatible with the central-place scheme, an empirical fit of the Pareto curve hardly validates central-place theory in detail. (For further discussion of interpretations of the rank-size relationship, see Berry and Garrison, 1958a.)

The final approach to the urban hierarchy listed at the outset is the study of functional correlates of community size. Investigators taking this approach (e.g., Ogburn, 1937; Schettler, 1943; Duncan, 1951; Duncan and Reiss, 1956) have simply regarded community size as an independent variable and examined whether various social and economic characteristics of communities manifest a significant regression on size. This work typically has relied on no deductive scheme of a hierarchy; it has employed no prior empirical classification of communities in terms of levels in a hierarchy (except as size may be regarded as a basis for such classification); and it has not been directed specifically toward the statement of regularities in mathematical summary form. There is, nonetheless, a convergence of the community-size studies with the other approaches (Duncan 1957b, 1959b). On the one side, it may be observed that all approaches concede at least a rough correspondence between community size and level in the hierarchy, although in an empirical classification like that of Smailes (discussed previously) there would be considerable overlapping of sizes as between levels in the hierarchy. On the other side, the interpretations of correlations between community size and various dependent variables which have been suggested, often have involved the kind of assumptions that theorists of the urban hierarchy have developed more systematically. The matter may perhaps be put this way: If social and economic characteristics of cities can be shown to vary with community size in a systematic fashion, any viable theory of urban hierarchy must be able to account for such relationships or at least show that they are not incompatible with assumptions of the theory. It is perhaps by careful study of the correlates of community size that we can most readily come to appreciate limitations on present ideas concerning hierarchic systems. Accordingly, the following sections of this chapter set forth in some detail a body of data on variation in industry structure by size of community and offer some observations on the relevance of these data for the notion of an urban hierarchy.

INDUSTRY DISTRIBUTION AND CITY SIZE

The data with which we shall be working in most of this chapter are the labor force industry statistics of the *1950 Census of Population.* It is necessary to consider at the outset some problems of classification that arise in using these data. The industry statistics published in the population census are shown in varying detail. The basic classification, which consists of nearly 150 items (industry titles), is used in the tabulations shown for the United States as a whole, individual states, and standard metropolitan areas. It is this "detailed classification" which we employ in working with standard metropolitan areas in Parts III and IV. The statistics for urbanized areas, smaller urban places, and counties are published in the form of a "condensed classification," each of whose 41 items is a combination of the titles in the detailed classification. In this chapter, where we are concerned with the industry structure of all sizes of urban communities, and in chapter 7, where the analysis deals with the parts of the country lying outside standard metropolitan areas, it is necessary to use the more highly aggregated condensed classification.

An important tool of the analysis in this chapter, as in chapter 7 and in Parts III and IV, is the grouping of industry titles by broad categories indicative of type of resource use (for the manufacturing industries) or local vs. non-local orientation (for the service industries). While the reasons for making this grouping are the same, the actual content of the broad categories used here and in chapter 7 is different from that of the categories used in the final parts of the study. This results from the dependence on the condensed industry statistics in the earlier chapters in contrast to the availability of the detailed statistics for the studies reported in the later chapters. In effect, the broad categories that will be described here are a crude approximation to those introduced in chapter 9.

The first of the broad categories, extractive industries, is defined in the same way in both contexts. It simply consists of agriculture, forestry and fisheries, and mining. As is explained more fully in chapter 9, the basis of grouping the manufacturing industries is a summary of the 1947 input-output tables developed by the Regional Studies Unit of Resources for the Future, Inc. (see Perloff *et al.,* 1960). This RFF table permits one to distinguish "first stage resource users" from all other industries. Unfortunately, the industries of the condensed classification used in the population census do not match those of the RFF table (which is based on some 200 industry titles) very precisely. The best we can do, therefore, is to classify as *processing* industries those industry groups a significant proportion of whose labor force is employed in industries identified as first stage resource users in the RFF table. All other manufacturing industries are placed in the category of *fabricating* industries. Neither of these terms, "processing" vs. "fabricating" industries, is to be understood in any precise technical sense. The terms are adopted simply for convenience in exposition, and to call attention to the fact that certain component industries in the former group do depend more or less directly on raw material inputs, while most of the industries in the latter group work mainly with materials that have already been through an initial processing stage in the flow of production.

The following industry groups of the condensed classification were grouped as *processing* industries; the titles in parentheses are those of the main first stage resource users included in the industry group:

- Furniture, and lumber and wood products (sawmills, planing, and veneer mills; plywood)
- Primary metal industries (blast furnaces; primary copper; primary lead; primary zinc; primary metals, not elsewhere classified)
- Food and kindred products (meat packing and whole poultry; processed dairy products; canning, preserving, and freezing; grain mill products; sugar; miscellaneous food products)
- Textile mill products (spinning, weaving, and dyeing)
- Other nondurable goods (tobacco manufacture; pulp mills; petroleum products; coke and byproducts).

Each of these groups, of course, includes industries which are not first stage resource users. For example, "furniture, and lumber and wood products" includes "furniture and fixtures," which is a fabricating industry; it also includes "logging," which is actually an extractive industry. Its classification here as a "processing" industry means only that an appreciable proportion of the employment in the industry group is in component industries classified as first stage resource users. There is no way to be sure that in any particular urban place the employment in "furniture, and lumber and wood products" actually represents the presence of processing industries; but this is the assumption that must be made in using the highly aggregated industry categories available for this study. Interpretations, of course, must be carefully qualified.

The remaining 9 categories of manufacturing industry in the condensed classification of the population census, here classified as *fabricating* industries, are as follows:

Fabricated metal industries, including not specified metal
Machinery, except electrical
Electrical machinery, equipment, and supplies
Motor vehicles and motor vehicle equipment
Transportation equipment, except motor vehicle
Other durable goods
Apparel and other fabricated textile products
Printing, publishing, and allied industries
Chemicals and allied products

Some of these "fabricating" industries do include components which are first stage resource users. The most conspicuous example is perhaps "chemicals and allied products." Our classification simply implies that the component industries of each of these groups are preponderantly not first stage resource users.

In regard to the service industries, for reasons indicated subsequently, we are most interested in distinguishing those believed to serve consumers (individuals and other industries) located predominantly within the local community from those assumed to have an appreciable or preponderant proportion of non-local customers. The component industries falling into each category are listed subsequently in table 9. "Local" services include retail trade, repair services, private household services, utilities and sanitary services, such personal services as laundering, cleaning, and dyeing ("other personal services") and such professional and related services as those of welfare, religious, and membership organizations and the legal and engineering professions ("other professional and related services"). The remaining services, classed as non-local, actually vary considerably in degree of dependence on non-local markets, as far as this may be guessed from their titles (listed later, in table 9). Most if not all undoubtedly have sizable local clienteles. However, when their representation in a community is disproportionately large, the presumption is that an appreciable part of the clientele is located outside the community. For example, "educational services, government" includes public elementary and high schools—clearly a local service for the most part. But where unusually large numbers are employed in this industry one can generally be sure of finding a municipal or state college or university in the community. Much the same kind of consideration governs the placement of the other "non-local" services in that category. It will be noted that the viewpoint taken in framing this classification tends to minimize the number of services assigned to the "local" category.

Two other categories are of no direct interest. "Construction" is placed in a separate category and largely ignored in the analysis, on the assumption that variation by city size in proportion of construction workers is more probably a reflection of differences in recent and current rates of growth than of a division of labor in terms of community size. "Industry not reported" is retained as a category only to simplify the statistical manipulations of the data.

The other major axis of classification is by size of community. Decisions concerning this classification actually were made prior to the conception of this volume at the time the industry data were aggregated into size groups. The main consideration at that point was to make the size classification as nearly comparable as possible with that used in a special report of the 1950 Census dealing with characteristics by size of place (industry tabulations were not included in that report) so that analysis of industry variation by community size could be matched with the study of variation in occupational composition reported by Duncan and Reiss (1956, chapter 8). We shall not be concerned here with the occupational data, although the longer report on which this chapter is largely based (Winsborough, 1959a) deals with the influence of industrial structure on variation in occupational composition by community size.

The size-of-place classification used in this chapter is shown in table 3, which gives the percentage distribution of the employed labor force by the seven broad industry categories described above. The size classification requires little comment, and the industry data may stand for the moment as simply indicating the relative magnitudes of the industry categories and the general tendencies of variation with city size. The extractive category diminishes in relative importance in ascending the size scale, as does the processing category (disregarding the rural-farm size class). By contrast, the relative numbers engaged in fabricating increase with increasing size of community. Within the urban size categories—i.e., excluding groups (8) and (9)—the two types of services manifest contrary tendencies: non-local services increase as a proportion of the labor force while local services decrease with increasing size of city. The relative variation within each category, however, is small as compared with that observed for processing and fabricating.

We next consider the question of how to recognize a tendency toward "hierarchy" in a distribution like that of table 3, or in a table

Table 3. Percentage Distribution of the Employed Labor Force by Broad Industry Categories, by Size of Place, for the United States: 1950

Size of place	All industries	Industry category						
		Extractive	Manufacturing		Services		Construction	Not reported[1]
			Processing	Fabricating	Local	Non-local		
Urbanized areas								
(1) 3,000,000 or more	100.0	0.67	9.58	21.69	27.20	33.89	5.27	1.70
(2) 1,000,000 to 3,000,000	100.0	0.55	11.00	21.10	26.90	33.17	5.69	1.59
(3) 250,000 to 1,000,000	100.0	1.39	11.15	16.42	29.43	33.84	6.26	1.51
(4) 50,000 to 250,000	100.0	1.58	13.54	17.05	29.25	31.01	6.18	1.39
Other urban places								
(5) 25,000 or more[2]	100.0	2.30	13.58	14.08	31.32	31.21	6.16	1.35
(6) 10,000 to 25,000	100.0	4.17	14.32	12.48	31.64	29.51	6.41	1.47
(7) 2,500 to 10,000	100.0	6.90	14.12	10.04	32.34	27.77	7.15	1.68
Rural territory								
(8) Nonfarm	100.0	14.08	14.65	10.76	25.86	23.62	8.90	2.13
(9) Farm	100.0	72.33	5.85	3.41	6.51	6.87	3.10	1.93

[1] Includes "not specified manufacturing industries" and "industry not reported."
[2] Of a total of 193 cities in this group 21 had populations somewhat in excess of 50,000 but were not recognized as urbanized areas.

SOURCE: Tabulated from data in State tables, vol. II, *1950 Census of Population*.

(which is too large to show here) giving such a distribution for the 41 industries of the condensed classification. Suppose we compared line (1) with line (5) in table 3 by subtracting each entry (except the total) in the latter from the corresponding entry in the former and summed separately the positive differences and the negative differences. Each sum would work out to 10.6 percentage points (disregarding the sign of the sum). A figure derived in this way is termed the "index of dissimilarity" of the two size groups with respect to their (seven-category) industry composition. Among other interpretations of this index, we may say that 10.6 per cent of the workers in size group (5) would have to shift to another industry category if the two size groups were made to match perfectly on a proportional basis.

Table 4. Indexes of Dissimilarity of Urban Size-of-Place Groups with Respect to Industry Composition, United States: 1950

(Upper right half of table, based on 41 industry groups; lower left on broad industry categories)

Size of place[1]	Size of place[1]						
	(1)	(2)	(3)	(4)	(5)	(6)	(7)
(1)	...	11.9	10.9	15.2	16.9	18.6	22.8
(2)	1.8	...	9.9	11.6	15.5	19.1	22.9
(3)	5.5	4.8	...	6.4	8.7	12.1	16.9
(4)	7.8	6.4	3.2	...	6.3	9.6	14.2
(5)	10.6	9.2	5.2	3.0	...	5.6	10.4
(6)	13.8	12.4	8.3	6.1	3.3	...	6.7
(7)	17.8	16.5	12.4	10.2	7.5	4.4	...

[1] See table 3 for identification of size-of-place groups.

SOURCE: See table 3.

Now, if industry distributions do fall into a hierarchic pattern and if the size classification of cities is accepted as a rough classification by levels in a hierarchy, we should expect the index of dissimilarity to be greater the greater the size difference involved in the comparison. Specifically, in an arrangement like that of table 4, showing indexes of dissimilarity for each pair of size groups, we should expect the indexes to increase, reading up or to the right from a point on the diagonal of empty cells (down or to the left, if we are studying the other set of figures). The two sets of indexes in table 4 conform quite well to this expectation. The indexes in the upper right half of the table, calculated from the distributions by 41 industry groups, depart from the expected pattern only in that the last two entries in row (1) are slightly too small in comparison with the entries just below them. The indexes in the lower left half of the table, based on the seven-category distributions (table 3), fit the expectation as to order perfectly.

Since the subsequent materials will introduce some potentially confusing details and since we shall devote most of our attention to departures from the neat pattern just described, it is perhaps well to dwell a moment on the significance of the results recorded in table 4. It should be noted first that the finding is not an artifact of the classification scheme—either that of the 41-item census condensed classification or our seven-category aggregation thereof. Indeed, the census classification probably works against the hypothesis. The condensed classification was designed by the census statisticians for the presentation of small-area data. They must quite deliberately have selected their industry groups in the expectation that most groups would show appreciable numbers employed in most tabulation areas, irrespective of size and type of community. Quite clearly they would not be interested in publishing long columns of ciphers in tables for towns and small cities simply to indicate the absence of industries found only in large cities. These industries, if there are any, would therefore have been grouped with others lacking so sharp a differentiation by size of place. The whole effect of such aggregation would be to dampen the variation by community size. The order that we have discovered, therefore, although expressed in terms of more or less arbitrary industry and community-size categories, depends in no essential way upon these categories. Instead, it supports the suggestion that the collection of urban communities existing in the United States in 1950 did constitute a *system*—a system manifesting a hierarchic principle of organization at least roughly correlated with community size. Quite evidently the statistics given in table 4 do not pertain to the characteristics of any particular city. We should be quite loath to undertake an explanation of the inter-city variance in industrial characteristics with only city size available as an explanatory factor. We do contend that a regular pattern of variation in industry structure with city size is a salient feature of the system as such.

The subsequent analysis, summarized in tables 5-8, has to do with decomposition of the pattern exhibited in table 4. We consider separately segments of the industry structure and a broad geographic breakdown of the system of cities to explore the basis of this pattern more fully.

It will be noted in table 4 that each index in the lower left panel is smaller than the corresponding one in the upper right panel. This reflects a mathematical property of the index of dissimilarity, for an index computed for $n - k$ categories ($n > k > 0$) can at most be no larger than an index computed for n categories, if the $n - k$ categories are combinations of the n categories. However, some interest does attach to the differences between the two sets of indexes. If we subtract each index in the lower left panel from the index in the upper right panel corresponding thereto, the difference represents dissimilarity of the underlying distributions *within* broad categories. If the pattern of these differences departs markedly from our hypothesized ordering, we shall conclude that the pattern exhibited by the 41-industry indexes is essentially due to city-size variation by the broad industry categories and not to the variation within these categories. Table 5 presents the differences in question. Obviously the pattern of these figures is by no means perfect, although one has the impression that some tendency toward realization of a perfect pattern is still present.

Table 5. Indexes of Dissimilarity of Urban Size-of-Place Groups with Respect to Industry Composition within Broad Industry Categories, United States: 1950

(Figures shown are differences between corresponding figures in the two halves of table 4; see text for explanation)

Size of place[1]	Size of place[1]						
	(1)	(2)	(3)	(4)	(5)	(6)	(7)
(1)	...						
(2)	10.1	...					
(3)	5.4	5.2	...				
(4)	7.4	5.2	3.2	...			
(5)	6.2	6.2	3.4	3.3	...		
(6)	4.7	6.7	3.8	3.5	2.3	...	
(7)	5.0	6.4	4.4	4.0	2.9	2.3	...

[1] See table 3 for identification of size-of-place groups.

SOURCE: See table 3.

We are unable to state categorically how much of a departure we can tolerate and still retain this impression. However, it is possible to objectify the formation of such an impression with a simple enumeration of the deviations from the hypothesized pattern. For each entry in the table, count the number of smaller entries lying below it in its column and the number of smaller entries lying to the left of it in its row. Sum these numbers over all entries to obtain i, the total number of "inversions" in the table. For a perfect pattern, of course, $i = 0$. If the table is completely reversed from the hypothesized pattern we should have, as the maximum of i, $N(N-1)(N-2)/3$, where N is the number of size groups, in this case 7. To obtain an index of ordinal arrangement of the table which varies between -1.0 (for complete reversal of pattern) and $+1.0$ (for a perfect pattern), we may compute $1 - 2i/\max(i) = 1 - 6i/N(N-1)(N-2)$. Computing this "index of ordinal arrangement" (for lack of a better term) for the matrix shown as table 5, we obtain a value of .54, which results from the occurrence of 16 inversions out of a possible 70 (one of the two ties in the table is broken in the favorable direction, the other in the unfavorable, when the indexes are computed to two decimal places).

Obtaining an index of ordinal arrangement of .54 for table 5 does not tell us whether that table may be accepted as evidence for the existence of a hierarchic pattern of the within-category variation in industry composition. However, with an index this low we should certainly not want to urge such a conclusion too strongly. Very tentatively, we might suggest that an index lower than .75 or .70 casts suspicion on the hierarchy hypothesis. One other feature of table 5 becomes evident in counting up the number of inversions: all but one of the entries disturbing the expected pattern are in column (1). If we omit the largest size group and recompute the index of ordinal arrangement for six city-size groups, we obtain a value of .95. If the matter were worth pursuing, we could inquire what peculiarity of the largest cities (New York, Chicago, and Los Angeles) produces this type of departure from the hypothesized pattern.

Another approach to decomposition of the pattern of table 4 is taken in table 6. Here the manufacturing industries are treated separately, the percentage distributions being calculated with total manufacturing employment as the base. The arrangement of the indexes of dissimilarity for the 14-industry distributions clearly suggests a hierarchic pattern: the index of ordinal arrangement for the figures in the upper right panel is .83. However, subtracting out the component of these indexes associated with the two broad categories, processing and fabricating, destroys the hierarchic pattern completely, and the index of ordinal arrangement in the lower left half of the table is −.14, or effectively zero. As far as we can determine with the data available, any tendency toward hierarchy in the manufacturing sector considered by itself is due solely to the fact that processing industries outweigh fabricating industries in volume of employment in small towns, whereas a preponderance of fabricating industries appears in the smaller cities and increases as city size increases.

Table 6. Indexes of Dissimilarity of Urban Size-of-Place Groups with Respect to Manufacturing Industry Composition, United States: 1950

(Upper right half of table based on 14 manufacturing industries; in lower left half indexes based on 2 broad manufacturing categories have been subtracted from corresponding indexes in upper right half of table)

Size of place[1]	Size of place[1]						
	(1)	(2)	(3)	(4)	(5)	(6)	(7)
(1)	...	21.6	16.7	24.3	23.2	24.0	28.2
(2)	17.9	...	17.6	18.0	22.4	28.6	33.5
(3)	6.9	11.4	...	10.4	11.8	17.2	24.0
(4)	10.7	8.0	6.6	...	8.9	15.0	20.4
(5)	4.7	7.6	3.2	4.1	...	9.8	15.7
(6)	1.2	9.4	4.2	5.8	5.5	...	10.0
(7)	0.4	9.3	6.0	6.2	6.3	5.0	...

[1] See table 3 for identification of size-of-place groups.

SOURCE: See table 3.

A similar kind of analysis for service industries is summarized in table 7. Note that the hierarchic pattern is perfectly realized for all 21 service industries. But when the component due to the broad categories, local vs. non-local services, is subtracted out, the index of ordinal arrangement falls to .29, certainly an unimpressive figure. Considering services separately, then, our conclusion—within the limits of inference imposed by the level of aggregation of the basic data—is that the hierarchic tendency is fully explained by the decreasing importance of local services, relative to non-local services, as size of community increases.

Table 7. Indexes of Dissimilarity of Urban Size-of-Place Groups with Respect to Service Industry Composition, United States: 1950

(Upper right half of table based on 21 service industries; in lower left half indexes based on 2 broad service categories have been subtracted from corresponding indexes in upper right half of table)

Size of place[1]	Size of place[1]						
	(1)	(2)	(3)	(4)	(5)	(6)	(7)
(1)	...	7.9	10.1	11.1	13.6	15.0	16.4
(2)	7.6	...	8.3	8.3	11.7	13.4	14.9
(3)	8.1	6.5	...	7.5	11.0	13.0	14.5
(4)	7.1	4.6	5.5	...	4.3	6.3	8.0
(5)	8.0	6.4	7.4	2.8	...	3.2	5.1
(6)	7.8	6.5	7.7	3.1	1.5	...	2.8
(7)	7.1	5.9	7.2	2.7	1.4	0.8	...

[1]See table 3 for identification of size-of-place groups.

SOURCE: See table 3.

The general conclusion from all three tables (5-7) is that the hierarchic pattern of variation revealed by a 41-industry classification is largely accounted for by the tendency of extractive, processing, and local service industries to relate inversely to city size and the complementary tendency of fabricating and non-local service industries to relate directly to city size. The conclusion must be phrased in terms of the particular industry classification used, however. There is evidence, for example, that a much more detailed breakdown of some categories of service industries than that afforded by the condensed classification will produce a hierarchic pattern, independent of the local vs. non-local grouping (Duncan, 1959b).

One further decomposition of the initial hierarchic pattern is considered in table 8, which gives a summary of results obtained by examining city-size group industry distributions within the four broad census regions. It should be stated at once that this particular regionalization corresponds to no particular hypothesis we have in mind. It, like the city-size categories, was introduced into the tabulations with a view toward comparability with the census size-of-place report. We may, if we like, think of the four regions as providing so many "replications" of our investigation for the United States. This view, however,

Table 8. Indexes of Ordinal Arrangement for Specified Matrixes of Index of Dissimilarity of Urban Size-of-Place Groups with Respect to Industry Composition, United States, by Census Regions: 1950

Census region	All industries			Manufacturing			Services		
	All (41) groups	7 categories	Residual	All (14) groups[2]	2 categories	Residual	All (21) groups	2 categories	Residual
Based on 7 size-of-place groups									
United States	.91	1.00	.54	.83	1.00	−.14	1.00	1.00	.29
Northeast	.91	.86	.37	.69	.54	−.06	.89	.54	.80
North Central	.63	.74	.40	.34	.17	.09	.91	.63	.66
South[1]	...	...	...	...	...	...	...	...	...
West	.94	.86	.60	.86	.83	−.23	.83	.26	.83
Based on 6 size-of-place groups									
United States	1.00	1.00	.95	1.00	1.00	.25	1.00	1.00	.25
Northeast	.95	.75	.35	.70	.35	.15	.85	.35	.80
North Central	.75	.75	.30	.55	.40	.00	.90	.50	.60
South	1.00	1.00	.45	1.00	1.00	.35	1.00	1.00	.55
West	1.00	.90	.50	.80	.75	−.45	.90	1.00	.70

[1] No places in size group (1) in the South.
[2] Excludes "not specified manufacturing industries."

SOURCE: See table 3.

may be inadequate, assuming the validity of our initial conclusion that the cities of the United States comprise a "system." There is no reason whatever to suppose that four arbitrary hunks of a system would each reproduce on a smaller scale all essential properties of that system. In fact, we can turn the argument around and suggest that if evidence for a hierarchic system is lacking when national data are subdivided by regions, but present at the national level of aggregation, then the system in question is in fact a national one and not a mere collection of similar regional systems.

The data in table 8 are in the form of indexes of ordinal arrangement pertaining to the tables already shown for the United States and to tables constructed in analogous fashion for each of the four regions. The analysis is a little messy, since one region lacks a city in the size group, 3,000,000 inhabitants or more. As an expedient to permit some comparison of other regions with the South, we show a panel of data based on the six categories of places smaller than this.

Considering first the data for all industries, we are impressed with the finding that each region, with the possible exception of the North Central, exhibits a strong or fairly strong hierarchic tendency, both in the indexes of dissimilarity based on 41 industry groups and in those based on seven broad categories. This tendency, however, weakens markedly when we test the pattern of the residuals of the 41-industry indexes from the 7-category indexes. Thus far, the regional breakdown confirms the national results, by way of replication.

For manufacturing (second three-column panel, table 8), the initial evidence for hierarchy within each region is not so consistent. In the South the pattern is perfect, both for the 14 manufacturing industries and the two broad categories thereof; in the West the hierarchic tendency is reasonably strong. Within the Northeast the hierarchic pattern weakens perceptibly, and in the North Central region it is not strong enough to be very interesting. In each region, as in the United States, little remains of the hierarchic pattern when the two-category indexes of dissimilarity are subtracted from the 14-industry indexes. Inspection of the original data pinpoints one source of the marked deviation from a hierarchic pattern in the North Central region. In this region there is a pronounced concentration of automobile manufacturing in city-size group (2)—Detroit—and in size group (4)—Flint, Lansing, Pontiac and South Bend. These two size groups are, therefore, unusually similar in manufacturing industry composition and differ considerably from the other size groups. (Note that the index of ordinal arrangement rises when the largest size group is omitted.) We are not using this interpretation of the results to "explain away" the lack of hierarchy for manufacturing industries in the North Central region. Instead, the conclusion is that one should not expect a very good approximation to hierarchy, as our methods reveal it, when dealing with a classification that is weighted heavily by a highly sporadic and highly localized industry like motor vehicle manufacturing.

Considering finally the service industries (last three columns of table 8), we observe that the hierarchic pattern is rather strong within each region, though perfect only in the South, as far as the distributions for all 21 service industries are concerned. There is little interregional consistency, however, in magnitudes of the index of ordinal arrangement for the indexes based on the two broad categories of services, local and non-local. The marked shift for the West between the results for six size groups and those for seven pinpoints the deviant behavior of the Los Angeles industrial profile. The significant factor is not, as one might imagine, that city's specialization in non-local entertainment and recreation services (this group includes the motion picture production industry), but rather the fact that it has exceptionally high proportions in all *local* services, as compared with city-size groups (2) to (5). Curiously enough, the residuals of the 21-group indexes from the two-category indexes manifest a weak tendency toward hierarchy in each region, though not in the United States as a whole, contrary to the finding for manufacturing, where there is no such tendency. To oversimplify the implications of these results for sake of a clean-cut conclusion, we are tempted to suggest that the urban hierarchy as far as manufacturing is concerned is truly national in scope while that for services is regional, in a broad sense, with the national hierarchy representing a summation of the regional ones with a few distinctively national features superimposed upon it.

At this point the reader—having been led through a tortuous sequence of problems of classification and the formation of indexes and of indexes to summarize the patterns of other indexes—may wonder what the fuss is all about. Our primary concern has been to give empirical content and support to the contention that the cities of the nation constitute a system. More specifically, we have tested the supposition that it is a hierarchic system and that the principle of hierarchy, whatever it may be, is more or less adequately indicated by city size. Our positive results on this count alone appear worthwhile, apart from subordinate conclusions. We need not recapitulate the latter here, but simply note that various of their implications are investigated at appropriate points throughout the remainder of the volume.

URBANIZATION OF INDUSTRY GROUPS

One implication of the foregoing results will be checked immediately. If there is a hierarchic pattern, and if a major aspect of the pattern is variation by size of city in such broad industry categories as extractive, processing, fabricating, local services, and non-local services, we should expect these categories of industries to group themselves rather distinctly in terms of their tendencies toward concentration in large or small urban communities. Such a grouping is evident in the array of industry groups by the index of urbanization within the five broad categories (excluding construction and industry not reported), shown in table 9. We shall comment further on these data after describing the rationale of the index of urbanization and its connection with the theoretical questions raised earlier.

While the previous section of this chapter investigated the industry composition of city-size groups, this section deals with the city-size distribution of industry groups. The viewpoint is changed although the data are the same. As the term is used here, urbanization refers to the extent to which an industry group is concentrated in cities of large size in comparison with the size-of-city distribution of the entire employed labor force. Figure 2 exhibits the urbanization curves of selected industries. These curves are constructed by plotting the cumulative percentage distribution of an industry group against the cumulated percentage distribution of all workers by size of city. The cumulation begins with the largest cities—size group (1)—and extends through the smallest—size group (7)—where the cumulated percentage is, of course, 100 for all industries. It is obvious on inspection that the apparel industry is concentrated in the largest cities, while mining is concentrated in the smallest. (Actually, the greater part of mining workers are found in rural areas, but we are considering only the urban labor force here.) In general, the farther the curve falls below the diagonal of proportional distribution the greater the degree of urbanization; the farther it lies above the curve, the less the urbanization. To reduce the comparisons to a numerical basis, one calculates the percentage of the area below the diagonal encompassed between the curve and the diagonal, using the convention that areas above the diagonal are negative in algebraic sign. The formula for this index of urbanization (an adaptation of the Gini concentration ratio for a Lorenz curve) is $(\Sigma X_{j-1} Y_j - \Sigma X_j Y_{j-1})/100$, where X_j is the cumulative percentage of employment in industry X through the jth city-size group, Y_j is the cumulative percentage of employment in all industries through the jth size group, and the summation is over all size groups. (The divisor, 100, is required to put the result in percentage form.) Because the industries differ somewhat in size of total employment, and thus in the proportions that they contribute to the total, comparisons between industries are less biased if the index of urbanization is adjusted. The adjustment is effected by dividing the index by one minus the proportion which the given industry forms of the total. This is tantamount to computing the index of urbanization as described

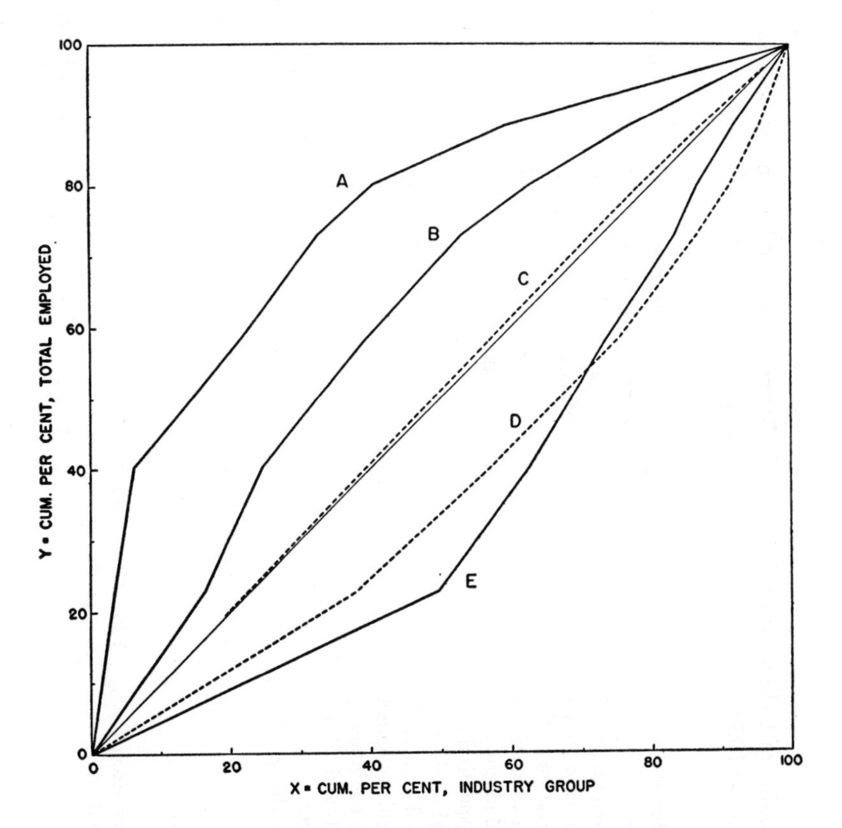

Figure 2. Urbanization Curves for Selected Industry Groups, based on Urban Size-of-Place Distributions, United States: 1950. (A—Mining; B—Furniture, and lumber and wood products; C—Food and dairy products stores and milk retailing; D—Business services; E—Apparel and other fabricated textile products.)

Table 9. Index of Urbanization for Each Industry, Based on Urban Size-of-Place Distributions, United States: 1950

Fabricating	Processing	Extractive	Local services	Non-local services
28 Apparel & other fabricated textile products				24 Business services
23 Transportation equipment, exc. motor veh.				19 Other transportation
18 Electrical machinery				
16 Printing, publishing & allied products				16 Finance, insurance and real estate
11 Fabricated metal ind.				
11 Motor vehicles & motor vehicle equipment				
7 Chemicals and allied products				7 Wholesale trade
6 Other durable goods			5 Other professional & related services	6 Entertainment & recreation services
				5 Telecommunications
	3 Primary metal ind.			3 Public administration
				2 Trucking service and warehousing
1 Machinery, except electrical	1 Food and kindred products			2 Educational services, private
			−1 Eating & drinkplaces	

		−2 Food & dairy prod. stores, and milk retailing	−2 Medical and other health services
		−3 Utilities and sanitary services	−3 Hotels and lodging places
−4 Other nondurable goods		−3 Other personal services	
		−5 Other retail trade	
		−9 Private households	−10 Railroads and railway express service
		−10 Repair services	−18 Educational services, government
−24 Furniture, & lumber & wood products			
−30 Textile mill products	−30 Forestry & fisheries		
	−43 Agriculture		
	−53 Mining		

NOTE: Construction (−5) and Manufacturing industries, not specified (16) are not shown.

SOURCE: See table 3.

above with Y as employment in all industries other than X, rather than in all industries. The indexes in table 9 were adjusted in this fashion. (For further discussion of the index of urbanization, see Duncan, 1952, 1959b; Winsborough, 1959b.)

Let us now consider reasons why urbanization indexes might be expected to show significant between-category variation. If in a hierarchic system "the populations of cities tend to be directly proportional to their maximum hinterlands" (Hoover, 1955, p. 197), we should expect to find industries with large non-local market areas concentrated in large cities. While we have no precise way of estimating the "range of a good" as applied to the industry groups under study here, we have attempted to distinguish crudely between services thought to have extensive non-local service areas and those assumed to be primarily local in orientation. Thus we expect non-local services to have higher urbanization indexes than local.

Extractive industries are not really "central" activities at all, but rather "field" activities. It should be remembered in this connection that the census labor force data are compiled on the basis of where people live, rather than where they work. Hence if persons engaged in mining or agriculture are found living in central places it does not necessarily follow that mining or agricultural activities are carried on in those places. We can be sure, however, that extractive activities are carried on where there is some resource that lends itself to extraction. If the resource is one that occurs sporadically (e.g., minerals), then (*ceteris paribus*) we expect to find that the central places most accessible thereto are more often small than large, since there are more small places than large ones. If the resource is relatively ubiquitous but covers extensive areas (e.g., agricultural land), the average accessibility of the resource to small places must be greater than to large places, for the same reason. Hence we expect that the residences of persons in the extractive sector of the labor force will show a very low degree of urbanization.

The classification of manufacturing industries—processing vs. fabricating—has to do with type of input rather than with what the location theorist calls "orientation" as such. Yet if there are industries oriented to raw materials, we should surely expect to find them among processing industries rather than among fabricating industries. The latter, we may presume, are more likely to be oriented to markets—either to final consumer markets or to other industries for which fabricated products constitute inputs. By analogy with extractive industries, therefore, we expect processing industries to show a low degree of urbanization, while fabricating industries would be expected to locate more often in large centers for convenient access to the concentrated markets afforded by these centers or to their nodal positions on long-distance transportation networks.

The foregoing expectations are realized by and large in the data shown in table 9. The lowest urbanization indexes appear for the three extractive industries, and this category barely overlaps that of the processing industries. Processing industries in turn have markedly lower urbanization indexes on the whole than fabricating industries, with the slight overlap involving only one industry in the latter category. The services are not quite so well behaved. We do find some relatively high urbanization indexes among non-local services, and none among local services. However, two of the non-local services have indexes as low as the lowest among local services. The lowest urbanization index for a service industry (—18 for educational services, government) is easily accounted for by the location of many state colleges in small towns and to some extent, perhaps, by a tendency of parochial (classified as "private") elementary and secondary schools to occur more often in large than in small cities. The low urbanization index for railroads and railway express service no doubt reflects the "sporadic occurrence" of railroad repair shops, division points, classification yards, etc., which have made "railroad towns" of some small and medium-sized cities (Alexandersson, 1956, p. 92). We must be careful, however, not to press too hard for an explanation of the finding that local and non-local services are only partly discriminated by the index of urbanization, in view of the crudeness of the initial classification itself.

We now raise the question of how consistently industries are differentiated by the index of urbanization from one broad census region to another, bearing in mind the qualifications placed on such a regional comparison in the previous section. Table 10 shows for selected sets of industries the (Pearsonian) correlation between the urbanization indexes of each pair of the four census regions. The correlation coefficients are all positive, which means that there is at least some tendency for industries with high urbanization indexes in one region to have high indexes in the other regions and for low urbanization indexes to be found among the industries of one region if the same industries have low indexes in other regions. However, the magnitude of some of the correlations is low, and five of the six coefficients for the manufacturing industries taken separately are too low to be statistically significant by the conventional test. The coefficients are materially higher for the service industries as a group. The pronounced difference between the results for manufacturing and those for services is consistent with the earlier finding that hierarchic tendencies in the industry distributions are more evident within regions for services than for manufacturing.

Table 10. Zero-Order Correlations of Adjusted Urbanization Indexes between Pairs of Regions, United States: 1950

Region	Region: North Central	South	West
	All groups (38 industries)[1]		
Northeast	.67**	.50**	.42**
North Central	...	.76**	.72**
South	...	...	.57**
	Manufacturing (14 industries)		
Northeast	.29	.22	.22
North Central	...	.20	.46*
South	...	...	.39
	Services (21 industries)		
Northeast	.74**	.43*	.80**
North Central	...	.70**	.59**
South	...	...	.56**

[1] Omits construction, not specified manufacturing industries, and industry not reported.

* Significantly different from zero at .05 level of probability.

** Significantly different from zero at .01 level of probability.

One point of interpretation is especially relevant to the manufacturing industries. As has been pointed out more than once already, the degree of aggregation is rather high in the industry groups of the condensed classification. Moreover, in making comparisons between regions we encounter the problem that the components of an industry group may differ markedly from region to region. For example, study of the detailed industry statistics in the census reveals that "furniture, and lumber and wood products" is heavily weighted with "furniture and fixtures" in the Northeast and North Central regions and with "sawmills, planing mills, and mill work" in the South and West. Only in the latter two regions, therefore, is "furniture, and lumber and wood products" primarily a processing industry; in the other two it is much more like a fabricating industry. Accordingly, we are not surprised that its index of urbanization varies from region to region as follows: Northeast, —12; North Central, —16; South, —27; and West, —26.

We illustrate some further ramifications of the aggregation problem and simultaneously bring out some additional substantive points in the presentation of the final body of data to be considered in this chapter. These data concern the detailed industries making up the "business services" group in the condensed classification. It is recalled from table 9 that the business services group has a comparatively high index of urbanization, 24; its index is also rather consistently high in all regions, ranging from 15 in the West to 26 in the Northeast. The detailed breakdown of business services comes from a quite different source from that of the labor force statistics, and the form of the data differs in a number of significant details. The source is the *1954 Census of Business*. Data pertain to volume of receipts of business services establishments (rather than employment). The city-size classification is based on political cities rather than urbanized areas, and the size categories are not the same as those we have been using up to now. Urbanization is measured in the way described previously, but in terms of the comparison between cumulated percentages of service receipts and cumulated percentages of resident population, rather than between two employment series. Consequently, the urbanization indexes cannot be compared directly with those given previously; only comparisons internal to table 11 are legitimate.

In addition to the urbanization index for each business service industry, table 11 indicates a "critical size of city" for each. This is simply the size interval where the number of business service establishments reported in the *Census of Business* falls below the number of cities in the interval. At larger sizes, where the number of establishments exceeds the number of cities, we can assume that virtually every city has at least one establishment, although this may not be strictly true. Our first observation is that none of the kinds of business shown in table 11 appears regularly below a city-size limit of 10,000 inhabitants. (The "other, n.e.c." category—actually a congeries of quite diverse industries—is disregarded in the foregoing statement.) At least two of the business services, "news syndicates" and "advertising agencies," undoubtedly are representatives of a class of "central" services which occur characteristically quite high in the urban hierarchy. (Although the critical city size for "advertising agencies" is correctly identified as

10,000–25,000, the agencies found in the smaller cities and towns are quite small in average size as compared with the major agencies located in big cities.)

Table 11. Index of Urbanization and Critical City Size for Each Kind of Business Services, United States: 1954

Kind of business	Critical city size (1,000's)	Index of urbanization
News syndicates	250–500	80
Advertising agencies	10–25	76
Outdoor advertising services	25–50	52
Miscellaneous advertising	50–100	68
Detective agencies	50–100	69
Duplicating, addressing, mailing, stenographic services	10–25	65
Private employment agencies	25–50	63
Blueprinting, photocopying services	50–100	62
Window display service	50–100	59*
Services to dwellings, other buildings:		
Window cleaning	10–25	59
Disinfecting, exterminating	10–25	45
Miscellaneous	10–25	59
Telephone answering service	25–50	56
Consumer, mercantile credit; adjustment, collection agencies	10–25	55
Photofinishing laboratories	25–50	55*
Interior decorating service	25–50	45
Sign painting shops	25–50	40
Coin-operated machine rental, repair services	100–250	33
Auctioneers' establishments (service only)	100–250	21
Other business services (n. e. c.)	2.5–5	44

* Estimate subject to minor error (data withheld on disclosure rule).

SOURCE: Duncan (1959b, table 2), based on data from the *1954 Census of Business.*

It is uncertain how many of the remaining kinds of business should be recognized as examples of the central-place principle. The fact that several are found regularly in cities of around 25,000 population suggests the possibility that some of them serve units located in smaller towns as well as local concerns, but we lack data on the extent to which this may be the case. Yet, it seems unlikely that such an enterprise as "telephone answering" involves services to a non-local clientele to any great degree. We are tempted to think that the primary principle accounting for the urbanization of most of the business services is that a specialized demand arises in larger places when enough local business units requiring such services are present.

In fact, these data appear to point up fairly severe limitations on the ability of strict central-place theory to account for variation in degree of urbanization among business service industries. To bring out these limitations, we must first recall that "one important element in central place theory is the notion of the *range* of a good"; and, according to Berry and Garrison (1958c, p. 304), "this range marks out the zone or tributary area around a central place (urban center) from which persons travel to the center to purchase the good." This formulation, of course, is closely related to Lösch's (1954) concept of the "market area," provided we include the possibility of shipment of goods outward from the center to the market area or the provision of services in that area by units located at the center, irrespective of whether customers actually travel to the center. Now, implicit or explicit in the central-place scheme is the supposition that an entire regional or national economy may be subdivided into the market areas for a particular good, service, or class of goods or services. Thus if we know which centers provide the good or service in question, we can calculate the average size of market area and say something about its structure. For example, if a given service is performed by all towns and cities of 18,000 inhabitants or more and only by such centers, we know that the market areas for this service include towns smaller than 18,000, villages, and open country territory.

Our evidence, summarized by means of urbanization indexes and critical city sizes, does not directly test the assumption involved in the centrality principle. However, table 11 shows that there are numerous kinds of business identified in census statistics on service trades that do not appear often enough in small towns for one to suppose that their "ranges" or "market areas" are made up primarily of village and open country areas, while many of the more highly urbanized services do not appear *prima facie* to be kinds of activity for which the market areas would include the numerous towns and cities of smaller size lacking such service establishments. Two of the business services examined do indeed represent the centrality or hierarchy principle: news syndicates and advertising agencies. It may be that we have failed to recognize some others which likewise exemplify this principle. Yet it seems most unlikely that all the service trades with moderately high or high urbanization indexes and critical city sizes of, say, 25,000–50,000 or more actually have "ranges" encompassing towns lower down in the hierarchy as well as villages and open country areas. In short, *the differentiation and specialization of service trades with increasing city size can be explained to only a small degree by principles stemming from the central-place scheme.*

Admittedly, central-place theory has not attempted to explain all aspects of urban structural differentiation. Yet in reading the literature dealing with the urban hierarchy it is difficult not to form the impression that centrality is supposed to account for much if not all of the variation in economic structure observed to be correlated with size of center. The proponents of the hierarchy idea have not felt it necessary to recognize other principles. The theory of central places suggests that large cities specialize in economic activities which have broad market areas. But we may note at least three supplementary principles which must be added to account for forms of specialization for which this explanation does not hold but which are, nevertheless, observed in large cities:

(1) Conditions of life in large cities generate certain "needs" or "tastes" not typical of small cities.

(2) As city size increases, certain services performed by households or business units for themselves are demanded in sufficient quantity to support specialized units supplying them. This is the familiar principle of "external economies of scale." The important thing to notice, however, is that the emergence of such services with increasing city size does not require one to think in terms of sizable non-local market areas. (Incidentally, this illustrates one of the difficulties with the economic base idea. If, for example, a manufacturing establishment engaged in producing for "export" hires janitors to wash windows, their wages appear in the value added for basic industries. But if the services of an establishment specializing in window cleaning are purchased, receipts from these services appear in totals for "non-basic" industries.)

(3) With increasing city size, services performed by generalized units are taken over in part by units specialized in a restricted line of services. This division of labor with increase in the extent of the local market does not presuppose either an increase in the per capita volume of the particular service performed by all types of unit combined or an

extension of the market area for the service—although both these factors may be concomitants, to be sure.

In short, intensive examination of urbanization indexes for detailed industries leads us to place some qualifications on the earlier conclusion that a hierarchic tendency is clear in city-size comparisons of industry distributions. That there is such a tendency cannot be denied. Nor is there any question that size of community is somehow closely connected with whatever it is that produces a hierarchy. Yet we have found enough evidence of conflicting results from different bodies of evidence that we should probably reopen the issue stated at the outset as to whether an urban hierarchy can be depicted realistically in terms of a single dimension of variation. Moreover, we have discovered a number of kinds of industrial variation by city size that cannot be accounted for on the basis of deductions from the central-place scheme. Therefore, the urban hierarchy that one might delineate empirically, taking account of city size, would not necessarily be a central-place hierarchy. Valuable as it is, the central-place model is only one tool for the understanding of a system of cities. Few of the other available tools boast so elegant a form; nevertheless, they must be used if we are to understand the salient properties of the system.

CHAPTER 4

Metropolitanism and Metropolitan Areas

There is, of course, no possibility of determining what a metropolis "really is," statistically or otherwise, because "metropolis" is a category, concept, or construct devised by social scientists to order their data, and the category is given different contents by different investigators. To make an intelligent choice among alternative versions of the concept, it is necessary to understand how these differences arise. In reviewing various outstanding discussions of metropolitanism we are not undertaking a semantic exercise for its own sake; instead, we are trying to identify quickly some salient features of the structure of contemporary communities which have led numerous research workers to seize upon "metropolis" and "metropolitan" as classificatory and heuristic concepts.

CRITERIA OF METROPOLITANISM

The concept of "metropolis" does not belong to any one writer or school of thought; it has been used so widely and diffusely that every investigator has both the liberty and the responsibility to define it in a way that seems suitable for his purposes. However, a starting point for much of the recent discussion of metropolitanism is the work of

N.S.B. Gras (1922a, b). His formulations were stated so generally that several varieties of specific, operational constructs have seemed consistent with them.

Gras (1926, pp. 183-189) proposed an account of economic evolution which recognizes

> five forms of general economic organization. These are collectional economy, cultural nomadic economy, settled village economy, town economy, and now, in modern times, metropolitan economy. . . . The new metropolitan economy was based upon an internal organization of productive forces and an external relationship with other units either of the same order or of more primitive form. Internally the new unit was made up of a great commercial city as nucleus and a large surrounding area as *hinterland*. . . . In the big surrounding area of the unit were the towns and the farms, the railroads and the mines, the canals and the forests. . . . The dependence of center and area might be great, but it did not preclude a further dependence on other metropolitan units or on distant-town economic units, where the latter still existed. Indeed, one of the chief functions of the great commercial center was to establish and maintain connections with the rest of the world . . . in the metropolitan center, are the specializing agencies which manage the exchange of the whole group. . . . Generally speaking . . . a metropolitan community arises at a favorable conjunction of two circumstances, the economic development of the *hinterland* and the rise of business ability and organization in the center.

It is worth noting that, although this formulation identifies the metropolitan area as a spatial unit and suggests a considerable size as a salient feature, neither spatial structure nor size of population, but rather function is identified as the touchstone of metropolitanism. Thus Gras (1922a, p. 294) suggests as "criteria of a fully developed metropolis" the following:

> The population of the metropolis would be large, as compared with the population of other cities in the district. This comparative advantage, however, would be suggestive, not final. The metropolis would have a relatively large proportion of workers engaged in wholesaling and relatively few in manufacture, when compared with other large cities in the district. And there would be a lack of any marked dependence on a neighboring center for trade and transportation. . . . If statistics proved that its loans to the surrounding area were large (especially its discounts of commercial paper), then it would be classed as a fully developed (in function) metropolitan center. Or we may put it this way: that city is a full-fledged metropolis when most kinds of products of the district concentrate in it for trade as well as transit; when these products are paid for by wares

> that radiate from it; and when the necessary financial transactions involved in this exchange are provided by it.

Although we are not here concerned with the validity of Gras's account of economic evolution, we may take note of his scheme of "phases" in the emergence of metropolitan economy, because these indicate the major classes of functions he attributed to a developed metropolis. The four phases are (1) organizing the market, (2) industrial development, (3) development of transportation, and (4) development of financial organization.

Because Gras and other writers speak of the "dominance" of the metropolis, and some critics have charged them with regarding "dominance" as a unilateral exercise of influence, it is well to point out that no sophisticated writer on metropolitanism has ever conceived of "dominance" as other than a form of mutual interdependence. In the words of Gras (1922a, p. 187),

> It is true that in studying this organization we are inclined to emphasize the great metropolitan center; but to forget the large dependent district would be fatal to a correct understanding of the subject. Perhaps, indeed, it is somewhat incorrect to speak of the area as dependent upon the center, for, though that is true, the center is also dependent upon the outlying area with its towns, villages, and scattered homesteads. Interdependence of the parts is really the key to the whole situation.

The concept of "metropolitan community" developed by McKenzie (1933), although related to and partly derived from Gras's formulation, placed greater emphasis upon settlement pattern and the role of automobile transportation in integrating the elements of the metropolitan region. In general, McKenzie's "metropolitan community" or "metropolitan region" is a much more limited areal unit than Gras's "hinterland." The following statements convey the essential points:

> This new type of regional community that is emerging from the former pattern of semi-independent units of settlement is, of course, the direct result of motor transportation and its revolutionary effect upon local spatial relations. . . . The coming of the motor vehicle and the paved highway, the expansion of the press and other agencies of communication have brought the city and its hinterland into a closer functional relation. . . . The metropolitan region . . . is primarily a functional entity. Geographically it extends as far as the city exerts a dominant influence. It is essentially an expanded pattern of local communal life based upon motor transportation. . . . The metropolitan region represents a constellation of centers, the interrelations of which are characterized by dominance and subordi-

> nation. Every region is organized around a central city or focal point of dominance in which are located the institutions and services that cater to the region as a whole and integrate it with other regions. . . . Certain functions, notably communications, finance, management, and the more specialized commercial and professional services, are becoming more highly concentrated in or near the center of the dominant city. (McKenzie, 1933, pp. 69-71.)

Bogue (1949) was apparently influenced by this emphasis on "local spatial relations" in his definitive study of metropolitan dominance. This emphasis leads to a focus of attention on the internal structure of the metropolitan community, as is apparent in the following summary of Bogue's interpretation of findings:

> The metropolitan community thus appears to be an organization of many mutually interdependent and inter-functioning subcommunities oriented about the hinterland cities, which, in turn, are subdominant to and interdependent with the dominant metropolis, and inter-function with it. The entire community organization appears to be held together by a system of community specialization in, and exchange of, locally produced surpluses to fill those needs which cannot be most efficiently satisfied by local institutions. (Bogue, 1949, p. 59.)

A considerable portion of Bogue's study rests upon the comparison of metropolitan centers with hinterland zones in respect to levels of production or activity in manufactures, trade, and service industries. On the basis of regressions of "indexes of specialization" in these "sustenance activities" on "distance from the nearest metropolis," Bogue (1949, p. 40) concludes that "every zone in the hinterland is dependent upon the metropolis for wholesale trade and services, and that the outer zones are dependent upon the metropolis and the inner zones for manufacturing." One must be very careful not to misinterpret this result. On the face of it, the author appears to be asserting that each metropolitan community is structured in terms of a division of labor among metropolitan center, inner zones, and outer zones, such that the center performs wholesale and service functions not only for itself but also for the inner and outer zones, while the center and inner zones combined perform manufacturing for the entire community. From such a portrayal, one gains the impression that the implicit model is that of von Thünen's "isolated state" (see Melamid, 1955) wherein center and outlying zones constitute a self-sufficient system. Bogue was aware that his research design was inadequate to distinguish between intra-metropolitan and inter-metropolitan division of labor and specialization, for he remarks that his scheme implicitly assumes

> that each metropolis provides all of the dominance which may exist in its surrounding hinterland. This, of course, is not strictly true. . . . Metropolitan influence, apparently, can extend completely across several intervening metropolitan areas. In other words, beyond the metropolitan economy there is the intermetropolitan or national economy, in which each of the various metropolitan centers diffuses its dominance over the entire nation and in which each center is itself but a unit joined with other metropolises in a division of labor. (Bogue, 1949, p. 27.)

Certainly we know that some "metropolitan centers" (as Bogue defines them) and their contiguous zones do not produce all the manufactured goods sold in their more distant zones. In fact, as material in later chapters illustrates abundantly, the division of labor in respect to manufactures is rather seldom on an intra-metropolitan community basis. The major import of Bogue's results, therefore, is the demonstration of a division of labor between metropolitan (central) and nonmetropolitan (hinterland) parts of the total national economy rather than simply between each metropolitan center and its own hinterland.

Thus, from the review of McKenzie and Bogue we gain an impression of the danger in overemphasizing one criterion of metropolitanism: that a metropolis is a city which dominates its hinterland. Or, to put it another way, the category of "dominance" must not be construed to apply solely to metropolis-hinterland relationships within a hypothetically self-sufficient metropolitan region; instead, a major subcategory of the functions considered as expressions of dominance embraces those wherein the metropolis mediates relationships between the metropolitan region and other parts of the national, or even international, economy. (See especially Pappenfort, 1959, and our discussion thereof in chapter 7.)

The discussion of the metropolis by Florence (1955) interests us for two particular reasons; first, it places uncommon emphasis on size as a criterion of metropolitan status; second, it explicitly relates the concept of metropolis to that of the urban hierarchy (see our discussion of the latter in chapter 3). Florence uses the term "metropolis" to refer to the biggest city in a country, but applies the adjective "metropolitan" to the next few largest cities or areal concentrations of population. He suggests that populations of one or two million might be used to identify metropolitan cities and metropolitan areas, respectively, on an absolute size criterion. Actually, not much of the discussion is given over to a defense of these suggestions; rather, the author is concerned to gauge the economic efficiency of the metropolis and to ascertain its characteristic and distinctive functions. Analyzing employment data by means of location quotients, Florence (1955, p. 110ff.) concludes that the following are among the more significant metropolitan functions: "acting as headquarters of finance and of certain business services like accounting and technical advice"; communication, "represented by the publishing of newspapers and of periodicals and books and by various publishing and printing services"; and "leading scientific progress"—all of which functions "suggest that the metropolis is a clearinghouse as well as a reserve or pool of distributable resources and a brain and nerve center for economic action." But the metropolis also excels in economic activities catering to cultured and luxury tastes; it is a center of entertainment and specialized recreational services; and it provides a wide range of specialized professional services: "The variety of activities of a metropolis . . . includes highly special activities which only it performs on any substantial scale." In summary of his conclusions, Florence (1955, p. 116) presents the following scheme of "the hierarchy of city functions":

Metropolitan Area (over 1,000,000 population)
Finance and business services
Book and periodical publishing and printing services
Science
Arts
Applied arts
Entertainment

Large City (200,000 to 1,000,000 population)
Wholesaling
Public services
Newspaper publishing

Middling City (25,000 to 200,000 population)
Public utilities
Commercial printing
Baking and bottling of beverages
Construction activities
Professional services (school teachers, general practitioners, and so on)
Eating and drinking locals
Retailing

In this scheme it is considered that the metropolitan area performs not only its own functions, but also those attributed to the large city and the middling city; whereas the large city performs functions of the middling city as well as those distinguishing it from the latter. No firm basis is given for the classifications in this scheme; but it does illustrate the possibility of treating metropolitan status as a particular level of functional specialization in an urban hierarchy. We may note, too, that there appears to be an implicit assumption that population size is a reliable indicator of a city's place in the hierarchy. Friedmann (1956) presents a somewhat more elaborate statement of the place of the metropolis in the urban hierarchy, based in part on the statement by Florence.

The notion of hierarchy is worked out in a more taxonomic fashion by Vance and Smith (1954); however, this is but one noteworthy feature of their work, which has value, among other things, as a summary of previous efforts to identify metropolitan centers in the United States. The authors make a critical distinction at the outset of their study of metropolitan dominance and integration in the southern states:

> Whereas urbanization may refer to any aspect of population agglomeration, metropolitanism should be reserved for the organizational component that great cities impose upon the urbanization process. Any city with a large population is usually referred to as a metropolis, but it may be well to point out that while all metropolises are large cities, not all large cities are metropolises. Population size is a concomitant; function is the keynote.

As a preliminary to classifying southern cities by metropolitan status, Vance and Smith devised an index of dominance, which is a weighted sum of six variables selected as indicators, on the one hand, of "high-level distribution, specialization, and control" and, on the other hand, of "the gross underpinnings a city has for building its market and amassing wealth." The six variables are wholesale sales, business services receipts, number of manufacturing branch offices, retail sales, bank clearings, and value added by manufacturing. Although each of these variables is expressed in absolute, rather than per capita form, it is found that the composite index by no means correlates perfectly with population size. The accompanying diagram (figure 3) will serve both to identify the categories of metropolitan status suggested by Vance and Smith on the basis of their index and to indicate the way in which they chose to depict their notions of metropolitan integration. Unfortunately, they are not very explicit about the meaning of "major lines of integration" nor their procedures for recognizing same.

The distinction by Vance and Smith between "national" and "super" types of metropolis and the remaining levels is reminiscent of an earlier discussion which may be noted here:

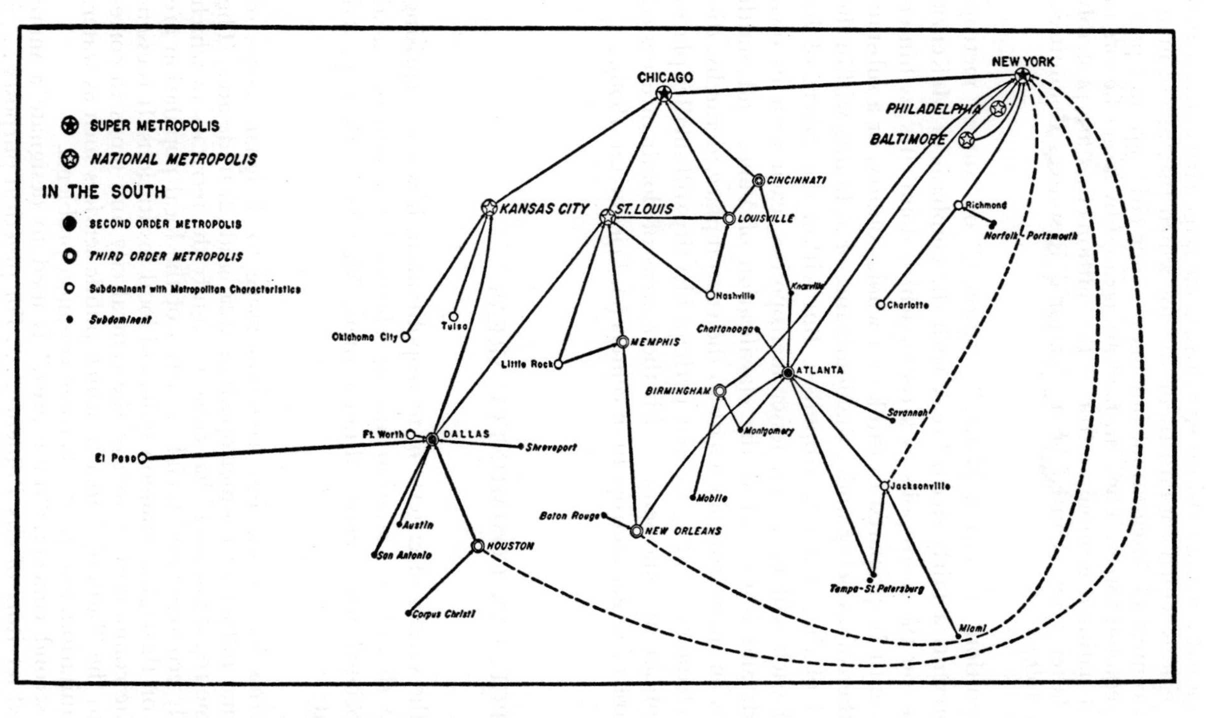

Figure 3. Metropolitan Organization of the South, with Orders of Dominance and Major Lines of Integration, According to Vance and Smith (1954)

> Metropoli [sic] are geographically of two kinds—regional foci and supraregional creations. In other words, some large cities are created by the regions which contain them and for which they are in many respects centers of integration, but many other cities are not products of regional forces. These instead are created by larger factors in the total national economy. Most of the million-cities are probably of this latter type. (United States National Resources Committee, 1935, p. 159.)

The recognition of "supraregional," "national," or "super" metropolises represents a fairly sharp break with the emphasis of McKenzie and Bogue on the metropolis as a center which dominates its hinterland. We must be prepared to think of a whole country, or a substantial part thereof, as being under the dominance or as falling within the hinterland of these giant metropolises. But within the sphere of influence of each will be found lesser metropolises, each with its own hinterland; and if we follow the classification of Vance and Smith (which has an interesting similarity to the central-place hierarchy, discussed in chapters 2 and 3), we may perhaps identify still smaller places —metropolitan in some sense—with their areas of dominance nested within those of larger metropolitan centers (cf. Friedmann, 1956).

METROPOLITAN COMMUNITY AREAS

Given the variety of criteria of metropolitanism, it is not surprising that there should be variation among schemes for delimiting areal units associated with metropolitan centers. McKenzie (1933, p. 84) noted that

> Two terms have come into common usage to designate zones of communal influence: (1) metropolitan area; and (2) trade area. The term "metropolitan area" has come to signify the territory in which the daily economic and social activities of the local population are carried on through a common system of local institutions. It is essentially the commutation area of the central city and tends to correspond to the "built-up" area in which public services such as water, light, sanitation, and power become common problems.
>
> The second concept, "trade area," is used to designate a more extended territory of city influence. . . . For practical purposes . . . a city's trade area may be defined . . . as "the surrounding geographical territory economically tributary to a city and for which such city provides the chief market and financial center."

Hawley (1950, pp. 245-258) gives a careful discussion of the problem of identifying "community areas," which emphasizes the "varying degrees of distinctness" of boundaries, their temporal instability, and the interpenetration of community areas; the implication is that a community may have more than one boundary, depending on the functions under scrutiny. He suggests a useful, though somewhat abstract, distinction among "primary," "secondary," and "tertiary" community areas. A somewhat similar distinction is employed by L. P. Green (1957, pp. 709-710), whose formulation is interesting for its attempt to link the concept of economic base (see chapter 2) with the problem of identifying the metropolitan area:

> Intensive study of the economies of metropolitan regions shows that their economic functions may be classed as either basic or non-basic. The basic functions are those performed for markets mainly outside the region, such as mining or steel-making, where the product is exported to earn regional imports rather than consumed locally within the region. The non-basic functions are those performed for markets mainly within the region, such as the running of departmental and provision stores, whose supplies are not normally exported. The wealth and prosperity of the region ultimately depend upon its basic economic functions. Its boundaries depend very much upon the service areas of its non-basic economic functions . . . most metropolitan regions today seem to have two main boundaries and one subsidiary boundary. At the centre is the city hub or central business district, with its great buildings, soaring land values and congested traffic. Outside the subsidiary boundary of this hub is the rest of the metropolitan zone proper embracing a population in daily contact with the hub and whose limits determine the first of the two main boundaries. Beyond the metropolitan zone proper lies an extensive and expanding zone embracing more remote areas whose inhabitants, although not in daily contact, are economically dependent on the hub for many specialized services. Its boundary, in itself an indeterminate and shifting zone, marks the confines of the metropolitan region and the limit of the hub's regional attraction.

This formulation calls attention to the interregional functions of metropolises as well as the functions they perform directly for their hinterlands; it explicitly avoids any suggestion that the metropolitan region is a self-sufficient economy. By discussing the economic base of the entire metropolitan region, however, it bypasses the question of the economic base of the metropolis proper, in which many writers would include "functions performed for markets within the region" insofar as these markets lie outside the metropolitan center.

Beginning with the economic and population censuses of 1947-50, government statistical agencies have made extensive use of the concept of "standard metropolitan area" (SMA). Because many statistical series are now reported for these units, we shall be using them extensively throughout the present study. Although, like any general-purpose set of tabulation units, SMA's have deficiencies and offer analytical inconveniences of one kind or another (see Duncan, 1956a), they have gained widespread acceptance (Shryock, 1957). The SMA concept had a number of predecessors in previous attempts to delimit statistical areas, recognizing functional entities extending beyond the corporate boundaries of large cities; however, we need not review the evolution of the concept here (see Shryock, 1957). The SMA is essentially an operational specification for what McKenzie called the "metropolitan area" and Green the "metropolitan zone proper" (in the quotations given earlier).

> In essence . . . an S.M.A. starts out with a city of 50,000 or more. It includes the whole county containing that city. It also includes any contiguous county that meets the criteria of a metropolitan character and of economic and social integration with the central county. (Shryock, 1957, p. 165.)

The "metropolitan character" of counties was ascertained from the numbers and proportions of nonagricultural workers; their "integration" with the center was inferred from information on commutation and telephone calls between central and outlying counties. Roughly speaking, then, the SMA may be interpreted as a commutation area, a housing market area, and, perhaps most important here, as a labor market area. The last interpretation has been widely accepted; thus Mattila and Thompson (1955, p. 215) state: "the labor market for most local industries is conceived as being roughly coincident with the metropolitan area." Figure 4 shows the location of the 151 SMA's which, in 1950, had populations of 100,000 or more. An additional 17 SMA's with populations between 50,000 and 100,000 were recognized in the 1950 Census; but there is considerable question as to their "metropolitan" qualifications as judged by any criterion other than the rather liberal one of a mere 50,000 population in the central city. Some of the vagaries of the SMA system, occasioned by its delimitation (except in New England) on the basis of county units, are evident from the map.

Although difficult problems are encountered and arbitrary proce-

---

Figure 4 (opposite). Standard Metropolitan Areas with Populations of 100,000 or More: 1950. (Based on a map by the United States Bureau of the Census.)

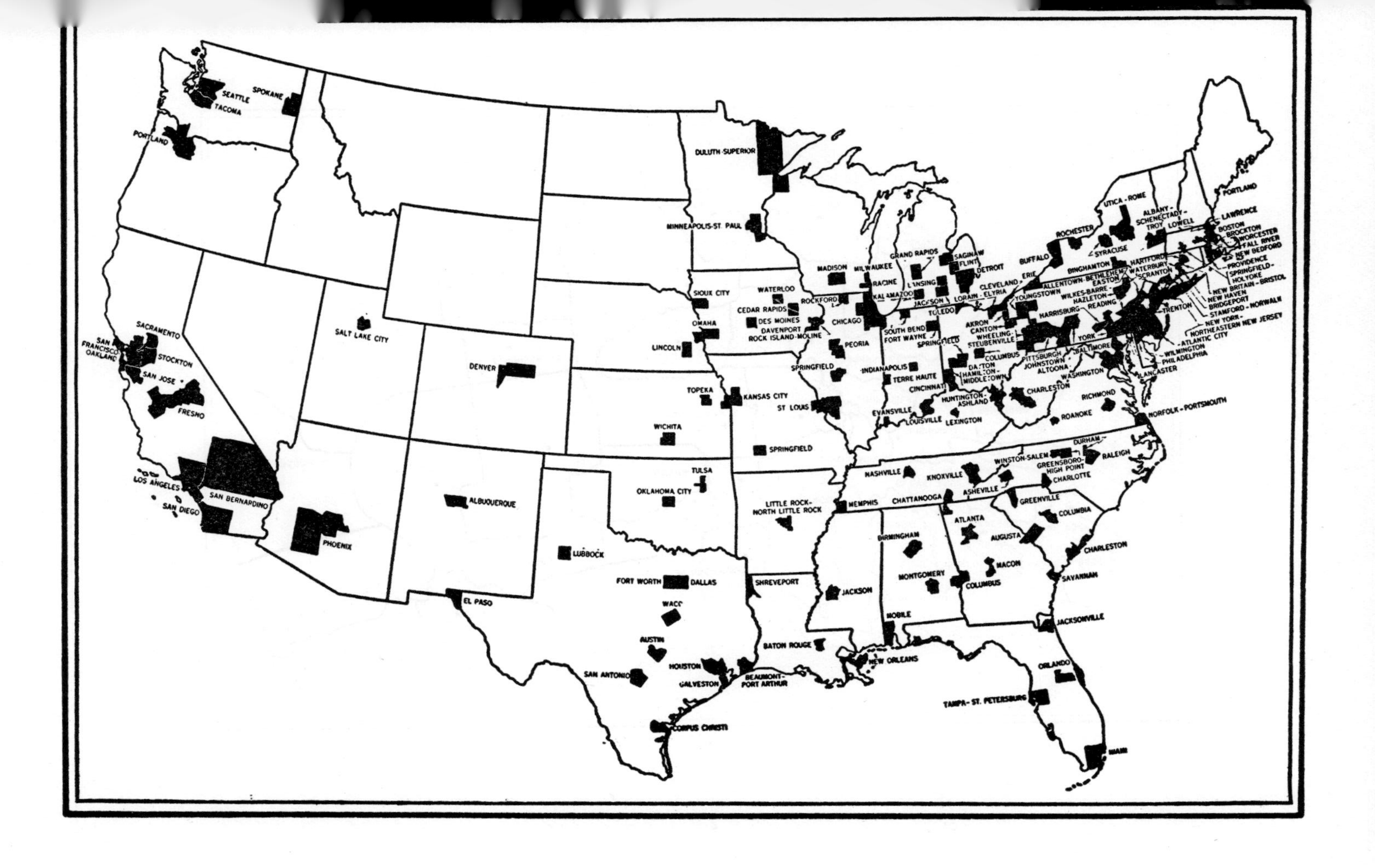
SEATTLE
TACOMA
SPOKANE
PORTLAND
SACRAMENTO
SAN FRANCISCO OAKLAND
STOCKTON
SAN JOSE
FRESNO
LOS ANGELES
SAN BERNARDINO
SAN DIEGO
PHOENIX
SALT LAKE CITY
DENVER
ALBUQUERQUE
EL PASO
LUBBOCK
FORT WORTH
DALLAS
WACO
AUSTIN
SAN ANTONIO
HOUSTON
GALVESTON
CORPUS CHRISTI
BEAUMONT-PORT ARTHUR
DULUTH-SUPERIOR
MINNEAPOLIS-ST. PAUL
SIOUX CITY
OMAHA
LINCOLN
TOPEKA
KANSAS CITY
WICHITA
TULSA
OKLAHOMA CITY
WATERLOO
CEDAR RAPIDS
DES MOINES
DAVENPORT ROCK ISLAND-MOLINE
ST LOUIS
SPRINGFIELD
LITTLE ROCK-NORTH LITTLE ROCK
SHREVEPORT
BATON ROUGE
NEW ORLEANS
MADISON
MILWAUKEE
RACINE
ROCKFORD
CHICAGO
PEORIA
SPRINGFIELD
GRAND RAPIDS
KALAMAZOO
LANSING
JACKSON
SAGINAW
FLINT
DETROIT
TOLEDO
SOUTH BEND
FORT WAYNE
INDIANAPOLIS
TERRE HAUTE
EVANSVILLE
LOUISVILLE
LEXINGTON
CINCINNATI
DAYTON
HAMILTON-MIDDLETOWN
SPRINGFIELD
COLUMBUS
HUNTINGTON-ASHLAND
CHARLESTON
CLEVELAND
LORAIN-ELYRIA
AKRON
CANTON
WHEELING-STEUBENVILLE
YOUNGSTOWN
PITTSBURGH
JOHNSTOWN
ALTOONA
ERIE
BUFFALO
ROCHESTER
SYRACUSE
UTICA-ROME
ALBANY-SCHENECTADY-TROY
BINGHAMTON
ALLENTOWN-BETHLEHEM-EASTON
WILKES-BARRE-HAZLETON
SCRANTON
READING
HARRISBURG
YORK
LANCASTER
BALTIMORE
WASHINGTON
TRENTON
PHILADELPHIA
WILMINGTON
ATLANTIC CITY
NORTHEASTERN NEW JERSEY
NEW YORK-
STAMFORD-NORWALK
BRIDGEPORT
NEW HAVEN
NEW BRITAIN-BRISTOL
WATERBURY
HARTFORD
SPRINGFIELD-HOLYOKE
PROVIDENCE
NEW BEDFORD
FALL RIVER
WORCESTER
BROCKTON
BOSTON
LOWELL
LAWRENCE
PORTLAND
RICHMOND
ROANOKE
NORFOLK-PORTSMOUTH
DURHAM
RALEIGH
WINSTON-SALEM
GREENSBORO-HIGH POINT
CHARLOTTE
ASHEVILLE
KNOXVILLE
NASHVILLE
CHATTANOOGA
MEMPHIS
GREENVILLE
COLUMBIA
CHARLESTON
ATLANTA
AUGUSTA
MACON
COLUMBUS
SAVANNAH
BIRMINGHAM
MONTGOMERY
JACKSON
MOBILE
JACKSONVILLE
ORLANDO
TAMPA-ST. PETERSBURG
MIAMI

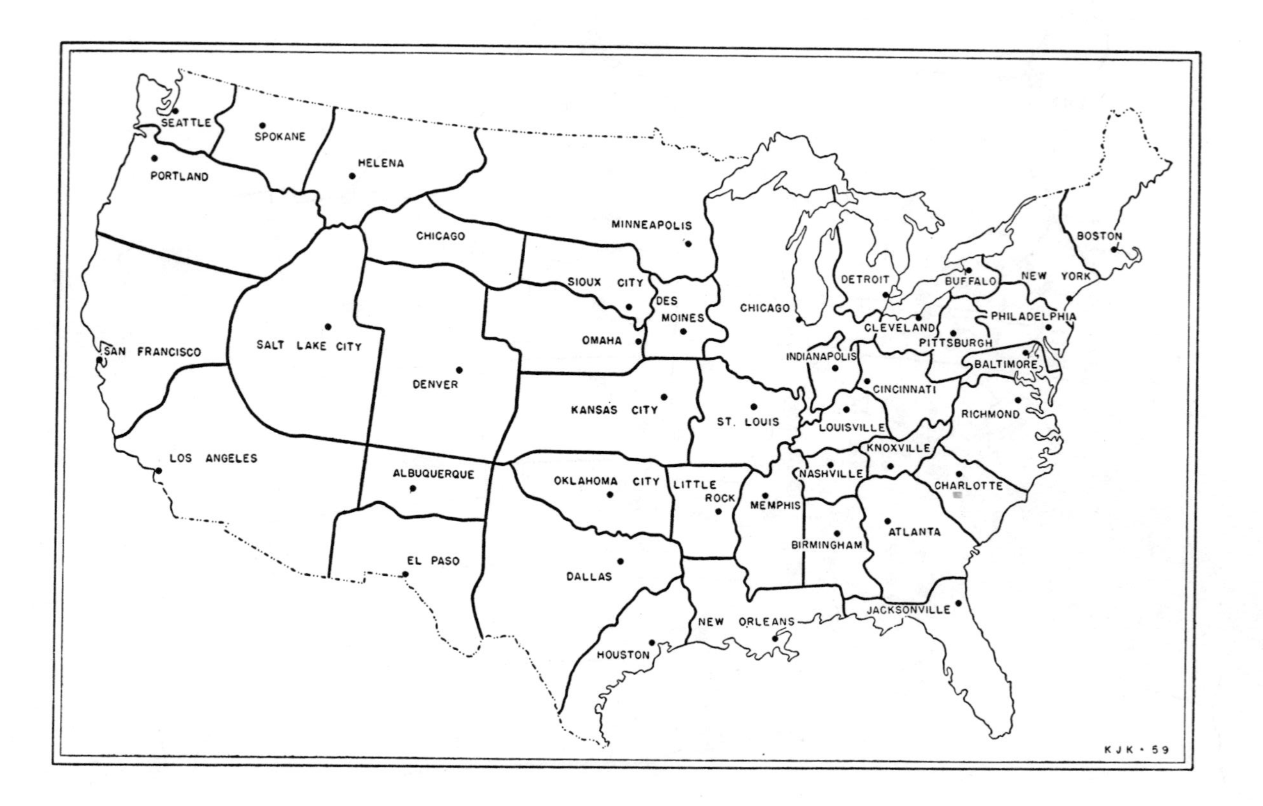
SEATTLE
SPOKANE
HELENA
PORTLAND
CHICAGO
MINNEAPOLIS
BOSTON
SIOUX CITY
DES MOINES
CHICAGO
DETROIT
BUFFALO
NEW YORK
SALT LAKE CITY
OMAHA
CLEVELAND
PHILADELPHIA
SAN FRANCISCO
PITTSBURGH
INDIANAPOLIS
BALTIMORE
DENVER
CINCINNATI
KANSAS CITY
ST. LOUIS
RICHMOND
LOUISVILLE
KNOXVILLE
LOS ANGELES
ALBUQUERQUE
OKLAHOMA CITY
LITTLE ROCK
NASHVILLE
CHARLOTTE
MEMPHIS
ATLANTA
BIRMINGHAM
EL PASO
DALLAS
NEW ORLEANS
JACKSONVILLE
HOUSTON
KJK • 59

dures must be used in delimiting "metropolitan areas" in McKenzie's sense of the commutation area of the central city, there is an even wider range of inviting alternatives when it comes to the delineation of the broader "trade areas." One of the best known schemes of "metropolitan regions," that developed by Park and Newcomb, appeared in McKenzie's monograph (1933, chapter VIII). Park and Newcomb suggested that circulation areas of metropolitan newspapers serve as general-purpose trade areas because the "similarity of the newspaper to other articles of commerce together with its advertising function makes for distribution of newspapers, like other commodities, from local centers of trade, and the limits within which they circulate tend to coincide with the trade area." Although Park and Newcomb plotted boundaries of metropolitan regions on the basis of circulation statistics, they did not use such statistics as an independent criterion of metropolitanism. Instead, they made up a list of metropolises merely by adding a few cities to the list of cities having a Federal Reserve Bank or Branch Bank, inasmuch as "the Federal Reserve cities . . . had already been selected to perform one type of regional service." Figure 5 shows the Park-Newcomb metropolitan regions for 1929. It is unfortunate that their work has not been repeated for a more recent date. They noted some minor but perhaps significant changes between 1920 and 1929, and one might suppose that further changes have occurred in the subsequent three decades.

Other investigators besides Park and Newcomb have relied on the territorial units of the Federal Reserve System as a starting point for delimiting metropolitan regions or community areas; hence it will be well to describe those units briefly. Figure 6 shows a recent map of the districts and branch territories of the Federal Reserve System. There have been minor changes in these territorial units from time to time since they were delimited in 1914; however, the twelve Federal Reserve Bank Cities are the same as those originally designated. The Reserve Bank Organization Committee, although it did not use those terms, was concerned in considerable part with metropolitan functions and metropolitan areas. This committee collected extensive evidence from some 37 cities concerning their qualifications to serve as Bank Cities and it polled banks in all parts of the country to ascertain their preferences as to location of Reserve District headquarters. Two of the committee's

---

Figure 5 (opposite). Metropolitan Regions in the United States as Defined by Park and Newcomb on the Basis of Daily Newspaper Circulation: 1929 (after McKenzie, 1933, Chapter VIII)

criteria "in determining the respective districts and the selection of the cities" were the following: "mercantile, industrial, and financial connections existing in each district and the relations between the various portions of the district and the city selected for the location of the Federal reserve bank"; and "general geographical situation of the district, transportation lines, and the facilities for speedy communication between the Federal reserve bank and all portions of the district" (United States Senate, 1914, p. 361). The establishment of the districts and branch territories is doubly significant from our standpoint. First, the Organization Committee was concerned to describe metropolitan structure as it then existed; even if its work had been merely academic, it would still be useful today, on the assumption that such structure tends to persist. But the work was not wholly academic; instead, the establishment of the Federal Reserve System no doubt tended to maintain the positions of financial dominance of the Federal Reserve Bank Cities against the competition of cities that might later have arisen to challenge them—for example the 25 cities that lost out to them when the system was set up.

A study which depended heavily on the Federal Reserve areas in delimiting trade areas was conducted by the National Recovery Administration in the 1930's. The following excerpts from the report (United States Office of the National Recovery Administration, 1936, pp. 12, 15-16) indicate the methods employed:

> A careful analysis of the location of the borders of the 37 Federal Reserve territories revealed that these dividing lines reflected natural major wholesale areas to a remarkable degree. This result is probably due to the fact that evidence concerning the movement of trade was examined when the main banks were established years ago and it is logical to suppose that the location of these banks has exerted some influence on the general flow of trade.
>
> There are, of course, certain areas which seem to have been improperly allocated at the outset or in which considerable economic change has occurred. These are the areas where the Division of Research and Planning has made several major and numerous minor "flow of trade" adjustments. . . .
>
> In approaching the problems of actually drawing the border lines many "flow of trade" factors are examined comparatively for every section of the country. Their effect on commerce is then graphically plotted on maps. The actual delineation of the boundary line is then a matter of impartial, experienced judgment.

Figure 6 (opposite). Boundaries of Federal Reserve Districts and their Branch Territories: 1954

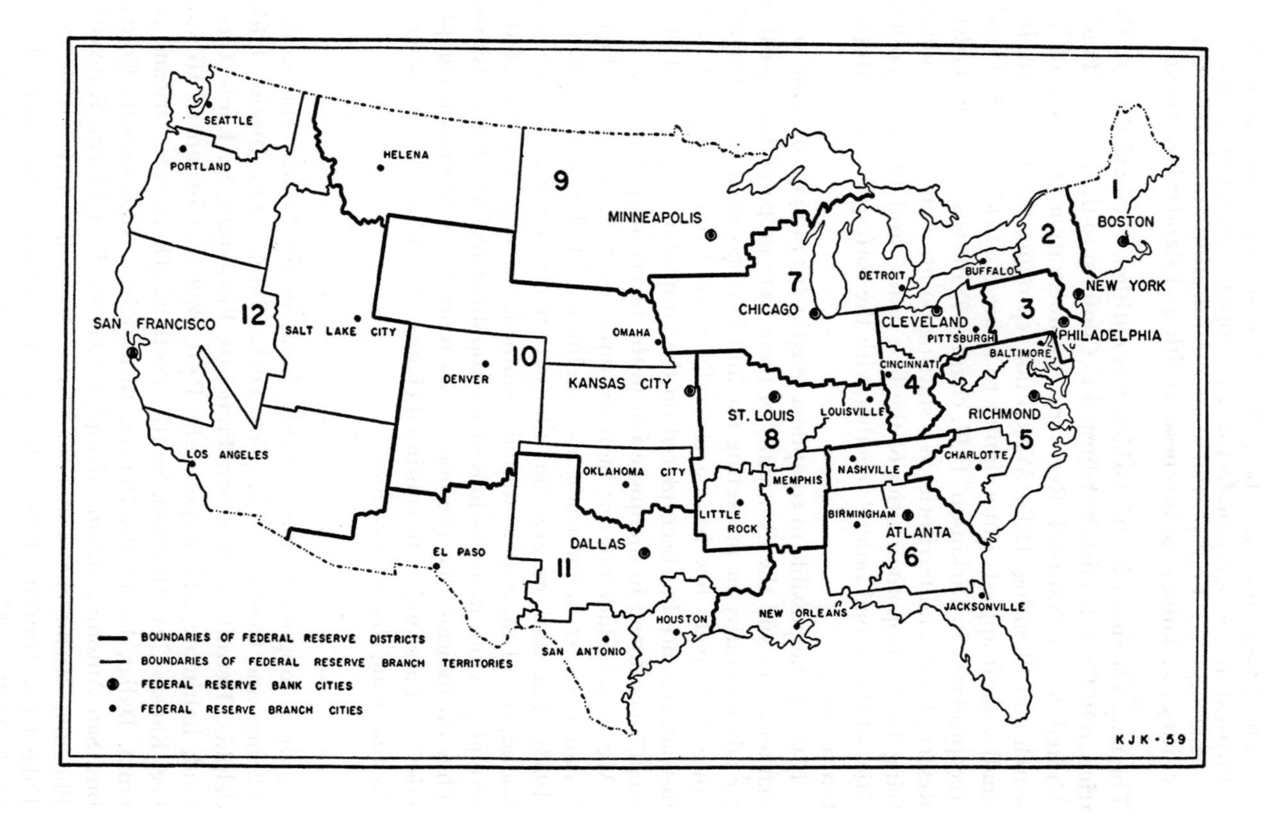
1
BOSTON
2
NEW YORK
BUFFALO
3
PHILADELPHIA
PITTSBURGH
BALTIMORE
4
CLEVELAND
CINCINNATI
DETROIT
5
RICHMOND
CHARLOTTE
6
ATLANTA
BIRMINGHAM
NASHVILLE
JACKSONVILLE
NEW ORLEANS
7
CHICAGO
8
ST. LOUIS
LOUISVILLE
MEMPHIS
LITTLE ROCK
9
MINNEAPOLIS
HELENA
10
KANSAS CITY
OMAHA
DENVER
OKLAHOMA CITY
11
DALLAS
EL PASO
HOUSTON
SAN ANTONIO
12
SAN FRANCISCO
SEATTLE
PORTLAND
SALT LAKE CITY
LOS ANGELES
BOUNDARIES OF FEDERAL RESERVE DISTRICTS
BOUNDARIES OF FEDERAL RESERVE BRANCH TERRITORIES
FEDERAL RESERVE BANK CITIES
FEDERAL RESERVE BRANCH CITIES
KJK-59

> The factors used can be grouped under four general headings: Physical and geographic factors . . . Population, families and home ownership . . . Transportation, communication and distributive facilities . . . Volume of business, wealth and standard of living.

The map produced in this fashion was entitled, "Federal Reserve Districts and Their Branches, Adjusted to Conform to the Flow of Trade" (United States National Recovery Administration, Division of Research and Planning, 1935). We do not reproduce this map, since in a small scale it appears quite similar to figure 6. Dickinson's 1934 study (recapitulated in Dickinson, 1947, chapter 7) likewise used the Federal Reserve Cities and territories as a starting point; it ended up by identifying 18 "metropolitan cities of the first order" and 12 "metropolitan cities of the second order," together with the corresponding metropolitan regions.

It would be possible to compile a lengthy list of maps of trade areas, market areas, and the like. Many of them were prepared for a particular administrative or marketing use and have no great general significance. Relatively few have a carefully worked out theoretical basis; instead, reliance has been placed on the "impartial, experienced judgment" mentioned in the quotation in the preceding paragraph.

We shall include but one more example of a trade area map. Figure 7 shows the 52 major trade areas delimited by Thomas and Crisler (1953). The authors give no information on how the number and boundaries of these areas were determined, although it is implied that several previous delimitations of metropolitan regions were consulted. They do indicate that the boundaries represent a "statistical compromise" and are subject to continual change. As an "ideal" they propose the following characterization:

Figure 7 (opposite). Major Trade Areas of the United States, after Thomas and Crisler (1953). (New York, Chicago, Los Angeles, Philadelphia, Detroit, Boston, San Francisco, Pittsburgh, St. Louis, Cleveland, Baltimore, Minneapolis – St. Paul, Buffalo, Cincinnati, Milwaukee, Kansas City, Houston, Seattle, Portland (Ore.), New Orleans, Atlanta, Dallas, Louisville, Denver, Birmingham, Indianapolis, Columbus, San Antonio, Miami, Memphis, Omaha, Fort Worth, Knoxville, Phoenix, Richmond, Oklahoma City, Nashville, Jacksonville, Salt Lake City, Duluth, Tulsa, Des Moines, Spokane, Charlotte, Little Rock, El Paso, Shreveport, Albuquerque, Portland (Me.), Sioux City, Amarillo, and Great Falls.)

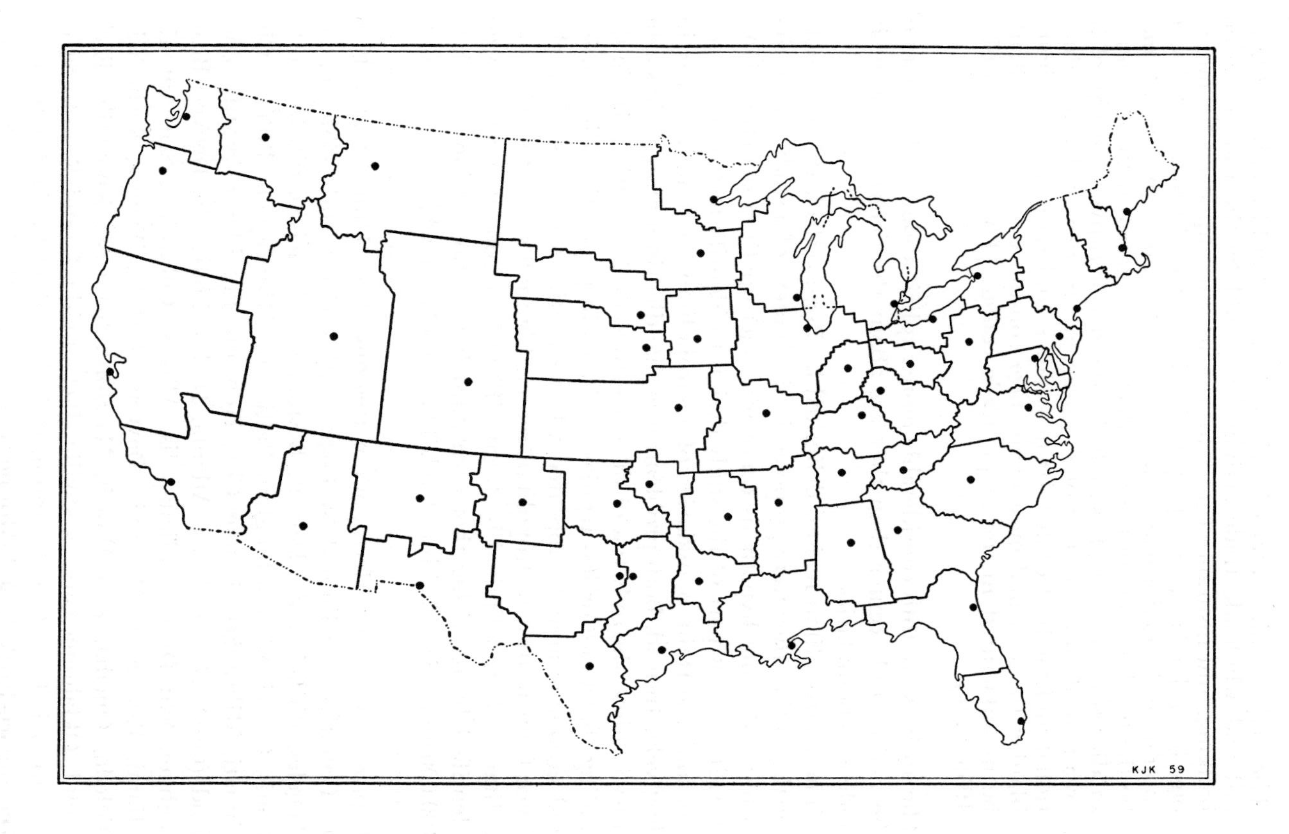
KJK 59

> The major trade center of each trade area should dominate the retail and wholesale trade activity. It should be the transportation, banking, and insurance center for the area, headquarters for numerous federal offices, and play a dominant role in area politics. It should be the major marketing center for the area's products. It may be the headquarters of big manufacturing concerns with factories in smaller trade centers. It should be the major convention city of its area and often the recreational, music, art, literary, religious, educational and medical center. Its newspapers and radio stations should blanket the area and most of the beer consumed in the area should be manufactured in the major trade center. (Thomas and Crisler, 1953, p. 9.)

The authors are thus considerably more explicit about the functions of the major trade center than they are about the determination of its trade area boundaries.

The metropolitan regions delimited by Bogue (1949, 1955) are noteworthy in that they were proposed in the context of a study attempting to test a definite hypothesis concerning metropolitan structure. However, it was not part of the study design to identify metropolitan centers and ascertain boundaries of metropolitan community areas inductively. Instead, both problems were handled in a more or less arbitrary fashion; the only test of the correctness of the solutions lay in the finding that more or less regular gradients in population distribution and economic activity appeared when counties were ordered by distance from nearest metropolitan center. Figure 8 shows the 67 metropolitan regions delimited by Bogue. The 67 metropolitan centers were identified by requiring that each must have a population of at least 100,000 and a sizeable hinterland. The boundaries, which follow county

---

Figure 8 (opposite). Metropolitan Regions of the United States, 1948, as Tentatively Delimited by Bogue (1949). (New York, Chicago, Los Angeles, Philadelphia, Detroit, Boston, San Francisco, Pittsburgh, St. Louis, Cleveland, Washington, Baltimore, Minneapolis, Buffalo, Cincinnati, Milwaukee, Kansas City, Houston, Providence, Seattle, Portland (Ore.), New Orleans, Atlanta, Dallas, Louisville, Denver, Birmingham, San Diego, Indianapolis, Albany, Columbus, San Antonio, Miami, Rochester, Memphis, Dayton, Norfolk, Tampa, Springfield, Toledo, Omaha, Fort Worth, Hartford, Syracuse, Knoxville, Richmond, Oklahoma City, Nashville, Jacksonville, Grand Rapids, Sacramento, Salt Lake City, Scranton, Duluth, Tulsa, Peoria, Chattanooga, Davenport–Rock Island–Moline, Des Moines, Wichita, Spokane, Erie, South Bend, Charlotte, El Paso, Fort Wayne, and Evansville.)

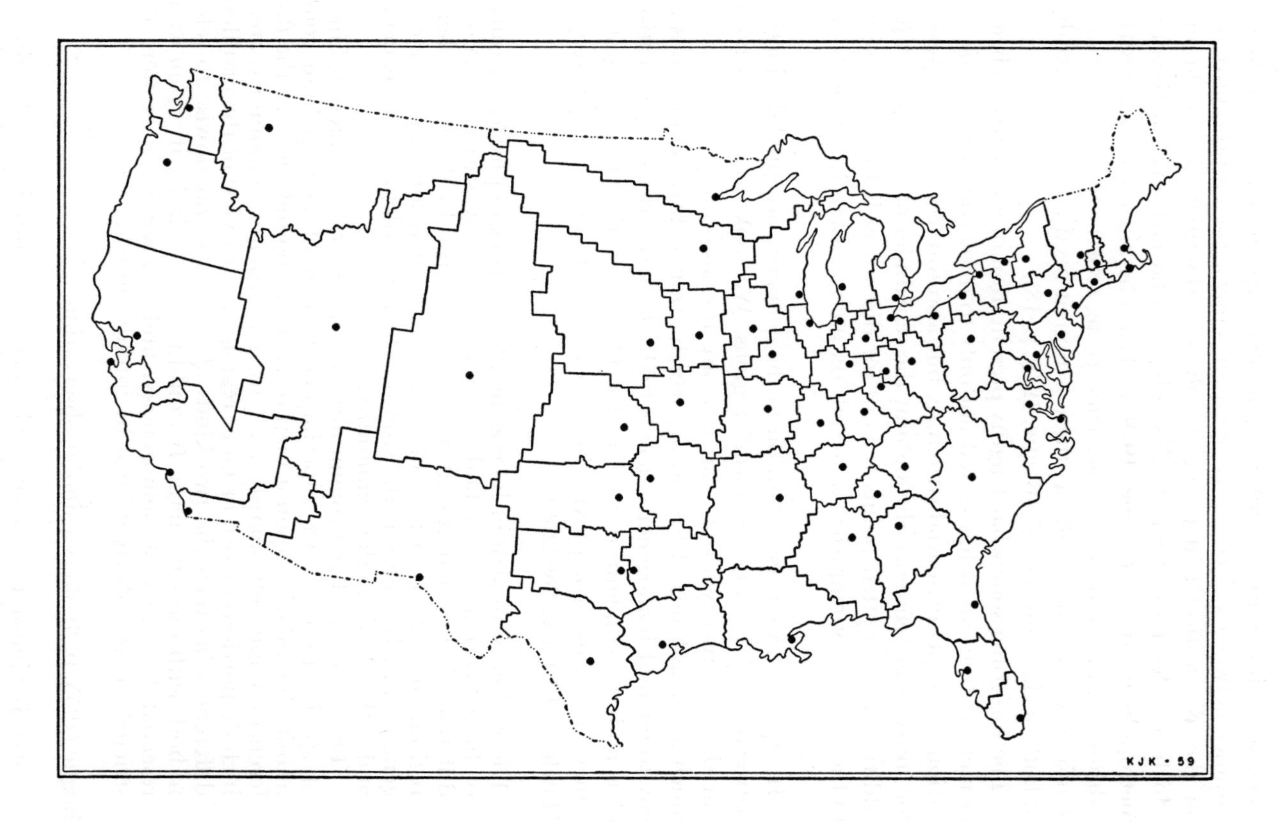
KJK • 59

lines, were drawn in such a way as to bisect (approximately) the airline distance between adjacent metropolitan centers. Such a procedure rests on the assumption that a "metropolis can dominate all of the area which lies closer to it than to any other similar city, even if the other metropolis is larger" (Bogue, 1949, p. 17). The author recognizes that "although . . . the rough guesses concerning centers and boundaries of dominance are fairly realistic, there is urgent need for detailed studies of both of these problems" (Bogue, 1949, p. 18).

The foregoing somewhat lengthy presentation of alternative schemes of metropolitan areas has served not only to draw contrasts among the various concepts of spatial structure, but also to record some materials for convenient reference throughout the remainder of our study. A few additional conceptual points remain for discussion before we proceed to the analysis of empirical materials on metropolitan functions (chapter 5).

In chapter 2 we drew attention to the generally accepted distinction between "nodal" and "uniform" regions. We took occasion to point out that the two types of areal unit are not absolutely distinct, inasmuch as some kinds of uniformity which are not direct expressions of environmental homogeneity may actually be responses to the location of a node or configuration of nodes. Our view, therefore, suggests a somewhat greater complexity in the situation than that expressed by Hawley (1950, pp. 260-262):

> The region is an area of homogeneity in respect to physical features or human occupancy or both . . . the community area is actually a different kind of spatial unit from that described by the geographer's region. Instead of an area of homogeneity, it is an area of heterogeneity. . . . Diversity is the stuff of which interdependence is made and is thus basic to the community.
>
> The region and the community area are therefore different kinds of spatial units. If we superimpose a map of metropolitan community boundaries upon a map of regional boundaries . . . the differences stand out sharply . . . in many places community areas include portions of two or more regions. . . . In view of the manifest differences between the two kinds of area, it seems unwise to refer to both with the same term. It would make for clarity if *region* were reserved for areas of homogeneity, and *community area* were restricted to areas distinguished by interdependence.

Bogue (1955, p. 3) offers a similar observation:

> There is almost no agreement between the boundaries of uniform regions and nodal regions. In fact, there is a remarkable tendency for nodal centers to be located near the boundary of a uniform re-

> gion, or a subregion. This means that the boundaries of uniform regions tend to bisect the territory of nodal regions. Thus, one outstanding characteristic of the nodal region is a tendency toward internal diversity rather than toward homogeneity. Clearly, the distinction between nodal and uniform regions is not merely verbal, but reflects two different ways of conceptualizing an area.

While we are not disposed to deny the distinction emphasized in these remarks—though it may be symptomatic that Hawley's suggestion as to terminology has not won general acceptance—we wish to point out that this distinction by itself is not a sufficient basis for proceeding to identify the functions of metropolises with regard to either "uniform" or "nodal" regions. In the first place, as we have already noted, in respect to the metropolitan (nodal) region, the metropolis performs both intra- and interregional functions. Secondly, in respect to the uniform region, we find that the regional relationships of the metropolis take on a variety of forms. For example, despite the observation that metropolitan centers frequently lie near the boundary of a uniform region, there are also striking instances in which they are centrally located with respect to uniform regions. Such is particularly likely to be the case with "central-place" cities (see chapter 2). In instances where the metropolitan region contains segments of two highly diverse uniform regions, it may have the function of mediating exchange between those regions. There are also cases in which the metropolitan center lies on a boundary of a uniform region, but most of its metropolitan region lies within the area of supposed uniformity; here again the metropolis is likely to perform "inter-regional" functions. To give but one more example, a "uniform" region may actually emerge as a combination of hinterlands of several metropolitan centers.

We offer the scheme in table 12 in the hope that it may encourage a more thorough exploration of metropolis-region relationships than has yet been undertaken. It should be made clear that the "uniform regions" with which we are here concerned are what have been called "single-factor regions," as opposed to "composite" regions (see United States National Resources Committee, 1935, pp. 151-152). Whereas there is a relatively clear meaning to the notion of a region as an extended area in which some factor is more or less uniformly present to a specified degree, the idea of a multi-factor region of relative homogeneity is one that defies operational specification and invokes questionable or obscure methodological premises (see Duncan, Cuzzort, and Duncan, 1960). It may well be that the whole attempt to describe the spatial plan of an economy in "regional" terms represents but a stage of methodological development whose ultimate successor will dispense with the "region" concept almost entirely. If and when we have adequate measures of the "factors" said to define regions and of the parameters governing the spatial orientation of nodal functions, it may prove possible to combine this information in multivariate mathematical models of spatial structure in which "regional" boundaries do not appear as such. Crude and tentative models incorporating this point of view already have been proposed; the future will no doubt resolve issues as to the range of their descriptive and explanatory utility.

Table 12. Schematic Relations between Uniform Regions and Nodal Spatial Structure

Type of factor defining uniform region	Example of uniform region	Possible relations to nodal structure
Environmental	Physiographic region Climatic region Soil type region Mineral resource region	(a) Central-place or resource-exploiting city may be oriented to uniform region and its nodal region may be contained within or coextensive with uniform region. (b) Nodal region may overlap distinct types of uniform region.
Combination of environmental and functional factors	Type-of-farming region	Uniform region may be oriented to a node or configuration of nodes, as well as representing a response to relatively homogeneous environmental conditions.
Functional	Manufacturing zone	Uniform region is likely to be oriented to a configuration of nodes.

CHAPTER 5

Major Economic Functions

Following the conceptual development of criteria of metropolitanism in the previous chapter, we present here some empirical analyses of data pertaining to three broad classes of functions: financial, commercial, and industrial. The treatment is highly selective in terms of the indicators with which we deal. This results both from limitations of the available data and from the need to keep the discussion within a manageable scope. In the chapter following, we present a somewhat more formal treatment of a single global indicator of inter-regional functions of metropolitan centers. Here we deal first with one aspect of the financial functions of the metropolis and then turn to summary measures of commercial and industrial activity.

BANK LOANS

Gras, as we have mentioned in chapter 4, laid considerable stress on financial functions as being distinctive of the metropolis and considered a city to be a "fully developed" metropolitan center only if it performed important financial functions for the surrounding area. Despite this emphasis, which came early in the literature, little has been done by students of metropolitanism to advance our understanding of the financial role of the metropolis. For their part, specialists in the study of banking seemingly have had little interest in the spatial structure of financial activities or in concepts like those dealt with in previous chapters of this volume. J. Q. Stewart (1950) presents an analysis of population and distance effects on the flow of bank checks into New York, and Lösch (1954, pp. 462-466) gives some pieces of information indicating a tendency for interest rates to rise with distance from metropolitan centers. Such data provide significant preliminary evidence on the financial dominance of the metropolis. It is to be hoped that the availability of the English translation of Lösch's work will stimulate further empirical exploration of this important problem. Such data on financial functions as we shall present here are likewise incomplete and fragmentary, but they suggest that the metropolis does indeed play a key role in the organization of financial activities.

In 1955 the Board of Governors of the Federal Reserve System conducted a sample survey of commercial and industrial loans of member banks. This survey obtained unique information on the location of borrowers along with data on size of loans, size of banks, size and business of borrower, and the like. (For a description of the survey design and a summary of national findings, see Eckert, 1956.) Unfortunately, much of the analysis of this material was decentralized to the research staffs of the twelve Federal Reserve Banks; a few of them published fairly complete reports while the others made relatively little use of the data. Our own study falls short of realizing the potential value of the survey data, even though we make use of certain unpublished figures secured by correspondence. It is unfortunate that apparently no provision has been made for a full-scale analysis of these data from the standpoint of metropolitan functions and inter-regional relationships. It has been observed that

> The ability to shift funds readily from one part of the country to another is one of the important functions of the nation's banking system. Banks located in New York and Chicago have long been recognized as an important source of funds for business throughout the nation. To a lesser extent, banks in other large cities have been known to provide loan facilities to distant borrowers. In neither case, however, has there been a statistical basis for appraising the inter-regional flow of funds generated by business demands in excess of the volume of credit available at local banks. The 1955 Survey provided for the first time a body of quantitative data on the volume of bank lending to nonlocal borrowers. (Processing difficulties delayed the availability of these data until recently and led to the omission of similar data from the coverage of the 1957 Survey.) [Federal Reserve Bank of Cleveland, 1958, p. 9.]

In considering metropolitan financial functions, it is appropriate to begin by acknowledging the pre-eminent role of New York. New York

Table 13. Commercial Loans Made by Second (New York) Federal Reserve District Member Banks as Percentage of Commercial Loans by All Federal Reserve Member Banks in the United States, by Business of Borrower: 1955 and 1946

(Based on amounts of loans outstanding, October 5, 1955, and November 20, 1946)

Business of borrower	1955	1946
Total, all borrowers	34.3	35.0
Manufacturing and mining, total	40.8	38.7
Food, liquor and tobacco	34.7	39.5
Textiles, apparel, and leather	60.7	46.3
Metals and metal products	34.5	37.3
Petroleum, coal, chemicals, and rubber	47.3	43.2
Other	30.7	31.2
Trade, total	25.5	29.6
Wholesale trade and commodity dealers	31.8	33.9
Retail trade	19.9	22.6
Other, total	33.2	34.8
Sales finance companies	31.5	39.5
Transportation, communication, and other public utilities	52.8	47.5
Construction	21.4	13.0
Service firms	24.2	26.9
All other borrowers[1]	28.9	27.0

[1] Includes real estate operators, owners, agents, brokers, and subdividers and developers of real property.

SOURCE: Federal Reserve Bank of New York (1957, table V); Eckert (1956, table 1).

City's population amounts to only five per cent of the nation's total; with its Standard Metropolitan Area, New York's share of population is about eight per cent. But 29 per cent of the commercial loans by Federal Reserve System member banks outstanding on October 5, 1955, were made by banks located in New York City (see source for table 13). Table 13 gives a pretty good indication of New York's share of the credit market, inasmuch as 85 per cent of the loans (in terms of dollar amounts) in the Second District were made by New York City banks. (The Second District consists essentially of the New York metropolitan area, extending into northern New Jersey and southwestern Connecticut, plus all of up-state New York.) It is significant that there was little change between 1946 and 1955 in the Second District's share of loans: in both years somewhat more than one-third of the amount of loans outstanding was accounted for by Second District banks. We need not attempt a detailed explanation of the variation by type of business around this average. The Second District's share is low for loans to borrowers in retail trade, as one would expect from the comparatively small scale of this business and its dispersion throughout the United States. The high proportion of loans by Second District banks to the textile, apparel, and leather industries no doubt reflects the localization of the apparel industry in New York City. We have no ready explanation for the changes, by kind of business, in the Second District's share of loans over the nine-year period. In some cases, e.g. construction, it may be that an increase in the proportion of loans made by Second District banks is related to a change in the current rate of activity in the industry. For most of the categories of business, the Second District's share was much the same in the two years.

Table 14 suggests a fairly clear pattern of allocation of financial functions among cities; the comparisons concern the principal metropolitan centers in the Second District and the distribution of the loans made by banks in these cities over their "hinterlands." In marked contrast to banks anywhere else in the Second District, New York City banks made nearly half (46 per cent) of their loans to borrowers outside the district. The nearest comparable figure was 22 per cent for Buffalo banks. At the same time, the New York City banks were making loans to borrowers within the city in about the proportion one would expect from the proportion of intra-city loans elsewhere in the district. A quite small proportion of loans by New York City banks, therefore, went to borrowers in the New York metropolitan area but outside the city limits or to borrowers in other parts of the Second District. One-third of the loans made to borrowers in the New York metropolitan area outside the city proper were made by banks in the large New Jersey suburbs, over half of whose loans were to borrowers outside their own city limits but within the New York metropolitan area. There was some variation in pattern among the major up-state cities, but in each case around one-fourth to one-third of the loans were made to borrowers outside the city and its metropolitan area but within the Second District. Buffalo (a Federal Reserve Branch City) and Albany-Schenectady-Troy banks made considerably higher proportions of their loans outside the Second District than did Rochester or Syracuse banks; but their activity in this field was small as compared

Table 14. Per Cent Distribution of Business Loans and Average Size of Loans Outstanding on October 5, 1955, by Location of Borrowers and of Lending Banks in the Second (New York) Federal Reserve District

Location of business borrower	Location of lending bank: Total Second District	New York City	Cities[1] in New Jersey	Buffalo	Rochester	Syracuse	Albany, Schenectady, and Troy	Remainder of Second District
Total amount of loans ($1,000,000)[2]	10,366	8,752	235	296	105	99	91	789
			Per cent of total amount					
All locations[2]	100.0	99.9	100.0	100.0	100.0	100.0	100.1	100.0
Within same city	47.0	47.3	34.9	43.2	63.8	58.0	35.6	46.6
Outside city but within same metropolitan area or county	9.0	4.8	55.3	9.5	1.9	6.0	11.1	41.7
Elsewhere in Second District	3.7	1.7	0.9	25.3	29.5	30.0	36.7	7.9
Outside Second District, but within United States	40.3	46.1	8.9	22.0	4.8	6.0	16.7	3.8
			Mean size of loan ($1,000)					
All locations[2]	45	97	17	33	23	19	17	8
Within same city	33	56	15	25	22	22	11	7
Outside city but within same metropolitan area or county	16	50	18	11	7	10	12	8
Elsewhere in Second District	31	15	20	75	26	16	21	11
Outside Second District, but within United States	431	576	52	325	50	60	150	17

[1] Newark, Jersey City, Paterson, and Passaic.

[2] Includes loans to borrowers in United States territories, but excludes loans to borrowers outside the United States and its territories.

SOURCE: Federal Reserve Bank of New York (1957, table I).

with New York City banks. Finally, it may be noted that banks in the smaller cities of the Second District (shown in table 14 as a single "remainder") had a lending pattern somewhat like the New Jersey suburbs of New York; i.e., an overwhelming proportion of their loans was made to borrowers located within their own boundaries or immediate environs.

It is likely that the data in table 14 understate the importance of the national (i.e., outside Second District) lending function of New York City banks. It is pointed out that "many national concerns have headquarters in New York City, and, although they may disburse their borrowed funds in other parts of the country, loans to such businesses were classified for purposes of the survey as loans to local borrowers" (Federal Reserve Bank of New York, 1957, p. 4).

Figures on the average size of loans (lower panel of table 14) supplement the foregoing description. For banks at all locations, the loans to borrowers outside the Second District were much larger on the average than those to intra-district borrowers. Loans by New York City banks, however, were far larger in average amount than those made to borrowers outside the district by banks at the other locations. For the up-state cities, the non-local (outside the city and its metropolitan area or county) loans within the Second District were larger than the local loans, for the most part. This was not true of New York City loans; but, again, it must be remembered that many of New York's "local loans" are in effect loans to businesses operating outside the city.

The figures in table 14 include loans to borrowers in United States territories, but exclude loans to borrowers in foreign countries. The latter were appreciable in amount only for New York City banks; foreign loans accounted for a little over two per cent of all commercial loans of New York City banks.

Table 15 brings out a significant aspect of the lending pattern: the participation of more than one bank in the making of a loan. This comes about in the following manner:

> Banks who have customer requests for loans that are larger than they can or wish to handle alone may share the loan with other banks in one of two ways. The first is a pool-type arrangement in which two or more banks share a loan; in their negotiations with the borrower the participating banks may operate through a syndicate leader or they may jointly or separately work out the loan details with the borrower. This method is most often used by large banks in connection with loans to large borrowers. The second is an excess or "overline" arrangement in which the initiating bank offers another bank that part of a loan which exceeds the bank's legal limit

for loans to a single customer, or which exceeds the line of credit which the bank wishes to extend to the customer concerned [Federal Reserve Bank of New York, 1957, p. 15].

Table 15. Per Cent of Amount of Commercial Loans (Outstanding on October 5, 1955) Made by Second (New York) District Member Banks with Participation of Other Banks, by Location of Borrowers and of Lending Banks

	Location of lending bank				
Location of borrower	All Second District member banks	Central reserve New York City banks	Other member banks in New York City	Member banks in other major cities[1]	All other member banks in Second District
All locations	25.3	28.9	1.9	11.8	6.0
Within same city, metropolitan area, or county	16.1	19.6	2.0	6.8	5.0
Elsewhere in Second District	21.9	24.0	...[2]	24.8	10.4
Outside Second District	37.8	38.6[3]	...[2]	16.7	19.0

[1] Newark, Jersey City, Paterson, Passaic, Buffalo, Rochester, Syracuse, Albany, Schenectady, and Troy.

[2] Too few loans to yield a representative figure.

[3] Includes loans to borrowers outside the United States, 11.9 per cent of the amount of which were made with participation of other banks.

SOURCE: Federal Reserve Bank of New York (1957, table XIII).

We have omitted the detail on types of "participated loans" (for which see source) in order to bring out the major finding: the making of participated loans is much more common among the central reserve New York City banks than among banks elsewhere in the Second District (nearly 98 per cent of the loans made by member banks in New York City were made by the central reserve New York City banks). At all locations participated loans were a much higher fraction of nonlocal than of local loans; and for the central reserve New York City banks, participated loans were a much higher proportion of loans made to borrowers outside the Second District than of loans to intra-district borrowers. These differences, of course, are consistent with the differences previously observed in average size of loan, and they serve to point up the complexity of financial organization at the core of the credit market and the important integrative function performed by the large banks located there.

Table 16. Per Cent Distribution of Business Loans and Average Size of Loans Outstanding on October 5, 1955, by Location of Borrowers and of Lending Banks in the Fourth (Cleveland) Federal Reserve District

Location of business borrower	Location of lending bank					
		Major cities				
	Total Fourth District	Cleveland	Cincinnati	Pittsburgh	Others[1]	Smaller centers
Total amount of loans ($1,000,000)[2]	1,916	335	283	642	195	461
	Per cent of total amount					
All locations[2]	100.0	100.0	100.0	100.0	100.0	100.0
In Fourth District						
Local[3]						
Major city	36.6	55.9	60.0	31.5	72.9	...
Smaller center	21.3	...	...	...	...	88.7
Nonlocal						
Major city	4.2	9.7	4.6	3.6	2.4	1.6
Smaller center	10.3	15.6	8.1	11.1	11.9	5.9
Outside District[2]	27.6	18.8	27.3	53.8	12.8	3.8
	Mean size of loan ($1,000)					
All locations[2]	23	36	55	84	27	8
In Fourth District						
Local[3]						
Major city	28	24	39	33	22	...
Smaller center	8	...	...	...	...	8
Nonlocal						
Major city	84	119	108	546	165	15
Smaller center	30	55	71	99	44	7
Outside district[2]	220	232	202	508	140	20

[1] Akron, Columbus, Dayton, and Toledo, Ohio.
[2] Excludes loans to borrowers outside the United States.
[3] In same metropolitan area as major city or in same county as smaller center.
SOURCE: Federal Reserve Bank of Cleveland (1958, table 3).

Another Federal Reserve District for which a fairly detailed analysis of the loan survey data has been published is the Fourth (Cleveland) District. The data in table 16 summarize information on the differentiation of centers in this district according to lending functions. It should be noted at once that although the Federal Reserve Bank is located in Cleveland, a much larger volume of lending is done by the banks of Pittsburgh, which is a Branch City. It would appear that Cleveland banks specialize to a greater degree in lending to "regional" borrowers (i.e., those located in the Fourth District), whereas Pittsburgh is much more of a "national" financial center. Indeed, as is noted subsequently, Pittsburgh ranks fourth among cities of the United States (after New York and Chicago and close behind San Francisco) in absolute amount of non-local loans. The large size of Pittsburgh loans also is suggestive: the average size of its inter-district loans is roughly comparable with the corresponding figure for New York (table 14). The fact that a higher proportion of Cincinnati's than of Cleveland's loans are outside the Fourth District may not be significant, inasmuch as the former center is located near the boundary of the district. We note that the average size of out-of-district loans is smaller for Cincinnati than for Cleveland, and a somewhat higher proportion of its loans are local (i.e., within the metropolitan area). But on the whole, Cincinnati and Cleveland appear rather similar in respect to their lending functions. As was true in the Second District, the banks in smaller places in the Fourth District do the bulk of their lending to local businesses (within the same county or metropolitan area). In both districts the average size of non-local loans is substantially greater than that of local loans.

The remainder of the discussion concerns data compiled on a national basis (unpublished tabulations from the 1955 survey were kindly supplied by the Division of Research and Statistics, Board of Governors, Federal Reserve System). Our purpose is merely to sketch some gross features of the system of commercial lending, as revealed by the survey data. (Some additional material on business loans is presented in the next section of this chapter.)

The bulk of all loans are made to borrowers located in the same Federal Reserve Districts as the lending banks. Nevertheless, a little over one-fifth of the amounts lent were to borrowers in different districts. Since the districts are quite sizeable, it is evident that an appreciable proportion of lending involves considerable distances between borrowers and lenders. The data in table 17 indicate that over half (in terms of amount) of all inter-district loans were made by Second

(New York) District banks; and the inter-district loans of these banks were nearly five times greater in amount than the inter-district loans received by borrowers in this district. Only two other districts—the First (Boston) and Fourth (Cleveland)—lent more money than they borrowed. The remaining nine districts were net borrowers; there was appreciable variation among them in the degree to which they were dependent upon inter-district loans. In contrast to the net lenders, the Fifth (Richmond) and Ninth (Minneapolis) Districts lent only about one-eighth or one-seventh as much to other districts as they borrowed from them, and the magnitude of their inter-district borrowing was quite substantial as compared with that of intra-district borrowing.

Table 17. Summary of Business Loans by Federal Reserve District Location of Lending Bank and of Borrowers, Based on Amounts of Loans Outstanding, October 5, 1955

Federal Reserve District	Amount of loans ($100 million)[1]			Ratio of inter-district lending to borrowing[2]	Ratio of actual to "expected"[3] intra-district loans
	Intra-district	Inter-district			
		Lending	Borrowing		
Total, all districts	228.1	76.6	76.6	1.00	5.5
1 (Boston)	13.2	4.4	2.0	2.22	15.1
2 (New York)	61.6	41.5	8.6	4.84	2.6
3 (Philadelphia)	13.1	2.8	4.5	0.62	14.2
4 (Cleveland)	13.9	5.3	4.7	1.11	11.8
5 (Richmond)	10.5	1.1	7.8	0.15	15.0
6 (Atlanta)	13.2	1.3	3.5	0.37	16.6
7 (Chicago)	30.5	10.3	12.9	0.79	5.2
8 (St. Louis)	8.1	2.2	3.4	0.67	20.9
9 (Minneapolis)	5.5	0.5	3.7	0.13	30.3
10 (Kansas City)	9.5	1.7	6.2	0.27	16.4
11 (Dallas)	16.9	2.3	10.2	0.23	9.9
12 (San Francisco)	32.1	3.2	9.1	0.35	6.7

[1] These amounts may differ slightly from totals shown in publications of the several Federal Reserve Banks owing to minor variations in processing of the data; excludes loans to borrowers outside the continental United States.

[2] Computed before rounding loan amounts to $100 millions.

[3] See text.

SOURCE: Unpublished tabulations from the 1955 Survey of Bank Loans for Commercial and Industrial Purposes (supplied by the Division of Research and Statistics, Board of Governors, Federal Reserve System).

The available data permit the construction of a table showing loans from each district to each district. Aside from the marked variation in the roles of the several districts already suggested, perhaps the most striking pattern revealed by this table is the influence of distance on lending. To bring out the distance effect, it is necessary to standardize the data for variation between districts in amounts lent and borrowed. The reasoning followed here may be illustrated as follows. From table 17 it appears that 16.7 (13.2 plus 3.5) hundred million dollars of loans were made to borrowers in the Sixth District, which amounts to 5.5 per cent of all loans reported in the United States. Now, if lending were independent of the relative location of banks and borrowers and of the distances separating them, we should expect 5.5 per cent of loans made in each district to be to Sixth District borrowers. Thus, the "expected" amount of loans from Seventh District banks to Sixth District borrowers would be 5.5 per cent of 40.8 (30.5 plus 10.3) hundred million dollars, or $2.2 hundred million. The actual amount of Seventh District loans to Sixth District borrowers, $0.44 hundred million, is only one-fifth this expected amount. Similar ratios of actual to "expected" loans were computed for the 144-cell (12 $\times$ 12 districts) table.

The distance effect is revealed most clearly in the fact that intra-district loans are uniformly much greater than "expected." Over the whole table, the ratio of actual to "expected" intra-district loans is 5.5. For the Second (New York) District, the ratio is only 2.6, reflecting that district's position as the principal national credit market. At the other extreme, the ratio of actual to "expected" intra-district loans was 30.3 for the Ninth (Minneapolis) District. Also suggestive of a distance effect is the finding that the actual-to-"expected" ratio is 0.35 for loans between contiguous Federal Reserve Districts as compared with 0.27 for non-contiguous districts. However, contiguity is an exceedingly crude indicator of distance here, and the distance effect is brought out better by considering ratios for individual pairs of districts.

Table 18 reports rank correlations between the ratios of actual to "expected" loans and distances separating the Federal Reserve Bank Cities of the respective districts. For example, the table shows that the ratio of actual to "expected" loans from the First District has a rank correlation of —.31 with the distances of the districts from the First, taking the First District itself as the nearest. (As a crude approximation, distances between districts were taken as the main line railroad distances between their Federal Reserve Bank Cities.) All the rank correlations computed in this fashion are negative, as are those computed by correlating ranks of the ratios of actual to "expected" loans with distances of a given district from the districts from which it is borrowing. If the intra-district loans are disregarded, the corresponding correlations, shown in table 18 as set (b), are somewhat smaller in magnitude, but still negative with one exception. That exception is no doubt a significant one, for it applies to the Second (New York) District, the amounts of whose inter-district loans are seen to be virtually independent of distance once a standardization is made for the total amounts borrowed by the other districts. The fact that both correlations for the Twelfth (San Francisco) District are comparatively small may indicate that for some reason distance fails to differentiate greatly among the borrowers from and lenders to the western United States. However, it is also entirely possible that the result merely reflects the extremely crude approximation of distance being used.

Table 18. Rank Correlations of Ratios of Actual to "Expected" Loans with Distances between Federal Reserve Districts: 1955

Federal Reserve District	Lending, by distance of borrower[1]		Borrowing, by distance of lender[1]	
	(a)	(b)	(a)	(b)
1 (Boston)	−.31	−.10	−.87	−.83
2 (New York)	−.17	.08	−.80	−.74
3 (Philadelphia)	−.87	−.83	−.78	−.71
4 (Cleveland)	−.63	−.52	−.58	−.45
5 (Richmond)	−.56	−.43	−.91	−.88
6 (Atlanta)	−.84	−.79	−.60	−.48
7 (Chicago)	−.69	−.59	−.45	−.29
8 (St. Louis)	−.92	−.89	−.63	−.52
9 (Minneapolis)	−.44	−.27	−.54	−.40
10 (Kansas City)	−.76	−.68	−.62	−.50
11 (Dallas)	−.48	−.32	−.40	−.22
12 (San Francisco)	−.33	−.13	−.32	−.12

[1] Correlations in set (a) are based on ranks for all 12 districts, while those in set (b) are based on ranks for inter-district loans only.

SOURCE: See table 17.

Turning to information on lending by specific cities, we find that for thirteen cities non-local loans amounting, in total, to one hundred million dollars or more were reported (non-local loans are to borrowers outside the respective metropolitan areas). These cities, with amounts of non-local loans in $100 million, are as follows:

New York	44
Chicago	12
San Francisco	4.9
Pittsburgh	4.4
Boston	3.9
Philadelphia	3.4
Dallas	2.7
St. Louis	1.7
Detroit	1.6
Cleveland	1.5
Buffalo	1.4
Cincinnati	1.1
Milwaukee	1.1

If we were to list non-local loans of all major cities it would be obvious that there is a strong correlation between city size and absolute amount of non-local lending. However, the foregoing tally of the principal lending cities exhibits some significant departures from a perfect correlation with size. San Francisco and Pittsburgh rank third and fourth, respectively, in terms of amount of non-local loans; but their SMA populations place them in ranks seven and eight on population size in 1950. Dallas similarly shows up more strongly on lending (seventh place) than would be expected from its 1950 SMA population rank of 24. By contrast, Los Angeles, the third largest SMA in 1950, ranks 18th in respect to amount of non-local loans; Washington and Baltimore, with SMA size ranks of 11 and 12, stand at ranks 24 and 25, respectively, on non-local loans; and Detroit's rank of tenth on non-local loans is well below its population rank of fifth. Evidently, non-local lending is a function in which metropolitan centers may specialize to some extent independently of population size.

Table 19 presents a schematic summary of a substantial portion of the available data on inter-city lending. The table is restricted to central cities of SMA's which in 1950 had populations exceeding a half million (arranged in order of population size of SMA). Data are lacking for only two metropolitan centers (Albany-Schenectady-Troy and Youngstown) falling in this size range, but for smaller centers the tabulations are much less complete and the amounts of loans typically are much smaller. In interpreting this table it should be quite clear that neither the total amount of lending nor the total amount of borrowing done by any of the cities is covered. The table indicates only the cases where the total amount of loans was $1,000,000 or more and excludes loans involving cities other than those shown. In some cases substantial amounts of loans were made by smaller cities to cities shown in the table. In table 19 the three leading lending cities are identified and ranked with respect to the amounts lent to each specified borrowing city. For example, the table shows that six cities made loans of $1,000,000 or more to Denver borrowers, with New York the leading lender to Denver, Chicago second, and Fort Worth (identified in the notes) third. It is necessary to remember that this ranking shows only the relative importance of lending cities in terms of the loans to a specific borrowing city; it says nothing about the relative amounts of loans obtained by different cities. Perhaps the most important caution concerns the nature of the underlying data. They are based in part on samples rather than complete enumerations of banks and of loans; and they pertain to a single point in time. We should expect that another survey taken on the same date with a different sampling procedure would have shown somewhat different results. Moreover, we can be sure that the volume of inter-city lending is subject to short-run temporal fluctuations as well as long-run trends, although we do not know how much change in the pattern of table 19 would be expected if similar data were compiled year after year. To be conservative, then, it is well to focus attention on the general aspects of the pattern of inter-city lending revealed here, rather than on close comparisons of individual pairs of cities or on the precise amounts of the loans.

If the reader bears the foregoing warnings in mind, he will be repaid by some careful study of table 19. First and foremost, it brings out the extent to which commercial lending by banks is an inter-metropolitan activity. Banks in large cities do not merely meet the demand for credit in their "hinterlands"; they typically also lend money in large amounts to other large cities, oftentimes to quite distant ones. If lending cities were ranked in terms of the geographic dispersion of their borrowers, the ranking would be much the same as that previously given for amounts of non-local loans, although the two bases of ranking would not give identical results.

Table 19 serves to highlight once again the dominant position of New York. Twenty-three of the other thirty large cities borrow more from New York banks than from banks in any other city (always excepting local loans). The instances in which New York fails to rank first are instructive. Without exception, they concern cities compara-

City location of borrower[1]	City location of lending bank (see stub)[2]																															Notes[3]	Classification[4]
	NY	Cg	LA	Pa	Dt	Bo	SF	Pi	SL	Cl	Wa	Ba	Mp	Bu	Ci	MI	KC	Ho	Pr	Se	Po	NO	At	Dl	Lo	De	Bi	SD	In	Co	SA		
New York	–	1	x	3	x	2	x	x	x	x	x	x	x	x	x	x	x	x	x	x	–	x	x	x	x	x	–	–	x	x	–		A
Chicago	1	–	x	x	x	3	2	x	x	x	–	x	x	x	x	x	x	x	x	x	x	x	x	x	x	–	–	–	x	–	–		A
Los Angeles	1	3	–	x	x	x	2	x	x	x	–	–	–	x	x	–	x	x	–	x	x	–	–	x	–	–	–	–	–	–	x		B
Philadelphia	1	2	–	–	–	x	x	x	x	–	x	–	–	–	–	–	x	–	–	–	–	–	–	–	–	–	–	–	–	–	–	a	A
Detroit	1	2	–	x	–	x	x	3	–	x	–	–	–	–	–	x	–	–	–	–	–	–	–	–	–	–	–	–	x	–	–		B
Boston	1	3	–	2	–	–	–	–	–	–	–	–	–	–	–	–	–	–	x	–	–	–	–	–	–	–	–	–	–	–	–		A
San Francisco–Oakland	1	3	x	x	–	x	–	2	–	–	x	–	–	x	–	–	–	–	–	x	x	–	–	–	–	–	–	–	–	–	–		A
Pittsburgh	1	–	2	3	–	x	–	–	–	x	–	–	–	–	–	–	–	x	–	–	–	–	–	–	–	–	–	–	–	–	–		A
St. Louis	1	2	x	x	x	x	x	3	–	x	–	–	x	x	–	–	–	–	x	–	–	–	–	–	–	–	–	–	–	–	–		B
Cleveland	1	2	–	x	x	–	–	3	–	–	–	–	–	–	x	–	–	–	–	–	–	–	–	–	–	–	–	–	x	–	–		B
Washington	1	–	–	3	–	x	–	2	–	–	–	x	–	–	–	–	–	–	–	–	–	–	–	–	–	–	–	–	–	–	–		B
Baltimore	1	2	x	3	x	x	x	x	x	x	x	–	–	x	x	x	x	x	x	x	x	–	x	–	x	–	–	–	x	–	–		B
Minneapolis–St. Paul	1	2	–	x	x	x	3	x	x	x	–	x	–	x	x	x	x	–	–	–	–	–	–	–	x	–	–	–	–	–	–		B
Buffalo	1	–	–	–	–	2	–	3	–	–	–	–	x	–	–	–	–	–	–	–	–	–	–	–	–	–	–	–	–	–	–		B
Cincinnati	1	2	–	–	x	–	–	x	x	–	–	–	–	–	–	–	3	–	–	–	–	–	–	–	–	–	–	–	x	–	–		C(i)
Milwaukee	2	1	–	–	–	x	–	3	–	–	–	–	–	–	–	–	–	–	–	–	–	–	–	–	–	–	–	–	–	–	–		B
Kansas City	1	2	–	–	x	x	–	3	x	–	–	–	–	–	x	–	–	x	–	–	–	–	–	x	x	–	–	–	–	–	x		B
Houston	1	3	–	–	x	x	x	x	x	–	–	–	x	–	–	–	x	–	–	–	–	–	x	2	–	–	–	–	–	–	x		C(i)
Providence	2	–	–	x	–	1	–	3	–	–	–	–	–	–	–	–	–	–	–	–	–	–	–	–	–	–	–	–	–	–	–		B
Seattle	1	3	–	–	–	–	2	x	–	–	–	–	–	–	–	–	–	–	–	–	–	–	–	–	–	–	–	–	–	–	–		B
Portland, Ore.	2	3	–	–	–	x	1	–	–	–	–	–	–	–	–	–	–	–	–	x	–	–	–	–	–	–	–	–	–	–	–		B
New Orleans	1	2	–	–	–	x	–	x	x	x	–	–	–	–	–	–	–	x	–	–	–	–	x	–	–	–	–	–	–	–	–	b	C(ii)
Atlanta	1	x	–	–	–	x	–	x	–	–	–	–	–	–	–	–	x	–	–	–	–	x	–	–	–	–	2	–	–	–	–	c	C–D
Dallas	1	3	–	x	x	2	x	x	x	–	–	–	–	–	–	–	x	x	–	–	–	–	–	–	–	x	–	–	–	–	x		B
Louisville	2	1	–	–	–	–	–	–	x	–	–	–	–	–	3	–	–	–	–	–	–	–	x	–	–	–	–	–	–	x	–		C(ii)
Denver	1	2	–	–	–	–	–	–	–	–	–	–	x	–	–	–	x	–	–	x	–	–	–	–	–	–	–	–	–	–	–	d	C(ii)
Birmingham	1	–	–	–	–	–	–	–	–	–	–	–	–	–	–	–	–	–	–	–	–	–	–	–	–	–	–	–	–	–	–	e	D
San Diego	x	–	x	–	–	–	1	–	–	–	–	–	–	–	–	–	–	–	–	–	–	–	–	2	–	–	–	–	–	–	–	f	D
Indianapolis	2	1	–	–	–	x	–	x	x	–	–	–	–	–	x	–	–	–	–	3	–	–	–	x	–	–	–	–	–	–	–		C(i)
Columbus	1	x	–	x	–	–	–	3	–	2	–	–	–	–	x	–	–	–	–	–	–	–	–	–	–	–	–	–	–	–	–		C(i)
San Antonio	2	x	–	–	–	–	–	–	x	–	–	–	–	–	–	–	–	1	–	–	–	–	–	x	–	–	–	–	–	–	–	g	D

[1] Central cities of SMA's with 1950 populations of 500,000 or more (except Albany–Schenectady–Troy and Youngstown).
[2] Symbols: Ranks (1, 2, 3) identify cities with largest amounts of loans to specified city; x—refers to total loan amount of $1,000,000 or more.
[3] Notes: a—third ranking city is Wilmington, Del.; b—third ranking city is Memphis, Tenn.; c—third ranking city is Jacksonville; Fla.; d—third ranking city is Fort Worth, Texas; e—only one city lending $1,000,000 or more; f—third ranking city is Phoenix, Ariz.; g—third ranking city is Tulsa, Okla.
[4] See text.

SOURCE: Unpublished tabulations from the 1955 Survey of Bank Loans for Commercial and Industrial Purposes (supplied by the Division of Research and Statistics, Board of Governors, Federal Reserve System).

tively close to another important financial center. Thus New York loses first place to Chicago only with respect to Milwaukee, Indianapolis, and Louisville; to Boston with respect to Providence; to Houston with respect to San Antonio; and to San Francisco with respect to Portland and San Diego. Only in the case of San Diego, where New York ranks behind Dallas, Phoenix, and Los Angeles, as well as San Francisco, does New York fail to place in second rank.

Chicago's position in second place seems almost equally unambiguous; for 21 of the 30 other cities it ranks first, second, or third in respect to amount of loans. The instances where it fails to show up in a leading position are mostly those where the city in question is much more highly accessible to a competing major center than to Chicago. The importance of relative accessibility can be illustrated in a comparison of actual amounts of loans made by New York and Chicago to the remaining cities. If we measure the distance of New York and that of Chicago to a given city (called "X"), the higher the ratio of the X-to-New York distance to the X-to-Chicago distance, the greater the relative advantage of Chicago with respect to distance. Similarly, we may measure the relative dependence of city X on the two centers by the ratio of Chicago-loans-to-X to New York-loans-to-X. We find that on the average, the greater is Chicago's advantage with respect to the accessibility of a city, the heavier is that city's dependence on Chicago for loans, as compared with New York. The rank correlation for the 12 largest cities (those, save New York and Chicago, with 1950 SMA populations exceeding one million) is .58; for the remaining cities listed in table 19, the rank correlation is .82. This finding is only apparently in disagreement with the one reported earlier, to the effect that Second District loans to other districts vary more or less independently of distance, given a standardization for total amounts borrowed by those districts. What evidently happens is that at varying distances from New York there is a succession of lesser centers competing relatively effectively with New York; but at all distances New York retains an appreciable share of the lending, while each of its competitors enjoys a relatively high position only within a somewhat more circumscribed territory. We have not carried out further correlation analysis of the effect of accessibility on competition between lending centers, but inspection of table 19 makes it seem quite plausible that distance, among other factors, plays an important role in allocating borrowers among cities with funds to lend.

The information in table 19 permits some further comments regarding the cities previously identified as leaders in respect to amount of non-local loans. Both San Francisco and Pittsburgh can justifiably be regarded as centers of national importance on the basis of the spatial dispersion of their lending as well as the total amount thereof. Both lend extensively to the largest cities and to smaller centers scattered over the country. However, San Francisco shows up the stronger in regard to the western cities and Pittsburgh is the more important center for loans east of the Mississippi (roughly). Comparing Pittsburgh and Philadelphia, one sees that the latter is fully as important in respect to loans to the cities of one million or more inhabitants; but Pittsburgh has the greater volume of business among cities between a half and one million. There is a good deal of resemblance between the spatial patterns of lending by Pittsburgh and Boston, although the former has a slightly larger total volume of non-local loans. Dallas, whose position in seventh place with respect to total amount of non-local lending is quite remarkable in view of its population size, is seen to have a much greater geographic concentration of its loans than do the centers ranking higher. Apart from loans to the three largest metropolises, the lending business of Dallas is strongly channeled toward the rapidly developing Southwest.

Looking at table 19 from the viewpoint of the borrowing city, one kind of pattern can be brought out by suggesting a typology of cities based on the credit markets on which they depend most heavily. Let us arbitrarily designate as the "national" credit market the combination of six cities with the largest amounts of non-local loans (New York, Chicago, San Francisco, Pittsburgh, Boston, and Philadelphia). It may be seen that all the 14 largest cities (those with SMA populations over 1,000,000) find their three ranking lending centers in this "national" market, with one exception. (That exception is the rank of third assigned to Wilmington in respect to loans to Philadelphia.) The same can be said of a number of somewhat smaller cities: Milwaukee, Kansas City, Providence, Seattle, Portland, and Dallas. We have next a group of cities that might be said to depend on a "national-regional" credit market, in that one of their three largest suppliers of loans is outside the "national" market. Cities in this group (with the "regional" center indicated in parentheses) are the following: Cincinnati (Kansas City), Houston (Dallas), Indianapolis (Seattle), Columbus (Cleveland), Denver (Fort Worth), New Orleans (Memphis), and Louisville (Cincinnati). This group may be subdivided, placing the first four in one subgroup and the last three in another. The difference is that the city given as source of loans in the former case is itself dependent on the "national" market for its three leading lenders, whereas in the latter case it is not. A borderline case is that of Atlanta, both the second and third ranking lenders to which are in its own Federal Reserve district and outside any of the foregoing categories. However, Atlanta does get substantial loans from Chicago, Boston, and Pittsburgh, as well as New York. There are three clear instances of cities depending on "regional-national" credit markets. San Diego, San Antonio, and Birmingham each have one of their largest lenders among cities comprising the "national" market, but they are heavily dependent otherwise on "regional" centers. Actually the only city reporting loans to Birmingham in an amount exceeding $1,000,000 was New York; its other major source of funds is identified only as places in the Sixth Federal Reserve District (in which Birmingham is located) but outside the principal cities in that district (Atlanta, Jacksonville, Miami, Nashville, and New Orleans). Other examples of cities depending on "national-regional" and "regional-national" lending centers would be easy to find if we considered cities in metropolitan areas of less than a half million inhabitants. For example, the ranking lenders to Wichita, Kansas, are St. Louis, New York, Kansas City, Chicago, Oklahoma City, and Tulsa. To find an example of a city depending on "regional" centers solely we must again look at smaller cities. Little Rock, Arkansas, for example, was reported as obtaining loans totaling $1,000,000 or more from only two centers, Memphis and St. Louis, and from places outside the principal cities of the Eighth Federal Reserve District.

To recapitulate, the data suggest a rough hierarchical ordering in terms of the following categories, codes for which are entered in the last column of table 19:

A. the "national" credit market;
B. cities (except A) whose principal lenders are in the "national" market;
C. cities whose principal lenders comprise a "national-regional" market—
   (i) principal lenders all in categories A and B, and
   (ii) one principal lender in category C or lower;
D. cities whose principal lenders comprise a "regional-national" market; and
E. cities whose principal lenders comprise a "regional" market (not represented in table 19, but Little Rock given as an example).

We do not wish to place too heavy a stress on the possibility of using these categories for empirical taxonomic purposes (although they seem quite appropriate as far as the present data go) because of the crude and qualitative fashion in which we have measured dependence on a lending city and because of probable instability in the loan data themselves.

COMMERCE AND MANUFACTURING

As we have seen in earlier chapters, writers on "metropolitanism" have usually accorded much greater importance to trade and the organization of commerce than to industrial production as a distinguishing characteristic of the metropolis. This is not to overlook the industrial basis of much of the urban growth in the nineteenth century nor to neglect the fact that some cities of considerable size and importance have based their development on pre-eminence in manufacturing. But the consensus among students of metropolitanism is that the exercise of commercial dominance is much more diagnostic of the organizational role of the metropolis than is the sheer volume of goods produced. It will be of interest to see how the data examined here and in later chapters fit in with this point of view.

Before describing the variables analyzed here, it is well to indicate some that are deliberately omitted. We shall give no special attention to the retail trade function. All metropolises have fairly well developed if not highly specialized retail facilities for servicing their own populations. There is a goodly number of kinds of retail business that are fairly highly concentrated in metropolitan centers as opposed to smaller places. Many of these are somewhat specialized types of retail outlet requiring populations of metropolitan proportions for an adequate basis of support (Hawley, 1941; Duncan, 1952). Some of these, no doubt, draw retail customers from a fairly extended hinterland (see Pfanner, 1940); but the volume of trade handled by such outlets is a comparatively small proportion of the total of the metropolitan center. The major inference from Bogue's (1949) data on retail specialization in the metropolitan community seems to be that the metropolitan center captures a substantial proportion of the retail trade of customers living in the immediately surrounding ("suburban") zone, but a comparatively small part of the trade of residents of zones further from the center. Moreover, if one examines the more detailed data compiled by Isard and Whitney (1949), it becomes apparent that metropolitan centers draw retail trade from the suburbs in large proportions only in certain kinds of business. There is clearly a need for more detailed studies of metropolitan retail trade functions than have yet been made; but we shall forego such investigation here in favor of a concentration on matters that seem to require more immediate attention. We shall further omit from consideration in this chapter the personal and professional services, some of which represent significant types of metropolitan functional specialization. These have been treated to some extent in chapter 3 and will receive further attention in Part III. Actually, in both chapter 3 and Part III use is made of complete industrial classifications of the labor force. Hence we feel free to single out a few categories of special interest for treatment here.

As representatives of "commercial" functions, we consider the volume of wholesale trade and of receipts of establishments providing business services; both are expressed in dollars per capita. "Business services," as defined in the *Census of Business,* is a somewhat heterogeneous aggregate, including advertising; consumer credit reporting agencies; duplicating, addressing, blueprinting, etc.; private employment agencies; news syndicates; services to buildings; and a wide variety of miscellaneous types of services. The largest single component is advertising, which in 1948 accounted for 40 per cent of the total receipts of all business services establishments in the United States. As a global measure of "industrial" functions, we use value added by manufacture, per capita, with no breakdown by kind of manufacturing. (Such a breakdown plays a prominent role in the analyses in Part III.) Some technical notes on these indicators are supplied in the Appendix. Our choice of these particular indicators for intensive study was motivated primarily by the ready accessibility of the statistics. However, we would be well advised in any case—other considerations being equal—to maintain some continuity with such previous studies as those of Bogue (1949) and Vance and Smith (1954).

Table 20 presents per capita wholesale, business services, and manufactures statistics for standard metropolitan areas (SMA's) classified by size. In earlier discussions we have noted the views of some writers that size does not afford a decisive criterion of a city's status as a "metropolis." However, it has to be conceded that large size is presumptive evidence of a claim to metropolitan status, and that if a quick judgment on the point is required, size probably serves about as well as any other single variable. In fact, we are willing to propose that any variable which does not show at least a moderately high correlation with city size is probably a poor indicator of metropolitanism: large size is a necessary, though not sufficient, criterion. On this criterion, per capita wholesale sales and business services receipts appear

Table 20. Average Per Capita Wholesale Sales, Business Services Receipts, and Value Added by Manufacture, for Standard Metropolitan Areas of 100,000 or More, by Size and Federal Reserve System Classification: 1947-48

Size and classification[1] of Standard Metropolitan Areas	Number of SMA's	Wholesale sales, 1948	Business services receipts, 1948	Value added by manufacture, 1947
		Mean[2] per capita value in dollars		
1,000,000 or more	14	2,027	20	716
Bank city	8	2,514	22	754
Branch city	5	1,463	17	786
Other	1	951	11	71
500,000 to 1,000,000	19	2,033	12	598
Bank city	3	3,875	20	466
Branch city	9	1,985	12	494
Other	7	1,306	10	789
300,000 to 500,000	23	1,477	11	588
Bank city	1	2,047	15	785
Branch city	5	2,983	14	371
Other	17	1,000	10	641
250,000 to 300,000	21	1,036	8	637
Branch city	1	1,984	13	227
Other	20	989	8	658
150,000 to 250,000	36	1,121	8	655
Branch city	3	2,624	8	272
Other	33	984	8	690
100,000 to 150,000	38	1,056	7	581

[1] Classification of largest central city in SMA.
[2] Unweighted mean of per capita values for SMA's in each group.

SOURCE: United States census reports (see Appendix).

to have value in discriminating between metropolitan and not-so-metropolitan cities, whereas per capita value added by manufacture has little such value. Taking the extreme size classes in table 20, the largest SMA's had per capita wholesale sales nearly double those of the smallest SMA's and per capita business services receipts nearly three times as large. The relative differences by size in respect to per capita value added by manufacture were much smaller and, moreover, did not vary nearly so regularly by size. It should be mentioned that there is some bias in the size comparisons in that the smaller SMA's, on the average, have somewhat larger proportions of rural population, who perhaps should not be included in the denominators of the per capita ratios. An adjustment for this bias might change the comparisons for manufacturing; it would hardly alter the pattern of size differences for wholesale and business services, although it would diminish somewhat the magnitude of the differences.

In addition to the size classification, there is a classification of SMA's in table 20 according to whether the principal central city is a Federal Reserve Bank City, a Branch City, or has no bank or branch of the Federal Reserve System. If this classification may be taken as an indication of metropolitanism, then it is significant that there are positive correlations between Federal Reserve status and both per capita wholesale sales and per capita business services receipts, as well as a positive correlation between size and Federal Reserve status. By contrast, per capita value added by manufacture is negatively related to Federal Reserve status. In regard to size, 8 of the 14 SMA's of 1,000,000 or more, but only three of the 19 SMA's of 500,000 to 1,000,000 and one of the 23 SMA's of 300,000 to 500,000 are Federal Reserve Bank Cities; a similar relationship to size for Branch Cities can be discerned upon elimination of the Bank Cities from consideration. (One Branch City—Helena, Mont.—is not large enough to qualify as an SMA.)

Further light on interrelationships of commercial and industrial functions is shed by the statistical analysis summarized in table 21. Here are presented intercorrelations of the three indicators, by size groups. Among the larger SMA's there is a substantial positive correlation between per capita wholesale sales and per capita business services receipts; within the three smaller size groups this correlation, while still positive and appreciable, is smaller. Only within the largest size group is per capita value added by manufacture positively correlated with either wholesale or business services, and the reliability of these two coefficients is questionable, with only 14 SMA's. At the other extreme of the size scale, manufacturing correlates negatively with wholesale and business services. At intermediate sizes the correlation is essentially nil with business services and negative but small with wholesale. These data, together with those in table 20, seemingly justify the use of wholesale and business services as indicators of metropolitanism, but lend no support to the supposition that manufacturing is a distinctively metropolitan function.

In the lower panels of table 21 are shown correlations of the three variables with measures of location. Population potential was intro-

Table 21. Rank Correlations Among Selected Economic and Locational Variables, for Standard Metropolitan Areas of 100,000 or More, by Size: 1947-48

Variables[1] correlated	Size of SMA					
	1,000,000 or more	500,000 to 1,000,000	300,000 to 500,000	250,000 to 300,000	150,000 to 250,000	100,000 to 150,000
Number of SMA's	14	19	23	21	36	38
Wholesale with—						
Business services	.63	.88	.75	.49	.57	.39
Manufacturing	.31	−.07	−.19	−.20	−.35	−.56
Business services with manufacturing	.33	.01	.01	.03	.03	−.33
Population potential with—						
Distance[2]	.67[3]	.69	.67	.59	.67	.67
Wholesale	−.13	−.23	−.53	−.11	−.34	−.58
Business services	−.11	−.20	−.40	−.23	−.01	−.35
Manufacturing	.29	.81	.72	.56	.70	.52
Distance[2] with—						
Wholesale	−.38[3]	−.58	−.36	−.43	−.59	−.75
Business services	−.46[3]	−.43	−.21	−.19	−.22	−.49
Manufacturing	.09[3]	.69	.80	.37	.57	.79

[1] Wholesale sales, business services receipts, and value added by manufacture in per capita form.

[2] Distance from nearest larger SMA; ranked from low to high.

[3] New York SMA excluded.

duced in chapter 2 as an index of accessibility (see also the Appendix). We may note that the configuration of population distribution which determines the pattern of isopotential lines (see the map, figure 1, chapter 2) is in large measure a function of where the major metropolitan centers are located. Hence, in characterizing an SMA in terms of the population potential in its vicinity, we are, in effect, characterizing it in terms of its generalized accessibility to other metropolitan areas. An alternative indicator, which we selected primarily because of its simplicity, is the railroad distance, ranked from low to high, of an SMA to the nearest larger SMA (see Appendix). As is shown in table

21, there is a fairly high correlation between these two locational variables, and one which is remarkably constant from one size group to another. (The population potential values for SMA's on which the correlations in table 21 are based are highly approximate. They were estimated from a map like that shown as figure 1, chapter 2. This map was constructed to give fairly accurate values of potential in the *non*metropolitan parts of the United States, but the isolines of potential cannot be considered accurate in the immediate vicinity of metropolitan centers. Hence the potential values we used represent the general level of population potential somewhere in the neighborhood of each SMA, but not the potential value that would be found at its center if a direct calculation were made.)

The striking result from the analysis of commercial and industrial functions in relation to these locational variables is that, within each size group, SMA's with high accessibility tend to have higher levels of manufacturing activity than those with low accessibility, whereas both wholesale and business services are negatively correlated with accessibility. On the whole the correlations for manufacturing are larger in absolute value than for the two indicators of commercial functions, and larger in absolute value for wholesale than for business services. Broadly speaking, we may interpret these results as showing the market orientation of manufacturing: an SMA tends to have a good deal of manufacturing if it is situated near concentrations of population. But for wholesaling and business services, accessibility to other SMA's seemingly implies competition from those SMA's for hinterland trade. As Vance and Smith (1954, p. 115) put it, for a city to emerge as a metropolis, "there must be a 'respectful' distance from other great cities." This gives us what is perhaps the most significant qualification on the use of sheer population size as an indicator of metropolitanism: a city of a given size is more likely to have metropolitan features if it has room to establish a sizable hinterland than if it lies in the shadow of a larger city. Interestingly enough, Bogue (1949) was forced to modify his size criterion for recognizing metropolitan centers in the part of the country where population potential rises to its highest levels. Another implication of our results is that the commercial and industrial functions of a metropolis—however defined—reflect not only its relationships with its hinterland—however delineated—but also its position in the more inclusive inter-metropolitan complex. We thus come back to the observation of chapter 2 that to understand what a city does we need to know where it is; but we have now given the "where" a somewhat more concrete interpretation.

An interesting detail in table 21 is that in five out of six comparisons for wholesale and four out of six for business services the absolute size of the correlation with distance is greater than that with potential. However, for manufacturing the correlation with potential is the higher in four of the six comparisons. Thus, while both potential and distance are related to the dependent variables and the two are rather highly intercorrelated, they do seem to get at slightly different aspects of accessibility. Some analogous findings are noted in chapters 7 and 8.

We may consider, finally, the interrelations of the commercial and industrial functions under examination with the financial function discussed earlier. The significance of non-local lending by metropolitan banks in supporting the economic activity of the "hinterland" is suggested in the following observations:

> Chicago—by virtue of its size—is the dominant Midwestern supplier and user of bank funds for business. Half the volume of business loans made by Chicago banks goes to nonlocal borrowers, if nonlocal borrowers are defined as those headquartered beyond the borders of counties adjoining the lender's metropolitan area or county. . . . In the smaller urban banks the proportion of out-of-town to total business loans averages about 13 per cent, and in rural banks it averages about 5 per cent. In general, the smaller the bank and the smaller the center in which it is located, the greater is the proportion of local loans in its portfolio.
>
> A variety of reasons may contribute to this tendency. In some small industrially oriented cities and towns, demands for loans on the part of the firms within the community are more than sufficient to absorb all the funds the local banks are willing to lend to business. In other cases, smaller banks find themselves without the contacts and servicing facilities to attract distant borrowers, even if they desire to do so. Moreover, the cost to small banks of making business loans outside their area may be relatively high. In these circumstances, many a small bank finds it more advantageous to gain balance in its earning assets by increasing its investment holdings rather than seeking out-of-town loans. (Federal Reserve Bank of Chicago, 1957, pp. 11-12.)

Table 22 summarizes correlations expressing relationships between per capita volume of business ("commercial") lending and the variables previously considered. It should be noted that conclusions drawn from these figures are not wholly reliable, for several reasons. First, the loan data are for 1955, and the base populations are for 1950. Second, the loan amounts are given only for central cities of SMA's rather than for all banks in the SMA's. This probably biases the figures on total business loans worse than those on non-local loans, since it is primarily the banks in central cities which make non-local loans, as was pointed out earlier in the case of the New York SMA. (In a few instances, loan data are available for important suburban cities, and these figures were combined with those for the respective central cities.) Third, loan data are not available for two SMA's in the 500,000—1,000,000 population size class and for eight SMA's in the 300,000—500,000 class. Omission of these SMA's probably distorts the results, since the omitted areas, in general, are those with relatively low levels of banking activity.

Although the results must be interpreted with caution, they fall into an interesting pattern: per capita measures of bank lending correlate rather consistently with per capita wholesale trade; they are positively but somewhat erratically correlated with per capita business services receipts; they are not significantly correlated with per capita value added by manufacture or with the locational variables (population potential and distance to nearest larger SMA) that are fairly closely related to manufacturing. The suggested conclusion is that banking activities "hang together" with commercial activities while manufacturing varies somewhat independently of both.

The correlation results give no clear indication of whether per capita volume of total loans or of non-local loans considered separately is the preferable measure of "metropolitan" banking functions. Aside from the bias mentioned above, it must be recalled that the distinction between local and non-local loans is misleading or unreliable in some cases. It is pertinent to observe that a much more readily available indicator of banking functions—per capita demand deposits (see Appendix)—apparently provides a fairly effective surrogate for the loan variables. The bottom panel of table 22 shows that in the two larger size groups per capita demand deposits is fairly highly correlated with both loan variables and shows a pattern of relationships with the other variables similar to that noted for the loan variables. The correlations for SMA's of 300,000—500,000 also are instructive, for the information on deposits is available for all areas in this class. It may be seen that the omission of eight SMA's attenuates the correlations of the commercial indicators with bank deposits; these eight SMA's are known to have comparatively small amounts of deposits and may be assumed to engage in lending on a relatively small scale.

The foregoing analysis is not meant to characterize the interrelations of commercial and financial activities in any close detail. The indicators used are quite gross and each is an aggregate of more or less heterogeneous components. The assessment of relationships was deliberately based on the non-parametric technique of rank correlation to avoid any temptation to become excessively preoccupied with the mathematical form of the relationships.

Table 22. Rank Correlations of Selected Banking Variables with Selected Economic and Locational Variables, for Standard Metropolitan Areas of 300,000 or More, by Size

Variables[1] correlated	Size of SMA		
	1,000,000 or more	500,000 to 1,000,000[3]	300,000 to 500,000[4]
Number of SMA's	14	17	15 (23)
Total business loans (1955) with—			
Wholesale (1948)	.67	.71	.78
Business services (1948)	.24	.75	.34
Manufacturing (1947)	−.05	.10	−.30
Potential (1950)	−.01	−.24	−.08
Distance (1950)	−.43[2]	−.47	−.19
Non-local business loans (1955) with—			
Wholesale	.57	.76	.81
Business services	.25	.81	.26
Manufacturing	.22	.42	−.21
Potential	.17	.17	−.09
Distance	−.29[2]	−.17	−.07
Demand deposits (1950) with—			
Wholesale	.62	.86	.49 (.75)
Business services	.45	.76	.61 (.86)
Manufacturing	.15	.26	−.23 (.00)
Potential	.29	−.01	−.13 (−.38)
Distance	−.26[2]	−.39	−.13 (−.12)
Total business loans	.68	.76	.58
Non-local business loans	.72	.85	.34

[1] All variables except potential and distance to nearest larger SMA are expressed per capita; base population is 1950 census figure for banking variables and estimated 1948 figure for wholesale sales, business services receipts, and value added by manufacture. Distance ranked from low to high, other variables high to low.

[2] New York SMA excluded.

[3] Albany–Schenectady–Troy and Youngstown SMA's excluded; loan data not available.

[4] Figures in parentheses are for all 23 SMA's in size group. Other figures exclude Allentown–Bethlehem–Easton, Charleston (W. Va.), Knoxville, Norfolk–Portsmouth, Springfield–Holyoke, Tampa–St. Petersburg, Wheeling–Steubenville, and Wilkes-Barre–Hazleton SMA's; loan data not available.

SOURCE: *1947 Census of Manufactures, 1948 Census of Business, 1952 County Data Book,* unpublished loan data supplied by Division of Research and Statistics, Board of Governors, Federal Reserve System.

Despite all necessary qualifications, the findings reported in this chapter are not without significance, even if that significance lies primarily in documenting relationships hitherto largely assumed rather than demonstrated to exist. It was shown that bank lending is indeed an activity with "metropolitan" characteristics. Large cities are differentiated in terms of their relative importance with respect to this activity and fall into a roughly hierarchical pattern of inter-city financial relationships. On the whole, highly developed financial facilities are found in conjunction with high levels of the kind of trade activity thought to be characteristic of "metropolises." But industrial activity varies more or less independently of these financial and commercial functions. A "metropolis" defined by its commercial and financial characteristics may or may not have a comparatively high level of manufacturing activity—the two possibilities are about equally probable.

None of the materials in this or preceding chapters suggests a unique formal criterion for distinguishing between cities which are metropolitan centers and those which are not. No rigid distinction of this sort is needed, in all probability. For particular analyses, classifications of convenience can be devised with some assurance that any "reasonable" scheme is not likely to look materially more or less arbitrary than some reasonable alternative. We can, however, say something about the nature of the metropolis on the basis of our findings. (Compare with our discussion of Gras's criteria, summarized at the outset of chapter 4.) If one were setting out to identify metropolitan centers he would first look at cities of relatively large size. He would then discriminate among them in terms of level of commercial activity, expecting with some reason that cities ranking high in this respect would be those wherein such activity is supported by well developed financial facilities and services. Such a commercial-financial center is more likely to be found at some distance from competing centers of comparable size than in locations near numerous competitors. Cities with the foregoing metropolitan characteristics may have rather highly developed manufacturing activities, though this is not especially likely to be the case, for the conditions favoring manufacturing—access to the markets afforded by major population concentrations—are not greatly favorable to high development of the commercial-financial functions. Whatever the functions that are proposed as distinctive characteristics of metropolises, they should be studied not only with reference to the "hinterland" being served directly—if such can be identified—but also in the context of the large intermetropolitan system which so profoundly influences the spatial structure of the whole national economy.

CHAPTER 6

Interregional Flow of Funds

As we have suggested in previous chapters, an important class of metropolitan functions comprises those of mediating interregional exchanges. Although this type of function has been widely recognized, relatively little research has been done to delineate the role of metropolitan centers in interregional relationships. The major reason for this gap in the literature is doubtless the lack of pertinent data. Recently it has been pointed out that a potentially important source of information on the subject has been neglected, i.e., the records of flows of funds maintained by the Federal Reserve System:

> The flows of funds between regions of the United States are concrete evidences of important economic processes. Data on these flows between Reserve districts or zones, unlike most economic data, are extremely current and are available as a by-product of the Federal Reserve accounting system. . . . The bulk of check or wire transfers of funds between regions is collected through the Federal Reserve System. In addition, virtually all other inter-regional payments, such as checks or wires which are collected through correspondents or in other ways, are ultimately reflected in their net amount on the Reserve Banks' books. Records of the Interdistrict Settlement Fund, adjusted to include transfers of funds by the United States Treasury and inter-Reserve Bank transactions, furnish a picture of the flow of commercial and financial payments and receipts between each of the 36 head office and branch zones of the Federal Reserve System. Data on commercial and financial transactions reveal a number of definite patterns in the interdistrict movements in funds. These patterns may be viewed from the standpoint of a structural geographic

> pattern of flows or of specific seasonal and trend relationships between individual districts. (Bowsher, Daane, and Einzig, 1957, pp. 139-140.)

The function of collecting, clearing, and transferring funds performed by the Federal Reserve Banks and Branch Banks in 36 cities (most of which are commonly recognized as "metropolitan centers") has become a vital part of the total process of exchange of goods and services, as is indicated by the rapid and continuing growth in numbers of checks cleared by Reserve Banks (United States Board of Governors of the Federal Reserve System, 1954, p. 157). The transfer of funds, therefore, is a "metropolitan" function par excellence.

DATA AND MODELS

Certain conceptual problems are recognized to render the meaning of data on Interdistrict Settlement Fund (ISF) clearings obscure for some purposes:

> (1) the payments flows and the flow of goods and services may not coincide in time or as between the same districts; (2) the gross payments and receipts figures exclude correspondent bank clearings and are thus incomplete and perhaps unrepresentative in the short run; (3) mixed in with commercial transactions are financial transactions; and (4) the financial transactions cover such a gamut of exchanges that in the aggregate they are not useful for purposes of economic analysis. (Daane, Einzig, and Bowsher, 1955, p. 32.)

We, therefore, approach the analysis of a sample of ISF data with some trepidation, in view of the acknowledged difficulties of interpreting results, and given the limited exploration of these data up to now. (For a comprehensive statement on the nature and limitations of the ISF data, see Daane, Einzig, and Bowsher, 1955.) However, we point out that we are concerned not with the anatomy of the financial mechanisms involved nor with the meaning of the results for Federal Reserve System policy nor with any of a large number of other problems best left to competent specialists in money and banking. We merely wish to investigate some aspects of the "structural geographic pattern of flows" in a preliminary fashion. For our purposes it is not necessary to specify what transactions underlie the flows of payments if only we may assume that the payments records are, indeed, "concrete evidence of important economic processes," and not pure artifacts of bookkeeping. Any evidence of pattern or structure in the flows will then be acceptable evidence that some aspect or aspects of the economy are organized around metropolitan centers and the banking functions performed in those centers. Our general point of view is in conformity with what we understand to be the major methodological premises of Rutledge Vining's program of research on "the spatial structure of an economic system." In Vining's research it was necessary to resort to the use of data whose "distributions conform only roughly to the idea" of a spatial structure oriented to a system of centers, whose units of measurement are not of a kind that might be desirable, but which are "illustrative nevertheless" (Vining, 1953, pp. 57-59). Vining's inductive procedures have as an objective

> to present an idea of spatial structure and to present materials that empirically outline its form and features. . . . It is to be taken for granted that in continuing the work that I describe I do not already know all of the essential features of the form and structure of an economic system. Thus, my problem is not a mere problem of computation and estimation. This is one of my quarrels with much of empirical economic research—essences and natures are already presumed to be known and all that remains to be done consists of computation and estimation. The emphasis of my point of view is placed otherwise. The discovery of essences and natures of structures and processes is the principal objective, and the concern . . . is the nature of the spatial structure of a human economy. (Vining, 1952b, p. 479.)

It is entirely possible that the kinds of conceptual and analytical refinements that might be proposed for the treatment of flow data will differ according to whether one takes as a starting point some *a priori* conception of the meaning the data should have or, alternatively, begins with some preliminary evidence of pattern in the data and seeks to understand anomalous features of that pattern or observed systematic departures from it.

Data on ISF clearings are compiled weekly by the Board of Governors of the Federal Reserve System and distributed to the 36 Reserve Bank offices in the form of photocopies. Through the co-operation of the Research Department of the Federal Reserve Bank of Chicago, we gained access to a sample of these weekly records. The sample consists of the aggregated records for four weeks in 1957: January 24-30, April 25 to May 1, July 25-31, and October 24-30. These weeks were selected arbitrarily rather than at random, with some thought of trying to avoid weeks involving unusually large volumes of income tax payments and of roughly averaging out the seasonal patterns known to exist in the ISF data (see Bowsher, Daane, and Einzig, 1957). The weekly ISF report is in the form of a 36 × 36 table showing payments from each of the 36 Federal Reserve Banks and Branch Banks to each of the other 35; actually a few cells in the table are missing, as we indicate presently. We shall use the term "zones" to refer to the 36 territorial units in the Federal Reserve System (see the map in chapter 4, figure 6).

Our analysis concerns gross volume of flows between each pair of zones; e.g., we added the payments from New Orleans to Cincinnati to the payments from Cincinnati to New Orleans to obtain a measure of the gross flow or interchange between the two zones, abstracting from the direction of flow and from the net balance of flows in whichever direction it occurred. Some feeling for the magnitudes involved may be conveyed by the observation that the largest gross flow (total for the four sample weeks) was $6.4 billion, between the New York and Chicago zones, and the smallest was $6 thousand, between the Memphis and Helena zones. Data on gross flow (as here defined) were not available for Detroit-Chicago nor for intra-district clearings in the Twelfth (San Francisco) Federal Reserve District. For lack of a suitable basis of estimation, we arbitrarily set the Detroit-Chicago gross flow approximately equal to the Detroit-New York gross flow. Data for an earlier year were used to estimate roughly the gross flows within the Twelfth District. Altogether, 11 of the 630 streams of gross flow were thus estimated. (For details on the estimates, see the Appendix.)

Our table of gross flows between 630, i.e., (36)(35)/2, pairs of zones resembles in form the kinds of data used hitherto in studies of intercity airline passenger traffic, telephone calls, and like interchanges. Hence it seemed appropriate to work with the so-called "gravity model" employed in many of these studies. (For a comprehensive survey of applications of gravity models, see Carrothers, 1956.) In its simplest form the gravity model for interchanges between pairs of territorial units postulates that the volume of interchange is directly proportional to the product of the populations of the two units and inversely proportional to the distance separating them. Thus, if H_{ij} is the gross flow between the ith and the jth zones, P_i and P_j are the respective populations of the zones, and D_{ij} is the distance between them (presumably measured from some appropriate central point within each zone), then the gravity model is of the form, $H_{ij} = KP_iP_j/D_{ij}$, with K as a constant of proportionality.

A cursory inspection of our flow data reveals that this model will not provide an acceptable fit. We therefore considered two alternatives, both generalizations of the simple gravity model. Model I is of the form, $H_{ij} = A(P_iP_j/D_{ij})^b$, or $\log H_{ij} = a + b \log (P_iP_j/D_{ij})$, where A and b are constants to be determined from the data and $a = \log A$. Model II is of the form, $H_{ij}/P_iP_j = C/D_{ij}^d$, or $\log (H_{ij}/P_iP_j) = c - d \log D_{ij}$, where $c = \log C$. Whereas there is a feeling among some proponents of gravity models that the simple model (with exponent unity for population and distance) can be given a theoretical rationalization, Models I and II have been used simply as empirical or "curve fitting" functions. Iklé (1954) claims that no meaningful interpretation can be given a function in which population has an exponent different from unity, but believes that the exponent of distance should be determined empirically rather than assumed to be unity (Hammer and Iklé, 1957); hence he favors Model II. Warntz (1957, p. 128) following Stewart, takes a contrary position in stating a strong preference for clinging "to purely physical notions," in which "space and time are to be recognized as dimensions of the economic system and hence to be treated isomorphically in the rigid pattern of mathematical physics"; Warntz would presumably seek means of improving the fit of the simple gravity model other than altering its unit exponents. There is controversy as well regarding the means of fitting data to these models (Iklé, 1955; Anderson, 1955b). The simplest procedure, other than graphic estimation, is perhaps to use least squares regression techniques with the logarithmic versions of the models, which are linear in form, although objections to this procedure have been stated (Anderson, 1955b).

RESULTS

Without trying to resolve the foregoing issues, we fitted both models, employing conventional regression methods with the logarithms of the variables. For Model I, with flow (H_{ij}) in dollars, population (P_i and P_j) in 1,000's of inhabitants (in 1950) and distance (D_{ij}) in miles of railroad distance between the Federal Reserve Bank and Branch Cities (see Appendix), the constants were found to be $a = 1.69$ and $b = 1.37$; the correlation coefficient was .82. For Model II, the constants were $c = 4.61$ and $d = 1.22$; the correlation coefficient was $-.54$. Thus, in both models distance has an exponent appreciably greater than unity in absolute value. But, as we shall point out, it is likely that both models are incomplete in that pertinent variables affecting the volume of flows have been omitted. This being the case, it should be remembered "that any maximizing estimate of b is only an approximation to the 'best' value of b since the addition of another variable to the formula . . . can be expected to change the value of the estimate of b" (Anderson, 1955b, p. 715). The present evidence, therefore, does not adjudicate the controversy as to the exponent of distance.

In interpreting the correlation coefficients it must be remembered that the regression technique used here minimizes sums of squares of errors in the logarithm of flows, not in the flows in dollar units. The fact that the correlation for Model II is smaller in absolute value (the difference in sign is an artifact of the way we wrote the equations) than the correlation for Model I must not be misunderstood. The correlation coefficient for Model I is like a multiple correlation, in the sense that flow (the dependent variable) is related to population and distance (a combination of two independent variables), whereas that for Model II is like a partial correlation in the sense that flow is related to distance, with population held constant. What we should probably conclude from the comparison of the two coefficients is that the volume of flow varies inversely with distance independently of population size and directly with population size independently of distance. Since we have no theoretical basis for preferring one model to the other, we continue the discussion in terms of the results for Model I only.

The first point we wish to emphasize is that this modified gravity model gives a pretty good first approximation to the spatial structure of the system of flows. Model I accounts for two-thirds of the variation in the logarithms of gross flows between pairs of zones. Although we shall dwell at some length on inadequacies of the model, it is well to keep in mind that no possible refinement of the model could lead to more than a 50 per cent increase in the proportion of variation "explained."

The residual variation not accounted for by Model I may be regarded as a net sum of variation due to random and systematic errors of measurement of the variables in the model plus variation attributable to variables omitted from the model. Possible errors of measurement include the following: (1) There may be a random error of measurement due to the selection of a sample of only four out of 52 weeks in the year. The sampling procedure may have introduced a systematic error as well if the spacing of the sample weeks was not such as to average out seasonal patterns of variation in flows. (2) There is some systematic error in the measurement of population in that we had to use 1950 populations, whereas the flow data are for 1957. The average change in population size since 1950 would affect only the constant A (or a) of the model, but differential growth means that we systematically understated the population of rapidly growing areas. Some evidence bearing on this point is given subsequently. (3) The measure of distance used here is crude. It was assumed that railroad distance was more pertinent than airline or highway distance for most transactions, but this plainly would not be the case for all. Moreover, our distances were ascertained for the 36 cities, and these may be biased as compared with average distances separating the populations of the respective zones. Stewart and Warntz (1958a) have shown that Federal Reserve Bank Cities uniformly are located eccentrically with respect to the geographic centers of their districts, in the direction of increasing population potential (this effect might be less noticeable if measured with respect to centers of population rather than area). We assume that any bias arising from this source is relatively small, given that we are working with the 36 zones rather than the 12 districts of the Federal Reserve System.

As to errors arising from omission of relevant variables—which are probably more serious than those arising from imprecise or inaccurate measurements—we offer a distinction between two cases. First, the "system" of flows may not be in equilibrium, i.e., the volume or directional pattern of flows may be subject to cyclical changes or secular trends which were of necessity ignored in the analysis. Second, even if the "system" is in equilibrium, we surely have not included all the elements of its structure in our rudimentary model. Among the more interesting possibilities of variables omitted are the following: (1) Our variable, population size, should probably be regarded as a surrogate for a variable, "economic size," or "capacity to generate flows." Although it is hard to suggest a convenient indicator of the latter, one can give reasons why population size may be a defective indicator. The populations of the 36 zones differ in level of urbanization, average income, type of economic activity, and degree of dependence on extralocal resources and markets. (2) The model, in introducing distance as the only factor in spatial orientation, abstracts from the two-dimensional spatial patterning or geographic arrangement of the zones. It is possible that two zones at a given distance apart will have a greater flow if they are adjacent than if they are separated by another zone. Students of migratory population flows have suggested "intervening opportunities" as a refinement of "distance," although it is still uncertain whether this is a worthwhile or important refinement (Anderson, 1955a). There may be still other spatial or geographic factors acting to channel flows somewhat independently of distance; these might differ according to the mode of transportation. (3) It could be that the mechanism by which the ISF operates or the uses to which it is put by the U. S. Treasury, for example, operate to generate flows between certain zones rather than others. We have no specific indication that this is the case, but there is pertinent evidence of non-random departure from the model according to the classification of zones (see below). (4) Since the foregoing enumeration is no doubt incomplete, we must recognize the possible relevance of additional but unsuspected variables.

Because our analysis of flows represented by the ISF clearings is only preliminary, we have not sought to refine the model or the variables entering into it. We merely wish to conclude our discussion of the model by pointing to some evidence of systematic error; possibly this evidence will furnish a starting point to investigators interested in a more thorough analysis. We inserted the population and distance values into the model to calculate the flow for each pair of zones from the computed constants of the model. The actual flow minus the calculated flow (both in logarithmic form) is our measure of error.

First we may note that only 42 per cent of the errors are positive and 58 per cent are negative; hence the positive deviations from the estimating equation are larger on the average than are the negative deviations. The discrepancy from the expected value of 50 per cent (if the errors were random) seems too great to attribute to chance. It is possible that this effect could be removed by fitting a model involving a nonlinear function of the logarithm of P_iP_j/D_{ij}; we did not investigate this possibility, since we regard it as more likely that the skew distribution of deviations is produced by one of the sources of systematic error suggested previously.

We counted the positive and negative deviations for the 35 streams of flow associated with each of the 36 zones and characterized each zone as having a majority of positive deviations or a majority of negative deviations. (In this procedure, of course, each deviation is counted twice—one for each member of the pair of zones.) There is an unmistakable geographic pattern of the deviations. In the Ninth (Minneapolis), Tenth (Kansas City), Eleventh (Dallas) and Twelfth (San Francisco) Federal Reserve Districts are found 15 of the 36 zones. For only three of these 15 zones was there a preponderance of negative deviations (Minneapolis, Omaha, and San Antonio). By contrast, of the 21 zones in the eight districts to the east, there were only two (New York and Pittsburgh) for which the positive outnumbered the negative deviations. (The reader is reminded that some of these flows were crudely estimated.)

On the basis of current population estimates by states, we tried to guess which zones increased in population more rapidly than the country as a whole between 1950 and 1957 (using estimates in United States Bureau of the Census, *Current Population Reports,* "Population Estimates," Series P-25, No. 168). The term "guess" is used advisedly, for the official state estimates are themselves subject to error, and we had to resort to intuition and analogy with 1940-50 growth rates in the numerous cases where a zone did not coincide with a state but included parts of one or more states. Of the 15 zones assumed to have increased at above-average rates, 9 had an excess of positive over negative deviations; of the 21 zones with below-average growth rates, only 5 had an excess of positive over negative deviations. This presumably significant departure from a random pattern is not independent of the previously noted geographic pattern of deviations, inasmuch as many of the rapidly growing zones are in the West. Approaching the problem a little differently, we note that there are three categories in which a pair of zones involved in an interchange may fall: both zones of the pair grew more rapidly than the average; one did and the other did not; and neither did. For a random sample of 50 pairs of zones we tabulated the number of pairs according to these three categories with a cross-classification of the deviation of actual from expected flow as positive or negative. The chi-square for the 2×3 table is not significant. However, if we remove from the sample the 18 pairs of zones concerning whose growth-rate classification we feel least confident, the chi-square is significant at the .05 level. In this reduced sample, the fractions of pairs with positive deviations are 3/3 for both zones growing rapidly, 9/18 for one of the pair with rapid growth, and 2/11 for neither with rapid growth.

The indication of systematic error introduced by bias in our population figures may be open to more than one interpretation. While it is certain that we would reduce or eliminate some of the excessively large deviations by entering the model with current rather than out-of-date population figures, a cursory inspection of the data suggests that there probably would remain some systematic departure from the model on the part of rapidly growing zones. If this proved to be true, we should have to conclude that the "system" of flows is not in equilibrium, or that part of the flows are generated in response to growth occurring at a given time; to include this effect one would have to construct a "dynamic" model.

The 36 zones of the Federal Reserve System are of two types: those containing a Federal Reserve Bank and those with a branch of the

Federal Reserve Bank of the district in which the zone is located (see figure 6, chapter 4). If the bank-branch distinction is crossed by the distinction between flows within a district and those across district boundaries, we obtain the five categories shown in table 23. That table gives the proportion of positive deviations (actual minus computed flows from Model I) for each of the five types of flow. There is a clear departure from the expectation of only random variation in proportion of positive deviations over the five types; chi-square for the table is 37.9, which, with four degrees of freedom, is significant at the .001 level. It will be recalled that for lack of data we had to estimate intra-district flows for 11 pairs of zones: 5 bank-branch pairs and 6 branch-branch pairs. It happens that all 11 of the estimated figures are higher than the values computed from Model I. This may mean that our estimates were too high; or it may merely be that the missing data happen to be for zones which tend to have larger flows than those predicted by the model. In any event, if these 11 cases are removed, the proportion of positive deviations remains as high as 78.9 per cent for intra-district bank-branch flows and 58.8 per cent for intra-district branch-branch flows. Moreover, if we compute chi-square for the inter-district flows only (last three lines of table 23), it remains significant at the .01 level. It seems clear that there are systematic deviations from the model associated with type of flow.

Table 23. Deviations from Model I of Interdistrict Settlement Fund Flows, by Type of Flow

Type of flow	Number of pairs of zones	Per cent of positive deviations
All types	630	42.2
Intra-district		
Bank-branch	24	83.3
Branch-branch	23	69.6
Interdistrict		
Bank-bank	66	42.4
Bank-branch	264	46.4
Branch-branch	253	31.4

SOURCE: Unpublished data furnished by Chicago Federal Reserve Bank.

This source of systematic departure from the model is not, of course, independent of those previously identified. For example, the number of zones per district is 3.75 in the four westernmost Federal Reserve Districts and only 2.625 in the eight districts to the east; hence, the five categories in table 23 have differing representation of the two "regions." We have not tried to distinguish a "regional" from a "type-of-flow" effect, but it did seem expedient to make one further check on the latter. This consisted of recomputing the constants of Model I separately for each of the three types of interdistrict flow; the results are shown in table 24. (We did not make a similar computation for intra-district flows, because of the uncertain validity of our estimated figures in this group.) It appears that the constants of the model differ appreciably according to type of flow considered. In particular, flows between branch territories fall off more rapidly with distance than do flows between bank territories, inasmuch as the exponent of distance rises from 0.96 to 1.31 in going from the latter to the former group. In further analysis of these data using similar models, it would be well to begin with an investigation of features of the Federal Reserve System or of the ISF that may explain the differences among types of flow in the relation of flow to distance.

Table 24. Computed Constants for Model I, by Type of Gross Flow

Type of flow	Number of pairs *N*	Regression constants[1] *a*	Regression constants[1] *b*	Correlation coefficient *r*
All flows[2]	630	1.69	1.37	.82
Interdistrict flows				
Bank-bank	66	3.70	0.96	.65
Bank-branch	264	2.50	1.17	.72
Branch-branch	253	1.79	1.31	.75

[1] For equation, computed $\log H_{ij} = a + b \log (P_iP_j/D_{ij})$, where H_{ij} is gross flow in dollars, P_i or P_j is population in 1,000's of inhabitants, and D_{ij} is distance in miles.

[2] Includes intra-district flows (47 pairs of zones).

SOURCE: Unpublished data furnished by Chicago Federal Reserve Bank.

EXAMPLES

We now present in cartographic form some further information on patterns of deviation from Model I (figure 9). For selected pairs of zones we make comparisons showing with which other zones the first member of the pair has the larger gross flow and with which zones the second has the larger flow. These actual differences are shown on the maps by connecting lines. The expected differences are indicated by shading the area within which one member of the pair is expected to have the larger flows. As long as we are comparing zones of the same type (both contain a Federal Reserve Bank City or both contain a Branch City), Model I as originally computed and the revised versions of the model in table 24 lead to the same expectation. Thus if we are comparing Zones 1 and 2 in regard to their respective flows with Zone 3, Zone 1 is expected to have the larger flow if P_1/D_{13} is greater than P_2/D_{23}.

Most of our examples concern comparisons where there were several departures from the model; but since they were chosen to highlight such departures it should be remembered that the model is not as bad as it may look. Figure 9A, for example, depicts a comparison for which the model worked rather well. The Boston zone has a considerably larger population than the Minneapolis zone (8.8 vs. 5.1 million). Its total gross flow (sum of Boston gross flow with 35 other zones) bears an even higher ratio to that of Minneapolis ($7.6 vs. $3.2 billion). But 72 per cent of Boston's flow is with New York, and 78 per cent is with New York and Chicago combined, whereas only 34 per cent of the Minneapolis flow is with New York and 61 per cent with New York and Chicago combined. The map reveals two zones with which Boston had the larger flow contrary to expectation—both on the periphery of the area within which Minneapolis was expected to have the larger flow. Similarly, there are two zones on the periphery of Boston's

---

Figure 9 A–F (on following pages). Comparisons of Selected Pairs of Federal Reserve Zones with Respect to Relative Size of Gross Flows (Interdistrict Settlement Fund Clearings): 1957. Each outlying zone is connected with the one of the pair with which it has the larger gross flow. The shaded area covers zones with which one of the pair is expected to have the larger gross flow, according to Model I. (Source: Unpublished data furnished by Chicago Federal Reserve Bank.)

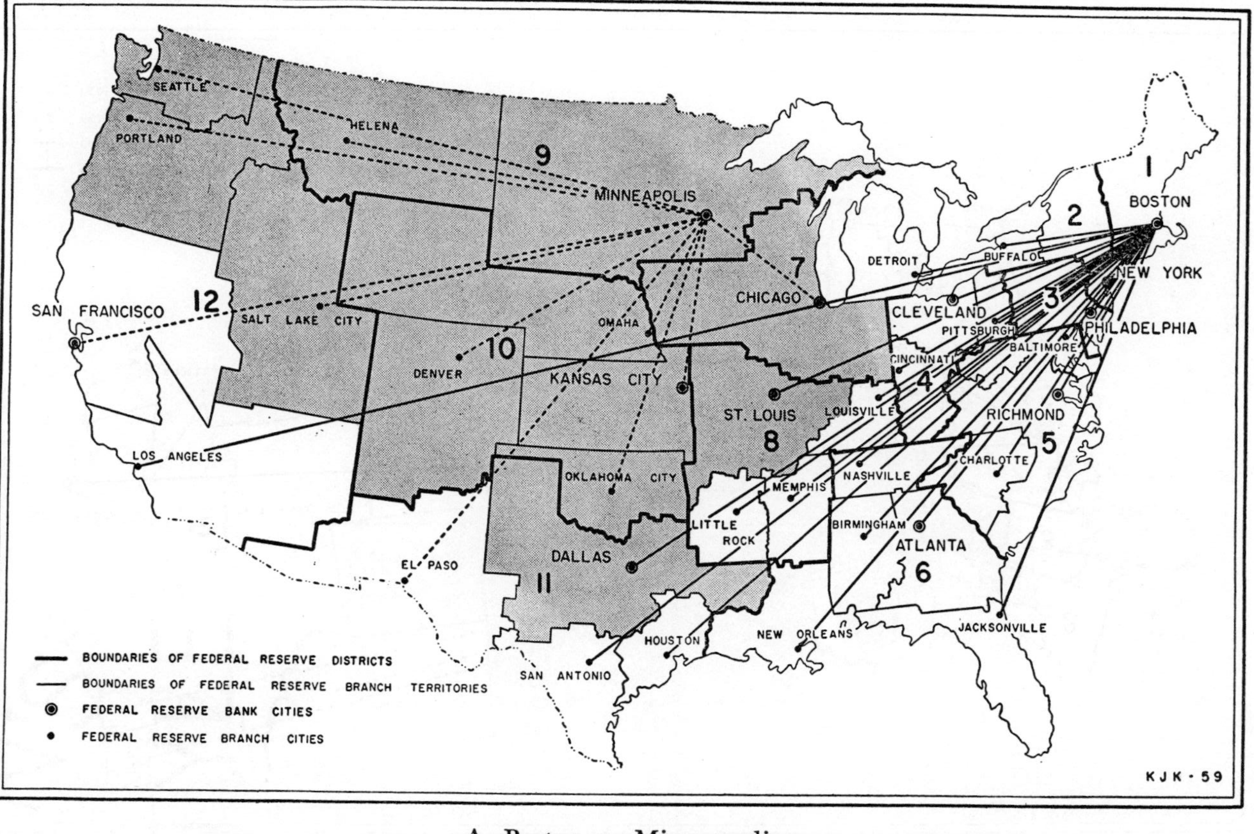

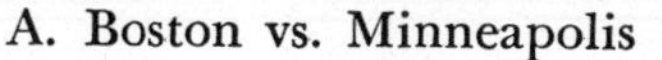
A. Boston vs. Minneapolis

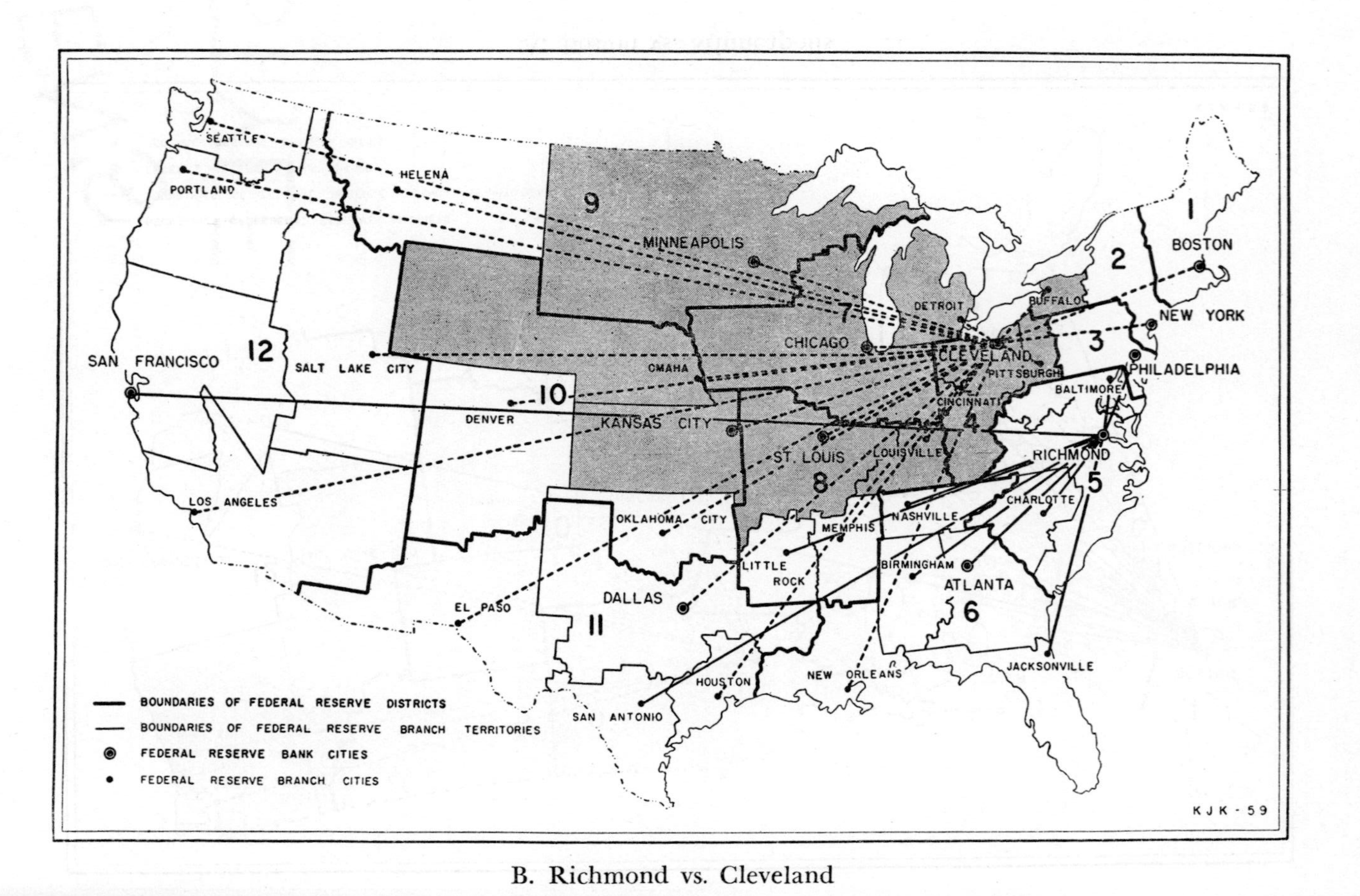

B. Richmond vs. Cleveland

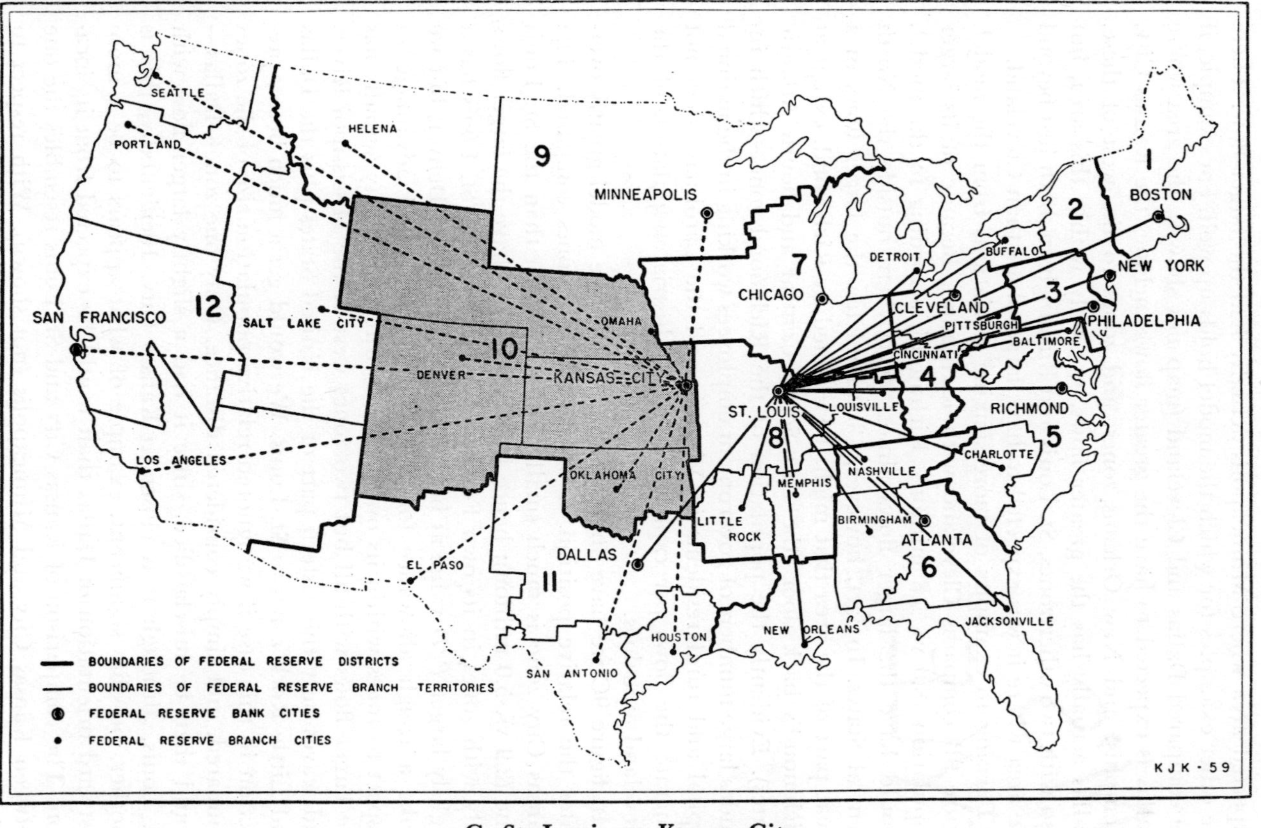

C. St. Louis vs. Kansas City

expected area where Minneapolis actually had the larger flow. There are other examples for which the model holds up well. For example, if we compared Dallas and Cleveland (map not shown), the area where Dallas is expected to have the greater flows includes the Kansas City, Memphis, and New Orleans zones, and zones to the west of these. Dallas actually has the greater flows, not only within this area, but also with two other zones, St. Louis and Birmingham, both just beyond the area where it was expected to have larger flows than Cleveland.

Turning to examples of more striking deviations from the model, figure 9B compares Cleveland with Richmond. Because of its larger population (8.0 vs. 5.8 million), Richmond, according to the model, should have the larger flows almost everywhere outside the North Central States. In fact, however, Cleveland has the larger flows in a great part of the area that might be claimed by Richmond, except at Richmond's back door (the East South Central and South Atlantic States). Evidently the population of the Richmond zone—which includes large numbers of government employees working in the national capital and rural residents in Virginia and the Carolinas—does not generate the flows per capita that the industrial population of the Cleveland zone does.

In figure 9C we have an instance in which the model greatly overstates the relative position of one of the two zones compared. The Kansas City zone is much smaller in population than the St. Louis zone (2.9 vs. 5.0 million); hence it is expected to have the larger flows only with zones in its own Federal Reserve District. (St. Louis has a slightly larger P/D value at both Oklahoma City and Denver, but we make a rough allowance for Kansas City's presumed advantage in respect to zones within its own district.) But Kansas City actually has the larger flows with all but two zones west of the Mississippi River, and leaves only the eastern part of the United States plus the Dallas and Little Rock zones to St. Louis. We would get a much better prediction in this case if we ignored relative population size of the zones compared, and simply considered distance. Only one zone—Dallas—would then be misclassified, since it had a slightly larger flow with St. Louis, although it is closer to Kansas City. Incidentally, this is another, possibly significant, example of what appears to be a more eastward orientation of Dallas than would be expected from its location. The comparison of Kansas City and St. Louis resembles the one between Kansas City and Minneapolis (not shown). With respect to Minneapolis, Kansas City is expected to have the larger flows with only six zones in the heart of the continent. But it actually had the higher

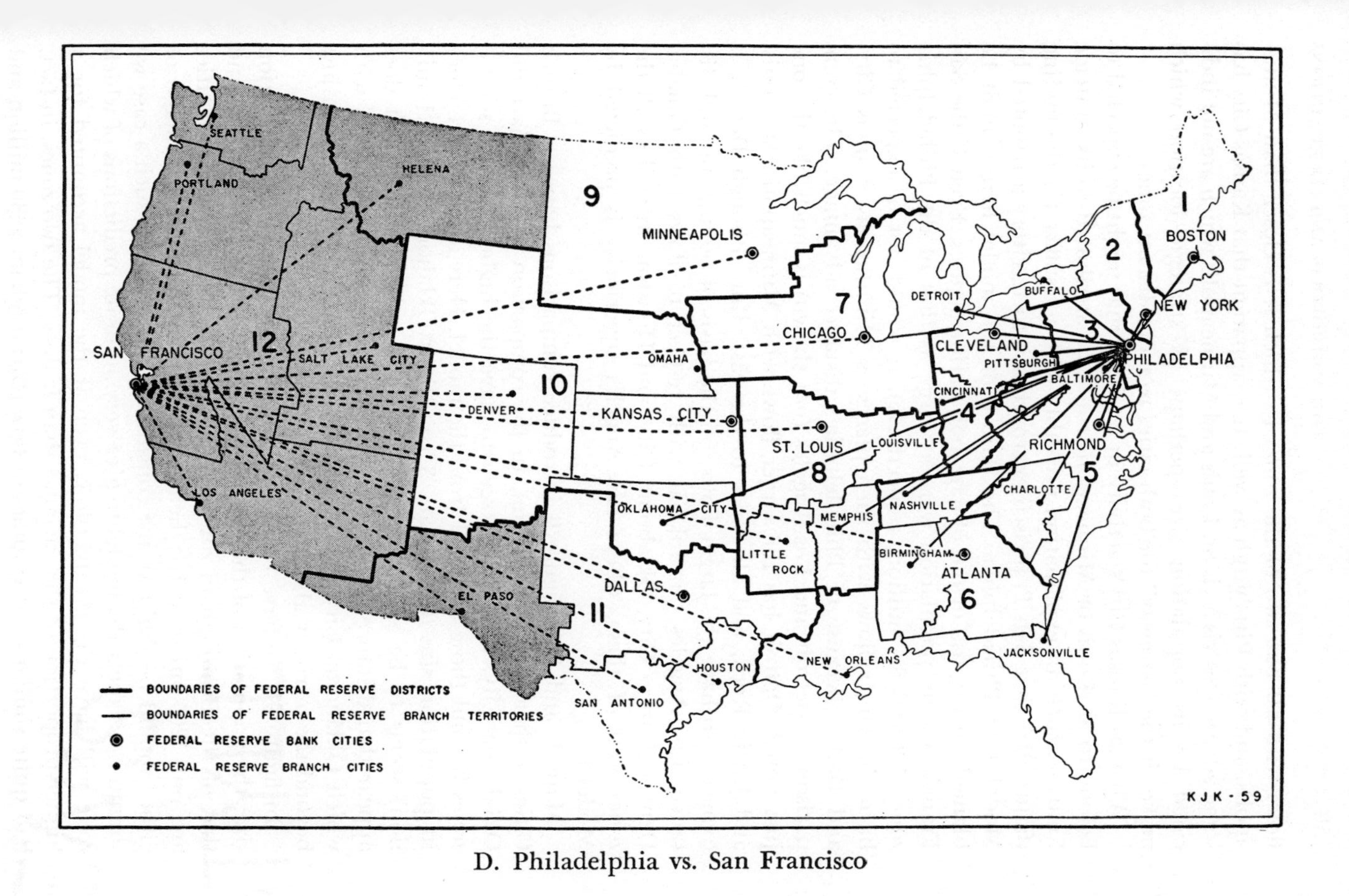

D. Philadelphia vs. San Francisco

flows with all but two of the zones to which it is closer than Minneapolis, and with Pittsburgh as well. It is apparent that Kansas City has some advantages vis-à-vis St. Louis and Minneapolis which are not indicated by its population size—perhaps its strategic location which makes it the "gateway" for both cities to more distant zones.

Whereas Kansas City's activity in territory that might be expected to belong to St. Louis or Minneapolis could be attributed to its strategic location, such an explanation probably will not suffice for the finding (figure 9D) that San Francisco encroaches into territory attributed by Model I to Philadelphia. The failure of the model here cannot be blamed on the use of out-of-date population figures. Even if the San Francisco zone population were as large as that of the Philadelphia zone (5.0 and 8.4 million, respectively), it would not be expected to have the larger flows with such places as Minneapolis, Kansas City, and Dallas, because of Philadelphia's distance advantage. The comparison of Detroit and Los Angeles (not shown) is much like the one just noted. Detroit has the larger flows with Minneapolis, St. Louis, and Little Rock, and all zones to the east. But although Detroit is expected to have the larger flows, on the basis of population and distance, Los Angeles outranks it with respect to flows with Omaha, Denver, Kansas City, Oklahoma City, and Houston, as well as all the zones west of these, where Los Angeles superiority is predicted by Model I.

Maps E and F in figure 9 introduce comparisons between Branch Cities, rather than Bank Cities. In the comparison of Cincinnati and Oklahoma City, the latter is seen to have the higher flows in several zones beyond those expected from the model. Here again, discrepancy in population size (Cincinnati, 3.5 million; Oklahoma City, 2.1 million) seems to be a poor guide to relative volume of flows. It does appear that distance is operating, however, for most of the zones with which Oklahoma City unexpectedly has the larger flows are ones just beyond the territory allocated to it by Model I.

In figure 9F we have two zones of approximately equal population size; the population of the Nashville zone was 2.2 million in 1950 and that of the Birmingham zone was 2.5 million in 1950. The two cities are only 205 miles apart; hence the relative distance advantage of either should be slight at any considerable distance. In such a case we should not expect the model to give very accurate predictions of which zone will have the greater flow, even if the model accounted for a higher proportion of the variance than it does. The two zones, in fact, had quite similar total volumes of flow (Birmingham $880 million and

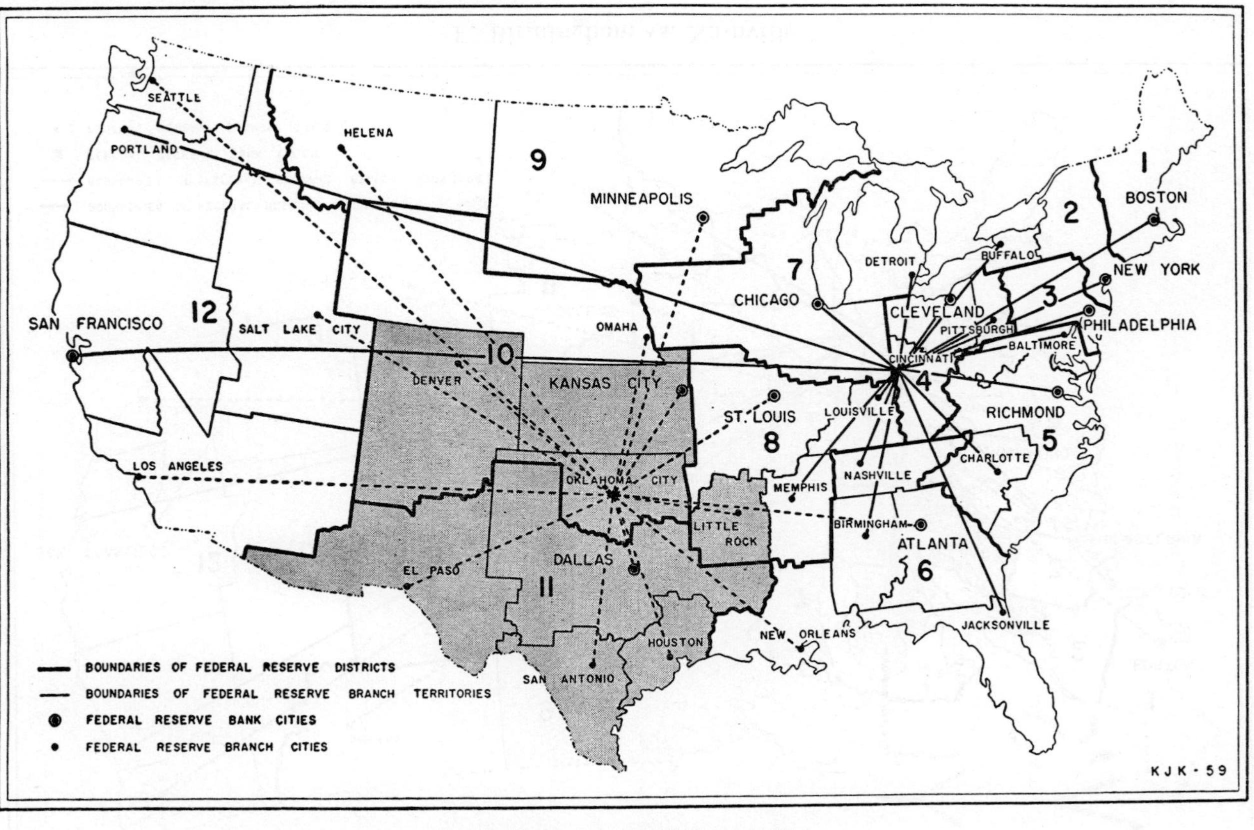

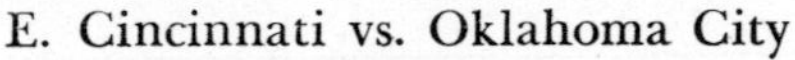

E. Cincinnati vs. Oklahoma City

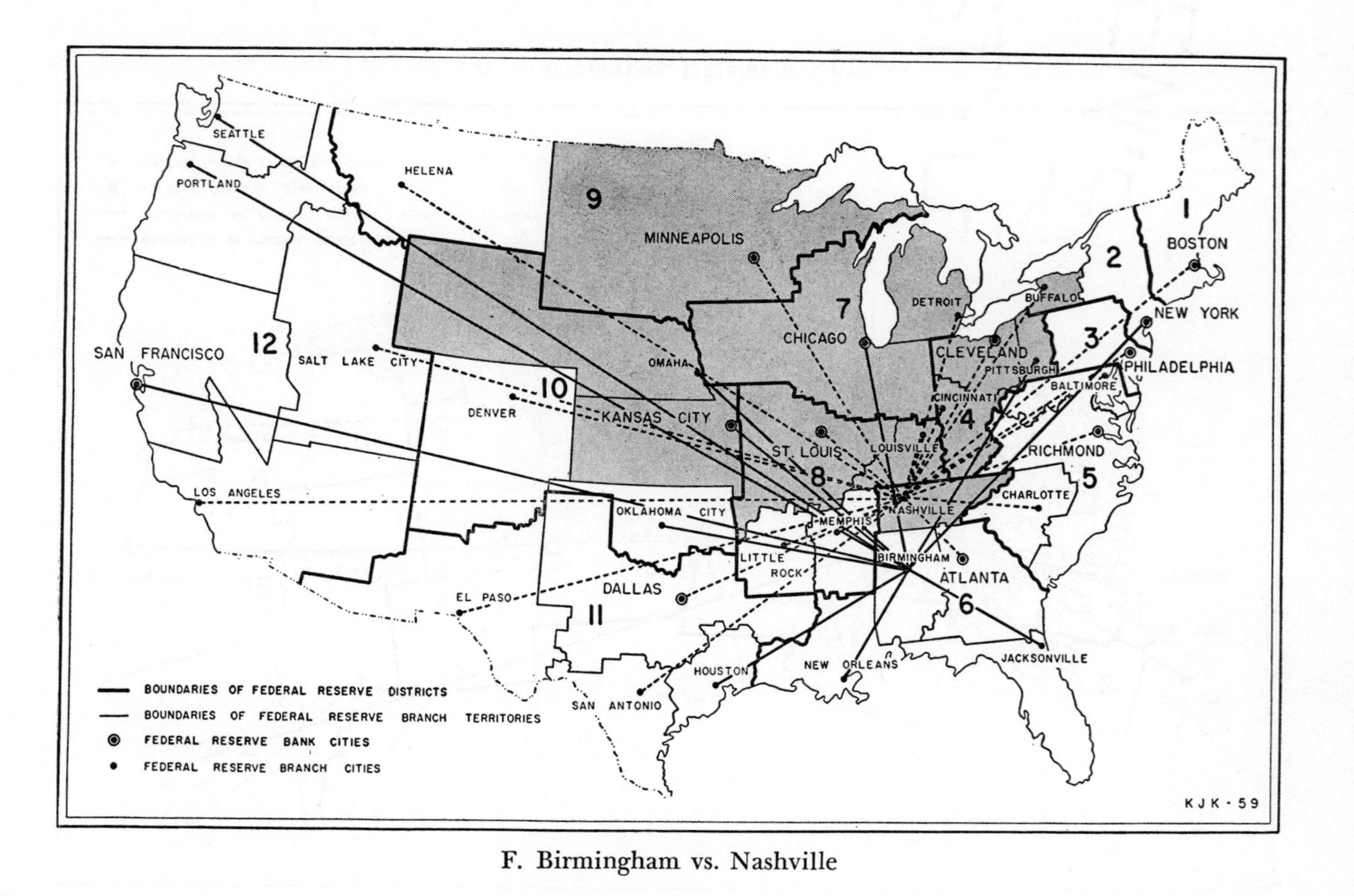

F. Birmingham vs. Nashville

Nashville $876 million). Nashville had the larger flow with more zones, but Birmingham had larger flows with several of the most important centers: New York, San Francisco, Kansas City, and Chicago, of which the last two are within the area where Nashville should have the larger flows on the basis of the model. There is perhaps some patterning here in terms of type of economic activity or other factors that we have not investigated.

We may summarize some implications of these examples, bearing in mind that they are not a representative sample of the performance of the model. It seems clear that distance effects are pervasive, although the model seemingly does not always give the proper weight to distance. Or, to put it another way, the weight given to population sometimes seems excessive. This suggests that an improved model must incorporate some better indicator of "economic size" or "capacity to generate flows"—perhaps population weighted by income—than sheer number of inhabitants. In several instances, there appear to be significant locational effects, above and beyond those accounted for by distance alone. As it stands, the model makes no provision for such effects, and it is not wholly clear how a "location" factor could be introduced into the model conveniently. Finally, where population, distance, and location do not seem of decisive importance in accounting for differences in the flows of two zones, it may be that still other, but as yet unidentified, factors take on some importance.

While our attention has been given to the investigation of gross flows by means of a simple gravity-type model, there are numerous other possibilities for the analysis of such flows—not to mention those arising from the consideration of directions of flow and net balances of flows. It seems conceivable that one could work out a pretty clear picture of a hierarchy of metropolitan centers on the basis of such flow data, although for this purpose it would be desirable to have a somewhat larger sample of time periods than we used, to insure stability of observed patterns. The flow data, like other banking statistics, make it evident that New York is at the top of the hierarchy. Of the 35 other zones, 29 had larger flows with New York than with any other zone. Only one—Omaha—had a larger flow with Chicago than with New York. At the bottom of the hierarchy are found five branch territories with small total flows each of which had a larger flow with the zone containing the Bank City of its Federal Reserve District than with New York; these are the San Antonio, Salt Lake City, El Paso, Little Rock, and Helena zones. Chicago's position as second to New York in the hierarchy is fairly plain, though by no means as plain as New York's top position. San Francisco and Philadelphia are near the top, but Detroit, although it has a large flow with New York and (presumably) with Chicago, is by no means a major center as measured by the flow of funds. Figure 10 offers some documentation for the statements just made, as well as additional details; it shows all pairs of zones between which there was a gross flow of $100 million or more in the aggregate of four sample weeks in 1957, with the New York and Chicago zones omitted. New York had a flow this large with each zone except Little Rock, Helena, and El Paso. There were 10 zones whose flow with Chicago was below $100 million—all Branch City rather than Bank City zones. It is interesting to compare the map of flows with figure 3 in chapter 4, which gives the conception of Vance and Smith (1954) of "major lines of integration" in the South. It is possible that the study of flows will provide an objective means of testing such hypotheses as theirs.

Figure 10 (opposite). Interdistrict Settlement Fund Gross Flows of $100,000,000 or More (Total of Four Weeks in 1957), Excluding New York and Chicago Zones. (Source: Unpublished data furnished by Chicago Federal Reserve Bank.)

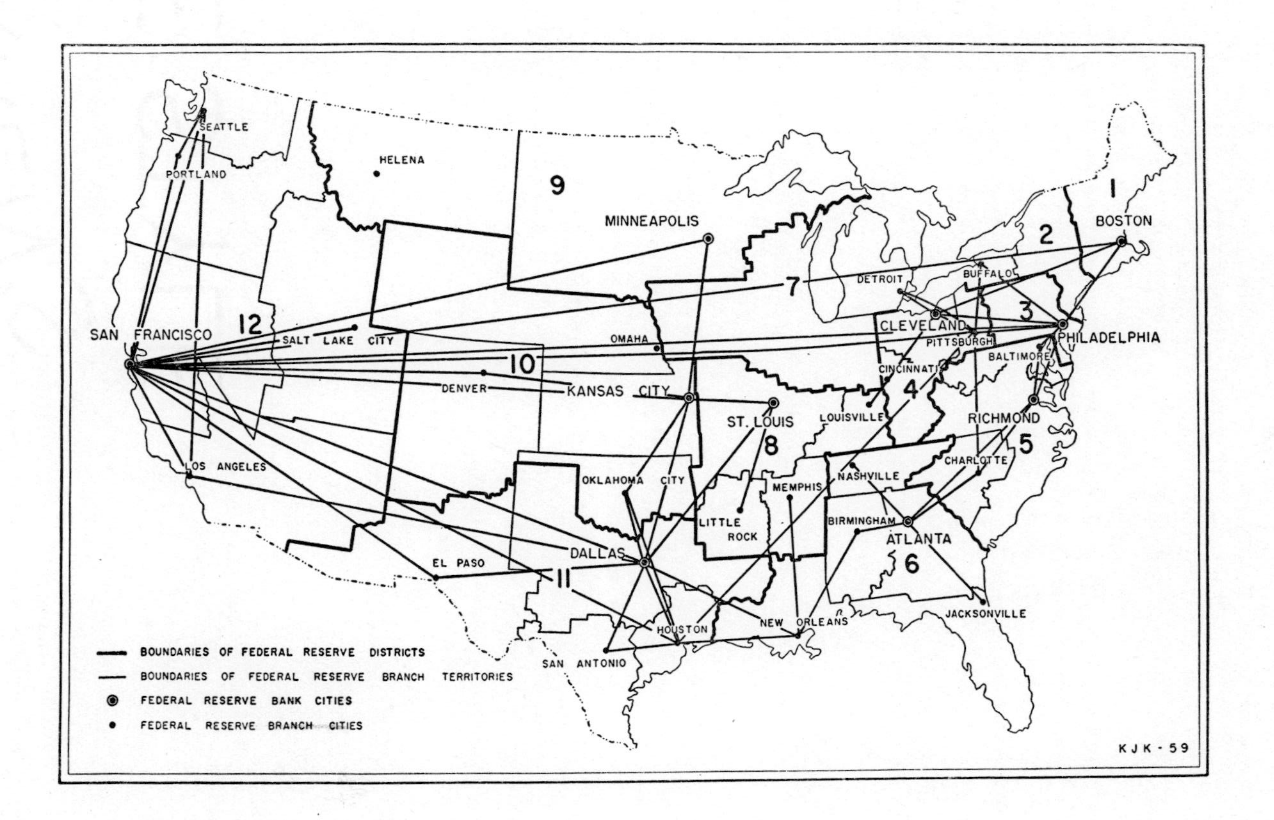
SEATTLE
PORTLAND
HELENA
9
MINNEAPOLIS
1
BOSTON
2
7
DETROIT
BUFFALO
3
12
SAN FRANCISCO
SALT LAKE CITY
OMAHA
CLEVELAND
PITTSBURGH
PHILADELPHIA
BALTIMORE
10
DENVER
KANSAS CITY
CINCINNATI
4
ST. LOUIS
LOUISVILLE
RICHMOND
8
5
LOS ANGELES
OKLAHOMA CITY
MEMPHIS
NASHVILLE
CHARLOTTE
LITTLE ROCK
BIRMINGHAM
ATLANTA
DALLAS
EL PASO
11
6
HOUSTON
NEW ORLEANS
JACKSONVILLE
SAN ANTONIO
BOUNDARIES OF FEDERAL RESERVE DISTRICTS
BOUNDARIES OF FEDERAL RESERVE BRANCH TERRITORIES
FEDERAL RESERVE BANK CITIES
FEDERAL RESERVE BRANCH CITIES
KJK-59

PART II

METROPOLITAN DOMINANCE: HINTERLAND ACTIVITIES

A developing human community, no less than a plant community, transforms its habitat. It changes the face and modifies the pattern of "places" or areas. . . . When we note the regularities and recurrences of settlement patterns and kindred phenomena, we may feel at times that we are dealing with phenomena not fundamentally different in type from those of the plant and animal ecologists.

—S. W. Wooldridge and W. Gordon East

CHAPTER 7

Manufacturing Outside Metropolitan Areas

One of the classic statements on metropolitanism—McKenzie's *Metropolitan Community* (1933)—developed the idea of a metropolis primarily in terms of the large city which "dominates" its hinterland. The emphasis on metropolis-hinterland relationships within the metropolitan community was carried over into Bogue's (1949) influential monograph on metropolitan dominance. In his study, dominance, regarded as a "special kind of control over a community of interfunctioning units," was inferred from gradients describing the change in population density and intensity of broad classes of "sustenance activities" with distance from the metropolitan center.

Although we have taken no specific exception to the McKenzie-Bogue approach, our own discussion has emphasized rather more strongly the concept, developed by Gras, of the metropolis as implicated in a system of inter-metropolitan relationships. We have shown that to account for the performance of distinctively metropolitan functions by a city one must pay attention to that city's situation within the larger inter-metropolitan complex. In some respects the point of view we have sought to stress derives less from the literature on the "metropolitan community" than from such work as that of Vining (1953, 1955), the key concept in whose frame of reference is the "system of cities" or the "spatial structure of the economy," rather than the metropolis as such.

In coming to a direct examination of the role of the metropolis in structuring hinterland activities, we find in the literature an excellent formulation of the general hypothesis guiding our analyses:

> Research . . . directed at relationships between the metropolis and surrounding territories has demonstrated an urban-oriented structure as a basis of contemporary ecological organization.
>
> However, studies of the metropolitan community have not sufficiently emphasized equally important intercommunity relations that characterize ecological organization. A "community"—whether the concept is applied to plants, animals, or human beings and their institutions—by definition is not a discrete entity. It is an identifiable set of symbiotic relationships which necessarily are involved with and have implications for other such identifiable sets. Several or many such communities constitute an ecological "field," which is the fundamental unit of analysis. Hypotheses and methods used in the study of several communities or even a single community need to be predicated upon a process of abstraction from the more inclusive area. Attention should be directed at relations between contiguous metropolitan communities and to those between more widely separated areas. If metropolises are central dominants for hinterlands, their simultaneous, as well as independent, influences may affect the structure of the metropolitan community. (Pappenfort, 1959, p. 380.)

Pappenfort's empirical materials concern the location of branch plants of manufacturing concerns in the State of Illinois. In contrast to the global inferences about dominance possible in such a study as Bogue's, the analysis of manufacturing operating combinations permits conclusions about a specific, relatively homogeneous type of control. Pappenfort's findings are concisely summarized as follows:

> The spatial distribution of the production and administrative units of operating combinations falls into a consistent pattern in relation to Chicago which justifies defining that metropolitan area as a central dominant for the state. At the same time, the joint influence of the metropolitan centers of St. Louis and Chicago is related to the distributions of certain subgroups of operating combinations. Finally, when the home office of an Illinois factory is in another state, the administration is situated in a region which is related to the production unit's location in Illinois. (Pappenfort, 1959, pp. 380-81.)

The third finding may be given in a little more detail:

> Home offices in 23 states other than Illinois administered 335 manufacturing establishments in Illinois. . . . The factories with administrative offices in the Industrial Belt are located differently in Illinois from the remainder with offices in other states. For example, 64 per cent of plants controlled from the Industrial Belt are in the Chicago Metropolitan Area, and 36 per cent are in the hinterland.

> Those with administrative offices elsewhere in the United States reverse the pattern: only 30 per cent are in the Chicago Metropolitan Area, while 70 per cent are in nonmetropolitan counties. (Pappenfort, 1959, p. 384.)

Thus Chicago's functions both as a manufacturing center in its own right and as a locus for the control of manufacturing activities in its hinterland are influenced by its situation with respect to the inter-metropolitan complex.

Following up the suggestion that "dominance" is manifested not only in metropolis-hinterland relationships but also in the orientation of hinterland activities to an inter-metropolitan "ecological field," in this chapter and the next we examine three types of activity—manufacturing, mining, and agriculture—in the nonmetropolitan United States. The areal units in the analysis are the nonmetropolitan state economic areas (SEA's), of which there were 351 in the system devised for use in the 1950 Census. (There were variant SEA systems for the different types of census tabulations; the system we use is based on the SEA's delimited for agricultural tabulations, but with metropolitan components excluded.)

In this chapter and the next we have employed a more elaborate form of multiple variable statistical analysis than is used anywhere else in the volume, in order to bring out the complicated joint and net relationships among our "dependent variables"—those representing levels of economic activity in the nonmetropolitan United States—and our "explanatory variables"—those indicating the position of nonmetropolitan areal units within the total spatial framework of the economy. We have made the presentation of statistical technicalities rather terse, for those conversant with the techniques. By skimming over these technicalities, however, the reader who is not familiar with multiple regression techniques can glean the major results from the verbal descriptions. Attention may be called to the highly condensed summary presented in chapter 1 (pp. 11-14), which may also be consulted if the argument becomes difficult to follow.

MANUFACTURING: MAJOR PATTERNS

Manufacturing activity tends to be concentrated in metropolitan centers and their immediate environs. Nearly a third of the 1950 metropolitan labor force was in manufacturing, as compared with about a fourth of the nonfarm, nonmetropolitan labor force and a tenth of the farm labor force. Nonetheless, a substantial proportion of the nation's manufacturing activity, perhaps three-tenths, took place outside metropolitan areas of 100,000 or more, assuming that the residential distribution of manufacturing employees is an adequate indication.

For the analysis reported here, percentage of the 1950 employed labor force in manufacturing is taken as an indicator of level of manufacturing activity. The mean (unweighted) proportion in manufacturing is 16.4 per cent for a systematic sample of 100 nonmetropolitan state economic areas (see Appendix for description of sample). The standard deviation of 11.1 per cent and the sample range from 2.1 to 44.9 per cent are indicative of substantial areal variation in level of manufacturing activity.

Certain characteristic features of the metropolis, identified in previous chapters, suggest that proximity to a metropolitan center or centers should be conducive to high levels of manufacturing activity. For example, the metropolis is a focal point for intra-regional and intermetropolitan lines of transport and communication. The large number of consuming units localized in the metropolitan center(s) may constitute a sizable market for goods produced in the hinterland.

In the conventional research design for an investigation of metropolitan dominance in the hinterland, each nonmetropolitan territorial unit is classified by distance to nearest metropolitan center. Systematic variation in level of manufacturing activity by distance to nearest metropolitan center is taken as an indication of metropolitan dominance on manufacturing activity in the hinterland. There is, indeed, a significant inverse relationship between proportion in manufacturing and the logarithm of distance in miles to nearest metropolitan center; $r = -.53$ for the sample of 100 non-metropolitan SEA's (see Appendix for description of distance variable). In figure 11 it will be noted that a disproportionate number of the areas with "high" levels of manufacturing are located at the lesser distances from a metropolitan center.

But on the basis of our earlier discussion it might be hypothesized that position with respect to the national configuration of metropolitan centers rather than position with respect to the nearest metropolis influences the level of manufacturing activity (see Harris, 1954). Population potential (see Appendix) provides a convenient summary measure of proximity to the configuration of metropolitan centers, or accessibility to the national market. There is a significant direct relationship between proportion in manufacturing and population potential; $r = .46$ for the sample of 100 nonmetropolitan areas. In the scattergram (figure 11), a disproportionate number of the areas with "high" levels of manufacturing have above-average population potentials.

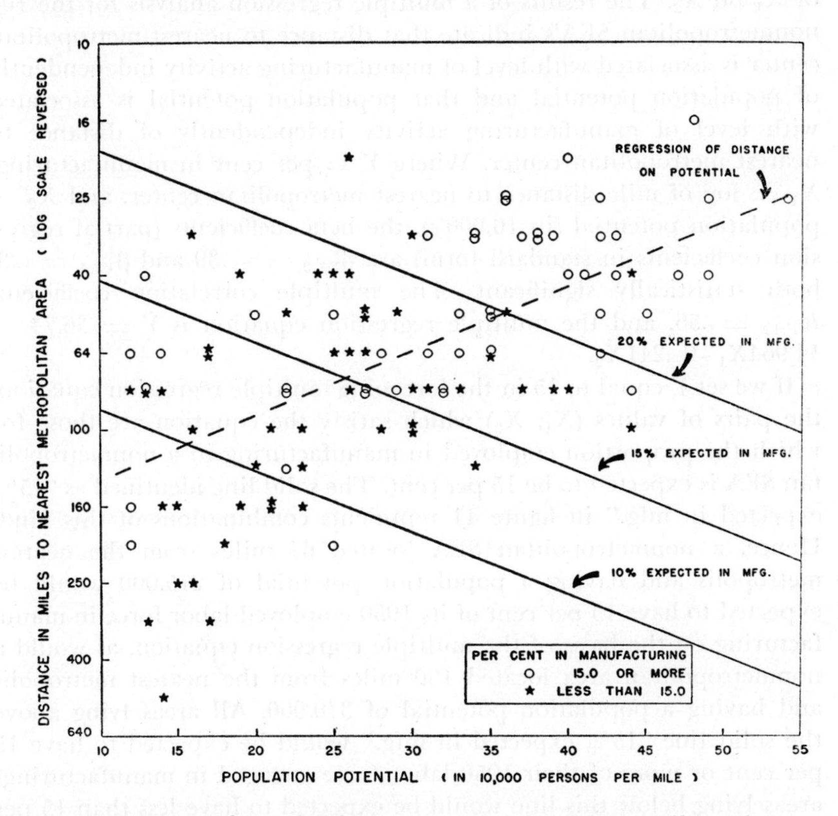

Figure 11. Regression of Distance to Nearest Metropolitan Area on Population Potential, and Relation of Manufacturing Employment to Distance and Potential, for Sample of 100 Nonmetropolitan State Economic Areas: 1950

These two results are not wholly independent, for the scattergram also shows that areas of above-average population potential tend to be located at the lesser distances from a metropolitan center, and areas of below-average potential tend to be located at the greater distances from a metropolitan center. (Note that the distance scale is reversed on the graph, so as to show "proximity" to a metropolitan center varying directly with potential.) In fact, where X_1 = log of mile distance to nearest metropolitan center and X_2 = population potential (in 10,-000's), $r_{12} = -.60$ and $\hat{X}_1 = 2.29 - .016X_2$ for the sample of 100 non-metropolitan areas. The dashed line in figure 11 shows the regression of X_1 on X_2. The results of a multiple regression analysis for the 100 nonmetropolitan SEA's indicate that distance to nearest metropolitan center is associated with level of manufacturing activity independently of population potential and that population potential is associated with level of manufacturing activity independently of distance to nearest metropolitan center. Where Y = per cent in manufacturing, X_1 = log of mile distance to nearest metropolitan center, and X_2 = population potential (in 10,000's), the beta coefficients (partial regression coefficients in standard form) are $\beta_{Y1.2} = -.39$ and $\beta_{Y2.1} = .23$, both statistically significant. The multiple correlation coefficient, $R_{Y.12} = .56$, and the multiple regression equation is $\hat{Y} = 36.74 - 14.964X_1 + .241X_2$.

If we set $\hat{Y}$ equal to 15 in the foregoing multiple regression equation, the pairs of values (X_1, X_2) which satisfy the equation are those for which the proportion employed in manufacturing in a nonmetropolitan SEA is expected to be 15 per cent. The solid line identified as "15% expected in mfg." in figure 11 represents combinations of this kind. Hence, a nonmetropolitan SEA located 64 miles from the nearest metropolis and having a population potential of 215,000 would be expected to have 15 per cent of its 1950 employed labor force in manufacturing on the basis of the multiple regression equation, as would a nonmetropolitan area located 100 miles from the nearest metropolis and having a population potential of 340,000. All areas lying above the solid line "15% expected in mfg." would be expected to have 15 per cent or more of their 1950 labor force engaged in manufacturing; areas lying below this line would be expected to have less than 15 per cent of their 1950 labor force in manufacturing. Of the 62 areas lying above this line, 38 have 15 per cent or more in manufacturing and 24 have less than 15 per cent in manufacturing; of the 38 areas lying below this line, 11 have 15 per cent or more in manufacturing and 27 have less than 15 per cent in manufacturing. The solid lines identified as "10% expected in mfg." and "20% expected in mfg." were obtained in a similar fashion when $\hat{Y}$ was set equal to 10 and 20 respectively.

The influence of lesser, "submetropolitan" or "subdominant" population nodes on level of manufacturing activity in nonmetropolitan SEA's may be inferred from a further analysis. If X_3 = index of local urbanization (a summary measure of the size-of-place distribution of population in the nonmetropolitan SEA itself, defined in the Appendix), then $r_{Y3} = .28$. The index of local urbanization is virtually independent of distance to nearest metropolitan center and population potential ($r_{13} = .02$ and $r_{23} = -.13$). Results of a multiple regression analysis for the 100 nonmetropolitan SEA's indicate that local urbanization is associated with level of manufacturing activity independently of distance to nearest metropolitan center and population potential, that distance to nearest metropolitan center is associated with level of manufacturing activity independently of local urbanization and population potential, and that population potential is associated with level of manufacturing activity independently of local urbanization and distance to nearest metropolitan center. The beta coefficients (partial regression coefficients in standard form) are $\beta_{Y3.12} = .32$, $\beta_{Y1.23} = -.36$ and $\beta_{Y2.13} = .29$, each statistically significant. Unfortunately, we lack separate data on the nonfarm employment structure in nonmetropolitan SEA's. Hence the weight attributed to local urbanization may, in large part, be a function of varying proportions of farm population. Yet the analysis is pertinent in demonstrating that the influence of potential and distance to metropolis cannot be explained by any joint association with local urbanization.

The manufacturing industries can be subdivided into "processing" industries, a substantial proportion of whose inputs are raw materials, and "fabricating" industries, the bulk of whose inputs are processed materials. The processing industries presumably are more resource oriented than the fabricating industries, whereas the latter are more market oriented than the former. (The classification of industries as processing or fabricating is outlined in chapter 3.)

The proportion of the employed labor force in processing industries tends to decrease as distance from nearest metropolitan center increases ($r = -.22$ for the sample of 100 nonmetropolitan SEA's); however, the proportion of workers in processing industries is largely independent of population potential and position with respect to "submetropolitan" population nodes (r's of .10 and .17 respectively). In combination, log of mile distance to nearest metropolitan area, population potential, and the index of local urbanization account for only eight per cent of the inter-area variance in level of processing activity ($R = .28$); and in the multiple regression equation, only distance to a metropolitan center makes a significant, independent contribution in accounting for this variance.

The proportion of the employed labor force in fabricating industries, by contrast, not only decreases as distance from nearest metropolitan center increases ($r = -.50$ for the sample of 100 nonmetropolitan SEA's); it also increases markedly as population potential increases ($r = .67$); and it tends to increase as urbanization in the local area increases ($r = .24$). In combination, these three variables account for 56 per cent of the inter-area variance in level of fabricating activity ($R = .75$ for the sample of 100 nonmetropolitan SEA's); and the multiple regression analysis indicates that population potential and local urbanization make statistically significant, independent contributions in accounting for the variance among areas.

The contrast between the two types (processing and fabricating) signifies that much of the orientation of manufacturing as a whole to the national configuration of metropolitan centers is accounted for by such an orientation on the part of fabricating industries—those least directly dependent on the extraction of raw materials. This gives us an important refinement of the earlier conclusion that there is a direct relationship between proportion of employment in manufacturing and population potential.

MANUFACTURING: DETAILED ANALYSIS

A general tendency for manufacturing activity to be concentrated toward population nodes frequently has been noted. For example, Florence and Friedson (U. S. National Resources Planning Board, 1943, p. 63) state:

> While immobility of population, differential reproduction rates, and various other factors have resulted in a distribution of population not directly related to productive activity, differences in population density serve as a rough index of the relative extent of economic activity among various areas. A high density usually points to intensity of production and often to the development of peculiarly "urban" activities, mainly manufacturing and services.

Harris (1954) indicates that the "manufacturing belt" in the northeastern United States coincides with the area of highest "market potential," a summary measure of accessibility to consumers and analogous to population potential. Harris (1954, pp. 315-16) also points out:

> A large and very significant fraction of manufacturing in the United States is not tied to local raw materials, local markets, or to current regional differences in power or labor costs; this segment . . . appears to be concentrated in areas having maximum accessibility to national or regional markets for such products.

There is a paucity of empirical studies dealing specifically with the distribution of manufacturing activity in the nonmetropolitan United States. The typical focus of such studies is either the distribution of manufacturing over the entire nation, which is in large part a function of the distribution of metropolitan centers, or the distribution of manufacturing among and within the metropolitan centers themselves. However, observations such as those just quoted, though based on consideration of the total economy rather than its nonmetropolitan sector, indicate that manufacturing employment tends to be high in areas which are densely populated and/or have high accessibility to a sizable market.

In the nation as a whole, the proportion of the resident labor force in manufacturing tends to vary directly with the "urbanization" of the area. For example, in 1950 manufacturing accounted for about 30.7 per cent of the resident employment in all urbanized areas; outside urbanized areas the proportions were 27.8 per cent in cities of 25,000 or more, 25.4 per cent in towns of 2,500 to 25,000, 25.6 per cent in villages and other rural-nonfarm areas, and only 9.4 per cent in the rural-farm population. (See chapter 3 for a fuller discussion of the urbanization of manufacturing employment.) Thus, we suspect that the proportion of the labor force in manufacturing will increase as the degree of urbanization in a nonmetropolitan SEA increases. And should a direct relationship obtain between a nonmetropolitan SEA's urbanization and its population potential or proximity to a metropolitan center, covariation of manufacturing activity with potential or proximity would be observed.

In the remainder of this chapter, the previously stated relationships among manufacturing employment, population potential, proximity to a metropolitan center, and local urbanization are elaborated. Extrapolating the results of analyses based on the total economy, we hypothesize that manufacturing employment varies directly with the population potential, proximity to metropolitan centers, and urbanization of hinterland areas.

A systematic sample of 100 nonmetropolitan SEA's (described in the Appendix) is employed in most of the analyses in chapters 7 and 8. For each SEA falling in the sample, we have available three measures of population distribution (described in the Appendix) indicating its position in the "spatial structure of the economy" or the ecological "field." The first is population potential in 10,000's; the second is the logarithm of mile distance to nearest metropolitan SEA; the third is an index of local urbanization based on the size-of-place distribution of population within the nonmetropolitan SEA. A correlation analysis based on the sample of 100 SEA's indicates a significant inverse relationship between potential and distance to nearest metropolitan center ($r = -.60$), or a significant direct relationship between potential and proximity to a metropolitan center. But local urbanization is largely independent of both potential and distance to metropolitan center (r's of $-.13$ and .02 respectively). (The inter-correlations among the three measures will be reconsidered in chapter 8. At this point, it is sufficient to note that on an SEA-by-SEA basis local urbanization is largely independent of population potential or distance to nearest metropolitan SEA.)

For the sample of nonmetropolitan SEA's, manufacturing employment (proportion of the 1950 employed labor force in manufacturing) varies directly with population potential, proximity to a metropolitan center, and local urbanization. In terms of zero-order correlations, population potential accounts for 21 per cent of the SEA-to-SEA variance in manufacturing employment, proximity (as measured by log of mile distance to nearest metropolitan SEA) accounts for 28 per cent of the variance, and local urbanization accounts for eight per cent. In combination, the three nodal indicators account for 41 per cent of the inter-SEA variance in manufacturing employment, with each making a significant, and roughly equal, independent contribution to the explanation of the variance among SEA's. (The zero-order and multiple regression analyses are summarized in table 25.)

The proportion of workers employed in manufacturing is, of course, the sum of the proportions of workers employed in the several individual manufacturing industries. There is strong reason to suspect that the locational pattern of manufacturing industries whose operations call for large inputs of unprocessed materials will be influenced to a greater extent by the distribution of these materials or natural resources than is that of the manufacturing industries principally engaged in fabricating products from processed materials. The locational pattern of the fabricating industries probably is influenced more by the distribution of the market. If there were no marked association between the abundance of natural resources and accessibility to the market on a small area basis, manufacturing employment in processing industries would be less closely associated with the nodal indicators—population potential, proximity to a metropolitan center, and local urbanization—than would that in fabricating industries. In checking this hypothesis, we employ the crude distinction between "processing" and "fabricating" industries set forth in chapter 3, again calling attention to the fact that it serves only very roughly to identify industries with important raw materials inputs as opposed to those whose material inputs are largely in semi-manufactured form.

Table 25. Zero-Order and Multiple Correlations Relating Manufacturing Employment to Indicators of Population Distribution, for a Sample of 100 Nonmetropolitan State Economic Areas: 1950

Dependent variable: Per cent employed in—	Multiple corre-lation	Independent variable: Population potential	Distance to metropolitan center	Local urbani-zation
			Zero-order correlation	
All manufacturing	...	.46**	−.53**	.28**
Processing industries	...	.10	−.22*	.17
Fabricating industries	...	.67**	−.50**	.24*
			Beta coefficient	
All manufacturing	.64**	.29**	−.36**	.32**
Processing industries	.28*	−.03	−.24*	.17
Fabricating industries	.75**	.63**	−.13	.33**

* Significant at .05 level of probability.
** Significant at .01 level of probability.

For the sample of nonmetropolitan SEA's, employment in processing industries is largely independent of population potential and local urbanization on an SEA-by-SEA basis. Employment in processing industries tends to vary directly with proximity to a metropolitan center; however, only five per cent of the inter-SEA variance in processing employment is accounted for by proximity. In combination, the three nodal indicators account for only eight per cent of the inter-SEA variance, and only proximity to a metropolitan center makes a significant independent contribution to the explanation of variance.

On the other hand, employment in fabricating industries varies directly with population potential, proximity to a metropolitan center, and local urbanization. Population potential accounts for 45 per cent of the SEA-to-SEA variance in fabricating employment, proximity accounts for 25 per cent of the variance, and local urbanization accounts for six per cent. In combination, the nodal indicators account for 56 per cent of the SEA-to-SEA variance in fabricating employment, with population potential and local urbanization making significant independent contributions to the explanation of variance.

It is worth noting that employment in processing industries has its highest correlation with proximity to a metropolitan center, whereas for fabricating industries the highest correlation is with population potential. The evidence suggests that the metropolis sometimes serves as a sizable market for "regional" raw materials and that proximity to a metropolis may lead a nonmetropolitan area to exploit the natural resources which are present and to develop a relatively high level of manufacturing activity in processing industries.

It is somewhat surprising that the relationship between manufacturing employment and local urbanization is not stronger, for an increase in the urbanization index implies an increase in the proportion of the labor force in nonfarm industries, of which an important component is manufacturing. The urbanization index accounts for only eight per cent of the inter-SEA variance in manufacturing employment, six per cent of the variance in fabricating employment, and three per cent of the variance in processing employment. However, the fabricating-processing differential is consistent with the fact that fabricating industries are more highly urbanized than are processing industries (chapter 3).

We have seen that the relationship between processing employment and the indicators of population distribution is quite different from the relationship between fabricating employment and the nodal indexes. Because we suspect that there are important differences within the two broad categories of manufacturing, the analysis turns to the individual industry groups. These individual "industries," however, are themselves somewhat heterogeneous aggregates in some instances.

The regression techniques employed in the foregoing analysis are not altogether suitable for the analysis of relationships between employment in an individual manufacturing industry and the nodal indexes. For most manufacturing industries, a relatively few nonmetropolitan SEA's have high proportions employed in the given industry, whereas a relatively large number of SEA's have virtually no employment in the industry. The distribution of SEA's by employment in the industry, then, is skewed; but regression and correlation results are more readily interpreted when there is an approximately symmetrical distribution with respect to the dependent variable.

For the individual manufacturing industries, our approach is to classify each SEA falling in the sample as "specialized" or "nonspecialized" in the given industry and as "high" or "low" in terms of population potential, distance to nearest metropolitan center, or local urbanization. In 1950 roughly two per cent of the employed labor force in the country as a whole was in each of the 14 manufacturing industries of the "condensed classification" with which we are working. Hence, an SEA with two per cent or more of its workers in a given industry may be regarded as "specialized" in that industry. With respect to the nodal indicators, the "high" category includes about half the SEA's in each case. To test the association between specialization in a given manufacturing industry and a nodal indicator, we use chi-square, which provides an alternative test of association which requires no assumption about the form of the distributions of variables. However, it may happen that the relationship between employment in an individual manufacturing industry and a nodal indicator is too complex to be described adequately by any single summary measure of association. An example is the relationship between employment in the furniture, lumber, and wood products industry and population potential.

Half the sample of nonmetropolitan SEA's are classified as specialized in the furniture, lumber, and wood products industry. Of the 50 specialized SEA's, 33 are classified as high population potential, whereas only 18 of the 50 nonspecialized SEA's are classified as high population potential. On the basis of this classification, we conclude that there is a positive association between specialization in the furniture, lumber, and wood products industry and high population potential (chi-square is 7.8, significant at the .01 level).

However, a scattergram depicting the relationship between employment in the furniture, lumber, and wood products industry and population potential takes on a roughly triangular form, i.e., the range in employment in the industry is much less among SEA's with high potential values than among SEA's with low potential values. This pattern is brought out by the following tabulation.

Per cent employed in furniture, lumber, and wood products	*All sample SEA's*	*Population potential in 10,000's*	
		28 or more	*27 or less*
All sample SEA's	100	51	49
10.0 or more	12	2	10
2.0 to 9.9	38	31	7
1.9 or less	50	18	32

A least squares regression line fitted to the data for the 100 SEA's has a slope of —0.11, indicating an average tendency for employment in furniture, lumber, and wood products to decrease as population potential increases; the correlation coefficient is —.21, significant at the .05 level. But because of the skewed distribution of employment in the industry, there is some doubt about the reliability of the association.

We already have indicated that for the 2 × 2 table: per cent in industry, 2.0 or more and 1.9 or less versus potential, 28 or more and 27 or less, chi-square is 7.8 (significant at the .01 level) and the direction of association is positive. However, for the 2 × 2 table: per cent in industry, 10.0 or more and 9.9 or less versus potential, 28 or more and 27 or less, chi-square is 5.0 (significant at the .05 level) and the direction of association is negative. The complex nature of the relationship is not disclosed by either of the crude classifications.

Detailed inspection of the scattergram indicates that six of the sample SEA's, all located in the Pacific Coast or Mountain regions, have very low potential values (120,000 to 140,000) and very high proportions employed in furniture, lumber, and wood products (14 to 29 per cent). The only other sample SEA with as many as 14 per cent of its employed workers in the industry is in Alabama; the potential value for the SEA is 280,000, or about the same as for the average nonmetropolitan SEA. Some 19 sample SEA's, 16 of which are in the South, have high proportions in the industry (5 to 12 per cent); potential values for the 19 areas range from 220,000 to 400,000. The remaining 74 SEA's, each with less than 5 per cent employed in the industry, range from 120,000 to 540,000 in population potential.

There are, then, two distinct spatial groupings of nonmetropolitan SEA's specializing in furniture, lumber, and wood products—one group in the Pacific Coast and Mountain regions, characterized by very high specialization and low population potential; the second, in the South, characterized by high specialization and moderate to high population potentials. By no means all SEA's falling in these broad regions are specialized in the industry; and not all SEA's specializing in the industry are found in these regions.

Employment in the furniture, lumber, and wood products industry appears to be largely independent of proximity to a metropolitan center or local urbanization; its relationship with population potential has been described in some detail. Cursory inspection of maps showing the distribution of forest land (e.g., United States National Resources Board, 1934, Figs. 26-33) suggests that the location of appropriate natural resources is closely related to the spatial pattern of specialization in the industry.

A third of the sample nonmetropolitan SEA's are classified as specialized in the food and kindred products industry. Neither the chi-square calculations nor inspection of graphic materials suggests a relationship between specialization in this processing industry and any of the nodal indicators.

Nearly a third of the sample SEA's are classified as specialized in "other nondurable" goods manufacturing, which includes such diverse activities as tobacco manufactures, paper and allied products, petroleum and coal products, rubber products, and leather and leather products. Specialization in the industry appears to be positively associated with population potential (chi-square is 6.1, significant at the .05 level) and with local urbanization (chi-square is 4.3, significant at the .05 level).

A sixth of the nonmetropolitan SEA's in our sample are classified as specialized in the textile mill products industry. Specialization in the textiles industry appears to be associated positively with population potential (chi-square is 10.7, significant at the .01 level) and negatively with distance to nearest metropolitan center (chi-square is 6.2, significant at the .05 level). This result indicates that the nonmetropolitan SEA's specializing in the textile industry, nearly all of which are located in the eastern part of the nation, are relatively accessible to both the national market and to "regional" centers.

A tenth of the sample SEA's are specialized in the primary metals industry. Neither the chi-square calculations nor inspection of graphic materials suggests a relationship between employment in primary metals and any of the nodal indicators. Nonmetropolitan SEA's specializing in the industry are found in the mountain states, in Alabama, and in states often identified as part of the "Northeastern Manufacturing Belt."

It will be recalled that processing employment was found to be largely independent of population potential and local urbanization and to vary inversely with distance from a metropolitan center. None of the five individual processing industries exhibits this particular pattern of relationships with the nodal indicators. (See summary in table 26.) However, the relationship between aggregate processing employment and distance to a metropolitan center was loose. Employment in furniture, lumber, and wood products shows no simple, significant relationship with any one of the nodal indicators; and a cursory analysis suggests that employment in the industry is more closely related to natural resources, i.e., the abundance of forested lands, than to the nodal indicators. Employment in textiles varies directly with population potential and inversely with distance to nearest metropolitan center; and employment in "other nondurable" goods appears directly related to population potential and local urbanization. Nonmetropolitan specialization in both the food and the primary metals industries seems to be largely independent of the nodal indicators.

Table 26. Patterns of Association of Specialization in Individual Manufacturing Industries with Indicators of Population Distribution, for a Sample of 100 Nonmetropolitan State Economic Areas: 1950

Industry	Number of SEA's specializing in industry	Independent variable: Population potential	Independent variable: Distance to metropolitan center	Independent variable: Local urbanization
		Kind of association[2]		
Processing industries				
Furniture, and lumber and wood products	50	?[3]	0	0
Food and kindred products	32	0	0	0
Other nondurable goods	31	+	0	+
Textile mill products	15	++	–	0
Primary metals	10	0	0	0
Fabricating industries				
Transportation equipment except motor vehicle[1]	3	...	...	...
Printing, publishing, and allied industries[1]	4	...	...	...
Chemicals and allied products[1]	5	...	...	...
Motor vehicles and motor vehicle equipment	6	+	0	0
Fabricated metals	8	+	–	0
Electrical machinery, equipment and supplies	8	+	–	0
Apparel and other fabricated textiles	11	++	0	0
Machinery, except electrical	12	++	– –	0
Other durable goods	17	++	–	0

[1] Instances of specialization too few for analysis of association.

[2] ++, positive association significant at .01 level of probability; +, positive association significant at .05 level; 0, association not significant; –, negative association significant at .05 level; – –, negative association significant at .01 level.

[3] Association not consistent as to sign (see text).

Nonmetropolitan specialization in a fabricating industry occurs relatively infrequently. Less than five per cent of the sample SEA's are classified as specialized in the transportation equipment, printing and publishing, and chemicals industries respectively; the low frequency of specialization precludes detailed analysis for these industries. The percentage of specialized SEA's ranges from 6 to 17 for the remaining six individual fabricating industries—motor vehicles, fabricated metals, electrical machinery, apparel, nonelectrical machinery, and "other durable" goods.

A direct association between specialization in the industry and population potential is observed for each of the six individual fabricating industries. A negative association between specialization in the industry and distance to nearest metropolitan center is observed for four of the six fabricating industries—fabricated metals, electrical machinery, nonelectrical machinery, and "other durable" goods. Specialization in the industry appears to be independent of local urbanization for each of the six fabricating industries.

It will be recalled that fabricating employment as a whole was found to vary directly with population potential and local urbanization and inversely with distance to nearest metropolitan center. None of the six individual fabricating industries examined exhibits this particular pattern of relationships with the nodal indicators. However, employment in each of the six individual fabricating industries is directly associated with population potential; about 45 per cent of the variance in aggregate fabricating employment was accounted for by potential. Employment in four of the six fabricating industries is negatively associated with distance to nearest metropolitan center; about 25 per cent of the variance in aggregate fabricating employment was accounted for by distance to metropolitan center. No association is found between employment and local urbanization for an individual fabricating industry; roughly five per cent of the variance in aggregate fabricating employment was accounted for by local urbanization.

These exploratory analyses of the relationship between employment in an industry and the nodal indicators suggest that individual fabricating industries are more likely to be oriented toward metropolitan centers than are individual processing industries. This, of course, was the general conclusion with respect to fabricating and processing industries taken as groups.

The major patterns revealed by the study of manufacturing in nonmetropolitan areas already have been summarized at the beginning of this chapter. However, it may be useful to take a final synoptic view of the relation between manufacturing activity and aggregate accessibility to the nation's population, as indexed by population potential. Table 27 reduces the information to a five-category classification of SEA's by kind and degree of "specialization" in manufacturing, shown in relation to population potential. Here, as in the foregoing discussion, an SEA is said to be "specialized" in a given industry if two per cent or more of its labor force is employed in that industry. This table, unlike the previous presentations, is based on data for all the 351 nonmetropolitan SEA's in the United States rather than a sample thereof.

Table 27. Percentage Distribution of Nonmetropolitan State Economic Areas by Type of Manufacturing Specialization and Population Potential: 1950

Type of specialization	All nonmetropolitan SEA's	Population potential (10,000 persons/mile) 40 and over	30 to 39.9	20 to 29.9	Under 20
Number of SEA's	351	68	97	100	86
		Per cent of SEA's			
All types	100.0	100.0	100.0	100.0	100.0
Not specialized	16.8	1.5	3.1	19.0	41.9
Single specialization, processing	21.9	7.3	12.4	33.0	31.4
Multiple specialization, all processing	20.2	2.9	25.8	28.0	18.6
Multiple specialization, predominantly processing	18.8	22.1	35.0	15.0	2.3
Specialization mostly or wholly fabricating	22.2	66.2	23.7	5.0	5.8

The pertinent relationships stand out rather clearly in Table 27. An area of low population potential is somewhat unlikely to be specialized in any manufacturing industry; if it is specialized, it is very probable that the specialization will be in one or more processing industries rather than in fabricating industries. By contrast, areas of high population potential almost uniformly have some specialization in manufacturing, and quite typically this specialization is partly or wholly in fabricating industries rather than in processing industries. The areas of intermediate levels of population potential are likewise in an intermediate position as to pattern of specialization in manufacturing.

CHAPTER 8

Extractive Activities In Nonmetropolitan Areas

Extrapolating from the results reported in the preceding chapter, one might reason that if resource-using manufacturing industries are less clearly oriented to the metropolitan complex than are manufactures for which resources have only indirect significance, then resource-extracting industries are unlikely to exhibit a locational pattern suggesting metropolitan dominance. Such, however, is not the case, as will be made clear in an analysis of two major resource extractors, coal mining and agriculture.

COAL MINING

Of the 351 nonmetropolitan state economic areas, 122 were identified as areas with recoverable coal reserves in 1950 (see map in Perloff *et al.*, 1960). Production of coal in 1949 was reported in 94 of these nonmetropolitan SEA's. The scattergram (figure 12) shows that the nonproducing areas tend to have relatively small recoverable reserves and relatively low population potentials as compared with the producing areas. (See Appendix for description of data and estimates of coal reserves and production.)

The logarithm of the estimated recoverable coal reserves in 10^{14}

British thermal units and production status (producing vs. nonproducing) have a point biserial correlation coefficient of .48 for the 122 nonmetropolitan areas with coal reserves. Population potential and production status have a point biserial correlation coefficient of .20 for the same set of areas. Volume of reserves (log of estimated recoverable reserves in 10^{14} Btu's) is largely independent of population potential on an area-by-area basis ($r = -.12$).

Let X_1 = log of recoverable reserves in 10^{14} Btu's and X_2 = population potential (in 10,000's); we can then set up a linear discriminant function of the type, $Z = k_1X_1 + k_2X_2$. To determine the value of the

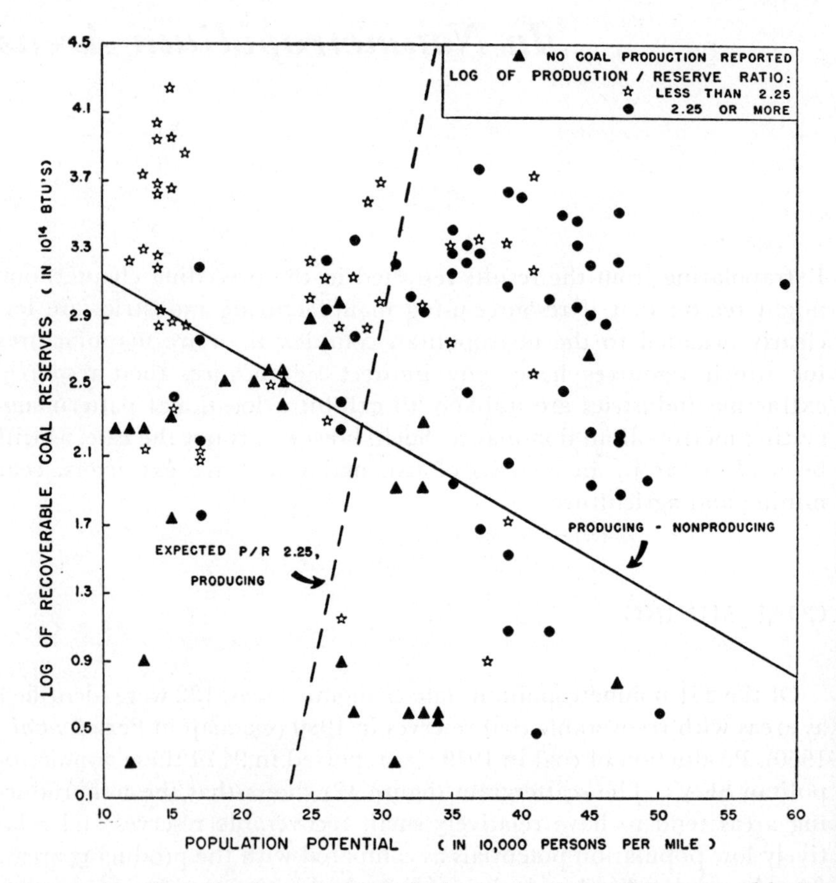

Figure 12. Coal Production in Relation to Estimated Recoverable Reserves and Population Potential, for 122 State Economic Areas with Known Reserves: 1949

function which "best" separates producing from nonproducing areas, we set $Z = k_1 (\bar{X}_{1p} + \bar{X}_{1n})/2 + k_2 (\bar{X}_{2p} + \bar{X}_{2n})/2$, where the subscripts p and n refer respectively to producing and nonproducing areas. Solution of systems of equations determining the k-values yields the following estimates: $k_1 = .202$ and $k_2 = .009$. The calculated Z-value is, then, .730. The solid line identified "Producing-Nonproducing" in figure 12 represents combinations of X_1 and X_2 which lie within the range of the data and yield a Z-value of .730. Areas falling above the "Producing-Nonproducing" line are expected to be in production; those falling below the line are expected not to be in production. Of the 79 areas lying above the line, 71 reported production in 1949 and 8 reported no production; of the 43 areas lying below the line, 23 reported production in 1949 and 20 reported no production. This discriminant function, then, classifies the 122 SEA's in regard to producing-nonproducing status with only 28 errors. This is somewhat better than the performance of either variable—log of recoverable reserves or population potential—alone. Regarding each as a single-variable discriminator, we have 35 errors of classification using the log of amount of reserves and 50 errors using population potential.

In summary, although resource endowment is clearly the more important determinant, it appears that population potential may make a small, independent contribution to the determination of whether an SEA produces coal or not. Resources are necessary, but not quite sufficient. It should be noted that quality of reserves is only roughly standardized in this analysis. The different types of deposits—anthracite, bituminous, subbituminous, and lignite—were equated on the basis of conventional Btu's-per-ton ratios. However, the actual quality of the reserves (as well as the amounts, of course) is subject to unknown errors of estimate (see Appendix).

Availability of the required resource, then, is the major determinant of whether coal production takes place. Moreover, we should expect to find production in large amounts where coal deposits are extensive and in small amounts where they are not. But if we standardize production for extent of available reserves, it is possible to highlight the effect of other variables affecting amount produced. In particular, if we measure "intensity" of production relative to resources by a production/reserve ratio, the significance of location with respect to the intermetropolitan complex becomes clear. Restricting the analysis to the 94 nonmetropolitan SEA's reporting production in 1949, we find a strong direct relationship between log of the production/reserve ratio and population potential ($r = .65$). The correlation between log of production/reserve ratio and log of estimated recoverable reserves is —.27; and we also note an inverse relationship between log of recoverable reserves and population potential ($r = -.26$). Multiple regression analysis indicates a significant direct relationship between log of production/reserve ratio and population potential, independently of log of recoverable reserves (partial regression coefficient of .63), but no significant relationship between log of production/reserve ratio and log of recoverable reserves independently of population potential (partial regression coefficient of —.10). The multiple regression equation is $\hat{Y}$ || $1.22 - .111X_1 + .045X_2$. The dashed line in figure 12 identified "Expected p/r 2.25, producing" represents combinations of X_1 and X_2 falling within the range of the data which yield $\hat{Y}$'s of 2.25. Producing areas lying to the right of the line are expected to have production/reserve ratios, the log of which exceeds 2.25; producing areas lying to the left of the line are expected to have production/reserve ratios, the log of which is less than 2.25. Of the 51 areas falling to the right of the line, 40 have high production/reserve ratios and 11 have low production/reserve ratios; of the 43 areas falling to the left of the line, 11 have high production/reserve ratios and 32 have low production/reserve ratios. This discrimination, of course, is essentially due to population potential alone.

In the foregoing analysis no attention was given to distance from nearest metropolis as an indicator of metropolitan dominance, because cursory examination disclosed that it has no influence on amount of coal production independently of its association with population potential. There are 28 SEA's with reported coal production in the systematic sample of 100 nonmetropolitan SEA's used in the other analyses described here. For these 28 SEA's the partial correlation between log of production/reserve ratio and distance, holding constant potential, is only .06 (note the reversal in sign from the zero-order correlation of —.44); whereas the partial correlation between log of production/reserve ratio and potential, holding constant distance is .62 (as compared with the zero-order r of .71 for the sample of 28 producing SEA's).

AGRICULTURE: MAJOR PATTERNS

Turning to agriculture, we find relationships somewhat analogous to those for coal mining. (See Appendix for full description of the variables studied.) In considering the extent to which farmland is put into crops, the quality of the basic resource receives heavy weight in the regression equation while location also is important. But in studying output in relation to the amount of the resource, e.g., the per-acre value of products sold, location is the prominent explanatory variable. The agricultural data are of interest in another respect: these two dependent variables show different patterns of response to the two locational indicators, distance from a metropolis and population potential.

Within the nonmetropolitan United States, there is a general tendency for the per-acre value of farm products sold to be high in the environs of metropolitan areas and low in the more remote parts of the hinterland. In fact, the coefficient of correlation between per-acre value of farm products sold in 1949 (dollars) and the logarithm of distance to nearest metropolitan center was —.52 for the sample of 100 nonmetropolitan SEA's. (See Appendix for description of sample.) A weaker tendency for the per-acre value of products sold to be high in areas of high population potential and low in areas of lesser potential also is evident ($r = .39$).

The pattern of areal variation in per-acre value of products sold apparently cannot be accounted for in terms of inter-area differences in soil quality, at least insofar as these differences are reflected in the index used here, based on estimates of ground conductivity ($r = .05$ for the sample of 100 SEA's). The methods used are outlined later in this chapter on pages 185-87, and in the Appendix, pages 557-59.

We also note that on the average, areas in which the economic environment, or accessibility to markets, is most favorable to agricultural production are those in which the natural resources for agricultural production are not necessarily highly favorable. For the sample of 100 SEA's, the coefficient of correlation between the log of mile distance to nearest metropolitan area and the soil quality index was a statistically nonsignificant .14 and that between population potential and the soil quality index was —.23.

In combination, log of mile distance to nearest metropolitan center, population potential, and the soil quality index account for 30 per cent of the inter-area variance in per-acre value of farm products sold in 1949 ($R = .55$). But in the multiple regression equation the only statistically significant partial regression coefficient is that of per-acre value of products on log of distance to metropolitan area, holding constant population potential and the soil quality index ($\beta = -.44$).

The percentage of farmland in cropland in the nonmetropolitan United States also tends to increase as distance to nearest metropolitan center decreases; where Y = per cent of farmland in cropland and X_1 = the logarithm of mile distance to nearest metropolitan area, $r_{Y1} = -.27$ for a sample of 100 nonmetropolitan SEA's. A direct relationship between percentage of farmland in cropland and population potential (X_2) also is evident ($r_{Y2} = .35$). And the percentage of farmland in cropland tends to be high in areas of estimated high soil quality and low in areas where the index of soil quality (X_3) is low ($r_{Y3} = .46$).

For the sample of 100 nonmetropolitan SEA's, the mean (unweighted) proportion of farmland in cropland was 46.2 per cent. The standard deviation was 20.9 percentage points; and the proportion of farmland in cropland ranged from 1 to 88 per cent over the 100 sample nonmetropolitan SEA's. In combination, population potential, log of mile distance to nearest metropolitan area, and the soil quality index account for 44 per cent of the inter-area variance in proportion of farmland in cropland ($R_{Y.123} = .66$). The betas, or partial regression coefficients in standard form, indicate a direct relationship between proportion of farmland in cropland and population potential holding constant distance to metropolitan area and soil quality, and a direct relationship between proportion of farmland in cropland and the soil quality index holding constant population potential and distance to metropolitan area ($\beta_{Y2.13} = .42$ and $\beta_{Y3.12} = .57$). However, there is no statistically significant relationship between proportion of farmland in cropland and log of mile distance to nearest metropolitan area when population potential and the ground conductivity index are taken into account ($\beta_{Y1.23} = -.11$).

The two indicators of agricultural activity—per-acre value of farm products sold and proportion of farmland in cropland—either of which might conceivably be taken as an indicator of "intensity" of agricultural activity, are associated with indicators of the "economic" and "natural" environments in strikingly different ways. Inter-area differences in per-acre value of farm products sold are associated primarily with differences among nonmetropolitan SEA's in proximity to nearest metropolis; inter-area differences in proportion of farmland in cropland are associated primarily with differences among areas in population potential and soil quality.

The second of these relationships is shown graphically in figure 13. Nonmetropolitan SEA's in which the proportion of farmland in cropland is relatively low tend to be areas in which both population potential and the soil quality index are relatively low; i.e., they tend to cluster in the lower left quadrant of the scattergram. Nonmetropolitan SEA's in which the proportion of farmland in cropland is relatively high tend to be areas in which population potential or the soil quality index or both is relatively high.

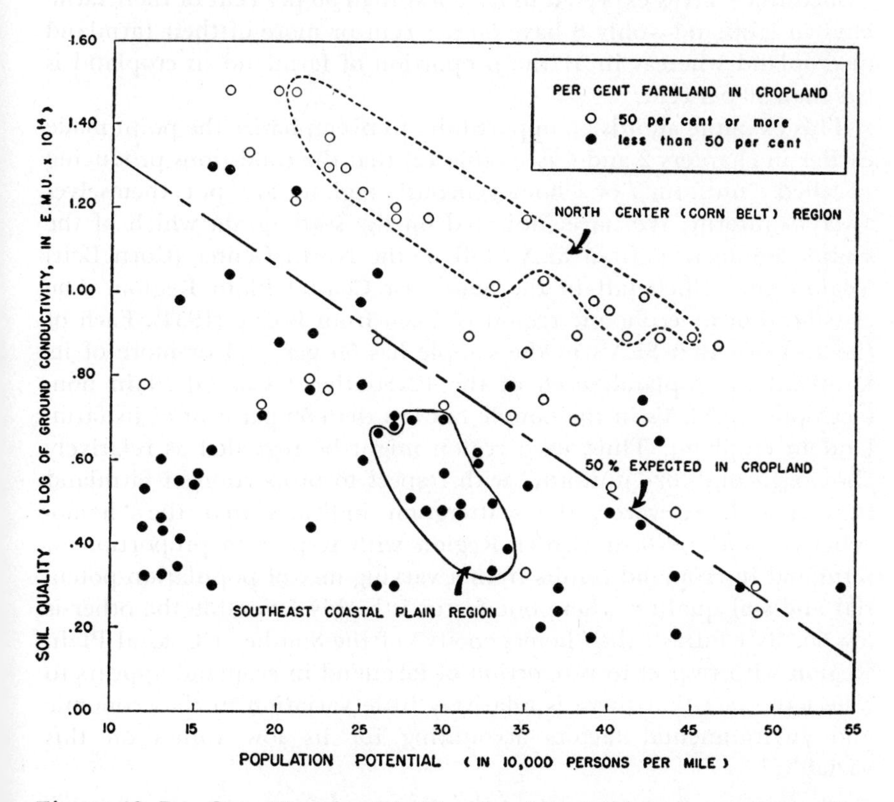

Figure 13. Per Cent Farmland in Cropland, in Relation to Soil Quality and Population Potential, for Sample of 100 Nonmetropolitan State Economic Areas: 1950

We have calculated the multiple regression equation, $\hat{Y} = -6.67 + .951X_1 + 35.398X_2$, where Y = per cent of farmland in cropland, X_1 = population potential in 10,000 persons per mile, and X_2 = the logarithm of ground conductivity (in electromagnetic units $\times 10^{14}$). If $\hat{Y}$ is set equal to 50, values of (X_1, X_2) which satisfy the foregoing equation lie on the dashed line, "50% expected in cropland," shown in figure 13. Nonmetropolitan SEA's falling above the dashed line are expected to have proportions of farmland in cropland of 50 per cent or more. Of the 41 SEA's falling above the dashed line, 33 have proportions of farmland in cropland of 50 per cent or more and 8 have proportions of less than 50 per cent. Of the 59 areas falling below the dashed line—areas expected to have less than 50 per cent of their farmland in cropland—only 8 have 50 per cent or more of their farmland in cropland whereas in 51 the proportion of farmland in cropland is less than 50 per cent.

This example affords an opportunity to re-emphasize the point made earlier in chapters 2 and 4 (see table 12) that the conditions producing so-called "uniform" or "homogeneous" regions are not themselves always uniform. We have indicated on the scattergram which of the sample nonmetropolitan SEA's fall in the North Center (Corn Belt) Region and which fall in the Southeast Coastal Plain Region. The classification by economic region is taken from Bogue (1954). Each of the 15 Corn Belt SEA's in the sample has 50 per cent or more of its farmland in cropland; each of the 12 Southeast Coastal Plain nonmetropolitan SEA's in the sample has less than 50 per cent of its farmland in cropland. Thus, each region might be regarded as relatively "homogeneous" or "uniform" with respect to proportion of farmland in cropland. However, the scattergram indicates that the "homogeneity" of the North Center Region with respect to proportion of farmland in cropland results from a varying mix of population potential and soil quality; where one factor is highly favorable the other is less so. By contrast, the "homogeneity" of the Southeast Coastal Plain Region with respect to proportion of farmland in cropland appears to reflect the fact that there is relatively little variation in the economic and environmental factors accounting for its low values on this variable.

AGRICULTURE: DETAILED ANALYSIS

The agricultural sector of the economy is, of course, resource oriented, but accessibility to consumers of agricultural products also is essential. The form and level of agricultural activity respond to the economic as well as the physical environment. The following analyses focus on relationships obtaining between agricultural activity in a nonmetropolitan area and the area's accessibility to the national market, a "regional" market, and a local market—as indicated by selected aspects of population distribution—when gross inter-area differences in quality of the resource are taken into account.

One of the better-known formulations of the relationship between agricultural activity and population nodes is the classical statement of von Thünen. In general, the von Thünen model assumes a single center and deduces that the intensity of agricultural production will decrease as distance from this center increases. Like any abstract model, this one cannot purport to be an accurate and detailed description of the relationship in all situations; but it continues to serve as a useful framework for organizing and examining data (see, for example, Melamid, 1955). On the empirical side, influences of the metropolitan center and the hinterland city, respectively, on some characteristics of the rural-farm population and of agricultural organization have been examined by Duncan (1956b, c). Anderson and Collier (1956) demonstrated the influence of both the metropolitan center and the hinterland city on agricultural activity within a segment of the national economy.

Research of this type, along with the formulations of students of location theory, suggests that an area's position in the spatial framework of the economy, as well as its natural resources, is a determinant of the form and level of agricultural activity in the area. As in the analysis of manufacturing (chapter 7) we consider three facets of this spatial framework: first, population potential, or accessibility to the national market; second, distance to nearest metropolitan center; and third, the extent of urbanization within the nonmetropolitan area itself. These variables are described formally in the Appendix.

In formulating an investigation of areal variation in agricultural activity, when it is clear intuitively that concentrated agricultural activity can occur only if the physical environment is permissive initially or is modified in its prohibitive aspects, some index of the "quality" of the physical environment seems essential. An index might be based on the observed agricultural productivity of the area under a specified set of inputs, a specified type of management, and a specified schedule of prices which permits aggregation of the production statistics for different commodities into a summary figure. Kendall (1939) has described an interesting attempt to derive a single index of "crop productivity" for 48 counties in England by means of a multivariate analysis of observed yields of ten crops. But using an index of this type to "explain" inter-area differences in agricultural activity involves circular reasoning. On the other hand, any effort to obtain a measure of the suitability of natural resources for agricultural activity, independent of observed production, would require voluminous and detailed data on the physical and chemical properties of the soil, the growing season, topographic features, the rate of evapotranspiration, and indicators of other relevant aspects of the environment; the "index" would probably involve several dimensions. One crude approximation to such an "index" was presented for states in the reports of the United States National Resources Board (1934, p. 127). The total acreage of each state was allocated to one of five "land productivity classes," which were developed by considering "the principal physical conditions influencing productivity, such as soil type, topography, rainfall, and temperature" and assuming "that the input of labor and capital will be that most nearly capable of maintaining the natural level of productivity, but without irrigation, additional drainage, or the addition of lime fertilizer or other amendments except nitrogen-fixing legumes" (United States National Resources Planning Board, 1943, pp. 36-37). The classification, however, is not available for areal units smaller than states; and it was based on relatively incomplete data.

For the purposes of this study, the ground conductivity map prepared by the Federal Communications Commission in 1938 appears to offer the most usable of the imperfect data that are available. On the basis of the relationship between ground conductivity and soil type in areas where measurements of radio signal attenuation in the standard broadcast band were available, a ground conductivity map for the United States was prepared from the soil type maps of the United States Department of Agriculture (information obtained from correspondence with the Federal Communications Commission and their report, T.R.R. 2.1.4.). In effect, the various types of soil were ranked by the FCC analysts in terms of quality on the basis of their estimated average ground conductivity; the ranking is independent of past or current agricultural production, which depends on the schedule of inputs as well as on the character of the natural resources. (See Appendix for further discussion.) Consequently, an index of "soil quality" based on "ground conductivity" was selected as at least a crude indicator of the suitability of natural resources for agricultural activity. Such an index, of course, can hardly reflect all aspects of the physical environment which are associated with agricultural productivity; and the suitability of the natural resource itself for agricultural production cannot be measured directly except in relation to a given schedule of inputs. As is true of the "land productivity classes," the ground conductivity index has not been carefully validated as an indicator of "soil quality" or suitability of the physical environment for agricultural activity. However, aside from its convenience, the usefulness of the ground conductivity index is suggested by recent statements of Albrecht (1956, 1957); he points out that areas of good radio reception or high ground conductivity have soils in which the combination of moisture and salts is similar to that required for agricultural production. Furthermore, the index of soil quality is used in the analysis primarily as a rough "control factor" in investigating inter-area differences in agricultural activity; certainly no attempt is made to evaluate economic returns to the resource.

There are available, then, three indicators of accessibility—population potential, distance to a metropolitan center, and local urbanization—and an indicator of the physical environment—the soil quality index. The zero-order correlations among these four variables are summarized in table 28. Looking first at the inter-correlations among the indicators of accessibility, we note a substantial degree of empirical independence as well as theoretical independence among the three variables. For the sample of 100 nonmetropolitan SEA's, population potential is inversely related to distance from a metropolitan center ($r = -.60$). In the northeastern United States, where population potentials are highest, metropolitan centers are more closely spaced than in other parts of the nation; in view of this, it is not surprising that areas of relatively high potential, on the average, are located closer to a metropolitan center than are areas of low potential. On the other hand, both population potential and distance to metropolitan center are largely independent of urbanization within the area itself. All three nodal indicators are retained in the subsequent analysis, for they apparently are sensitive to somewhat different aspects of the national and regional patterns of population distribution.

In the last column of table 28, the zero-order correlations between each of the nodal indicators and the index of soil quality are presented. Population potential is inversely related to soil quality ($r = -.23$); this suggests that, on the average, the areas with greatest accessibility to the national market have relatively poor natural resources for agricultural production. Distance to a metropolitan center and local urbanization are largely independent of the index of soil quality.

Agricultural production, of course, cannot be concentrated areally as can industrial production. From the standpoint of agricultural production alone, the most favorable areal pattern for both producers and consumers of agricultural commodities would be a relatively even distribution over the arable land. But considering only industrial production, the most favorable areal pattern for both the producers and consumers of industrial goods would be one of unevenness or concentration. In a highly industrialized economy, the areal pattern of population distribution or the distribution of consumers tends to be dominated by the industrial sector and to be uneven. (See Lösch, 1954, pp. 98-99.) The areal pattern of agricultural production which emerges under these conditions might be thought of as a resultant of two sometimes conflicting "pulls"—the concentration of the consumers of agricultural products and the dispersion of areas where the combination of natural resources is favorable for agricultural production.

Table 28. Zero-Order Correlation Matrix for Indexes of Accessibility and Soil Quality, for Sample of 100 Nonmetropolitan State Economic Areas: 1950

Variable	Variable		
	Distance to metropolitan center	Urbanization in local area	Index of soil quality
Population potential	−.60**	−.13	−.23*
Distance to metropolitan center	...	.02	.14
Urbanization in local area	...	...	.03

* Significant at .05 level.
** Significant at .01 level.

Not all arable land is included in farms. Whether or not the arable or potentially arable land actually is used for agricultural production depends on the economic environment in large part. Hawley (1950, p. 358) in discussing the reorganization of land uses accompanying expansion, notes that the productivity of the now-abandoned New England farm land did not decrease, but "as in so many other instances, its productivity simply proved inadequate to the competition offered by western lands," when the efficiency of interregional transportation increased.

For the sample of 100 nonmetropolitan SEA's, land in farms as a proportion of all land varies from a low of 8 per cent to a high of 98 per cent; the mean (unweighted) proportion is 68 per cent with a standard deviation of 24 percentage points. The proportion of land in farms varies directly with the soil quality index; and this index accounts for about 45 per cent of the inter-area differences in the proportion of land in farms. The zero-order correlations (summarized in table 29) between the proportion of land in farms and each of the three nodal indicators indicate that there is little relationship on an area-by-area basis between the proportion of farmland and potential, distance to metropolitan center, or local urbanization.

Table 29. Zero-Order Correlations of Six Aspects of Agricultural Activity with Indexes of Accessibility and Soil Quality, for Sample of 100 Nonmetropolitan State Economic Areas: 1950

	Independent variable			
Dependent variable	Population potential	Distance to metropolis	Local urbanization	Index of soil quality
Per cent of land in farms	.09	−.06	−.10	.67**
Per cent of farmland in cropland	.35**	−.27**	−.15	.46**
Per-acre value of products sold	.39**	−.52**	.08	.05
Per-acre value of land and buildings	.34**	−.56**	.06	.05
Rural-farm population density	.54**	−.36**	−.30**	−.46**
Per cent part-time and residential farms	.24*	−.21*	.06	−.72**

* Significant at .05 level.
** Significant at .01 level.

The multiple regression model permits an assessment of the proportion of the inter-area variance in the dependent variable which is explained by the independent variables in combination and provides an indication of the relative importance of each independent variable in accounting for the variation in the dependent variable. The coefficient of multiple correlation is .72; 52 per cent of the inter-SEA variance in proportion of land in farms is accounted for by the three nodal indicators and the soil quality index in combination. The latter is the major "explanatory" factor; in areas of high ground conductivity, a relatively high proportion of the land is in farms. But population potential also makes a significant contribution to the "explanation" of inter-area differences in the proportion of land in farms (as shown by its significant Beta coefficient in table 30); high population potential or relatively easy access to the national market is conducive to a high proportion of land in farms. Little additional information is contributed by the other independent variables—distance to metropolitan center and local urbanization (as shown by their nonsignificant Beta coefficients). Theoretically, then, a combination of high population potential and high ground conductivity would be most likely to produce a relatively high proportion of land in farms; however, in view of the negative association between potential and ground conductivity in the nonmetropolitan United States, this combination is somewhat unlikely to occur.

Table 30. Summary of Multiple Regressions of Six Aspects of Agricultural Activity on Indexes of Accessibility and Soil Quality, for Sample of 100 Nonmetropolitan State Economic Areas: 1950

	Independent variable				
Dependent variable	All variables	Population potential	Distance to metropolis	Local urbanization	Index of soil quality
	R	*Beta coefficients*			
Per cent of land in farms	.72**	.23*	−.02	−.09	.73**
Per cent of farmland in cropland	.67**	.40**	−.12	−.11	.57**
Per-acre value of products sold	.56**	.18	−.43**	.11	.15
Per-acre value of land and buildings	.58**	.05	−.55**	.07	.13
Rural-farm population density	.68**	.39**	−.07	−.24**	−.36**
Per cent part-time and residential farms	.73**	.03	−.10	.08	−.70**

* Significant at .05 level.
** Significant at .01 level.

In the zero-order correlation analysis, no significant relationship between the proportion of land in farms and any one of the three nodal indicators was discerned; but within the multiple regression framework, when gross inter-area differences in soil quality are controlled statistically, the positive association of proportion farmland with potential is observed. The major determinants of proportion farmland, among the four variables considered here, are soil quality and population potential. A partial correlation, then, can be computed to evaluate the relationship between proportion farmland and population potential independent of soil quality, i.e., the correlation between proportion farmland and potential when gross inter-area differences in ground conductivity have been eliminated statistically. The coefficient of partial correlation between proportion farmland and potential, holding constant ground conductivity, is .33 (significant at the .01 level), a considerable increase over the zero-order correlation of .09 between proportion farmland and population potential.

Another aspect of the land use pattern is the proportion of the land in farms which is classified as cropland. That part of the land in farms which is used as cropland, as opposed to pasture or woodland, has been called "the most productive part of the nation's land resources" (*United States Census of Agriculture: 1950,* Vol. V, Part 4, p. 30). The mean (unweighted) proportion of farmland in cropland for the sample of SEA's is 46 per cent, with a standard deviation of 21 percentage points; the proportion ranges from about 1 per cent to 88 per cent.

The proportion of farmland in cropland is related directly to ground conductivity and to population potential and varies inversely with distance to a metropolitan center (see table 29). About 21 per cent of the inter-SEA variance in the proportion of farmland in cropland is accounted for by the index of soil quality, about 12 per cent by population potential, and about 8 per cent by distance to nearest metropolitan center. In combination, the three nodal indicators and the soil quality index account for 45 per cent of the inter-SEA variance in proportion of farmland in cropland. The soil quality index and population potential make significant independent contributions to the explanation of inter-area differences in the proportion of farmland used as cropland; little additional information is contributed by the other independent variables—distance from a metropolitan center and local urbanization.

The coefficient of partial correlation between proportion of farmland in cropland and population potential, holding constant soil quality, is .53 (significant at the .01 level), as compared with the zero-order correlation of .35 between the proportion of farmland in cropland and potential. Thus, when inter-area differences in the suitability of the physical environment for agricultural activity are crudely controlled, areas of high population potential, on the average, have relatively large proportions of their acreage devoted to farmland and high proportions of their farmland used as cropland or in a relatively intensive form of agricultural land use. The relationship between potential and proportion of farmland in cropland is somewhat stronger than that between potential and the proportion of land in farms.

It is perhaps worth noting that the proportion of land in farms was more highly correlated with the soil quality index than was the proportion of farmland in cropland. The explanation of this finding probably lies in the fact that by restricting the denominator of the proportion to farmland rather than total acreage a partial control on "soil quality" enters the dependent variable.

The per-acre value of products sold is probably the most direct indicator of agricultural productivity available among the items reported in the *1950 Census of Agriculture*. For the 100 sample SEA's, the average (unweighted) value of products sold per acre was $24, with a standard deviation of $17. For individual SEA's in the sample, the per-acre value of products sold varied from about one dollar to $88.

Looking at the zero-order correlations summarized in table 29, one sees that the per-acre value of products sold varies inversely with distance to a metropolitan center and directly with population potential; inter-area differences in this measure of intensity of production appear to be largely independent of inter-SEA variation in local urbanization or soil quality. For the sample of SEA's, 27 per cent of the inter-SEA variance in per-acre value of products sold is accounted for by distance to nearest metropolitan center and 16 per cent by population potential. The three nodal indicators and the soil quality index, in combination, account for 32 per cent of the inter-SEA differences in the per-acre value of products sold. The coefficient of multiple correlation is only slightly higher than the zero-order correlation between the per-acre value of products sold and distance to nearest metropolitan center; and within the multiple regression framework, only the latter variable contributes significantly to the "explanation" of inter-SEA variance in per-acre value of products sold.

The patterns of relationship between the per-acre value of land and buildings and the indexes of accessibility and soil quality are similar to those between the per-acre value of products sold and the nodal indicators and soil quality. The per-acre value of land and buildings, of course, reflects the productivity of the land as well as the investment in buildings and improvements. For the sample of SEA's, the average (unweighted) value of land and buildings per acre was $78, with a standard deviation of $51. The per-acre value of land and buildings ranged from less than $10 to about $250. It seems likely that areas differ in respect to the relative contributions of land and of buildings to the over-all value figure; however, the value of land and buildings cannot be broken into its component parts with the available data.

The per-acre value of land and buildings varies inversely with distance to a metropolitan center and directly with population potential; on an area-by-area basis, it is largely independent of local urbanization and soil quality. For the sample of SEA's, 31 per cent of the inter-SEA variance in per-acre value of land and buildings is accounted for by distance to a metropolitan center and 11 per cent by population potential. The three nodal indicators and soil quality, in combination, account for 33 per cent of the inter-SEA variance in per-acre value of land and buildings. The proportion of variance explained by the indexes of accessibility and soil quality in combination is only 2 percentage points greater than that explained by distance to nearest metropolitan center alone; and within the multiple regression framework, only distance to a metropolitan center contributes significantly to the "explanation" of inter-SEA variance in per-acre value of land and buildings.

The findings on per-acre value of products and of farms are generally consistent with the von Thünen model—intensity of agricultural production decreases as distance from a population node increases. Access to markets presumably is conducive to intensive agricultural activity. But access to a "regional" market, or metropolitan center, rather than access to the national market is associated with high per-acre values of products sold and of land and buildings. In part, the demand for perishable commodities in the metropolitan center of a "regional" market may be sufficient to bring about intensive production in the nearby nonmetropolitan areas; but with a high level of technology in food preserving and transport, proximity to the national market should be nearly as important as proximity to a "regional" market. A somewhat different line of reasoning might lead to the conclusion that the high values per acre observed in proximity to metropolitan centers reflect a greater competition for land among alternative uses, and that agricultural uses can compete successfully only if they use the land intensively and yield a substantial net return to the land. These suggestions necessarily are speculative. The statistical results, however, clearly indicate that dimensions of the national distribution of population other than the over-all configuration of nodes influence some aspects of the organization of economic activity in the nonmetropolitan United States.

Another aspect of agricultural activity is the adjustment of the farm population to the land. The population residing on farms, as defined by the Bureau of the Census, is not synonymous with the population dependent on agriculture for a livelihood; some rural-farm residents secure part or all of their income from nonagricultural sources, and, on the other hand, not all persons deriving their income from agricultural sources reside on farms. Consequently, the rural-farm population per 1,000 acres of land in farms only approximates a measure of the population dependent on agriculture per unit of land in agricultural use or its inverse, the land-man ratio. The rural-farm density figure, however, reflects accurately the settlement pattern or habitation ratio in the rural-farm areas. (For an analysis of "habitation ratios," based on total land rather than land in farms, in relation to distance from a metropolitan center, see Bogue, 1949.)

For the sample of SEA's, the mean (unweighted) rural-farm population density was 31 per 1,000 acres of land in farms, with a standard deviation of 22; and in this sample, rural-farm density ranged from one person per 1,000 acres of farmland to 110 persons per 1,000 acres of farmland. The zero-order correlations summarized in table 29 reveal that rural-farm density is directly related to population potential and inversely related to soil quality, distance to metropolitan center, and local urbanization. About 29 per cent of the inter-SEA variance in rural-farm density is accounted for by population potential; habitation ratios in the rural-farm sector are, on the average, highest in areas of high population potential. On the other hand, about 21 per cent of the inter-SEA variance in rural-farm density is accounted for by the soil quality index; rural-farm habitation ratios are, on the average, highest in areas where the physical environment is not particularly well-suited for agricultural activity. Inter-area differences in distance to a metropolitan center account for 13 per cent of the inter-SEA variance in rural-farm density; rural-farm habitation ratios are, on the average, high in nonmetropolitan areas which lie relatively close to a metropolitan center. Nine per cent of the inter-SEA variance in rural-farm density is accounted for by differences among areas in the extent to which they are "urbanized." Habitation ratios for the rural-farm population are relatively low in the more highly "urbanized" areas. (There is some circularity in this last result owing to the fact that the proportion of population classed as rural-farm enters into the definition of the urbanization index; see Appendix for this definition.)

Within the multiple regression framework, population potential, local urbanization, and the soil quality index each contributes independently to the "explanation" of area-to-area differences in rural-farm population density. Distance to a metropolitan center contributes relatively little additional information. The indexes of accessibility and soil quality in combination account for 47 per cent of the inter-SEA variance in rural-farm density. High population potential, poor soil quality, and a low degree of urbanization in the local area are the combination of factors most likely to be associated with high population density in the rural-farm sector. At any rate, it seems fairly clear that the rural-farm population is distributed unevenly with respect to agricultural resources on an area-by-area basis, and that its pattern of distribution is shaped in part by that of the nonfarm sector of the economy.

Analysis of areal variation in the proportion of farms operated on a part-time or residential basis suggests that farm residence coupled with off-farm work is one way in which relatively high rural-farm densities are maintained in areas of limited agricultural resources. The mean (unweighted) proportion of farms classified as part-time or residential was 32 per cent for the sample of SEA's; and the standard deviation was 20 percentage points, with the proportion of part-time and residential farms ranging from less than 5 per cent to 92 per cent.

The relationship between the proportion of part-time and residential farms and the soil quality index is inverse ($r = -.72$); areas in which a high proportion of the farms are operated on a part-time or residential basis are, on the average, areas of limited agricultural resources. The proportion of part-time and residential farms varies directly with population potential ($r = .24$) and inversely with distance to a metropolitan center ($r = -.22$); it is largely independent of urbanization in the local area. The direction of relationship between proportion of farms operated on a part-time or residential basis and distance to a metropolitan center might be anticipated from findings about metropolitan-nonmetropolitan differentials in the proportion of part-time and residential farms. In the immediate vicinity of large metropolitan centers (within Standard Metropolitan Areas with a central city of 250,000 or more), 42 per cent of the farms were operated on this basis in 1950, as were 39 per cent of the farms in the immediate vicinity of smaller metropolitan centers. In counties containing a sizable hinterland city, 33 per cent of the farms were classified as part-time or residential; and in counties outside the immediate influence of a metropolitan center or sizable hinterland city, only 30 per cent of the farms were operated on a part-time or residential basis (Duncan, 1956b, c). However, a direct relationship between proportion of part-time and residential farms and local urbanization also is suggested by these findings; and no such relationship emerges in the regression analysis. It should be noted, however, that the earlier findings reveal the greatest difference between metropolitan and nonmetropolitan counties, while the present analysis is confined to nonmetropolitan areas. About 54 per cent of the inter-SEA variance in proportion of part-time and residential farms is accounted for by the indexes of accessibility and soil quality in combination; 52 per cent is accounted for by the soil quality index alone. Apparently position in the spatial framework of the economy is relatively unimportant in "explaining" inter-area differences in the proportion of farms operated on a part-time or residential basis outside metropolitan areas.

To recapitulate, it will be recalled that 45 to 54 per cent of the areal variation in two indicators of patterns of land utilization (per cent of land in farms and per cent of farmland in cropland) and in two indicators of the adjustment of the rural population to their environment (the rural-farm population per 1,000 acres of land in farms and the proportion of farms operated on a part-time or residential basis) was accounted for by the indicators of accessibility and soil quality in combination. About 33 per cent of the areal variation in two measures reflecting intensity of production—per-acre value of products sold and per-acre value of land and buildings—was accounted for by the four independent variables in combination.

Of course, the indicators of the physical environment and accessibility employed here account for only a part of the areal variation in agricultural activity obtaining in the nonmetropolitan United States. On the other hand, the proportions of variance accounted for by the three nodal indicators and soil quality are significant—especially so in view of the fact that neither the pattern of population distribution over the nation nor the general pattern of areal variation in agricultural resources is likely to be modified extensively in the short run. To the extent that these persistent distributional patterns are the "basic" determinants of areal variation in agricultural activity, the existing pattern of inter-area differences in agricultural activity can be expected to continue.

PART III

INDUSTRY STRUCTURE AND REGIONAL RELATIONSHIPS

The concepts of ecology in the study of the complex interrelationships within communities might illuminate some of the foundations for the prosperity of plants, industrial as well as botanical.

—Chauncy D. Harris

CHAPTER 9

Industry Structure: Overview

In the remainder of the study we shall be concerned with the analysis of the industry structure of standard metropolitan areas (SMA's) in terms of the relationship between that structure and the "regional" situation of the SMA. The detailed and sometimes complex analyses to follow represent variations on our original theme, that "what a city does depends on where it is." We expect to add substance and refinement to this formulation by devising a classification of industry structure, analyzing variations among SMA's in industry structure according to this classification, and exploring interrelationships between the industry structure of the metropolitan area and activities carried on in the remainder of the economy.

Materials available for our basic classification and for making more detailed characterizations of the industry structures of individual SMA's include the labor force data of the *1950 Census of Population* and the employment data of the *1947 Census of Manufactures.* (We relied on the pre-1950 economic censuses rather than on those taken recently so as to keep our data from different sources more nearly comparable with respect to time.) There is a problem that must be acknowledged immediately and that affects even the most detailed census information. For the most part, census classifications of industries are based on distinctions as to type of product—e.g., the classification of manufacturing industries according to whether they produce durable or nondurable goods. The census classifications do not emphasize the differences among industries with respect to type of locational tendency nor with respect to stages in the production sequence (from extraction of raw materials and their initial processing to fabrication in the form of goods for final consumers). There is, of course, some information of the latter type in the census. We are given the broad distinction between mining, manufacturing, and the distributive industries; and within manufacturing there are such classifications as primary versus fabricated metals. But often a census industry group combines industries at the first stages of production with those at the final stages. These defects in the census classifications—from our point of view—mean that all our classifications are unavoidably crude. By working with the most detailed information available we seek to avoid gross errors in our conclusions; but it is too much to expect that the manipulation of census data will give a sharply etched picture of the industry structure of an SMA with the aspects relevant to the present inquiry clearly in the foreground.

In the brief reference to the interregional input-output model of Walter Isard (1951) in chapter 2, we indicated that the model is one of potentially great complexity and that data for implementing the model for any considerable number of metropolitan areas are not available. We have kept this model in mind as a general conceptual framework, but our classification procedures are quite crude as compared with those required by the model in its fully developed mathematical form. What we did attempt with our industry classification was to gain a judgment of the extent to which the industries in an SMA are directly or immediately dependent upon resource-extracting industries as opposed to the later stages of fabricating goods or the performance of services for final consumers. We also wished to obtain clues as to the extent to which service industries in the metropolitan area are of a type likely to be performed for a metropolitan hinterland as opposed to those directed largely to the maintenance of the local metropolitan population.

INDUSTRY CATEGORIES

Given the emphasis in the study on comparative analysis, it was desirable to define the universe of units to be compared quite comprehensively. In this chapter we are, therefore, concerned with all 151 SMA's with 1950 populations of 100,000 or more. The best source of relatively detailed industry data for all these areas is the labor force industry tabulations of the *1950 Census of Population*. The economic censuses do not include all industries, and, although the *Census of Manufactures* has rather more detailed industry classifications than the population census, it gives these only for SMA's with 40,000 or more manufacturing employees. The excellent materials in *County Business Patterns* (issued from time to time by the Bureau of the Census and the Bureau of Old Age and Survivors Insurance) do not add materially to the detail available in the population census and are not presented in quite so convenient a form for analysis of SMA's. The "detailed industrial classification" of the population census comprises 148 items; the number of employed persons in each of the 148 industries is given for each SMA of 100,000 or more inhabitants.

Our first problem was to arrange these industries in categories reflecting—albeit crudely—the type and degree of their relationship to natural resource extraction. Pertinent information is contained in the *1947 Interindustry Relations Study* of the United States Bureau of Labor Statistics. (We shall not attempt an exposition of the principles and results of "interindustry" or "input-output" research, since excellent non-technical as well as technical statements are readily available —see especially Glaser, 1951; University of Maryland, Bureau of Business and Economic Research, 1954; Cumberland, 1956; and references given in these sources.) However, we did not need to consult the "200 Sector Tables" of the study directly. The Regional Studies Unit of Resources for the Future, Inc., has compiled a table of "Important Input-Output Relationships for Primary Resource Extractors and 1st and 2nd Stage Resource Users, 1947," based on the *1947 Interindustry Relations Study*. This RFF table (as we shall refer to it) divides industries into four groups: (1) 21 "primary resource extractors," including such industries as agriculture and mining (each subdivided into several categories); (2) 27 "1st stage resource users," including among others various kinds of food packing and processing, primary metal industries, and processing of lumber; (3) 32 "second stage resource users," made up of textile, apparel, chemical, furniture, metal rolling, and like industries; and (4) 109 "industries for which resources have the most indirect significance," including 25 "service industries" and such manufacturing industries as paper, rubber, and glass products, fabricated metals, and machinery and parts in a rather detailed breakdown. Thus the industries classified as first stage resource users are distinguished from others by their relatively high degree of dependence on raw material inputs. The second stage resource users have among their major inputs the outputs of the first stage resource users. The last group of industries, those for which resources are quite indirectly involved, obtain very small proportions of their inputs from primary resource extractors or first stage resource users. (For further discussion of the RFF table, see Perloff *et al.,* 1960; we are indebted to Perloff and associates for the opportunity to make use of this material prior to publication.)

There are two important limitations on the RFF table which are inherent in the method and source on which it is based. First, to describe an industry, for example, as a "first stage resource user" is to give only a partial description of its inputs: the industries in this category range in proportion of inputs obtained from primary resource extractors from 9 to 76 per cent. The remaining inputs include labor, of course, and often major inputs from the first stage resource-using industry itself as well as from other industries. Second, in adapting the RFF categories to our use, it was necessary to match the "sectors" of the interindustry relations study with the industry titles of the population census, and this could not always be done with precision. In particular, in cases wherein one census industry was broken down into several sectors in the RFF table, and the latter fell into different resource-use categories, it was necessary to assign the census industry to that category which included the larger or more important sector(s). This determination was made on the basis of value added by manufacture or, where this information was not disclosed, on the basis of value of products shipped, as reported in the *1947 Census of Manufactures.* For example, one of the census industry titles is "blast furnaces, steel works, and rolling mills." In the RFF table, this is broken down into "blast furnaces," classified as a first stage resource user, and "steel works and rolling mills," grouped with the second stage resource users. The respective amounts of value added in 1947 were $328 million and $2,276 million; hence the census title was placed under second stage resource users on the basis of the greater importance of "steel works and rolling mills." We have no way of knowing from the population census data that the relative importance of the two components in a given SMA is the same as in the United States as a whole; in some instances, therefore, the classification should perhaps be different, and in all instances it is crude. This kind of roughness characterizes all the data given in terms of the industry categories described in this chapter. However, in our intensive studies of the individual SMA's (Part IV) we were able to make use of the more detailed industry classification of the *Census of Manufactures* where available.

Our other major use of the RFF table was to group census industry titles on the basis of type of market for outputs. Industries in any of the four groups may dispose of their products to other industries for further processing or fabricating, or they may have their outputs going directly to "final demand."

> Final demand consists of households and state and local government. This figure for some industries such as autos and new construction may be misleadingly low, because the output was arbitrarily assigned to "gross private capital formation." The figure is also misleading for coal, as the private consumption was arbitrarily assigned to "real estate and rentals." (Footnote to RFF table.)

We arbitrarily classified each industry, more than 50 per cent of whose output goes to final demand, as "producing for final market," and each industry with less than 50 per cent of its output going to final demand as "producing for non-final market." Difficulties in classifying census industry titles were handled in the way previously described. The crude nature of this classification and its arbitrary basis in some instances mean that it is not as informative in actual application as we had hoped it would be. It is retained, nevertheless, because it proved useful as a rough guide to the investigation of market areas for outputs.

The combination of these two principles of classification—type of resource-use and market for outputs—leads to the following set of categories, disregarding service industries and construction:

Resource use	*Type of market* Non-final	*Type of market* Final
Primary resource extractors	(1)	. . .
First stage resource users	(2)	(3)
Second stage resource users	(4)	(5)
Industries for which resources have the most indirect significance	(6)	(7)

Although it is logically possible for a primary resource extractor to produce for final markets, there was no industry falling in such a category under our procedures.

The classification of service industries was accomplished even more summarily and perhaps more crudely. Type of resource use does not enter the classification, of course. The residual category, service industries, includes a variety of activities concerned with distributive and commercial functions as well as personal and professional services to individuals and various services to other economic units. For our purposes, the most relevant basis of classification is whether the services are performed for local populations or establishments (those residing or located within the SMA) or for non-local clienteles. The census provides no such information, and, of course, many industries perform both local and non-local functions. Lacking facilities for careful study of the problem we had to guess at which industries might be expected to perform local, maintenance functions primarily and which were most likely to have significant extra-local functions. In some cases it seemed probable that an industry, if relatively small, might be largely local, but if large might well be serving extensive non-local populations; insurance, hospitals, entertainment, recreation, and educational services are industries of this kind. Accordingly, we have three categories of service industries; (8) service industries, local; (9) service industries, non-local; and (10) service industries, may be local or non-local. Such a classification could have only the most approximate validity at best, and it is quite possible that some industries were improperly classified on even an approximate basis. To some extent, our procedure for analyzing the industry data protects us from the consequences of a misclassification and provides indirect tests of the validity of the classification; such evidence is presented subsequently.

Two census industry titles, "construction" and "industry not reported," remain to be accounted for. These were placed in separate categories, (11) and (12) respectively, and for the most part ignored in the subsequent analysis. The reasoning behind this special treatment for construction was as follows. Our analysis is almost wholly static or cross-sectional; we are concerned with "structure" rather than "dynamics," if that distinction be allowed. But the volume of construction and, consequently, the proportion of the labor force employed in the construction industry are in large part determined by the current growth or expansion of a community. We computed the rank correlation between the rate of population increase, 1940-50, for SMA's and the proportions of their labor force in construction, with the following results for population size groups of SMA's:

Size	*Rank correlation*
1,000,000 or more (N = 14)	.50
500,000 to 1,000,000 (19)	.90
300,000 to 500,000 (23)	.75
250,000 to 300,000 (21)	.81
150,000 to 250,000 (36)	.58
100,000 to 150,000 (38)	.63

Whether or not a metropolitan area might meaningfully be described as specializing in construction, in a fashion analogous to "non-local services," it is apparent that this could not be determined without standardizing for rate of growth. To put it another way, it seems likely that the locational and situational factors responsible for high employment in construction would be somewhat different from those relevant to other aspects of the industry profile. It is probably true that there are other industries posing analogous problems, but there is none for which the case seems as clear.

In summary, the twelve categories of our classification are as follows:

(1) Primary resource extractors; production for non-final market
(2) First stage resource users; production for non-final market
(3) First stage resource users; production for final market
(4) Second stage resource users; production for non-final market
(5) Second stage resource users; production for final market
(6) Resources of indirect significance; production for non-final market
(7) Resources of indirect significance; production for final market
(8) Service industries; local
(9) Service industries; non-local
(10) Service industries; may be local or non-local
(11) Construction
(12) Industry not reported.

The industry titles of the population census assigned to each of these categories in accordance with the foregoing criteria are indicated in the tabulation below. Most of these industry titles are drawn from the detailed industrial classification rather than the more highly aggregated ("intermediate" and "condensed") systems; see United States Bureau of the Census, *Census of Population: 1950,* vol. II, *Characteristics of the Population,* part 1, United States Summary, List C—"Relationships among Condensed, Intermediate and Detailed Industrial Classification Systems Used in the 1950 Census of Population," pp. 58-59 (Washington: Government Printing Office, 1953). But in those cases where all the detailed industries subsumed under a title in the condensed system fell in one of our broad categories, only the industry title from the condensed system is shown; such cases are identified by an asterisk (*). Retail trade (**) comprises three titles from the condensed system: "food and dairy products stores, and milk retailing"; "eating and drinking places"; and "other retail trade."

Category 1: Primary resource extractors; production for non-final market
- Agriculture
- *Forestry and fisheries
- *Mining
- Logging

Category 2: First stage resource users; production for non-final market
- Sawmills, planing mills, and mill work
- Structural clay products
- Miscellaneous nonmetallic mineral and stone products
- Grain mill products
- Dyeing and finishing textiles, except knit goods
- Petroleum refining

Category 3: First stage resource users; production for final market
- Meat products
- Dairy products
- Canning and preserving fruits, vegetables, and sea foods
- Confectionery and related products
- Beverage industries
- Miscellaneous food preparations and kindred products
- Not specified food industries
- Tobacco manufactures

Category 4: Second stage resource users; production for non-final market
- Miscellaneous wood products
- Blast furnaces, steel works, and rolling mills
- Other primary iron and steel industries
- Cement, and concrete, gypsum, and plaster products
- Yarn, thread, and fabric mills
- Miscellaneous textile mill products
- Synthetic fibers
- Paints, varnishes, and related products
- Miscellaneous chemicals and allied products
- Pulp, paper, and paperboard mills
- Miscellaneous petroleum and coal products

Category 5: Second stage resource users; production for final market
- Furniture and fixtures
- Bakery products
- Knitting mills

Carpets, rugs, and other floor coverings
*Apparel and other fabricated textile products

Category 6: Resources of indirect significance; production for non-final market
Primary nonferrous industries
*Fabricated metal industries (incl. not specified metal)
*Machinery, except electrical
Electrical machinery, equipment, and supplies
Motor vehicles and motor vehicle equipment
Ship and boat building and repairing
Railroad and miscellaneous transportation equipment
Glass and glass products
Pottery and related products
Professional equipment and supplies
Photographic equipment and supplies
Printing, publishing, and allied industries
Drugs and medicines
Paperboard containers and boxes
Miscellaneous paper and pulp products
Rubber products
Leather: tanned, curried, and finished
Not specified manufacturing industries

Category 7: Resources of indirect significance; production for final market
Aircraft and parts
Watches, clocks, and clockwork-operated devices
Miscellaneous manufacturing industries
Footwear, except rubber
Leather products, except footwear

Category 8: Service industries; local
Street railways and bus lines
Taxicab service
Telephone (wire and radio)
Electric light and power, and electric-gas utilities
Gas and steam supply systems
Water supply
Sanitary services
**Retail trade
Real estate (incl. real estate-insurance-law offices)

Accounting, auditing, and bookkeeping services
Miscellaneous business services
*Repair services
Private households
*Other personal services
Theaters and motion pictures
Bowling alleys, and billiard and pool parlors
Medical and other health services, except hospitals
Welfare and religious services
Nonprofit membership organizations
Legal services
Engineering and architectural services
Postal service
Local public administration

Category 9: Service industries; non-local
Railroads and railway express service
*Trucking service and warehousing
Water transportation
Air transportation
Petroleum and gasoline pipe lines
Services incidental to transportation
Telegraph (wire and radio)
Other and not specified utilities
*Wholesale trade
Banking and credit agencies
Security and commodity brokerage, and investment companies
Advertising
Hotels and lodging places
Radio broadcasting and television
Miscellaneous professional and related services
Federal public administration
State public administration

Category 10: Service industries; may be local or non-local
Insurance
Miscellaneous entertainment and recreation services
Hospitals
Educational services, government
Educational services, private

Category 11: Construction
Construction

Category 12: Industry not reported
  Industry not reported

VARIATION IN INDUSTRY STRUCTURE

The first steps in analyzing the industry structure of SMA's were to aggregate the detailed industry statistics for each SMA into the twelve categories and to compute the percentage distribution of the employed labor force by these categories. An example of the latter is shown in Table 31, column (b), for the Milwaukee SMA, along with the distribution of the total labor force of the United States in column (a) for comparison. While inspection of the two distributions suffices to identify the categories for which the Milwaukee distribution diverges from the United States distribution markedly, somewhat more precise comparisons are afforded by the location quotients. These are obtained by dividing the percentages in the SMA distribution by corresponding percentages in the United States distribution, as illustrated in table 31. One can see at a glance, then, that Milwaukee is rather highly specialized in industries classed as first stage resource users producing for the final market and as those for which resources are of only indirect significance, producing for non-final markets; and it should perhaps be regarded as somewhat specialized in industries for which resources are of indirect significance, producing for final markets.

Other things being equal, it is tempting to assume that these three categories include the bulk of Milwaukee's "export" industries and hence comprise the better part of its "economic base." Methods for identifying the economic base by means of location quotients—although on the basis of less highly aggregated industry categories—have, indeed, been proposed (e.g., Hildebrand and Mace, 1950); and this method has been worked out in rather elaborate form (Mattila and Thompson, 1955). The method, however, has been subjected to severe criticism in terms of its implicit assumptions concerning areal or regional uniformity of the earnings of the factors of production, production functions and economies of scale, and patterns of consumption, as well as the assumptions that no products are exported by an industry until local needs are met and that goods produced by a given industry group are homogeneous. In the opinion of Leven (1956, p. 255), "the shortcomings of this technique render it useless as a quantitative measure of basic activity in an area." Some of these objections are granted

Table 31. Illustrative Computation of Location Quotients and Index of Dissimilarity for Industry Category Distribution, Milwaukee Standard Metropolitan Area: 1950

Industry category[1]	Per cent of employed labor force: United States distribution (a)	Per cent of employed labor force: Milwaukee distribution (b)	Location quotient (b)/(a)	Difference between distributions (b) − (a): +	Difference between distributions (b) − (a): −
(1)	14.4	0.7	0.05		13.7
(2)	2.1	0.5	0.24		1.6
(3)	2.0	4.1	2.09	2.1	
(4)	5.2	4.2	0.80		1.0
(5)	3.4	3.0	0.89		0.4
(6)	10.9	28.8	2.63	17.9	
(7)	1.9	2.2	1.13	0.3	
(8)	32.5	32.4	1.00		0.1
(9)	12.8	11.2	0.87		1.6
(10)	7.2	6.7	0.94		0.5
(11)	6.1	5.1	0.83		1.0
(12)	1.5	1.2	0.78		0.3
All categories	100.0	100.1	...	20.3	20.2

Adjustment of Index of Dissimilarity:
Milwaukee employment/United States employment = 374,655/56,225,340 = .0067
Adjusted index = 20.3/(1 − .0067) = 20.4
NOTE: Original calculations carried out with two decimals in per cent distributions.

[1] See p. 205 for identification.

SOURCE: *1950 Census of Population.*

in principle by the exponents of location-quotient techniques, and it is pointed out that "strictly interpreted, the *index of local specialization* is really a measure of labor force specialization *per se,* and only by successively more tenuous inferences may it be extended to the role of an index of product specialization and, ultimately, product-market orientation of local industry" (Mattila and Thompson, 1955, p. 218). Fortunately, for our purposes we need not assess the validity of some of the more refined inferences attempted by the location-quotient technique; nor is it necessary for us to claim that this technique identifies the "economic base" in any technical sense of the term. We are satisfied that the technique is sensitive to major axes of specialization in the industry structure of a metropolitan area. We are seeking a feasible method for characterizing the "profiles of specialization" of SMA's for comparative analysis, not an inexpensive substitute for the field work required actually to measure the economic base of a particular metropolis. Our decision to work initially with highly aggregated industry categories reflects an interest in a gross sort of variation. Although later we go into industry structure in more detail, we are still looking for ways to characterize "profiles" in summary terms, rather than indexes, say, of the relative size of "export" industries.

Besides giving the location quotients for industry categories, table 31 also illustrates the computation of an overall measure of the divergence of the SMA distribution from the United States distribution, the index of dissimilarity. This index is calculated by taking differences between the two distributions, category by category, and summing either the positive or the negative differences. The index of dissimilarity for Milwaukee is 20.3 per cent; to make Milwaukee's distribution the same as that of the United States, therefore, it would be necessary to shift one-fifth of the Milwaukee labor force to different categories. The adjustment shown in table 31 converts the index of dissimilarity from a measure of the divergence of the Milwaukee from the United States distribution to a measure of the divergence of Milwaukee's distribution from that of the rest of the United States, excluding Milwaukee. This adjustment, of course, is appreciable in size only for the largest SMA's.

Table 32. Quartiles of Distribution of Standard Metropolitan Areas on Adjusted Index of Dissimilarity to United States Industry Category Distribution, by Size: 1950

Size of SMA	Number of SMA's	Q_1	Median	Q_3	$Q_3 - Q_1$
1,000,000 or more	14	16.6	17.4	19.2	2.6
500,000 to 1,000,000	19	16.0	19.4	23.6	7.6
300,000 to 500,000	23	17.7	22.0	24.4	6.7
250,000 to 300,000	21	16.4	18.8	24.6	8.2
150,000 to 250,000	36	17.8	20.9	24.3	6.5
100,000 to 150,000	38	19.2	21.6	26.9	7.7

In chapter 2 we suggested that large metropolitan centers tend to be more diversified, i.e., less specialized, in their industry structures than smaller places. Although it is only a general tendency, the data in table 32 support this generalization, if the index of dissimilarity is accepted as a measure of degree of specialization. For example, the median (adjusted) index of dissimilarity for SMA's of 1,000,000 or more is 17.4 as compared with 21.6 for SMA's of 100,000 to 150,000. Moreover, the interquartile range of the indexes is much smaller for the largest SMA's than for the SMA's of lesser size. There is some interruption of the gradient at sizes 250,000 to 300,000 and 300,000 to 500,000 but the tendency remains as indicated.

Since we are comparing SMA's with the United States, we would expect almost all of them to be "specialized" in some degree, if only because metropolitan areas typically have small proportions engaged in extractive activities. The lowest indexes of dissimilarity are, in fact, found for SMA's that have unusually large proportions of workers in mining or whose boundaries (which must follow county lines) are so drawn as to include sizable agricultural populations. The five SMA's with indexes below 13 (Charleston, S. C., Duluth, Minn. – Superior, Wis., Huntington, W. Va. – Ashland, Ky., Knoxville, Tenn., and Scranton, Pa.) are cases in point. At the other extreme of high specialization are typically found SMA's specializing in manufacturing. This is true of eight SMA's with indexes exceeding 29 (Akron, Ohio, Detroit, Mich., Flint, Mich., Fall River, Mass., Lawrence, Mass., New Britain – Bristol, Conn., South Bend, Ind., and Waterbury, Conn.). Two others with this extreme degree of specialization (Miami, Fla., and Washington, D. C.) have concentrations of employment in the service industries.

The indexes of dissimilarity on which the foregoing statements are based are set out in table 33, along with the location quotients for the several industry categories. As is explained in chapter 10, the location quotients serve as the initial basis for identifying the "industry profiles" of the SMA's studied individually in Part IV. In the remainder of the present chapter we summarize some findings on variation in location quotients among SMA's.

We are not especially concerned with community-size variation in industry structure at this point, since that subject was taken up in some detail in chapter 3. However, it is pertinent to consider whether there are marked and regular variations by size in the relative importance of the broad categories in our classification. Table 34 summarizes size variation in location quotients obtained from the industry distributions when the data for all SMA's in each size group are aggregated. In table

Table 33. Location Quotients of Industry Categories and Index of Dissimilarity to United States Distribution, for Each Standard Metropolitan Area of 100,000 or More: 1950

(See text for description of industry categories)

Standard Metropolitan Area	Industry category[1]											Index of dissim-ilarity[2]
	(1)	(2)	(3)	(4)	(5)	(6)	(7)	(8)	(9)	(10)	(11)	
SMA's of 1,000,000 or more												
New York–Northeastern New Jersey	0.05	0.56	0.83	0.64	2.56	1.09	1.90	1.18	1.23	1.10	0.85	19.6
Chicago, Ill.	0.07	0.69	1.79	1.32	0.95	1.85	1.09	1.05	1.17	0.94	0.75	17.2
Los Angeles, Calif.	0.21	0.88	0.88	0.38	1.15	0.93	2.72	1.29	1.04	1.14	1.24	16.7
Philadelphia, Pa.	0.15	1.17	1.32	1.25	2.08	1.48	0.82	1.06	0.93	1.03	1.00	13.8
Detroit, Mich.	0.06	0.28	0.60	0.70	0.30	3.63	0.41	0.96	0.70	0.84	0.79	29.4
Boston, Mass.	0.06	0.31	1.04	0.55	1.10	1.46	1.69	1.19	1.11	1.49	0.95	18.1
San Francisco–Oakland, Calif.	0.15	0.96	1.32	0.52	0.60	0.92	0.28	1.22	1.61	1.33	1.16	19.2
Pittsburgh, Pa.	0.37	0.47	0.88	3.63	0.32	1.33	0.28	0.98	0.94	0.93	0.89	17.6
St. Louis, Mo.	0.17	0.88	2.05	1.02	1.10	1.34	2.15	1.04	1.28	0.94	0.85	13.7
Cleveland, Ohio	0.06	0.40	0.59	1.63	0.92	2.22	1.29	1.02	1.00	0.94	0.84	18.0
Washington, D. C.	0.10	0.12	0.27	0.06	0.12	0.52	0.07	1.18	2.83	1.10	1.22	31.6
Baltimore, Md.	0.11	0.55	1.34	1.55	1.12	1.05	1.30	1.13	1.20	1.14	1.16	14.0
Minneapolis–St. Paul, Minn.	0.15	0.94	1.62	0.40	0.90	1.21	0.85	1.13	1.52	1.35	0.94	17.0
Buffalo, N. Y.	0.15	1.28	0.77	2.52	0.69	1.68	1.16	0.98	1.02	0.96	0.82	16.6
SMA's of 500,000 to 1,000,000												
Cincinnati, Ohio	0.10	0.43	1.35	1.02	1.10	1.57	1.61	1.13	1.14	1.02	0.95	14.8

[1] Industry category (12), "Industry not reported," is omitted. See p. 205 for identification of categories.
[2] Adjusted for proportion of United States employment in SMA.

Table 33. Continued

Standard Metropolitan Area	Industry category[1]											Index of dissim-ilarity[2]
	(1)	(2)	(3)	(4)	(5)	(6)	(7)	(8)	(9)	(10)	(11)	
SMA's of 500,000 to 1,000,000—Cont.												
Milwaukee, Wis.	0.05	0.24	2.09	0.80	0.89	2.63	1.13	1.00	0.88	0.94	0.83	20.4
Kansas City, Mo.	0.17	1.00	1.81	0.65	0.98	0.96	0.55	1.19	1.51	1.02	1.08	15.3
Houston, Texas	0.26	3.23	0.69	0.82	0.48	0.73	0.15	1.22	1.26	0.96	1.67	19.4
Providence, R. I.	0.09	1.06	0.45	3.40	0.65	1.26	5.11	0.91	0.72	0.92	0.86	23.6
Seattle, Wash.	0.25	1.10	0.84	0.34	0.50	0.57	3.18	1.22	1.53	1.24	1.17	21.3
Portland, Oreg.	0.55	1.56	0.79	0.86	0.73	0.56	0.28	1.20	1.38	1.16	1.24	15.1
New Orleans, La.	0.13	0.61	1.85	0.58	0.82	0.42	0.14	1.30	1.78	1.30	1.19	24.6
Atlanta, Ga.	0.14	0.52	0.92	0.95	1.16	0.61	0.43	1.32	1.44	1.12	1.30	19.2
Dallas, Texas	0.19	0.49	0.97	0.34	1.21	0.65	1.34	1.32	1.34	1.13	1.56	20.4
Louisville, Ky.	0.18	1.08	3.34	0.87	1.03	1.22	0.29	1.08	1.30	1.05	1.01	14.2
Denver, Colo.	0.25	0.58	1.33	0.34	0.53	0.73	0.59	1.24	1.61	1.31	1.35	20.6
Birmingham, Ala.	0.65	0.80	0.60	3.18	0.40	0.44	0.14	1.16	1.04	0.98	0.98	17.0
San Diego, Calif.	0.54	0.14	1.08	0.09	0.31	0.29	3.61	1.31	1.38	1.18	1.32	23.6
Indianapolis, Ind.	0.08	0.36	1.45	0.55	0.70	1.96	1.30	1.10	1.20	1.10	0.90	18.8
Youngstown, Ohio	0.27	0.33	0.29	5.17	0.81	1.59	0.16	0.84	0.71	0.76	0.72	28.4
Albany–Schenectady–Troy, N. Y.	0.16	0.67	0.79	0.97	1.30	1.78	0.39	0.98	1.47	0.96	0.90	16.0
Columbus, Ohio	0.14	0.21	1.02	0.48	0.54	1.38	1.58	1.09	1.50	1.43	0.96	18.6
San Antonio, Texas	0.26	0.40	1.44	0.18	0.78	0.34	0.21	1.32	1.92	1.04	1.46	26.2
SMA's of 300,000 to 500,000												
Miami, Fla.	0.21	0.22	0.53	0.13	0.71	0.27	0.23	1.54	1.57	1.04	1.73	29.5
Rochester, N. Y.	0.15	0.14	1.35	0.31	1.78	2.88	1.23	0.96	0.69	1.00	0.78	24.4
Memphis, Tenn.	0.33	1.24	1.14	0.61	0.80	0.78	0.21	1.27	1.41	1.08	1.18	16.6

SMA's of 300,000 to 500,000—Cont.												
Dayton, Ohio	0.21	0.18	0.41	0.75	0.42	3.05	0.78	0.90	1.17	0.80	0.74	24.7
Norfolk–Portsmouth, Va.	0.21	0.40	0.75	0.52	0.38	0.89	0.16	1.25	2.02	0.88	1.12	21.8
Allentown–Bethlehem–Easton, Pa.	0.35	0.65	0.95	3.98	3.60	1.05	0.74	0.80	0.65	0.77	0.82	25.2
Akron, Ohio	0.08	0.52	0.42	0.49	0.26	3.70	1.50	0.95	0.66	0.82	0.67	30.6
Tampa–St. Petersburg, Fla.	0.54	0.39	3.52	0.35	0.37	0.32	0.16	1.36	1.18	0.97	1.61	22.9
Springfield–Holyoke, Mass.	0.10	0.22	0.62	1.86	1.65	2.02	2.40	0.95	0.77	1.18	0.76	22.0
Toledo, Ohio	0.11	1.12	0.64	0.54	0.54	2.68	0.52	0.99	1.20	0.84	0.80	21.2
Wilkes-Barre–Hazleton, Pa.	1.70	0.19	1.88	1.25	3.36	0.37	0.55	0.84	0.72	0.90	0.67	21.2
Omaha, Nebr.	0.40	0.52	4.12	0.24	0.56	0.48	0.33	1.10	1.79	1.32	1.01	22.2
Fort Worth, Texas	0.22	0.84	2.06	0.29	0.79	0.41	5.50	1.22	1.23	0.95	1.36	23.0
Hartford, Conn.	0.16	0.12	0.77	0.60	0.53	1.57	4.63	0.97	0.82	2.32	0.89	22.8
Wheeling, W. Va.–Steubenville, Ohio	0.96	0.64	0.68	4.40	0.35	0.88	0.46	0.90	0.68	0.76	0.68	17.9
Syracuse, N. Y.	0.21	0.19	0.69	1.11	0.53	2.22	0.81	1.04	1.02	1.26	0.83	17.4
Knoxville, Tenn.	0.54	0.98	0.70	1.91	1.37	0.84	0.22	1.02	0.97	1.11	1.57	10.9
Phoenix, Ariz.	0.92	0.35	0.89	0.21	0.24	0.41	0.15	1.26	1.36	1.24	1.42	17.7
Richmond, Va.	0.11	0.57	3.45	1.14	0.84	0.50	0.20	1.20	1.47	1.35	1.24	21.9
Oklahoma City, Okla.	0.38	0.59	1.32	0.19	0.37	0.42	0.22	1.28	1.86	1.07	1.50	24.2
Charleston, W. Va.	1.52	0.54	0.29	2.62	0.18	0.54	0.07	0.98	0.85	0.88	0.95	16.0
Nashville, Tenn.	0.16	0.59	1.13	1.15	1.20	0.58	1.38	1.20	1.26	1.46	1.37	17.7
Jacksonville, Fla.	0.13	0.56	1.59	0.46	0.41	0.40	0.14	1.35	1.91	0.98	1.40	26.8
SMA's of 250,000 to 300,000												
Harrisburg, Pa.	0.36	0.31	1.61	1.37	1.66	0.39	1.43	0.90	2.18	0.89	1.07	21.8
Johnstown, Pa.	1.99	0.68	0.45	3.08	1.12	0.24	0.07	0.82	0.69	0.80	0.66	25.6
San Jose, Calif.	0.76	0.50	3.70	0.37	0.27	0.64	0.22	1.14	1.00	1.42	1.54	16.3
Grand Rapids, Mich.	0.27	0.47	0.51	0.46	2.57	2.22	1.00	0.98	0.94	0.90	0.86	18.8
Utica–Rome, N. Y.	0.51	0.58	0.90	1.43	1.61	1.64	2.39	0.93	0.84	1.09	0.72	14.7
Canton, Ohio	0.24	1.00	0.43	3.29	0.49	2.20	0.31	0.91	0.76	0.76	0.70	25.1
San Bernardino, Calif.	0.78	0.35	0.95	1.49	0.34	0.32	0.26	1.06	1.60	1.15	1.45	16.0

Table 33. Continued

Standard Metropolitan Area	Industry category[1]											Index of dissimilarity[2]
	(1)	(2)	(3)	(4)	(5)	(6)	(7)	(8)	(9)	(10)	(11)	
SMA's of 250,000 to 300,000—Cont.												
Sacramento, Calif.	0.49	0.43	2.21	0.13	0.23	0.26	0.11	1.06	2.52	0.93	1.42	26.4
Fresno, Calif.	1.73	0.43	1.85	0.25	0.23	0.25	0.09	1.09	0.98	1.07	1.40	18.0
Worcester, Mass.	0.10	1.70	0.38	1.79	1.16	1.78	3.15	0.97	0.68	1.30	0.79	21.1
Tacoma, Wash.	0.47	3.54	1.21	0.49	0.70	0.45	0.47	1.14	1.36	1.23	1.29	18.4
Salt Lake City, Utah	0.54	0.82	0.86	0.29	0.52	0.64	0.19	1.19	1.65	1.27	1.39	18.8
Flint, Mich.	0.16	0.09	0.27	0.18	0.15	4.88	0.10	0.80	0.44	0.74	0.58	42.6
Wilmington, Del.	0.34	0.79	0.60	3.79	0.79	0.95	0.45	0.95	0.86	0.99	1.28	16.5
New Haven, Conn.	0.09	0.29	0.78	0.76	1.67	1.77	2.10	1.04	1.02	1.32	0.91	16.9
Bridgeport, Conn.	0.06	0.60	0.35	0.93	1.42	3.10	1.96	0.92	0.61	0.75	0.90	26.3
Scranton, Pa.	1.04	0.18	1.00	1.06	3.46	0.60	1.38	0.92	1.07	1.07	0.64	11.6
Reading, Pa.	0.36	0.51	1.29	1.80	5.51	1.33	1.10	0.78	0.70	0.80	0.89	24.1
Duluth, Minn.–Superior, Wis.	1.21	0.30	0.69	1.02	0.72	0.45	0.27	1.01	1.61	1.11	0.82	12.1
Tulsa, Okla.	0.57	2.79	0.44	0.54	0.21	0.69	0.37	1.24	1.25	0.98	1.43	17.3
Peoria, Ill.	0.43	0.32	3.60	0.58	0.37	2.37	0.12	0.95	0.90	0.89	0.94	20.2
SMA's of 150,000 to 250,000												
Chattanooga, Tenn.	0.32	1.16	0.79	2.79	2.07	0.90	0.20	1.04	0.93	0.96	0.94	14.5
Huntington, W. Va.–Ashland, Ky.	0.69	1.44	0.68	1.67	0.96	0.83	0.48	0.97	1.36	1.01	1.02	9.2
Lancaster, Pa.	0.85	1.01	1.83	0.98	3.48	0.99	3.41	0.78	0.76	0.67	1.07	15.3
Davenport, Iowa–Rock Island–Moline, Ill.	0.38	0.51	0.89	0.44	0.46	3.00	0.26	0.96	0.80	1.00	0.76	22.0
Mobile, Ala.	0.33	1.21	0.64	1.14	0.50	0.57	0.05	1.14	1.81	0.88	1.05	19.5
Trenton, N. J.	0.15	0.49	0.81	0.93	1.22	2.20	1.40	0.93	1.03	1.26	0.96	16.9

SMA's of 150,000 to 250,000—Cont.												
Des Moines, Iowa	0.26	0.35	1.14	0.36	0.60	1.10	0.74	1.20	1.38	1.60	1.04	17.3
Wichita, Kans.	0.33	1.04	1.23	0.24	0.28	0.60	7.03	1.16	1.11	1.03	1.35	21.0
Spokane, Wash.	0.40	1.54	1.04	0.29	0.32	0.63	0.24	1.28	1.54	1.23	1.21	20.2
Erie, Pa.	0.34	0.30	0.71	1.33	0.54	2.85	2.18	0.85	0.76	0.84	0.69	24.3
South Bend, Ind.	0.17	0.17	0.64	0.25	0.82	3.55	2.89	0.84	0.65	0.91	0.61	31.6
York, Pa.	0.60	0.58	2.23	1.22	3.44	1.83	1.52	0.77	0.66	0.54	0.99	23.1
Stockton, Calif.	1.59	0.41	2.54	0.30	0.16	0.41	0.23	0.98	1.32	1.04	1.04	16.4
Charlotte, N. C.	0.26	0.59	0.87	1.72	1.62	0.50	0.18	1.27	1.25	0.96	1.21	19.2
Little Rock–North Little Rock, Ark.	0.38	1.17	0.67	0.43	0.84	0.41	0.61	1.24	1.57	1.49	1.27	20.5
Stamford–Norwalk, Conn.	0.12	0.25	0.43	1.01	1.35	1.88	1.70	1.13	0.82	0.91	1.27	18.3
Beaumont–Port Arthur, Texas	0.23	10.86	0.40	0.58	0.16	0.39	0.05	1.18	0.90	0.87	1.36	28.7
El Paso, Texas	0.46	0.70	0.98	0.21	0.68	0.41	0.12	1.28	1.74	1.00	1.46	21.9
Greensboro–High Point, N. C.	0.41	1.00	0.56	2.65	4.76	0.34	0.16	0.99	0.74	1.10	1.04	22.5
Binghamton, N. Y.	0.24	0.25	0.48	0.27	0.73	1.76	11.02	0.91	0.64	1.02	0.78	27.9
Fort Wayne, Ind.	0.35	0.26	1.02	0.22	0.90	2.89	0.20	0.95	1.01	0.92	0.77	20.8
Shreveport, La.	0.93	1.34	0.59	0.27	0.35	0.39	0.16	1.35	1.16	0.99	1.31	16.3
Lansing, Mich.	0.30	0.09	0.32	0.42	0.14	2.47	0.15	1.00	0.93	1.79	0.91	22.4
Columbus, Ga.	0.51	1.20	1.40	3.77	0.76	0.24	0.07	1.22	0.70	0.72	1.22	24.2
Madison, Wis.	0.92	0.17	2.82	0.21	0.23	0.73	0.22	1.02	1.10	2.29	1.00	14.8
Greenville, S. C.	0.50	2.17	0.62	5.14	1.10	0.29	0.08	0.98	0.58	0.86	1.10	25.1
Corpus Christi, Texas	0.81	1.51	0.82	0.51	0.24	0.27	0.12	1.26	1.35	0.89	1.81	19.0
Charleston, S. C.	0.54	1.44	1.75	0.99	0.45	0.96	0.04	1.23	0.98	1.11	1.08	11.1
Augusta, Ga.	0.68	2.37	0.68	3.00	0.42	0.01	1.07	1.12	0.92	1.19	1.10	19.3
Austin, Texas	0.40	0.28	0.53	0.12	0.31	0.26	0.09	1.37	1.28	2.13	1.84	28.7
Evansville, Ind.	0.19	0.71	2.82	0.17	1.01	2.47	0.57	1.02	0.94	0.91	0.83	20.5
Baton Rouge, La.	0.22	6.35	0.52	1.18	0.25	0.27	0.05	1.21	0.86	1.53	1.67	26.9
Waterbury, Conn.	0.10	0.06	0.50	0.76	0.78	3.57	5.00	0.79	0.44	0.79	0.66	35.9
Saginaw, Mich.	0.55	0.43	0.83	2.38	0.68	2.16	0.26	0.91	0.77	0.81	0.72	21.0
Rockford, Ill.	0.27	0.31	0.40	0.76	1.68	3.36	0.97	0.85	0.56	0.76	0.79	28.2
Savannah, Ga.	0.14	0.91	1.61	1.63	0.25	0.68	0.04	1.33	1.45	0.88	1.12	21.6

Table 33. Continued

Standard Metropolitan Area	Industry category[1]											Index of dissim-ilarity[2]
	(1)	(2)	(3)	(4)	(5)	(6)	(7)	(8)	(9)	(10)	(11)	
SMA's of 100,000 to 150,000—Cont.												
Lorain–Elyria, Ohio	0.38	0.16	0.26	4.64	0.38	1.84	1.29	0.84	0.53	0.80	0.76	28.8
Hamilton–Middletown, Ohio	0.31	0.24	0.88	4.09	0.32	1.98	0.60	0.81	0.49	1.11	0.95	27.7
New Britain–Bristol, Conn.	0.08	0.13	0.27	0.33	0.67	4.32	4.00	0.71	0.38	0.87	0.69	42.2
Winston-Salem, N. C.	0.35	0.49	9.80	0.90	2.75	0.47	0.12	0.96	0.74	0.92	1.03	23.6
Albuquerque, N. Mex.	0.24	0.48	0.45	0.54	0.29	0.17	0.14	1.22	1.69	1.26	2.71	28.6
Columbia, S. C.	0.45	0.65	0.54	0.88	0.45	0.20	0.30	1.30	1.31	1.78	1.46	22.2
Jackson, Miss.	0.93	0.98	0.78	0.40	0.80	0.33	0.13	1.28	1.10	1.23	1.46	14.8
Altoona, Pa.	0.29	0.79	0.79	0.83	1.02	0.24	0.59	0.95	3.10	0.79	0.67	26.9
Montgomery, Ala.	0.66	1.06	1.05	0.53	0.45	0.22	0.04	1.33	1.50	1.16	1.27	20.3
New Bedford, Mass.	0.26	0.29	0.58	3.88	3.06	1.52	1.34	0.88	0.51	0.65	0.65	28.6
Fall River, Mass.	0.13	0.86	0.42	4.48	5.16	0.73	0.63	0.83	0.58	0.72	0.78	32.6
Raleigh, N. C.	1.24	0.94	0.63	0.53	0.27	0.19	0.05	1.14	1.17	1.71	1.27	16.8
Macon, Ga.	0.42	1.48	0.82	2.02	0.67	0.17	0.27	1.20	1.69	0.99	0.91	21.6
Lowell, Mass.	0.17	0.32	0.79	4.44	1.62	0.87	2.27	0.89	0.72	1.25	0.75	24.5
Roanoke, Va.	0.18	0.63	0.83	1.47	1.36	0.41	0.06	1.09	1.87	1.29	1.26	21.5
Atlantic City, N. J.	0.36	0.20	0.71	0.13	2.02	0.30	0.22	1.41	1.47	0.83	1.47	26.5
Springfield, Ill.	0.73	1.19	0.45	0.12	0.22	1.27	0.68	1.09	1.40	1.22	1.02	13.1
Waco, Texas	0.68	0.78	0.64	0.53	1.00	0.47	0.18	1.26	1.19	1.48	1.25	15.8
Brockton, Mass.	0.18	0.44	0.60	1.04	0.99	1.04	10.59	0.97	0.74	0.84	1.02	19.4
Kalamazoo, Mich.	0.32	0.27	0.53	2.13	0.44	2.18	0.97	0.90	0.69	1.41	1.03	21.8
Lawrence, Mass.	0.08	0.12	0.42	7.37	0.91	0.71	2.23	0.84	0.49	0.82	0.62	35.8
Asheville, N. C.	0.65	1.17	0.41	2.17	1.35	0.21	0.19	1.17	0.94	1.44	1.13	17.2

SMA's of 100,000 to 150,000—Cont.												
Portland, Maine	0.13	0.40	1.59	1.53	0.99	0.45	1.10	1.26	1.53	1.23	0.87	21.1
Lincoln, Nebr.	0.52	0.42	0.75	0.09	0.24	0.58	1.59	1.16	1.48	2.02	1.14	20.5
Orlando, Fla.	0.84	0.37	1.47	0.24	0.24	0.27	0.09	1.38	1.22	1.06	1.52	20.0
Galveston, Texas	0.35	2.78	0.83	1.05	0.10	0.57	0.09	1.12	1.46	1.54	1.23	19.2
Springfield, Ohio	0.36	0.23	0.32	0.40	0.37	2.98	1.10	0.93	1.07	0.82	0.73	22.8
Racine, Wis.	0.44	0.20	0.70	1.24	0.52	3.52	0.69	0.84	0.49	0.72	0.66	28.9
Jackson, Mich.	0.46	0.56	0.41	0.33	0.73	2.60	0.42	1.05	0.99	0.75	0.70	19.3
Topeka, Kans.	0.39	0.38	2.20	0.08	0.22	0.66	0.09	1.06	1.95	1.84	1.15	23.4
Terre Haute, Ind.	0.61	0.24	3.59	1.30	0.51	0.57	0.45	1.12	1.47	1.05	0.70	17.0
Springfield, Mo.	0.69	0.61	1.33	0.21	1.11	0.43	0.19	1.17	1.61	1.34	1.12	17.4
Cedar Rapids, Iowa	0.78	1.72	3.79	0.22	0.31	1.47	0.13	1.03	0.94	1.05	0.90	13.3
Sioux City, Iowa	0.69	0.44	5.13	0.10	0.53	0.61	0.18	1.14	1.45	1.08	0.86	19.0
Durham, N. C.	0.34	0.60	7.71	1.25	1.18	0.24	0.03	1.05	0.56	2.02	1.48	26.9
Lubbock, Texas	0.91	0.29	0.66	0.25	0.38	0.24	0.09	1.28	1.30	1.22	1.89	19.8
Lexington, Ky.	0.67	0.25	1.37	0.06	0.42	0.34	0.17	1.28	1.10	2.20	1.38	22.0
Waterloo, Iowa	0.57	0.21	6.80	0.26	0.52	1.92	0.32	0.92	0.83	0.92	0.82	21.5

Table 34. Location Quotients of Industry Categories for Standard Metropolitan Areas Aggregated by Size Groups and for the Nonmetropolitan United States: 1950

Size group of SMA's	Number of SMA's	Industry category[2]									
		(1)	(2)	(3)	(4)	(5)	(6)	(7)	(8)	(9)	(10)
Total, 100,000 or more	151	0.23	0.72	1.15	1.06	1.22	1.33	1.25	1.11	1.19	1.08
1,000,000 or more	14	0.11	0.66	1.08	0.98	1.43	1.44	1.39	1.12	1.20	1.08
500,000 to 1,000,000	19	0.22	0.84	1.24	1.11	0.80	1.09	1.20	1.15	1.30	1.08
300,000 to 500,000	23	0.38	0.50	1.28	1.06	0.97	1.27	1.02	1.10	1.17	1.08
250,000 to 300,000	21	0.57	0.77	1.14	1.21	1.23	1.34	0.86	0.99	1.13	1.02
150,000 to 250,000	36	0.44	1.18	1.02	1.09	1.04	1.33	1.31	1.06	1.02	1.07
100,000 to 150,000	38	0.46	0.61	1.57	1.47	0.96	1.01	0.94	1.07	1.13	1.18
Nonmetropolitan United States[1]	...	2.08	1.40	0.79	0.92	0.69	0.54	0.65	0.85	0.74	0.89

[1] Includes 17 SMA's with populations of 50,000 to 100,000.

[2] Category (11), "Construction," and category (12), "Industry not reported," are omitted. See p. 205 for identification of categories.

35 we show size variation in terms of the proportion of SMA's having location quotients of unity or greater, the median location quotient for each size group, and the interquartile range of the location quotients for each size group. It is evident from these data that the distributions of location quotients are positively skewed in most cases. The explanation for this is simply that there is a "floor" of zero under the location quotients, but the "ceiling" is quite high, i.e., in most categories it is quite possible for an SMA to have several times the average proportion employed in the category. It is in line with an earlier observation to find that the two top size groups generally have smaller interquartile ranges of location quotients than the smaller size groups. Large SMA's less frequently exhibit extreme degrees of specialization than smaller SMA's. But there is little in the way of a regular size gradient in average location quotients or frequency of specialization (location quotient of one or more) by industry categories. The fact that large SMA's have lower location quotients in category (1) is at least partly an artificial result of the way in which SMA's are delineated. Such an outstandingly high mean location quotient as the 1.44 for SMA's of 1,000,000 or more in category (6) must likewise be discounted, because this category includes the manufacture of motor vehicles which is somewhat misleadingly classified in the RFF table as producing for non-final demand. In sum, when industries are aggregated into broad categories such as we are using here, the distributions no longer manifest clearly a tendency toward "hierarchy" like that described in chapter 3. Other essentially artificial reasons for this finding may be the use of a more detailed size classification here, the truncation of the range of sizes at 100,000 inhabitants, and the fact that SMA's include, in varying degrees, some population classified as rural.

Tables 34 and 35, however, exhibit certain other kinds of regularity. In all size groups, SMA's have quite low location quotients for category (1), the resource extracting industries; this finding requires no comment. Comparing the two categories of first stage resource using industries, we find that those producing for final markets, category (3), tend to have higher location quotients in metropolitan areas than those producing for non-final markets, category (2). The comparison is reversed at the more advanced stages of processing and fabricating. Among second stage resource users and among industries for which resources are most indirectly significant, the producers for non-final markets tend to have higher location quotients in metropolitan areas than the producers for final markets; i.e., location quotients are higher for category (4) than for category (5), and higher for category (6) than for category

Table 35. Measures of the Distributions of Location Quotients for Industry Categories, by Size Groups of Standard Metropolitan Areas: 1950

Size group of SMA's	Number of SMA's	Industry category[1] (1)	(2)	(3)	(4)	(5)	(6)	(7)	(8)	(9)	(10)
		Median location quotient									
1,000,000 or more	14	0.13	0.62	0.96	0.86	0.94	1.33	1.12	1.09	1.14	1.06
500,000 to 1,000,000	19	0.18	0.58	1.02	0.80	0.78	0.73	0.55	1.19	1.38	1.05
300,000 to 500,000	23	0.21	0.52	0.89	0.60	0.54	0.78	0.46	1.04	1.18	1.00
250,000 to 300,000	21	0.47	0.50	0.86	0.93	0.72	0.69	0.37	0.97	0.98	0.99
150,000 to 250,000	36	0.36	0.71	0.80	0.76	0.68	0.78	0.23	1.03	0.94	0.97
100,000 to 150,000	38	0.41	0.44	0.77	0.69	0.53	0.57	0.29	1.09	1.14	1.14
		Interquartile range of location quotients									
1,000,000 or more	14	0.09	0.54	0.57	1.03	0.53	0.63	1.28	0.16	0.28	0.20
500,000 to 1,000,000	19	0.13	0.69	0.66	0.62	0.50	1.01	1.37	0.21	0.38	0.22
300,000 to 500,000	23	0.38	0.42	0.94	0.94	0.82	1.61	1.04	0.30	0.69	0.36
250,000 to 300,000	21	0.51	0.49	1.01	1.22	1.33	1.57	1.25	0.16	0.76	0.35
150,000 to 250,000	36	0.29	0.98	0.61	1.20	0.74	1.78	1.11	0.28	0.54	0.28
100,000 to 150,000	38	0.38	0.54	0.84	1.28	0.65	1.20	0.84	0.31	0.75	0.57
		Per cent of SMA's with location quotients ≥ 1.0									
1,000,000 or more	14	0	14	50	50	43	79	57	79	79	57
500,000 to 1,000,000	19	0	32	53	21	26	42	42	84	84	68
300,000 to 500,000	23	9	9	43	39	26	35	26	57	61	52
250,000 to 300,000	21	19	19	38	48	43	43	38	43	48	48
150,000 to 250,000	36	3	44	33	39	28	39	28	58	44	47
100,000 to 150,000	38	3	16	32	42	29	32	24	63	58	63

[1] Category (11), "Construction," and category (12), "Industry not reported," are omitted. See p. 205 for identification of categories.

(7). There are some size groups of SMA's that constitute exceptions to these summary statements; hence the latter only represent general tendencies. But it is clear that processing of natural resources for use in other industries is an atypical metropolitan specialty. Moreover, at the more advanced stages of production metropolitan areas are more likely to specialize in producing things that will become inputs for other industries than in production of goods ready for the final consumer.

With respect to services, we note that specialization in "non-local" services, category (9), is more frequent or more pronounced than specialization in "local" services, category (8), or in services that may be local or non-local, category (10). The variation among the three categories of services in respect to frequency or degree of specialization is more evident among large than among small SMA's. We are inclined to interpret the fairly high location quotients for "local" services among large SMA's as evidence that these large centers need or provide more of these kinds of services for their local populations rather than as an indication that they have larger non-local markets for the ostensibly local services.

Since the broad industry categories reveal no very marked variation in pattern of specialization by size of SMA, we can be confident that other factors related to such variation operate on the whole independently of size. In table 36 we return to a consideration of two such factors descriptive of the locational situation of SMA's—population potential and distance to nearest larger SMA. (These variables are defined in the Appendix.) Table 36 shows rank correlations of proportions (or location quotients) in each category with potential and distance. We find that the patterns exhibited by the two sets of correlations are quite similar; moreover, neither distance (ranked inversely) nor potential consistently correlates higher with industry structure than the other. This result in large part follows from the high intercorrelation of the two variables (see chapter 7). We may therefore discuss the relationship of industry structure to accessibility in general terms, without specifying which of the two indicators thereof is under examination.

With but few exceptions, the correlations are negative for categories (1) to (3) and (8) to (10) and positive for categories (4) to (7). Thus the proportion of the labor force engaged in resource extraction or first stage resource-using industries is inversely related to accessibility, as is the proportion in any of the three categories of services, whereas the proportions in the second stage resource using industries and in indus-

Table 36. Rank Correlations of Proportions in Industry Categories with Population Potential and Distance to Nearest Larger Metropolitan Area, for Standard Metropolitan Areas, by Size: 1950

Size group of SMA's	Number of SMA's	Industry category[1] (1)	(2)	(3)	(4)	(5)	(6)	(7)	(8)	(9)	(10)
		Correlation with population potential									
1,000,000 or more	14	−.43	−.30	−.31	.46	.18	.18	−.16	−.31	−.31	−.42
500,000 to 1,000,000	19	−.61	−.32	−.02	.62	.31	.75	.14	−.76	−.61	−.47
300,000 to 500,000	23	−.17	−.12	−.35	.73	.29	.62	.48	−.87	−.76	−.26
250,000 to 300,000	21	−.47	−.19	−.30	.56	.66	.38	.49	−.72	−.46	−.46
150,000 to 250,000	36	−.28	−.53	−.13	.21	.64	.69	.59	−.64	−.60	−.30
100,000 to 150,000	38	−.46	−.44	−.37	.32	.36	.48	.55	−.56	−.46	−.53
		Correlation with distance to larger SMA[2]									
1,000,000 or more[3]	13	−.45	−.19	−.32	.34	.12	.18	−.03	−.27	−.20	−.13
500,000 to 1,000,000	19	−.22	−.42	−.03	.37	.04	.51	.17	−.72	−.62	−.44
300,000 to 500,000	23	−.29	.03	−.19	.37	.21	.65	.74	−.78	−.67	−.40
250,000 to 300,000	21	−.41	.14	−.22	.56	.40	.29	.52	−.41	−.42	−.09
150,000 to 250,000	36	−.15	−.51	−.22	.09	.21	.40	.39	−.69	−.51	−.16
100,000 to 150,000	38	−.59	−.42	−.29	.38	.18	.68	.58	−.85	−.69	−.49

[1] Category (11), "Construction," and category (12), "Industry not reported," are omitted. See p. 205 for identification of categories.

[2] Signs of correlation coefficients are reversed.

[3] Excluding the New York–Northeastern New Jersey SMA.

tries for which resources are least directly relevant are directly related to accessibility. The discovery of contrary tendencies among the six categories of manufacturing permits an important refinement of Harris's (1954) thesis on the market orientation of manufacturing in the United States. It will be recalled that a similar discovery in regard to the nonmetropolitan United States was reported in chapter 7, although the industry categories used there are even broader than those under scrutiny here.

The consistency of differences in the magnitudes of the correlation coefficients allows a couple of additional generalizations. On the whole, the inverse relationship with accessibility is more pronounced for the resource-extracting industries than for either category of first stage resource users; there is no consistent difference between the latter two in their response to accessibility. Over all comparisons, the category with the most marked negative relationship with accessibility is local services, category (8); its correlations are higher in absolute value than those of any of the other five categories with negative coefficients in the overwhelming majority of comparisons.

It is possibly this last finding which places the greatest strain on the acceptability of our initial classification of these service industries as "local." It is hard to see why the demand of a population for truly "local" or "maintenance" services should be a function of accessibility. However, the interpretation of the finding is complicated. For one thing, category (8) is by far the largest of our categories in terms of total employment (see table 31). It is, therefore, presumably subject to "random" fluctuation to a lesser degree than the other service categories. It must be remembered, too, that we are concerned with a distribution over a set of categories with a fixed total of 100 per cent. Hence if one category has a positive correlation with accessibility at least one other category must have a negative correlation. It would appear that "local" services are most clearly in a substitutive relationship with the manufacturing categories, (4) to (7). It seems entirely possible that highly accessible metropolitan centers specializing in fabricating industries actually "import" some of their maintenance or "local" services, e.g., retail trade, where "importing" would take the form of shopping trips to nearby centers. But no very secure diagnosis of the situation can be made without further investigation, and such investigation would doubtlessly result in a refinement of our service industry categories.

In completing the discussion of table 36 we observe that there is no clear tendency for the industry structures of smaller SMA's to respond more markedly to accessibility than those of the larger SMA's. The differences in magnitudes of the correlations within industry categories are certainly not in the contrary direction, but with the techniques used here it is not possible to demonstrate a connection between size of SMA and the degree to which industry structure is associated with distance or potential.

The foregoing analysis has several implications. If we think of a metropolis as a large city specializing in services provided for a "hinterland" population, we are likely to find specialization in "metropolitan" functions in cities protected by appreciable distances from the competition of other potential metropolises. Moreover if we think of a metropolis-region relationship as a division of labor in respect to the extraction and processing of natural resources, the attainment of "metropolitan" status would be favored by the same circumstance. But on the basis of our findings to this point there is little support for a characterization of the metropolis as a center for non-resource-oriented industries whose markets are in its hinterland. Instead, it would be more consistent to hypothesize that other metropolises are the major markets for metropolitan industries classified as second stage resource users or as industries for which resources are least directly significant. A careful consideration of industry structure and its variation according to locational situation, therefore, calls attention both to metropolis-hinterland and to intermetropolitan symbiotic relationships. As for methodological implications, it is clear that scrutiny of statistics on industry structure by itself can yield only indirect inferences about the relationships between metropolitan centers and outlying areas—however plausible such inferences may be. Unfortunately, the kind of direct evidence we need is not available in standardized form on a mass basis. The expedients we have devised for dealing with the problem are outlined in the following chapter.

CHAPTER 10

Industry Profiles and Regional Relationships

The discussion of variation in industry structure of standard metropolitan areas in the preceding chapter prepares the way for the more intensive examination of the industry profiles of individual SMA's which takes up most of the remainder of the volume. This chapter is largely concerned with the procedures employed in this examination. It will be necessary to expound and illustrate these procedures in some detail, but the general plan of the investigation is a simple one. It consists of the following steps: (1) establish which industries make up the "industry profile" of the SMA; (2) determine what the major inputs of the profile industries are and where they come from; (3) determine what the major outputs of the profile industries are and where they go; and (4) characterize the regional relationships of the SMA in terms of the supply and market or service areas of its profile industries. The materials collected in this fashion are set forth for a selection of individual SMA's (those with 1950 populations of 300,000 to 3,000,000) in Part IV; the comparative analysis of these materials is presented in chapter 11.

OUTLINE OF PROCEDURES

In chapter 9 we gave the rationale for a grouping of industries into broad categories and indicated how location quotients may be used to identify the general type of industry specialization that is characteristic of an SMA. But since these categories are quite broad, two SMA's could have a similar pattern of specialization in terms of major categories of industries but yet differ considerably in industry structure within categories. To arrive at the "industry profile" of an SMA, we proceed to identify the individual industries of the population census "detailed classification" which contribute to the SMA's specialization by broad categories; certain other industries are included in the "profile" even though they do not fall in a category of specialization, and others are excluded from the "profile" irrespective of the evidence provided by location quotients.

We indicate, first, the procedures for identifying profile industries among those in the first seven of our industry categories as described in chapter 9—i.e., the resource-extracting and manufacturing industries. For categories with a location quotient greater than one, component industries were considered part of the profile if their own individual location quotients were 2.00 or greater, or if their location quotients were 1.50 or greater and their numbers of employees relatively large. For industries falling in a category with a location quotient below unity, the test for inclusion in the profile was a location quotient of 2.00 or more and an employment amounting to at least 2 per cent of the SMA's employed labor force. Actually, it is comparatively uncommon to find such a profile industry outside of the major categories in which the SMA specializes.

With reference to the three categories of service industries, the procedure was somewhat different. Category (8), "service industries, local," and its component individual industries were disregarded entirely. The entirety of category (9), "service industries, non-local," was considered part of the profile, irrespective of location quotients. However, industries within this category with particularly high location quotients were identified and subjected to separate study. Finally, the criteria for including industries of category (10), "service industries, may be local or non-local," in the profile were the same as those for the resource-extracting and manufacturing industries.

As was mentioned in chapter 9, category (11), "construction," and category (12), "industry not reported," were eliminated from the investigation of industry structures.

No justification for these particular procedures and criteria is offered, other than the kinds of pragmatic considerations set forth in the preceding chapter. In particular, no claim is made that the "industry profile" as here identified is synonymous with the "economic base" as identified by other kinds of procedures—though it would be surprising if the composition of the economic base were not somewhat similar to that of the industry profile in most cases. Clearly, we could not substantiate a claim that all "export industries" of an SMA are included in its industry profile, nor a contention that the entire output of the profile industries is exported; neither proposition would be correct in most instances. Nevertheless, we do find evidence in many cases that the profile industries are "exporting," as would be expected on the basis of their relatively high location quotients or—in the case of nonlocal services—on the basis of the character of their outputs. An important exception is the profile industry which, so to speak, "exports" to other industries in the same SMA; this type of relationship is overlooked in conventional presentations of economic base theory, and, if our earlier speculations are correct, it probably turns up with increasing frequency as one ascends the city-size scale. That our procedure does not yield a precise estimate of the "economic base" is not necessarily to its discredit. So-called economic base theory is still in rather unsatisfactory shape, as is emphasized by its critics (Blumenfeld, 1955; Pfouts, 1957; Pfouts and Curtis, 1958) and acknowledged by its exponents (Andrews, 1953-56; Tiebout, 1956). The thing we are after is a fairly sharp delineation of what is distinctive about the industry structure of an SMA. Although our somewhat mechanical routine unquestionably leads to some errors of both inclusion and exclusion, it is apparently fairly successful on this criterion. The very rigidity of the procedures for identifying industry profiles is not an unmitigated disadvantage, where the ulterior purpose is comparative analysis.

Having identified profile industries, we needed to ascertain as precisely as possible what the inputs and outputs of those industries are. Wherever detailed industry statistics from the *Census of Manufactures* were available, these were examined for clues as to the nature of outputs. The *1947 Census of Manufactures* was ordinarily used for this purpose rather than the *1954 Census of Manufactures,* because it seemed desirable to work with the source closest in time to the *1950 Census of Population* and our other sources. Moreover, the 1947 figures are often available for somewhat more detailed industry categories than are the 1954 figures. It should be observed that figures on the number of employed persons in an industry as reported in the population census are not strictly comparable with the numbers reported in the manufacturing census, and sometimes the discrepancy between the two is appreciable. The two were taken at different times. In the *Census of Manufactures* employees are reported on the basis of the location of the establishments where they work but in the *Census of Population* on the basis of place of residence; however, with SMA's as the areal unit, this discrepancy may not be too serious in most cases. The employment reported in the statistics on manufacturing represents the average number of all full- and part-time employees who worked or received compensation in any of the twelve payroll periods covered in the census year, whereas the labor force statistics in the population census include all persons employed in a given industry during the calendar week prior to the enumeration. Because the manufacturing data are reported by establishments and the labor force data by individual respondents, the two are subject to different types of response and classification errors. Whereas labor force industry statistics are available in the "detailed classification" for all SMA's of 100,000 population or more, the detailed industry breakdowns of the *Census of Manufactures* are shown for only about one-third of these SMA's—those reporting 40,000 manufacturing employees or more. (Similar information is given for "principal industrial counties," those reporting 20,000 or more manufacturing employees.) Moreover, in a fairly large number of instances part of the detailed statistics are withheld to avoid disclosure of information for individual establishments.

Even the most detailed industry classification of the *Census of Manufactures* may group under a single title establishments making rather different sorts of products. Hence in discussing outputs of a given SMA, reference was always made to specific, localized information, where such was available. The use of such sources is described further, below.

In respect to inputs, the RFF table (described in chapter 9) based on the *1947 Interindustry Relations Study* was useful in providing general leads as to major inputs. But this table is based on aggregate national statistics and consequently required checking and supplementation with more detailed information of local relevance. Unfortunately, there is no comprehensive source of such local information and recourse must be had to a variety of incomplete and imprecise compilations of descriptive information. To all intents and purposes we ignored one major category of inputs, i.e., labor inputs; or rather, we assumed in effect that all labor inputs in an SMA's industries come from the SMA itself. This is in accord with the prevailing opinion, cited earlier, that the SMA is a good approximation to the "labor market area" in the short run. Another category of inputs, fuels, oftentimes cannot be associated with a particular industry on a small-area basis and has to be treated for each SMA in a general fashion.

Both in ascertaining the specific inputs and outputs of profile industries and, especially, in determining their origins and destinations it was necessary to rely heavily on literature of a monographic and fugitive character. Certain general texts in economic geography proved useful, as did some of the available regional geographies. Publications of economic and business research bureaus were used fairly frequently; these usually dealt with a particular group of industries, e.g., iron and steel, natural gas, and the like. Some monographs on particular cities were found to contain pertinent and sufficiently specific information; special mention may be made of the fact that the series of dissertations on industrial and urban geography carried out over the years in the Department of Geography of the University of Chicago contains much valuable information. Reports of city planning commissions and like bodies were generally disappointing, for our purposes. As to periodical literature, *Economic Geography* was perhaps the journal most frequently consulted. Various federal statistical publications, apart from censuses, were found to contain relevant information.

It is evident that no small scale search of this type of literature could be exhaustive. On the other hand, even the most thorough canvass would still leave many gaps in the information sought. Thus our information is uneven in quantity; moreover, its quality is somewhat variable. The general treatises consulted sometimes provided details of admirable specificity and evident validity; but more often they provide rather broad generalizations undocumented by statistical or other definite evidence. The more specialized regional geographies and similar texts sometimes give materials based on some sort of definite quantitative or qualitative evidence, although they are known, on occasion, to provide speculations and conjectures not clearly identified as such. Monographic sources and specialized periodical articles are, along with official compilations of statistics, the most likely sources for fully documented and adequately detailed data of the kind sought. Naturally, such sources were drawn upon whenever possible; but their very specialization made them more difficult to locate and more limited in scope. This forced a reliance upon more general materials in many cases where the only alternative was to forego description entirely. It may be that a by-product of our investigation will be to call attention to the rather grave scarcity of information available for depicting the regional relationships of metropolises in any reliable and comprehensive fashion.

Our reports on individual SMA's present such specific information on origins of inputs and destinations of outputs as we were able to uncover. However, there is the problem of reducing these bits of data to some order—a problem made difficult by the fact that they are of such varying specificity and reliability. The working solution to the problem took the form of a tentative classification of areas related to the metropolis. In this classification, "Area A" corresponds to the "metropolitan area" concept of McKenzie (see chapter 4); operationally, it is simply the SMA itself. "Area B" corresponds to McKenzie's "trade area," of which the most relevant operational versions have been presented in chapter 4. In locating an origin or destination in "Area B," we matched as best we could our specific information on this point with the several schemes of trade areas or metropolitan regions presented in the maps in chapter 4. If the origin or destination appears, on the basis of a rough judgment, to fall within the trade area or metropolitan region of the SMA, as identified on any of these maps, we coded it as "Area B." Thus our "Area B" is not a neatly delimited contiguous hinterland; but the "Area B" code is applied where it seems likely that a reasonable investigator might find the origin or destination to be in such a "hinterland" of the SMA. Given the limited precision of the available information, it was hardly possible to do more; and it is plain, even so, that different investigators might take issue with many of our "Area B" classifications. "Area C" is a residual category in the classification, embracing all origins and destinations not fairly clearly localized in "Areas A or B." For some SMA's, depending on the industry concerned, "Area C" might include several states, the entire nation, or, indeed, extensive foreign areas.

We seek with this classification to characterize the "regional relationships" of the SMA in terms of those which conform to the model of a hinterland dominated by a metropolis and those whose spatial pattern is much more extended and ramified than is suggested by this model. Inputs received from "Area B" and outputs going to "Area B" are those at least roughly classifiable as falling into the metropolis-hinterland pattern. "Area C" origins and destinations, on the other hand, imply some other type of pattern. This residual category, as would be expected, is highly heterogeneous. In some cases the "Area C" relationship appears to be an inter-metropolitan one; in others it extends over a multi-state "region" of resource-extracting or manufacturing activity; in still others there is no evident "regionalization" of the relationship, which may be national in extension; or the "region" in question may actually lie outside the territorial universe under investigation—the continental United States. (Chapter 11 reviews the major types of "Area C" relationships which we found.)

As is true of the other elements of our procedure, it seems best to base an evaluation not only on the general description of the procedure, as presented in the foregoing paragraphs, but also on an inspection of the results it produces, as set forth subsequently.

ILLUSTRATIVE ANALYSIS FOR MILWAUKEE

It will make the foregoing description of procedures clearer to present an example of their application to a particular SMA; at the same time, such a presentation will enable us to introduce the format in which all the individual analyses are presented in Part IV. The example chosen is one where the sources were unusually full. Hence, in effect it tests the procedure in the case where there are materials to work on. In the absence of adequate materials it matters little what the form of the analysis is.

The 1950 population of the Milwaukee SMA (consisting of Milwaukee County, Wis.) was 871,047, of which the central city population of 637,392 made up the larger proportion. We note as an important feature of Milwaukee's location that it is a port on Lake Michigan.

Table 31 in chapter 9 shows the proportion of the Milwaukee SMA's employed labor force within each of the 12 broad industry categories. Also shown are the location quotients obtained by dividing each of these percentages by the corresponding proportion of the total United States employed labor force falling within each of these categories. An index of dissimilarity is computed to provide a summary measure of the contrast between the two percentage distributions. This index is 20.3 for Milwaukee, indicating that about one-fifth of Milwaukee's employed persons would have to be redistributed among the several categories if this SMA's industry category profile were to be made to correspond exactly to that of the total United States. This is a fairly high degree of specialization, on the norms provided by table 32 in the preceding chapter.

Inspection of the location quotients indicates that in three of the 12 categories, Milwaukee has a greater percentage concentration of its employees than does the United States. It is assumed that these categories contain a large portion of Milwaukee's specialized industries, such specialization suggesting that the products of these industries are probably involved in non-local trade. The specialized categories, (3), (6), and (7), are similar in that all fall into a group that may be broadly designated as "manufacturing" as opposed to a "service" industry grouping. Two of the three are alike in that they are classified as third stage resource users, industries requiring primarily processed materials as inputs.

We now wish to isolate the important component industries for these three specialized categories, since not all of the industries classified within a given category make a substantial contribution to that category of specialization. We may isolate some of the important industries in the Milwaukee SMA by indicating for each of the specialized categories which of their constituent industries have relatively high location quotients. These location quotients for industries are obtained by dividing the per cent employed in the Milwaukee SMA in a given industry by the per cent employed in that industry for the United States. The more or less arbitrary criteria by which "specialized" industries were isolated are: (a) those industries possessing a location quotient of 2.00 or greater; and (b) those industries possessing a relatively large total employment and a location quotient of 1.50 or greater. Industries meeting these specifications are shown in table 37 listed under categories (3), (6), and (7).

Other industries important to Milwaukee's economy may not be included in one of these specialized categories. Two criteria are applied in order to isolate these industries: (a) Milwaukee's employment in the various industries is scanned to determine whether all industries employing two per cent or more of the employed labor force have been included in our first list of important industries; (b) if such an industry is found, and is not a part of category (8), "local services," it is next determined whether this industry shows a location quotient of 2.00 or greater when compared with the proportion employed in this industry for the United States. If *both* these criteria are met, the industry is included in our list of profile industries found in table 37. An examination of this table for Milwaukee indicates that the entry, "other primary iron and steel industries," is the one example of such an industry. Note also that the category of which it is a part is in parentheses to indicate that the category as a whole is not a specialty of Milwaukee.

Included also in table 37 is category (9), "non-local services," since it is assumed that all employment in this category will have relevance for the metropolitan functions of the SMA.

In general then, table 37 contains a listing of those industries, both manufacturing and service, which appear to be serving a primarily non-local market, either because of their specialization as revealed by high location quotients computed by comparing the SMA's percentage employment with that of the total United States for the same industry, or because the industry is considered by definition to be serving non-local areas—category (9) industries. These industries make up the "industrial profile" for the SMA under study. Table 37 presents this profile and provides for each of the industries the per cent the industry employs of the SMA's total employed labor force as well as the location quotient for the industry.

Table 37. Industrial Profile, Milwaukee: 1950

Category and industry	Location quotient	Per cent of employed labor force	Inputs primarily from area:	Outputs primarily to area:
(3) *First stage resource users; production for final market*				
Meat products	2.00	1.0	B	B, C
Beverage industries	6.33	2.3	C	C
(4) (*Second stage resource users; production for non-final market*)				
Other primary iron and steel industries	4.49	2.3	A, C	A, B, C
(6) *Resources of indirect significance; production for non-final market*				
Fabricated metal industries	2.32	3.5	A, C	A, B, C
Machinery, except electrical	4.98	11.5	A, C	C
Electrical machinery, equipment and supplies	2.96	4.2	A, C	C
Motor vehicles and motor vehicle equipment	2.15	3.3	C	C
Railroad and miscellaneous transportation equipment	3.89	0.4	C	C
Paperboard containers and boxes	2.87	0.6	B?	B?
Leather: tanned, curried and finished	5.88	0.1	C	A?
(7) *Resources of indirect significance; production for final market*				
Footwear, except rubber	1.92	0.9	A?	B, C?
Leather products, except footwear	2.24	0.3	A?	B, C?
(9) *Service industries; non-local*	0.88	11.2	*	B
Total in profile industries	...	41.6	...	...

* Inputs other than labor not considered.

Table 37 also presents a brief shorthand description of the areas from which inputs for these important industries are obtained and of the areas serving as markets for the outputs or products of these same industries. The assumption underlying this aspect of our material is that it is important to know whether the materials required by the important industries of an SMA are received from its "hinterland" or from more distant areas; likewise it is important to know the approximate location and extent of the market served by the products of these same industries. Our industry classification system provides us with information on the general nature of the inputs required—whether they are raw, processed, or fabricated materials; what we seek to determine now is their source and the market for the final product—to find which industries depend largely upon local or hinterland (Areas A or B) sources for inputs or markets as opposed to those dependent on more distant areas (Area C).

We must now explain by what methods we determined the areas from which important inputs were obtained or to which products were sent. On what basis, for example, did we decide that Milwaukee received most of its important inputs for its meat products industries from Area B, its "hinterland"? And on what basis did we decide that the products of this same industry were largely marketed in Areas B and C? In general, the procedure was to determine as specifically as possible for each industry included in the profile the important types of activity carried on by the industry within the SMA under study. Often we were able to do this by turning to the *Census of Manufactures* which frequently provides more detailed statistics on the components of the industry in a particular SMA. The limitations of this source, as noted earlier, should be recalled. In spite of these limitations, this source frequently provided valuable data. For the example of meat products, table 38 indicates that this industry includes both establishments engaged in wholesale meat packing and those engaged in the processing of prepared meats; the *Census of Manufactures* employment figures indicate that by far the more important of these are the wholesale meat packing establishments. In the summaries for 50 SMA's in Part IV we do not show a table comparable to table 38. However, in all cases where this information was available, we made use of it to ascertain as specifically as possible what the outputs of profile industries were.

The RFF table provides a list of some of the more important kinds of inputs necessary for the various types of manufacturing. This table indicates that the major inputs for the wholesale meat packing indus-

Table 38. Detailed Manufacturing Industries, Milwaukee: 1947

Category number and industry	1950 Employed labor force		1947 Manufacturing employment
	Per cent of total	Number	
(3) *Meat products*	1.0	3,668	4,026
Meat packing, wholesale			3,385
Prepared meats			613
Beverage industries	2.3	8,554	8,325
Bottled soft drinks			560
Malt liquors			7,130
Malt			569
(4) *Other primary iron and steel industries*	2.3	8,565	11,312
Iron and steel foundries			7,202
Gray iron foundries			3,850
Miscellaneous primary metal industries			4,110
(6) *Fabricated metal industries*	3.5	12,949	12,957
Cutlery, hand tools and hardware			1,378
Heating and plumbing equipment			1,835
Metal stamping and coating			2,189
Lighting fixtures			209
Miscellaneous fabricated metal products			1,087
Machinery, except electrical	11.5	43,119	53,690
Engines and turbines			11,249
Construction and mining machinery			8,972
Metalworking machinery			6,106
Special-industry machinery			4,916
General-industry machinery			7,371
Refrigeration machinery			956
Miscellaneous machinery parts			3,532
Electrical machinery, equipment and supplies	4.2	15,548	20,679
Electrical industrial apparatus			17,282
Motors and generators			6,025
Electrical control apparatus			9,754
Miscellaneous electrical products			1,451
(7) *Leather products, except footwear*	0.3	1,008	NA
Leather gloves and mittens			1,125

NA: Not available.

try are raw materials in the form of meat animals and poultry. The final step then was to determine whether or not certain types of meat were more important for the Milwaukee packing houses and where the major source for these materials was located relative to Milwaukee. For this information, specific monographic sources dealing with Milwaukee industries were consulted. Following then is a discussion of what was learned from this material, first taking up the wholesale meat industries and then the other important industries in the order listed in table 37, the industrial profile. First the sources of inputs are discussed, then the location of markets. It is on the basis of this material that the area designations in table 37 were estimated.

INPUTS AND SUPPLY AREAS FOR MILWAUKEE'S PROFILE INDUSTRIES

Meat products: Milwaukee is an important center for the production of veal. (Garland, 1955, p. 129.) Market figures for 1950 indicate that Milwaukee ranked as the second largest calf market in the United States, being outranked only by St. Paul, Minnesota. (United States Department of Agriculture, Production and Marketing Administration, 1951, pp. 7-10.)

Milwaukee received in that year 331,995 salable calves, 95 per cent of which were "driven in," i.e., received by truck rather than by rail shipments. Since rail shipments tend to occur over longer distances, this high percentage of driven-in receipts indicates that most of the calf receipts originate in areas relatively close to Milwaukee. In addition to these calves, Milwaukee received 209,446 cattle (88 per cent of which were driven in); 348,378 hogs (91 per cent of which were driven in); and 39,353 sheep (86 per cent of which were driven in). (*Ibid.*, pp. 7-10.) The best information we have indicates that the bulk of these inputs arrive from the farms of Wisconsin and eastern Minnesota, that is, Area B. (Garland, 1955, p. 149.)

Beverage industries: Table 38 indicates that malt liquor and malt industries account for most of the employment here. Chief inputs to these industries are again raw materials—particularly grains. Barley is the grain of greatest importance since malt (partially germinated barley) is essential to the brewing of beer and is also used in the manufacture of other alcoholic liquors. (Nielsen, 1950, p. 228.) Barley is received in Milwaukee by rail from the North Central states—particularly the Dakotas, Montana, and Nebraska—and is also received in large quantities by water from Port Arthur and Fort William, Canada. (Hamming, 1952, pp. 99-100.) Hops, another raw material input essential to the brewing industry, are grown in this country almost entirely on the West Coast—Oregon, Washington, and California. (*Encyclopedia Americana,* 1957, vol. 4, p. 480.) Thus, the chief raw materials for this industry may be said to originate in Area C.

Other primary iron and steel industries: These are included as contributing importantly to Milwaukee's economy (even though their category does not show specialization) because (a) this industry group includes more than 2.0 per cent of the employed persons of Milwaukee (2.29 per cent) and (b) its location quotient (4.49) is greater than 2.0.

Important inputs for this industry group are products of blast furnaces, scrap iron and steel, coke, products of steel works and rolling mills, limestone, and alloys. It is clear that the Milwaukee primary iron and steel industries are not concerned with the reduction of iron ore, primarily because there are no local coal resources. (Henning, 1953, p. 47.) The primary source for pig iron utilized is the Chicago-Gary area, although Cleveland supplies considerable amounts. The major source for scrap iron and steel inputs is the Milwaukee area itself. Milwaukee produces all of its coke requirements. Bituminous coal for this purpose is mined in western Pennsylvania and arrives by boat from Cleveland. (*Ibid.,* p. 49.) High-calcium limestone mined in Manistique, Mich., is shipped from Port Inland to Milwaukee by lake carrier. Dolomite limestone is secured from Waukesha, Wis. Sources for alloys are widely scattered. Silicon ore is secured from Niagara Falls, N. Y., Philo, Ohio, and Pittsburgh, Pa.; manganese from Alloy, W. Va. and Philo, Ohio; and chrome ore from Niagara Falls and Pittsburgh. Nickel alloys originate in Sudbery, Canada. In general, truck is used in preference to rail for alloy shipments. Sand for foundry castings is supplied from the dune areas near Grand Haven, Mich., arriving in a processed state via car ferry. (*Ibid.,* pp. 49-50.)

Taking up industries included in category (6), table 38 indicates that none of the subdivisions of these industries is large enough to dominate any of the industry groupings. Thus we may be justified in treating these groupings in their more generalized form while discussing their inputs.

Fabricated metal industries: The RFF input-output table indicates that major inputs of the fabricated metal industry include such processed materials as steel plates, sheets, bars, etc., from steel works and rolling mills; products from metal stamping industries; boiler shop products; nuts, bolts, and screw machine products; and other products of a similar nature. Carbon steel products come largely from the Chicago-Gary area by rail; the primary source of special alloy and stainless steels is the Pittsburgh area. (Henning, 1953, pp. 50-51.) Indications are that most of the iron and steel castings come from other industries located in Milwaukee's primary metropolitan area, although about one-fourth of the steel castings come from nearby Chicago. Likewise metal stampings and forgings are provided by industries of the immediate Milwaukee area. (*Ibid.*, pp. 55-57.)

Machinery, except electrical: Important inputs for the machinery industries include engines and turbines, motors and generators, boiler shop products, iron and steel castings, products from iron and steel foundries, and internal combustion engines. Sources for the castings and forgings are discussed above. Electrical motors are obtained principally from Illinois, Ohio, and New York state although Milwaukee itself provides about one-third of the supply. Engines are received from Chicago, Peoria, and Harvey, Ill., Waukesha, Wis., and from Milwaukee's own metropolitan area. (*Ibid.*, p. 57.)

Electrical machinery, equipment and supplies: The primary inputs for the electrical machinery and equipment industries include iron and steel castings, products from iron and steel foundries, metal stampings, products of nonferrous foundries, copper rolling and drawing plant products, motors and generators, and electrical control apparatus. Sources for castings, foundry products, stampings, and motors and generators are described above. Products of nonferrous foundries are obtained mostly from within the Milwaukee metropolitan area; however, some nonferrous castings are obtained from Chicago and Waukegan, Ill. and Pittsburgh, Pa. Copper castings come primarily from Kenosha, Wis., and electrical control apparatus is provided mostly by the Milwaukee area itself. (*Ibid.*, pp. 55-57.)

Motor vehicle and motor vehicle equipment: The motor vehicle industries require considerable and varied inputs. From second stage resource users come iron and steel castings, iron foundry products, and tires and tubes. From third stage resource users come metal stampings and machine shop products. The source for most of these inputs is discussed above. The origin of many tires and tubes used in Milwaukee is Akron, Ohio. Important specific sources of industry requirements are batteries from Milwaukee itself; bearings from Toledo, Detroit, Cleveland, and the eastern states; carburetors from Decatur, Ill., Detroit, and Indianapolis; magnetos from Beloit, Wis., Galesburg, Ill., and Springfield, Mass.; spark plugs from Toledo and Detroit; and transmissions from Detroit. (*Ibid.*, pp. 57-58.)

Railroad and miscellaneous transportation equipment: The inputs of importance for these industries have all been discussed above as to source. These inputs include iron and steel castings, tires and inner tubes, and products of the motor vehicles industries.

Paperboard containers and boxes: Inputs for the paperboard containers and boxes industry come primarily from paper and board mills. The exact location for wood pulp and paper supplies used in Milwaukee was not determined. However, it is known that many pulp and paper mills utilizing wood grown in the Fox River valley (east-central Wisconsin), northern Wisconsin and Canada, are located in Milwaukee's hinterland principally at Green Bay, Appleton, Neenah and Menasha, Wis. (Garland, 1955, pp. 136-137.) Presumably some of this pulp and paper is shipped to Milwaukee for paperboard use. Then too, some quantities of paper and wood pulp are received via the port from various foreign countries and from Canada. (See table 39.)

Leather: tanned, curried and finished: The final industry group to be considered in category (6) is that comprising establishments engaged in the tanning and finishing of leather. Primary inputs here are hides, skins, gum, wood, and chemicals. Chief sources of the skins and hides utilized in the leather industries appear to be the packing houses of the Chicago and Milwaukee area. Tanbark, which was an essential ingredient in the past for tanning operations, was obtained from the forests of Wisconsin and Minnesota. However, this material is no longer in great demand, having been replaced by chemical substitutes. (Whitbeck and Finch, 1941, pp. 193-197.) Milwaukee obtains most of its chemical supplies from Chicago and from Hammond, Ind. (Henning, 1953, p. 58.)

Footwear, except rubber; Leather products, except footwear: Category (7) contains two specialized industries. The two industries are similar in their inputs and so may be considered together. Important inputs for these industries are the products of the leather tanning and finishing industries, the products of the spinning, weaving, and dyeing mills, and various chemicals. The source of chemicals is discussed above. Although we have no direct evidence, it would seem a safe assumption that the local tanning industries furnish a large quantity of the leather materials. No information could be found concerning the origin of the textile inputs.

Fuel inputs: A discussion of inputs for a highly industrialized area such as Milwaukee would be incomplete without some consideration of the major sources for the fuels consumed in the area. It is difficult to determine which industries utilize which types of fuel and to separate industrial from domestic use; therefore, we will confine our attention to a general discussion of fuels consumed in the area and to their principal sources. Coal is Milwaukee's principal fuel, more than 90 per cent of the heat, light, and power used in the city being supplied by coal or by electricity manufactured from coal. About nine-tenths of the coal received is obtained from the Appalachian coal fields and is shipped to Milwaukee by boat from Lake Erie ports, principally Toledo and Sandusky, Ohio. Considerable quantities of anthracite are imported from eastern Pennsylvania, chiefly through the port of Buffalo, N. Y., but virtually all of this coal is used for the heating of homes. Coal is also received in Milwaukee by all rail shipment, largely from the fields of Indiana and southern Illinois. Also considerable amounts of coal are shipped entirely by rail from the Appalachian fields. (Reith, 1949, pp. 71-77; also, Ballert, 1953, pp. 48-50.) Fuel oil coming originally from Kansas and Oklahoma fields is refined in Whiting, Ind. (part of the Chicago SMA), for use in Milwaukee. Lighter fuels are shipped by boat to Milwaukee while the heavier residual fuels, used mainly by industry, arrive principally in tank cars. Natural gas is piped into Milwaukee from Hugoton Field located near Hansford, Texas. Electricity is manufactured in the area from coal. (Henning, 1953, pp. 60-61.)

Labor: In the Milwaukee and all other SMA's considered in this study, the primary source of labor supply is assumed to be the standard metropolitan area itself. In the case of Milwaukee it is perhaps worth noting the suggestion that the northwest European (particularly German) origin of many of the early Milwaukee residents goes a long way toward explaining the development of the brewing, skilled machine and leather industries in Milwaukee. (Alexandersson, 1956, p. 90; Henning, 1953, pp. 69-70.)

OUTPUTS AND SERVICE AREAS OF MILWAUKEE'S PROFILE INDUSTRIES

The preceding section has shown some of the important ways in which Milwaukee's important industries rest upon various "foreign" economies as the source for many of their basic material inputs. However, only half of the story has been told to this point since Milwaukee must find outside markets for the products of its specialized industries. We shall consider now the nature and destination of some of these products. Unfortunately, less precise and less complete information is available to us in this important area.

The industries will be taken up in the same order used in discussing inputs, beginning with the industries of category (3). The most important meat product produced in the Milwaukee area is veal. No information is available as to its market distribution, but a good guess would be that it includes much of the central portions of the United States. The chief product of the beverage industry is beer and its distribution is undoubtedly to a national market.

Outputs of the primary iron and steel industries find their principal markets within the Milwaukee area itself, with some products being distributed to the Wisconsin area in general and others being marketed in the Chicago area. (Henning, 1953, p. 62.)

With regard to the distribution of products of industries within category (6), only illustrative materials are available. Such products of the fabricated metal industries as beer cans and bottle caps find a large local market, while vegetable and milk cans, outboard motor parts and furnaces have a state-wide distribution. Radiators have a national distribution although most of them go to the western half of the manufacturing zone. Such items as padlocks have a world market. (*Ibid.*, pp. 62-63.)

Machinery produced in Milwaukee has both a national and world market depending on the particular type of machinery under consideration. For example, agricultural machinery goes largely to the states of Illinois, Iowa, Nebraska, Kansas, and Missouri; industrial machinery is sent in large quantities to the western half of the manufacturing zone as is electrical machinery. Transportation equipment goes largely to Kenosha, Wis., Detroit, Mich., and other parts of the Midwest, while mining and construction equipment find a national and even world market. (*Ibid.*, 63-67.) Many of the latter types of machinery are exported from the port of Milwaukee, finding their way to foreign markets via the St. Lawrence River. (See table 39.)

No information is available on the distribution of the products of the paperboard industries or of the leather tanning industries. However, the latter industry's products are no doubt in large part utilized by local leather and shoe industries.

Turning to category (7), again no direct evidence is available to us; however, we would assume that many of the shoe, glove and other leather products produced in Milwaukee find their market in the central United States.

The low location quotient for category (9), non-local services, indicates that the Milwaukee SMA is not highly specialized in this area and is possibly dependent upon other areas for some of these services. Nevertheless the total employment in wholesale trade is considerable and there are indications that some wholesale functions are performed by Milwaukee for the state of Wisconsin. (McCarty, 1940, p. 670.) As far as commercial and financial services are concerned, it appears that Milwaukee lies well within the long shadow cast by Chicago.

Table 39. Port Statistics, Milwaukee: 1950

Origin or destination	Commodity	Quantity shipped (short tons)
Imports, by origin		
Foreign (via the St. Lawrence River)	Fish and fish products	839
	Metals and manufactures	1,466
	Non-metallic minerals	2,075
	Wood and paper	979
	All other	1,695
Canadian	Newsprint paper	30,850
	Barley and rye	187,825
	All other	11,783
Domestic (Lakewise plus internal via Illinois waterway)	Anthracite coal	275,975
	Bituminous coal	3,329,007
	Gas, oil and distillate	340,629
	Motor fuel	859,245
	Kerosene	30,766
	Building cement	307,968
	Limestone	94,517
	Sand and gravel	164,971
	Machinery and vehicles	168,717
	All other	44,549
Exports, by destination		
Foreign	Machinery and parts	5,600
	All other	15,891
Canadian	Grains	25,109
	Iron and steel scrap	11,200
	All other	790
Domestic	Corn	16,604
	Barley and rye	14,188
	Wheat	51,272
	Machinery and vehicles	338
	All other	7,012

SOURCE: United States Board of Engineers for Rivers and Harbors (1953, No. 8, pp. 125–128).

Although water transportation does not show up in our employment statistics as a specialized industry in Milwaukee, we have already seen that the port is an important adjunct to several of the profile industries. Accordingly, the available data on the commerce of the port may be considered conveniently at this point. Table 39 presents a summary of the commodities handled at the port. The origins of these commodities and their destinations will be considered only in general terms, since many of these data are unavailable or, if available, have been covered in the preceding discussion. Moreover, whether the goods arriving at Milwaukee's port are utilized in the Milwaukee area or are transshipped to other areas is not known. In the same way, whether goods shipped from the port have originated in the immediate Milwaukee area or in more remote places remains an unknown.

But in spite of these many blank spaces in our report, what *is* revealed by the port data is the amount and type of material moving through this area. And this information has an importance of its own. The transshipment of commodities is one of the important functions of a metropolis, regardless of how this function is related to the important industries of that area, and to neglect this aspect would be to neglect an important part of the linkage between the city and outlying areas.

From table 39 it is clear that while Milwaukee's port commerce is somewhat diversified, coal receiving and grain shipping functions dominate. In 1950 approximately 3,600,000 tons of coal (mostly bituminous) were received via lake traffic. Petroleum products amounting to approximately one million tons were also received. Other important imports included 190,000 tons of barley and rye from Canada, 300,000 tons of building cement, 160,000 tons of sand and gravel and 170,000 tons of machinery and vehicles. Exports were in comparatively insignificant amounts, the largest single item being 100,000 tons of grain destined for Canadian and domestic ports. (United States Board of Engineers for Rivers and Harbors, 1953, No. 8, pp. 125-128.) Sources of the coal received in Milwaukee have already been discussed in detail. By far the largest United States receiver of grain shipped from Milwaukee is Buffalo, N. Y.; some corn is shipped to Oswego, N. Y. (Lake Carriers' Association, 1950, p. 93.) Considerable amounts of corn shipped from Milwaukee are also destined for the Canadian ports of Port Colborne and nearby Humberstone as well as the ports of the St. Lawrence River. (*Ibid.*, p. 94.)

From table 39, it is also clear that domestic lakewise traffic constitutes the bulk of the port's traffic. Moreover, table 39 treats only the general vessel traffic. In addition to the approximately 5.5 million tons of commodities moved on the Great Lakes by general vessels, an additional three million tons is transported by car ferry. These ferries—operated by three different railroad companies—link Milwaukee on the west side of Lake Michigan with the ports of Ludington and Muskegon, Mich., on the east side. The principal commodities involved in the eastbound traffic via car ferry are grain, manufactured products (beer, auto parts, agricultural implements, machinery, and advanced manufactures of iron and steel), dairy products and forest products. Moving westward are coal, manufactured products (bottles, containers, chemicals and semi-manufactures of iron and steel) and salt. (Hamming, 1952, pp. 68-76.)

While we do not reproduce a table like table 39 for the port cities described in Part IV, this information was consulted in each instance and an appropriate summary is given in the text.

SUMMARY FOR MILWAUKEE

It is clear that Milwaukee does not perform those large-scale financial or business functions which give it a sizable service hinterland. Undoubtedly, some central-place functions are provided for its surrounding area, but generally speaking Milwaukee must bow here to the dominance of nearby Chicago to the south and to Minneapolis-St. Paul to the northwest.

However, with regard to certain functions—e.g., as a barley and calf market—Milwaukee may be said to serve a large part of southeast Wisconsin. (This area may approximately correspond to Milwaukee's region as delimited by Bogue and has been referred to as "Area B.") With regard to other functions—e.g., as a specialized machinery fabricator and as a leather goods manufacturer—it may gather needed materials from the general Chicago area. This supply area we have included in "Area C," as being clearly beyond any "hinterland" that Milwaukee might be said to "dominate," although relatively nearby. In order to obtain certain specialized materials and its fuels, Milwaukee is obliged to range far outside of its immediate environs, utilizing national and even world-wide sources (Area C). Thus, this summary should make clear that only in terms of certain specialized functions can Milwaukee be said to enjoy a "regional dominance."

The same conclusions hold even more strongly in examining the location of Milwaukee's markets. As the title of category (6) indicates, the great majority of products turned out here are not destined for final consumption, but are fed into other industries for further processing. Thus it is most difficult to specify that geographical area wherein Milwaukee's products "dominate."

CHAPTER 11

Regional Relationships and Metropolitan Functions

The procedures for constructing "industry profiles" and for describing regional relationships which were expounded in the two preceding chapters have been applied to all Standard Metropolitan Areas (SMA's) with 1950 populations between 300,000 and 3,000,000. The results for each SMA are given in Part IV. Our task in this chapter is to summarize certain major implications of this material for identifying "metropolises" and characterizing their "regional situations." While some of the data upon which the discussion rests are given here in summary form, full support for empirical generalizations will be found only in the individual SMA reports in Part IV.

VARIETIES OF REGIONAL RELATIONSHIPS

In working with the concept of a "nodal region" consisting of a metropolis and its hinterland, two general procedures are available: one procedure takes the viewpoint of the hinterland; the other assumes the perspective of the metropolitan center. In the former, it is assumed that metropolitan centers have been identified on some explicit criterion. Then for every unit of area outside these centers a determination is made as to which center it "belongs" with. Thus, in chapter 4, we noted that Park and Newcomb assigned every part of the United States to one or another metropolitan newspaper circulation region; that "trade areas" typically are drawn so as to yield a set of exhaustive and mutually exclusive territories; and that Bogue constructed "metropolitan communities" by placing each county of the United States in the metropolitan community of the nearest metropolitan center. This general procedure may be said to embody an "administrative principle," for its clearest exemplification is the allocation of hinterland areas to regional headquarters, as in the case of the twelve Federal Reserve Districts or thirty-six Federal Reserve zones comprising districts and their branch territories. This "administrative principle" is most accurate as a description of nodal regions when there is actually a formal, legal, or quasi-legal arrangement which determines the boundaries. In the case of newspaper circulation regions, trade areas, and the like, however, it is recognized that the boundaries are impossible to determine with complete precision. Still, it is a fundamental assumption of the method that each part of the outlying territory can, in principle, be assigned to that center with which it is most closely related or upon which it is most heavily dependent. Moreover, the "metropolitan regions" yielded by this method are normally compact and continuous areas, approximately concentric to the metropolis.

Under the alternative procedure of attacking the problem from the standpoint of the metropolitan center, the objective is somewhat different. The investigator attempts to ascertain what outlying areas are important to the center and assigns to the center's "hinterland" those areas which have a sufficiently important relationship with the center. It is clear that this procedure can lead to radically different results from the "administrative principle." For one thing, the fact that, say, an outlying county is more closely related to center X than to center Y does not mean that it is an especially important part of X's hinterland. It may well be that no important function of X would be jeopardized if that county were lost completely to Y. This hypothetical case also illustrates another important possibility: two centers may have overlapping hinterlands—a contingency that cannot be reflected in delimitations made according to the strict "administrative principle." Moreover, a center's hinterland may be discontinuous, and the extent and boundaries of the hinterland may differ greatly from one central function to another.

It is no doubt significant that the second procedure has been used most extensively in case studies of individual metropolitan areas—see, for example, the work of Harris on Salt Lake City, summarized along with other examples by Dickinson (1947, chapter 6). When comparative studies are undertaken, recourse is had to the "administrative principle," since it offers a drastic simplification of the problem of delimiting metropolitan units. It is doubtful, for example, whether even the more important regional relationships of the fifty cities treated in Part IV could be presented on a single map (even if requisite data were available in full), because the network of center-hinterland connections would be much too complex to show diagramatically. A second consideration is that it is relatively easy to assemble data characterizing hinterlands when they have been delimited on the "administrative principle," but rather difficult to do so when the more flexible alternative procedure has been followed. Since we have chosen not to adhere to the "administrative principle," we cannot submit a simple formula for finding the "hinterland" of a metropolitan center, nor can we offer a compendium of data to use in comparing one hinterland with another. However, we can—and we feel this may be useful—point out some of the typical kinds of center-region relationship and offer a heuristic classification of centers in which such relationships enter as one basis of classification.

The 51 SMA's studied individually include several instances of centers with one or more industries important enough to be included in the "profile," where such industries are based on resources located in the immediate environs of the center. Specialization in coal mining based on activity carried on within the SMA is found in Pittsburgh, Wilkes-Barre, Wheeling-Steubenville, Charleston (W. Va.), and Birmingham. Birmingham, in addition, shows specialization in metal mining. Oklahoma City and Houston specialize in extraction of petroleum and natural gas. In several of these cases, other profile industries in the SMA depend upon the local extractive activities for inputs. However, they need not depend solely upon them; the petroleum refining industry in Houston, for example, draws upon distant as well as local sources of crude petroleum, and Pittsburgh's primary metals industry requires shipments of coal, as well as ores, from outside the SMA.

The foregoing accounts for all cities actually having an extractive industry in their profile. However, close linkages with extractive activities carried on in the vicinity of the SMA are observed in several other profiles. For example, New Orleans and San Diego have canning industries based upon fishing in adjacent coastal waters. (Incidentally, although it is paradoxical to classify water as "land," these waters might well be said to be important parts of the "hinterlands" of the respective centers.)

It is not especially common for a single center to enjoy complete "dominance" of a resource region, even when it is strategically located within that region. For example, both Seattle and Portland (Ore.) have lumber mill profile industries based on the timber resources of the northwest. The supply areas for cities with "tobacco manufactures" as a profile industry (Richmond, Tampa, Louisville, Wilkes-Barre–Hazleton, Jacksonville, and Memphis) likewise appear to overlap to some extent; moreover, several of these centers import tobacco from abroad as well as obtain it from domestic areas beyond their proximate "hinterlands." Perhaps the clearest case of inter-city competition for the output of a resource region concerns the twelve centers with "meat products" as a profile industry (Omaha, Fort Worth, Kansas City, Oklahoma City, Minneapolis – St. Paul, St. Louis, Indianapolis, Denver, San Antonio, Milwaukee, Columbus, and Nashville). The locations of these centers are shown in figure 14 in relation to data outlining roughly the extent of the livestock farming region. Indications are that each of these centers draws most heavily on the area in its immediate vicinity. Moreover, there are local specializations which are based on differentiation of livestock supply areas—for example, the relative concentration of Milwaukee's meat products industry in veal, that of Columbus in pork, and that of Denver in lamb. Nevertheless, certain of the centers are known to have supply areas overlapping those of other centers; and it would be a considerable oversimplification to draw boundaries in such a way as to allocate a unique and nonoverlapping territory to each center.

We have not yet exhausted the kinds of center-region relationships based on the linkage of a resource-using to a resource-extracting industry. Some cities owe a profile industry to their location within a productive region of specialized agriculture: witness the fruit and/or vegetable processing industries of Tampa, San Francisco, and Rochester, and Denver's sugar beet refining industry. But specialization in food processing and preparation does not require contiguity to the region where the raw materials are cultivated or collected. Baltimore, New Orleans, and San Francisco have profile food industries based, at least in part, on imports from foreign areas. Several of the half-dozen or so cities specializing in production of malt beverages apparently are supplied with certain basic inputs from rather distant sources. The beverage industry, of course, is consumer-market oriented; hence the localization of beverage production has no close relationship to the spatial distribution of inputs.

The foregoing discussion has referred to most of the instances of specialization in industry categories (2) and (3)—the resource using industries. The remaining examples likewise exhibit a diversity of city-region relationships. Memphis specializes in cottonseed oil processing on the basis of proximity to the "cotton belt"; but Buffalo's grain mill products industry is based largely on cheap water transportation from the distant grain producing region in the Great Plains and Canada. It appears that at least some of the cities specializing in processing of wood products draw inputs from sources located well beyond their "hinterlands" as delimited on the basis of "trade area" or "administrative" principles; but there are equally clear examples of profile industries based on mineral and energy inputs available in the immediate vicinity of the center. Most of the cities whose industry profiles reveal emphasis on resource-using industries are situated within regions producing at least some of the raw material inputs. The cases where such a relationship is least evident—Boston, Buffalo, Baltimore, and Providence—are ones with quite favorable water transportation facilities that, in effect, broaden their hinterlands considerably. But the relationship of a center to a resource region also is frequently one that involves linkages extending beyond the immediate "trade area"—i.e., one that must be classified as of the "Area C" type in the individual SMA analyses of Part IV.

Broadening the discussion to include all manufacturing profile industries—categories (4) to (7) as well as (2) and (3)—we find additional evidence of a considerable variety of center-region relationships in terms of the industries' inputs. Perhaps the easiest way to summarize this evidence is to suggest some salient types of relationship covered by the "Area C" category in the SMA reports in Part IV. (a) In some cases —the meat products industry of Denver is a good example—inputs are drawn not only from the surrounding area (the "hinterland" in the trade area sense) but from a much broader, but more or less contiguous region. Often the key to such a situation seems to be that the center enjoys advantages of relative accessibility to such a region, even if it is

---

Figure 14 (opposite). Standard Metropolitan Areas of 300,000–3,000,000 Inhabitants Having "Meat Products" as a Profile Industry, Located in Relation to Distribution of Livestock Farms: 1950. (Each small dot represents 100 livestock farms, other than dairy and poultry. Large dots show approximate locations of Columbus, Denver, Fort Worth, Indianapolis, Kansas City, Milwaukee, Minneapolis – St. Paul, Nashville, Oklahoma City, Omaha, St. Louis, and San Antonio Standard Metropolitan Areas. Based on maps by the United States Bureau of the Census.)

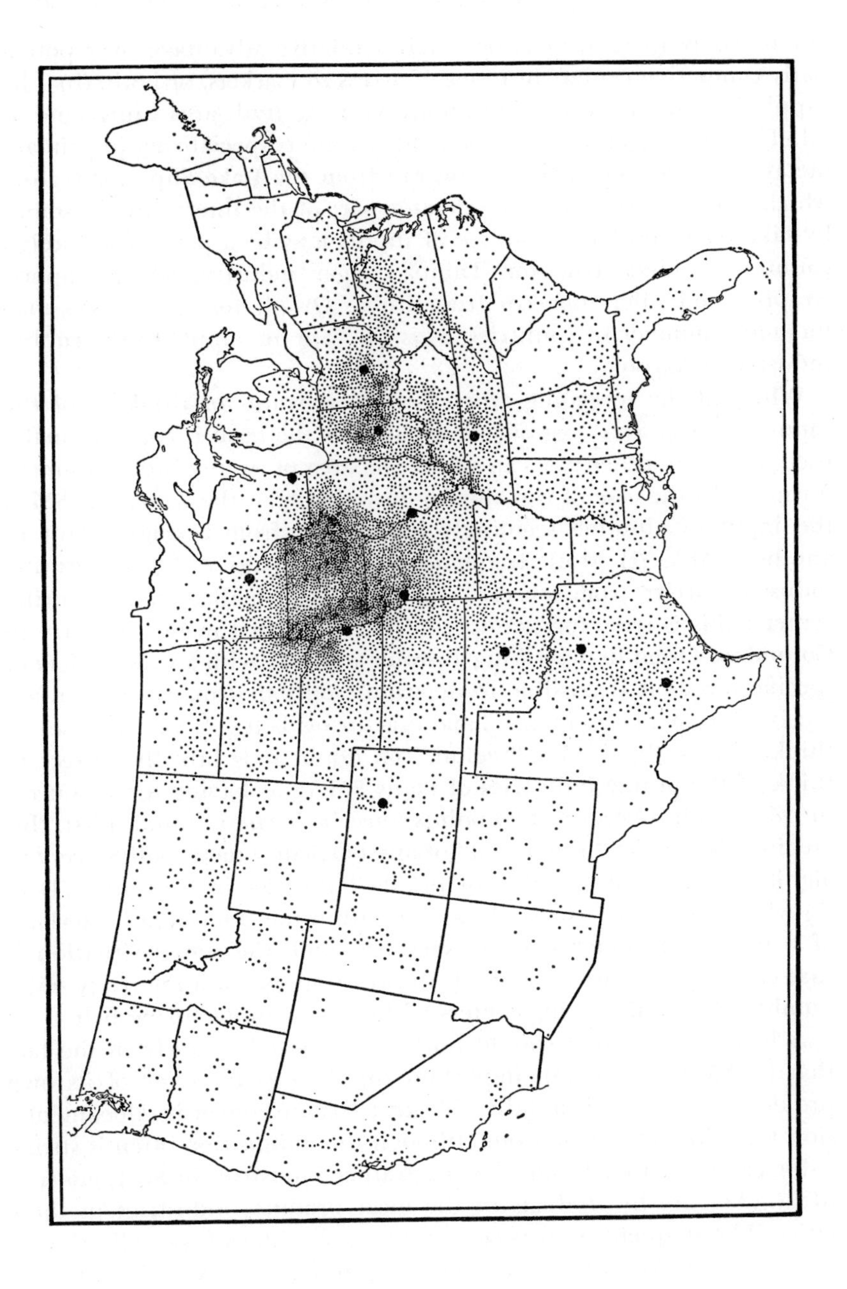

not precisely in its center, or it has a relative advantage over potentially competing centers in terms of access to markets, or both. (b) The supply area need not be continuous with the trade-area hinterland at all. Thus Youngstown—like some other centers specializing in primary metals—has depended upon iron ore from the Lake Superior region, which is transported over the greater part of the intervening distance by lake boats. (c) Such a source of inputs may be a particular foreign country, as holds true for Tampa's cigar industry, which imports wrapper and filler tobaccos from Cuba. Or (d) foreign sources may include a number of countries, as is the case for inputs to the rubber industry in Akron.

While in the foregoing types there is warrant for thinking of the input source(s) as a "region" or regions, as the term is conventionally used, there are other types in which the area of supply is quasi-punctiform. (e) In the case of the aluminum industry in the Knoxville SMA, the input of alumina seemingly is obtained from a single plant in another SMA. (f) More frequently, perhaps, inputs for fabricating industries arrive from several other SMA's or smaller manufacturing centers; this is true, for example, of the fabricated metals industry in Columbus. Often in describing a profile industry with a wide variety of specific inputs it is possible to determine only that many of them are received from places in the "manufacturing belt." If one chooses to think of this "belt" as a "region," no doubt it is broadly correct to think of the profile industries of many SMA's as having input sources in this region. However, two points must be borne in mind. First, this "region" is not the "hinterland" of any particular metropolitan center. Significantly, the proportion of profile industries in categories (4) to (7) whose inputs are clearly localized within the trade-area hinterland of a particular center is quite small. Second, the actual situation is that each type of input usually is drawn from one or a relatively small number of manufacturing centers within the manufacturing belt.

A final type (g) that should not be overlooked arises from the fact that an SMA may be an important supply area for some of its own profile industries. It is usually difficult to secure conclusive documentation that this is the situation, although the implication often is strong—for example, that inputs for the leather industries in St. Louis and Milwaukee are by-products of the meat products industries in those cities. The frequent joint occurrence in one center of specialization in two industries known to have a close input-output linkage is pertinent, if indirect, evidence. For example, there are 15 centers (among the 51 SMA's with populations between 300,000 and 3,000,000) with "fabricated metals" as a profile industry. There are 14 similarly specialized in "electrical machinery," of which 9 are found in a center specialized in fabricated metals. Exactly the same degree of association between fabricated metals and "machinery, except electrical" is observed, while 7 of the 10 cities with an "aircraft and parts" profile industry are likewise specialized in fabricated metals. Sometimes the suspicion is strong that intra-city input-output linkage is more significant for a particular profile industry than is any center-region relationship of similar functional type.

Thus far, center-region relationships have been viewed primarily from the standpoint of inputs to profile industries. If attention is focused on outputs of those industries a comparable variety of relationships is observed. Many of these, of course, are but the obverse of relationships already noted. For balance of emphasis, however, it seems well to list the main types suggested by the summary materials. (a) Conceivably an industry located in a center may find the whole of its market within the "trade area" or immediately contiguous hinterland of that center. However, this possibility seldom materializes when inquiry is limited to what we have called "profile" industries—i.e., those in which an SMA is relatively specialized in terms of employment. In order to support the degree of specialization required to characterize it as a "profile industry," the market for the industry seemingly must be more extensive. This observation must be qualified for profile industries closely linked to other industries in the same SMA which absorb much of their outputs. But the linked industries then would be expected to require rather extensive markets. No doubt there are many industries found in major cities whose markets are primarily local or more or less coincident with a tributary "trade area"—baking may be one example, and manufacture of beverages (where not a profile industry) may be another. Hence we retain this as a real and important type, though one not brought to light by our own methods of analysis. (b) A type that is clearly represented in our data involves a market inclusive not only of the "trade area" as conventionally delimited but a much broader, though generally contiguous region. Certain of the cities specializing in beverage manufactures, e.g., Minneapolis – St. Paul, appear to have such market areas. Oftentimes this kind of market area can be described only as "sub-national," for want of precise information as to its limits. The implication is then that the whole territory of the nation may be divided up into a relatively few "sub-national" markets dominated by a correspondingly small number of centers. It is doubtful that the margins of such market areas are clearly defined. Moreover, centers of only local importance may carve out small market areas within these broad "sub-national" regions. (c) By further extension, strong profile industries in major centers may have virtually "national" markets—e.g., the footwear industry of St. Louis—or even (d) international markets, as illustrated by the manufacture of cash registers in Dayton.

Where outputs are primarily to other industries—as in categories (2), (4), and (6)—rather than to ultimate consumers, the market areas may be more nearly punctiform than "regional" in character. In type (e) we have the situation that one SMA provides virtually the entire market for the output of a profile industry in another SMA. The automobile parts manufactured in Toledo (other than those used in local automobile assembly plants) are shipped primarily to Detroit. (f) By extension, the destinations of outputs may include a number of other centers; this is typical of a good many profile industries of cities located in or with accessibility to the manufacturing belt. (g) In some cases the distribution is so wide—albeit to specific manufacturing centers—that the market area is national or even international in scope though highly localized by the concentration of customers in particular centers.

It is evident that most of the foregoing types are such that market areas of a given center are likely to overlap or intersect with those of other centers. Again, the "administrative principle" seems poorly adapted to a description of center-region relationships as defined by markets—and even the notion of the market area as a "region" may involve a rather extreme extension of the idea of "region." Our findings support the observation of Vance and Smith (1954, p. 126) that "efforts to mark off the areal limits of dominance by either trade or the closely associated newspaper circulation [have] meant too literal a tie to territory for the different contingencies on space involved in metropolitan influence."

Turning from manufacturing industries to the broad gamut of "services," there is perhaps greater justification for use of the "administrative principle" in deriving a first approximation to center-region relationships. There are, of course, services which are explicitly organized on this principle. An important category of these is "state public administration." There are fifteen state capitals among the fifty-one SMA's under examination, all but three of which show up as specialized in state public administration. Significantly, these three are among the largest SMA's in the group—Baltimore (whose SMA includes the Maryland capital at Annapolis), Minneapolis – St. Paul, and Providence. We have already alluded to the organization of Federal Reserve Districts on the "administrative principle," and many federal agencies are similarly "regionalized." In the case of the nation's capital, the "service area," of course, includes the entire country. In a sense the same is probably true of centers like Norfolk, San Antonio, Oklahoma City, San Diego, and Dayton, a large share of whose federal public administration employment is directly or indirectly related to national defense establishments. There is little basis for assuming that such military centers divide the country up into "market areas," although it is true that some aspects of military administration employ "regional" divisions. There would probably be some justification for recognizing the applicability of the "administrative principle" to educational and hospital services and the like, although our materials seldom permit the delimitation of the service areas with any precision. Manifestly, such areas do not have sharp boundaries; there are both medical and educational centers that draw their clientele from all over the United States. But the fact that the "drawing power" of even the most eminent and best known educational institutions falls off with distance from their location (J. Q. Stewart, 1947a) implies that the greater part of their services are rendered to populations within a relatively circumscribed area.

The possibility of delimiting meaningful though necessarily arbitrary service or market areas for financial services and trade is implied by results reported in chapters 5 and 6. Data on flow of funds between Federal Reserve zones (chapter 6) show that every part of the country trades with or has financial transactions with every other part. However, the volume of such transactions, standardizing for the sizes of the populations involved, does fall off rather consistently with distance. As a consequence, we may infer that each center of any importance enjoys a relative dominance over a roughly concentric adjacent area, as compared with competing centers. A delimitation of such areas of dominance would possibly result in a set of "regions" such that a large proportion of all transactions could be described as intra-regional. Such a simplified description of patterns, apart from other distortions, could not bring out one of the most salient findings, i.e., that some centers do an essentially "national" business and compete effectively in all parts of the country or large sections thereof with the more strictly "regional" centers. Wholesale trade areas conventionally have been taken as the prototype of the "trade area" concept of center-region relationship. However, a close examination of the variety of functions subsumed under "wholesaling" would show that any single set of such areas can at best be regarded as a kind of average of the trade territories of the several functions. In actuality the wholesale trade territories of different centers are interpenetrating and overlapping.

Among transportation services, trucking is probably the mode of transportation which is most conducive to the establishment of center-region relationships on a pattern somewhat like that supposed by the "administrative principle." Trucking competes most effectively with other modes of transportation for short-haul business. In several of the reports (Part IV) dealing with centers specialized in meat products, attention is drawn to the high proportion of livestock receipts which are driven in by truck. Of the seven SMA's with trucking as a profile industry, six are identified as "regional capitals" or "regional metropolises" in the classification developed subsequently in this chapter.

By contrast, rail, water, and air transportation play important roles in opening up city-region relationships spanning much greater distances than the radius of a typical "trade area." Specialization in water transportation, as revealed by our industry profiles, occurs in eleven SMA's in the size group 300,000-3,000,000. All of these but Toledo, a port on the Great Lakes, are ocean ports; there is no instance of specialization in water transportation on the part of centers located inland on rivers, although evidence of the advantages of such locations is available in some cases. Aside from coastal trade, it is obvious that the "hinterland" of an ocean port is partly overseas. In the case of all the ocean ports specialized in water transportation and all but two or three of the remaining ocean ports, the monographic materials in Part IV establish a clear relation between the commerce of the port and other industries in the industry profile. When the port traffic is examined in detail, it often appears as well, however, that the kinds of commodities handled are determined neither by the character of the profile industries nor by the economic activities of the immediate hinterland. Thus Baltimore exports large quantities of grain, but is not located in an important grain producing region and has no profile industry other than beverage manufacture based on grain. The explanation here and doubtless in other analogous cases lies in the advantages of relative accessibility to sources and markets of commodities.

Specialization in rail transportation occurs in 15 SMA's, of which only two (Toledo and Jacksonville) also have water transportation in their industry profile. It may be suggested that rail transportation functions with respect to the interior much like water transportation with respect to overseas areas. It is a characteristically long-distance, bulk-cargo medium of transportation. It is most likely to provide important support for profile industries that draw inputs from far-flung areas or that find distant or widely dispersed markets.

This brief discussion of the contrasting roles of trucking and rail or water transportation is consonant with the emphasis which McKenzie placed on the function of automotive vehicles in integrating the "metropolitan community." As was pointed out in chapter 4, McKenzie thought of the metropolitan community primarily in terms of "trade areas" and analogous territorial bases of integration.

Our data indicate a specialization in air transportation for some 17 SMA's. By far the highest degree of specialization is manifested by Miami; this may be related in part to its functions as a tourist center with a sub-national if not national service area, as well as its advantageous location with respect to the Latin American traffic. Review of the remaining instances of industry profiles including air transportation points to no particular linkages worthy of note. It may simply be observed that such specialization is not characteristic of highly developed manufacturing centers. The inference drawn by Taaffe (1952, pp. 157-58) is hardly contradicted by our data:

> In general, air transportation seems to have followed rather than to have re-shaped regional ties. This is indicated in the airlines' business traffic by the prominence of the wholesale cities and larger diversified cities in air traffic generation. . . . It is possible that the concentration of air traffic on large centers may tend to increase the primacy of those cities. It is also possible, however, that air transportation has, to date, largely represented those activities which were already concentrated on large centers.

It hardly needs to be pointed out that air transportation assumes its greatest importance not in relating a center to its proximate, contiguous hinterland, but in facilitating relationships among widely separated centers. Appearance of specialization in air transportation, therefore, may be accepted as *prima facie* evidence of significant "national" or at least "inter-regional" functions.

AN APPROACH TO CLASSIFICATION

The detailed materials surveyed in this volume do not lend themselves to compact summary. Nevertheless, it seems possible to integrate most of the major themes of the several discussions by suggesting a classification of the SMA's studied most intensively—a classification which aims to embody criteria of metropolitanism and salient aspects of center-region relationships, as well as some of the ideas about "hierarchy" surveyed in chapter 3. It should be made clear at once that the approach to such a classification is typological and not taxonomic. We are less interested in getting each center into its proper category than in showing concretely how cities are differentiated in terms of metropolitan functions and regional relationships. It may be doubted that a rigid taxonomy is empirically justifiable, at least in the present state of knowledge and in the absence of developmental studies fully as intensive as our cross-sectional investigation. The use of a typological approach permits us to work with several axes of classification simultaneously without increasing the number of categories in geometric progression; in other words, the typology is understood to be multidimensional.

Table 40 provides a convenient display of some of the most important information on each of the SMA's in our classification. The first column of data concerns population size. This leading position is appropriate, for as we have pointed out, in absence of other indications, large size is presumptive evidence of functions describable as "metropolitan." In fact, size must be kept in mind at every stage in designing and evaluating the classification. Given two centers otherwise similar, the larger is assumed to be the more important—more "metropolitan" if you will—on the face of the matter. This comes out in a significant manner in connection with the per capita indicators shown in the remaining five columns of numerical data. At first sight it may seem awkward to deal simultaneously with absolute size and with per capita measures of activity, when it would be simpler to use absolute measures of the latter. Yet the juxtaposition of population size and per capita indicators provides a critical insight. Expressing a measure of economic activity in per capita form permits comparisons among cities as to "intensity" or as to the importance of the activity to the respective cities. If two cities have the same total of value added by manufacture, but differing sizes of population, it may be inferred that manufacturing is less important to the economy of the larger city. This is precisely the finding that is quickly revealed by the per capita comparison. But if two cities differing in size have identical per capita levels of value added, it is inferred that the larger city is likely to be supplying the larger non-local market. Comparing Chicago with Omaha on per capita wholesale sales we see from the per capita figures ($2,791 and $4,378, respectively) that Omaha is much the more highly specialized trading center. But when we reckon with Chicago's much larger size, it appears that it must have by far the larger wholesale trade area.

A simple graphic presentation of two of the indicators in table 40 provides a convenient starting point. Figure 15 shows the scatter dia-

Table 40. Selected Indicators of Metropolitan Functions, Standard Metropolitan Areas of 300,000 or More Inhabitants in 1950

Standard Metropolitan Area	Ab-brev-iation	Popu-lation, 1950 (1,000's)	Per capita economic-financial statistics[1] Value added by manufac-ture, 1947 (dollars)	Whole-sale sales, 1948 (dollars)	Business services receipts, 1948 (dollars)	Non-local commercial loans, 1955 (dollars)	Demand deposits, 1950 (dollars)	Remarks[2]	Classi-fication[3]
New York–Northeastern New Jersey	NY	12,912	735	3,294	41.24	342	1,612	B	N
Chicago	Cg	5,495	1,023	2,791	32.80	220	1,063	A, B	N
Los Angeles	LA	4,368	494	1,427	24.16	19	654	A, Br	Nd
Philadelphia	Pa	3,671	785	1,606	12.83	93	775	B	Nd
Detroit	Dt	3,016	1,000	1,671	24.08	52	644	Br	Nm
Boston	Bo	2,370	485	1,860	12.88	165	894	B	Dn
San Francisco–Oakland	SF	2,241	482	2,300	22.33	220	829	B, H	Rn
Pittsburgh	Pi	2,213	791	1,439	11.14	201	856	Br, H+	Dn
St. Louis	SL	1,681	794	2,444	16.35	104	791	A, B, H+	D
Cleveland	Cl	1,466	1,059	2,395	24.26	101	918	B, H	D

(NA): Not available.

* Figure based partly on estimate.

[1] Population base for manufacture, wholesale, and business services, 1948 estimate; for loans and deposits, 1950 census. See Appendix for sources of data.

[2] A: Per capita sales of wholesale assemblers of farm products exceeded the average for all SMA's in 1948. B: Federal Reserve Bank City; Br: Federal Reserve Branch City. H: Hinterland or regional resource base for profile manufacturing industry; H+ signifies unusual importance (not shown for SMA's of 3,000,000 or more inhabitants).

[3] See text and figure 16.

Table 40. Continued

Standard Metropolitan Area	Ab-brev-iation	Popu-lation, 1950 (1,000's)	Per capita economic-financial statistics[1]					Remarks[2]	Classi-fication[3]
			Value added by manufac-ture, 1947 (dollars)	Whole-sale sales, 1948 (dollars)	Business services receipts, 1948 (dollars)	Non-local commercial loans, 1955 (dollars)	Demand deposits, 1950 (dollars)		
Washington	Wa	1,464	71	951	10.89	24	667	...	S
Baltimore	Ba	1,337	671	1,324	13.79	25	535	Br	D−
Minneapolis–St. Paul	Mp	1,117	669	3,420	16.47	86	766	A, B, H	R
Buffalo	Bu	1,089	972	1,452	11.66	129	487	Br	D
Cincinnati	Ci	904	869	2,566	14.26	125	739	Br, H+	D
Milwaukee	Ml	871	1,163	1,797	15.50	124	736	H	D−
Kansas City	KC	814	602	4,174	16.58	120	932	A, B, H	R
Houston	Ho	807	491	2,229	12.88	108	1,062	Br, H+	C
Providence	Pr	737	957	973	8.71	41	547	...	M
Seattle	Se	733	381	2,132	14.15	120	718	Br, H	R
Portland	Po	705	483	2,165	16.19	58	655	A, Br, H	R
New Orleans	NO	685	335	2,111	11.08	42	585	Br, H	C
Atlanta	At	672	383	3,582	19.78	108	702	B, H	R
Dallas	Dl	615	413	3,870	23.32	443	1,158	A, B	R
Louisville	Lo	577	875	1,746	11.49	87	619	A, Br, H+	Cd
Denver	De	564	352*	2,338	13.12	46	788	A, Br, H	R
Birmingham	Bi	559	520	1,603	7.49	33	446	Br, H+	Cm
San Diego	SD	557	201	514	7.66	1	370	H	S
Indianapolis	In	552	890	2,720	13.73	122	857	A, H	Cd

Youngstown	Yo	528	1,098	534	4.30	(NA)	376	H	M
Albany–Schenectady–Troy	Ab	514	651	1,137	9.92	(NA)	414	H	D–
Columbus	Co	503	564	1,465	11.08	45	586	H	Cd
San Antonio	SA	500	140	976	6.22	35	520	Br, H	S
Miami	Mm	495	102	959	16.88	18	674	...	S
Rochester	Ro	488	1,069	1,013	39.39	74	549	H	M
Memphis	Me	482	456	4,522	10.01	139	613	Br, H	C
Dayton	Dn	457	1,096	902	7.89	13	446	A	M
Norfolk–Portsmouth	NP	446	213	1,114	4.76	(NA)	307	...	S
Allentown–Bethlehem–Easton	Al	438	820	540	3.84	(NA)	385	H	M
Akron	Ak	410	1,118	822	7.34	34	406	H	M
Tampa–St. Petersburg	Ta	409	175	925	8.85	(NA)	491	A, H	S
Springfield–Holyoke	SH	407	933	690	7.01	(NA)	458	H	M
Toledo	To	396	979	1,323	11.63	26	658	H	D–
Wilkes-Barre–Hazleton	WB	392	324	557	3.28	(NA)	247	H+	S
Omaha	Om	366	481	4,378	18.72	93	815	A, Br, H+	C
Fort Worth	FW	361	425	1,915	9.18	139	679	A, H	C
Hartford	Ha	358	869	1,313	16.62	65	1,185	...	D–
Wheeling–Steubenville	WS	354	757	515	2.78	(NA)	272	H+	M
Syracuse	Sr	342	854	1,698	14.55	105	445	H	D–
Knoxville	Kn	337	346*	827	4.45	(NA)	323	H	S
Phoenix	Px	332	136	996	8.88	23	516	A	S
Richmond	Ri	328	785	2,047	14.70	157	732	B, H+	Cd
Oklahoma City	Ok	325	248	2,390	18.83	149	699	A, Br, H+	C
Charleston, W. Va.	Ch	322	673	891	3.77*	(NA)	369	H+	M
Nashville	Na	322	439	1,462	12.34	96	532	Br, H+	C
Jacksonville	Ja	304	231	2,164	10.47	98	547	Br, H	C

gram of per capita value added by manufacture versus per capita wholesale sales for the 56 SMA's with populations exceeding 300,000. As the analysis in chapter 5 revealed, these two variables have low correlations in each size group of SMA's. The scatter diagram shows clearly that they vary nearly independently of one another. We have already mentioned the conclusion that if wholesaling is regarded as a characteristic metropolitan function, then a "metropolis" may have a high level of manufacturing activity or it may not—both contingencies are clearly in evidence.

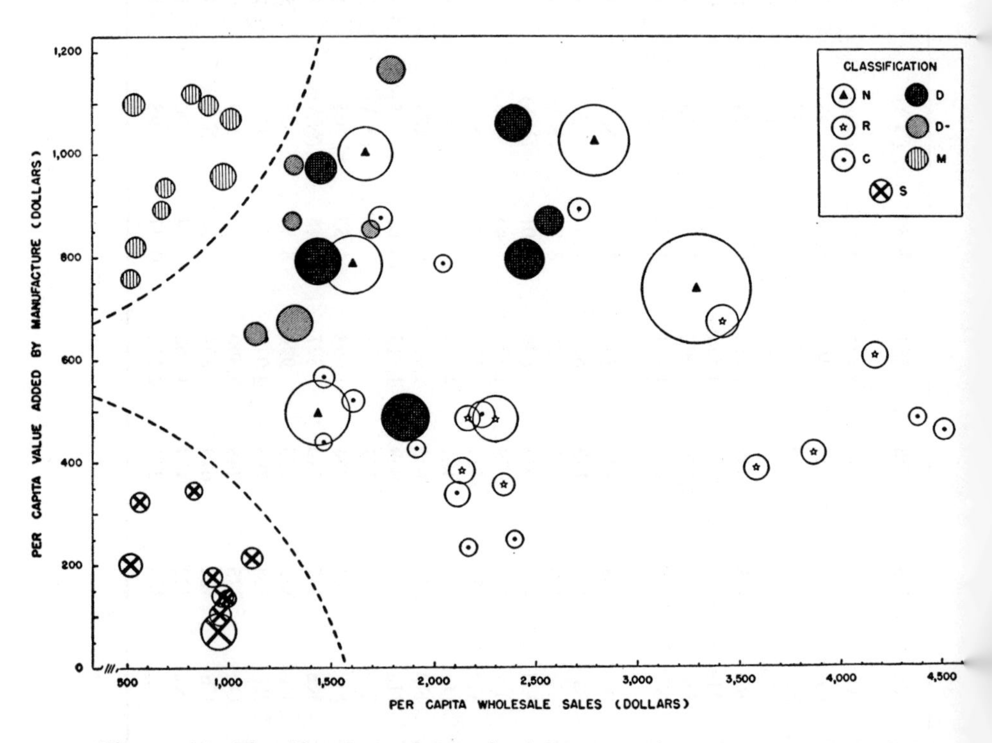

Figure 15. Classification of Standard Metropolitan Areas in Relation to Population Size, Per Capita Value Added by Manufacture, and Per Capita Wholesale Sales

N = National Metropolis
R = Regional Metropolis
C = Regional Capital, Submetropolitan
D = Diversified Manufacturing with Metropolitan Functions
D– = Diversified Manufacturing with few Metropolitan Functions
M = Specialized Manufacturing
S = Special Cases

Figure 15 immediately brings to light three fairly distinct groups of extreme cases. First, there are five SMA's with extremely high per capita wholesale sales, i.e., $3,500 or more, and moderately low per capita value added by manufacture. We shall disregard this group for the moment. Second, there is a group of nine SMA's with quite low per capita wholesale sales (below $1,200) but moderately high to quite high per capita value added by manufacture ($750 and above). Since these centers evidently have nearly minimal trading functions but are intensively engaged in manufacturing, we may call them "specialized manufacturing centers." Third, there is a group of nine SMA's with quite low levels of both per capita wholesale sales (under $1,200) and per capita value added by manufacture (under $400). On the face of it one would assume that such centers must have some function other than trade or manufacture rather highly developed. However, as it will appear, these nine SMA's are somewhat heterogeneous among themselves, so we shall simply call them "special cases," for convenience of reference. Having "sliced off" the nine "specialized manufacturing" and nine "special cases," we are left with 38 SMA's to classify. This large group contains great variation within it, of course, but all its members have levels of both trade and manufacturing activity above a bare minimum. Although we expect to find that some are more "metropolitan" than others, still there would probably be no great harm in regarding all as metropolitan or at least near-metropolitan centers in some sense.

On the next "slice" we single out the five largest SMA's, those with populations exceeding 3,000,000, designating them as "national metropolises." We have not studied these as intensively as the remaining SMA's above 300,000, and no individual reports on them appear in Part IV. Their regional relationships manifest greater complexities than we were prepared to investigate, given the limitations of time and resources for the study. However, references to these cities have been made in earlier chapters and several indicators are readily available for them. Emphasis was placed on the national financial functions of New York and on Chicago's position second only to New York in this respect. Reference was made to Detroit's high degree of specialization due to its prominence in automobile manufacturing for a national and world market. Los Angeles, although noted or notorious as a site for the motion picture industry, actually has a quite diversified industry profile. The same is true of Philadelphia, a major center of manufacturing and trade. Philadelphia, because of its close proximity to New York, apparently is subordinate to that "primate city" in many respects; the same is true of the remaining three giant SMA's, though perhaps to a somewhat lesser degree, since each of them is somewhat distant from New York. In chapter 4 we called attention to the view that the "million-cities" (referring to central-city rather than SMA populations and identical with the five SMA's examined here) are "not products of regional forces" but are "created by larger factors in the total national economy."

It is no doubt advisable to beware of overemphasizing sheer size. Yet, in a modern and reasonably efficient economy, cities do not attain great size without good reason. On balance of impressions and for lack of an appealing alternative, the decision to keep the five largest SMA's in a distinct category stands. However, it is recognized that the "national metropolises" are not identical in function. On per capita wholesale sales, business services receipts, non-local loans, and demand deposits (see table 40), New York and Chicago clearly stand apart from the remaining three. In the final classification, therefore, the latter are identified as being in a sort of transitional position between "national metropolises" and other types (as is explained presently).

The distinctions which remain to be set forth cannot be described by criteria as simple as those determining the recognition of "specialized manufacturing" centers, "special cases," and "national metropolises." The considerations entering into the remaining distinctions are, of course, of the same kinds as those previously emphasized: population size, per capita levels of manufacturing and trade, indicators (principally financial) of "metropolitan" functions, and character of industry profiles and regional relationships (as revealed by the individual studies in Part IV). But the relative weights and particular combinations of variables regarded as crucial, shift somewhat from category to category, and perhaps from instance to instance. This is only to concede that impressionism and judgment have been allowed to play a role. But it should be noted that even the most "objective" kind of classification inevitably would involve setting criteria which were arbitrary in some degree and themselves expressive of judgment or impressions. In any event, the reader has conveniently at hand virtually the entire body of evidence on which judgments are based and may modify them accordingly. We reiterate that our objective is not to produce a classification for its own sake, but to suggest some principles determining the structure of a system of cities.

We first pick out a group of SMA's rather closely akin to the "specialized manufacturing" centers. Baltimore, Milwaukee, Albany-Schenectady-Troy, Toledo, Hartford, and Syracuse have moderately high to very high levels of manufacturing activity as indicated by per capita value added. None of them is exceptionally high on per capita wholesale trade, though each is higher on this variable than any of the "specialized manufacturing" centers. None appears to have a full repertoire of "metropolitan" functions, though several do have one or a few characteristics of a metropolitan center. Baltimore, though a Federal Reserve Branch City, does not rate especially high on financial indicators; although the SMA includes the state capital and thus has administrative functions, it does not show up as specialized in same; and evidence for a large contiguous hinterland closely integrated with the center is not great. Milwaukee shows up with unexpected strength on financial indicators and has certain profile industries based on relationships with its "hinterland"; but this aspect of its profile is not highly developed and evidence suggests that its proximity to Chicago inhibits potential development of "metropolitan" characteristics. Albany-Schenectady-Troy shows specialization in state public administration and is favored by rail transportation; but otherwise its "metropolitan" characteristics are not highly developed and it does not manifest an exceptionally important role as focus for a metropolitan region. Toledo has primarily its slight superiority in wholesale trade to differentiate it from the "specialized manufacturing" centers. Hartford has one strong "metropolitan" function, i.e., its national insurance business; but it is clearly no major trade center and shows no high development of other characteristics indicative of metropolitanism. Finally, Syracuse, like Toledo, differs most obviously from the "specialized manufacturing" class with respect to its volume of wholesale trade per capita.

The group just enumerated is designated "diversified manufacturing centers with few metropolitan functions." Their characterization as "manufacturing centers" is amply justified by their positions on the value added indicator. The qualifier "diversified" follows in part from the evidence of trade functions somewhat more highly developed than those of the "specialized" manufacturing centers. Supporting evidence is found in the indexes of dissimilarity between SMA twelve-category industry distributions and that of the United States (see table 33, chapter 9). For the "specialized" manufacturing centers these indexes are arrayed as follows: 30.6, 28.4, 25.2, 24.7, 24.4, 23.6, 22.0, 17.9, and 16.0. The last two, for Wheeling-Steubenville and Charleston (W. Va.), respectively, are diminished by the relatively high proportions in extractive industries. By contrast, the indexes of dissimilarity for the "diversified" centers enumerated above are 22.8, 21.2, 20.4, 17.4, 16.0, and 14.0; note that none is above 23.5, whereas six of the nine "specialized" centers have higher indexes than this. In fact, except for four of the "special cases," only three other SMA's in the size range 300,000—3,000,000 have indexes of dissimilarity above 23.5: Jacksonville, Oklahoma City, and New Orleans. Perusal of the individual studies (Part IV) brings to light only one SMA among the "specialized" manufacturing centers that lacks a definite concentration in one or two manufacturing industries—the profile for Springfield-Holyoke does suggest some diversification. Specialization is clear for the remainder: textiles in Providence; heavy metals in Youngstown; photographic equipment in Rochester; machinery in Dayton; heavy metals, textiles and apparel in Allentown-Bethlehem-Easton; rubber in Akron; heavy metals in Wheeling-Steubenville; and chemicals in Charleston (with emphasis on coal mining as well in the last two).

The foregoing states the case for distinguishing "specialized manufacturing" centers from "diversified manufacturing centers with few metropolitan functions." The latter is now to be distinguished from a class of "diversified manufacturing centers with metropolitan functions." These combine a moderate to high emphasis on manufacturing with a considerable range and strength of metropolitan functions. They are notable for their large population sizes, ranging from 904,000 to over 2,000,000 as compared with 342,000–1,337,000 for the less metropolitan "diversified" manufacturing centers and 322,000–737,000 for the "specialized" manufacturing centers. (Compare the earlier discussion of size and diversification, chapter 2.) As suggested earlier, their large sizes require that added weight be given any evidence of high levels of trade, financial, and like activities. In fact, at the upper end of the size range in this category are found highly developed metropolitan functions that are clearly reminiscent of the "national" functions attributed to the largest SMA's. Both Boston and Pittsburgh are highly developed financial centers with wide geographic dispersion of the areas served (chapter 5). Another significant observation is that, unlike the less metropolitan "diversified" manufacturing centers, the six SMA's in question—Boston, Pittsburgh, St. Louis, Cleveland, Buffalo, and Cincinnati—all show considerable evidence of strong relationships with at least moderately large contiguous hinterlands. It must be acknowledged, however, that each encounters strong competition for the "dominance" of such hinterlands on the part of major centers at only moderate distances away.

Establishing the foregoing categories accounts for all but five SMA's in figure 15 having levels of per capita value added by manufacture in excess of $600, as well as a couple with slightly lower levels. Reasons for placing emphasis on non-manufacturing functions for the remaining five are indicated presently. It may simply be kept in mind that for the most part the two final categories consist of SMA's in which manufacturing is not exceptionally highly developed, although all have some measurable manufacturing activity.

In the two categories now to be described are placed cities which are rather highly specialized, for the most part, in industries representing "metropolitan" functions. Trade functions are moderately to highly developed. Typically, though not without exception, there are profile manufacturing industries depending for important inputs on resource-extracting activities in the hinterland or a broader but still contiguous "region." Trade areas of moderate to large size can be more or less realistically identified, and there is clear evidence of the role of the center in integrating activities of such areas.

The distinction between the "regional metropolis" and the "regional capital" (with "submetropolitan" characteristics)—as the two categories are named—turns in good measure on size. Denver, the smallest of the eight "regional metropolises," has a population of 564,000, while only three of the 13 "regional capitals" are this large. All the "regional metropolises" have per capita wholesale sales in excess of $2,100, while 6 of the "regional capitals" fall below this figure (see figure 15). However, the two groups are not perfectly distinguished on this criterion, for Omaha and Memphis have the highest per capita wholesale volume among the 56 SMA's. Their extreme development in this direction is partially discounted as a criterion of metropolitanism, since they are somewhat smaller than the "regional capitals" with most nearly comparable per capita wholesale activity.

Perhaps the easiest way to indicate how the size criterion was supplemented in distinguishing "metropolis" from "capital" is to indicate the relevant considerations for the three largest "capitals" and three smallest "metropolises." New Orleans and Atlanta are of virtually the same size, but Atlanta leads in all indicators listed in table 40 and is a Federal Reserve Bank city whereas New Orleans is a branch city. Houston, though somewhat larger than Dallas, is clearly second to Dallas as a trade and financial center, both on the basis of statistical indicators and in status in the Federal Reserve System. Louisville and Denver are of about the same size; both are Federal Reserve Branch cities and they are not greatly different on financial indicators, although Denver leads by a considerable margin in wholesale trade. However, the crucial evidence is that which suggests a much larger relative role for Denver as a center of a metropolitan region. Louisville is too close to Cincinnati and other competitors for its orbit of dominance to be greatly extended. In fact, in this respect and in regard to its manufacturing function Louisville is more like a "diversified manufacturing" center than any of the other "regional capitals"; this is taken into account in qualifying its placement in the latter category. Admittedly the case for classifying Denver as a "regional metropolis" would be stronger if the area it dominates were more highly developed.

The complete classification of the 56 SMA's is set forth schematically in figure 16, which also serves to identify the abbreviations for the seven categories used henceforth and in the last column of table 40. These abbreviations are particularly convenient for identifying the eleven centers which most obviously are marginal between two types. Thus the symbol "Nd" identifies a "national metropolis" which in some respects strongly resembles a "D" metropolis; the two "Dn" centers are in a similar transitional position. The "m" added to Detroit's "N" classification and to Birmingham's "C" classification signifies that specialized manufacturing is an outstanding characteristic of both places, although other functions account for their respective primary classifications. San Francisco, with an "Rn" designation, is a "regional metropolis" with certain functions—especially financial—nearly strong enough to qualify it as a "national metropolis." Several of the "regional capitals" are sufficiently strong in manufacturing or weak in trade that their resemblance in these respects to "D" centers deserves special notice. The minus sign in the abbreviation "D—" is to indicate the resemblance to "D" centers in manufacturing functions but the lesser degree of development of characteristically metropolitan functions.

The position of the "S" centers at the bottom of the diagram is meant only to set them apart for special attention. The arrangement of the remaining boxes, however, suggests a quasi-hierarchical structure. Obviously it is not a unidimensional one, nor is it possible to posit equivalent ranks for centers on opposite sides of the diagram at about the same distance from the top. The basis of ranking within categories is population size; but overlaps of size between groups have been pointed out. Finally, the diagram must not be interpreted as showing that centers low on the diagram are necessarily "subdominant" to one or more centers in boxes directly above them, although this may well be true in some instances, particularly as far as the "C" centers are concerned.

Had the classification in figure 16 been available at the beginning of

Figure 16. Classification of Standard Metropolitan Areas of 300,000 or More Inhabitants According to Metropolitan Functions and Regional Relationships

National Metropolis (N)
- New York
- Chicago
- Los Angeles (Nd)
- Philadelphia (Nd)
- Detroit (Nm)

Diversified Manufacturing with Metropolitan Functions (D)
- Boston (Dn)
- Pittsburgh (Dn)
- St. Louis
- Cleveland
- Buffalo
- Cincinnati

Diversified Manufacturing with few Metropolitan Functions (D–)
- Baltimore
- Milwaukee
- Albany–Schenectady–Troy
- Toledo
- Hartford
- Syracuse

Specialized Manufacturing (M)
- Providence
- Youngstown
- Rochester
- Dayton
- Allentown–Bethlehem–Easton
- Akron
- Springfield–Holyoke
- Wheeling–Steubenville
- Charleston, W. Va.

Regional Metropolis (R)
- San Francisco (Rn)
- Minneapolis – St. Paul
- Kansas City
- Seattle
- Portland
- Atlanta
- Dallas
- Denver

Regional Capital, Submetropolitan (C)
- Houston
- New Orleans
- Louisville (Cd)
- Birmingham (Cm)
- Indianapolis (Cd)
- Columbus (Cd)
- Memphis
- Omaha
- Fort Worth
- Richmond (Cd)
- Oklahoma City
- Nashville
- Jacksonville

Special Cases (S)
- Washington
- San Diego
- San Antonio
- Miami
- Norfolk–Portsmouth
- Wilkes-Barre – Hazleton
- Tampa – St. Petersburg
- Knoxville
- Phoenix

our research, it would have been possible to explore inter-category differences systematically in connection with each body of data analyzed. Here we can only suggest that this kind of systematic study might be worth while. In regard to transportation we note that not a single "N," "D," or "D—" center lacks access to water transportation; all are ports on ocean, lake or river. By contrast, 5 of the 13 "C" centers are landlocked. A situational factor of indubitable importance is relative location of the several types. All but one of the nine "M" centers are within 70 miles or less of an "N," "R," or "D" center. All of the "D—" centers are within 150 miles or less of a center in one of these three top classifications. By contrast, only two "R" centers are as close as 200 miles to another "R" or to an "N" or a "D" center. "C" centers likewise maintain "respectful" distances: five are 100-200 miles and seven are 200-500 miles from the nearest "R," "N," or "D" center. The lone exception, Fort Worth (located 32 miles from Dallas), raises an interesting point. In many respects Fort Worth and Dallas have complementary functions. If they had been located a little closer together, or if they had merely been in the same county at their present distance, we would be treating them as a single twin-city entity—one which would rival the twin cities to the north in pre-eminence as a "regional metropolis."

We must now explain how as many as nine SMA's came to be set aside in the anomalous "S" category. This group is a conglomerate of cities with highly distinctive and unusual functions and those for which the uniform procedures of the study run up against difficulties of interpretation. First let it be noted that the "S" centers do include some rather deviant cases. Four of them have comparatively high indexes of dissimilarity to the national industry category distribution. The "S" group includes the only four instances among SMA's of 300,000 or more inhabitants in which none of the location quotients for categories (2) to (7) inclusive (manufacturing) rises to unity or above.

The "S" center most obviously differentiated from all others is the Washington SMA. Either as an "historical accident" or for more intelligible reasons, the national capital never developed industrial, commercial, financial, or "metropolitan" service functions commensurate with the size given it by the concentration of federal employment in the area. From comparative studies we know this is not necessarily true of national capitals—witness London, long the world's leading metropolis and prototype of the very concept of metropolis. There are other national capitals in the world, however, that bear closer comparison with Washington. In any event, in a strictly national study, Washington can only be treated as the exception to all rules.

San Diego, San Antonio, and Norfolk-Portsmouth are SMA's that seem underdeveloped industrially and commercially on the basis of their size. If they were reduced to the sizes they would have attained without the stimulus of major military installations and associated activities, they probably would not have appeared in our group of SMA's of 300,000 and over and they surely would have shown up with higher per capita values on trade, financial, and manufacturing indicators.

Miami stands alone among cities of comparable size with its extreme specialization in the tourist trade. It is also rather exceptional for its extremely high growth rate in both the decades, 1930-1940 and 1940-1950. It is probable that high growth produces effects on the industry profile that are not adequately allowed for in our procedures. In chapter 9 we justified omission of construction from the detailed analysis of profiles on the ground that employment in this industry strongly reflects current growth. But there are other industries in a growing city which seemingly respond to rapid growth (Duncan and Reiss, 1956, chapter 15). In the case of Miami, we have rapid growth superimposed on the response to the tourist trade on the part of industries like those we have called "local services." In a tourist center, a considerable share of such services is, in effect, "exported" to non-local consumers. In short, Miami appears to require an analytical approach somewhat different from the kind we developed. Be it noted, however, that such special treatment would be appropriate primarily because Miami is, in fact, a "special case."

The outstanding characteristic of the Wilkes-Barre – Hazleton SMA is the extreme concentration of its employment in coal mining, a most unusual specialization for a large SMA. Had we proceeded by eliminating extractive activities from the employment distributions before computing profiles, this one manifestly would have looked rather different. This procedure could be justified in an inquiry directed to the discovery of distinctively "metropolitan" characteristics—of which extractive industry surely is not an example. Under such a procedure, however, the number of employed persons in this SMA's industry profile would have entitled it to a much lower rank on size than it has on the basis of total population, and it might well have been excluded from consideration with the present group of centers.

Three of the "special cases" illustrate some problems of units and classification that arise when uniform procedures are applied in broad comparative analyses. (See Duncan, 1956a, for a general statement on problems arising in using SMA data in comparative studies.) Among the SMA's of 300,000-500,000 population, Tampa – St. Petersburg, Knoxville, and Phoenix are somewhat unusual for their comparatively high percentages employed in agriculture, forestry, and fisheries (7.2, 12.7, and 6.0 per cent, respectively). Each of them has a location quotient of 0.5 or higher in category (1), primary resource extractors, as a consequence. The only SMA's in this size class with higher location quotients are those having appreciable employment in mining. A second common characteristic of the three SMA's is their relatively high proportions in construction (9.9, 8.7, and 9.6 per cent, respectively, as compared with 6.1 per cent in the country as a whole). All were rapidly growing SMA's between 1940 and 1950. As a consequence of the concentration in agriculture and construction—neither of which can be a "profile industry" under our procedures—relatively few other industries show up in sufficient proportions to be classed as profile industries. Consequently, the profiles for these three areas are not as informative as they might be under somewhat different procedures. It should be noted that the inclusion of substantial agricultural employment in an SMA is somewhat fortuitous, since it results from the use of whole counties in delimiting metropolitan areas. Where an SMA includes sizable agricultural areas whose "metropolitan" character is questionable, not only are employment figures somewhat distorted, but per capita measures of economic activity tend to be understated. Another way in which rapid growth doubtlessly affects the interpretation of industry structure should be mentioned. It is probable that a good many of what we have called "local services" are temporarily stimulated by rapid growth. This would not be reflected in our profiles, however, since we have excluded local services from the profile by definition.

While the somewhat anomalous character of these three SMA's is undoubtedly explained in part by defects in our procedures, there is another relevant consideration. Had we computed our profiles after subtracting out employment in agriculture and construction and possibly some other industries responding to current growth rates, these SMA's would have been smaller, relative to the others considered here, than they appear on the basis of total populations. In particular, Phoenix and Knoxville might no longer be classed with the SMA's of 300,000-500,000. To put the matter another way, it appears that all three cities could be regarded as nascent "regional capitals," and their position as such may be clear in the light of, say, 1960 data. At that time, however, there will probably be other emerging "regional capitals" which will prove equally difficult to classify in routine fashion.

Perhaps the most important general conclusion concerning the "S" centers is that they appear anomalous primarily because we were working with a restricted range of population size—SMA's of 300,000 or more inhabitants. In general terms we can anticipate what would be the outcome of extending our procedures to smaller places. We would find numerous additional "M" centers. There would also be a number of places with characteristics and functions like our "C" centers, but typically with smaller trade-area hinterlands and, with decreasing size, progressively weaker evidence of distinctively "metropolitan" functions. We can be fairly confident that there are no "N," "D," or "R" centers at the smaller sizes. But the relative frequency of places like our "S" centers would surely increase, and some additional types of highly specialized places would appear: college towns, mining towns, and an occasional highly specialized transportation center like Altoona, Pa., for example. There would be more cases of rather highly specialized resort centers, military centers, and cities whose profiles reflect primarily their services as state capitals. At the smallest sizes conventionally regarded as "urban," there would be not only many examples of these types, but many towns which could only be described as country trade centers, providing retail outlets, consumer services, and agricultural markets.

Perhaps it is not too wild an extrapolation to suggest that in the United States of 1950 an SMA size of roughly 300,000 inhabitants marked a transition point where distinctively "metropolitan" characteristics first begin to appear. Adequately to describe the base of the "urban hierarchy"—consisting of almost all urban centers smaller than this size—one would have to shift the emphasis from "metropolitanism" to other principles of functional differentiation. One thing seems certain: any realistic delineation of an "urban hierarchy" would have to reckon with a variety of types of "horizontal" differentiation as well as the "vertical" integration of lower- with higher-order centers and of centers with their hinterlands. Completion of the research required to turn these suggestions into verified empirical generalizations would provide a worthwhile contribution to our understanding of urban structure and the spatial pattern of the economy.

PART IV

FIFTY MAJOR CITIES AND THEIR REGIONAL RELATIONSHIPS

The unique functions which individual metropolitan centers perform are determined, in no small part, by the unique characteristics of their hinterlands; unless these unique features are known, it is difficult to comprehend how or why a particular metropolis performs the combination of functions it does.

—Donald J. Bogue

NOTE: The remaining chapters are based on the information we have gathered on some 50 of the nation's largest standard metropolitan areas (SMA's). The presentation, being arranged according to categories of the typological classification suggested in the previous chapter, will serve to support that classification as well as to indicate the range of variation included within each category. The materials not only supply documentation and illustration of the earlier discussion but also suggest a number of subsidiary hypotheses not hitherto mentioned. In addition, they may be of value for reference purposes, since, to our knowledge, no similar compilation of information is readily available. In this connection, it is well to reiterate some of the limitations to which the information is subject. Manifestly, we are able to mention only the "highlights." By design, our attention is focused on what we have called profile industries—those that make the economy of the SMA somewhat distinctive—and we have disregarded or taken for granted the many auxiliary activities that any large city must have. Since our purpose is to provide a mid-century cross-section for use, among other things, as a bench mark, we give no systematic information on historical developments, current rates of growth, changes since the period to which our statistical data refer, or prospects for the future, although relevant points are sometimes mentioned. To the reader seeking information of this kind, we can only plead that we had to tailor our task to the resources available for completing it, and we chose to emphasize what seemed to us the most natural starting point for a comprehensive description of the metropolitan economy of the United States. Finally, in examining the data to follow, it is well to bear in mind the comments made earlier (chapter 10) as to variation in quality and quantity of the information available to us.

CHAPTER 12

Metropolitan Centers

This chapter deals with the two categories of SMA's that, apart from the "national metropolises," have the clearest claim to the status of major metropolitan centers—"diversified manufacturing centers with metropolitan functions" and "regional metropolises." For both groups we have already given summary evidence of strong metropolitan functions and clearly recognizable relationships to metropolitan hinterlands. SMA's in the first group, which average somewhat larger in population size, combine the metropolitan functions with important and varied manufacturing functions; in the second group, on the whole, trade relations are found to be more highly developed, on a relative basis.

DIVERSIFIED MANUFACTURING WITH METROPOLITAN FUNCTIONS

Boston	*Cleveland*
Pittsburgh	*Buffalo*
St. Louis	*Cincinnati*

The industrial profiles of the cities included in this group are alike in having industries falling into at least two, and usually more, of our six broad categories of manufacturing. Moreover, there are usually several individual industries listed under each category. Each center exhibits employment specialization in one or more non-local services, and each is readily identified as a financial center of some importance by its status in the Federal Reserve System. The cities are somewhat homogeneous in that 34-44 per cent of the total employment in each is accounted for by profile industries. Their individuality is apparent from the situational factors identified as being related to the actual makeup of their profiles.

BOSTON

SMA consists of Suffolk and parts of Essex, Middlesex, Norfolk, and Plymouth Counties, Massachusetts
1950 population: central city, 801,444; SMA, 2,369,986
Important location feature: port on Atlantic Ocean
Other important features: Capital of Massachusetts; Federal Reserve Bank city

INPUTS AND SUPPLY AREAS FOR BOSTON'S PROFILE INDUSTRIES

Confectionary and related products: The major inputs are sugar, chocolate, and various nuts. Sugar is presumably obtained from local refineries since the SMA imports large quantities of raw sugar from Cuba and Puerto Rico. Cocoa beans and shells are also imported, with Brazil an important source (United States Board of Engineers for Rivers and Harbors, 1957, No. 3, pp. 244-46.) Nuts and other ingredients are probably from various Area C sources.

Miscellaneous fabricated textile products: Input sources were not determined but presumably are within the great string of textile towns stretching from New England to the southern Appalachian Piedmonts. (See Alexandersson, 1956, fig. 12, p. 66.)

Electrical machinery, equipment, and supplies: A wide range of products are manufactured by industries in this category and inputs can be discussed only in general terms. Various high grade metal and glass products are probably important inputs and are presumably obtained from local, hinterland, and Area C sources. For New England electronics manufacturers in general, about 50 to 60 per cent of the inputs are from New England sources. Research and development work is an important activity in the SMA's electronics industry. (Federal Reserve Bank of Boston, 1956b, pp. 3-4.)

Ship and boat building and repairing: Shipbuilding is essentially an

Table 41. Industrial Profile, Boston: 1950

Category and industry	Location quotient	Per cent of employed labor force	Inputs primarily from area:	Outputs primarily to area:
(3) *First stage resource users; production for final market*				
Confectionary and related products	4.79	0.7	A, C	B, C
(5) *Second stage resource users; production for final market*				
Miscellaneous fabricated textile products	1.53	0.2	B?, C?	C?
(6) *Resources of indirect significance; production for non-final market*				
Electrical machinery, equipment, and supplies	2.66	3.7	A, B, C	B, C
Ship and boat building and repairing	5.14	1.4	C	C
Professional equipment and supplies	1.67	0.4	A, B, C	C
Printing, publishing, and allied industries	1.65	2.5	A?, B, C	B, C
Paperboard containers and boxes	2.30	0.5	B, C	A, B, C?
Miscellaneous paper and pulp products	2.27	0.5	B, C	?
Rubber products	2.64	1.1	B, C	C
Leather: tanned, curried, and finished	11.44	1.0	C	A, B, C
(7) *Resources of indirect significance; production for final market*				
Watches, clocks, and clockwork-operated devices	2.17	0.1	A, B	C
Footwear, except rubber	3.92	1.9	A, B, C	C
Leather products, except footwear	1.83	0.2	A, B, C	C
(9) *Service industries; non-local*	1.11	14.2	*	B, C
Banking and credit agencies	1.55	(1.5)	*	C
Security and commodity brokerage, and investment companies	2.62	(0.4)	*	A, B, C
Advertising	1.50	(0.3)	*	A, B
Miscellaneous professional and related services	1.75	(0.2)	*	A, B, C
State public administration	1.79	(0.8)	*	A, B
(10) *Service industries; may be local or non-local*				
Insurance	2.07	2.8	*	C
Hospitals	1.74	3.0	*	A, B
Educational services, private	2.52	2.4	*	A, B, C
Total in profile industries	...	36.6	...	...

* Inputs other than labor not considered.

assembling and finishing industry. A great array of manufactured parts no doubt come from many sources in the industrial belt. However, the basic material purchased is iron and steel forms and heavy machinery, and on these modern shipbuilding is absolutely dependent. (Jones and Darkenwald, 1954, p. 467.) These iron and steel inputs are probably obtained from eastern steel producers outside the hinterland. New England was a great center for shipbuilding until the Civil War. Timber resources were important. But "with the advent of iron and steel as basic raw materials and with mechanical power for propulsion, New England lost some of its former advantages for shipbuilding." (*Ibid.*, p. 468.)

Professional equipment and supplies: Major products include medical instruments and supplies, optical instruments and supplies, and mechanical measuring instruments. No doubt for many of these products skilled workers and technicians are important and transportation costs negligible. Access to material inputs is not the major factor in the localization of this industry in the Boston area, since raw material and shipping costs are relatively inconsequential. The industry does, however, require technically trained people and skilled labor. (Federal Reserve Bank of Boston, 1953a, p. 7.)

Printing, publishing, and allied industries: Although it concerns the printing and publishing industry of all New England, the following statement is probably relevant to the Boston SMA:

> Much of its needs for paper are met by the many regional concerns turning out specialty papers and by the newsprint plants in New England and Eastern Canada. Other supplies are also readily available locally. (Federal Reserve Bank of Boston, 1953b, p. 3.)

Paperboard containers and boxes; miscellaneous paper and pulp products: While much of New England is forest, not all of the region's lumber inputs are obtained from hinterland sources. "While most of the present pulpwood supply comes from New England forests, eastern Canada has been shipping in about one-third of the pulpwood or its pulp equivalent which New England mills consume." (National Planning Association, Committee of New England, 1954, p. 26.) In addition, wastepaper is an important raw material for the paperboard industry and this is abundant in the densely populated parts of the country. (Alderfer and Michl, 1957, p. 293.)

Rubber products: In 1955, nearly 70,000 tons of crude rubber were received by the port of Boston. The major sources were Malaya and Indonesia, with Thailand, Viet-Nam, Laos, and Cambodia also shipping crude rubber. (United States Board of Engineers for Rivers and Harbors and Maritime Administration, 1957, No. 3, p. 245.) Presumably the fabrics used in rubber footwear are obtained from hinterland sources.

Leather: tanned, curried, and finished: Leather tanning is an early New England industry which was originally based on local inputs. In the early days, hides were taken to small tanneries located near timber where bark was available. When chemical tanning was introduced, it became possible to locate larger plants near the coast in closer proximity to the labor supply and transport facilities. (McCarty, 1940, p. 572.) According to Hoover (1937, p. 115), there are three important materials used in tanning: hides or skins, water, and a tanning agent. Water is largely irrelevant as a location determinant in a broad sense, because streams and lakes are more or less ubiquitous. Owing to technological changes, the locational importance of tanning agents was reduced and tanneries became free to locate near the plentiful supplies of hides at slaughtering centers. These changes in the economics of the industry have had varied effects.

> In the case of the lighter leathers, the new situation was not so clearly defined. Much more labor and power and a greater variety of materials are necessary. The advantages acquired from long situation in one place and from the proximity of similar enterprises are much more important in the goatskin and sheepskin branches of the business. Furthermore, the goatskins and a considerable part of the other skins have always been imported, so the optimum location with reference to material supply is on the seaboard. For all these reasons the manufacture of lighter leathers, and particularly that of kid, has remained concentrated in two districts along the Atlantic coast: one practically suburban to Boston, and the other extending from Newark to Wilmington. (*Ibid.*, p. 260.)

In addition to hides and skins obtained from foreign sources, the light leather industry uses chromate salts in the process which are obtained from British and Portuguese Africa, Greece, Brazil, and French Oceania. (Alderfer and Michl, 1957, p. 463.) Probably heavy leather tanning takes place in the SMA also; the subsidiary of a major meat packer has a tannery in the SMA. (Moody's Investors Service, 1950a, p. 936.)

Watches, clocks, and clockwork-operated devices: Metal parts for spring-driven and electric clocks and timers are probably obtained from fabricators in the SMA and the hinterland. For example, a local watch manufacturer also produces watch and clock parts (*ibid.*, p.

2968), although the proportion of components it manufactured was not determined. Similarly, a national electrical company which manufactures clocks and timers in the SMA, has a plant in another SMA in Massachusetts which manufactures clock and timer parts as well as clocks and motors. (*Ibid.*, p. 2376.) New England is a significant producer of synchronous motors used in electric clocks. (Federal Reserve Bank of Boston, 1953a, p. 8.) In recent years part of this industry has shifted to the manufacture of precision parts for the electronics and missiles industries.

Footwear, except rubber; Leather products, except footwear: Shoe machinery is manufactured in the SMA. (Alexandersson, 1956, p. 45.) Leather inputs are no doubt supplied by local and hinterland tanneries. Leather is probably also obtained from Area C tanneries, since sales offices of tanneries located outside the hinterland are maintained in Boston. (Moody's Investors Service, 1950a, pp. 646, 2690.) Although the leather and shoe industries are concentrated in New England, the relative importance of the area has declined for a number of reasons, including increased mechanization of the industry and consequent declining importance of skilled labor, the industry's search for nonunion labor to reduce large wage costs, the depletion of eastern tanning materials, and the growing importance of the Middle West as a supplier of hides and leather. (Alderfer and Michl, 1957, p. 478.)

OUTPUTS AND SERVICE AREAS OF BOSTON'S PROFILE INDUSTRIES

Confectionary and related products: Distribution is mainly to hinterland and sub-national markets. However, there is at least one national producer in the SMA.

Miscellaneous fabricated textile products: Curtains, draperies and other housefurnishings are the most important products. Distribution was not determined, but it is supposed that a sub-national market is served.

Electrical machinery, equipment, and supplies: Electronic tubes, radio sets, electric lamps, and motors are part of the wide range of products manufactured by this rapidly growing industry. (*1947 Census of Manufactures;* Moody's Investors Service, 1950a, pp. 401, 1009, 2376.) The electronics industry is apparently the fastest growing industry in New England, and Boston has grown faster than the remainder of the area. The following discussion of New England's industry is probably applicable to the SMA:

> New England's electronics producers specialize in industrial products or consumer product component parts that concentrate a high value in a small product, such as transistors, tubes, instruments and switches. For example, none of the major television producers have assembly plants in New England, but New England firms make a large portion of the small tubes and other components for television sets. This specialization arises out of special competence in the research, development and engineering phases of the industry in contrast with the material assembly, production, and consumer marketing functions of the industry.
>
> Sales of New England electronics manufacturers are about evenly divided between the northeastern states and the rest of the United States. The typical concern ships one-fifth of its products to other companies located in New England, one-fourth to concerns in New York and New Jersey, and almost one-half of its total output to concerns located in other parts of the United States. . . . The New England market is of greater importance to electronics manufacturers located in the Boston area than to those located in other parts of New England. (Federal Reserve Bank of Boston, 1953c, p. 2.)

With national growth of aircraft and missiles industries, distribution of Boston's electronic products is becoming more widespread. A survey of New England electronics manufacturers found that "An adequate supply of skilled workers was the most frequently listed advantage." The second most frequently mentioned advantage for Boston's manufacturers is that

> . . . education and research institutions in Boston and surrounding communities have done much to foster the growth of the electronics business in the area. Boston area manufacturers listed the availability of research facilities and nearness to large numbers of technical experts. (*Ibid.*, pp. 2-3.)

The government is an important consumer of these SMA products. Distribution is apparently largely by truck with railroads a poor second. (Federal Reserve Bank of Boston, 1956b, p. 4.)

Ship and boat building and repairing: Although shipyards are important, they play a subordinate role in the Boston SMA's economy. Quincy, Mass., is the major shipbuilding site in New England with its yards equipped with ways, wharves, foundries and other facilities for the construction of all types of naval and merchant vessels. With the recent advent of nuclear-powered ships, the Fore River Shipyard in Quincy has taken on added significance. In addition, the port of Boston has ample facilities for repairing vessels of all sizes. Most New England plants are now "engaged chiefly in the manufacture of small ships, yachts, torpedo boats, schooners, and motorboats, in which speed is a significant factor." (Jones and Darkenwald, 1954, p. 468.)

Professional equipment and supplies: The products of this industry, which include mechanical measuring instruments, optical instruments and supplies, and medical instruments and supplies, are probably distributed to a broad national market.

Printing, publishing, and allied industries: In the emergence of book and periodical publishing in America during the nineteenth century New York became the center (Alexandersson, 1956, p. 86), but Boston has maintained an active position in book printing and publishing. (Federal Reserve Bank of Boston, 1953b, p. 2.) In addition to books, which are distributed nationally, one of the newspapers has an Area C distribution (*Encyclopedia Americana,* 1953, vol. 4, p. 295) and greeting cards are probably distributed to a national or broad subnational market.

Paperboard containers and boxes: Paperboard boxes are the major product of this industry, and the SMA and hinterland manufacturers of such products as shoes and clocks no doubt provide important markets. Distribution to Area C markets was not determined.

Miscellaneous paper and pulp products: Distribution was not determined.

Rubber products: Distribution of rubber footwear produced in the SMA (McCarty, 1940, p. 572; Moody's Investors Service, 1950a, p. 1850) is no doubt to a national market, since "the rubber footwear industry is concentrated in the shoe manufacturing district of New England, with Massachusetts as the leading state." (Alexandersson, 1956, p. 80.) In addition, rubber and cotton hose and belting as well as a general line of mechanical rubber goods are produced in the SMA. Distribution is apparently to a national market since sales offices are located in a number of Area C cities. (Moody's Investors Service, 1950a, p. 84.)

Leather: tanned, curried, and finished: About 80 per cent of the leather industry's output is used by shoe manufacturers. (Alderfer and Michl, 1957, p. 458.) The shoe producers located in the SMA and in the hinterland are important markets. Furthermore, other leather products are produced in these areas and form markets for the outputs of the SMA's tanneries. In addition, markets in C areas are probably found for some of the specialized leathers produced in the SMA. The declining markets of the leather industry have been attributed to the growing use of leather substitutes—cloth, rubber, and plastics. (*Ibid.,* p. 469.)

Watches, clocks, and clockwork-operated devices: National markets are no doubt served. Foreign competition in the assembling of movements is an important factor in the watch segment of the industry. (Federal Reserve Bank of Boston, 1953a, pp. 7-8.) Recent shifts in this industry were noted above.

Footwear, except rubber: New England and, presumably, Boston shoe manufacturers concentrate in the production of men's and women's shoes with juvenile, infants', and babies' shoes relatively less important. (Federal Reserve Bank of Boston, 1953d, p. 2.) The industry in New England faces the problem of the growth of new competitive areas in the South and West and the shift of markets toward the West. (United States Council of Economic Advisers, Committee on the New England Economy, 1951, p. 173.) The organization of the industry in New England presents problems since there is a "predominance of small firms operating plants of less than optimum size. This has been particularly true in Massachusetts, where the industry got its start in the days when optimum size was much smaller than it is today." (*Ibid.*, p. 179.) Furthermore, there are marketing problems associated with the highly seasonal pattern of production and the failure of the small firms to get their products into the most effective marketing channels.

Leather products, except footwear: Handbags and small leather goods, luggage, and industrial leather belting are among the products of this industry. Distribution is assumed to be sub-national.

Non-local services: According to McCarty (1940, p. 577), Boston is the "focal point for commerce and finance" in New England. Its wholesale and banking facilities serve much of New England, although it should be noted that southern New England is in some respects more closely linked to New York City than to Boston. (Green, 1955, p. 299.)

> Boston is the principal port of New England and the commercial capital of one of the most heavily populated and highly industrialized regions of the United States. The New England area, all of which, except the southern part of Connecticut, can be considered part of Boston's economic hinterland, comprises only about 2 per cent of the country's area, but contains over 6 per cent of the population and draws nearly 7 per cent of the national income. (United States Board of Engineers for Rivers and Harbors and Maritime Administration, 1957, No. 3, p. 239.)

The port of Boston is closer to northwest Europe than other major eastern ports. However, the port primarily serves the New England portion of the nation, since the competing ports of New York, Philadelphia, and Baltimore are closer to the Middle West. Because rail rates are higher than water rates, it is cheaper to ship from inland points through the port of Philadelphia or Baltimore than through Boston. Thus McCarty (1940, p. 578) observes that the port "handles comparatively little of the nation's wheat export," and that Boston's handicap in the shipment of goods produced in the Middle West and the lack of bulky goods produced in New England for shipment combine to minimize shipments from the port. For example, in 1955 foreign imports amounted to roughly 4.6 million tons, but exports to only 0.5 million. (United States Board of Engineers for Rivers and Harbors and Maritime Administration, 1957, No. 3, p. 241.) Recently, "more than three-fourths of all New England-made foreign exports have been shipped through the Port of New York," although hope for improvement of the Boston port's position is seen in the equalization in the early 1950's of the export grain rates of railroads. (National Planning Association, Committee of New England, 1954, pp. 468-69.)

The major foreign imports and exports are described below:

> Over 77 per cent of the import tonnage originated in the Caribbean area. . . .
>
> The principal import commodities were petroleum and petroleum products, sugar, iron ore, gypsum, wood and paper, textile products and fibres, vegetable food products other than sugar, crude rubber, and chemicals and chemical products.
>
> . . . Over 41 per cent of the export tonnage was destined for the United Kingdom and Ireland. Ports in the Netherlands, Belgium, West Germany range received 17 per cent. About 24 per cent was shipped to the Mediterranean area.
>
> Leading commodities were iron and steel scrap and grain, which accounted for 51 per cent, respectively, of all exports. Newsprint, other paper products, chemicals and chemical products, rubber manufactures, animal products such as dried milk, animal oils, and leather manufactures, and industrial machinery were also important in the export trade. (United States Board of Engineers for Rivers and Harbors and Maritime Administration, 1957, No. 3, pp. 244-45.)

Noncontiguous and intercoastal trade were relatively small, and involved receipts of sugar from Puerto Rico, canned and dried fruits from Hawaii, and lumber, shingles, and canned fruits and vegetables from the Pacific coast. (*Ibid.*, p. 246.) Domestic trade with Atlantic and Gulf coast ports was important and also involved receipts far in excess of shipments:

> Bituminous coal to a total of 2,016,530 tons, and 1,016,393 tons of petroleum products were the leading commodities inbound from other Atlantic ports. In the outbound Atlantic coastwise category petroleum products totaling 618,836 tons were most important.
>
> Petroleum, both crude and processed, was dominant in the trade

> with Gulf ports. Over 7,000,000 tons of Boston's receipts from the Gulf area consisted of various petroleum products. (*Ibid.*, p. 247.)

As the figures above indicate, the SMA and New England in general are dependent on fuel inputs from distant sources. "The almost total lack of fuel resources in New England has inevitably raised the delivered prices of most types of fuel above the national average." (National Planning Association, Committee of New England, 1954, p. 188.) This conclusion may not apply to fuel oil.

Boston serves the nation's wool industry by providing an important wool market and there are significant relationships between the marketing of wool and the SMA's financial institutions:

> The Boston wool market is the largest in the United States and second only to London in world importance. It is no mere pit in which wool is bought and sold. For when one speaks of the Boston wool market, one thinks of huge warehouses, sufficient in size to store an entire year's clip of wool in the United States, of dealers and brokers, and of Boston bankers who finance most of the wool manufacturers of the United States. (McCarty, 1940, p. 570.)

Specific profile services are indicated below:

Banking and credit agencies: The Boston Federal Reserve District includes all of New England except for one county in Connecticut. However there is evidence that "major cities in the area look toward the financial capital of the country rather than to the regional center at Boston." (Green, 1955, p. 297.) Nevertheless Boston's banks serve much of New England as well as borrowers throughout the nation. McCarty (1940, pp. 579-580) discerns a connection between conservative credit policies and separation of ownership from management in New England and the region's decline. In an effort to obtain new industries and more diversification of industry, Boston's bankers, "formerly willing to finance only certain types of industries, now seek more diversified portfolios." (*Ibid.*, p. 577.) Whether New England's credit institutions are adequately supplying capital for new and smaller industries is apparently questionable. It has been claimed that "Boston banking interests have deliberately discouraged investments in New England and promoted emigration of capital to other regions." (National Planning Association, Committee of New England, 1954, p. 439; see also pp. 397-441.) For whatever reason, it does seem to be true that Boston banks make extensive non-local investments.

Security and commodity brokerage, and investment companies: Boston is outstanding as the location of open-ended investment companies. In June 1953, there were twenty-nine such companies in Boston and 83 significant companies in the rest of the United States and Canada. (Fiduciary Publishers, 1954, pp. 129-132.) "The Boston-domiciled open-end companies comprise over 40% of the industry, as measured by net assets." (National Planning Association, Committee of New England, 1954, pp. 415-416.) These companies are of limited direct benefit to the financial requirements of the SMA or its hinterland since

> the investment companies must confine their operations to trading existing or new issues of the better stocks. They also tend to stress the selling end of their business more than the investing end, and this works against new ventures. (*Ibid.*, p. 416.)

A national market is no doubt served by these organizations since "Many open-end investment companies now have nationwide sales programs." (Federal Reserve Bank of Boston, 1956a, p. 3.) The SMA has pioneered in the recent development of venture-capital organizations.

> There are only a few such organizations in the United States, and most of them are but a few years old. Most of them are also "private" organizations, based upon the wealth of an individual or family. The two New England venture-capital organizations are located in Boston. (National Planning Association, Committee of New England, 1954, p. 417.)

In addition, the SMA no doubt provides a wide array of security and investment services. Massachusetts is the fifth ranking state in the nation in the number of shareholders and shares held in publicly owned companies. (*Ibid.*, p. 404.) The total New England region also ranks high and no doubt the SMA's brokers have important hinterland functions.

Advertising: Boston's important position with respect to much of New England suggests that advertising organizations in the SMA serve hinterland as well as local businesses.

Miscellaneous professional and related services: The SMA is "one of the leading research and development centers in the Nation" (United States Department of Labor, 1957, p. 118), and this industry has contributed greatly to the development of new industries in the SMA and the hinterland. Two of the SMA's educational institutions are among the national leaders in research expenditures. (National Planning Association, Committee of New England, 1954, p. 579.) Although much of the research is under federal sponsorship, facilities are also available for industrial services.

State public administration: Boston is the state capital and consequently performs administrative functions for Massachusetts.

Insurance: Boston is one of the most important insurance centers in the nation with the head offices of many national companies. (See for example, Moody's Investors Service, 1950c, pp. 1077, 1096, 1121, 1141, 1478, 1489.)

Hospitals: Boston has an unusually large percentage of its population engaged in medical services. With some of the outstanding hospitals in the nation located in the SMA, services are probably rendered to the New England hinterland as well as the local population.

Educational services, private: A large number of educational institutions are located in the SMA. They no doubt vary from student bodies composed primarily of residents of the SMA to schools such as Massachusetts Institute of Technology and Harvard University which draw students from the entire nation and foreign countries. Many of these institutions perform research functions which are of benefit to the SMA:

> During the last few years a whole new generation of research-based enterprises has come into existence, frequently to exploit new scientific and engineering knowledge acquired during World War II. A large number of such companies . . . have settled and grown near their spawning ground in Cambridge, Massachusetts. (National Planning Association, Committee of New England, 1954, p. 559.)

SUMMARY: BOSTON

Our analysis confirms the impression that the "outstanding characteristic of this area is its diversity; virtually every kind of economic activity is represented to some extent." (United States Department of Labor, 1957, p. 118.) Many of the profile industries were established in the SMA at a time when the distribution of raw materials or markets was considerably different from the present and when skilled workers were more important. As a consequence the SMA, like much of New England, has been faced with an increasing difficulty in maintaining its competitive position in a number of industries which are more suitably located elsewhere. Its competitive position is best in those industries where the transportation costs of raw materials and finished products are a relatively small part of the production costs and where highly skilled labor and technical knowledge are important. The SMA performs important non-local services which vary in distribution from national (e.g., insurance) to regional (e.g., wholesaling).

PITTSBURGH

SMA consists of Allegheny, Beaver, Washington, and Westmoreland Counties, Pennsylvania
1950 population: central city, 676,806; SMA, 2,213,236
Important location feature: port at the junction of the Allegheny, Monongahela and Ohio rivers
Other important feature: Federal Reserve Branch city

INPUTS AND SUPPLY AREAS
FOR PITTSBURGH'S PROFILE INDUSTRIES

Coal mining: The SMA "lies at the heart of the largest and most productive coal field on the continent" (*Encyclopedia Americana,* 1953, vol. 22, p. 126). Nearly one-third of the bituminous coal mined in Pennsylvania in 1954 was accounted for by the 23 million tons produced within the SMA. (Federal Reserve Bank of Cleveland, 1957b, p. 5.) Because SMA's generally do not specialize in extractive industries, the distribution within the SMA of the labor force in this industry is considered. Of roughly 30,000 men employed in the SMA's coal mining industry, less than 1,000 reside in the city of Pittsburgh. Roughly 7,500 reside in Allegheny County outside the central city. Washington and Westmoreland Counties account for the majority with approximately 13,000 and 8,000, respectively. Thus mining employment in the SMA is concentrated away from the central city.

Blast furnaces, steel works, and rolling mills: Among thirteen selected blast furnace locations, Pittsburgh enjoys the lowest assembly cost for coal—one of the major inputs in the steel industry. (Alderfer and Michl, 1957, p. 67.) Prior to the development of the by-product coking process, the unusual suitability of nearby Connellsville coal for coking, together with ready accessibility of cheap coal by river transport facilities, was a factor favoring growth of the Pittsburgh steel industry. (Zimmermann, 1951, p. 661.) In the early days, the industry was based on local iron ores, and Pittsburgh's rolling mills received pig iron by river from furnaces near the coal mines. However, changes in the nature of the market for pig iron forced the Pittsburgh rolling mills to control the production of pig iron, and after 1860 blast furnaces were built in connection with local rolling mills. These plants turned to the high grade ore of the Lake Superior region. The city's advantage with respect to nearby coal supplies and relatively low freight costs for ore shipments via Lake Erie led to the industry's first

Table 42. Industrial Profile, Pittsburgh: 1950

Category and industry	Location quotient	Per cent of employed labor force	Inputs primarily from area:	Outputs primarily to area:
(1) (*Primary resource extractors; production for non-final market*)				
Coal mining	4.03	3.7	A	A, C
(4) *Second stage resource users; production for non-final market*				
Blast furnaces, steel works, and rolling mills	14.01	16.5	A, B, C	A, B, C
Other primary iron and steel industries	1.90	1.0	A, B	A?
Miscellaneous petroleum and coal products	6.00	0.3	A, B	A, B, C
(6) *Resources of indirect significance; production for non-final market*				
Primary nonferrous industries	2.16	0.8	C	A, B, C
Fabricated metal industries	1.82	2.7	A	A, C
Electrical machinery, equipment, and supplies	2.73	3.8	A	C
Railroad and miscellaneous transportation equipment	5.00	0.5	A	C
Glass and glass products	7.72	1.9	A, B, C?	C
Pottery and related products	2.70	0.3	A, B, C	C
Professional equipment and supplies	2.14	0.5	A?	C
(9) *Service industries; non-local*	0.94	12.0	*	B, C
Railroads and railway express service	1.62	(4.0)	*	C
Total in profile industries	...	44.0	...	...

* Inputs other than labor not considered.

becoming integrated in Pittsburgh. (McLaughlin, 1938, pp. 304-5.) At present, iron ore is received from Great Lakes sources by such Lake Erie ports as Conneaut, Ohio, where "iron ore, the predominant commodity received, is transshipped by rail to the Pittsburgh steel district and intermediate points" (United States Board of Engineers for Rivers and Harbors, 1951, No. 2, p. 44). Although railroad transportation facilities between Lake Erie and the Pittsburgh SMA are unusually efficient, it costs more to move ore the distance of roughly 100 miles from Lake Erie to the SMA than to move it between Lake Superior sources and Lake Erie ports. (Alderfer and Michl, 1957, p. 65.) Because of changes in technology, scrap has increased rapidly in importance (Zimmermann, 1951, p. 665) and the SMA apparently obtains this input from an extensive region that includes Area C sources. The cost of scrap is consequently relatively high "in spite of the tendency for deficit areas to minimize their use of scrap" (Isard and Capron, 1949, p. 124). The increasing importance of scrap is a factor in the rise of competing steel centers:

> The relative decline of Pittsburgh has, in part, been due to the persistent scarcity of scrap. Pittsburgh's productive capacity has always far exceeded its consumptive ability. Consequently, its local market supplies a smaller proportion of scrap in terms of production needs than do other areas. Chicago, on the other hand, has greater accessibility to scrap supplies. As a result, the price (including transport expense) which Chicago pays for scrap is significantly lower than is Pittsburgh's. This partially explains the relatively greater growth of Chicago. The sizable development of steel production in the Detroit area in recent years is another instance where a large steel-consuming market and a large scrap-originating site have coincided. (Isard, 1948, p. 215.)

The primary source of limestone is Pennsylvania. (Chapman, 1953, p. 21.) The most important Pennsylvania producer in 1952 was a county adjoining the SMA. (United States Bureau of Mines, Regional Mineral Industry Divisions, 1955, p. 801.) According to Chapman (1953, p. 33) fluxing materials are "usually available at low cost to all iron and steel centers." Consequently, this is probably not a primary factor in Pittsburgh's competitive position. Alloys no doubt are obtained from a number of domestic and foreign sources.

Other primary iron and steel industries: Inputs are presumably from local and hinterland blast furnaces and mills.

Miscellaneous petroleum and coal products: Coal sources, as noted earlier, are located in the SMA and the hinterland. While petroleum refining takes place in the SMA, it is surmised that Pittsburgh's standing in this industry is due to coal by-products obtained in coking operations for the steel industry. Although Pittsburgh's rise to prominence in the steel industry was based to an important degree on the suitability of its coal for beehive coke ovens, the SMA adopted the process which produced more coke as well as by-products—although not as rapidly as other parts of the nation. (Murphy and Murphy, 1937, pp. 492-494.) It is said that a single by-product coke plant in the Pittsburgh area uses nearly one per cent of the world's total coal production. Most of the by-product coke ovens in the nation are built by a Pittsburgh company. (*Encyclopedia Americana,* vol. 22, 1953, pp. 126-127.)

Primary nonferrous industries: It is assumed that zinc ore is currently obtained from Area C sources since, in the middle thirties, the tri-state area of Kansas, Missouri, and Oklahoma supplied the zinc inputs. (Murphy and Murphy, 1937, p. 490.) Copper sources were not determined and it is assumed they are outside the hinterland. Bronze and brass inputs presumably are from local and Area C sources. The SMA, headquarters for the largest aluminum company in the nation, has a large aluminum fabricating plant. The importance of the SMA in the development of the industry is indicated below:

> The first [electrolytic] plant was erected in Pittsburgh, but it was only a few months before it was moved to New Kensington [within the SMA]. . . . After aluminum was produced commercially a market for the new metal had to be developed so the producers turned to kitchen utensils, tubing, and metal sheets. Aluminum decreased in price as its production and uses increased.
>
> At the time the aluminum industry was founded, the securing of capital was most important in establishing its location. As long as the industry remained small the bauxite ore could be shipped from Arkansas and there was sufficient electrical power for its conversion into metal. However, as production increased more ore was needed and greater quantities of electricity were used, so the industry is installing its new operations outside the district . . . where cheap water power is available. No longer is ore converted to metal in New Kensington and the plant is entirely a fabricating unit. (Miller, 1943, p. 400.)

Aluminum inputs are from Area C sources. (See map, Alderfer and Michl, 1957, p. 111.)

Fabricated metal industries: Inputs are no doubt primarily from the SMA itself since "Steel rolling mills in the Pittsburgh area turn out every line of steel products, ranging from heavy structural components to fine wire." (Federal Reserve Bank of Cleveland, 1957b, p. 4.) Garland (1955, p. 64) and Alexandersson (1956, p. 43) have emphasized the tendency for satellite steel-using industries to be attracted to the suppliers of their basic materials, leading to a situation in which all industries in a particular production chain may be found within a single community.

Electrical machinery, equipment, and supplies: Steel and iron inputs presumably are largely obtained from sources within the SMA. A copper rolling mill is operated by one of the companies in this industry

(Moody's Investors Service, 1950a, p. 2709) and other nonferrous metal inputs are presumably obtained in part from local producers discussed above.

Railroad and miscellaneous transportation equipment: Access to steel and properly trained labor are major factors in the location of producers of rolling stock. (Alexandersson, 1956, p. 58.) Metal inputs for the production of railroad equipment are no doubt provided by local sources.

Glass and glass products: The importance of cheap fuel as a determinant of the location of the glass industry is indicated by Miller (1943, pp. 400-401):

> The natural resources of Pittsburgh and its vicinity offered unusual advantages for the development of this infant industry. The abundance of glass sand and wood for charcoal as the first fuel, and later coal on the Monongahela River resulted in the centering of the glass industry along this valley. An important glass industry did not develop along the Allegheny until natural gas became the principal furnace fuel. The discovery of natural gas permitted the glass industry to spread throughout the region.

Recently, gas sources from the Midcontinent Field have become available by pipeline, although this does not promise to increase significantly the size of the industry in the area. (Alexandersson, 1956, p. 62.) Sand inputs are presumably from sources in Areas A and B.

Pottery and related products: The SMA is on the fringe of the major pottery producing region centered in East Liverpool, Ohio. Fuel inputs are presumably from local sources and clay inputs are apparently obtained from local, hinterland, and Area C sources. (Alexandersson, 1956, p. 60.)

Professional equipment and supplies: Metal inputs are presumably obtained from local producers.

OUTPUTS AND SERVICE AREAS OF PITTSBURGH'S PROFILE INDUSTRIES

Coal mining: As indicated earlier, the SMA is a major producer of bituminous coal. In addition to the considerable amount of coal consumed by local industries, the SMA sends coal to Area C users by boat and rail. Shipments of coal by rail from Pittsburgh to lower Lake Erie ports balance the large quantities of ore moved from these ports to the SMA. With the addition of steel products sent by rail to these Lake ports, the net effect is unusually low cost railroad transportation. (Zimmermann, 1951, p. 663.)

Blast furnaces, steel works, and rolling mills: The importance of steel is indicated by the SMA's percentage of national capacity. "Blast furnaces account for about 17½ per cent of national pig iron capacity; steel furnaces in the area represent about 15 per cent of the nation's basic steel capacity." (Federal Reserve Bank of Cleveland, 1957b, p. 4.) Located within the SMA are the headquarters of the largest steel producer as well as a number of other producers of national importance. In addition to the important local market provided by the metal-using industries discussed below, other local industries such as non-electrical machinery are no doubt significant.

Pittsburgh's position with respect to Area C markets has declined in relative terms, although the SMA still has important non-local markets. The factors leading to a decrease in the SMA's proportion of the national production of steel have been examined by a number of writers. In addition to the changes in coking technology and the increase in importance of scrap as an input, the now defunct Pittsburgh-plus system has received considerable attention as a factor maintaining the SMA's position in the industry at a level above that which would have been produced had the competitive factor been the only one at work. (Alderfer and Michl, 1957, p. 66; Adams, 1950, pp. 148-98.) Of importance in the working of this system was the existence of a Pittsburgh based company which dominated the production of steel in the United States. However, caution in estimating the significance attributed to this factor in the steel industry of Pittsburgh is suggested by Isard and Capron (1949, pp. 131-133):

> Theoretically, the choice of a particular pricing system—whether an f.o.b. mill, a single basing-point, or a multiple basing-point with or without differentials—has little impact upon the location of basic steel capacity. The fundamental problem is to select the location that minimizes the cost of production, including the freight charge to the market. . . .
>
> The basing-point system may only have veiled a partially obsolete locational structure which an f.o.b. mill system would have brought to light.
>
> The presence of inefficiency as well as a rigid entrepreneurship within the industry can greatly modify the trends we have suggested —namely, relative if not absolute decline of the western Pennsylvania and Youngstown area steel industry and growth of the Detroit area, eastern seaboard, and Pacific Coast. The iron and steel industry, burdened with a huge investment in plant facilities and surrounded by a host of dependent industries, is a notably inflexible one. Historically, strong resistance to change of location has always been experienced.

Isard and Capron (1949, p. 124) note the decline in Pittsburgh's eastern markets caused by the superior locations of steel producers in Bethlehem, Buffalo, and Baltimore. The westward movement of steel markets has been a factor in Chicago's challenge of Pittsburgh's position.

Other primary iron and steel industries: It is assumed that local metal-using industries comprise a major market for the foundry products and forgings produced by these industries.

Miscellaneous petroleum and coal products: Creosote, phenol, cresol, and other by-product coke chemicals are produced in the SMA. (Moody's Investors Service, 1950a, p. 2666.) These products presumably have important local, hinterland, and Area C markets.

Primary nonferrous industries: Zinc, sheet copper, brass, bronze, and aluminum basic shapes are produced in the SMA. (Federal Reserve Bank of Cleveland, 1957b, p. 4.) Zinc produced in the SMA has important markets in western Pennsylvania because it is used in galvanized wire. The market in western Pennsylvania for the sulphuric acid obtained in zinc smelting was a factor in the SMA's selection as a site for smelting. (Murphy and Murphy, 1937, p. 490.) The markets for the other nonferrous metals probably range from local to Area C in distribution.

Fabricated metal industries: Products of this category—including cutlery, hand tools, hardware, plumbing fixtures and fittings, structural metal products, springs, bolts, nuts, and rivets, among others (*1947 Census of Manufactures*)—no doubt vary from local to national distribution.

Electrical machinery, equipment, and supplies: Specific products are indicated below:

> Included in this group is the largest single plant in the greater Pittsburgh area, which produces switchgear, generators, and other electrical equipment for industrial use. Other plants employing more than 1,000 people produce transformers, electric cables and wire, radios and record-players, and electric control devices. Switchgear, pole line hardware and electric insulation are manufactured at two somewhat smaller plants. (Federal Reserve Bank of Cleveland, 1957b, p. 4.)

The location of the offices and main plants of the nation's second most important electrical producer makes "electrical machine manufacturing the most important of the secondary metal products industries in the steel city." (Alexandersson, 1956, p. 48.) Facilities for the production of large electrical equipment, such as generators, and the research laboratories are located in the SMA. (Moody's Investors Service, 1950a,

p. 2709.) However household appliances are largely produced by this company in other parts of the nation. Alexandersson (1956, p. 48) also notes a similar distribution of facilities for the other major national electrical producer which has its headquarters in Schenectady, New York.

> Often the two big companies develop new products at their home plants but manufacture them elsewhere, frequently in smaller centers affording lower taxes, cheaper sites, lower labor costs, or a combination of these advantages. (*Ibid.*, pp. 48-49.)

In illustrating such decentralization, McLaughlin (1938, p. 220) cites "the transfer . . . often soon after experimental work had turned out satisfactory products, of the making of electric refrigerators and electric household appliances from the East Pittsburgh plant to the plant in Mansfield, Ohio." The distribution of the products of this industry is to national and international markets.

Railroad and miscellaneous transportation equipment: Railroad air brake equipment, train signaling and control equipment are included in the railroad equipment manufactured in the SMA. (Moody's Investors Service, 1950a, p. 2435.) They are distributed to national markets.

Glass and glass products: Plate glass is the most important glass product of the SMA. (Miller, 1943, p. 401.) Factors leading to the concentration of this industry and to large facilities are indicated below:

> The flat glass branch is characterized by very large plants, among the largest of any manufacturing industry. . . . The economy of large-scale production partly explains why the glass industry is geographically concentrated in spite of its bulky and relatively cheap products made from raw materials and fuels, available in scattered localities all over the continent. (Alexandersson, 1956, p. 62.)

Window glass, tableware, decorative glass, bottles, and jars also are manufactured. (Miller, 1943, p. 401.) The factors which lead to a concentration of glass production also lead to wide-spread distribution and, no doubt, the SMA's markets are at least sub-national.

Pottery and related products: It is assumed that pottery products are distributed to a large market primarily in Area C.

Professional equipment and supplies: Automatic temperature controls are manufactured in the SMA and research facilities are also located in Pittsburgh. (Moody's Investors Service, 1950a, p. 1138.) Distribution of these products is no doubt national.

Non-local services: Important non-local functions are performed by Pittsburgh. McCarty (1940, p. 549) indicates that its trade area includes "the coal areas of Pennsylvania and West Virginia as well as a considerable section of southeast Ohio." Although financial functions are not reflected clearly in the employment statistics, the SMA is also a major banking center with a high proportion of non-local loans which are distributed nationally. (See chapter 5.) The location in Pittsburgh of the headquarters of a number of important national manufacturers indicates that important administrative functions are performed in the SMA for Area C plants. The administrative importance for its hinterland is indicated below:

> Corporations with their main administrative or operating offices in Pittsburgh dominate manufacturing localities in western Pennsylvania, the panhandle of West Virginia, and east central Ohio. In general, these sections make up a homogeneous area specializing in the production of coal, iron and steel, heavy machinery, and glass and clay products. From a broad economic point of view the Wheeling and Youngstown industrial areas form a continuation of the Pittsburgh manufacturing district. With respect to financial control, however, Youngstown is more closely tied to Cleveland than to Pittsburgh. (McLaughlin, 1938, pp. 237-238.)

The location of Pittsburgh at the junction of three navigable rivers has been a key factor in its hinterland relationships. The total waterborne commerce of the port is possibly the highest of any inland port in the country and compares favorably with that of many lake and ocean ports. The Monongahela River gives access to the great coal fields of northern West Virginia, the Allegheny to the oil and coal fields of upper western Pennsylvania, and the Ohio to the Middle West and South, not to mention the Gulf of Mexico and the oceans of the world. (*Encyclopedia Americana,* 1953, vol. 22, p. 126.) Coal accounts for most of the tonnage shipped on all three rivers. (Federal Reserve Bank of Cleveland, 1957b, p. 5.) Sand, gravel, crushed rock, and petroleum products are also important receipts via the Ohio River. Important shipments from Pittsburgh on the Ohio River include rolled and finished steel mill products, bituminous coal, coal-tar products, and petroleum products. (United States Department of the Army, Corps of Engineers, [1956], Part 2, pp. 162-63.) The importance of the river in the early development of Pittsburgh is discussed below:

> At Pittsburgh, river routes and land routes converge. Consequently, the city early became the trading center for western Pennsylvania as well as the fitting-out point for settlers who were moving farther west.

> . . . Much of the great westward movement of population in the latter part of the eighteenth century and during the first half of the nineteenth century was down the Ohio River to the lands in the southern parts of Ohio, Indiana, and Illinois, and the northern part of Kentucky. Most of the early movement of people into the old Northwest Territory after it was released by the proprietor states for settlement came by way of this route. . . . Pittsburgh benefited materially by this population shift. The city became one of the main trade and distribution centers in the New West.
>
> Furthermore, the early importance of manufacturing at Pittsburgh resulted from the fact that its geographic position facilitated the assembly of raw, and partially worked, materials. Its location at the junction of the Allegheny and Monongahela rivers early led to the bringing together at that point of the materials for making hardware and other iron products. (McLaughlin, 1938, pp. 303-304.)

The specific non-local service in which Pittsburgh shows specialization is railroads and railway express service. Five major trunk lines and a large number of switching or terminal lines serve Pittsburgh. (*Encyclopaedia Britannica,* 1955, vol. 17, p. 979.)

> Railroads are an important factor in the economy of the Pittsburgh area because of heavy shipments of such bulky commodities as iron ore and coal into the region. Several important East-West railroad lines converge here. (Federal Reserve Bank of Cleveland, 1957b, p. 5.)

The important railroad interchange of coal and iron ore between Lake Erie and the SMA was discussed earlier. A line between Pittsburgh and New York has "the heaviest traffic in America." (Alexandersson, 1956, p. 93.)

SUMMARY: PITTSBURGH

The iron and steel facilities of the SMA are based on raw materials from local, hinterland, and Area C sources. Many of the profile industries of the SMA depend directly or indirectly on steel and other metal products of the SMA for their major inputs. In addition, the presence of cheap coal and natural gas has attracted industries which are particularly dependent on low-cost fuels. Products of the SMA are distributed to very wide markets, no doubt in many cases national and international. Shifts in technology and the westward movement of population and manufacturing have reduced the SMA's advantages as a steel and iron producer. However its position is still very important and the location of important steel consuming industries in the SMA as well as the considerable investment in plants and facilities has helped maintain its industrial importance.

ST. LOUIS

SMA consists of St. Louis city, St. Louis and St. Charles Counties, Missouri, and Madison and St. Clair Counties, Illinois
1950 population: central city, 856,796; SMA, 1,681,281
Important location feature: port on Mississippi River
Other important location feature: Federal Reserve Bank city

INPUTS AND SUPPLY AREAS FOR ST. LOUIS' PROFILE INDUSTRIES

Meat products: The movement of the meat packers westward has benefited the SMA. (Alexandersson, 1956, p. 87.) In 1950 the public stockyards ranked first in hogs, third in calves, sixth in cattle, and ninth in sheep and lambs. (United States Department of Agriculture, Production and Marketing Administration, 1951, pp. 7-9.) In the late 'twenties, Missouri, southern Illinois, Arkansas, Mississippi, and western Tennessee compromised the supply area for hogs and cattle. (Duddy and Revzan, 1931, pp. 16, 26.)

Beverage industries: Barley, an important input for breweries, is grown extensively in the northern spring wheat region in the Dakotas and Minnesota (Jones and Darkenwald, 1954, p. 259) and presumably such sources are used. Rice is grown in the United States as a highly localized commercial crop. One of the few areas is in eastern Arkansas and is, presumably, the source used by the brewers in the SMA. (The most important brewer in the SMA claims to be one of the few United States beer producers using rice as an adjunct grain.)

Other primary iron and steel industries: Coal is mined in southern Illinois, although it is apparently "not of the best quality, for metallurgical purposes" (Dicken, 1949, p. 415); it is used in steel manufacture, blended with West Virginia coal. Iron ore is obtained from Great Lakes sources by rail. (Garland, 1955, p. 116.) Fluorspar is used as a flux and is mined in southern Illinois. (United States Bureau of Mines, Regional Mineral Industry Divisions, 1955, p. 309.) The SMA was, at least in the 'twenties, in a good location for obtaining scrap iron relatively cheaply via rail, and Thomas (1927, pp. 88-89) observed:

> The possibility of East St. Louis' future as a steel center has been considerably enhanced by the discovery of a process whereby coke, suitable for manufacturing steel, can be made from Illinois coal. To

Table 43. Industrial Profile, St. Louis: 1950

Category and industry	Location quotient	Per cent of employed labor force	Inputs primarily from area:	Outputs primarily to area:
(3) *First stage resource users; production for final market*				
Meat products	3.12	1.5	B, C?	C
Beverage industries	4.14	1.5	C	C
(4) *Second stage resource users; production for non-final market*				
Other primary iron and steel industries	2.96	1.5	B, C	A, C
Miscellaneous textile mill products	1.50	0.2	C?	C?
Paints, varnishes, and related products	2.70	0.3	A, C	C?
Miscellaneous chemicals and allied products	2.08	1.8	A, B, C	A, C
Miscellaneous petroleum and coal products	2.80	0.1	B, C	?
(5) *Second stage resource users; production for final market*				
Miscellaneous fabricated textiles	2.13	0.3	C	A
(6) *Resources of indirect significance; production for non-final market*				
Primary nonferrous industries	1.61	0.6	B, C?	A, C
Fabricated metal industries	1.85	2.8	A, C	A, C
Electrical machinery, equipment, and supplies	1.84	2.6	A, C	C
Railroad and miscellaneous transportation equipment	3.27	0.4	A, C	C
Glass and glass products	2.40	0.6	B, C	C
Drugs and medicines	2.10	0.2	A, C	C
Paperboard containers and boxes	2.25	0.4	C	A?
Miscellaneous paper and pulp products	1.59	0.3	B, C	?
(7) *Resources of indirect significance; production for final market*				
Aircraft and parts	1.65	0.8	A, C	C
Footwear, except rubber	4.67	2.2	A, C	C
Leather products, except footwear	1.58	0.2	A, C	?
(9) *Service industries; non-local*	1.28	16.3	*	B, C
Railroads and railway express service	1.59	(3.9)	*	C
Services incidental to transportation	2.29	(0.2)	*	C?
Telegraph (wire and radio)	1.50	(0.1)	*	A, B
Total in profile industries	...	34.6	...	...

* Inputs other than labor not considered.

> the present time but little pig iron has been manufactured exclusively from iron ores. In the past, many attempts by many people have been made to coke Illinois coal for blast furnace use, but none of them proved successful until the perfection of the Roberts Process. . . . This accomplishment represents a step in the rapid development of the steel industries in the Middle West. Apparently steel can be made as cheaply or even more cheaply in St. Louis and Chicago than in Pittsburgh.

Apparently Chicago was able to capitalize on these changes to a greater extent than St. Louis, owing to its advantageous position with respect to Great Lakes ore movements.

Miscellaneous textile mill products: Hats comprise a major product of this industry. Although inputs were not determined, the SMA is an important fur market.

Paints, varnishes, and related products: Linseed oil is produced from flaxseed which is grown primarily in Minnesota and North Dakota. (Zimmermann, 1951, p. 278.) Soybean oil is also used in paints and varnishes and its extensive cultivation in Illinois suggests this as a possible input. Lead and zinc pigments used in paints are obtained from the lead refineries located in the SMA. (United States Bureau of Mines, 1953, p. 692.)

Miscellaneous chemicals and allied products: Large quantities of sulphur are received via the Mississippi River (United States Department of the Army, Corps of Engineers, [1956], Part 2, p. 199); these shipments are from southern sulphur sources for use in the chemical industry. Soybeans are used in the chemical industry and are presumably supplied from Illinois sources. The smelting of nonferrous metals such as lead and zinc in the SMA no doubt leads to important by-products which are utilized by the chemical industry. Fluorspar, which can be used to produce hydrofluoric acid and sodium fluoride, is mined in southern Illinois. (United States Bureau of Mines, 1953, pp. 524, 528.) Missouri was the second largest producer of primary barite in the nation in 1950. Barite is used in producing barium chemicals, lithopone, and drilling mud for oil drilling. By-products in the production of steel also contribute liquors and tars from coke to the chemical industry.

Miscellaneous petroleum and coal products: The extensive refining of petroleum and the location of the southern Illinois coal fields contribute to this industry. Southern Illinois is also a producer of oil. (Alexandersson, 1956, p. 31.)

Miscellaneous fabricated textiles: Textile bags are the most important of the several products in this category. Presumably, such fibers as jute are used in this industry and they are obtained via Mississippi River transportation. (United States Department of the Army, Corps of Engineers [1956], Part 2, p. 199.)

Primary nonferrous industries: Missouri ranked first among states in the production of lead with southeastern Missouri supplying 31 per cent of the domestic output. (United States Bureau of Mines, 1953, p. 686.) Lead is smelted and refined in the SMA from ores obtained from the mines just to the south. (*Ibid.*, p. 692.) The SMA is also important in determining lead prices:

> The two major markets for lead in the United States are New York and St. Louis. Much of the lead produced domestically is sold at prices normally based upon quotation in these markets. Since suspension of trading on the London Metal Exchange in September 1939, the London market has had no direct influence on New York quotations, and the differential between St. Louis and New York prices has remained 0.2 cent a pound, an amount approximating the freight charges between the two cities. (*Ibid.*, p. 697.)

Zinc reduction plants are located in the SMA and use ores mined in the Tri-State area of southeastern Kansas, southwestern Missouri, and northeastern Oklahoma. (*Ibid.*, pp. 1280, 1288-1290.) Also, secondary copper refining is performed in East St. Louis. (Alderfer and Michl, 1950, p. 91.) The input sources are found both within and outside the hinterland.

Fabricated metal industries: The metal inputs for this industry are supplied by the steel and nonferrous metal producers located in the SMA as well as from other sources in the industrial belt.

Electrical machinery, equipment, and supplies: Metal inputs are presumably from local sources as well as producers of parts elsewhere in the industrial belt.

Railroad and miscellaneous transportation equipment: In addition to Area C producers, local metal sources are used. For example, one large producer has its own rolling mills and iron foundry. (Moody's Investors Service, 1950a, p. 1.)

Glass and glass products: At least one source is located in the SMA and a nearby county:

> Sand used in making glass, and for other special purposes, is obtained from outcrops of the St. Peter formation in St. Charles, Jefferson, and St. Louis Counties. Much of it is produced by underground mining methods. (United States Bureau of Mines, Regional Mineral Industry Divisions, 1955, p. 517.)

Fluorspar is used in glass production and is mined in southern Illinois. (*Ibid.*, p. 309.) Barite is used somewhat in the glass industry and is mined in Missouri. (United States Bureau of Mines, 1953, p. 161.) Fuel is a major cost factor in the glass industry (Alexandersson, 1956, p. 61), which uses natural gas from Louisiana.

Drugs and medicines: Historical factors in the development of this industry are indicated below:

> Many of the . . . firms located in the Wholesale District date back to the all-river or river-rail epochs, when there was flourishing business in providing stocks of drugs and medicines for the pioneers who were pushing west. As towns were founded farther west and drug stores established in them, St. Louis wholesale merchants supplied them with drugs because it was practicable to ship goods along the routes taken by the settlers. Furthermore, because of the numerous routes leading to St. Louis, it has been economical to assemble the necessary materials for manufacturing drugs and medicines. The transition from merchant druggists to manufacturing druggists was accomplished relatively early in St. Louis. (Thomas, 1927, pp. 73-74.)

Inputs are probably from the heavy chemical producers and other industries often producing by-products useful to this industry, e.g., meat packers and coke producers. Other inputs and sources were not determined, but it is assumed that inputs are also obtained from Area C.

Paperboard containers; miscellaneous paper and pulp products: Pulp inputs, aside from local straw and waste paper, are from southern sources beyond the hinterland.

Aircraft and parts: Inputs for the airframe assembly operations come from many parts of the industrial East and from airplane parts producers on the West Coast. Parts produced in the SMA have their metal inputs supplied from local and Area C sources.

Footwear, except rubber: The leather inputs are supplied by meat slaughtering operations in the SMA as well as from other Midwestern sources. Inputs vary according to the type and quality of shoe produced.

> For all types and kinds of shoes, however, the labor and leather inputs are by far the most important input (or cost) items. A considerable part of the history of the shoe industry can be explained in terms of the effort to effect savings on these particular cost items. (Freutel, 1951, p. 155.)

The industry in the nation was monopolized by New England when skilled labor was necessary for the production of shoes. However, the development of shoe machinery in the 1860's

> enabled the substitution of unskilled labor inputs for higher priced skilled labor in a number of important processes. There was a growing supply of unskilled labor in the expanding west. This substitution permitted a reduction in shoe prices and a consequent expansion of the market, particularly for cheap shoes. . . .
>
> At about the same time the supply of tanning material in the East was becoming depleted, forcing leather tanners westward into new forest areas and increasing the cost of the leather input to Eastern shoe producers. The Midwest was becoming an increasingly important source of hide supplies, a factor further reducing the cost of the leather input to Midwestern manufacturers.
>
> The development of new tanning processes in the latter part of the nineteenth century . . . encouraged a shift in hide tanning toward the stockyard cities of the Midwest. Thus, technological change in an industry supplying one of its inputs also encouraged the westward shift of the shoe industry. . . .
>
> The large industrial areas of the East with their available supply of skilled labor were strongly attractive to new high-productivity manufacturing industries and the pressure on wage levels was steadily upward. The development of shoe machinery had given the industry considerable mobility, both because . . . the system of leasing machinery on a royalty basis made capital requirements low and new entry relatively easy and because of reduced dependence on the presence of a skilled labor supply. (Freutel, 1951, p. 156.)

Leather products, except footwear: Leather inputs are supplied by sources in the SMA and areas outside the hinterland.

OUTPUTS AND SERVICE AREAS OF ST. LOUIS' PROFILE INDUSTRIES

Meat products: Distribution is to a large market beyond the hinterland. Apparently it is to the economic advantage of the packers to locate in East St. Louis on the eastern side of the Mississippi River. Packers west of the river, i.e., in St. Louis, are in a better position to supply local metropolitan markets.

> It may well be supposed that St. Louis constitutes a large market for meat products. This market is almost completely supplied by West Side packers, and by East Side packers from West Side branches. The major portion of the meat products packed in the East Side are destined to points east of the Mississippi River. . . . the National Stock Yards, East Side, are adjusted to large-scale Eastern business, while the West Side plants are adjusted to a smaller local consumption. (Thomas, 1927, pp. 64-65.)

Beverage industries: The SMA has several breweries with extensive distribution. In 1958, two of the beers produced in the SMA were distributed nationally. However, these companies have established several branches in other parts of the country in order to reduce shipping costs. The future growth of this industry in the SMA is therefore probably limited to meeting demand occasioned by population growth.

Other primary iron and steel industries: Local manufacturing and fabricating provide an important market for products of iron and steel foundries. The fact that steel is shipped via the Mississippi (United States Department of the Army, Corps of Engineers, [1956], Part 2, p. 199) suggests that there are other markets. For example, one SMA steel producer has fabricating plants in Dallas and Beaumont, Texas, and New Orleans. (Moody's Investor Service, 1950a, p. 1172.)

Miscellaneous textile mill products: Hats possibly have a sub-national market.

Paints, varnishes, and related products: It is assumed that distribution is to a sub-national market.

Miscellaneous chemicals and allied products: Presumably local and sub-national markets are important users of the chemicals produced. Alumina, formerly produced in the SMA, was distributed to aluminum reduction plants outside the SMA. The East St. Louis plant "was the leading producer of commercial aluminum trihydrate and other special aluminas not to be reduced to metal." (United States Bureau of Mines, 1953, p. 175.) Other chemicals manufactured for medicinal and pharmaceutical purposes (Moody's Investors Service, 1954, p. 1266) probably have important local and sub-national markets. Inorganic industrial chemicals are also probably distributed to local and sub-national consumers.

Miscellaneous petroleum and coal products: Distribution of these products was not determined.

Miscellaneous fabricated textiles: The local clothing industry is important (Alexandersson, 1956, p. 72) and probably provides the major market for fabricated textiles. Probably the textile bags manufactured in the SMA are used for packaging by the grain mills and processors located there.

Primary nonferrous industries: Local metal fabricators, machinery manufacturers, transportation equipment producers, and other industries in the SMA are important markets. The important position which the SMA and portions of the hinterland have in the domestic production of lead and zinc suggests that there are also significant markets beyond the hinterland for these metals.

Fabricated metal industries: The variety of products produced in this category includes tin cans and tinware, cutlery, hand tools and other hardware, boiler shop products, metal stampings, lighting fixtures, and wirework, among others (*1947 Census of Manufactures*). It is assumed that the SMA, located on the edge of the manufacturing belt, is in a good position for supplying hinterland, southern, and southwestern markets in addition to its own local consumers.

Electrical machinery, equipment, and supplies: Industrial electrical apparatus is probably distributed to a sub-national market. All types of electrical motors are manufactured for use in refrigerators, washing machines, phonographs, and other appliances (Moody's Investor Service, 1950a, p. 265) as well as for general industrial purposes.

Railroad and miscellaneous transportation equipment: The SMA is well situated for this industry with a large number of railroads located in the area. Products include passenger and freight cars, diesel electric motor cars, city and interurban electric railway cars, and general railway supplies. (Moody's Investor Service, 1950b, pp. 2904, 1.) Markets are extensive, although possibly varying according to the item.

Glass and glass products: Glass containers are produced in the SMA by a branch of at least one large national producer. (United States Department of Labor, 1957, p. 166.) This suggests that a sub-national market is possibly served.

Drugs and medicines: Distribution is probably to sub-national and national markets since "light chemical industries, exemplified by pharmaceutical preparations, make expensive products relative to weight and can locate themselves with regard to the national market." (Alexandersson, 1956, p. 73.)

Paperboard containers and boxes: The distribution of paper boxes was not determined, although the SMA no doubt uses an important portion of the output.

Miscellaneous paper and pulp products: The market for envelopes and other products was not determined.

Aircraft and parts: In 1950, airplanes, helicopters, guided missiles, and jet engines were produced for national use. (Moody's Investors Service, 1950a, p. 115.)

Footwear, except rubber: Shoes are distributed to a national market.

> In 1950, five out of the six leading women's shoe advertisers, four out of ten leading men's advertisers, and the first five children's advertisers were St. Louis branded lines. Nearly half of the branded lines made in this country are manufactured in this area. (Freutel, 1951, p. 158.)

Leather products, except footwear: The distribution of luggage and other leather products manufactured in the SMA was not determined.

Non-local services: St. Louis, the leading middle western rail center outside Chicago, has an extensive wholesale trade area. Its wholesale grocery area is identified by McCarty (1940, p. 432) as including the eastern half of Missouri and the southwestern quarter of Illinois; trade areas for other lines of goods are larger. A portion of the Southwest is served by the SMA's wholesalers. (Garland, 1955, p. 115.) However the commercial importance of the SMA declined in competition with Chicago after the expansion of the railroads.

> A hundred years ago her citizens did not doubt that St. Louis would be the principal city of the Midwest, if not of the country. Providentially situated where the trade of the upper Mississippi River terminated and that of the lower river began, St. Louis held a strategic economic position. St. Louis was the northern terminus for the large steamboats of the lower river and the southern terminus for the smaller steamboats of the upper river, and it was here that cargoes were unloaded and reloaded for further shipment. There seemed little doubt that the commerce of the Mississippi Valley would continue in a predominantly north-south direction and that it would hinge on St. Louis. Moreover, it appeared that the future physical expansion of the United States would take place with St. Louis, a natural gateway to the West and Southwest, as the base of operations.
>
> St. Louis' hope of primacy gradually disappeared as technological change removed the great obstacle to the development of Chicago. Possessed of facilities for water transportation eastward, Chicago's chief problem had been to tap the rich territory to the west. The advent of the railroad meant that Chicago, with its more favorable location for east-west rail traffic, could break the commercial hold of St. Louis on the upper Mississippi Valley. Yet despite the economic losses sustained by St. Louis and the impetus given to the growth of Chicago as a result of the Civil War, St. Louis by a narrow margin remained the third largest American city in the census of 1870. During the 1870's, however, as Chicago achieved trade supremacy in the great region to the north, St. Louis was forced to look to the area lying roughly in the quadrant to the southwest for her future markets.
>
> Even thus restricted, St. Louis for more than three decades enjoyed a kind of golden age. . . . St. Louis firms specialized in the manufacture of products much in demand in communities on the rapidly closing frontier, and even as the era of the steamboat merged into the railroad age, the city remained a primary transportation center. But it was as a commercial center, her great full-line, full-service wholesalers distributing an endless stream of goods to the whole of the growing Southwest, that St. Louis could lay claim to pre-eminence. (Robertson, 1954, p. 86.)

The SMA, a Federal Reserve Bank city, is important as a financial center. However, earlier efforts to increase its importance permanently on a national level were unsuccessful; the episode is recounted by Robertson (1954, pp. 88-92):

> In seeking to become a group of ultimate holders of bank reserves, St. Louis banks were taking a calculated risk. At one stroke they were required to double their own cash reserves, and balances due from New York would no longer count in the computation of their reserve position. The main objective was to attract balances from reserve cities, which would presumably grow in number; there was the further likelihood that country banks would increase their accounts as St. Louis became a more important money center.
>
> St. Louis banks, by requesting central reserve city status, hastened their own growth. St. Louis banks in 1887 reported 3 per cent of all bankers' balances held by the central reserve city group; between 1902 and 1914 the figure was never below 9 per cent and was as high as 11 per cent. . . . Both Chicago and St. Louis banks attracted accounts from banks in contiguous states, and a part of the sharp increase in balances at these cities was attributable to the geographic expansion of the country. It seems apparent, however, that both cities, and especially St. Louis, took business away from New York by gaining accounts in the West and Southwest that had formerly been held in New York. . . .
>
> Both Chicago and St. Louis banks behaved under stress like banks of reserve cities rather than of central reserve cities, rapidly drawing down their New York balances, contracting their own loans, and unduly conserving their cash. . . . St. Louis, like the reserve cities, responded to both seasonal and cyclical pressures by turning to New York for funds.
>
> It was commonly thought in 1914 that the establishment of the Federal Reserve System would lead to large declines in bankers' balances. . . . When, with the onset of the depression of 1920-21, bankers' balances fell well below their 1914 levels, it was apparent that St. Louis banks had suffered a much greater loss of correspondent business than had banks generally. There was no longer a legal reason why reserve city banks should keep balances with central reserve city banks if it were not entirely convenient to do so. No full-fledged money market had developed in St. Louis. In the absence of legal compulsion, many banks in the West and Southwest simply found their interests better served by keeping their correspondent balances in one of the rapidly growing new cities of the area.
>
> St. Louis bankers soon came to the realization that central reserve city status was no longer beneficial. Such additional prestige as the classification afforded was far more than offset by a legal reserve requirement of 13 per cent as compared with 10 per cent for banks in reserve cities. . . .
>
> Thus was concluded a little known episode in the financial history of America. In an effort to lift themselves by their own bootstraps to positions of greater power and prestige, St. Louis banks requested central reserve city status when the financial importance of the city did not warrant it. As holders of a portion of the ultimate reserves

of the banking system, St. Louis banks doubtless experienced a growth which they would not have had as a reserve city. The capital resources thus attracted may well have given impetus to the expansion of the Southwest. Yet St. Louis banks were never able to accept responsibility for guiding and aiding the commercial banking system as New York banks were able to do. Because they could not actually supply central reserve city services, there was no reason for them to bear a greater share of the reserve burden than less venturesome banks in sister cities.

The port is an important receiving and shipping center for grains, particularly corn and wheat. Coal and petroleum products are received in extensive amounts and the latter is also shipped out in large quantities. Steel mill products are shipped into and out of the SMA. (United States Department of the Army, Corps of Engineers, [1956], Part 2, pp. 198-200.) The proximity of the SMA to the soybean growing areas probably accounts for extensive shipments of this product. The river location was important in the early development and growth of the SMA. While railroads later diminished the importance of the river, it is still highly significant.

Non-local services in which St. Louis showed specialization are discussed below.

Railroads and railway express service: St. Louis, one of the most important railroad centers in the nation, has 18 railroads linking it with other parts of the country. "Railroads concentrate on the St. Louis metropolitan district and cross the Mississippi at the place where major river traffic from the south extends farthest into the same region." (Garland, 1955, p. 115.) In addition to this important position with respect to Mississippi River freight movements, St. Louis is also "at the junction of east-west and southwest-northeast flow." (Garland, 1955, p. 87.)

Services incidental to transportation: Presumably this activity is related to the extensive railroad and shipping activities in the SMA.

Telegraph (wire and radio): An automatic high-speed message center is located in the SMA to serve Missouri and Illinois. (*Encyclopedia Americana,* 1957, vol. 26, pp. 345, 347.)

SUMMARY: ST. LOUIS

St. Louis is able to draw many important inputs such as lead, coal, oil, livestock, and other agricultural products from its hinterland and this is reflected in its becoming "one of the most diversified manufacturing centers in the United States." (Alexandersson, 1956, p. 100.) Located on the western edge of the manufacturing belt and possessing excellent transportation facilities, the SMA has an active wholesaling trade as well as a good position for supplying markets in Area C with its products.

CLEVELAND

SMA consists of Cuyahoga and Lake Counties, Ohio
1950 population: central city, 914,808; SMA, 1,465,511
Important location feature: port on Lake Erie
Other important feature: Federal Reserve Bank city

INPUTS AND SUPPLY AREAS FOR CLEVELAND'S PROFILE INDUSTRIES

Blast furnaces, steel works, and rolling mills; other primary iron and steel industries: Iron ore is obtained from Lake Superior sources via the Great Lakes. Indicative of Cleveland's excellent location with respect to this input is the fact that not all of the ore received is used locally. It is also sent inland by rail to an extensive area "embracing steel mills, foundries, and paint and pigment manufacturers in the states of Kentucky, Maryland, New Jersey, New York, Ohio, Pennsylvania, and West Virginia." (United States Board of Engineers for Rivers and Harbors, 1951, No. 3, p. 37.) Coking coal is obtained from Pennsylvania and limestone from sources in Ohio and Michigan. (Garland, 1955, p. 134.) Limestone is second only to iron ore in tonnage received by the port of Cleveland. (United States Board of Engineers for Rivers and Harbors, 1951, No. 3, pp. 106-109.)

Synthetic fibers: Rayon is produced in the SMA. The principal raw ingredients are bleached sulphite wood pulp, caustic soda, carbon bisulphide, sulfuric acid, zinc sulphate, and coning oil. (Moody's Investors Service, 1950a, p. 1518.) Presumably many of the chemicals are produced locally and the pulp sources are outside of the hinterland.

Paints, varnishes, and related products: An important input is linseed oil which is produced from flaxseed. Flaxseed is received, at least in part, via water transportation. (United States Board of Engineers for Rivers and Harbors, 1951, No. 3, p. 67.) The major sources of flaxseed in the United States are the Dakotas, Minnesota, and Montana. (Bengtson and Van Royen, 1950, p. 250.)

Miscellaneous chemicals and allied products: Ohio is an important source for salt, particularly brine which is obtained within the SMA and utilized in the production of alkalies. Along with limestone, "alkali plants require cheap fuel. Therefore they are located on the northeastern brines within reach of the coal fields of Ohio, West Virginia, and Pennsylvania." (Zimmermann, 1951, p. 785.) The specific factors in the location of the alkali industry in the SMA serve to illustrate Alexandersson's (1956, p. 75) general statement:

> A relatively new chemical district stretches along the southern shore of Lake Erie with Cleveland as the main center. The advantages for heavy chemical manufacturing are here the same as for the primary iron and steel industry: an excellent market location and low assembly costs for raw materials.

Miscellaneous petroleum and coal products: These products are assumed to be, in part, by-products of the extensive industrial consumption of coal in the SMA from Ohio, Pennsylvania, and West Virginia mines and the refining activities of the SMA.

Primary nonferrous industries: There are numerous nonferrous foundries and forges in this SMA. The SMA has "an aluminum foundry and forge plant which is one of the largest of its industry. Also, there is one large brass mill." (Federal Reserve Bank of Cleveland, 1957a, p. 5.) The sources for these metals were not determined but are assumed to be outside of the hinterland.

Fabricated metal industries: Presumably the SMA itself supplies a considerable portion of the metal inputs of this industry.

Machinery, except electrical: The inputs for this industry are assumed to involve metal products produced in the SMA and other parts of the industrial belt.

Electrical machinery, equipment, and supplies: The inputs are probably supplied by the SMA and other sources in the industrial belt.

Motor vehicles and motor vehicle equipment: Parts such as axles, automobile stampings, lined bearings, engine parts, transmissions, and metal panels are produced in the SMA. (United States Department of Labor, 1957, p. 226; Moody's Investors Service, 1950a, p. 1337.) These parts presumably are made from metals processed in the SMA. In addition, automobiles are assembled and trucks and busses are manufactured in the SMA. (United States Department of Labor, 1957, p. 226.) It is assumed that components from other parts of the industrial belt are used as well as products from the SMA.

Railroad and miscellaneous transportation equipment: Parts and appliances are produced for the railroad industry. (Moody's Investors Service, 1950a, p. 1069.) Metal inputs are presumably from local sources, at least in part.

Professional equipment and supplies: Mechanical measuring instruments and medical instruments and supplies are produced. However, the inputs were not determined.

Paperboard containers and boxes: Sources were not ascertained but are assumed to be outside the hinterland.

Table 44. Industrial Profile, Cleveland: 1950

Category and industry	Location quotient	Per cent of employed labor force	Inputs primarily from area:	Outputs primarily to area:
(4) *Second stage resource users; production for non-final market*				
Blast furnaces, steel works, and rolling mills	2.91	3.4	C	A, B?, C
Other primary iron and steel industries	3.45	1.8	C	A, B?, C
Synthetic fibers	3.11	0.3	A, C	A, C
Paints, varnishes, and related products	6.80	0.7	C	C
Miscellaneous chemicals and allied products	1.60	1.4	B, C	A, C
Miscellaneous petroleum and coal products	1.40	0.1	C	A, C?
(6) *Resources of indirect significance; production for non-final market*				
Primary nonferrous industries	3.39	1.3	C	A, B?
Fabricated metal industries	3.01	4.5	A	C
Machinery, except electrical	2.83	6.5	A, C	C
Electrical machinery, equipment and supplies	2.32	3.3	A, C	C
Motor vehicles and motor vehicle equipment	2.76	4.3	A, C	C
Railroad and miscellaneous transportation equipment	2.27	0.2	A	?
Professional equipment and supplies	1.86	0.4	?	C?
Paperboard containers and boxes	1.70	0.3	C	A?
(7) *Resources of indirect significance; production for final market*				
Aircraft and parts	3.20	1.5	A	C
(9) *Service industries; non-local*	1.00	12.7	*	B
Advertising	1.85	(0.4)	*	?
Total in profile industries	...	42.7	...	...

* Inputs other than labor not considered.

Aircraft and parts: Parts such as bushings and aircraft electric equipment are produced in the SMA. This industry is assumed to use metals produced in the SMA, at least in part.

OUTPUTS AND SERVICE AREAS OF CLEVELAND'S PROFILE INDUSTRIES

Blast furnaces, steel works, and rolling mills: The SMA itself is an important market for iron and steel because of its extensive metal working, fabricating, and machinery industries. Sheet steel is trucked to Michigan and other points in Ohio. (United States Board of Engineers for Rivers and Harbors, 1951, No. 3, p. 103.) Pig iron and other steel products are also shipped via the Great Lakes. (*Ibid.*, p. 109.)

Other primary iron and steel industries: The many producers of metal products in the SMA provide at least part of the market for the foundry and forging industries.

Synthetic fibers: Yarns for tires and textiles are produced. (Moody's Investors Service, 1950a, p. 1518.) Presumably the apparel industry in the SMA uses rayon, and it is assumed that tire producers in Akron and other Ohio cities are users of the rayon produced for the manufacture of tires.

Paints, varnishes, and related products: Since several national producers of paints and varnishes maintain plants in the SMA (Moody's Investors Service, 1950a, pp. 329, 736, 1018), it is assumed that the output is distributed to at least a sub-national market.

Miscellaneous chemicals and allied products: In addition to alkalies, magnesium compounds, chlorine, and sulfuric acid are produced in the SMA. (United States Department of Labor, 1957, p. 226; United States Board of Engineers for Rivers and Harbors, 1951, No. 3, p. 97; United States Bureau of Mines, Regional Mineral Industry Divisions, 1955, p. 727.) The SMA provides an important market for industrial chemicals. Distribution to points outside the local area was not determined except that sulfuric acid is apparently sent by rail to points in Ohio and Pennsylvania. (United States Board of Engineers for Rivers and Harbors, 1951, No. 3, p. 97.)

Miscellaneous petroleum and coal products: Coke oven by-products include tar, sulfate of ammonia, light oil derivatives, gas, and other coal chemicals. (Zimmermann, 1951, p. 491.) The distribution of these products was not determined and it is assumed that they have markets outside of the hinterland as well as in the SMA.

Primary nonferrous industries: In addition to the important metal using markets in the SMA, it is assumed that the products of nonferrous foundries are distributed at least to industrial cities in the hinterland.

Fabricated metal industries: The numerous products of these industries include heating and plumbing equipment, sheet metal work, metal stampings, fabricated wire products, lighting fixtures, bolts, nuts, washers, and rivets, among others (*1947 Census of Manufactures*). They probably range in distribution from sub-national to national markets. It is said that more steel wire, wire nails and bolts and nuts are manufactured in Cleveland than in any other city on earth. (*Encyclopedia Britannica*, 1957, vol. 5, p. 809.) Cleveland's central location for distribution within the industrial belt is probably an important factor in its activity in this industry.

Machinery, except electrical: According to Alexandersson (1956, p. 48), the most important factor affecting the location of the machine manufacturing industry is the market. Cleveland is well situated in the industrial belt for distribution of its machine tools and general industrial machinery. In addition, special industry machinery such as that used in the mining industry is produced. The distribution of these products is probably sub-national and national. Similarly, household appliances probably have wide markets.

Electrical machinery, equipment, and supplies: Motors, generators, electrical control apparatus, communication equipment and other electrical products comprise the outputs of this industry. Presumably such products are distributed to sub-national and national markets.

Motor vehicles and motor vehicle equipment: Trucks and busses are distributed to a national market. Assemblies are probably to a sub-national market. Automobile plants in Michigan and assemblers throughout the United States are probably markets for the components produced in the SMA.

Railroad and miscellaneous transportation equipment: The distribution was not determined.

Professional equipment and supplies: It is assumed that these products have sub-national and national markets.

Paperboard containers and boxes: Distribution was not determined, but it is assumed that the SMA is an extensive user of such products.

Aircraft and parts: Parts produced in the SMA are probably distributed to assembly plants throughout the nation.

Non-local services: Cleveland is the site of the Fourth District Federal Reserve Bank and plays a financial role in the area. However, as a financial center, Cleveland is second to Pittsburgh, a Federal Reserve

Branch city in its district. Cincinnati also has a relatively important function in intra-district financing. The only non-local service showing specialization in terms of employment is advertising; the specific functions performed by the Cleveland advertising industry were not determined. In wholesaling, Cleveland "serves as a commercial, wholesale, and distribution point for the north-central part of Ohio within 50 to 75 miles of Cleveland and for other lake-front cities on Lake Erie." (United States Board of Engineers for Rivers and Harbors, 1951, No. 3, p. 1.) Steamship companies accounting for about 80 per cent of the domestic tonnage in the Great Lakes have headquarters in the SMA. Movements of iron ore and coal between Great Lakes ports is co-ordinated by the Ore and Coal Exchange, which is also located in Cleveland. It is thus possible to increase the efficiency of shipping and railroad facilities by co-ordination of all movements of lake cargo coal and ore. (*Ibid.*, pp. 78-81.) As to the waterborne commerce of Cleveland itself, bulk commodities comprise roughly 75 per cent of the port's tonnage.

> Most of Cleveland's commerce is composed of such bulk commodities as iron and concentrates; bituminous coal and lignite; limestone; and sand, gravel and crushed stone. The location of this important Great Lakes port on the south shore of Lake Erie places it in proximity to the coal fields and to highly productive steel mills and industrial areas; therefore the harbor serves as a natural gateway for the movement of commodities to or from these areas. Movements of petroleum products, automobiles, and manufactured iron and steel articles also contribute greatly to the port's lake traffic. (*Ibid.*, p. 105.)

The port of Fairport, Ohio, is located within the SMA. Its major commerce consists of receipts of limestone and shipments of coal from Pennsylvania, West Virginia, and Ohio to lake markets on either side of the International Boundary. (United States Board of Engineers for Rivers and Harbors, 1951, No. 2, pp. 103, 112.)

SUMMARY: CLEVELAND

Cleveland is highly diversified in manufacturing. These industrial activities are dependent on the iron and steel produced in the SMA from raw materials mined outside of the hinterland. The raw materials can be transported relatively cheaply by water on the Great Lakes and by rail from relatively close sources. The manufactured products of the SMA can then be shipped to the industrial and consumer markets of the urbanized and industrialized belt in which Cleveland is centrally located. McCarty (1940, p. 551) has neatly summarized the city's situation:

> Cleveland stands today in one of the best commercial locations in America. Railroads have come and skirted the lake, placing Cleveland on the busiest transportation route in the country. Lake Superior ores were discovered and Cleveland has become the operating center for three-quarters of all Great Lakes shipping. With ore and coal shipments passing through her harbor, Cleveland has become a strategic crossroads for American commerce. And where such crossroads develop there also grow important commercial cities.

BUFFALO

SMA consists of Erie and Niagara Counties, New York
1950 population: central city, 580,132; SMA, 1,089,230
Important location features: port on Lake Erie, Niagara River, New York State Barge Canal, Welland Canal
Other important feature: Federal Reserve Branch city

INPUTS AND SUPPLY AREAS FOR BUFFALO'S PROFILE INDUSTRIES

Miscellaneous nonmetallic mineral and stone products: "The production of aluminum oxide in the United States and Canada is largely concentrated in the Niagara Falls area. . . . The larger part of the silicon carbide production is also in the Niagara region." (United States Bureau of Mines, 1953, p. 105.) The sources for the aluminum oxide and silicon carbide, while not determined, are probably not in the Buffalo hinterland.

Grain mill products: Buffalo is an important center for the receipt, processing, and transmission of wheat and other grains from the Midwest and Canada. The importance of the transportation cost factor in the location of the grain processing and handling industry in Buffalo is indicated below:

> The growth of Buffalo as a flour milling center was materially aided by certain regulations requiring the railroads to withdraw, from the western millers, the free storage privilege for flour at the city. Milling interests were then faced with the problem of continued milling at Minneapolis and upper Mississippi Valley points and then moving the flour through to New England and areas east of Buffalo, N. Y., and Pittsburgh, Pa., at the higher freight rates inci-

dental to flour shipments than applied to grain, or to move the mills eastward. Therefore, to serve the great eastern markets with a minimum of transportation costs, it was obvious that the grain should be shipped as far east as feasible and there milled into flour for further rail movement. A prerequisite for the port to be selected would be its proximity to the grain producing areas—nearer than the ports on Lake Ontario—so that large grain freighters could make more frequent call. Least distances to such Atlantic Coast exporting ports as New York, Philadelphia, and Baltimore were also important. Buffalo, at the eastern extremity of Lake Erie, was the ideal location to be endowed with ensuing rate economies. (United States Board of Engineers for Rivers and Harbors, 1952, No. 1, pp. 89-90.)

Wheat and other grains are brought into Buffalo along the Great Lakes from sources in the Midwest. Duluth is a particularly important shipping point in the movement of spring wheat to Buffalo. (Nielsen, 1950, p. 213.) Duluth-Superior also sends large quantities of corn, barley, and oats to Buffalo. Chicago sent wheat and corn and Milwaukee wheat in excess of one million bushels during the 1950 season. The Canadian ports of Fort William and Port Arthur also sent considerable quantities of wheat, oats, and rye to Buffalo. (Lake Carriers' Association, 1950, p. 93.) Canadian wheat can be sent without import duties when it is milled under bond for export. (Dicken, 1949, p. 410.)

Blast furnaces, steel works, and rolling mills: Buffalo's steel industry is aided by the economical access to raw materials primarily via lake transportation. Iron ore is shipped cheaply from Lake Superior sources via the Great Lakes. Limestone is also shipped from Great Lakes quarries. Calcite, Michigan, is an important source of fluxing limestone (Garland, 1955, p. 166), although it is not clear whether it is the major source for Buffalo's steel industry. The coal is obtained by water and rail from northern Appalachian sources. (Bengtson and Van Royen, 1950, p. 428.) The additional inputs necessary for the production of ferro-alloys such as ferrotitanium, ferrophosphorous, ferrosilicon—to name a few—were not determined. However, it seems reasonable to assume that they are primarily from the C area.

Other primary iron and steel industries: The inputs are generally the same as that for the steel industry discussed above. Sand, which is used by the foundries, is shipped in by water transportation. (United States Board of Engineers for Rivers and Harbors, 1952, No. 1, p. 36.)

Cement, and concrete, gypsum, and plaster products: Cement is made from about 75 to 80 per cent limestone and 20 to 25 per cent clay or shale. (Zimmermann, 1951, p. 772.) Slag can also be used in cement making. The sources for limestone are quarries along the Great Lakes;

Table 45. Industrial Profile, Buffalo: 1950

Category and industry	Location quotient	Per cent of employed labor force	Inputs primarily from area:	Outputs primarily to area:
(2) ***First stage resource users; production for non-final market***				
Miscellaneous nonmetallic mineral and stone products	7.07	1.1	C?	C
Grain mill products	5.19	1.1	C	B, C
(4) ***Second stage resource users; production for non-final market***				
Blast furnaces, steel works, and rolling mills	5.09	6.0	C	A, C
Other primary iron and steel industries	2.45	1.3	C	A, C
Cement, and concrete, gypsum, and plaster products	1.84	0.3	A, C	C
Synthetic fibers	2.89	0.3	A, C	A, C?
Miscellaneous chemicals and allied products	3.89	3.4	C	A, C
Pulp, paper and paperboard mills	2.34	1.0	C	A?
Miscellaneous petroleum and coal products	4.60	0.2	C	C
(6) ***Resources of indirect significance; production for non-final market***				
Primary nonferrous industries	2.53	1.0	C?	A, C?
Fabricated metal industries (incl. not specified metal)	1.70	2.5	A, C?	C
Electrical machinery, equipment, and supplies	2.28	3.2	A, C?	C
Motor vehicles and motor vehicle equipment	2.80	4.3	A, C	C
Professional equipment and supplies	2.00	0.4	?	?
Paperboard containers and boxes	2.40	0.5	A?	?
Miscellaneous paper and pulp products	1.73	0.4	A?	C
Rubber products	1.93	0.8	C	C?
(7) ***Resources of indirect significance; production for final market***				
Aircraft and parts	2.72	1.2	A, C	C
(9) ***Service industries; non-local***	1.02	13.0	*	B, C
Railroads and railway express service	1.61	(4.0)	*	C
Air transportation	1.51	(0.6)	*	C
Total in profile industries	...	42.0	...	...

* Inputs other than labor not considered.

it is shipped to Buffalo via lake transportation. (United States Board of Engineers for Rivers and Harbors, 1952, No. 1, p. 36.) Shale was mined within the SMA by at least one Buffalo cement producer. Gypsum is mined within the Buffalo SMA and in counties close to the SMA. (United States Bureau of Mines, Regional Mineral Industry Divisions, 1955, pp. 658, 667.)

Synthetic fibers: Viscose rayon is manufactured in Buffalo. Wood pulp, sulphuric acid, and caustic soda are important materials necessary for its manufacture. The source of the wood pulp was not ascertained, but it is doubtlessly nonlocal. The chemical industry is important in the SMA and produces the necessary chemicals. (See below.)

Miscellaneous chemical and allied products: Because of the existence of sufficient and cheap water power, based on the great resources of Niagara Falls, Buffalo is active in the chemical industry. (Federal Reserve Bank of New York, 1952, p. 135.) The first major hydroelectric development in America, Niagara attracted the so-called electrochemical and electrometallurgical industries, for whom power is a major cost item. (McCarty, 1940, p. 611.) The material inputs for the great array of organic and inorganic industrial chemicals and other chemical products were not determined. However, probably most of the raw materials are not in the immediate vicinity of Buffalo.

Pulp, paper, and paperboard mills: The lumber sources were not determined but are assumed to be nonlocal. Pulp and paper processing involves the use of various chemicals, depending on the process, such as sulphites, sulphates, and caustic soda. (Jones and Darkenwald, 1941, pp. 88-89.)

Miscellaneous petroleum and coal products: Petroleum is received from Great Lakes tankers, and through shipments via the New York State Barge Canal. (United States Board of Engineers for Rivers and Harbors, 1952, No. 1, p. 102.) A pipe line connects Buffalo with the eastern seaboard. (Colby and Foster, 1947, p. 345.) Coal is received by water and rail transportation from fields in the Northern Appalachians.

Primary nonferrous industries: Niagara Falls, an early site for the location of an aluminum reduction plant, lost the industry in 1949 because of the same factor which originally had led to its selection—cheap and sufficient power. Other industries can afford to pay higher rates for power. (Alderfer and Michl, 1957, p. 111.) The inputs for the primary nonferrous industry were not determined; however an important portion of the labor force in this category were employed in nonferrous foundries.

Fabricated metal industries: At least some of the steel and iron inputs are produced locally.

Electric machinery, equipment, and supplies: Presumably some of the metal inputs are produced in the local area.

Motor vehicles and motor vehicle equipment: Various parts, stampings, and assemblies are manufactured in Buffalo for the automobile industry. (United States Department of Labor, 1957, p. 196.) The source for the metals probably is the local industries, and parts used in the assembly of automobiles are shipped in from Detroit, Toledo, and Cleveland. (McCarty, 1940, p. 611.)

Professional equipment and supplies: Inputs were not determined.

Paperboard containers and boxes: Paperboard mills, located within the SMA, presumably supply the paper inputs.

Miscellaneous paper and pulp products: Paper and pulp mills are located in the area.

Rubber products: The sources for the rubber inputs were not determined. However it is assumed that they are not from the hinterland. Cord fabric used in tires comes from Utica, New York. (Moody's Investors Service, 1950a, p. 2176.)

Aircraft and parts: Helicopters and planes are assembled in Buffalo. The industrial northeast is a major source for parts. Sources for the metal frames are probably local.

OUTPUTS AND SERVICE AREAS OF BUFFALO'S PROFILE INDUSTRIES

Miscellaneous nonmetallic mineral and stone products: Aluminum oxide and silicon carbide are used to produce artificial abrasives and probably have a national market. (United States Bureau of Mines, 1953, p. 105.)

Grain mill products: As indicated earlier, Buffalo is conveniently located for supplying grain to the Atlantic coast ports for export. For domestic purposes, flour is distributed by railroad and motor vehicles to the eastern section of the United States and to areas as far west as the Mississippi River. (United States Board of Engineers for Rivers and Harbors, 1952, No. 1, p. 115.) The milling of grains is facilitated by the availability of cheap power. In addition to flour, animal feeds and human breakfast cereals also are processed. At least one cereal is distributed nationally. (Gray, 1954, p. 215.) The dairy region in western New York is a market for the feed. (Alderfer and Michl, 1950, p. 516.)

Blast furnaces, steel works, and rolling mills: Buffalo itself is an important market for its iron and steel products. (Bengtson and Van Royen, 1950, p. 428.) Steel is also trucked to Detroit and shipped by canal barge to New York City. (Garland, 1955, p. 136.)

Other primary iron and steel industries: Various fabricating industries within the Buffalo area are doubtlessly important markets for the output of the foundry industries; it is assumed that other markets are scattered over the manufacturing zone.

Cement, and concrete, gypsum, and plaster products: Cement is produced for more than the local market since cement clinkers are shipped out. (United States Board of Engineers for Rivers and Harbors, 1952, No. 1, p. 36.) Gypsum is used for various building purposes. The existence of at least one national building supply manufacturer and the fact that the gypsum deposits are the "most easterly in location of any such deposits in the United States" suggests that products of this industry serve a sub-national market. (United States Bureau of Mines, Regional Mineral Industry Divisions, 1955, p. 658.)

Synthetic fibers: Rayon is used in the apparel industry and in tires. The existence of a tire factory in Buffalo and the area's location with respect to the rubber plants of Akron and the textile mills of New England, suggest that the output is distributed to a sub-national market.

Miscellaneous chemicals and allied products: There exists an important market with the Buffalo SMA as well as elsewhere in the manufacturing belt. According to Alexandersson (1956, p. 73), heavy chemicals often are manufactured in port cities in the market areas. The complicated technology of the chemical industry, the diverse uses found for many chemicals, and the fact that much of the chemical industry output is utilized by other segments of the chemical industry (see Alderfer and Michl, 1957, p. 242) make it difficult to analyze the outputs and markets in detail. The uses and markets for the acids, salts, sodas, synthetic flavors, dyes, cellophane, chlorine, perfumes, soaps, sodium, and other chemical products of the SMA (*Encyclopedia Americana*, 1953, vol. 20, p. 689) no doubt vary from local to sub-national and national markets and from one specific end product to a considerable range of end products.

Pulp, paper, and paperboard mills: It is assumed that the local paper and paperboard industries receive at least part of the output of the pulp mills, and that part of the output of the paperboard industry goes to local manufacturers of paperboard containers and boxes.

Miscellaneous petroleum and coal products: Coal is an important raw material for the chemical industry. Further, the manufacture of coke for the local steel industry produces such important by-products as ammonium sulphate, tars, and other chemicals. (Jones and Darkenwald, 1941, p. 426.) Similarly, the refining of crude petroleum yields a number of products in addition to gasoline and fuel oil.

Primary nonferrous industries: The products of the primary nonferrous industries probably have a market in the Buffalo SMA and in other cities in the industrial belt.

Fabricated metal industries: Cutlery, hand tools, presses, and other products typical of the industrial belt probably are distributed to a sub-national market.

Electrical machinery, equipment, and supplies: Electrical industrial apparatus and appliances probably are distributed to at least a sub-national market. Arc welders and batteries are two of the specific outputs in this category. (*Encyclopedia Americana,* 1953, vol. 4., p. 295.)

Motor vehicles and motor vehicle equipment: Probably the parts produced and not used in local assemblies are shipped eastward and westward to other assembly plants. Automobiles from Detroit are shipped to Buffalo for shipment to eastern markets. (United States Board of Engineers for Rivers and Harbors, 1952, No. 1, pp. 129-130.)

Professional equipment and supplies: Outputs were not determined.

Paperboard containers and boxes: Although distribution was not determined, industries in the local area, such as breakfast cereal manufactures, are users of such products.

Miscellaneous paper and pulp products: Building paper and wallpaper are two of the products produced. (*Encyclopedia Americana,* 1953, vol. 4, p. 295.) It is assumed that they have sub-national distribution.

Rubber products: The tires and tubes probably have a national distribution since the company mentioned in the source did not appear to have any other factories in the United States. (Moody's Investors Service, 1950a, p. 2176.) It is interesting to speculate on the fact that it is located in Buffalo rather than Akron. Since the company does not have a significant original equipment market in the United States, it is perhaps more influenced in locating with reference to the national replacement market than are the companies which, besides producing for automobile manufacturers, also manufacture tires and tubes for the replacement market in several cities.

Aircraft and parts: The helicopters are produced for both military and commercial purposes and have at least a national distribution. (Cunningham, 1951, p. 156.) The airplanes are also probably for a national market.

Non-local services: Buffalo wholesale houses are said to have a rich trade territory in northwestern New York and adjacent parts of Canada. (McCarty, 1940, p. 612.) Buffalo is a Federal Reserve Branch city and the territory of the branch, ten counties in western New York, is roughly similar to the trade area just described. Niagara Falls is a tourist attraction as well as a power source. Two of the non-local service industries have especially high location quotients, i.e., railroads and railway express service, and air transportation.

Railroads and railway express service: As a rail center, Buffalo is

> considered to be the second largest in the United States being served by ten trunk lines, representing nearly one third of the total railroad mileage of the United States and Canada, and two switching lines. These rail carriers maintain twelve freight and five passenger terminals. Because of its boundary location (between Eastern Trunk Line and Central Freight Association Territories), Buffalo is a western terminus with resultant complicated rate structures; its location is within economical distance of several of the important Atlantic coast ports. (United States Board of Engineers for Rivers and Harbors, 1952, No. 1, p. 142.)

Air transportation: Five air carriers maintain passenger service and freight service. (United States Board of Engineers for Rivers and Harbors, 1952, No. 1, p. 142.) In 1950, 192,817 passengers and 5,447 tons of cargo were carried an average distance of 364 miles. (United States Department of Commerce, Civil Aeronautics Administration, 1951, p. 14.)

Although the port does not directly generate enough employment to classify Buffalo as specialized in water transportation, we have noted that the lake commerce is vital to several of the basic industries. Buffalo has been characterized as the "major eastern gateway to the Midwest" (Garland, 1955, p. 135) on the basis of its situation at the eastern end of Lake Erie and at the end of two major canals. The principal items coming into the SMA via the port are Canadian and domestic grains, coal, limestone, iron ores, and scrap metal. The inbound commerce greatly exceeds the outbound, but the latter includes important shipments of iron, steel, and metal products, among other items. (United States Board of Engineers for Rivers and Harbors, 1952, No. 1, pp. 134-38.)

SUMMARY: BUFFALO

Although it lacks important raw materials in its metropolitan area and hinterland, apart from water and some nonmetallic minerals, Buffalo is able to obtain needed raw materials from other sources because of economical transportation made possible by its location. For example, Buffalo is the only part of the "Eastern Steel District" which can economically use ores from Lake Superior. The inputs for its resource-using industries come primarily from Area C. Several of these industries serve as sources of inputs for fabricating industries in Buffalo as well as other parts of the manufacturing belt. Aside from these industrial linkages within the SMA, both supply and market areas are much more extensive than the metropolitan hinterland proper. Buffalo is a financial center for its hinterland area.

CINCINNATI

SMA consists of Hamilton County, Ohio, and Campbell and Kenton Counties, Kentucky
1950 population: central city, 503,998; SMA, 904,402
Important location feature: port on Ohio River
Other important feature: Federal Reserve Branch city

INPUTS AND SUPPLY AREAS FOR CINCINNATI'S PROFILE INDUSTRIES

Beverage industries: The malt liquor industry accounts for a large part of Cincinnati's specialization in this industry group. Important inputs for this industry are grains and hops. The important grain, barley, is produced largely in the north central states and so must be shipped considerable distances to Cincinnati. However, corn, wheat, and some barley are grown in the lower Ohio valley largely to serve the beverage industries. (Garland, 1955, p. 205.) Hops are grown in this country largely on the West Coast (*Encyclopedia Americana,* 1957, vol. 4, p. 480) and considerable amounts are imported from European countries. (United States Brewers Foundation, 1958, p. 84.)

Paints, varnishes, and related products: Inputs for this industry group can be described only in general terms since the specific sources of inputs utilized in Cincinnati were not determined. Important inputs here are vegetable oils, lead products, petroleum products, and industrial inorganic and organic chemicals. The important vegetable oil input is linseed oil made from flaxseed. Flaxseed is grown in the central northern states, particularly Minnesota, and large quantities of the seeds are imported from Argentina. (Nielsen, 1950, p. 365.) Lead is mined in this country chiefly in southeast Missouri, Idaho and the tri-state district—Missouri, Kansas, and Oklahoma. (Zimmermann, 1951, p. 736.) Petroleum processing industries are located within the SMA as are manufacturers of chemical products. (See below.) Inputs may arrive from these industries.

Table 46. Industrial Profile, Cincinnati: 1950

Category and industry	Location quotient	Per cent of employed labor force	Inputs primarily from area:	Outputs primarily to area:
(3) *First stage resource users; production for final market*				
Beverage industries	3.58	1.3	B, C	C
(4) *Second stage resource users; production for non-final market*				
Paints, varnishes, and related products	1.90	0.2	A, C	C
Miscellaneous chemicals and allied products	3.11	2.7	A, B, C	A, C
Miscellaneous petroleum and coal products	4.00	0.2	B, C	C?
(5) *Second stage resource users; production for final market*				
Furniture and fixtures	1.78	1.0	B	C?
(6) *Resources of indirect significance; production for non-final market*				
Fabricated metal industries	1.61	2.4	A, B, C	A, C
Machinery, except electrical	2.17	5.0	A, C	C
Printing, publishing, and allied industries	1.95	3.0	A, C	A, C
Paperboard containers and boxes	2.50	0.5	B	A
Miscellaneous paper and pulp products	4.00	0.9	B	C?
(7) *Resources of indirect significance; production for final market*				
Watches, clocks, and clockwork operated devices	5.67	0.3	A, C	C
Miscellaneous manufacturing industries	2.39	2.0	A, C	C
(9) *Service industries; non-local*	1.14	14.5	*	B, C
Railroads and railway express service	1.54	(3.8)	*	C
Telegraph	2.00	(0.2)	*	B, C
Advertising	2.25	(0.4)	*	A, C
Total in profile industries	...	34.0	...	...

* Inputs other than labor not considered.

Miscellaneous chemicals and allied products: Among the miscellaneous chemical products produced in Cincinnati, soap is of greatest importance. (City Planning Commission of Cincinnati, 1946, p. 14.) Important inputs for this industry are vegetable oils, various industrial organic chemicals, animal oils and various paper products. Probably the most important source of vegetable oils is cotton seed, the inedible oils of which are utilized in the making of soap. (Whitbeck and Finch, 1941, p. 110.) Cotton is grown in the southern portion of Kentucky and Tennessee; cotton acreage constitutes 12 per cent of the total crop acreage in the lower Ohio valley. (Garland, 1955, p. 207.) The crushing seed mills are probably located near the production centers since the seed is bulky. (Whitbeck and Finch, 1941, p. 110.) It is assumed that cotton-seed oil is obtained from this general area and shipped to Cincinnati soap factories. Some inorganic industrial chemicals are produced within the SMA (City Planning Commission, 1946, p. 14); others no doubt arrive from other cities of the manufacturing zone. Various animal oils are no doubt obtained from the meat packing industries of Cincinnati and other cities of the Corn Belt. Paper inputs are available in the local SMA. (See below.)

Miscellaneous petroleum and coal products: Again inputs can be discussed only in general terms. General sources of coal utilized in Ohio include (in order of importance) West Virginia, Ohio itself, eastern Kentucky, Pennsylvania, and Virginia. (Haynes, 1955, p. 15.) Oil and oil products are received from the Gulf states and from the Mid-Continent producing fields, although some quantities are available locally. (Garland, 1955, p. 209.) In 1955 over 4 million tons of bituminous coal and 51,000 tons of crude petroleum were received via the port. (United States Department of the Army, Corps of Engineers [1956], Part 2, p. 162.)

Furniture and fixtures: Important inputs for this industry are lumber and lumber products. Large quantities of both hard and soft woods are available in the hinterland (the lower Ohio valley). Commercial hardwoods available include ash, beech, hickory, maple, oak, red gum, walnut, and several others. (Garland, 1955, p. 209.) Sources of inputs (other than wood and wood products) for the screen and blind manufacturers within this industry group were not determined.

Fabricated metal industries; machinery, except electrical: Important inputs include processed and fabricated metals and metal products of all kinds. Specific sources for these inputs include locations in Kentucky and Ohio. Other inputs no doubt arrive from other industries within the SMA. Important sources for primary metal inputs are Chicago and Pittsburgh. Fabricated metals and parts no doubt arrive from many of the cities of the manufacturing zone. (See Garland, 1955, pp. 60-63.)

Sources for fuels utilized in Cincinnati may be discussed here. Sources for coal and petroleum have been indicated above. Natural gas is available within Ohio, but large amounts also arrive by pipeline from the Mid-Continent field and from Kentucky and Mississippi. (Stockton, 1952, pp. 169-170; Garland, 1955, p. 209.)

Printing, publishing, and allied industries: Important inputs for this industry group are paper and inks. Paper products no doubt arrive from other industries within the SMA as well as nearby SMA's such as Louisville. (See Garland, 1955, p. 210.) Printer's ink is produced by local chemical firms.

Paperboard containers and boxes; Miscellaneous paper and pulp products: Important inputs for these industries are paper and pulp products from softwood forests. Softwoods are available in the hinterland area from the lower Ohio valley. (*Ibid.*, p. 209.)

Watches, clocks, and clockwork operated devices: Raw materials for these industries play only a minor part, since these are high labor and low raw material cost industries. (Alexandersson, 1956, p. 62.) The specialization in this industry group around 1950 was due almost entirely to the location in Cincinnati of a large watch manufacturer. Watch cases were manufactured by the plant with the movements being produced in Switzerland, but timed, adjusted, regulated, and cased at this Cincinnati plant. (Moody's Investors Service, 1950a, p. 158.) We understand that this activity has been discontinued since 1950.

Miscellaneous manufacturing industries: Inputs include fabricated metals and metal parts of all types. Some processing of nonferrous metals is done within the SMA (City Planning Commission, 1946, p. 14) and inputs may arrive from these industries; however undoubtedly many inputs arrive from other parts of the manufacturing zone.

OUTPUTS AND SERVICE AREAS OF CINCINNATI'S PROFILE INDUSTRIES

Beverage industries: Chief outputs of the Cincinnati beverage industries are beers and ales. Since several of these companies are quite large, their products no doubt enjoy a large market, extending at least over the central United States. (Thomas and Crisler, 1953, p. 65.)

Paints, varnishes, and related products: A large paint company producing a variety of paints and paint products is located in Cincinnati and undoubtedly serves at least a sub-national market area.

Miscellaneous chemicals and allied products: The *1954 Census of Manufactures* indicates that about one-fourth of the employment in this industry group is engaged in the manufacture of inorganic chemicals, that another fourth is engaged in the production of soap and related products and that also important for this SMA is employment in the production of organic chemicals and miscellaneous chemical products. Nature and distribution of the inorganic and organic chemicals produced in Cincinnati were not determined; undoubtedly a local market is being served as well as more distant parts of the manufacturing zone. Large companies engaged in the production of many types of soaps, lotions and cosmetics are located in Cincinnati and undoubtedly serve a national or even an international market. (Thomas and Crisler, 1953, p. 64.) Perhaps significant among the employment in miscellaneous chemicals is the rather large group engaged in the production of printing ink. As Cincinnati is an important printing and publishing center (see below), no doubt a good share of the output of this industry goes to the local market. Plastics are also produced in Cincinnati and depending on the specific product enjoy a sub-national or a national market. (City Planning Commission, 1946, p. 14.)

Miscellaneous petroleum and coal products: Apparently petroleum asphalt products are one important output of this industry. In 1955 over 130,000 tons were shipped from Cincinnati via port traffic. (United States Department of the Army, Corps of Engineers [1956], Part 2, p. 162.)

Furniture and fixtures: The largest share of this employment was engaged in the production of household furniture, second in importance being the production of screens, shades and blinds, particularly Venetian blinds. Distribution of these products is assumed to be to a sub-national market.

Fabricated metal industries: Products of this industry group were quite varied, the most important products being heating and plumbing equipment, structural metal products, and metal stampings. Distribution no doubt varies with the individual products and markets range from local to national in scope.

Machinery, except electrical: Here again the output is quite varied. Specific products include machine tools, general industry machinery, and special industry machinery such as milling machines and laundry machines. (Thomas and Crisler, 1953, p. 65.) Distribution varies with the products but in many cases a national market is being served. Alexandersson (1956, p. 45) comments briefly on the history and present importance of the machine tool industry in Cincinnati:

> The machine tool industry used to be dominated by New England with its manufacturing tradition and skilled labor. The center of production has, however, moved to the leading metal manufacturing states of the Middle West. Ohio is the largest producer but also Michigan, Wisconsin and Illinois have a considerable output of these products, which are of strategic importance in all machine manufacturing. Cincinnati is by far the largest single machine tool manufacturing center but also Cleveland, Detroit, Milwaukee and Chicago are large centers.

Printing, publishing, and allied industries: Cincinnati obtained an early start in this industry group, becoming important with the publishing of McGuffey Readers. (Thomas and Crisler, 1953, p. 65.) Those branches of this industry group tending to serve primarily a national market include the publishers of books, the printers of greeting cards and the printers of playing cards. (Thomas and Crisler, 1953, p. 64; McCarty, 1940, p. 432.)

Paperboard containers and boxes: According to the *1947 Census of Manufactures,* the majority of employment in this industry group is engaged in the production of paperboard boxes. It is assumed that a large share of this production is marketed in the local area, chiefly serving the manufacturers of soaps and related products.

Miscellaneous paper and pulp products: Among the outputs of this industry are envelopes and paper sacks. Distribution of these products is no doubt to a sub-national area. (City Planning Commission of Cincinnati, 1946, p. 14.)

Watches, clocks, and clockwork operated devices: Outputs of the watch industry include chiefly watches in all price fields. Since one of the world's largest companies operated in Cincinnati as of the time covered by our data, the distribution of these products undoubtedly was nation- and perhaps world-wide. (Thomas and Crisler, 1953, p. 64.)

Miscellaneous manufacturing industries: Outputs here include such varied products as golf and other sporting goods equipment, pianos and organs, and advertising signs, and jewelry. (*1947 Census of Manufactures;* Thomas and Crisler, 1953, pp. 64-65.) The companies producing sports equipment and pianos and organs are quite large and undoubtedly serve a national market. Markets for the other products were not determined.

Non-local services: As well as having a large complement of manufacturing employment, Cincinnati is an important commercial city.

McCarty (1940, pp. 432-33) indicates that Cincinnati first became prominent as a supply point for settlers going west and later as a market and transshipment point for their pork products. The city is often described as a "gateway" or "crossroads," owing to its location on the Ohio river at the focus of 7 railroads and as many major highways. (Garland, 1955, p. 210.) The commercial significance of the river port is suggested by the fact that in 1955 Cincinnati received approximately 6½ million tons of materials and shipped approximately 1½ million tons. Chief receipts were coal, steel products, and petroleum and products, while the chief exports consisted of motor fuel, gasoline, and petroleum asphalt. (United States Department of the Army, Corps of Engineers, [1956], Part 2, pp. 162-63.) According to McCarty (1940, p. 433), Cincinnati's trade territory extends over much of the Kentucky Blue Grass district and the lower Miami Valley. The same writer indicates that Cincinnati's banking and wholesale trade interests are not limited to southwest Ohio, but cover much of Kentucky and penetrate southeastern Indiana. Particular services in which Cincinnati shows specialization are described below.

Railroads and railway express service: This specialization is accounted for by the earlier general discussion of non-local services. It has been pointed out that Cincinnati lies at an important junction between the northern manufacturing zone cities and the South. It also is part of the network which connects the cities of the Ohio River with the industrial cities of the Great Lakes. (Garland, 1955, p. 88.)

Telegraph: The most important reason for Cincinnati's specialization in telegraph services is no doubt the location in Cincinnati of one of Western Union's 15 automatic, high-speed message centers. The center located in Cincinnati serves the states of Ohio, West Virginia, Kentucky, and Tennessee. (*Encyclopedia Americana,* 1957, vol. 26, pp. 345, 347.) Specialization in telegraph services is also probably related to Cincinnati's commercial functions and to the location there of a Federal Reserve System Branch Bank.

Advertising: Specialization in this service category may be related to the manufacturing of advertising signs and displays in Cincinnati. Probably a sub-national area is served by this employment in addition to the local SMA.

SUMMARY: CINCINNATI

Cincinnati reveals a diversified industrial structure with its manufacturing industries concentrated on fabricating functions. Raw materials utilized by local industries and available from the hinterland area include grains produced for the beverage industries, cotton seed for the soap industries and wood inputs for the furniture industry. There seems to be considerable linkage between industries within the SMA, with chemicals, metal products, and paper products finding an important market as inputs for other industries located within the SMA. However, important segments of the economy appear to depend almost entirely on Area C for both inputs and markets. Non-local services of a commercial and financial nature are performed for the immediate hinterland, while Cincinnati's railroads and Ohio River traffic no doubt link it with more distant national areas.

REGIONAL METROPOLISES

San Francisco – Oakland	*Portland (Oregon)*
Minneapolis – St. Paul	*Atlanta*
Kansas City	*Dallas*
Seattle	*Denver*

The eight SMA's in this group are alike in being centers of commercial activity and nodal points for rather extensive hinterlands over which they enjoy relatively uncontested dominance. In many instances, they have developed profile industries which collect, process, and tranship the outputs of extractive activities carried on in their vicinity, although none has a concentration of employment in manufacturing. All these metropolises exceed a half million population on an SMA basis. An interesting sidelight on their regional and interregional functions is provided by statistics of airline passenger traffic. The United States Civil Aeronautics Administration (1951) computes a "domestic airline traffic passenger index," the number of passengers enplaned at a station during 1950 per 1,000 of the community's population. All of the "regional metropolises" have scores of 250 or more on this index; the range is from 266 for Minneapolis – St. Paul to 724 for Dallas. Of all the remaining 25 SMA's with populations over 500,000, only Chicago, Washington, Houston, and New Orleans have indexes as high as 250. The regional metropolis, it appears, is in a good position to take advantage of the latest major phase in transportation technology, given its relatively great distance from competing centers of equal or higher rank.

SAN FRANCISCO – OAKLAND

SMA consists of Alameda, Contra Costa, Marin, San Francisco, San Mateo, and Solano Counties, California

1950 population: central cities, 1,159,932 (San Francisco, 775,357; Oakland, 384,575); SMA, 2,240,767

Important location feature: port on Pacific Ocean

Other important feature: Federal Reserve Bank city

INPUTS AND SUPPLY AREAS FOR SAN FRANCISCO – OAKLAND'S PROFILE INDUSTRIES

Canning and preserving fruits, vegetables, and sea foods: Most of the canning activities are apparently located in the Alameda County portion of the SMA. (*1947 Census of Manufactures.*) Situated near parts of the great fruit and vegetable producing regions of California, the food processing plants of Oakland use agricultural products from southern Alameda county and adjacent communities. (*Encyclopaedia Britannica,* 1955, vol. 16, p. 661.) The "rich and productive Santa Clara Valley and . . . the delta lands of the Sacramento and San Joaquin rivers" supply fruits and vegetables to canneries in the San Francisco Bay area. (Zierer, 1956, p. 253.) No doubt a wide variety of fruits and vegetables are canned and dried, although the specific foods were not determined. Fish canning, a relatively minor component of this industry category in the SMA, is based on frozen tuna imported from Japan (*ibid.,* p. 255) and fish caught by the local fleet.

> Small piers . . . are owned and operated by various fish canning companies. Most of these piers have a specially designed sardine conveyor extending from its face to the cannery in the rear. The operation of the canneries is seasonal and also depends on the size of the catches. (United States Board of Engineers for Rivers and Harbors and Maritime Administration, 1952, No. 30, pp. 14-15.)

Can inputs are probably primarily from local sources since several major can producers are located in the SMA. (Moody's Investors Service, 1950a, pp. 1636, 2623.) Although the canning industry is a small scale operation because of seasonality and perishability, there are several large companies in the industry that have administrative functions performed in the SMA. One company has its offices, as well as laboratories and general warehouse, in the SMA (Moody's Investors Service, 1950a, p. 287) and another has its western offices located in San Francisco. (Thomas and Crisler, 1953, p. 137.)

Table 47. Industrial Profile, San Francisco – Oakland: 1950

Category and industry	Location quotient	Per cent of employed labor force	Inputs primarily from area:	Outputs primarily to area:
(3) *First stage resource users; production for final market*				
Canning and preserving fruits, vegetables, and sea foods	2.92	0.8	A, B	C
Miscellaneous food preparations and kindred products	2.35	0.5	C	B, C
Not specified food industries	1.57	0.1	...	...
(9) *Service industries; non-local*	1.61	20.6	*	B, C
Warehousing and storage	1.94	(0.3)	*	B, C
Water transportation	4.65	(1.7)	*	B, C
Air transportation	4.06	(0.7)	*	C
Services incidental to transportation	2.00	(0.1)	*	B, C
Telegraph (wire and radio)	2.25	(0.2)	*	B, C
Wholesale trade	1.50	(5.3)	*	B, C
Banking and credit agencies	1.60	(1.5)	*	B, C
Security and commodity brokerage, and investment companies	1.69	(0.3)	*	A, B, C
Advertising	1.75	(0.3)	*	A, B, C
Miscellaneous professional and related services	1.75	(0.2)	*	?
Federal public administration	2.47	(4.4)	*	C
(10) *Service industries; may be local or non-local*				
Insurance	1.97	2.7	*	C
Miscellaneous entertainment and recreation services	1.76	0.7	*	B, C
Total in profile industries	...	25.4	...	...

* Inputs other than labor not considered.

Miscellaneous food preparations and kindred products: The importance of San Francisco's coffee imports and processing are described below:

> On the Pacific Coast, San Francisco is the principal port of entry for imports of green coffee. From 1950 to 1952, San Francisco accounted for almost three-fourths of total Pacific Coast imports by weight, compared with somewhat less than 70 per cent in the prewar years.

> Coffee is the largest single import of the San Francisco customs district. Los Angeles is the second ranking coffee importing port on the Coast, but her share was only 20 per cent in 1938 and 16 per cent in 1952. Portland, Seattle, and Tacoma import the remaining share.
>
> The concentration of approximately 15 per cent of United States coffee imports on the Pacific Coast is partly accounted for by the fact that West Coast markets are more or less geographically isolated from the eastern roasting centers, so that the establishment of a coffee industry in this area was a logical development. The proximity of Pacific Coast ports to Central American markets, moreover, helps to assure an adequate supply of green coffee for Pacific Coast roasters. (Federal Reserve Bank of San Francisco, 1953, p. 124.)

The SMA's important position in importing and roasting coffee is due to its development as a significant port before other West Coast cities. Employment in this industry is relatively small since coffee roasting is highly mechanized. (*Ibid.*, pp. 125-26.)

The SMA is active in both the cane and beet segments of the sugar industry. San Francisco is the nearest major port to the Hawaiian cane sugar sources. (Zierer, 1956, p. 256.)

> The refinery at Crockett [in the SMA] with 12 per cent of the nation's cane-refining capacity handles 85 per cent of Hawaii's sugar. . . . The Crockett refinery, which turns out 13 million bags of refined sugar a year, is said to be the third largest in the country. The refining is done in California rather than in the Islands because the United States restricts offshore refining for the American market. (*Ibid.*, p. 256.)

California is the largest producer of sugar beets in the nation (Federal Reserve Bank of San Francisco, 1951, p. 1), and the SMA's hinterland is apparently a source of sugar beets. (Alderfer and Michl, 1957, Fig. 29-2, p. 533.) Factories are located close to the producing areas to economize on transportation costs since "Only about one-sixth of the weight of the beets is represented by the sugar extracted." (Hoover, 1948, p. 35.)

The SMA is an important spice importer (Thomas and Crisler, 1953, p. 137) and it is assumed that these inputs are obtained from a number of foreign areas.

OUTPUTS AND SERVICE AREAS OF SAN FRANCISCO – OAKLAND'S PROFILE INDUSTRIES

Canning and preserving fruits, vegetables, and sea foods: Distribution is no doubt to a broad national market. Although analyzing the growing competitive difficulties of canners in the total San Francisco Federal Reserve District, the following quotation is probably relevant to the SMA:

> An increasingly serious problem for western canners, especially of vegetable products, is the mounting cost of shipping to distant markets. In spite of rapid and continuing population growth in the Pacific region, the principal market outlets for most District cannery products are still to be found in the central and eastern states. . . . increases in spread between Pacific Coast points and other competitive areas have resulted from the flat percentage method of increasing freight rates which has been applied in recent years. . . .
>
> There can be no doubt that many [District canners] . . . have been seriously restricted in their market areas by the resulting higher costs of distribution. This applies more particularly to canners of vegetable products, which are packed in widely different parts of the country; the leading Pacific Coast fruit packs enjoy something approaching a monopoly of their respective fields, though they are not free from the competition of other varieties of fresh and processed fruits. (Federal Reserve Bank of San Francisco, 1949, p. 70.)

A declining position in national markets and decentralization of the canners were suggested as probable future developments in the canning industry of the District. (*Ibid.*, pp. 70-71.)

Miscellaneous food preparations and kindred products: Since the SMA accounts for the major portion of coffee imported in its Federal Reserve District, figures for the District are probably applicable to the SMA.

> About 85 to 90 per cent of the green coffee that is roasted in the District is consumed in the District. This percentage, however, does not hold true for individual roasters. If the individual companies maintain roasting plants in other parts of the United States, almost 100 per cent of their roast is consumed here in the seven western states; other plants send about 15 per cent of their roast to points outside the District. (Federal Reserve Bank of San Francisco, 1953, p. 126.)

The SMA presumably markets coffee primarily to a sub-national western market. Description of the sugar markets is complicated by differences in distribution between cane and beet sugars. According to Alexandersson (1956, p. 88), the two sugars "do not normally compete on a national scale" because cane sugar is distributed from coastal sources while beet sugar production is concentrated in the interior. The markets for California beet sugar producers are described below:

> The principal markets for California beet sugar companies are located in the Pacific Coast states. The larger companies who pro-

> duce more than can be sold in these areas must sell their excess in the southwestern states and in the St. Louis-Chicago area where competition from Intermountain and New Orleans processors is keen. (Federal Reserve Bank of San Francisco, 1951, p. 11.)

A factor handicapping beet sugar producers is the consumer preference shown for cane sugar. Beet sugar in the Twelfth Federal Reserve District has industrial and institutional markets that are more important than its consumer markets. In addition beet sugar is sold at a lower price than cane sugar. There are also two important by-products of sugar beets. Both beet tops, obtained during harvesting, and beet pulp, obtained during the manufacture of sugar, are used as livestock feeds. (Zierer, 1956, p. 163.) It is assumed that the pulp is consumed by livestock in the hinterland. Cane sugar refined in the SMA is distributed to an extensive sub-national market consisting of 25 states west of Chicago, and to Alaska and Hawaii. (United States Board of Engineers for Rivers and Harbors and Maritime Administration, 1953, No. 31, p. 253.)

> Although California is a large sugar market (this is particularly true since it is the principal fruit- and vegetable-canning state), the cane sugar must compete with beet sugar. About twice as much sugar is refined west of the Rockies as is consumed there. (Zierer, 1956, p. 256.)

Both cane and beet sugar are marketed from eight basing points in the United States. While this presumably does not directly affect the SMA producers, since San Francisco is the sole West Coast point for calculating freight charges, the location of other producers on the West Coast who must use freight charges based on shipment from San Francisco no doubt complicates the distribution of sugar. Spices are presumably ground and distributed to sub-national and national markets.

Non-local services: In addition to its industrial activities, San Francisco is the financial, commercial, and management center of the Pacific Coast. (*Encyclopedia Americana,* 1953, vol. 24, p. 234.) Its hinterland varies in terms of function, but the Central Pacific Coast area is apparently most intensely served by the SMA. This area "includes forty-eight of California's wealthy counties and extends from San Luis Obispo to the Oregon line." (United States Board of Engineers for Rivers and Harbors and Maritime Administration, 1952, No. 30, p. 193.)

> San Francisco is called the hub of the Central Pacific Coast Area, which contains 77% of California's farm acreage and comprises many of the richest agricultural valleys of California. Rail lines, highways and waterways, branch out to connect the port with the

> Sacramento, San Joaquin, Salinas, Santa Clara, Pajara, Sonoma and Napa valleys—rich irrigated soil basins that produce the major part of California agriculture. This is the local market or jobbing area in which, in competition with other large Pacific Coast ports, Bay Area shippers and distributors have a freight-rate advantage. It has been estimated that 90% of the imports entering San Francisco Bay are for use in this area, and that an equal percentage of exports originates there. (*Ibid.*, pp. 192-193.)

Non-local services in which the SMA is specialized are discussed below.

Warehousing and storage: Activity in this industry is no doubt associated with the important wholesaling functions discussed below. The SMA is a major distribution center for the coastal and mountain states and this no doubt contributes to its activity in warehousing. In addition, at least one major canner maintains its general warehouses in the SMA. (Moody's Investors Service, 1950a, p. 287.) Furthermore, there are important facilities used in connection with the activities of the port. (See United States Board of Engineers for Rivers and Harbors and Maritime Administration, 1952, No. 30, p. 50; 1953, No. 31, pp. 63-64.)

Water transportation: Historical factors in the development of the port's importance are indicated below:

> Upon completion of the first transcontinental rail line in 1869, San Francisco became the focal point for the determination of rates to be charged for rail movements from East coast and inland points to the West coast. The factors which placed San Francisco in a favored position were its natural harbor, and its central location on the Pacific coast of the United States, a preponderant advantage in distance and time consumed in trading with the Orient as compared with sailings from eastern seaboard and Gulf coast ports. Much has already been said of its harbor, and therefore, mention is made that it is commonly recognized as one of the world's foremost, protected deep-water harbors. (United States Board of Engineers for Rivers and Harbors and Maritime Administration, 1952, No. 30, p. 96.)

After the Panama Canal was built, railroads received competition from water carriers for transcontinental freight.

> This water route offered attractive services to the shipper at lower costs and became a keen factor in determining the transcontinental all-rail rates to the Pacific ports. The transcontinental lines, in order to procure a share of the traffic, were obliged to bring their rates into a close relationship with those of the water carriers. In fact, the water competitive factor obliged the railroads to publish rates to the Pacific ports which were materially cheaper than those prevailing to intermediate inland points. . . . This resulted in the "back

> haul" situation and enabled the water carriers to publish rates to compete for business to these inland points by routing shipments by water to the Pacific ports and thence inland by rail. (*Ibid.*, p. 96.)

Although not a profile industry, shipbuilding and repair functions are present (*ibid.*, p. 116) and employment in this industry has been volatile (United States Department of Labor 1957, p. 26), reflecting international developments.

The SMA is an important center for the receipt and shipment of petroleum and petroleum products. Oil from the San Joaquin Valley is shipped from Port Estero, near San Luis Obispo, to the SMA refineries. (Zierer, 1956, p. 324.) Refined petroleum is shipped to points along the California coast, the Pacific Northwest, Alaska, and Hawaii. Coffee is an important import and is obtained from Central and South American sources. (*Ibid.*, p. 325.) Sugar and canned pineapple are both obtained from Hawaii. Foreign trade, at least of the port of San Francisco, is primarily with the Orient.

> During 1950 over 66 per cent of cargoes exported over the piers at San Francisco moved westward across the Pacific. Of the 608,027 tons exported approximately 44 per cent was destined to Japan and the Republic of the Philippines.
>
> The southward route from San Francisco to trade areas of the Caribbean, and South and Central America was the second most important artery for exports. Over 101,000 tons or 16 per cent of the port's total exports moved over this route. (United States Board of Engineers for Rivers and Harbors and Maritime Administration, 1952, No. 30, p. 195.)

A great variety of products were involved in these exports. In addition to coffee imports, bananas were obtained from Costa Rica and Panama, meat products from Argentina, copra and nuts from the Philippines, and newsprint paper from Canada and the Baltic countries. Midwestern and Eastern United States trade with the Orient through the ports of the SMA has declined because of factors indicated below:

> During recent years, the volume of traffic moving from points east of the Rocky Mountains for export, via the port of San Francisco to destinations in the Far East, has declined greatly. Contributing factors to this decline are: economic and political disturbances in the Far East and incidental prohibitory trade regulations, increased rail costs from interior points to Pacific coast ports, and strong competition offered by favorable commodity rate structures applying from the midwest to Atlantic seaboard and Gulf ports. (*Ibid.*, pp. 103-104.)

In an effort to compensate for this decline, emphasis has been placed upon the development of exportable products from western sources.

These new sources involve shorter land trips to the port and have been dominated by truckers.

> Reliable economic surveys have ascertained that approximately 80 per cent of the tonnage exported from the port is transported to the port by motor freight carriers. The proximity of the fertile areas of the great Central Valley, which produces an annual crop of agricultural products valued at approximately one billion dollars; the immense surpluses of grain, fruits, and nuts; and the easy access of the motor trucks to storage bins and curing plants have all materially aided the motor carrier industry to become the chief mode of transportation. (*Ibid.*, p. 104.)

Air transportation: A number of important airlines serve San Francisco and Oakland Municipal Airports, including several transpacific airlines. The maintenance and operational headquarters for several lines are located in the SMA. (United States Board of Engineers for Rivers and Harbors and Maritime Administration, 1952, No. 30, p. 107.) Air freight movements are extensive, as the discussion of the port of Oakland suggests:

> A great portion of the cargo moved to, from, and via the port area is transported by air freight. Both foreign and domestic cargoes, including clothing, machinery, electrical equipment, flowers, fruit, drugs, and photographic supplies move from the port in regularly scheduled flights to cities in almost every continent. (United States Board of Engineers for Rivers and Harbors and Maritime Administration, 1953, No. 31, p. 111.)

In 1950, seven domestic airlines made 50,101 departures and flew 633,181 passengers an average distance of 924 miles. In addition, 12,712 tons of cargo were carried. (United States Department of Commerce, Civil Aeronautics Administration, 1951, p. 5.) Four international airlines flew 25,546 passengers and 355 tons of cargo in 1,185 departures. (*Ibid.*, p. 22.)

Services incidental to transportation: Activity in this industry is no doubt related to the extensive water, rail, and air shipments and transshipments. A large number of freight forwarders are located in the San Francisco port area. (United States Board of Engineers for Rivers and Harbors and Maritime Administration, 1952, No. 30, p. 103.)

Telegraph (wire and radio): The SMA is a major international communication center, according to the *Encyclopedia Americana* (1953, vol. 24, p. 237), with four trans-Pacific radio communication systems maintaining regional headquarters in San Francisco. The telegraph companies which connect the West with the remainder of the nation also have headquarters in the SMA. In addition there are naval, army, and airline communication centers in the SMA. (*Ibid.*, p. 237.) Western Union's automatic, high speed message center in Oakland serves California and Nevada. (*Encyclopedia Americana,* 1957, vol. 26, pp. 345, 347.)

Wholesale trade: McCarty (1940, pp. 89-90) states that San Francisco wholesalers serve the northern two-thirds of California and parts of Nevada, Oregon, and Idaho. It was noted earlier that the most intensively served area is the Central Pacific Coast. Doubtlessly, the SMA also distributes manufactured goods to much of the West on a less intensive basis.

Banking and credit agencies: The Twelfth District Federal Reserve Bank is located in San Francisco and serves the three Pacific Coast states, Idaho, Nevada, Utah, and part of Arizona. The territory served directly by San Francisco rather than by one of the four Branch cities in the Twelfth District includes all but nine counties of California and eastern and central Nevada. The SMA is a major national banking center and is the most important financial center of the West. The largest private bank in the nation has headquarters in San Francisco. It maintained over 500 branches in California at the beginning of 1950 as well as offices in London, Manila, Tokyo, Yokohama, Kobe, Shanghai, Bangkok, and representatives in New York, Paris, Milan, and Zurich. (Moody's Investors Service, 1950c, p. 493.) There are other important large banks in the SMA. (*Encyclopedia Americana,* 1953, vol. 24, p. 236.) In addition, a holding company maintained a majority interest in nearly 50 domestic banks "operating 132 banking offices in California, Oregon, Nevada, Washington, and Arizona." (Moody's Investors Service, 1950c, p. 977.)

Security and commodity brokerage, and investment companies: Although dwarfed by New York, the SMA is the "nation's second largest security market." (*Encyclopedia Americana,* 1953, vol. 24, p. 236.) A number of security brokers are no doubt in the SMA. Brokers for such commodities as coffee are presumably located in the SMA.

Advertising: A considerable number of the advertising companies located in San Francisco are branches of firms with headquarters in the East and the Midwest. (See Standard Advertising Register, 1955, p. 981.) This suggests that in addition to purely local advertising functions, broader regional advertising services are performed in the SMA.

Miscellaneous professional and related services: Specific services performed were not determined. Included in this category are nonprofit educational and scientific research agencies and such services as those performed by lecturers and writers.

Federal public administration: The SMA is important in defense and government administration. (United States Department of Labor, 1957, p. 26.) The armed forces maintain supply bases, air bases, and administrative units in the SMA. (*Encyclopedia Americana,* 1953, vol. 20, p. 528.) In addition, "There is a U. S. Mint here along with many other federal offices." (Thomas and Crisler, 1953, p. 137.)

Insurance: The SMA is the insurance capital of the West. (*Encyclopedia Americana,* 1953, vol. 24, p. 236.) No doubt at least broad subnational markets are served.

Miscellaneous entertainment and recreation services: San Francisco is an important tourist center which no doubt partially accounts for the SMA's activity in this industry.

SUMMARY: SAN FRANCISCO – OAKLAND

The profile manufacturing industries of the SMA are based on the agricultural products of its hinterland and of Area C sources. In addition, the SMA has a wide array of non-profile industrial activities which are growing in importance. However its most significant activities are the wide array of commercial, financial, and administrative functions performed for its great agricultural hinterland, and the Pacific and Intermountain states, Hawaii, and Asia. Between early 1940 and November 1955, more than 300,000 workers in the trade, service, and finance industries were added and the SMA "has retained its original complexion as a center of trade, service and finance" (United States Department of Labor, 1957, p. 26).

MINNEAPOLIS – ST. PAUL

SMA consists of Anoka, Dakota, Hennepin, and Ramsey Counties, Minnesota

1950 population: central cities, 833,067 (Minneapolis, 521,718; St. Paul, 311,349); SMA, 1,116,509

Important location feature: at the navigable head of the Mississippi River

Other important features: Federal Reserve Bank city (Minneapolis); Capital of Minnesota (St. Paul)

INPUTS AND SUPPLY AREAS FOR MINNEAPOLIS – ST. PAUL'S PROFILE INDUSTRIES

Meat products: The St. Paul Union Stockyards had the following receipts for 1950: 2.8 million hogs; 1.1 million cattle; 0.6 million sheep; and 0.5 million calves. (Lewis, 1952b, p. 10.) Roughly 12 per cent of

Table 48. Industrial Profile, Minneapolis – St. Paul: 1950

Category and industry	Location quotient	Per cent of employed labor force	Inputs primarily from area:	Outputs primarily to area:
(3) *First stage resource users; production for final market*				
Meat products	3.39	1.7	B	B, C
Beverage industries	1.72	0.6	B, C	B, C
(6) *Resources of indirect significance; production for non-final market*				
Machinery, except electrical	1.72	4.0	B?, C	B?, C?
Professional equipment and supplies	3.81	0.8	C?	C
Printing, publishing, and allied industries	1.78	2.7	B	C
Miscellaneous paper and pulp products	2.00	0.4	B	C
Not specified manufacturing industries	2.14	0.5	...[1]	...[1]
(9) *Service industries; non-local*	1.52	19.3	*	B, C
Railroads and railway express service	1.82	(4.5)	*	C
Warehousing	2.00	(0.3)	*	B
Air transportation	4.12	(0.7)	*	C
Telegraph (wire and radio)	1.88	(0.2)	*	C
Wholesale trade	1.74	(6.1)	*	B
Banking and credit agencies	1.66	(1.6)	*	B
Security and commodity brokerage, and investment companies	2.81	(0.4)	*	A, B?
Advertising	3.40	(0.7)	*	A, B
(10) *Service industries; may be local or non-local*				
Insurance	1.68	2.3	*	B, C
Hospitals	1.59	2.8	*	B?
Total in profile industries	...	35.4	...	...

* Inputs other than labor not considered.
[1] No information on inputs and outputs.

the receipts were by railroad shipment. Minnesota accounts for approximately 80 per cent of the St. Paul receipts. Southern Minnesota is an important shipper of hogs. (McCarty, 1940, p. 288.) According to Dickinson (1947, pp. 220-21), out-of-state livestock comes from an area which "extends west to the 'economic divide,' though in southern and western Montana live-stock shipments . . . are principally directed to

Chicago." According to Alexandersson (1956, p. 87), the increase in percentage of livestock shipped by truck has lessened the transportation advantage of Chicago, and meat packing has been migrating farther west, with centers closer to the producing areas gaining in importance.

Beverage industries: Barley is the single most important input for the brewing industry in terms of weight and accounts for about 70 per cent of the raw materials. (Alderfer and Michl, 1950, p. 615.) The SMA is located close to the most important barley growing region in the United States. (Smith and Phillips, 1946, p. 461.) The corn products probably come from the Area B portion in the corn belt, while the remaining inputs used by the brewing industry such as rice, sugar, sirups, and hops probably are produced in the C area. Although the specific sources for the soft drink industry were not determined, sirup is one of the most important inputs and it is assumed that it comes from sugar beet areas in the hinterland, although possibly Area C sugar sources are also used. (See Alderfer and Michl, 1957, p. 533.)

Machinery, except electrical: The inputs for this industry are assumed to include various primary and processed metal products. The steel inputs were not determined, although Duluth is a steel producing city. Montana is an important source in the United States for zinc and copper. Presumably, the manufacturing belt provides many of the inputs also.

Professional equipment and supplies: The SMA is an important producer of temperature controls and heat regulators. (Moody's Investors Service, 1950a, p. 2031.) The inputs for these and other instruments are assumed to be metals and high grade alloys. The sources were not determined.

Printing, publishing, and allied industries: The Minnesota portion of the hinterland is a producer of paper products which is the important material input for this industry.

Miscellaneous paper and pulp products: The SMA is an important producer of adhesive tapes. (Moody's Investors Service, 1950a, p. 879.) The paper inputs were not determined but are assumed to be at least partially from hinterland producers.

OUTPUTS AND SERVICE AREAS OF MINNEAPOLIS – ST. PAUL'S PROFILE INDUSTRIES

Meat products: Although a considerable portion of the St. Paul livestock receipts are slaughtered locally, it should be noted that animals are also shipped to packers in other parts of the state as well as in other states. Further, particularly for cattle and sheep, animals are shipped to feeders rather than slaughtered. (Lewis, 1952b, p. 10.) The animal shipments are made by rail and truck in roughly equal proportions. The meat slaughtered in the SMA has a large market. Data for the entire State of Minnesota indicate that the northeastern and north-central parts of the country were the two most important markets for fresh meats; western and northeastern markets were most important for cooked, cured, and dried meats; and southern and northeastern markets were the biggest users of edible packing house products. (Lewis, 1952b, p. 11.)

Beverage industries: One of the large brewers in the SMA has a sub-national distribution ranging from Wisconsin and Iowa through Montana and Wyoming. (Moody's Investors Service, 1950a, p. 1039.) Another SMA brewer markets its beer in the north central states. (Moody's Investor Service, 1954, p. 1079; 1955, p. 1236.)

Machinery, except electrical: Farm and industrial tractors, farm combines, corn shellers, corn pickers, hay balers, and other farm equipment are produced in the SMA. (Moody's Investors Service, 1950a, p. 958.) It is assumed that they have an important market in the hinterland as well as other parts of the country. Metalworking and industrial machinery products are assumed to have at least sub-national markets.

Professional equipment and supplies: The heating controls are probably distributed to at least a national market. Other instruments are produced in the area; what they are was not learned. (United States Department of Labor, 1957, p. 158.) Artificial limbs are manufactured and, although the distribution was not determined, it is assumed to be at least for a national market, since Minneapolis apparently is internationally known for the product. (*Encyclopedia Americana,* 1953, vol. 19, p. 160.)

Printing, publishing, and allied industries: Minneapolis has daily publications in the specialized fields of finance and commerce, building trades, farming, and grain dealing. (*Encyclopaedia Britannica,* 1955, vol. 15, p. 555.) St. Paul is said to be the largest publisher of law books in the world. (*Ibid.,* vol. 19, p. 852.) The SMA is also an important producer of various advertising novelties and some of them fall in this category, e.g., calendars. Regional and national markets are probably served by industries in this category.

Miscellaneous paper and pulp products: The cellophane adhesive tape has at least a national distribution.

Non-local services: The SMA performs non-local services for a considerable area. It is the commercial, industrial, and financial center for Minnesota, North and South Dakota, eastern Montana, and western Wisconsin. (*Ibid.*, vol. 15, p. 555.) St. Paul's trading area comprises northern and western Wisconsin and southeastern Minnesota; Minneapolis' region includes western Minnesota, North and South Dakota, and Montana. McCarty (1940, p. 287) concludes that "Minneapolis commercial interests are far-flung and regional while those of St. Paul are more highly localized. St. Paul has a smaller trade territory and serves it more thoroughly."

Railroads and railway express service: The SMA is a leading railroad center for the western Middle West. (Alexandersson, 1956, p. 94.) There are at least ten trunk railroad lines located in the SMA. Seven railroads have construction and repair functions performed in Minneapolis. (*Encyclopaedia Britannica,* 1955, vol. 15, p. 555.)

> Granger and transcontinental lines, which parallel each other in an east-west alignment, focus on Minneapolis-St. Paul and terminate in the Chicago area. Grain and lumber are the principal eastward-bound commodities, and manufactured goods are the westward-bound, although the industrial exchange between Minneapolis-St. Paul and Chicago is significant. (Garland, 1955, p. 86.)

Railroads have replaced the Mississippi as the significant transportation factor for the Twin Cities. The river freight traffic in 1950 included inbound barge shipments of 1.8 million tons, consisting primarily of oil and petroleum products (65 per cent of total tonnage) and bituminous coal (31 per cent). Outbound shipments were negligible by comparison; they amounted to about 30,000 tons. Since "less than 2 per cent of Minnesota's interstate freight traffic moves on the Mississippi River" (Lewis, 1952b, p. 35), it appears that the river is not an important factor in the total movement of goods of the SMA, although it was important in its early growth.

Warehousing: A study of public warehousing in Minneapolis-St. Paul, although made in the early thirties and covering only one type of warehousing, offers material that is probably relevant to the factors affecting the wholesaling and warehousing industries:

> The conditions requisite to the support of the public merchandise warehouses in Minneapolis and St. Paul are the same as those required for the fostering of the large jobbing trade, namely, excellent transportation systems entering and radiating to all points in a well-populated trade area and a favorable freight rate structure. The commercial development of the Twin Cities and the circumstances

favoring their growth well illustrate the importance of these factors. . . . The existence in a transportation center of both potential and actual water competition to the railroads is likely to result in favorable transportation rates. The jobbing trade and public warehouses depend upon a rate structure that allows a large enough margin between a combination of carload and l.c.l. rates and straight l.c.l. rates to make these services economical. In the case of warehouses, this differential must be great enough to equal or exceed the storage and handling charges. On the whole, the Twin Cities have enjoyed such rates. (Vaile and Nordstrom, 1932, p. 15.)

Air transportation: Five airlines operate in the Twin Cities. One of the airlines has international routes and the SMA is therefore a port of entry. (*Encyclopaedia Britannica,* 1955, vol. 15, p. 555.) In 1950, 295,029 passengers and 4,300 tons of cargo were carried an average distance of 598 miles by domestic airlines. (United States Department of Commerce, Civil Aeronautics Administration, 1951, p. 11.)

Telegraph: Specialization in this service is no doubt in part related to this SMA's function as a financial and commercial center. In addition Minneapolis is the location of one of Western Union's 15 automatic, high speed message centers and serves the following states: North Dakota, South Dakota, Minnesota, Iowa, and Wisconsin. (*Encyclopedia Americana,* 1957, vol. 26, pp. 345-347.)

Wholesale trade: The Minneapolis-St. Paul SMA ranked first among SMA's of 1,000,000 or more in respect to per capita wholesale sales in 1948. Its per capita figure was $1,000 higher than that of the second rank SMA among those of one to three million. The wholesale activities of the SMA are indicated below.

Lewis (1952a, p. 14) notes that sales of agricultural raw materials, particularly grain and livestock, constituted about one-third of wholesale sales in the area in 1948. The livestock functions of the SMA were discussed earlier; however grain mills failed to meet the location quotient requirements for inclusion. While Minneapolis is still an important flour milling center, its relative position has declined somewhat. According to Alexandersson (1956, pp. 87-88), after many years as the "flour city," Minneapolis declined in importance owing to decreasing yields in the spring wheat region and changes in transportation rates adverse to Minneapolis but favorable to Buffalo. The latter city enjoys proximity to eastern markets and its location in a dairy region affords a market for by-product mill feed. Kansas City likewise has grown as a milling center and rivals Minneapolis in volume of production. However, Minneapolis still retains its administrative and integrative function since the headquarters of the five largest flour milling companies are still in the city. (*Encyclopedia Americana,* 1953, vol. 19, p. 197.) Further, Minneapolis companies apparently have maintained control of much of the milling output in these competing centers. In 1931, Minneapolis companies owned 86 per cent of Buffalo's output and a quarter of Kansas City and Oklahoma output. (Pickett and Vaile, 1933, p. 67.)

Returning to the discussion of wholesale functions, it is worth noting that the wholesale distribution function of the SMA varies from item to item in the region served in the same manner as an SMA's manufacturing and financial hinterlands may be considerably different. Thus, while the sources for agricultural produce are roughly the Ninth Federal Reserve District (Lewis, 1952a, p. vi), "Several Twin Cities wholesalers, especially in groceries and automotive equipment, have established branches throughout the Upper Midwest." (*Ibid.,* p. 12.)

The following quotation, though based on an analysis of hardware wholesaling, suggests why the SMA's hinterland is primarily westward:

> The fundamental factor which determines a market pattern is the location of a given wholesale center with respect to competing wholesale centers and to the sources of supply. Each wholesale center is surrounded by an area in which its wholesalers have a cost advantage over firms located in other centers. Sources of supply affect the market pattern through the freight-rate structure. A wholesaler must be governed in his market coverage by the combined in and out freight rates of staple lines. He must make calculations for individual products or groups of products which will indicate the market he can reach profitably from his warehouse.
>
> Many basic hardware lines are manufactured for the most part north of the Ohio River and east of the Mississippi. This situation is a major determinant of the general shape of the Twin Cities wholesale hardware area. Twin Cities firms cannot backhaul, except for a short distance, against the competition of Wisconsin and Illinois wholesalers. Their market lies to the west where they can ship in l.c.l. quantities over long distances before meeting serious competition. (Lewis, 1952a, p. 41.)

Since one of the major wholesale functions performed by the SMA involves the distribution of manufactured goods from the industrial belt, it is clear why the hinterland extends much further in a westward direction than an eastward direction. A similar factor in the movement of agricultural products to the populous east was noted in the discussion earlier of meat packing. The distribution of beer, since it involves inputs primarily from the SMA's hinterland, is an illustration of a product which does not face backtracking expenses when shipped eastward. Thus at least one brewer is able to market in the Chicago area and another brewer, although distributing primarily in the metropolitan hinterland, also has markets in Iowa, Nebraska, and Wyoming.

Banking and credit agencies: Vance and Smith (1954, p. 123) have observed the association between financial and wholesale functions. Hartsough (1925, p. 143), writing in the 'twenties, discussed the financial functions of the SMA:

> A general survey of the situation indicates that the Twin Cities have just passed into the financial phase of their metropolitan development, and that the area for which they perform financial services is substantially the same as that from which they concentrate the grain and livestock, and for which they are the jobbing center. Their financial control is less dominant, however, than their control in the other branches of exchange, for it is of more recent development. Moreover, the Twin Cities themselves do not constitute a financial center that is independent in the sense of isolation. No city does, at the present time, for capital and credit facilities are too highly fluid. In our financial life we more nearly approach national economy than in any other aspect of our economic life. New York of course being the national center. Yet New York itself is by no means an independent center in this sense. The Twin Cities are dependent in an important degree upon other parts of the country, but their chief function—and it is a highly essential one—is to act as a nucleus where both demand and supply are concentrated, where the capital which comes in from other districts may be concentrated for distribution, and to which the rest of the district may look for satisfaction of its financial needs.

The importance of the Federal Reserve Bank location at Minneapolis also has been discussed by Hartsough (1925, p. 140), who notes that because of its rediscounting of commercial paper, "the Federal Reserve Bank brings the center into prominence as the chief source of loanable funds for the district." The association between financial and wholesaling functions was noted for at least the public merchandise segment of warehousing in the 'thirties:

> Products of industry or agriculture that must be stored and financed until sold seek distributing centers where both services are highly developed. . . . Most loans are made on seasonal commodities. The highly developed credit and distribution facilities in the Twin Cities attract large quantities of merchandise to their warehouses. (Vaile and Nordstrom, 1932, p. 39.)

Security and commodity brokerage, and investment companies: Markets and exchanges for grains and cattle exist in the SMA. A large national investment company is located in the SMA. (Fiduciary Publishers, 1954, p. 130.)

Advertising: Several New York advertising agencies have branches and there are a number of independent agencies. The location of general and special newspapers in the SMA may also be a factor.

Insurance: There is at least one insurance company in the SMA with a territory of roughly 25 states. (Moody's Investors Service, 1950c, p. 1145.)

Hospitals: There is a large veterans' hospital as well as University of Minnesota hospital facilities in the SMA. The area served by the SMA hospitals was not determined.

SUMMARY: MINNEAPOLIS – ST. PAUL

Located between the industrialized north central area and the agricultural great plains, the SMA serves as a market for agricultural products destined for consumption in the east and as a distributor to the northwest of the industrial products of the manufacturing belt. Its hinterland for many functions is quite extensive and includes Minnesota, northern and western Wisconsin, the Dakotas, and a part of Montana. The manufacturing functions performed in the SMA appear to have markets in an area much greater than its hinterland.

KANSAS CITY

SMA consists of Clay and Jackson Counties, Missouri and Wyandotte and Johnson Counties, Kansas
1950 population: central city, 456,622; SMA, 814,357
Location feature: port on Missouri River
Other important feature: Federal Reserve Bank city

INPUTS AND SUPPLY AREAS FOR KANSAS CITY'S PROFILE INDUSTRIES

Meat products: Important inputs for the meat packing industries are livestock of all kinds—cattle, sheep, horses, hogs, and mules. In 1950, Kansas City ranked fourth in the United States in number of salable cattle received in its public stockyards (1.2 million cattle received); fourth in the United States in number of sheep and lambs received (694,000); and seventh in the United States in number of calves received (135,000). In addition to these receipts, 624,000 hogs were received in 1950. (United States Department of Agriculture, Production and Marketing Administration, 1951, pp. 7-8.) Fifty-five per cent of the cattle received were driven in to market (arrived by means other than rail); 53 per cent of the calves, 81 per cent of the hogs and 27 per cent of the sheep and lambs. Since driven-in receipts usually indicate that relatively short distances are involved, these rather low percentages indicate that Kansas City's market extends considerably beyond its immediate surrounding area. (United States Department of Agriculture, Production and Marketing Administration, 1951, p. 10.)

Table 49. Industrial Profile, Kansas City: 1950

Category and industry	Location quotient	Per cent of employed labor force	Inputs primarily from area:	Outputs primarily to area:
(3) *First stage resource users; production for final market*				
Meat products	4.94	2.4	B, C	C
(9) *Service industries; non-local*	1.51	19.3	*	B, C
Railroads and railway express service	1.94	(4.8)	*	C
Trucking service	1.57	(1.7)	*	B, C
Warehousing and storage	2.05	(0.3)	*	B
Air transportation	7.18	(1.2)	*	C
Petroleum and gasoline pipe lines	2.38	(0.1)	*	C
Services incidental to transportation	2.61	(0.2)	*	B?
Telegraph (wire and radio)	2.32	(0.2)	*	C
Other and not specified utilities	2.17	(0.1)	*	B?
Wholesale trade	1.52	(5.3)	*	B
(10) *Service industries; may be local or non-local*				
Insurance	1.64	2.2	*	C
Total in profile industries	...	23.9	...	...

* Inputs other than labor not considered.

Points of origin for livestock (in 1939) included over half of the states, the receipts being almost entirely from west of the Mississippi. Major sources included Kansas, Missouri, Oklahoma, Nebraska, Colorado, Texas, and New Mexico. (Kansas City, City Plan Commission, 1945, pp. 19-20.) It was estimated that 12 per cent of all livestock produced in the first five states listed above, plus Arkansas, found their way to the Kansas City market, these inputs making up 63 per cent of Kansas City's total livestock receipts. (Kansas City, City Plan Commission, 1945, p. 4.) Kansas City and similar centers receive a large volume of feeder cattle, some of which are shipped to distant feeder lots. (Neff and Williams, 1954, p. 61.)

OUTPUTS AND SERVICE AREAS OF KANSAS CITY'S PROFILE INDUSTRIES

Meat products: Shipments from the meat products industry—chiefly meat products, hides, and miscellaneous by-products—were made to 37 states (chiefly the central and eastern sections, with Illinois, Missouri and Kansas receiving the largest amounts) and to some foreign countries. Eighty per cent of the shipments were by rail. (Kansas City, City Plan Commission, 1945, p. 22.)

Non-local services: Kansas City is first and foremost a service and commercial center, continuing a tradition established in early pioneer days. Neff and Williams (1954, p. 4) consider that agriculture

> brought income into the city and the surrounding area from distant markets where its products were sold. Thus agriculture and, to a lesser extent, other extractive industries such as metal mining and lumbering were for many years the backbone of the economy of Kansas City. Though few city dwellers could be classified as farmers or farm laborers, their jobs and income depended largely on agriculture.

The growth of most of Kansas City's profile industries not only depended on having a productive agricultural hinterland but also required the development of its transportation facilities. Neff and Williams (1954, p. 265) conclude that the city's "central location and excellent transportation facilities—rail, air, and truck—provide direct access to nearly every market in the nation." It may be noted that water transportation was not mentioned, although Kansas City is located on the Missouri River. The river, however, is navigable at this location only about eight months a year, and only one regularly scheduled barge line operates, although some corporations operate their own barges. The minor importance of water transportation is suggested by the estimate that no more than one per cent of the grain shipped from Kansas City goes by water. (*Ibid.*, p. 93.) Specific non-local services in which Kansas City is specialized are described below.

Railroads and railway express service: Twelve major railroads serve the Kansas City area. These operate over the entire western half of the United States and have direct connections north to Minneapolis – St. Paul, northeast to Chicago, east to St. Louis, southeast to Memphis, and south to New Orleans and other Gulf ports. Normal railroad freight service from Kansas City provides one-day service west to the Colorado line; north to southern Minnesota and across Illinois, including Chicago; and south to include Arkansas and most of Oklahoma. Four days in transit will reach all parts of the Atlantic Coast except New England, and normal six-day service includes the California coast as far north as San Francisco. (Neff and Williams, 1954, pp. 91-92.)

Trucking service: Kansas City is served by 145 truck lines. "Excellent highways from all parts of the plains states and to eastern and southern points have contributed to the rapid development of the trucking industry." (Kansas City, City Plan Commission, 1945, p. 16.) Neff and Williams (1954, p. 217) attribute the specialization in trucking to Kansas City's central geographic position and to the fact that several large local industries—stockyards, meat packers, wholesalers, and automobile assembly plants—make extensive use of trucking facilities.

Warehousing and storage: The livestock- and grain-gathering functions performed by Kansas City for its area necessitate the development of large warehouses for storage. In addition:

> Kansas City's importance as a distributing center and diversion point has resulted in the establishment of several large and important cold storage warehouses, where produce of many kinds (especially poultry, eggs and butter) is stored in large quantities. This produce may be stored for several months, whether 'in transit' to other parts of the country or for local consumption. (Kansas City, City Plan Commission, 1945, p. 13.)

Air transportation: Kansas City's position at the center of the United States takes on added significance in the air age. (Garland, 1955, p. 228.) In 1950 seven airlines were operating in Kansas City and in that year carried 288,060 passengers and 3,236 tons of air cargo an average distance of 546 miles. (United States Department of Commerce, Civil Aeronautics Administration, 1951, p. 11.) Specialization in this industry is due not only to the relatively high volume of air traffic but also to the presence of the overhaul base and most of the administrative offices of a major airline. (Neff and Williams, 1954, p. 217.)

Petroleum and gasoline pipe lines: According to Neff and Williams (*ibid.*, p. 65),

> Petroleum production became important in the Mid-Continent field about the turn of the century. Early production from eastern Kansas

> pools led to the establishment of a refinery in Kansas City in 1904 to process products for the trading area served by the city. Later discoveries shifted the center of production in the Mid-Continent field away from Kansas City into Oklahoma. . . . removed from the chief producing fields, Kansas City has benefited as a refining and transshipment point for Mid-Continent petroleum on its way to market. . . . Natural gas was associated with the early oil produced in eastern Kansas. It was recovered and piped for use in Kansas City. This original source of gas for the metropolitan area soon was depleted and the pipeline system was extended to the south and west to tap other supplies. Chief sources of natural gas for Kansas City now are the Hugoton field in southwestern Kansas, Oklahoma, and Texas, and the Panhandle field in Texas. These fields also supply a large surplus of gas for transmission to other urban markets in the midwestern states.

Services incidental to transportation: The specific nature of this employment was not determined.

Telegraph: Specialization in telegraph service is no doubt related to Kansas City's importance as a transportation center and to its commercial and financial activities. The city is the site of a regional office of the long lines division of the American Telephone and Telegraph Co.

Other and not specified utilities: The nature of this specialization for Kansas City was not determined.

Wholesale trade: Kansas City is one of several cities located near the climatically determined division zone between intensive agriculture to the east and extensive grazing and wheat farming to the west; all of these cities enjoy high wholesale trade employment (Alexandersson, 1956, p. 100.) Kansas City is an important assembler of farm products. Among the important farm products handled in addition to livestock are grains—chiefly wheat, corn, oats, rye, barley, and sorghums, arriving from the six states in the immediately surrounding area—Kansas, Missouri, Nebraska, Iowa, Arkansas, and Oklahoma; seeds—chiefly field—collected particularly from Kansas and Missouri; and poultry and eggs, again collected mostly from Kansas and Missouri. (Kansas City, City Plan Commission, 1945, pp. 28, 32, 33, 35.) Kansas City's wholesale trading area for many lines includes almost all of Kansas and western Missouri. For lines in which transportation costs are low, the trade area is larger, although it has contracted since the 1890's, when for some lines it included the entire western half of the United States. (Neff and Williams, 1954, pp. 209-10.)

Insurance: Kansas City has a "national reputation as an insurance center," according to Neff and Williams (1954, p. 220). Seven life insurance companies have home offices there and seventy maintain branch offices. The city is the home of the nation's largest reinsurance company. (*Idem.*)

SUMMARY: KANSAS CITY

Many of Kansas City's profile industries are directly or indirectly tied in with its extensive agricultural hinterland. "Surrounded by a rich agricultural region, with no other large city within a 250-mile radius, Kansas City is a major wholesale and retail trade center for this section of the country. . . . As the seat of the 10th Federal Reserve District, Kansas City is also the financial hub of an area comprising all or a portion of 7 states." (United States Department of Labor, 1957, p. 162.) Kansas City also functions as a transportation center for a large section of the Middle West.

SEATTLE

SMA consists of King County, Washington
1950 population: central city, 467,591; SMA, 732,992
Important location feature: port on Puget Sound off the Pacific Ocean
Other important feature: Federal Reserve Branch city

INPUTS AND SUPPLY AREAS FOR SEATTLE'S PROFILE INDUSTRIES

Sawmills, planing mills and mill work: Inputs for this industry consist principally of logs and other forest materials. The entire Pacific Northwest region has become an important supplier of forest materials for the nation.

> The forests which cover nearly one-half the land of the Pacific Northwest contain 46 per cent of the Nation's total sawtimber volume and 57 per cent of its softwood sawtimber, and in addition millions of acres of young, vigorously growing trees which will provide timber for future generations. The forests of the region supply 35 per cent of the Nation's annual cut of sawtimber. (Highsmith, [1953], p. 31.)

Several types of forests are found in the Pacific Northwest. The Douglas-fir type is the most extensive and commercially important forest type; also found are the spruce-hemlock type, ponderosa pine type, the

Western white pine type and the hardwood types. (*Ibid.*, pp. 29-30; Freeman and Martin, 1954, pp. 229-236.)

> 84 per cent of the Northwest's lumber production is from two species, Douglas-fir and Ponderosa pine . . . the great concentration of lumber production (primarily from Douglas-fir) is in western Oregon and western Washington. (Highsmith [1953], p. 93.)

Table 50. Industrial Profile, Seattle: 1950

Category and industry	Location quotient	Per cent of employed labor force	Inputs primarily from area:	Outputs primarily to area:
(2) *First stage resource users; production for non-final market*				
Sawmills, planing mills, and mill work	1.58	1.6	B, C?	C
(7) *Resources of indirect significance; production for final market*				
Aircraft and parts	12.57	5.8	B, C	C
(9) *Service industries; non-local*	1.53	19.6	*	B, C
Water transportation	5.73	(2.1)	*	C
Air transportation	3.58	(0.6)	*	C
Wholesale trade	1.58	(5.6)	*	B, C
Hotels and lodging places	1.60	(1.5)	*	C
Federal public administration	2.04	(3.7)	*	C
(10) *Service industries; may be local or non-local*				
Insurance	1.59	2.2	*	B, C?
Miscellaneous entertainment and recreation services	1.62	0.6	*	A, C
Total in profile industries	. . .	29.8	. . .	. . .

* Inputs other than labor not considered.

In the period 1945-1949, Washington was second to Oregon in the Pacific Northwest in the production of lumber. Approximately three billion board feet were turned out; this was slightly less than half of the production in Oregon. (Freeman and Martin, 1954, p. 244.) Turning to Seattle specifically, in the middle thirties Seeman (1935, pp. 22, 28-29) estimated that Seattle's timber hinterland consisted only of the forest areas immediately surrounding the city. He pointed out that transportation facilities demanded that lumber mills be located along navigable water, and this factor had scattered the industry all along the Puget Sound with the result that little of the surrounding timber got to Seattle for processing. Whether or not this is still the case could not be determined. McCarty (1940, p. 115) remarks that lumber has never played as important a part in Seattle's economic life as it has in the other cities of Puget Sound.

Aircraft and parts: Seattle, like other West Coast cities specializing in aircraft, is concentrated in airframe production and thus in final assembly. Inputs are almost entirely processed and fabricated materials. Processed materials include alloy steels, copper, aluminum sheet and tubing, aluminum castings and similar materials. Some of the processed materials are available in the hinterland—e.g., aluminum is processed in considerable quantities in plants located at Spokane and Vancouver, Washington; steel is produced in Seattle utilizing scrap, and copper is refined in Tacoma, Washington. (Highsmith, [1953], pp. 105-110.) Still only a part of the processed inputs come from the hinterland (Freeman and Martin, 1954, p. 422) and no specific information was found on the source of these inputs. However, it is known that California and Oregon account for many of the manufactured products shipped to Washington. (Ullman, 1957, p. 55.) Fabricated inputs include chiefly airplane engines and propellers. The specific source of these inputs utilized by Seattle's aircraft plants is also unknown; however important centers for the production of airplane engines are Hartford, Indianapolis, New York, and Boston, while New York, Hartford, and Dayton are propeller manufacturing centers. (Cunningham, 1951, pp. 225-226.) In 1950, the Seattle SMA accounted for 11.7 per cent of the United States total employment in airframe construction. (*Ibid.*, pp. 159-160.)

Fuel inputs for Seattle SMA may be discussed only in general terms. Electric power is of greatest importance, 91 per cent of it being produced for the Pacific Northwest in hydroelectric plants located in the area. (Highsmith [1953], p. 79.) Coal deposits are found on both flanks of the Cascades but it is necessary to import superior quality coal from Utah, British Columbia, Montana, and Wyoming. (Freeman and Martin, 1954, pp. 406-407.) This coal arrives by rail while quantities of petroleum arrive by water from western states. (Ullman, 1957, p. 50.)

OUTPUTS AND SERVICE AREAS
OF SEATTLE'S PROFILE INDUSTRIES

Sawmills, planing mills, and mill work: Outputs of the lumber industry tend to consist mostly of only partly finished or rather crude products. Highsmith [1953], p. 94, states:

> In the Northwest lumber industry the emphasis has been on the early stages of manufacture, with very little manufacture of products from the rough or planed lumber turned out by the mills of the region.

The heavy production of Douglas-fir lumber goes largely into the building trade. (McCarty, 1940, p. 107.) Other products of the industry include cedar shingles and plywood materials. (United States Department of Labor, 1957, p. 318.) Markets for Seattle lumber industries are unknown, but it is known that Washington lumber products are distributed throughout the United States (Renner, 1951, p. 297) with particularly large quantities being shipped to California and the states of the manufacturing zone. (Ullman, 1957, p. 54.) Lumber is a major export commodity from the port of Seattle with large quantities destined for the Atlantic Coast ports, Alaska, and Great Britain. (United States Board of Engineers for Rivers and Harbors and United States Maritime Administration, 1953, No. 36, pp. 200-202.)

Aircraft and parts: Military planes and transports are specialties of the Seattle aircraft plants and their distribution is international. (Freeman and Martin, 1954, p. 422.)

Non-local services: Seattle is described by McCarty (1940, p. 117) as a "commercial city" whose wealth is based on foreign and domestic trade. This description is not inappropriate in view of the particular non-local services in which Seattle is specialized.

Water transportation: Seattle became prominent as a port when it was established as the base of operations for the Alaskan trade at the end of the 19th century. Being nearer to the Orient than any of the other major ports, it was able to pre-empt a good share of the trade with the Orient, although its advantage was somewhat lessened with the opening of the Panama Canal. (McCarty, 1940, pp. 115-16.) In foreign trade Portland was for many years the unquestioned leader. But in 1950 Seattle took the lead. Portland surpassed Seattle in foreign exports but Seattle handled over ten times the tonnage reaching Portland in imports. (Freeman and Martin, 1954, pp. 429-30.) In 1951 Seattle's port carried on a total commerce of slightly over 12 million tons, 64 per cent of which were imports. Important types of export commodities were grains, particularly wheat; fruits; lumber and products; coal; petroleum products; and metals and manufactures. Imports included vegetable food products; petroleum and products; wood and products; fish; and sand, gravel, and crushed rock. (United States Board of Engineers for Rivers and Harbors and United States Maritime Administration, 1953, No. 36, pp. 204-213.)

In foreign trade, Seattle exports a little over twice as much tonnage as it imports. Its most important export commodity, wheat, went largely to India, Japan, Peru and other South American countries. Coal exports were all destined for Japan. The largest receiver of Seattle's domestic exports was Alaska. (*Ibid.*, p. 198.)

Pacific Canada shipped about one-third of all of the foreign goods received in Seattle, lumber, paper products and limestone being the chief commodities. Metals and manufactures were received from Belgium, Japan, the Philippines, and South American countries. Vegetable food products consisting chiefly of coffee and bananas were received from Brazil and Panama, respectively. Chemicals arrived principally from England. Domestic imports were dominated by petroleum products shipped from California ports. (*Ibid.*, pp. 198-201.) According to Carlson (1950, p. 151), entrepôt manufacturing—the processing of commercial materials passing through Seattle—is not great.

Air transportation: With regard to air transportation, data gathered for 1950 by the Civil Aeronautics Administration indicate that for Seattle and Tacoma combined, four domestic airlines operated carrying a total of 286,626 passengers and 3,698 tons of cargo an average distance of 729 miles. (United States Department of Commerce, Civil Aeronautics Administration, 1951, p. 20.) Seattle also had heavy international business, with two airlines operating carrying 40,830 passengers and 4,844 tons of cargo. (*Ibid.*, p. 23.) In air terms, Seattle is closer to the Orient via the Great Circle Route than any other major American city and is the gateway to Alaska. Regular flights serve all parts of the United States, Alaska, Canada, Hawaii, and the Orient. (United States Board of Engineers for Rivers and Harbors and United States Maritime Administration, 1953, No. 36, p. 197.)

Wholesale trade: The extent of Seattle's trade hinterland is commented upon by McCarty (1940, pp. 116-117):

> The Seattle trade territory includes not only the forest and farm lands of the Puget Sound Valley but also a vast productive area in eastern Washington and adjacent Idaho and Montana. To these lands Seattle acts as a gatherer and distributor. From this territory Seattle railroads gather wheat, fruit, flour, and animal and mineral products; to it they distribute manufactured goods and other articles for home consumption. Leadership in commercial development is almost invariably accompanied by leadership in finance. Seattle is banker not only to its own shipping interests, its lumbermen and fish merchants, but to Alaska and portions of interior Washington.

More specific information on the commodities involved indicates that Seattle's grain hinterland extends east to the Rocky Mountains (although Portland serves large areas of Idaho, Montana and southern Washington); its fruit hinterland includes the irrigated valleys east of the Cascades and the immediate Puget Sound fruit-producing region; and fish are brought from all waters extending from the Bering Sea to Puget Sound. (Seeman, 1935, pp. 22-24.) These plus timber (discussed above) are roughly the important areas serving Seattle's port commerce. Seattle's trade territory as delimited by Thomas and Crisler, Park and Newcomb, and Highsmith includes all of the western half of Washington with the exception of the few southernmost counties. This area, which is far smaller than the McCarty trade area, apparently is based on Seattle's timber and fruit hinterland and on the area to which products are distributed.

Hotels and lodging places: With its pleasant climate, nearness to the ocean, forests, Canada and Alaska, Seattle is an important tourist center. (See Freeman and Martin, 1954, pp. 270-281.) It is assumed that Seattle's specialization in this industry group is related to this tourist center function. Also relevant may be the military installation in Seattle as well as the seasonal nature of the lumber industry causing a flow of personnel through Seattle.

Federal public administration: Seattle's specialization in this industry group is no doubt chiefly related to the location in Seattle of the headquarters of the 13th Naval District and sizable United States Navy installations. (*Ibid.*, p. 461.)

Insurance: This specialization is no doubt related to the location in Seattle of a Federal Reserve System Branch Bank. One insurance company located in Seattle employed over 500 people in 1953, three companies employed over 250 persons and seven, over 100. Numerous other smaller units were also operated in this SMA. (*1953 County Business Patterns.*) It is assumed that a sub-national area is being served by these offices.

Miscellaneous entertainment and recreation services: It is assumed that this specialization, like that in hotels, is related to Seattle's functions as a tourist center and also to the location in Seattle of military personnel.

SUMMARY: SEATTLE

Seattle is fairly dependent upon its immediate hinterland for lumber and electrical power inputs. Also from this area come aluminum and copper for its aircraft industries as well as fruit and fish for its commerce. Seattle also performs important wholesale and financial functions for this area. From Area C come grains for the port commerce, coal and petroleum and various inputs including engines and propellers for its aircraft industries. In turn, Seattle sends to this area its finished aircraft and hinterland commodities—fruits, fish, and lumber. Financial (insurance), military, and recreation functions are also performed for Area C.

PORTLAND (OREGON)

SMA consists of Clackamas, Multnomah, and Washington Counties, Oregon and Clark County, Washington

1950 population: central city, 373,628; SMA, 704,829

Important location feature: port on the Columbia River connecting with the Pacific Ocean

Other important feature: Federal Reserve Branch city

INPUTS AND SUPPLY AREAS FOR PORTLAND'S PROFILE INDUSTRIES

Sawmills, planing mills, and mill work: The important inputs for these industries are timber and fuels. Timber inputs can only be discussed in general terms. Large stands of timber are available from Portland's hinterland but inputs no doubt arrive from all parts of the Pacific Northwest. (See map in Highsmith, [1953], p. 31.) The discussion of this timber region in the preceding (Seattle) section is applicable here. Since 1938, Oregon has been the leading lumber producing state in the nation. (United States Board of Engineers for Rivers and Harbors and United States Maritime Administration, 1954, No. 34, p. 135.) In 1949 Oregon produced over seven billion board feet of lumber, more than twice the amount turned out by its closest rival, Washington. (Freeman and Martin, 1954, p. 244.)

Turning to fuels, electricity produced from water power is the central source of power in the Pacific Northwest, over 98 per cent of the electricity produced in Washington, Oregon, and Idaho during 1950 being developed from this source. (Freeman and Martin, 1954, p. 209.) Some coal is available on both slopes of the Cascades; however, it is necessary to import superior quality coal from Utah, British Columbia, Montana, and Wyoming. (*Ibid.*, pp. 407-408.) Petroleum arrives from California ports, making up 96 per cent of Portland's coastwise imports.

Table 51. Industrial Profile, Portland, Oregon: 1950

Category and industry	Location quotient	Per cent of employed labor force	Inputs primarily from area:	Outputs primarily to area:
(2) *First stage resource users; production for non-final market*				
Sawmills, planing mills, and mill work	2.62	2.7	B, C	A, C
(9) *Service industries; non-local*	1.38	17.6	*	B, C
Warehousing and storage	1.59	(0.3)	*	B, C
Water transportation	3.08	(1.1)	*	C
Telegraph (wire and radio)	1.84	(0.1)	*	B, C
Wholesale trade	1.64	(5.8)	*	B, C
Total in profile industries	...	20.3	...	...

* Inputs other than labor not considered.

OUTPUTS AND SERVICE AREAS OF PORTLAND'S PROFILE INDUSTRIES

Sawmills, planing mills, and mill work: The lumber industry of the Northwest has emphasized the early, or processing, stages of manufacture, with little fabrication of products from the rough or planed lumber. The importance of the Pacific Northwest lumber industry is indicated by the following quotation:

> The United States depends heavily on the Northwest for softwood products. Since 1918 this region has been the nation's leading producer of lumber and during the past 7 years has supplied 44 per cent of the softwood lumber and 35 per cent of the total lumber, 64 per cent of the plywood, 17 per cent of the wood pulp, 8 per cent of the paper, 95 per cent of the shingles, and 66 per cent of the laths. Large size poles and piling come chiefly from the Northwest. Since 1946 over half of the nation's total lumber exports have originated in this region. Douglas-fir exports alone equal the exports of all other species combined; and Ponderosa pine is also a leading export species.
>
> The forest products industries employ 51 per cent of all persons engaged in manufacturing and pay 52 per cent of the region's industrial payroll. Forest products in 1950 received 54 per cent of the value added by manufacture within this region, and in 1949 provided 48 per cent of the railroad freight traffic originating in the

Northwest on Class I railroads and 57 per cent of the traffic on Class II railroads. (Highsmith, [1953], p. 93.)

Lumber products from Oregon find their way to virtually every state in the union with major amounts going to California, Texas, the North Central states, and the states of the manufacturing zone. (Ullman, 1957, p. 136.) Portland's share of the timber industries just described was not determined. However its initial "growth was based primarily upon forest resources; the transporting, manufacturing, and shipping of lumber, plywood, furniture, paper and other forest products are still the major activities." (Freeman and Martin, 1954, p. 451.) Thus sawmill products supply local furniture and paper industries as well as national markets. Lumber products also move from the port of Portland to many foreign countries.

Non-local services: According to Thomas and Crisler (1953, p. 132), "Portland is the financial, transportation, business, and industrial center of Oregon and parts of Washington and Idaho." Salient aspects of its situation are described as follows by Freeman and Martin (1954, pp. 215, 449):

> Portland, Oregon, with its 35-foot channel is strategically situated at the crossroads of the great east-west Columbia River waterway and the north-south Willamette-Puget trough. Thus the city has opportunity to serve the commerce of the world's oceans and the hinterlands of the Willamette Valley and the Inland Empire. . . .
>
> Its location on the banks of the navigable Willamette River near its confluence with the Columbia has been of major significance for urban development. Through Portland have passed the rich and varied products from the fertile Willamette Valley, the heavily forested slopes of the Cascades, and the semiarid farm- and rangelands to the east. Its natural crossroads position at the junction of the main north-south route from California to Puget Sound and the only water-level passage from the Columbia Basin to the coast has been a valuable asset throughout Portland's history. Down the gorge carved by the turbulent Columbia came the pioneers to claim the rich farmlands of Oregon. Train, truck, and barge, heavily freight-laden, all take advantage of this economical corridor through the Cascades.

The specific non-local services in which Portland is specialized reflect the influence of its regional situation and strategic location.

Warehousing and storage: This specialization is assumed to be directly related to Portland's functions as a port and wholesale center.

Water transportation: Portland boasts the only large fresh-water harbor on the Pacific Coast; this advantage has been enhanced by the improvement for navigation of the lower Columbia River. Portland is the leading wheat and lumber shipping port on the coast, ranking 24th in total commerce among all United States ports. (Thomas and Crisler, 1953, p. 132.) In 1951 the total commerce of the port of Portland amounted to a little over 12 million tons, approximately 60 per cent of which were imports. Although Seattle leads the Pacific Northwest ports in total foreign tonnage handled, Portland has the greater export tonnage, shipping to foreign ports four times as much wood and paper as either Seattle or Tacoma, as well as larger amounts of farm produce. (Freeman and Martin, 1954, pp. 429-430.) Over 70 per cent of Portland's foreign exports went across the Pacific, principally to India and Japan; 16 per cent moved east across the Atlantic while about 8 per cent went to South and Central America areas. (United States Board of Engineers for Rivers and Harbors and United States Maritime Administration, 1954, No. 34, p. 151.) Important export commodities included grains and grain products, logs and lumber, other wood and paper including newsprint, petroleum products and sand and gravel. (*Ibid.*, pp. 140-148.)

Foreign imports originated chiefly in the Far East and Western Europe. Turning to domestic traffic, petroleum products, chiefly from California ports, was the leading commodity inbound while lumber and canned goods comprised the principal commodities moving from the port of Portland. Receipts in Portland from traffic on the Columbia River were largely made up of lumber products, sand, gravel and rock and wheat; while shipments from Portland to river ports included lumber products, sand, gravel and rock, and petroleum products. (*Ibid.*, pp. 148, 151.)

Telegraph: Portland is the location of one of Western Union's 15 automatic, high speed message centers which serves the states of Washington, Oregon, Idaho, and Montana. (*Encyclopedia Americana*, 1957, vol. 26, pp. 345, 347.) It is assumed that this specialization is also related to Portland's functions as a port and as a wholesale and financial center.

Wholesale trade: Much of Portland's wholesale trade activity seems to be concentrated on the assembling of various commodities from surrounding areas. Portland is one of eight SMA's between one-half and three million population that is above average in per capita sales of assemblers of farm products according to statistics compiled from the *1948 Census of Business*. Products assembled in Portland show great diversity. Portland collects large quantities of wheat for local milling and for export from the areas of concentrated production in Oregon (the northeast corner), from southern Idaho, from Washington south of the Snake River, and from parts of Washington north of the Snake. (Seeman, 1935, p. 24.) From the rich Willamette Valley southwest of Portland comes a large variety of crops: hops (over half of America's total production), prunes, walnuts, filberts, strawberries, and truck farm products, as well as poultry, eggs and milk. (Freeman and Martin, 1954, pp. 292-300; Highsmith [1953], pp. 50, 62.) Apples are available from the area to the west of Portland. Sheep and cattle are gathered from all parts of the Pacific Northwest. Portland's lumber inputs have already been discussed. Many of these commodities are processed in Portland before being transshipped, Portland being a local center for flour milling, meat packing, the collection of wool and production of textiles, the packing, canning and freezing of fruits and vegetables, and the processing of timber. (Freeman and Martin, 1954, p. 451.) But of all these activities, only the timber industries (see above) are of such a size as to appear as a part of Portland's specialized industry profile.

Portland's wholesale trade area as delimited by Thomas and Crisler is similar to that assigned to Portland by McKenzie (1933, chapter 8). This area includes all of Oregon, a few of the southwest counties in Washington and a portion of west central Idaho. On the other hand Highsmith ([1953], p. 111) delimits Portland's wholesale trading area for manufactured goods and finds it to include a much smaller area—the same Washington Counties, but only a part of Oregon, the southeast corner being assigned to the trade area of Boise, Idaho. The discrepancy may be accounted for in part on the grounds that Portland's largest wholesale trade area is the one from which products are gathered rather than the one to which they are distributed. The above discussion of specific commodities indicates that for some products (sheep and cattle and lumber) the trade area is much more inclusive than any of the above delimitations.

SUMMARY: PORTLAND

Portland is chiefly a commercial center for the Pacific Northwest. Both financial and commercial (wholesaling, telegraphy, warehousing, and water transportation) functions are performed by this SMA for its immediate hinterland as well as more distant areas. Hinterland resources form the chief inputs for its most important industry group: wood processing industries. Outputs of wood products serve a local, national and international market. Power is also available in the local area in the form of water harnessed for the production of electricity.

ATLANTA

SMA consists of Cobb, De Kalb, and Fulton Counties, Georgia
1950 population: central city, 331,314; SMA, 671,797
Important features: Federal Reserve Bank city; state capital of Georgia

INPUTS AND SUPPLY AREAS FOR ATLANTA'S PROFILE INDUSTRIES

Furniture and fixtures: The manufacture of furniture requires the use of both hard and soft woods—the soft woods being used for the interior parts of the furniture and for crating furniture for shipment—and textile products for upholstery. (Whitbeck and Finch, 1941, pp. 146-147.) These materials are all readily available from Atlanta's trade area as oak and pine forests are relatively plentiful in this region (the southern Piedmont). (See map in United States National Resources Planning Board, 1943, p. 54.) However, there are also probably timber inputs from other parts of the country. (Whitbeck and Finch, 1941, p. 148.) Textile inputs are likewise available from nearby areas, the Piedmont area of Virginia, North and South Carolina, and Georgia producing large quantities of cotton textile products. (Alexandersson, 1956, pp. 65-67.)

Bakery products: Inputs for bakery products include grain mill products, miscellaneous food products, meat packing and poultry products, and sugar. Vegetable oil products and meat products are available from other industries within the SMA. (McCarty, 1940, p. 379; United States Department of Labor, 1957, p. 60.) Grain mill and other products probably arrive from other SMA's.

Miscellaneous fabricated textile products: Inputs are primarily from yarn, thread, and fabric mills. Sources can only be discussed in general terms. Cotton textile inputs are readily available from Georgia and surrounding states.

> North Carolina exceeds every other state in cotton-system spindles in place, having 5,927,000 or 25 per cent of the total for the United States in 1948; South Carolina is second with 5,642,000 or 24 per cent; and Georgia third with 3,217,000 or 13 per cent. (Hoover and Ratchford, 1951, p. 145.)

Atlanta itself has a substantial employment in yarn, thread, and fabric mills although not quite large enough to meet our criteria for specialization. Undoubtedly many inputs arrive from these SMA industries. Rayon textile inputs are likewise available from surrounding Southern states.

> In 1947, the South had about 60 per cent of the capacity of the industry (about 75 per cent if West Virginia is included) and the proportion is likely to increase in the future since most of the large plants built after the war are located in the South. Virginia, with six large plants, is the leading state of the Union and in 1947 produced about a third of the nation's total. Tennessee is second in the country with four plants and Georgia, North Carolina and South Carolina have one or more plants each. (*Ibid.*, p. 151.)

Table 52. Industrial Profile, Atlanta: 1950

Category and industry	Location quotient	Per cent of employed labor force	Inputs primarily from area:	Outputs primarily to area:
(5) *Second stage resource users; production for final market*				
Furniture and fixtures	1.68	1.0	B	C
Bakery products	2.00	1.0	A?, C	C
Miscellaneous fabricated textile products	1.61	0.2	A, B, C	C
(9) *Service industries; non-local*	1.44	18.4	*	B, C
Air transportation	3.72	(0.6)	*	C
Telegraph (wire and radio)	3.31	(0.3)	*	B, C
Wholesale trade	1.54	(5.4)	*	B
Federal public administration	1.84	(3.3)	*	C
(10) *Service industries; may be local or non-local*				
Insurance	1.96	2.6	*	B, C
Total in profile industries	...	23.2	...	...

* Inputs other than labor not considered.

OUTPUTS AND SERVICE AREAS
OF ATLANTA'S PROFILE INDUSTRIES

Furniture and fixtures: Outputs include household furniture, both plain and upholstered, and mattresses. (United States Department of Labor, 1957, p. 60.) Distribution of these products is no doubt to a sub-national area.

Bakery products: Specialization in this industry group is largely due to the location in Atlanta of a large wholesale baking company engaged in the manufacture of cookies, crackers, and similar products. (*Idem.*) Distribution of these products is no doubt to a sub-national market.

Miscellaneous fabricated textile products: Specific products of this industry group include cotton bags, tarpaulins, and other miscellaneous textile products. (*Idem.*) Distribution of these products is probably to a sub-national market.

Non-local services: Atlanta ranked first among all of the cities of the South on Vance and Smith's (1954, p. 128) metropolitan functions score. "It's strategic location and excellent transportation facilities make Atlanta a major center of commerce, finance, and distribution for this section of the country." (United States Department of Labor, 1957, p. 60.) With rail connections to the seacoast established before the middle of the 19th century, Atlanta was able to capitalize on its central location with respect to much of the Southeast. The city was already a crossroads of rail lines before the Civil War, during which it served as a supply depot and manufacturing center for the Confederacy. Recovering from its destruction during that conflict, Atlanta became a focus of major traffic currents and a regional headquarters for many national distributors. (Vance and Smith, 1954, pp. 121-22.) McCarty (1940, p. 378) emphasizes the city's strategic position in respect to transportation, identifying it as the "leading railroad center of the South." It is observed that its transportation facilities make Atlanta a good location for wholesale enterprises and financial institutions. McCarty indicates that Atlanta's wholesale trade area includes most of the Georgia Piedmont and that its banking interests serve an even wider territory. The specific non-local services in which Atlanta is specialized will be seen to accord with the foregoing descriptions.

Air transportation: In 1950, five airlines were carrying on domestic service in Atlanta, carrying 395,876 passengers and 4,366 tons of cargo an average distance of 423 miles. Its domestic airline traffic passenger index in 1950 was surpassed only by those of Miami and Dallas, among the larger SMA's. (United States Department of Commerce, Civil Aeronautics Administration, 1951.)

Telegraph: Atlanta was chosen by Western Union to be the location of one of their 15 automatic, high-speed message centers; Atlanta serves both Georgia and Florida. (*Encyclopedia Americana,* 1957, vol. 26, pp. 345, 347.) In addition Atlanta's specialization in telegraph no doubt reflects its important commercial functions.

Wholesale trade: Atlanta's specialization in this service received some comment above. Its trade area appears to include a large part of Georgia and the southwest portion of South Carolina. (See the Park and Newcomb and Thomas and Crisler maps.) Vance and Smith indicate that the rise of Atlanta as a major wholesale and commercial center illustrates a general ecological principle.

> As any region develops its own productivity and economic complexity, the locus of metropolitan development shifts from the "gateway" cities to those in the interior which the German theorists have called "central place" cities. This began to happen in the South before 1860 in the organization of distribution laid down by the railroads. It is in this trend that we see the beginnings of the phenomenal development of the two great regional metropolises, Atlanta first and later Dallas. (Vance and Smith, 1954, p. 121.)

Federal public administration: A large number of Federal offices are located in Atlanta. (Thomas and Crisler, 1953, p. 43.) Among these are the headquarters of the Third Army, Fort McPherson, and a large federal penitentiary. (*Encyclopedia Americana,* 1957, vol. 2, p. 502.)

Insurance: Atlanta is considered the leading financial center of the Southeast, an appropriate location for a Federal Reserve Bank. Specialization in insurance is probably related to its financial functions. In 1953 Atlanta contained one insurance company employing more than 500 persons, three companies employing between 250 and 500 persons, and 18 employing between 100 and 250 persons. (*County Business Patterns, 1953.*) Atlanta's Federal Reserve District includes the states of Georgia, Florida, Alabama, Tennessee, and the southern parts of Mississippi and Louisiana. Undoubtedly some insurance functions are performed for a roughly comparable area, but Atlanta by no means "dominates" all of this broad area to the exclusion of other metropolitan centers.

SUMMARY: ATLANTA

Atlanta's profile manufacturing industries gather the great majority of their inputs from the surrounding hinterland. Outputs of these industries appear to serve a larger area, at least the Southeast United States. This SMA is most important as a commercial and financial center, although it has undergone rapid expansion in manufacturing during the recent period not covered by our statistics. Transportation and financial services are performed for the Southeast. Wholesaling and state administrative functions are performed for a smaller area.

DALLAS

SMA consists of Dallas County, Texas
1950 population: central city, 434,462; SMA, 614,799
Important feature: Federal Reserve Bank city

INPUTS AND SUPPLY AREAS FOR DALLAS' PROFILE INDUSTRIES

Miscellaneous fabricated textile products: Inputs for this industry are products from textile mills and minor amounts of animal furs and hides. Most of the necessary inputs appear to come from producers in the Appalachian Piedmont area and from the Mid-Atlantic states. (McKnight, 1956, pp. 44-56.)

Aircraft and parts: Dallas, like most of the Western cities involved in the production of aircraft, concentrates primarily on airframe production and final assembly. (Cunningham, 1951, p. 226.) Processed inputs include alloy steels, copper, aluminum processed materials and fuels. Fabricated materials include chiefly airplane engines and propellers. Sources of the inputs are unknown, except that almost all of the materials arrive from outside of the state. (McKnight, 1956, pp. 44-56.) Much of the growth of the Dallas aircraft industry occurred as a result of World War II and the emphasis placed on a decentralization of the industry. Dallas was selected because of its labor supply, central location, favorable terrain and climate. (Cunningham, 1951, pp. 126, 131, 134.)

With regard to fuels, natural gas is readily available in the general area from both the Gulf Coast field to the south and from the Panhandle field to the northwest. (See map in Zimmermann, 1951, p. 561.) Light fuel products—gasoline, diesel fuel, etc.—are piped in from the Houston-Bayton area and from the Port Arthur – Beaumont area. (McKnight, 1956, pp. 139-140.)

OUTPUTS AND SERVICE AREAS OF DALLAS' PROFILE INDUSTRIES

Miscellaneous fabricated textile products: The specific nature of these products was not determined. However, they are probably closely related to the apparel industry in Dallas, an industry which is large enough to make Dallas an important fashion center. (Alexandersson,

1956, pp. 72-73.) Marketing of these apparel and fabricated textile products is reported to be: 10 per cent in Dallas, 30 per cent outside Dallas but within Texas and the remaining 60 per cent outside Texas. (McKnight, 1956, pp. 44-56.) Probably the majority of the business done outside Texas is limited to the Southwestern states.

Table 53. Industrial Profile, Dallas: 1950

Category and industry	Location quotient	Per cent of employed labor force	Inputs primarily from area:	Outputs primarily to area:
(5) *Second stage resource users; production for final market*				
Miscellaneous fabricated textile products	1.99	0.3	C	B, C
(7) *Resources of indirect significance; production for final market*				
Aircraft and parts	4.07	1.9	B, C	C
(9) *Service industries; non-local*	1.34	17.0	*	B, C
Trucking service	1.66	(1.8)	*	B, C
Warehousing and storage	1.55	(0.3)	*	B
Air transportation	4.76	(0.8)	*	C
Telegraph (wire and radio)	3.32	(0.3)	*	B, C
Wholesale trade	1.84	(6.5)	*	B
Banking and credit agencies	1.79	(1.7)	*	B, C
Security and commodity brokerage, and investment companies	2.31	(0.4)	*	B, C
(10) *Service industries; may be local or non-local*				
Insurance	2.61	3.5	*	B, C
Total in profile industries	...	22.7	...	...

* Inputs other than labor not considered.

Aircraft and parts: Aircraft produced in Dallas supply a national market and perhaps an international one, with most of the production going outside of the state. (McKnight, 1956, pp. 44-47.)

Non-local services: Dallas is a "major trade and distribution center and the leading banking center of the Southwest." (United States Department of Labor, 1957, p. 294.) Alexandersson (1956, p. 101) believes that Dallas' wholesale functions are concentrated on the distributive side with nearby Fort Worth serving as a collection center for some of the area, particularly for the range country to the west. The central location of Dallas in the Southwest is regarded as an important factor in its concentration on distribution functions. It is noted that

> Dallas in the Southwest . . . resembles Atlanta in its location and development. Growing up on broad flat plains in one of the most fertile sections of the Southwest, Dallas reached 10,000 population by 1880 and entered the census classification of cities over 100,000 in 1920. After Atlanta's old cotton lands had reached their maximum production, the lands of Dallas's sustenance area continued in their prime, and the riches of oil from under those soils did far more than cotton to make Dallas a major distribution center. (Vance and Smith, 1954, p. 122.)

Non-local services in which Dallas is specialized are discussed below.

Trucking service; Warehousing and storage: These services are closely related to Dallas' functions as a wholesale trade center. No doubt a considerable portion of the Southwest is served by these industry groups.

Air transportation: Civil Aeronautics Administration statistics for 1950 domestic traffic indicate that Dallas far exceeded its nearest Texas rival, Houston, in number of aircraft departures (34,465), number of passengers carried (442,450), and tons of cargo carried (6,170), although it was not an important center for international air service. (United States Department of Commerce, Civil Aeronautics Administration, 1951, p. 18.)

Telegraph: It is assumed that this service is closely related to commercial and financial functions. Located in Dallas is one of Western Union's 15 regional automatic high-speed message centers; it serves the state of Texas.

Wholesale trade: One delimitation of the wholesale trading area of Dallas includes all of northern Texas including almost all of the Panhandle, a large chunk of northern Louisiana, the southwest corner of Arkansas, the southeast corner of Oklahoma and the east central portion of New Mexico. (United States National Recovery Administration, 1935.) McCarty (1940, p. 386) estimates that Dallas' trade territory includes a large section of the cotton and oil country of northeast Texas.

Banking and credit agencies; Security and commodity brokerage and investment companies: These services are undoubtedly related to the fact that a Federal Reserve Bank is located in Dallas. Alexandersson (1956, p. 109) states that "Dallas is the leading financial center of Texas and the Southwest." Financial services are no doubt performed for the entire eleventh Federal Reserve District, which includes all of Texas, parts of New Mexico, Arizona, and Louisiana.

Insurance: Insurance is likewise related to the Federal Reserve Bank operations. Dallas is "one of the top insurance centers of the nation" and several large insurance companies have headquarters or branch offices here. (United States Department of Labor, 1957, p. 294.)

SUMMARY: DALLAS

Dallas ranks as a major Southern metropolitan center. Vance and Smith (1954, p. 128) find that Dallas ranks second only to Atlanta on their index of metropolitan functions for southern cities. Although fuels are available locally, Dallas does not show a high specialization in manufacturing industries. Dallas may be said to be chiefly a service center and performs important wholesale services for its hinterland and financial services for an even larger area.

DENVER

SMA consists of Adams, Arapahoe, Denver, and Jefferson Counties, Colorado

1950 population: central city, 415,786; SMA, 563,832

Important features: Federal Reserve Branch city; capital of Colorado

INPUTS AND SUPPLY AREAS FOR DENVER'S PROFILE INDUSTRIES

Meat products: Wholesale meat packing functions are of greatest importance for Denver's meat products industry. Denver ranked first in the nation as a lamb and sheep market in 1950 (one million salable lambs being received) and seventh as a cattle market (0.7 million salable cattle being received). (United States Department of Agriculture, Production and Marketing Administration, 1951, pp. 7-8.) Denver is the largest lamb market in the United States and the largest cattle market outside of the corn belt area of the country. (Henderson, 1954, p. 365.) Cattle are received from surrounding states in all directions but chiefly from the west (Mather, 1950, p. 91) while lambs arrive chiefly from the Pacific Northwest. (Denver Planning Office, 1953, p. 38.) Sixty-eight per cent of the cattle and 40 per cent of the sheep and lambs are trucked in. (United States Department of Agriculture, Production and Marketing Administration, 1951, p. 10.) The relatively high percentages hauled in by rail indicate that a sizable proportion of the shipments span a considerable distance.

Table 54. Industrial Profile, Denver: 1950

Category and industry	Location quotient	Per cent of employed labor force	Inputs primarily from area:	Outputs primarily to area:
(3) *First stage resource users; production for final market*				
Meat products	2.63	1.3	B, C	C
Miscellaneous food preparations and kindred products	1.58	0.3	B	B, C
(9) *Service industries; non-local*	1.61	20.6	*	B, C
Trucking service	1.62	(1.7)	*	B, C
Warehousing and storage	1.72	(0.3)	*	B
Air transportation	5.24	(0.9)	*	C
Other and not specified utilities	3.42	(0.2)	*	A, B?
Wholesale trade	1.63	(5.7)	*	B
Security and commodity brokerage and investment companies	1.76	(0.3)	*	B, C
Hotels	1.58	(1.5)	*	C
Federal public administration	1.96	(3.5)	*	C
State public administration	1.61	(0.8)	*	B
(10) *Service industries; may be local or non-local*				
Hospitals	1.79	3.1	*	B, C
Educational services, private	1.51	1.4	*	A, B, C
Total in profile industries	...	26.7	...	...

* Inputs other than labor not considered.

Miscellaneous food preparations and kindred products: Specialization in this industry in Denver appears to be largely due to the location there of industries engaged in the refining of sugar beets. Sugar beet refining is a prime example of an industry whose location is dominated by a single material. Plants are almost without exception located in areas of sugar beet production partly because of the great reduction in bulk of sugar beets in the process of extraction of the sugar content and partly because of their perishable nature. (United States National Resources Planning Board, 1943, p. 137.) According to McCarty (1940,

p. 238), Denver's trade area includes the irrigated sugar-beet section of northeast Colorado as well as the southeastern part of Wyoming and western Nebraska. A map of important sugar beet counties in the United States together with the location of sugar beet factories as of 1941 indicates that Denver's supply of sugar beets probably arrives largely from areas to the immediate northeast and south. (United States National Resources Planning Board, 1943, p. 137.)

Fuels: Petroleum is available from the state of Colorado as well as from neighboring states in considerable quantities, the quantity of regional production far exceeding regional consumption. (Denver Planning Office, 1953, pp. 40-42.) Natural gas is also available in the area; however considerable quantities are also received from both the Hugoton Gas Field in Kansas and from the Amarillo Gas Field of Texas. (Denver Planning Office, 1953, p. 116; Stockton, 1952, p. 170.) Coal is available from the hinterland area (Colorado, Wyoming, and New Mexico) in considerable quantities; however, its use as a fuel has been declining. (Denver Planning Office, 1953, p. 43.) Electric power is available from both steam and hydro-electric generating stations in the local area. (*Ibid.*, p. 108.)

OUTPUTS AND SERVICE AREAS OF DENVER'S PROFILE INDUSTRIES

Meat products: Important outputs include wholesale meat products. Meat packed in Denver has a market which extends as far as the West Coast and reaches some eastern points. However, for the most part, markets are limited to the western areas of the country because of the heavy competition from meat packing centers in the central states. (Denver Planning Office, 1953, p. 53.)

Miscellaneous food preparations and kindred products: Important products of the beet sugar refineries include sugar and animal feeds in bulk and cake form. (Nielsen, 1950, p. 273.) The specific market area served by Denver sugar refineries was not determined. However Alderfer and Michl (1957, p. 539) suggest that large areas may be involved. They explain:

> The competition between the beet and cane refiners is also keen. Beet sugar is produced in 16 states, from Ohio and Michigan westward to California, Washington, and Oregon. The Mountain states are not large consuming states because of sparse population and lack of sugar-using industries. Accordingly, to dispose of their production the beet refiners must market their sugar over wide areas, areas that

are also served by the cane refiners. It is not unusual for beet refiners to market sugar as far east as Buffalo and Pittsburgh. Thus, except for the Mountain states, where beet sugar accounts for 80 to 90 per cent of all the sugar consumed, and the Eastern seaboard and the Gulf, where no beet is used, the beet and cane refiners are in strong competition.

Non-local services: Denver performs important commercial, financial, and wholesale functions for a large area of Western United States. Alexandersson (1956, pp. 101-102) indicates that an important reason for Denver's prominence as a service and distribution center is its location at the contact point between the range land of the Great Plains and the irrigated area to the north of the city in the South Platte Valley. The irrigated land supplies forage crops for livestock, a considerable proportion of which spends time on the nearby range. The same writer indicates that Denver is the commercial center of a broad area in the Rocky Mountain states and identifies the city as the "major financial and administrative center between the Missouri River and the Pacific Coast."

Specific services in which Denver shows specialization are mentioned below.

Trucking service: Although in 1950 rail shipment accounted for a sizable amount of the livestock inputs for Denver (see above), trucks were nevertheless of importance for the livestock industry. More generally it is estimated that trucks bring to Denver 44 per cent of the inputs for the large manufacturing firms and carry out 64 per cent of the products; and that they bring 53 per cent of the inputs for the large wholesale firms and carry out 82 per cent of the products. (Denver Planning Office, 1953, pp. 100-101.)

Warehousing and storage: This specialization is assumed to be related to Denver's functions as a collection and distribution center for the Rocky Mountain and adjoining Plains region.

Air transportation: Denver is an important air terminal having in 1950 eight domestic airlines operating which carried a total of 243,437 passengers and 3,458 tons of cargo an average of 731 miles. (United States Department of Commerce, Civil Aeronautics Administration, 1951, p. 5.)

Other and not specified utilities: Specialization in this category appears to be due to the importance of irrigation employment in this area. The Denver SMA itself contained 140,188 acres of irrigated farm land in 1950. (United States Bureau of the Census, *United States Census of Agriculture: 1950, Irrigation of Agricultural Lands,* 1952, pp.

4-11, 4-12.) It could not be determined how large an area is served by the Denver employment, but in the counties immediately north of Denver (including Adams, Boulder, Morgan, Weld, and Larimer) hundreds of thousands of acres are under irrigation. In 1949 Colorado was second only to California in number of acres under irrigation; in that year 2,872,348 acres were irrigated. (*Ibid.*, pp. 3-5, 4-2.)

Wholesale trade: In line with its commercial dominance of a large portion of the Rocky Mountain area and the Colorado Great Plains, Denver is an important wholesale center for this area. (McCarty, 1940, pp. 199-200.) According to statistics compiled from the *1948 Census of Business,* Denver was one of eight SMA's between one-half million and three million population which were above the average for all SMA's in per capita sales for wholesale assemblers of farm products. It has already been noted above that Denver is an important livestock market and sugar refining center. In addition, fruits of all kinds are gathered from its irrigated hinterland.

Estimates of Denver's wholesale trade area vary somewhat but in general agree that all of Colorado and at least the southwest portion of Wyoming is included. Thomas and Crisler expand this area to include all but the westernmost part of Wyoming while Petersen's version includes, in addition to the above areas, the northern half of New Mexico, one or two counties in Kansas and two counties in Utah. (Petersen, 1936, p. 42.) This latter delimitation is based on a combination of several maps including retail shopping areas, wholesale grocery trade territories, and trade territories of representative Denver jobbers. (*Ibid.*, pp. 30-38.) The Denver Planning Office's delimitation is based upon data gathered from 151 Denver firms and suggests that the bulk of sales occurs in Colorado, Wyoming, and New Mexico, with small western portions of Kansas and Nebraska being included. (Denver Planning Office, 1953, pp. 70-72.)

Security and commodity brokerage and investment companies: It is assumed that this specialization is at least in part related to the location in Denver of a branch bank of the Federal Reserve System. McCarty (1940, p. 200) describes Denver as "the leading commercial and banking center between the Missouri River and the Pacific coast," so no doubt these services are performed for at least a sub-national area.

Hotels: Denver enjoys a flourishing tourist industry partly because of its climate and partly because of its location near the Colorado Rockies. (McCarty, 1940, pp. 198-199; and Thomas and Crisler, 1953, p. 116.)

Federal public administration: In addition to being the location for one of the three Federal mints in this country, Denver is the location for a great variety of Federal branch offices. The 225 or so bureaus and commissions are said to be more than are found in any other city outside Washington. (*Encyclopaedia Britannica,* 1957, vol. 7, p. 226.) One factor in the location of these offices in Denver may be the general tendency to reduce concentration of government offices on the two coasts for strategic reasons. In addition to these national government offices, Denver is the location of several military establishments including an Air Force Finance Center, Lowry Air Force Base, and Rocky Flats Atomic Plant. (United States Department of Labor, 1957, p. 32.)

State public administration: Denver is the capital of Colorado and is the location of many state-related offices.

Hospitals: Several hospitals in Denver serve primarily non-local patients. Children's, Colorado General and Psychopathic, Veterans Administration, Mount Airy, and St. Joseph's serve a regional clientele while Fitzsimons Army, Jewish Consumptive Relief Society, National Jewish, and Spears Chiropractic serve a national and international clientele. (Denver Planning Office, 1953, p. 129.)

Educational services, private: Among the larger private educational institutions in Denver are the University of Denver and Regis College. (Thomas and Crisler, 1953, p. 116.) These institutions both serve at least in part a non-local clientele.

SUMMARY: DENVER

Denver appears to be chiefly a commercial and financial SMA performing metropolitan functions for a large portion of the Mountain States. Some processing of resources is carried on—notably meat packing and sugar refining—and inputs appear to arrive from the immediate hinterland (Area B) in the case of sugar beets and from both hinterland and regional areas (B and C) for livestock. Transportation, wholesaling, irrigation, administrative, and educational services appear to be performed for a large but sparsely populated area (Area B) consisting chiefly of Colorado and parts of New Mexico and Wyoming, while financial, military and tourist functions are performed for a regional or national area.

CHAPTER 13

Regional Capitals

Houston	*Indianapolis*	*Fort Worth*
New Orleans	*Columbus*	*Richmond*
Louisville	*Memphis*	*Oklahoma City*
Birmingham	*Omaha*	*Nashville*
		Jacksonville

Ample justification for describing each of the thirteen cities in this group as a "regional capital" will be found in the summary materials to follow. In each instance important reciprocal regional relationships with an adjacent hinterland can be discerned readily. On the one hand, each city has one or more profile industries directly related to resource-extracting activities carried on in its hinterland. Petroleum is important for Houston and Oklahoma City; livestock for Omaha, Fort Worth, Oklahoma City, Indianapolis, Columbus, and Nashville; tobacco for Richmond, Louisville, and Jacksonville; grains for Memphis and Louisville; lumber and cotton for Memphis; sea food and sugar cane for New Orleans; and coal, iron ore, and limestone for Birmingham. On the other hand, each city is a center for commercial and personal services of first importance to its hinterland. Specialization in wholesale trade and/or one or more business services is typical. Nine of the cities are Branch cities in the Federal Reserve System and one is a Bank city. All but one of the thirteen exhibit specialization in one or more forms of transportation—an important symptom of the necessary access to a sizable hinterland.

Despite the regional prominence of each of these cities, it is clear that as far as distinctively "metropolitan" functions are concerned, they take second rank to the "regional metropolises" described in the previous chapter. Although there is some overlap of sizes, they are considerably smaller on the average. Hence a comparable degree of specialization suggests that regional relationships are on the average less extensive.

We may call attention to the fact that several of these regional capitals—Louisville, Birmingham, Indianapolis, Columbus, and Richmond in particular—have manufacturing functions relating them to a much larger segment of the national economy than their own hinterlands. In this regard they are transitional to the class of "diversified manufacturing centers" described in the preceding and the subsequent chapter or, in the case of Birmingham, to the class of "specialized manufacturing centers."

HOUSTON

SMA consists of Harris County, Texas
1950 population: central city, 596,163; SMA, 806,701
Important location feature: port on the Houston Ship Channel off the Gulf of Mexico
Other important feature: Federal Reserve Branch city

INPUTS AND SUPPLY AREAS FOR HOUSTON'S PROFILE INDUSTRIES

Crude petroleum and natural gas extraction: Houston lies within the productive Gulf Coast petroleum and gas fields. (See maps in Zimmermann, 1951, pp. 514, 561.) This joint occurrence is quite common since natural gas and petroleum often occur together and much of the gas produced in the United States is from petroleum wells. (Dicken, 1949, p. 297.) It is estimated that the "gas available in the five principal gas reserve fields within 50 miles of Houston . . . is adequate to supply the area with low cost industrial fuel at a rate of 100 million cubic feet per day for over 130 years." (Houston Chamber of Commerce, 1940, p. 52.) Since extraction is an unusual specialization for an SMA it will be worthwhile to point out the residence of the employees in this industry group. According to the *1950 Census of Population* about half of the approximately 7,000 employees in this group reside within the city of Houston, the other half residing in urban places within the county. Harris county is 90 per cent urban.

Table 55. Industrial Profile, Houston: 1950

Category and industry	Location quotient	Per cent of employed labor force	Inputs primarily from area:	Outputs primarily to area:
(1) (*Primary resource extractors; production for non-final market*)				
Crude petroleum and natural gas extraction	5.17	2.1	B	A, C?
(2) *First stage resource users; production for non-final market*				
Petroleum refining	12.76	5.9	A, B, C	C
(9) *Service industries; non-local*	1.26	16.1	*	B, C
Warehousing and storage	2.30	(0.4)	*	B, C
Water transportation	3.54	(1.3)	*	C
Air transportation	1.63	(0.3)	*	C
Petroleum and gasoline pipe lines	6.32	(0.2)	*	C
Wholesale trade	1.56	(5.5)	*	B
Total in profile industries	...	24.1	...	...

* Inputs other than labor not considered.

Petroleum refining: Chief inputs for petroleum refining industries are crude oil and natural gas. Crude oil is available in the immediate vicinity of Houston from the Gulf Coast field. In recent years 6 to 8 per cent of all crude oil produced in the United States and 11 or 12 per cent of all natural gas production came from 29 counties within a 100-mile radius of Houston. (Houston Chamber of Commerce [1958], pp. 13, 16.) However, Houston refineries serve a much more extended area, refining oil piped from the nearby East Texas field and Louisiana Gulf field, as well as the more distant fields of west and northwest Texas, the Mid-Continent field and even from fields as distant as Wyoming. (Nisco Basic Survey, 1935, p. ST B6; McCarty, 1940, pp. 364-367.) Crude petroleum is received in considerable quantities via the port.

OUTPUTS AND SERVICE AREAS OF HOUSTON'S PROFILE INDUSTRIES

Crude petroleum and natural gas extraction: In 1950 the total production of crude petroleum from the Gulf Coast fields totaled 198,139,-000 barrels. (United States Bureau of Mines, 1953, p. 908.) It could not be determined what proportion of this production was sent to local refineries and what proportion was piped to more distant areas.

Petroleum refining: Outputs of Gulf Coast refineries in 1950 totaled 502,939,000 barrels; major products included gasoline, fuel oils and kerosene. (United States Bureau of Mines, 1953, p. 942.) Output of refineries located in Houston itself was not determined. Houston would appear to have a good location with regard to oil shipment:

> Favorable locations for large refineries are tidewater points fairly close to the center of crude production. Tankers are the cheapest transport facilities and tidewater location has the advantage of sending different products in different directions with a minimum of backtracking. (Zimmermann, 1951, p. 541.)

Large amounts of refinery products are shipped from Houston's port to other parts of this country and to foreign countries, petroleum (including crude oil) making up approximately 80 per cent of all the tonnage handled through the port. (Houston Chamber of Commerce, 1940, p. 52.) Crude oil and oil products are also transported to all parts of Texas, the central states and the manufacturing zone by pipeline. (For maps, see Zimmermann, 1951, p. 529 and Dicken, 1949, p. 294.)

Non-local services: During the 80-year period from its founding until the period of the first world war, Houston developed an economy based largely on the range livestock, agriculture, and timber production of its hinterland, becoming especially important as a distribution center for the cotton region of south-central Texas. The completion of the Houston Ship Channel in 1915 roughly coincided with the sharp rise in demand for petroleum products occasioned by World War I and the beginning of the automobile age and with the period of rapid expansion of petroleum production in Texas and Louisiana. Houston's water transport facilities made it an excellent location for petroleum refining, an industry which has continued to expand and which, particularly in the post World War II period, has attracted the growing sister industry, petro-chemical manufactures. The steady increase in the port traffic in the early days reflected the rising volume of exports of cotton, but these reached a peak in the early 1930's, while petroleum and related products have continued to increase in volume. As a Federal Reserve Branch city, Houston has important financial functions. However, the industries in which it shows specialization are most clearly connected with the commercial functions performed for its hinterland and broader areas.

Warehousing and storage: This specialization is no doubt tied to

Houston's function as a cotton and oil collection-distribution center and to the activities of the port.

Water transportation: Houston lies at the end of the Houston Ship Channel which opens onto the Gulf of Mexico. An extensive trade area is involved in Houston's port commerce:

> The local territory served by Houston, in which the port enjoys a freight rate advantage over New Orleans, in general, includes the whole of Texas, eastern half of New Mexico, southwestern corner of Kansas, and all of Oklahoma west of Oklahoma City. Comprising a vast agricultural and oil producing region this area contributes the preponderance of Houston's export tonnage.
>
> Of the principal commodities produced within this area petroleum products, which originate almost entirely within the State of Texas, account for the bulk of Houston's outbound foreign cargo. Cotton, wheat and other grains which also make up a considerable portion of the port's exports, originate principally in Texas, Kansas, Oklahoma and New Mexico. The source of many other mineral and agricultural products contributing to Houston's export trade, lies within this local hinterland territory.
>
> Outside the local area, the port of Houston serves, on an equalized freight rate basis with Mobile and New Orleans, a territory embracing the Central States, including Minnesota and parts of Michigan, and extending west from the Mississippi River to California, and north to the Canadian border. (United States Board of Engineers for Rivers and Harbors and United States Maritime Commission, 1949, No. 24, p. 191.)

Petroleum and products, wheat, miscellaneous grains and flour, coal, and cotton comprised approximately 90 per cent of Houston's total export tonnage in 1948. About 40 per cent of the foreign commerce went to the United Kingdom, 18 per cent to the Bordeaux-Hamburg area, 14 per cent to the Azores, Mediterranean, and Black Sea area and smaller amounts to the Baltic, Scandinavian, Iceland and Greenland, Caribbean, North China and Japanese areas. (United States Board of Engineers for Rivers and Harbors and United States Maritime Commission, 1949, No. 24, pp. 191-192.) Important imports from foreign countries included coffee from Colombia and Panama, petroleum and products from Mexico, and newsprint paper from Newfoundland. Trade with United States Pacific Coast ports was relatively small; most of it consisted of petroleum imports from California. (*Ibid.,* p. 194.) The bulk of Houston's domestic petroleum exports were received by Atlantic coastal ports. (See map in Ullman, 1957, p. 176.)

Air transportation: Houston is second only to Dallas among Texas cities in number of passengers served. Like Dallas, Houston is served by seven airlines, and in 1950 Houston airlines carried 229,250 passengers and 1,277 tons of cargo an average distance of 584 miles. (United States Department of Commerce, Civil Aeronautics Administration, 1951, p. 18.)

Petroleum and gasoline pipelines: The importance of petroleum pipelines has been mentioned above under the topic of petroleum refining. In addition, Houston is an important focus of the network of natural gas pipelines transporting gas from the Gulf area to the Central and Eastern United States. (See map in Stockton, 1952, p. 157.)

Wholesale trade: Houston's trade area, as delimited by Bogue, comprises roughly the southeast corner of Texas. There is general agreement that the city's sphere of influence covers much of the Gulf Coast region of the state. Houston is outranked by Dallas in commercial and financial functions according to Vance and Smith (1954, p. 128), but ranks third among the cities of the South on their metropolitan function score. The most important part of Houston's commercial activity is tied in with its port functions and is discussed above.

SUMMARY: HOUSTON

Houston's profile industries appear to rest on services performed for a broad regional area. Extraction, processing, and distribution of petroleum and natural gas are functions relating Houston both to its local areas (gathering) and more distant ones (distribution). Wholesale functions and financial services are performed for its hinterland area; however the more specialized services—warehousing and storage, water transportation, air transportation and petroleum pipelines—involve relationships with numerous more distant parts of the national economy.

NEW ORLEANS

SMA consists of Jefferson, Orleans, and St. Bernard Parishes, Louisiana

1950 population: central city, 570,445; SMA, 685,405

Important location feature: port on the Mississippi River connecting with the Gulf of Mexico

Other important feature: Federal Reserve Branch city

INPUTS AND SUPPLY AREAS FOR NEW ORLEANS' PROFILE INDUSTRIES

Canning and preserving fruits, vegetables, and sea foods: The canning industry in New Orleans is concentrated on preparing the products of the Gulf fisheries—particularly shrimp and oysters, with smaller amounts of crabs, turtles, red snappers, pompanos, and various other salt and fresh water fish. (Louisiana Legislative Council, 1955, p. 207; Dicken, 1949, p. 55.) Shrimp are caught all along the coast of Louisiana from New Orleans west to the Texas line (Louisiana Legislative Council, 1955, p. 255), while oysters predominate to the east of New Orleans. (See map in Dicken, 1949, p. 51.)

Table 56. Industrial Profile, New Orleans: 1950

Category and industry	Location quotient	Per cent of employed labor force	Inputs primarily from area:	Outputs primarily to area:
(3) *First stage resource users; production for final market*				
Canning and preserving fruits, vegetables, and sea foods	1.82	0.5	B	C
Beverage industries	2.67	1.0	C	B, C
Miscellaneous food preparations and kindred products	5.45	1.1	B, C	C?
(9) *Service industries; non-local*	1.78	22.7	*	B, C
Warehousing and storage	2.74	(0.5)	*	B, C
Water transportation	12.78	(4.7)	*	B, C
Air transportation	2.04	(0.4)	*	C
Services incidental to transportation	2.99	(0.2)	*	C?
Telegraph (wire and radio)	2.32	(0.2)	*	B, C
Wholesale trade	1.82	(6.4)	*	B
Security and commodity brokerage, and investment companies	1.69	(0.3)	*	B
(10) *Service industries; may be local or non-local*				
Miscellaneous entertainment and recreation services	2.87	1.1	*	C
Hospitals	1.82	3.2	*	B, C
Total in profile industries	...	29.6	...	...

* Inputs other than labor not considered.

Beverage industries: Chief inputs for the malt liquor industry, which makes up a large share of the beverage industry's employment, are grains, particularly barley, and hops. Large quantities of fresh water are also used. Specific sources for these inputs were not determined.

However, it is known that considerable quantities of barley and other grains were received via the port from other Mississippi ports. These shipments of barley no doubt are transported down the Mississippi River from the heavy producing regions in the Dakotas and Minnesota. Hops are produced in this country chiefly in California and the Pacific Northwest (*Encyclopedia Americana,* 1957, vol. 4, p. 480) but considerable quantities are imported from European countries. (United States Brewers Foundation, 1958, p. 84.)

Miscellaneous food preparations and kindred products: Two food industries contributing heavily to New Orleans' specialization in this industry group are sugar refining and vegetable oil industries. (McCarty, 1940, p. 466.) Raw materials for sugar refining are readily available from New Orleans' hinterland; the lower Mississippi Valley provides nine-tenths of the sugar cane grown in the United States. (United States Bureau of Agricultural Economics and Bureau of the Census, 1952, p. 28; see also Vance, 1935, pp. 219-225.) It is probable that in addition cane sugar inputs in some form are received for refining via the port. (Alexandersson, 1956, p. 88.) Exact inputs necessary for the manufacture of vegetable oils were not determined, but it seems clear that the chief input for the New Orleans industries is cotton seed (see Whitbeck and Finch, 1941, p. 110.), which is available from the surrounding area but may arrive also from considerable distances. Other types of vegetable oils are received via the port and include coconut, cottonseed, palm and palm kernel, and soybean. (United States Board of Engineers for Rivers and Harbors and Maritime Commission, 1947, No. 20, pp. 194-195.) Major sources for these oils in 1941 were Argentina and the Philippines. (*Ibid.,* pp. 353-361.)

Fuel inputs for this SMA can be discussed only in general terms. Petroleum and natural gas are available in large quantities in Louisiana. In 1952 the state was second in the nation in the production of natural gas and third in the production of petroleum and natural gasoline. (United States Bureau of Mines, Regional Mineral Industry Divisions, 1955, p. 407.) Petroleum was produced in 57 of the 64 parishes in the state. In addition to these sources, some petroleum is received via the port from foreign countries and from coastal trade. The nearest sources of coal appear to be the states of Alabama, Oklahoma, and Texas. (See map 3 in Chapman, 1953, following p. 22.)

OUTPUTS AND SERVICE AREAS
OF NEW ORLEANS' PROFILE INDUSTRIES

Canning and preserving fruits, vegetables, and sea foods: Chief outputs include canned shrimp and oysters. Distribution is no doubt to a sub-national area.

Beverage industries: A large brewing company operates a plant described as "the largest brewery in the South" (Thomas and Crisler, 1953, p. 55). Distribution is no doubt to a sub-national market.

Miscellaneous food preparations and kindred products: Distribution of sugar refined in New Orleans was not determined but probably is to a sub-national market. Vance (1935, pp. 219-220) points out: "Were it not for the fact that the protective tariff enables Louisiana sugar to be sold for two or three times what it costs to produce sugar in Cuba, this exotic plant would be grown in the southern United States only for its sirup." Vegetable oils manufactured in New Orleans no doubt likewise serve a sub-national market.

Non-local services: New Orleans is an important commercial city with a long historical background of commercial eminence. Prior to the railroad era, the advantages of New Orleans were unmatched by any city save New York. However, New Orleans lost much of its commercial dominance when it failed to enter the railroad building race. "Now the difference in the economic position of New Orleans and Chicago can be gauged by the number of railroads entering each of the cities." (Vance and Smith, 1954, p. 119.) However, New Orleans still remains an important commercial city and specializes in several types of service functions.

Warehousing and storage: This specialization is no doubt related to New Orleans' function as a major cotton and sugar market and as one of the major ports of the United States.

Water transportation: Undoubtedly the port functions are of dominant importance for the economy of New Orleans. "One of the nation's leading domestic and foreign trading and distributing centers, New Orleans ranks high among the nation's ports in dollar volume of its foreign commerce." (United States Department of Labor, 1957, p. 110.) The hinterland served by the port varies with the commodity but may be generally described as follows:

> The port of New Orleans is a natural outlet to foreign markets for large quantities of agricultural and industrial products of its hinterland regions and it is a port of entry of raw materials which are important to the economic welfare of these areas.

> The extent of the tributary area of the port varies with the commodities moving, the type of commerce . . . and the direction of movement. The local tributary area extends as far north as Memphis. Although rail rates from this point to New Orleans are no lower than those to Mobile, the influence of the Mississippi River on freight traffic (which moves to and from Memphis) favors the port of New Orleans. On the east the limits are fixed by competition from the port of Mobile, and on the west by the western boundaries of Arkansas and Louisiana, beyond which competition with the Texas ports is encountered. (United States Board of Engineers for Rivers and Harbors and Maritime Commission, 1947, No. 20, pp. 340-341.)

In 1955 New Orleans' total port commerce was approximately 47 million tons, broken down as follows: 4 million tons, foreign imports; 7 million, foreign exports; 1 million, coastwise receipts; 9 million, coastwise shipments; 14 million, internal receipts; 7 million, internal shipments; and 5 million, local traffic. Thus New Orleans' import and export trade is fairly well balanced. The more important groups of commodities imported to New Orleans were the following: in foreign imports, sugar, bananas, coffee, inedible molasses, crude petroleum, and aluminum ores; in coastwise receipts, inedible molasses and petroleum products; in internal receipts, sea shells, grains, petroleum and products, building cement, sulphur, limestone and rock, iron products, and miscellaneous manufactures. Export trade included the following commodities: in foreign shipments, grains and grain products, soybeans, cotton and products, petroleum and products, sulphur, iron and products, and miscellaneous manufactures; in coastwise shipments, petroleum and products, sulphur and industrial chemicals; and in internal shipments, sugar, inedible molasses, petroleum and products, building cement, clays, sulphur, iron and products, and miscellaneous manufactures. (United States Department of the Army, Corps of Engineers [1956], Part 2, pp. 203-206.) It is clear from these statistics that New Orleans is closely tied to the states of the great Mississippi basin since almost half of its trade is carried on with the ports of the Mississippi. Water, joint barge-rail and rail-barge-rail services are offered between New Orleans and 40 of the states. (United States Board of Engineers for Rivers and Harbors and United States Maritime Commission, 1947, No. 20, p. 341.)

Data are available from 1947 on the specific sources and destinations of some of the important commodities involved in the New Orleans' port commerce. At that time, forest products were gathered largely from Louisiana, manufactures from the entire Southwest, products of agriculture from the Central and Southwest states, minerals from the same area (sulphur from near New Orleans, fluorspar from Kentucky and Illinois, bauxite from Missouri and Tennessee, iron ore from practically all mid-continent states, bituminous coal from all states bordering the Ohio and Mississippi Rivers, potash from Kansas and Oklahoma, gypsum from Michigan, Iowa, Texas, and Oklahoma, lead from Kansas, Missouri and Oklahoma), and petroleum and products from the Southwest. (*Ibid.,* pp. 342-344.) About 35 per cent of the New Orleans foreign exports went to the Caribbean area (grains, lumber, iron and steel, petroleum); 18 per cent to the United Kingdom (iron and steel, sulphur, woodpulp, lumber); 12 per cent to the Pacific countries (largely petroleum); 12 per cent to the east coast of South America (iron and steel, petroleum, asphalt, lumber); and smaller amounts of materials to Africa, Mexico, India, Canada, and other countries. (*Ibid.,* pp. 346-348.) Imports were as follows from foreign countries: Caribbean area, 73 per cent (mostly sugar and molasses; some ores, fruits and vegetables); east coast of South America, 10 per cent (mostly coffee and cocoa); the Oriental countries, 4 per cent (sugar and molasses, and copra) and small amounts from other countries. (*Ibid.,* pp. 349-350.) Receipts from the non-contiguous possessions of the United States (Alaska, Hawaii, and Puerto Rico) were largely sugar, molasses and canned fruits. Exports to these possessions consisted of grains, beverages, and petroleum.

Air transportation: Seven domestic airlines were operating in 1950 in New Orleans carrying 201,879 passengers and 1,955 tons of cargo an average distance of 617 miles. In addition three international lines operated carrying 19,347 passengers and 2,197 tons of cargo. (United States Department of Commerce, Civil Aeronautics Administration, 1951, pp. 9, 22.)

Services incidental to transportation: The specific nature of this specialization was not determined.

Telegraph: Specialization in telegraph services in New Orleans is most directly related to the location in this SMA of one of Western Union's 15 automatic, high-speed message centers. The center located in New Orleans serves the states of Arkansas, Louisiana, Mississippi, and Alabama. (*Encyclopedia Americana,* 1957, vol. 26, pp. 345, 347.) It is assumed that specialization in this service is also related to New Orleans' commercial and financial functions.

Wholesale trade: In 1935, New Orleans led all southern cities in volume of wholesale trade. This dominance has been lost but New Orleans still performs important wholesaling functions for southern Louisiana, including the sugar district, and for certain lines its territories stretch north to Memphis. (McCarty, 1940, p. 466.) The cotton territory served may be even larger.

Security and commodity brokerage, and investment companies: This specialization is undoubtedly related to the Federal Reserve Branch Bank located in New Orleans, whose territory includes the southern half of Louisiana and Mississippi.

Miscellaneous entertainment and recreation services: The concentration of employment in the miscellaneous entertainment and recreation services is no doubt closely related to New Orleans' reputation as a tourist center. The city is especially noted for the French Quarter, and the Mardi Gras attracts thousands of tourists annually. (Thomas and Crisler, 1953, p. 55; see also McCarty, 1940, p. 466.)

Hospitals: Among the hospitals in New Orleans serving primarily a non-local clientele are the United States Marine hospital, the United States Veterans hospital and a large railroad hospital. (*Encyclopaedia Britannica,* 1957, vol. 16, p. 323.)

SUMMARY: NEW ORLEANS

New Orleans depends on its surrounding hinterland for various food inputs (fish, cotton seeds, cane sugar) which are processed in the SMA and distributed to a sub-national market. New Orleans also performs important gathering, distribution, and financial services for its hinterland. This SMA is tied in with the national economy chiefly through the activities of its port. In addition recreation facilities undoubtedly serve a national market.

LOUISVILLE

SMA consists of Jefferson County, Kentucky, and Clark and Floyd Counties, Indiana

1950 population: central city, 369,129; SMA, 576,900

Important location feature: port on the Ohio River

Other important features: Federal Reserve System Branch city

INPUTS AND SUPPLY AREAS FOR LOUISVILLE'S PROFILE INDUSTRIES

Grain mill products: Important inputs for these industries are food grains and miscellaneous food products. Specific inputs and their sources were not determined; however it is known that Louisville enjoys a most productive agricultural hinterland (McCarty, 1940, p. 434) and probably numerous grain inputs arrive from this area. In general Kentucky receives her agricultural inputs from the following states: Illinois, Indiana, and Kentucky itself, with smaller amounts arriving from Kansas, Nebraska, Missouri, and numerous other more distant states. (Ullman, 1957, p. 74.)

Table 57. Industrial Profile, Louisville: 1950

Category and industry	Location quotient	Per cent of employed labor force	Inputs primarily from area:	Outputs primarily to area:
(2) *First stage resource users; production for non-final market*				
Grain mill products	1.72	0.4	B?	A?
(3) *First stage resource users; production for final market*				
Beverage industries	7.17	2.6	B	C
Tobacco manufactures	14.88	2.5	B	C
(5) *Second stage resource users; production for final market*				
Furniture and fixtures	2.80	1.6	A	B?
(6) *Resources of indirect significance; production for non-final market*				
Fabricated metal industries	2.41	3.6	A, C	A, C
Machinery, except electrical	1.70	3.9	C	B, C
(9) *Service industries; non-local*	1.30	16.6	*	B, C
Other and not specified utilities	2.38	(0.1)	*	B
Railroads and railway express service	1.85	(4.6)	*	C
(10) *Service industries; may be local or non-local*				
Miscellaneous entertainment and recreation services	1.63	0.6	*	C
Total in profile industries	...	31.8	...	...

* Inputs other than labor not considered.

Beverage industries: The most important component of this industry group is the distilled liquor industries. Inputs for these industries include chiefly corn, rye, malted barley and some other grains, and fuels. (*Encyclopedia Americana,* 1957, vol. 9, pp. 177-178.) Corn particularly is used in large quantities by the Kentucky distilleries, 727 million pounds being consumed in 1957. Other materials and amounts consumed by Kentucky distilleries in 1957 were as follows: 158 million pounds of rye; 125 million pounds of malt; 4 million pounds of wheat and 1 million gallons of molasses. (Data from tables made available by the Distilled Spirits Institute.) Specific sources for the grain inputs utilized in Louisville were not determined, but probably in general correspond with the sources described above for grain mill industries. Alderfer and Michl (1950, p. 621) feel that in general water supplies and tradition are among the more important determinants of location for this industry. Louisville's location on the Ohio River is thus probably of importance for this industry. Fuel inputs for this industry will be considered below.

Tobacco manufactures: Inputs for tobacco industries are chiefly tobacco and paper. Tobacco is available from the central and western parts of Kentucky and Tennessee, including small parts of Ohio and Indiana. (Dicken, 1949, pp. 236-237, 241.)

> Three broad types of tobacco are produced in this region, air-cured light burley in the northern part, fire-cured dark tobacco in the west and south, and dark air-cured tobacco in the middle section. Most of the light burley is used in the manufacture of cigarettes, the darker fire-cured types are exported, while the dark air-cured tobacco is used in the manufacture of chewing tobacco and snuff. (*Ibid.*, p. 243.)

Cigarette paper is made of a good grade of cellulose derived from linen, hemp, or ramie. Prior to the second world war, cigarette paper was imported from France. It is now being made from linseed-flax straw by a special paper mill recently set up in North Carolina. (Alderfer and Michl, 1950, p. 630.)

Furniture and fixtures: Inputs for this industry include chiefly timber products, particularly the hard woods. These inputs appear to be available from locally operated sawmills and planing mills which employ over 3,000 persons in the SMA. Forests in the surrounding area are rich in ash, beech, cypress, elm, hickory, maple, oak, red gum, and walnut. (Garland, 1955, p. 209.)

Fabricated metal industries: Major inputs for the fabricated metal industries come from processing and fabricating metal plants and include products of steel works and rolling mills, products from metal stamping industries, boiler shop products, miscellaneous fabricated products and fuels. As Louisville is relatively specialized in primary nonferrous metal production, some of these inputs probably are produced locally. One important source of iron and steel inputs is the Pittsburgh-Cincinnati area because their products may be shipped down the Ohio River to Louisville, although rail shipments are probably also important. (Garland, 1955, p. 88.) However, Chicago is not far distant and probably supplies large quantities of needed processed materials by rail. (*Ibid.,* pp. 62-63.) Fuel inputs are discussed below.

Machinery, except electrical: Important inputs for the machinery industries include engines and turbines, motors and generators, boiler shop products, iron and steel castings, products from iron and steel foundries and internal combustion engines. Again, the specific sources of these inputs were not determined. The majority no doubt arrive from near-by centers of production within the manufacturing zone. (See map in Ullman, 1957, p. 79.)

Fuels: As the Louisville SMA supports a fairly large manufacturing structure, fuel inputs are of considerable importance. Coal is received in Louisville mostly from the mines of western Kentucky, although considerable quantities arrive from the mines of eastern Kentucky and West Virginia. (Haynes, 1955, p. 16.) A large proportion of this coal goes into the manufacture of electricity. (*Ibid.,* p. 32.) Petroleum products consumed in Kentucky are also chiefly furnished from within the state, although some supplies arrive from the Gulf states, chiefly Texas, and from Illinois. (Ullman, 1957, p. 77.) Natural gas is likewise available from fields located within the state, chiefly in the eastern and southern areas. (See map, Zimmermann, 1951, p. 561.) However, about half of the gas consumed within the state arrives by pipeline from the Southwestern states. (Stockton, 1952, pp. 167, 170.)

OUTPUTS AND SERVICE AREAS OF LOUISVILLE'S PROFILE INDUSTRIES

Grain mill industries: Some of the grain mill products undoubtedly feed the local distilleries as well as other local industries (e.g., bakeries). Other markets were not determined.

Beverage industries: In 1957 Kentucky produced 87 million gallons of whiskey, about 73 per cent of the total amount produced in the United States. Other distilled spirits produced in Kentucky, and their amounts for 1957, were as follows: 967,000 gallons of rum; 248,000 gallons of gin; 109,000 gallons of vodka and 3 million gallons of other spirits. Kentucky's total production of distilled spirits accounted for about 41 per cent of the United States total production. (Data from tables made available by the Distilled Spirits Institute.) It was not possible to determine what portion of this total was accounted for by Louisville producers; however it is known that in the early 1950's Louisville distilleries produced about 25 per cent of the total United

States output of whiskey. Since many of the nation's largest distilleries are located here, the products of this industry may be said to enjoy a national distribution. (Thomas and Crisler, 1953, p. 69.)

Tobacco manufactures: Louisville is the home of several large tobacco companies manufacturing products distributed to a nation-wide market. (*Ibid.*, p. 69.) Cigarettes are the major tobacco product of these industries but chewing tobacco and snuff are also produced. (Whitbeck and Finch, 1941, p. 116.)

Furniture and fixtures: Outputs of the furniture industry include largely wooden house furniture; their market was not determined but probably includes most of Kentucky and parts of surrounding states.

Fabricated metal industries: Outputs of this industry group include plumbing supplies and fixtures, various aluminum products and miscellaneous fabricated steel products. (United States Department of Labor, 1957, p. 106.) Specific markets for these products were not determined. However, some of the fabricated steel products are no doubt fed into the machinery industries of the SMA, while the other types of products undoubtedly enjoy a wider distribution—both to other parts of the manufacturing zone and to consumers in near-by states.

Non-electrical machinery: The most important outputs of the machinery industry are agricultural machinery of various kinds, and tractors. (Thomas and Crisler, 1953, p. 69.) These products no doubt find a ready market in the surrounding corn belt territory as well as the more distant agricultural areas. Our figures do not reflect the recent growth of the household appliance industry (now a major employer in Louisville), which took place after 1950.

Non-local services: Of the many non-local services performed by Louisville for its surrounding area, employment figures indicate a particular specialization in three, which are discussed separately.

Other and not specified utilities: Concentration of employment in these utilities in Louisville could not be accounted for.

Railroads and railway express service: McCarty (1940, p. 434) has pointed out that there are relatively few railroad crossings of the Ohio River and that location at such a crossing gave a city like Louisville a commercial advantage, as the river traffic was partially diverted to railroads. In all, nine railroads serve the city of Louisville. (*Encyclopedia Americana,* 1959, vol. 17, p. 652.)

Miscellaneous entertainment and recreation services: This specialization in part reflects Kentucky's popularity with tourists in general (see Garland, 1955, p. 196) but more particularly the importance of horse racing in the city of Louisville. In addition to the Kentucky

Derby held at Churchill Downs, other horse races attract large numbers of visitors to the area every year. (*Ibid.*, p. 208.)

In general, it appears that Louisville is the dominant city of Kentucky, commercially as well as industrially. (McCarty, 1940, p. 435.) Park and Newcomb assigned to Louisville most of the state of Kentucky as its effective trade area. The location of a Federal Reserve Branch Bank in Louisville is no doubt an important factor in its commercial dominance in this area. Louisville's connections with its agricultural hinterland are reflected in its relatively high per capita value of sales by assemblers of farm products (see chapter 11). Its access to more distant areas is facilitated both by its position in the railroad network and by its location on the Ohio River. According to reports for 1955 (United States Department of the Army, Corps of Engineers [1956], Part 1, p. 18), its port commerce of some 5.5 million tons was comparable with that of Memphis (4.0 million tons), St. Louis (6.8 million tons), and Cincinnati (8.0 million tons).

SUMMARY: LOUISVILLE

Louisville's important industries may be said to depend in considerable measure directly or indirectly upon local natural resources—grains, tobacco, timber and abundant fuels—available from its surrounding hinterland (Area B). But in addition, an important segment of its economy, its metal fabricating and machinery industries, depends upon inputs from all parts of the manufacturing zone (included in Area C). Markets for its major products—whiskey, tobacco products, furniture, and machinery—are probably located primarily in Area C. Commercial and financial functions are performed for a fairly large surrounding area which includes most of Kentucky. Railroad services and entertainment functions (horse racing) are performed by this SMA for considerably larger areas (Area C).

BIRMINGHAM

SMA consists of Jefferson County, Alabama
1950 population: central city, 326,037; SMA, 558,928
Important feature: Federal Reserve System Branch city

INPUTS AND SUPPLY AREAS FOR BIRMINGHAM'S PROFILE INDUSTRIES

Metal mining: Birmingham's employment in this industry group is concentrated in the extraction of iron ore. (*Census of Mineral Industries, 1954*, Bul. M1-101, Table 4.)

> The Southeast has a large number of iron ore deposits which extend from below Bessemer, Alabama, on the south, to northern Tennessee and include northwest Georgia and western North Carolina. At one time or another, many of these deposits have been worked for the purpose of making iron, but the present industry is built principally on the resources of a restricted area in and around Birmingham, Alabama. (Chapman, 1953, p. 34; see also map 6, following p. 22.)

In 1950 Jefferson County had 11 active iron ore mines in operation with a total production of 6 million tons of usable ore. (United States Bureau of Mines, 1953, p. 630.) With regard to labor input, according to the *1950 Census of Population* only about one-fifth of those engaged in metal mining live within the city of Birmingham.

Table 58. Industrial Profile, Birmingham: 1950

Category and industry	Location quotient	Per cent of employed labor force	Inputs primarily from area:	Outputs primarily to area:
(1) (*Primary resource extractors; production for non-final market*)				
Metal mining	15.12	2.4	A, B	A
Coal mining	5.97	5.4	A, B	A, C
(4) *Second stage resource users; production for non-final market*				
Blast furnaces, steel works and rolling mills	9.47	11.2	A, B	A, C
Other primary iron and steel industries	5.73	2.9	A, B	A, C
Cement, and concrete, gypsum and plastic products	3.36	0.6	A, B	B
Miscellaneous petroleum and coal products	13.70	0.7	A, B	B
(9) *Service industries; non-local*	1.02	13.2	*	B, C
Railroads and railway express service	1.71	(4.2)	*	B, C
Total in profile industries	...	36.4	...	...

* Inputs other than labor not considered.

Coal mining: "The Warrior coal field lies to the west and southwest of Birmingham and is the most important source of coking coal in the Southeast." (Chapman, 1953, p. 54; see also map 7, following p. 22.) In 1949, 7,340,748 tons of bituminous coal were mined in Jefferson

County of which 6,983,350 tons were shipped by rail or water, 304,071 tons were shipped by truck and 53,327 tons were used at the mines. (United States Bureau of Mines, 1953, p. 309.) Of the almost 11,000 coal miners employed in Jefferson County only about 3,000 reside within the Birmingham city limits.

Blast furnaces, steel works and rolling mills: Major inputs for these industries are coke, iron ore, limestone and dolomite, manganese and alloying metals. Coal is available in the Birmingham area from the Warrior field deposits to the west and southwest of the city. This coal is shipped approximately 10 miles by rail to the furnaces and converted into coke and certain by-products. Iron ore is also available locally from the Red Mountain deposits and is shipped by rail about 10 miles to the factories. Flux (limestone or dolomite) is available from Birmingham Valley, and has to be shipped only six miles by rail. (Chapman, 1953, Table 6, p. 21.) Manganese ore is available in small quantities in North and South Carolina, Georgia, Tennessee, and Alabama. However, most inputs are obtained from foreign countries (India, Chile, Cuba and Mexico) via the port of Mobile. Alloying metals used in the production of special steels are needed only in small quantities and are obtained from outside of the southeastern United States for the most part, and indeed, frequently from outside of the country. (*Ibid.,* pp. 62-63, 85.)

Other primary iron and steel industries: Inputs for primary iron and steel industries include the products of blast furnaces, coke and products, and some waste products of iron and steel. The products of blast furnaces and waste products are readily available from industries within the SMA. Coke likewise is available from the SMA. (Chapman, 1953, pp. 182-183.)

Cement, and concrete, gypsum and plaster products: Important inputs for the cement industry are limestone (75 per cent), clay or shale (20 per cent), and small quantities of gypsum. The raw materials may be blast furnace slag, shells, rocks, or mixtures. (Zimmermann, 1951, p. 772.) Large deposits of limestone are available near Birmingham in a region that extends from the northern border of Tennessee to a point south of Birmingham. (Chapman, 1953, p. 61; see also map 8, following p. 22.) Blast furnace slag from the furnaces of Birmingham is also a source of limestone. (McCarty, 1940, p. 371.) Shale is found in quantities in the coal fields of this area. (Chapman, 1953, p. 54.) Gypsum is no doubt manufactured in the local area.

Miscellaneous coal and petroleum products: There is relatively little petroleum refining in Alabama and specialization in this industry reflects the further processing of the by-products of the coke ovens. Sources of coal inputs are described above.

OUTPUTS AND SERVICE AREAS OF BIRMINGHAM'S PROFILE INDUSTRIES

Metal mining: Alabama generally ranks behind Minnesota and Michigan in production of iron ore, with something like a tenth of the nation's output. The largest operations in the state are at Red Mountain, near Bessemer (within the Birmingham SMA). The product is mostly hematite and goes primarily to blast furnaces in Birmingham. (McCarty, 1940, p. 371.)

Coal mining: Although a major portion of the coal mined in the Birmingham area is used by local iron and steel industries, there is also a wide distribution throughout the South, particularly the eastern states of the Cotton Belt. The marketability of the coal is improved by cleaning. (*Ibid.,* pp. 370-371.)

Blast furnaces, steel works and rolling mills; Other primary iron and steel industries: The low assembly costs for the raw materials are counterbalanced by high transportation costs for the finished products when pig iron and steel are sold north of the Ohio River. (Alexandersson, 1956, p. 41.) Markets for the products of these industries are thus restricted geographically largely to the Southeastern United States. One possible exception to this statement is the pig iron and cast-iron pipe which were being produced in surplus within the South and thus have been forced to seek "outside" markets. (Chapman, 1953, p. 322.) "The foundry business in Birmingham specializes particularly in cast iron pressure pipe; it is claimed that here is the largest such center in the world, with 60 per cent of the North American production." (Tower, 1958, p. 41.) Blast furnaces coke their own coal. Most of this coke is utilized by local furnaces but some is shipped elsewhere. In fact, according to Chapman (1953, p. 185) even though only one-eighth of the coke produced in Alabama is shipped outside the state, Alabama has the most widespread out-of-state shipments of any of the coke-producing states. The availability of coke is an important factor not only in blast furnace activity but also in foundry and the metallurgical industries. Within the Southeast, Alabama and Tennessee show the highest employment in the iron and steel processing and fabricating industries within the South and it is likely that Birmingham furnishes a large share of the necessary inputs for these industries. (*Ibid.,* p. 278.) Vance and Smith (1954, p. 123) point out that because of its manufacturing activities, Birmingham can be its own best market.

Cement, and concrete, gypsum and plaster products: No information was discovered on the distribution of hydraulic cement produced in the Birmingham area; however, because of the bulk and relative low value per unit of weight of this product, its distribution costs are quite high. Moreover, the widespread distribution of limestone and cheap fuels makes it possible to locate the cement mills with primary consideration given to the market. (Alexandersson, 1956, pp. 59-60.) Thus, it is assumed that distribution of this product is limited largely to Alabama.

Miscellaneous petroleum and coal products: Products are largely composed of by-products of the coke industries. Those by-products which would be included in the industry under consideration are tars and crude light oils (other by-products are ammonia and gas). In 1948, 66 million gallons of coke oven tar were produced, 36 million gallons of which were sold to be refined into various tar products. Also in 1948, 23 million gallons of coke oven crude light oil were produced, most of which was refined on the premises of the producer to be sold to the manufacturers of motor fuel. Indications from statistics collected by Chapman (1953, pp. 185-89) are that the by-products of coal resulting from the production of coke are for the most part sold within Alabama.

Non-local services: McCarty (1940, p. 381) indicates that Birmingham's commercial interests serve the northern half of Alabama—a trade area delimitation that coincides approximately with those of Bogue and of Park and Newcomb (see chapter 4). Birmingham is the location of a Federal Reserve Branch Bank which serves the larger part of Alabama. Birmingham is also specialized in railroad services.

Railroads and railway express service: Railroads figure prominently in Birmingham's economy because of their importance in bringing raw materials to the iron and steel industries; most of the bulk shipments from basic iron and steel plants to their customers are by rail. (Chapman, 1953, p. 302.) In addition to the several large railroads operating through Birmingham, several of the larger iron and steel companies operate their own lines.

SUMMARY: BIRMINGHAM

Birmingham is quite obviously closely tied to its nearby hinterland (Areas A and B) for raw material inputs—iron ore, coal, flux—for its all-important iron and steel industries. In addition, materials for the cement industry—limestone, stone, and blast-furnace slag—are available from the hinterland and the SMA itself. Outputs of these industries provide important inputs for local and nearby manufacturing firms (Areas A and B); however, coal and metal outputs serve many parts of the southeastern United States. Birmingham also serves as a commercial and wholesale center for the northern half of the state of Alabama.

INDIANAPOLIS

SMA consists of Marion County, Indiana
1950 population: central city, 427,173; SMA, 551,777
Important feature: capital of Indiana

INPUTS AND SUPPLY AREAS FOR INDIANAPOLIS' PROFILE INDUSTRIES

Meat products: Indianapolis ranked fourth in the United States in 1950 as a market for the receipt of hogs, with over 2 million salable hogs received. Smaller quantities of cattle (340,000), calves (97,000) and sheep (191,000) were also received in 1950. (United States Department of Agriculture, Production and Marketing Administration, 1951, pp. 7-8.) Indications are that hogs arrive from nearby farming areas in Indiana and Ohio; 99 per cent of them are driven in to market. (*Ibid.*, p. 10.) The northeastern section of the east-central lowland (including most of Indiana and the northwest portion of Ohio) has long been important as the central corn-producing, hog-raising section in this country, and Indianapolis is situated right at its center. (Freeman, 1945, p. 95.) The cattle, calf and sheep receipts also arrive largely from the nearby areas, 94 per cent of the cattle, 93 per cent of the calves and 92 per cent of the lambs being driven in to market. (United States Department of Agriculture, Production and Marketing Administration, 1951, p. 10.)

Fabricated metal industries; Machinery, except electrical; Electrical machinery, equipment and supplies; and Motor vehicles and motor vehicle equipment: These several industry groups may be considered together because many of their inputs are similar in nature and because little specific information is available concerning the source of processed and fabricated metal inputs for this SMA. Concerning these metal-working industries, McCarthy (1940, p. 323) suggests that the Indianapolis – Fort Wayne district may be regarded as a segment of an "outer ring" of industrial cities specializing in machinery manufactures that has developed around the Chicago industrial center. Probably the basic iron and steel inputs arrive chiefly from Chicago while the multitude of fabricated metals and parts may arrive from any one of a number of nearby cities at the western end of the manufacturing zone. (See Garland, 1955, pp. 60-63.)

Table 59. Industrial Profile, Indianapolis: 1950

Category and industry	Location quotient	Per cent of employed labor force	Inputs primarily from area:	Outputs primarily to area:
(3) *First stage resource users; production for final market*				
Meat products	3.06	1.5	B	C
(6) *Resources of indirect significance; production for non-final market*				
Fabricated metal industries	1.80	2.7	C	C
Machinery, except electrical	1.77	4.1	C	C
Electrical machinery, equipment and supplies	3.14	4.4	C	C
Motor vehicles and motor vehicle equipment	2.06	3.2	C	C
Drugs and medicines	18.00	1.8	B, C	C
Paperboard containers and boxes	2.24	0.4	B?	A
Rubber products	2.25	0.9	B, C	C
(7) *Resources of indirect significance; production for final market*				
Aircraft and parts	3.89	1.8	C	C
(9) *Service industries; non-local*	1.20	15.3	*	B, C
Trucking service	1.67	(1.8)	*	B, C
Other and not specified utilities	2.17	(0.1)	*	?
State public administration	1.86	(0.9)	*	B
(10) *Service industries; may be local or non-local*				
Insurance	1.95	2.6	*	C
Total in profile industries	...	38.7	...	...

* Inputs other than labor not considered.

Fuels are naturally important for such an industrial district and can be discussed in general terms. Coal is available to Indianapolis from both the Eastern Interior field of Illinois, west Kentucky and southwest Indiana, and the Appalachian field of West Virginia, Ohio and eastern Kentucky. (See map 3 in Chapman, 1953, following p. 22.) Major supplies used in Indiana come from the state itself and from West Virginia. (Haynes, 1955, p. 15.) Natural gas arrives in Indianapolis by pipelines from fields in the Central and Southern producing regions of the United States. (Stockton, 1952, pp. 169-170.) Petroleum also arrives from this same general area, being piped in from the Mid-Continent and Gulf Coast fields to Indianapolis. (Garland, 1955, p. 115.)

Drugs and medicines: Inputs for drugs and medicine industries are chiefly chemicals. The input requirements for pharmaceutical preparations are quite expensive relative to weight and so the light chemical industries are found near to markets rather than to raw materials. (Alexandersson, 1956, p. 73.) Specific chemical inputs and their sources utilized in Indianapolis were not determined; however, Indiana is one of five states in which the production of drugs is concentrated and it is assumed that inputs arrive from other centers in the State and from nearby states. (See Jones and Darkenwald, 1954, p. 498.)

Paperboard containers and boxes: Wood pulp inputs for paperboard industries are available from forest areas in the southern and central portions of Indiana. (See map in U.S. National Resources Planning Board, 1943, p. 54.) Waste paper may also be used as a raw material. (Alderfer and Michl, 1957, p. 293.) Specific sources for inputs were not determined.

Rubber products: Inputs for rubber products industries include rubber—both crude and synthetic; products of textile mills; and chemicals. Sources of crude rubber utilized in the United States are chiefly the countries of Malaya, Indonesia, Thailand and Ceylon. Synthetic rubber plants are located in Texas, Louisiana, California, Pennsylvania, West Virginia, Connecticut, and Kentucky. The plants closest to Indianapolis are located in Louisville, Kentucky, and Akron, Ohio. (United States Department of Commerce, National Production Authority, 1952, p. VI-3.) Some textile inputs are available from the SMA itself. Sources of chemical inputs were not determined.

Aircraft and parts: Indianapolis is important to the airplane industry as a producer of engines; its importance in this field dates back to World War I. (Cunningham, 1951, pp. 37, 225). Specific sources of processed and fabricated metal inputs necessary for this industry were not determined; however, the majority no doubt arrive from centers within the manufacturing zone.

OUTPUTS AND SERVICE AREAS OF INDIANAPOLIS' PROFILE INDUSTRIES

Meat products: The meat products industries concentrate on wholesale meat packing. Two large plants operate in Indianapolis and probably serve a sub-national market area. (Federal Reserve Bank of Chicago, 1956, p. 18.)

Fabricated metal industries: Among the fabricated metal products produced in Indianapolis, roller chains, sprockets, structural metal products, roller bearings and transmissions for light and medium tanks and ordnance vehicles are important. Also manufactured are saws and saw blades, and cylinders for industrial gases. Distribution of these products is to a national market. (*Ibid.*, pp. 10-11.)

Machinery, except electrical: Power transmission equipment including power transmission chains and sprockets is a major item. Products from this particular industry "are sold to every major industry in the country" (*ibid.*, 1956, p. 11). Other machinery manufactured in this SMA includes construction equipment—motor graders, loaders, portable concrete mixers, excavators, and cranes—vertical turbines and hydrofoil pumps. Distribution of these products is also no doubt to a national market.

Electrical machinery, equipment and supplies: Electrical machinery produced in Indianapolis includes telephone sets, phonograph records (Indianapolis contains the world's largest phonograph record plant), television sets, electron tubes, residential heating and air-conditioning equipment, and miscellaneous radio parts, welding materials and multipurpose electrical contracts. (*Ibid.*, 15-16.) It would appear that the distribution of these products is nationwide.

Motor vehicles and motor vehicle equipment: Motor vehicle equipment produced in the SMA includes truck engines, truck bodies and cabs, large school bus and other special commercial vehicle chassis, and automatic transmissions and castings for motor blocks for passenger cars. (*Ibid.*, 1956, pp. 10-15.) Distribution of these products is to a national market.

Drugs and medicines: Indianapolis contains one of the country's largest manufacturers and developers of pharmaceutical products. This firm is a locally headquartered, locally owned international corporation and is internationally known as the first company to manufacture insulin and the Salk polio vaccine; it supplied approximately 70 per cent of the total vaccine for the 1955 and 1956 nationwide polio immunization programs. About four-fifths of this firm's manufacturing operations are in Indianapolis plants. (*Ibid.*, 1956, p. 16.) This industry group, then, may be said to serve a national market.

Paperboard containers and boxes: This industry is largely engaged in the manufacture of corrugated paper shipping containers for local food manufacturers. (*Ibid.*, p. 18.)

Rubber products: Products include inner tubes and tubeless tires as well as bicycle tubes and tires. (*Ibid.*, p. 14.) Distribution is to sub-national markets.

Aircraft and parts: Of greatest importance in this industry group is the production of airplane engines. Types produced in Indianapolis include the turbo-jet, the turbo-prop and other types of gas turbine engines. Other aircraft products include gears for aircraft engines and stainless steel alloy heat exchangers for jet aircraft. (*Ibid.*, pp. 9-10.) A national market is served.

Non-local services: Although it is clear from the manufacturing profile just described that Indianapolis is an important manufacturing center, it also performs important service functions. McCarty (1940, p. 324) indicates that Indianapolis is the major banking and commercial center for two-thirds of Indiana. The same author mentions that Indianapolis is the largest city in the United States not located on a navigable waterway; thus it developed early as a crossroads of overland routes. Indianapolis is one of seven SMA's between 500,000 and 3,000,000 inhabitants which were above the national SMA average on per capita sales of assemblers of farm products, according to the *1948 Census of Business*. "The central location and position as the State capital aided Indianapolis in becoming, early in its history, a trading center with markets for the livestock, grain and other agricultural products of the surrounding farm area." (U. S. Department of Labor, 1957, p. 90.) Specific non-local services in which Indianapolis specializes are mentioned below.

Trucking service: No doubt this service is related to Indianapolis' function as an assembler of farm products and to its position in the manufacturing zone.

Other and not specified utilities: The nature of employment in this service group was not determined.

State public administration: Indianapolis is the state capital of Indiana and is the center of many state-related offices and services.

Insurance: Indianapolis is "home town for 40 insurance companies, nearly all of whom do a regional as distinct from a national business." (Federal Reserve Bank of Chicago, 1956, p. 19.)

SUMMARY: INDIANAPOLIS

Indianapolis is related to its hinterland primarily as a city performing central-place functions, e.g., gathering products of agriculture from the rich surrounding farmlands and performing distributive and financial (insurance) and administrative services. Indianapolis is related to its larger environment through its tie-up with other cities in the manufacturing zone. Here Indianapolis performs largely fabricating functions, receiving raw materials and processed materials from other cities and turning out finished products or materials to be assembled in other manufacturing centers.

COLUMBUS

SMA consists of Franklin County, Ohio
1950 population: central city, 375,901; SMA, 503,410
Important feature: capital of Ohio

INPUTS AND SUPPLY AREAS FOR COLUMBUS' PROFILE INDUSTRIES

Meat products: Columbus meat products employment is concentrated in the wholesale meat packing industry. Columbus does not qualify as a ranking livestock center, but still received in 1950 considerable numbers of cattle (37,000), calves (17,000), hogs (127,000) and sheep (59,000). (United States Department of Agriculture, Production and Marketing Administration, 1951, pp. 7-8.) Obviously, there is a relative concentration in the handling and processing of hogs. Almost all of the hogs (99 per cent) and all of the calves received at Columbus were driven in while 91 per cent of the cattle and 89 per cent of the sheep were driven in. (*Ibid.,* p. 10.) This would seem to indicate that livestock, particularly hogs and calves, are chiefly drawn from nearby areas. Columbus is situated at the eastern edge of the corn-hog producing belt. (Garland, 1955, pp. 109-110.)

Fabricated metal industries: This industry group includes such varied establishments as those engaged in the production of structural steel, tools and implements, heating and cooling equipment, and metal stampings. Taking these industry groups up in this order, Pittsburgh is the principal source of structural, bar and sheet steel utilized by the Columbus industries. Smaller amounts arrive from Chicago, Cleveland, and Dayton. (Hunker, 1958, p. 110.) Steel used by the tool and implement industries is obtained from Pittsburgh, from Ohio, and from a company located in Washington, Pennsylvania. "For high-quality band saws, however, Swedish steel is purchased." (*Ibid.,* p. 122.) Wood for saw handles comes from Indiana, and for forks and hoes manufactured in this SMA ash wood available from the local area is utilized. Inputs for the heating equipment industries include the following: lightweight sheet steel is obtained from Pittsburgh; Weirton and Wheeling, West Virginia; Youngstown, Middletown, and Cleveland, Ohio; and Gary, Indiana.

> Gray iron castings are purchased locally and from foundries in Cleveland, Detroit, and Bloomington, Indiana . . . A variety of blowers and thermostats are used . . . for these, Minneapolis, Detroit, and Cleveland are supply centers. Brass valves and brass products . . . are obtained in Cleveland, Detroit, Pittsburgh, and Chicago. [An] organization in New Jersey supplies the asbestos required by the Columbus manufacturers. (*Ibid.,* pp. 137-139.)

Table 60. Industrial Profile, Columbus: 1950

Category and industry	Location quotient	Per cent of employed labor force	Inputs primarily from area:	Outputs primarily to area:
(3) *First stage resource users; production for final market*				
Meat products	1.75	0.9	B	C
(6) *Resources of indirect significance; production for non-final market*				
Fabricated metal industries	2.60	3.9	C	A, C
Machinery, except electrical	2.05	4.7	C	C
Railroad and miscellaneous transportation equipment	1.51	0.2	C	C
Glass and glass products	3.39	0.8	B, C	C
(7) *Resources of indirect significance; production for final market*				
Footwear, except rubber	2.75	1.3	C	C
(9) *Service industries; non-local*	1.50	19.1	*	B, C
Railroads and railway express service	1.90	(4.7)	*	C
Miscellaneous professional and related services	4.87	(0.6)	*	A, C
State public administration	5.30	(2.5)	*	B
(10) *Service industries; may be local or non-local*				
Insurance	2.25	3.0	*	C
Total in profile industries	...	33.9	...	...

* Inputs other than labor not considered.

The metal stampings industries have inputs and sources as follows:

> Raw materials are transported by truck in almost every instance. Steel products from Cleveland, Youngstown, Middletown, Sharon, Pittsburgh, Weirton, and Wheeling; brass from Detroit and New Jersey; and aluminum ingot and bar obtained . . . in Newark . . . are the basic raw materials. Plastics, obtained from chemical companies in the mid-west and east, are now being used to replace costly and scarce metals. (*Ibid.*, p. 108.)

Machinery, except electrical: Inputs are as follows:

> Raw materials are varied but less than 10 per cent are purchased in the city. Steel is most important. Columbus warehouses supply 8 companies, with Pittsburgh, Cleveland, Middletown, Chicago-Gary, and Youngstown the important supply centers for the others. Most iron castings are purchased in the city; some come from Marion . . . Less important are aluminum and brass castings which are supplied locally. (Hunker, 1958, p. 132.)

Motors and electric controls are purchased from the distributors of major American companies; however some local firms produce their own motors.

> Rubber products, such as belting and tubing, come from Akron or from local warehouses. Lumber has decreased in importance with changes in the industry but it is supplied from sources in the Appalachians or on the West Coast. (*Idem.*)

Approximately 75 per cent of the shipping is by truck but some of the larger companies prefer rail service. (*Idem.*)

Railroad and miscellaneous transportation equipment: Specialization in this industry group in Columbus was apparently largely the result of the location in that SMA of a large manufacturer of railroad cars. However in 1953 this company announced that it was suspending operations. (Hunker, 1958, p. 147.) Inputs for this company were much like those described above: steel was furnished by Pittsburgh mills and lumber came from the South. Some local foundry products were also utilized. (*Ibid.*, p. 148.)

Fuels: In an SMA in which manufacturing is as prominent an activity as in the case of Columbus, a discussion of the sources of fuel utilized would seem to be essential. In a discussion of raw materials in general available to the Columbus SMA, Hunker (1958, p. 216) explains:

> Coal, iron ore, natural gas, and timber were the basic raw materials which attracted industry to central Ohio from 1870 to 1900. Satisfactory deposits of these materials are no longer available locally nor

> have any other materials basic to modern industry taken their place. Consequently, there are few firms in central Ohio that are raw material oriented.

General sources of coal utilized in Columbus include eastern Kentucky, southern and eastern Ohio, Virginia, and West Virginia. Natural gas is available within Ohio, but most of the gas used in Columbus arrives by long-distance pipelines from the Southwest. Oil and oil products likewise are received from Ohio and Illinois sources, supplemented by shipments from the Gulf states by water to Cincinnati and thence by truck to Columbus.

Glass and glass products: Inputs include natural gas, glass, soda ash and lime. Only a limited supply of natural gas is available in the area (although this was a major reason for the location of the plants in the area) and gas piped from the Southwest is of increasing importance. Other raw materials must also be imported; however the position of Columbus is favorable in this respect compared with other glass centers. "Sand is purchased in the lake states and soda ash and lime in Ohio." (Hunker, 1958, p. 174.)

Footwear, except rubber: Tanned leather and miscellaneous textile products are essential inputs for the shoe industry.

> For a century or more, raw material supply centers have been in the New England and Eastern Seaboard states. Leather, cloth, and findings are still obtained there. Pennsylvania, Ohio, and Wisconsin have recently become important centers. St. Louis, probably the nation's leading shoe center, is another big supplier of findings. The scrap product used by the heel and fiber companies is difficult to obtain. It is found occasionally in this area but ordinarily it must be imported from the east.
>
> A large percentage of imported goods are carried by rail since the long haul of supplies and scrap is more economical this way. (Hunker, 1958, p. 198.)

OUTPUTS AND SERVICE AREAS OF COLUMBUS' PROFILE INDUSTRIES

Meat products: In 1953 two large meat packing companies employing over 500 persons each were operating in Columbus as well as three other packing plants employing over 100 persons. (*County Business Patterns 1953*.) It is assumed that plants as large as these are serving a sub-national market.

Fabricated metal industries: Most of the structural steel companies in this SMA are small and are limited in the distribution of their products to an Ohio market. However one firm employing around 400 workers specializes in the production of steel for aerials, towers, beacons, and hangars for the television, radio, and aircraft industries. Its products are distributed throughout the world. Two other plants, one producing porcelain steel and the other reinforced concrete frames, serve a national market. (Hunker, 1958, pp. 109-110.) Tools and implements produced in this SMA include saws and hand garden and farm tools. Markets served range in size from the central United States to the national. (*Ibid.*, pp. 121-122.) Turning to the heating equipment companies:

> Among the important products produced are domestic coal, gas and oil heating equipment. Various space and aircraft heaters, conversion burners, gas ranges, automatic and barometric draft controls, pipe fittings, and complete ventilating systems are also made. (*Ibid.*, p. 135.)

Markets are also discussed:

> The finished products are sold to a consumer market by dealers and jobbers. No company enters the retail trade, but sales are made to other manufacturers, to mail-order houses, . . . and to contractors. The sales territory is limited by the high-bulk, relatively low-value products. . . .
>
> In general, Columbus, at the junction of coal, gas and oil facilities, and near the population center of the nation, is an excellent location for marketing these commodities. . . .
>
> In addition to domestic and foreign sales, certain members of this industry have engaged in work on government contracts for space heaters for aircraft, tanks, and other military equipment. (*Ibid.*, pp. 135-136.)

Eleven of the firms in this industry group have good rail facilities "but they ship 75 per cent of their goods by truck since smaller than car-load lots make up the majority of their shipments." (*Ibid.*, p. 139.) Turning finally to the stamping companies located within this SMA, their major products include "automobile stampings, name plates, tin cans, pipe fittings, rollers, various types of aluminum extrusions, metal seals, and miscellaneous products for the automotive, electrical equipment, and construction industries." (*Ibid.*, p. 107.) Markets vary from local to national. Foreign markets are tapped but are not currently of importance. About 90 per cent of the shipment is by truck. (*Idem.*)

Machinery, except electrical: The most important types of machinery produced are of a general industrial nature. Portable industrial machinery includes wheelbarrows, conveyors, concrete mixing equipment, harvestors, and elevators; stationary machinery and equipment include scales, air purification systems, bakery machinery, hydraulic oil presses, roller bearings, nut and screw machines, and various testing devices. (Hunker, 1958, p. 124.) Distribution of products varies with the individual industry but in general a national or sub-national market is being served. (See *ibid.,* pp. 126-132.)

Railroad and miscellaneous transportation equipment: During the period covered by our study, the principal product of the major firm in this category was steel railroad cars. "The construction of railroad freight cars of all types was on a direct contract basis but, in recent years, the company did sub-contracting work for other shops." (Hunker, 1958, p. 147.)

Glass and glass products: Two large glass manufacturing firms are located in this SMA. One "employs over 1,000 workers and reaches a nationwide market with its table and miscellaneous glassware." (Hunker, 1958, p. 173.) The other employing over 1,500 is a subsidiary of a large national company and is engaged in the production of television tubes, again presumably for a national market. (*Idem.*)

Footwear, except rubber: Eight firms, the largest employing around 900 workers in 1953, are located in Columbus. Products include heels, platform shoes, quality women's dress and health shoes, and dance and ballet shoes. (Hunker, 1958, p. 196.) Markets vary with products. Three of the larger firms sell beyond the United States to South American and Pacific nations. Smaller firms are limited to the Central United States. Fifty per cent of one large heel manufacturer's sales "are in Ohio with neighboring states, Missouri (chiefly St. Louis), and the Pacific coast absorbing the remainder." (*Ibid.,* p. 198.)

Non-local services: McCarty (1940, p. 436) calls attention to the central position of Columbus within the state of Ohio, and indicates that the city is the commercial center for a trade territory producing corn, meat animals, sheep, wool, orchard fruits, clay products, and coal. Thomas and Crisler (1953, p. 62) assign to Columbus the central portion of the state of Ohio as a trade area. Specific services in which Columbus is specialized are listed below.

Railroads and railway express service: Coal from southeastern Ohio provided the first main incentive in 1870 for the development of railroad facilities in Columbus. (Hunker, 1958, p. 43.) Today five major railroads pass through the city and each maintains freight facilities in the SMA.

> Three of these provide both passenger and freight service; two are freight roads. These roads rank among the major lines of the east-north-central states. They carry more than 50 per cent of the bulk

goods coming to the city although more than 80 per cent of the finished products leave by truck. (*Ibid.,* p. 213.)

The three east-west routes connect Columbus with the raw materials centers to the east and the markets to the north and west. The two north-south routes . . . carry raw materials, primarily coal, toward northern markets. These lines are freight transporters as well. (*Ibid.,* p. 226.)

Miscellaneous professional and related services: This specialization is apparently due, at least in part, to the fact that Battelle Memorial Institute—one of the world's largest research agencies—is located at Columbus. (*Encyclopedia Americana,* 1957, vol. 7, p. 343.) Research work is carried on in connection with metals, rubber, coal, and various chemicals. (United States Department of Labor, 1957, p. 228.) Another research facility located in the SMA is the Research Foundation connected with Ohio State University. It has carried on important research in connection with the ceramic products industries. (Hunker, 1958, p. 212; the importance of both this foundation and the Battelle Institute for Columbus is discussed in this source, pp. 212-213.) It is claimed that in addition to aiding existing plants in the area through the development of improved processes, operations, machines, and plants, these organizations have been directly responsible for the establishment of four plants in the area and have influenced the location of many other concerns. (*Idem.*)

State public administration: Columbus is the capital of Ohio and is thus the location for many state-related offices and services.

Insurance: In 1953 one insurance company located in Columbus employed over 500 persons, three companies employed from 250 to 500 and ten between 100 and 250 persons. (*County Business Patterns 1953.*) Apparently a sub-national area is being served in most cases.

SUMMARY: COLUMBUS

Columbus is linked with its surrounding hinterland (Areas A and B) as a meat packing center depending on local livestock inputs; as a glass center depending somewhat on nearby supplies of natural gas and sand; and as a political center for the state of Ohio. On the other hand, however, fuels and processed materials to supply its manufacturing inputs arrive for the most part from outside the local area and immediate hinterland from various parts of the manufacturing zone (Area C), and its manufactured products are marketed in this area. In addition its large railroad employment is dependent upon trade originating largely in Area C, and insurance services located in Columbus apparently serve an area broader than the metropolitan hinterland proper.

It should be mentioned that the source information on input-output, supply-market relationships for Columbus is unusually full. Although we have drastically condensed this information, the picture of a complex set of relationships between the city and outlying areas should be convincing. Undoubtedly, a similar picture would emerge for many other cities if comparably detailed data were at hand.

MEMPHIS

SMA consists of Shelby County, Tenn.
1950 population: central city, 396,000; SMA, 482,393
Important location feature: port on the Mississippi River
Other important feature: Federal Reserve Branch city

INPUTS AND SUPPLY AREAS FOR MEMPHIS' PROFILE INDUSTRIES

Saw mills, planing mills and mill work: "Proximity to the oak, cypress, and gum forests of the Lower Mississippi Valley has made Memphis the country's leading hardwood center." (Thomas and Crisler, 1953, p. 53.)

Grain mill products: Grain inputs presumably come from the agricultural hinterland of Memphis.

Miscellaneous food preparations and kindred products: Included in this group are vegetable oil producing companies utilizing the oils from the grain mills. Moreover, as the "nation's largest inland cotton market" (*ibid.*, 1953, p. 53), drawing upon all the cotton-producing states of the South, Memphis is an important center for the processing of cottonseed products. Since the seed is bulky, the crushing mills are most advantageously located close to the supply of raw material.

Tobacco manufactures: Most of the tobacco inputs come from the burley regions of Tennessee and Kentucky.

Rubber products: Principal inputs for rubber products include rubber, cotton, chemicals, and coal. Sources of natural rubber are located in areas external to the United States. Much of the tire production in Memphis, however, is based on synthetic rubber produced in the United States. The cotton required is of the long staple variety produced in this country chiefly in South Carolina, Georgia, Florida, and Arizona. (Roterus, 1931, pp. 84-85.) Exact location of the sources utilized by the plants in Memphis was not determined. However, it seems clear that these inputs arrive from considerable distances. Nylon cord also is used, being obtained from various sources throughout the country.

Table 61. Industrial Profile, Memphis: 1950

Category and industry	Location quotient	Per cent of employed labor force	Inputs primarily from area:	Outputs primarily to area:
(2) *First stage resource users; production for non-final market*				
Saw mills, planing mills and mill work	1.65	1.7	B	C
Grain mill products	2.19	0.5	B	B?
(3) *First stage resource users; production for final market*				
Miscellaneous food preparations and kindred products	1.75	0.4	B, C	B, C
Tobacco manufactures	1.71	0.3	B	C
(6) (*Resources of indirect significance; production for non-final market*)				
Rubber products	5.12	2.2	C	C
(9) *Service industries; non-local*	1.41	18.0	*	B, C
Railroads and railway express service	1.51	(3.7)	*	C
Warehousing and storage	2.00	(0.3)	*	B
Air transportation	3.24	(0.6)	*	C
Wholesale trade	1.84	(6.5)	*	B
(10) *Service industries; may be local or non-local*				
Hospitals	1.84	3.2	*	B, C?
Total in profile industries	...	26.3	...	...

* Inputs other than labor not considered.

OUTPUTS AND SERVICE AREAS OF MEMPHIS' PROFILE INDUSTRIES

Saw mills, planing mills, and mill work: Products of these industries include various stages of processed hardwood lumber products, veneer, flooring and plywood. (U. S. Department of Labor, 1957, p. 284.) These processed materials no doubt enjoy a large market, chiefly in the central and eastern United States. (Ullman, 1957, p. 149.)

Grain mill products: Memphis' activity in this category is almost wholly confined to production of animal and poultry feeds rather than grain products for human consumption. It is surmised that the major market is the livestock industry in the Mid-South, which has shown impressive growth in recent decades.

Miscellaneous food preparations and kindred products: The principal product in this classification is cottonseed oil. Some of this oil is utilized by local companies for the production of vegetable oils, cottonseed cake, and chemicals. (Whitbeck and Finch, 1941, p. 110.) Non-local markets for this oil are no doubt significant too.

Tobacco manufactures: Memphis is the home of a large snuff company whose products enjoy wide distribution. (Thomas and Crisler, 1953, p. 53.)

Rubber products: A branch plant of the nation's largest tire and tube manufacturer is located in Memphis. Distribution of products is no doubt to a large section of the central and southern United States. (U. S. Department of Labor, 1957, p. 284.)

Non-local services: Memphis is the largest Mississippi port between St. Louis and New Orleans and serves as a commercial center for a wide region. (Alexandersson, 1956, p. 103.) Heavy river movements of steel, automobiles, chemicals, grains, lumber, and petroleum products tie Memphis to Kansas City, Minneapolis, Chicago, Pittsburgh, Houston, and New Orleans. Memphis ranked fifth among the southern cities on Vance and Smith's (1954, p. 128) metropolitan function score.

Railroads and railway express service: The importance of Memphis as a railroad city is in part a result of its site, since there are few places south of St. Louis where it has been feasible to construct railroad bridges across the Mississippi River. Important railroad shops also are located in Memphis. (McCarty, 1940, p. 382.)

Warehousing and storage: These services are no doubt closely linked with Memphis' functions as an important river port. Probably cotton and hardwood are among the chief commodities involved. Local sources claim that Memphis is the "world's largest interior cotton warehousing center."

Air transportation: Memphis is the most important air terminal in Tennessee, with six airlines operating services there. In 1950 there were 14,410 aircraft departures from Memphis carrying a total of 143,-662 passengers and 1,958 tons of cargo an average distance of 493 miles. (United States Department of Commerce, Civil Aeronautics Administration, 1951, p. 18.)

Wholesale trade: Memphis ranks among the nation's leaders in volume of wholesale sales. (United States Department of Labor, 1957, p. 284.) In general, Memphis appears to serve the western third of Tennessee, a portion of Arkansas and the northern half of Mississippi (McCarty, 1940, p. 382), although in some lines its trade area is appreciably larger.

Hospitals: Memphis is also relatively specialized in hospital service. In fact Memphis is described as "one of the foremost hospital centers of the South" with a total of 21 hospitals, having some 10,000 beds. (*Encyclopedia Americana,* 1957, vol. 18, pp. 617-618.) Large hospitals serving primarily non-local patients include St. Joseph's Crippled Adults and Crippled Children's hospitals, the United States Marine hospital, and a United States Veterans' hospital. (*Encyclopedia Americana,* 1957, vol. 18, p. 618.)

SUMMARY: MEMPHIS

Several of Memphis' important manufacturing industries rely heavily on inputs from local or surrounding areas—cotton, hardwoods, and tobacco. Certain of its products and services find national markets, but important central place functions also are provided for its immediate hinterland. Both the processing and the commercial functions have taken advantage of Memphis' strategic situation with respect to rail and inland waterway transportation.

OMAHA

SMA consists of Douglas and Sarpy Counties, Nebraska and Pottawattamie County, Iowa
1950 population: central city, 251,117; SMA, 366,395
Important feature: Federal Reserve Branch city

INPUTS AND SUPPLY AREAS FOR OMAHA'S PROFILE INDUSTRIES

Meat products: Chief inputs for this industry include livestock of many kinds—cattle, calves, sheep, and hogs. In 1950 Omaha ranked second only to Chicago in the number of cattle received at public stockyards; 1.6 million cattle were received in Omaha during 1950. In addition, Omaha ranked third in the nation as a market for sheep and lambs, 700,000 animals being received in 1950; and fifth in the nation as a hog market, 1.9 million hogs being received. In addition, 94,000 calves were received during that year. (United States Department of Agriculture, Production and Marketing Administration, 1951, pp. 7-8.) In recent years total volume of livestock receipts has been about the same as in Chicago. Ninety per cent of the hogs received in Omaha during 1950 were driven in by truck; this indicates that the animals arrived from relatively short distances. Among the other animals considered, 84 per cent of the cattle, 57 per cent of the calves and only 36 per cent of the sheep and lambs were driven in. (*Ibid.,* pp. 9-10.) The bulk of employment in this industry is made up of meat packing establishments; some of the largest United States companies operate plants in this city. (United States Department of Labor, 1957, p. 174.) According to recent reports of the Union Stockyards Company of Omaha, about nine-tenths of all livestock receipts originate in Iowa and Nebraska. Wyoming, South Dakota, and Kansas also are important sources. Mather (1950, p. 91) notes that "Omaha, Denver, Sioux City, Billings, and Ogden are the chief central markets for Wyoming cattle in order of importance." About three-fourths of all livestock received in Omaha are sold to local packers; some of these are shipped to other cities. The remainder are shipped to non-local packers or to country points, mostly in Iowa and Nebraska, for use as stockers and feeders.

OUTPUTS AND SERVICE AREAS OF OMAHA'S PROFILE INDUSTRIES

Meat products: Exact distribution of the products of the meat packing industries was not determined; however, the "Big Four" and some 14 or 15 other concerns have packing establishments in Omaha and the distribution of their products is clearly to a national and even a world market. (U. S. Department of Labor, 1957, p. 174.)

Non-local services: As well as the gathering and processing of meat animals Omaha performs other important services for its hinterland area. Omaha is one of the more important commercial centers of the American Midwest. (See Garland, 1955, pp. 239-240.) Some of the important services centered in Omaha are discussed below.

Railroads and railway express service: Omaha is served by nine major railroads and is the general headquarters for one, and location of western offices for two others. The early lead of Omaha over other potential centers of transportation and commerce north of Kansas City on the Missouri River is said to be related to the fact that the river's flood plain narrows at that point, making it feasible to bridge the river. Omaha is thus strategically located with respect to transcontinental routes and is situated as well at the focus of a fan-like system of rail lines covering most of Nebraska and parts of northern Kansas.

Table 62. Industrial Profile, Omaha: 1950

Category and industry	Location quotient	Per cent of employed labor force	Inputs primarily from area:	Outputs primarily to area:
(3) *First stage resource users; production for final market*				
Meat products	13.37	6.6	B, C	C
(9) *Service industries; non-local*	1.79	22.8	*	B, C
Railroads and railway express service	3.31	(8.2)	*	C
Trucking service	1.57	(1.7)	*	B
Warehousing and storage	3.53	(0.6)	*	B, C
Services incidental to transportation	4.86	(0.3)	*	B?
Other and not specified utilities	4.83	(0.3)	*	B?
Wholesale trade	1.66	(5.8)	*	B
Security and commodity brokerage and investment companies	2.00	(0.3)	*	B, C
(10) *Service industries; may be local or non-local*				
Insurance	2.81	3.8	*	B, C
Total in profile industries	...	33.2	...	...

* Inputs other than labor not considered.

Trucking service: Trucking in connection with the livestock industry has already been alluded to. Grains are another important commodity utilizing trucks in the Omaha area. (See Garland, 1955, pp. 237, 240.) In general trucks have become very strong competitors of the railroads for the local and hinterland traffic and for the intra-regional trade as well. (*Ibid.,* p. 86.)

Warehousing and storage: Omaha's specialization in warehousing and storage employment is no doubt related to its importance as a trucking and rail center. (*Ibid.,* p. 240.)

Services incidental to transportation: Specialization in this industry group is assumed to be related to Omaha's functions as a transportation center. Specific nature of this employment was not determined.

Other and not specified utilities: The nature of this specialization was not determined for Omaha.

Wholesale trade: Omaha is generally conceded to be the major wholesale trading center between Kansas City to the south and Minneapolis-St. Paul to the north (Alexandersson, 1956, p. 101). The state of Nebraska makes up a major portion of Omaha's trade area (McCarty, 1940, p. 320), although Omaha wholesalers also do business in western Iowa, northwestern Missouri, northern Kansas, eastern Wyoming, southern South Dakota, and even parts of Idaho and Montana. Omaha's specialization in wholesaling is partly due to the high volume of sales by assemblers of farm products (see chapter 11).

Security and commodity brokerage and investment companies: The Omaha Grain Exchange is the focus of one of the nation's major grain markets, serving a large regional area.

Insurance: Omaha is considered an important regional center for the insurance industry and one large national company has its general offices located within the city. (United States Department of Labor, 1957, p. 174.)

SUMMARY: OMAHA

Omaha's chief functions derive from her location in relation to the corn and winter wheat producing regions of the United States and the grazing lands of the Midwest, and to her position in the national rail network. Commodities, particularly livestock, are gathered from a broad region and (often after processing) are transshipped to eastern centers for consumption. Omaha also serves a smaller area as a distribution center for manufactured products received from the East. (Garland, 1955, p. 240.) Financial functions appear to be performed for a broader region than Omaha's immediate hinterland.

FORT WORTH

SMA consists of Tarrant County, Texas
1950 population: central city, 278,778; SMA, 361,253

INPUTS AND SUPPLY AREAS FOR FORT WORTH'S PROFILE INDUSTRIES

Meat products: In 1950 Fort Worth ranked second only to Denver as the nation's largest sheep and lamb market, 855,000 sheep being received at public stockyards in Fort Worth in that year. In addition Fort Worth ranked as the fourth largest calf market (224,000 calves received in 1950), and the tenth largest cattle market (426,000 cattle received in 1950), and was also an important market for hogs (237,000 hogs received in 1950). (United States Department of Agriculture, Production and Marketing Administration, 1951, pp. 7-8.) Eighty-seven per cent of the calves, 81 per cent of the sheep and lambs, 85 per cent of the cattle and 88 per cent of the hogs were driven in rather than received by rail. (*Ibid.*, p. 10.) Fort Worth is one of the dominant livestock markets of the country and its trade area appears to include much of the southwestern United States. (See McCarty, 1940, p. 240.) Talbert (1956, p. 140) indicates that while the majority of cattle inputs arrive from Texas, cattle are received also from Oklahoma, New Mexico, Arkansas, and Louisiana.

Table 63. Industrial Profile, Fort Worth: 1950

Category and industry	Location quotient	Per cent of employed labor force	Inputs primarily from area:	Outputs primarily to area:
(3) *First stage resource users; production for final market*				
Meat products	5.86	2.9	B, C	C
Confectionery and related products	2.21	0.3	C?	C?
(7) *Resources of indirect significance; production for final market*				
Aircraft and parts	22.28	10.2	C	C
(9) *Service industries; non-local*	1.23	15.6	*	B, C
Air transportation	3.18	(0.5)	*	C
Wholesale trade	1.58	(5.6)	*	B
Total in profile industries	...	29.0	...	...

* Inputs other than labor not considered.

Confectionery and related products: Inputs include sugar and miscellaneous food products. Specific sources were not determined but sugar cane is raised in the Gulf Coast states (Alexandersson, 1956, p. 88) and San Antonio is the center for the pecan shelling industry. (Billings, 1946, p. 226.)

Aircraft and parts: Fort Worth is the location of a large airframe assembly plant (Cunningham, 1951, p. 226) and this plant has been decisive in bringing in new aircraft-parts manufacturing to the SMA. (Talbert, 1956, p. 132.) Inputs include all manner of processed materials and fabricated parts which arrive from all parts of the country. (See Cunningham, 1951, p. 18.)

OUTPUTS AND SERVICE AREAS OF FORT WORTH'S PROFILE INDUSTRIES

Meat products: Meat products no doubt enjoy a wide distribution, as two of the country's leading meat packers have establishments in Fort Worth. (United States Department of Labor, 1957, p. 298.)

Confectionery and related products: A large firm manufacturing candy is located in Fort Worth. (*Ibid.,* p. 298.) Distribution of its products is no doubt to a regional area.

Aircraft and parts: Aircraft assembled in Fort Worth serve many parts of this country and of the world. Both airplanes and helicopters are manufactured in Fort Worth. (*Ibid.,* p. 298.)

Non-local services: Fort Worth, located only a few miles west of Dallas, is subordinate to Dallas in many service functions, particularly financial. (McCarty, 1940, p. 386.) Nevertheless, important non-local services are performed for a fairly extensive hinterland. Vance and Smith (1954, p. 128) call Fort Worth a "subdominant with metropolitan characteristics" and list it just below Richmond in their ranking of important cities of the South. They note that Fort Worth "has managed by organizing the hinterland to the north and west to resemble in dominance a traditional metropolis like Richmond. Dallas and Fort Worth taken together surpass all the cities of the Southeast in their potential." (*Ibid.,* p. 131.) Talbert (1956, pp. 137-39) describes the territory organized by Fort Worth as including Tarrant County, most of West Texas and a part of the Panhandle. This delimitation of the trade area is in general based on the circulation of the largest Fort Worth newspaper and on the distribution of out-of-town charge accounts at eleven Fort Worth retail stores. Fort Worth also serves as "a shipping and processing point for the vast northwest Texas agricultural sector" (United States Department of Labor, 1957, p. 298). Specialized non-local services performed by Fort Worth are discussed below.

Air transportation: Fort Worth is outranked by Dallas, Houston, and San Antonio in the number of airlines operated, but still is an important air transportation center for Texas. In 1950, six airlines operated services in Fort Worth carrying 50,375 passengers and 375 tons of cargo an average distance of 460 miles. (United States Department of Commerce, Civil Aeronautics Administration, 1951, p. 18.)

Wholesale trade: Fort Worth appears to serve the area to the west and northwest. However the area over which its dominance extends is limited by the location of Dallas to the east, Amarillo to the north and San Antonio to the south.

SUMMARY: FORT WORTH

Fort Worth's profile manufacturing industries appear to be dependent on a broader base than the immediate hinterland (Area B). Inputs for meat products, confectionery, and aircraft industries appear to arrive from considerable distances. Some non-local services are performed for Area B (chiefly wholesaling) but for financial services Fort Worth is dominated by near-by Dallas.

RICHMOND

SMA consists of Richmond city, Chesterfield and Henrico Counties, Virginia

1950 population: central city, 230,310; SMA, 328,050

Important location feature: port on James River

Other important features: Federal Reserve Bank city; capital of Virginia

INPUTS AND SUPPLY AREAS FOR RICHMOND'S PROFILE INDUSTRIES

Tobacco manufactures: Richmond lies on the northern edge of the Piedmont area of Virginia and North and South Carolina, an area specializing in the production of tobacco (northern Piedmont) and cotton (southern Piedmont). (McCarty, 1940, pp. 441-442.) The tobacco produced in the Richmond area is largely of the dark, fire-cured type. However, about three-fourths or more of this type of tobacco is exported to foreign markets, the remainder being used in this country for manufacturing chewing tobaccos. To the south of this area (apparently still within Richmond's hinterland) is a large region specializing in the production of bright, flue-cured tobaccos. These tobaccos are used primarily for the manufacture of plug tobacco, granulated smoking mixtures and cigarettes to be used in this country and also for export. To the north of Richmond (in Maryland) and to the west (western Virginia and western North Carolina) burley and light air-cured tobaccos are raised. (Jones and Darkenwald, 1954, pp. 309-310.) Most of the light burley is used in the manufacturing of cigarettes. (Dicken, 1949, p. 243.) Paper inputs for the industry apparently arrive from a special paper mill set up in North Carolina, or are imported. (Alderfer and Michl, 1950, p. 630.)

Miscellaneous textile mill products: Exact nature of the inputs utilized by this industry group was not determined. Cotton thread and fabric inputs no doubt arrive from other mills located throughout the Piedmont area. Synthetic fibers are produced within the Richmond SMA (see below). Other inputs were not determined.

Table 64. Industrial Profile, Richmond: 1950

Category and industry	Location quotient	Per cent of employed labor force	Inputs primarily from area:	Outputs primarily to area:
(3) *First stage resource users; production for final market*				
Tobacco manufactures	31.47	5.4	B, C	C
(4) *Second stage resource users; production for non-final market*				
Miscellaneous textile mill products	6.30	0.6	B?	C
Pulp, paper, and paperboard products	2.41	1.0	B?	A, C
Synthetic fibers	20.78	1.9	B, C	B, C
Miscellaneous chemicals and allied products	1.64	1.4	C?	C
(9) *Service industries; non-local*	1.47	18.7	*	B, C
Railroads and railway express service	1.66	(4.1)	*	C
Wholesale trade	1.50	(5.3)	*	B
Banking and credit agencies	1.88	(1.8)	*	B, C
State public administration	3.45	(1.6)	*	B
(10) *Service industries; may be local or non-local*				
Insurance	2.22	3.0	*	C
Hospitals	1.51	2.6	*	B
Total in profile industries	...	34.6	...	...

* Inputs other than labor not considered.

Pulp, paper, and paperboard products: Sources of paper and pulp inputs for this industry group were not determined. In general pulp resources of the general area are probably involved. (See Jones and Darkenwald, 1954, p. 84.)

Synthetic fibers: Rayon and industrial nylon are the most important of the synthetic fibers produced in Richmond. (United States Department of Labor, 1957, p. 314.) Inputs include cellulose from cotton linters or spruce wood, chemicals (sulphuric acid and caustic soda), and large quantities of soft water. (Jones and Darkenwald, 1954, pp. 528-529; Alderfer and Michl, 1950, pp. 406-407.) Wood pulp is available from the Appalachian forests and cotton linters arrive from the Cotton Belt. (Jones and Darkenwald, 1954, p. 529.) Water is available from the James River; sources of chemicals were not determined.

Miscellaneous chemicals and allied products: Inputs for this industry group are quite diversified and were not specifically determined. No doubt inputs arrive from many parts of the eastern and southern United States. The industry, it is said, was originally attracted to Richmond by the tidewater channel of the James River.

OUTPUTS AND SERVICE AREAS OF RICHMOND'S PROFILE INDUSTRIES

Tobacco manufactures: Several types of tobacco industries are represented in Richmond. Four large cigarette companies, one cigar, and two pipe tobacco companies are located in Richmond, all of them serving a national or sub-national market. (United States Department of Labor, 1957, p. 314; Thomas and Crisler, 1953, p. 38.)

Miscellaneous textile mill products: Varied outputs including hassocks, canvas products, and seat covers are produced. (United States Department of Labor, 1957, p. 314.) Distribution is probably to a sub-national market.

Pulp, paper and paperboard products: First attracted to Richmond by the tobacco industry, this industry now produces diversified products including paper cups, cartons, bags, and shipping containers. Many of the outputs still are utilized by local tobacco companies. (*Ibid.*, p. 314; Thomas and Crisler, 1953, p. 38.) Other outputs no doubt serve a sub-national area.

Synthetic fibers: Rayon and related outputs are no doubt fed into various textile plants both within the general Piedmont area and the New England area to the north.

Miscellaneous chemicals and allied products: Cellophane is probably the most important of the products of this industry. (United States Department of Labor, 1957, p. 314.) Distribution of this product is no doubt to a national or sub-national market. Other products include paints, varnishes, sulfuric acid, fertilizers, pharmaceuticals, insecticides, and fungicides.

Service industries, non-local: Richmond is considered the top ranking industrial and commercial center for the Virginia Piedmont. (McCarty, 1940, p. 442.) It is accessible for average-sized ocean-going vessels and has long been a leading tobacco market. (Alexandersson, 1956, p. 103.) The port commerce of Richmond is roughly comparable in volume to that of Washington, Wilmington, Charleston, Savannah, and Miami, though small, of course, in relation to such major ports as Baltimore and Norfolk. There is relatively little outbound traffic; in terms of tonnage, major receipts, largely from domestic sources, are petroleum products and sand, gravel, and crushed rock. (United States Department of the Army, Corps of Engineers [1956], Part 1, p. 302; Part 5, p. 17.) Vance and Smith (1954, p. 129) indicate that Richmond is declining as a commercial and service center, and its ranking on their index of metropolitan functions places it as a "subdominant with metropolitan characteristics." They suggest that its proximity to Baltimore, Philadelphia, and New York makes it subordinate to these centers in many functions, while it is encountering strong competition in the growth of Charlotte, North Carolina. Richmond shows specialization in several services performed for its hinterland and larger areas.

Railroads and railway express service: McCarty (1940, p. 442) notes the natural advantages of Richmond's location, where north-south coastal rail lines cross east-west routes leading to the harbors of the Virginia capes. The former are forced inland by the estuary of the James River.

Wholesale trade: Richmond's wholesale trade area appears to involve a large section of central Virginia. (McCarty, 1940, p. 442.) For some functions this area extends down into North Carolina (as shown on the map of newspaper circulation areas by Park and Newcomb); however it appears that recently Charlotte, North Carolina has become a strong competitor for this territory.

Banking and credit agencies: Richmond is the location of one of the 12 Federal Reserve System banks. Its specialization as a banking center is no doubt related to this fact and Richmond consequently performs financial services for a considerable area.

State public administration: Richmond is the capital of Virginia and is thus the location of many state offices.

Insurance: Richmond is the headquarters for 34 insurance firms. (United States Department of Labor, 1957, p. 314.) The dominance is in part related to the location in Richmond of the Federal Reserve Bank.

Hospitals: Richmond is the location of several large hospitals serving a largely regional clientele. The precise nature of the services available in Richmond was not determined. Richmond is a center of medical research related to tobacco and its use.

SUMMARY: RICHMOND

Richmond's profile industries appear to be closely related directly or indirectly with its hinterland (Area B). Many if not all tobacco inputs originate in this area as do wood products utilized in the manufacture of paper and rayon. Cotton fabric inputs probably also arrive from firms located in the hinterland. Outputs of Richmond industries are also related to the local and hinterland economy in that paper outputs feed the tobacco industries and rayon outputs the textile industries. However many outputs are destined for a national or subnational market, e.g., tobacco products, chemicals, and a portion of the rayon output. Wholesale and administrative services are performed for this hinterland while financial and transportation services are performed for a broader region (Area C) as well.

OKLAHOMA CITY

SMA consists of Oklahoma County, Oklahoma
1950 population: central city, 243,504; SMA, 325,352
Important features: Federal Reserve Branch city: capital of Oklahoma

INPUTS AND SUPPLY AREAS FOR OKLAHOMA CITY'S PROFILE INDUSTRIES

Crude petroleum and natural gas extraction: In 1952 Oklahoma was the third most important state in the volume of natural gas and LP-gases produced and the fourth largest producer of natural gasoline and crude petroleum. (United States Bureau of Mines, Regional Mineral Industry Divisions, 1955, p. 737.) In 1950 Oklahoma produced 164,-899,000 barrels of petroleum and between the periods 1941-1950 provided approximately eight per cent of the national production.

(United States Bureau of Mines, 1953, pp. 887, 893.) The natural gas production of Oklahoma in 1949 was 631,200 million cubic feet of which 373,200 million were from gas wells and 258,000 million were from oil wells. (*Ibid.*, p. 811.)

Table 65. Industrial Profile, Oklahoma City: 1950

Category and industry	Location quotient	Per cent of employed labor force	Inputs primarily from area:	Outputs primarily to area:
(1) (*Primary resource extractors; production for non-final market*)				
Crude petroleum and natural gas extraction	2.10	3.5	A, B	C
(3) *First stage resource users; production for final market*				
Meat products	3.88	1.9	B, C	C
(9) *Service industries; non-local*	1.86	23.8	*	B, C
Trucking service	1.76	(1.8)	*	B
Air transportation	1.59	(0.3)	*	C
Petroleum and gasoline pipe lines	2.00	(0.1)	*	C
Services incidental to transportation	2.29	(0.2)	*	?
Other and not specified utilities	2.50	(0.2)	*	B
Wholesale trade	1.55	(5.4)	*	B
Banking and credit agencies	1.59	(1.5)	*	B
Security and commodity brokerage and investment companies	2.31	(0.4)	*	B, C
Federal public administration	5.14	(9.2)	*	C
State public administration	2.74	(1.3)	*	B
(10) *Service industries; may be local or non-local*				
Insurance	1.52	2.0	*	B
Total in profile industries	...	31.2	...	...

* Inputs other than labor not considered.

In 1953, Oklahoma County (coterminous with the Oklahoma City SMA) was one of the five most productive counties in the state in the mining of petroleum. (United States Bureau of Mines, Regional Mineral Industry Divisions, 1955, p. 737.) The county is located at the approximate center of the huge, productive Mid-Continent gas and oil field which extends up into the center of Kansas and down into north-central Texas. (See map in Jones and Darkenwald, 1954, p. 406.) This field has been called "the largest and most productive oil-producing area in the world." (*Ibid.*, p. 404.)

> Large-scale commercial development began about 1906. Since then, production has mounted steadily, year by year, and apparently the maximum output has not yet been reached.
>
> The Mid-Continent Province produces practically all grades of oil. . . . The complexity of structural conditions, different sources of origin, and vast extent of the province are responsible for the pronounced diversity in the occurrence and in the quality of the oils. (Bengtson and Van Royen, 1950, p. 385.)

A word may be said here about the residential distribution of workers in this industry group within the SMA. Of the approximately 4,500 employees in this industry group approximately 3,500 resided in the urbanized area and, of these, 3,000 were within the central city in 1950.

Meat products: In 1950 Oklahoma City ranked ninth in this country as a market for cattle, 496,000 cattle being received at the public stockyards in that year. Other receipts included 87,000 calves, 235,000 hogs, and 94,000 sheep. It appears that the cattle and calves received in Oklahoma City come from relatively nearby since 98 per cent of the cattle and 97 per cent of the calves were driven in to market by truck. By contrast only 72 per cent of the hogs and 67 per cent of the sheep were driven in to market by truck in 1950. (United States Department of Agriculture, Production and Marketing Administration, 1951, pp. 7-8, 10.) The chief area of livestock raising in Oklahoma is on the dry, grassy western plains. (Oklahoma Planning and Resources Board, 1945, p. 20.) It appears that in addition to this area some animals are shipped from Kansas, Arizona, and Texas. (See map in Ullman, 1957, p. 126.)

OUTPUTS AND SERVICE AREAS OF OKLAHOMA CITY'S PROFILE INDUSTRIES

Crude petroleum and natural gas extraction: Petroleum products and natural gas are distributed from the Oklahoma City producing area to all parts of the nation. Only about 750 persons are employed in the SMA in petroleum refining industries as opposed to over 5,300 employed in the Tulsa SMA; so it is assumed that while some of the petroleum is refined in the SMA some may be shipped to Tulsa and elsewhere. There is general evidence that out-of-state refineries also are important. Thus for the state as a whole,

> Deliveries of crude to refineries in 1950 amounted to 141.4 million barrels, including 64.4 million to refineries in Oklahoma and 77.0

> million to other States. Interstate deliveries included 58.3 million barrels to the Indiana-Illinois refinery district, 11.4 million to Kansas and Missouri, 5.2 million to the Appalachian districts, and 2.1 million to Texas refineries. (United States Bureau of Mines, 1953, p. 919.)

As to the financial organization of the Mid-Continent field,

> The Mid-Continent Province is noted for the wide diversity of capital interests represented. Since it was the meeting ground of east and west and north and south, it was natural that capital from all of these sources should become interested in large-scale development there and, as a result, more different companies are exploiting oil in this province than in any other area in the world. These companies range all the way from those of world renown to those owned by a few people in some county or town. Contrary to popular opinion, no monopolistic condition prevails. (Bengtson and Van Royen, 1950, p. 385.)

Maps in Jones and Darkenwald (1954, pp. 406-407) show the network of pipelines (both crude and refinery products) connecting Oklahoma City with other producing centers and with distribution areas.

Natural gas is also distributed to a national market by means of pipe lines.

> Recent years have witnessed an enormous extension of pipe lines for the distribution of natural gas. Main lines now connect the gas fields of Louisiana, Texas, and Oklahoma with such distant cities as Minneapolis, Chicago, Detroit, and New York, and extend westward to Los Angeles. Some of the main lines are of huge diameters, from eighteen to thirty inches. (Bengtson and Van Royen, 1950, p. 392; a map of principal gas pipelines as of 1947 is also given.)

Meat products: Two large national companies have important packing houses in the SMA. (United States Department of Labor, 1957, p. 240.) Distribution of products is no doubt to a large part of the central and southwest United States. (See map in Ullman, 1957, p. 126.)

Non-local services: Alexandersson (1956, p. 101) indicates that the city's situation on the border between the Winter Wheat Belt and the Cotton Belt led to its growth as a commercial center for an area producing cattle, wheat and cotton. In connection with these activities, "State headquarters for grain, broomcorn, livestock, cotton, and other agricultural interests are maintained here." (Oklahoma Planning and Resources Board, 1945, p. 67.) It appears that the SMA and the state as a whole is to some extent dependent on non-local capital for the financing of industries.

> Most of the capital of the state is invested in land, forests, or mineral deposits. . . . Much of it is "outside" capital which has been invested in facilities to extract raw materials and minerals. (*Ibid.*, p. 55.)

Non-local service industries in which Oklahoma City is specialized point to important hinterland relationships.

Trucking service: This specialization is perhaps related to the importance of this SMA as a gathering center for agricultural products from the surrounding hinterland and as a distribution center for manufactured products to this same area.

Air transportation: In 1950 Oklahoma City had five airlines operating which carried a total of 98,695 passengers and 430 tons of cargo an average distance of 490 miles. (United States Department of Commerce, Civil Aeronautics Administration, 1951, p. 16.) There are 12 airports within a radius of about 20 miles of Oklahoma City. (*Encyclopedia Americana,* 1957, vol. 20, p. 699.)

Petroleum and gasoline pipe lines: This specialization has been given considerable attention in our discussion above of the distribution of petroleum and natural gas products mined in this area. A national market is served by this industry group.

Services incidental to transportation: Nature of this specialization was not determined.

Other and not specified utilities: This specialization is no doubt related to irrigation activities in the state of Oklahoma. In 1950 Oklahoma had 271,747 acres of farm land under irrigation representing an increase of 42 per cent over 1940. However, this figure still represented less than one per cent of the total farm land in Oklahoma. (United States Bureau of the Census, *United States Census of Agriculture: 1950, Irrigation of Agricultural Lands,* 1952, p. 37; for a map showing "present and proposed" irrigation projects as of 1942 in the state of Oklahoma, see Oklahoma Planning and Resources Board, 1945, p. 34.) None of the Oklahoma irrigation projects in the early 1940's was in the vicinity of Oklahoma City; however it is assumed that offices for some of these projects are located in Oklahoma City.

Wholesale trade: According to statistics compiled from the *1948 Census of Business,* Oklahoma City was one of six SMA's in the size group three to five hundred thousand which was above the national SMA average in per capita sales for assemblers of farm products. Thus here it can be pointed out that for all of Oklahoma's mineral wealth, as represented by its petroleum and natural gas industries, the value of its crop and livestock production exceeds that of its mineral and fuel output. (*Encyclopedia Americana,* 1957, vol. 20, p. 692.) The state ranks high, for example, in production of wheat, broomcorn, alfalfa seed, pecans and peanuts, and is a leading cotton producing state. According to McCarty (1940, p. 385) the most important of Oklahoma City's interests is cotton "for the Oklahoma City trade territory includes the rich red prairies of the southwest portion of the state." The Oklahoma Planning and Resources Board (1945, p. 67) describes the trade territory of the city as extending throughout Oklahoma and into the Texas Panhandle. Thomas and Crisler (1953, p. 102) are more conservative, assigning this SMA only the central and western portion of Oklahoma, with Tulsa dominating the northeastern section and Dallas and Fort Worth the Texas Panhandle. The *Encyclopaedia Britannica* (1957, vol. 16, p. 758) estimates that Oklahoma City performs nearly 50 per cent of the state's wholesaling activity.

Banking and credit agencies: Oklahoma City is the most important commercial and financial center in its state. Its branch bank in the Federal Reserve System has a district including all but the southeast corner of the state. No doubt banking interests are also related to the security and commodity brokers and the insurance companies located in this SMA.

Security and commodity brokerage and investment companies: Probably this employment specialization is quite directly tied in with the petroleum and natural gas interests of this area. According to the *Encyclopedia Americana* (1957, vol. 20, p. 693), the opening of oil, gas, and other mineral fields was a great stimulus to banking in Oklahoma. In addition some of this employment may be related to the SMA's importance as a cotton market.

Federal public administration: In 1957 it was estimated that over 27,000 persons in this SMA were employed by the federal government. (United States Department of Labor, 1957, p. 240.) The chief governmental employer in the area is the Oklahoma City Air Materiel Area which maintains "one of the Nation's largest air materiel supply depots." (*Idem.*) Another important government employer located in this SMA is the Civil Aeronautics Administration, which maintains an aeronautical center here for the training of technicians. (*Encyclopaedia Britannica,* 1957, vol. 16, p. 758.)

State public administration: Oklahoma City is the capital of the state of Oklahoma and thus many state-related offices are maintained here.

Insurance: According to the *1953 County Business Patterns* there were 278 units engaged in activity as insurance agents or carriers in this SMA. Two of the carrier units were large enough to employ between 100 and 250 employees. Indications are that these establishments are engaged largely in local and hinterland business. The *Encyclopaedia Britannica* (1957, vol. 16, p. 758) reports that this SMA is the home of insurance headquarters which clear over 75 per cent of the state's policies.

SUMMARY: OKLAHOMA CITY

The Oklahoma City SMA is closely tied to its local and hinterland areas for the supply of raw materials (livestock and petroleum and natural gas) for its profile manufacturing industries and because of the central place functions which it performs for an area including a large part of the state of Oklahoma. Although the extraction of petroleum and natural gas is a major employment group, the SMA functions chiefly as a commercial and financial center for this industry. The SMA is related to its agricultural hinterland as an important livestock and cotton market through its trucking services and wholesale trade functions. In addition financial (banking and insurance) and political functions are performed for this same area. In the distribution of its meat and petroleum and natural gas products and in its functions as a civilian air transportation center and materiel center for the Air Force, it is linked to the national economy.

NASHVILLE

SMA consists of Davidson County, Tennessee
1950 population: central city, 174,307; SMA, 321,758
Important location feature: on Cumberland River
Other important features: Federal Reserve Branch city; capital of Tennessee

INPUTS AND SUPPLY AREAS FOR NASHVILLE'S PROFILE INDUSTRIES

Meat products: 1950 receipts of livestock in Nashville were as follows: 139,000 cattle (99 per cent driven in), 38,000 calves (100 per cent driven in), 214,000 hogs (100 per cent driven in), and 66,000 sheep and lambs (99 per cent driven in). (United States Department of Agriculture, Production and Marketing Administration, 1951, pp. 7-8, 10.) The high proportion of livestock receipts driven in indicates that the livestock are being gathered from generally near-by areas. There appears to be a rather heavy concentration of swine and sheep and lambs raised in the central basin of Tennessee, (see maps A-9 and A-10, United States National Resources Committee, 1939, p. 342) and Nashville serves as the commercial center for this area. (McCarty, 1940, p. 437.)

Table 66. Industrial Profile, Nashville: 1950

Category and industry	Location quotient	Per cent of employed labor force	Inputs primarily from area:	Outputs primarily to area:
(3) *First stage resource users; production for final market*				
Meat products	1.71	0.8	B	C
(4) *Second stage resource users; production for non-final market*				
Synthetic fibers	24.67	2.2	B, C	C
Paints, varnishes and related products	2.00	0.2	C	B?
Miscellaneous chemicals and allied products	2.12	1.9	B, C	B, C
(5) *Second stage resource users; production for final market*				
Knitting mills	2.88	1.0	C	C
(7) *Resources of indirect significance; production for final market*				
Footwear, except rubber	4.60	2.2	C, A?	C
(9) *Service industries; non-local*	1.26	16.1	*	B, C
Warehousing and storage	1.88	(0.3)	*	B
Radio broadcasting and television	2.09	(0.2)	*	B, C
State public administration	2.68	(1.3)	*	B
(10) *Service industries; may be local or non-local*				
Insurance	1.73	2.3	*	C
Hospitals	1.61	2.8	*	B
Education services, private	2.43	2.3	*	B, C
Total in profile industries	...	31.8	...	...

* Inputs other than labor not considered.

Synthetic fibers: Rayon is the most important of the synthetic fibers produced in Nashville. (United States Department of Labor, 1957, p. 286.) Inputs necessary include cellulose (cotton linters or spruce wood), chemicals (sulphuric acid and caustic soda), and large quantities of soft water. (Jones and Darkenwald, 1954, pp. 528-529; Alderfer and Michl, 1950, pp. 406-407.) Specific sources of the cotton or spruce wood utilized were not determined. However, Nashville is on the edge of the Cotton Belt and spruce woods are available in near-by areas and farther to the south. (See Jones and Darkenwald, 1954, pp. 84-85.) Water is available from the Cumberland River. (United States Department of Labor, 1957, p. 286.) Sources for chemical inputs were not determined.

Paints, varnishes, and related products: This industry group requires inputs of vegetable oils (particularly linseed and tung oils), lead, petroleum products, and inorganic chemicals. Sources of inputs can only be discussed in general terms. Linseed oil derived from flaxseed is produced in this country chiefly in Minnesota and North Dakota. External sources include Argentina and Uruguay. (Zimmermann, 1951, pp. 277-278.) Tung oil is produced in this country along the Gulf of Mexico from Florida to eastern Texas; Mississippi is now the most important producer. However, domestic sources meet only a small part of the needs and large quantities of the oil are imported. (*Ibid.*, pp. 284-285.) Lead is mined in this country in the central and western states, particularly Missouri, Idaho, Kansas, and Oklahoma. (*Ibid.*, p. 736.) Sources of petroleum products and inorganic chemicals utilized by this industry group were not determined.

Miscellaneous chemicals and allied products: Many of the chemical products of this industry group utilize Tennessee phosphate, Nashville being an important center for this resource. (McCarty, 1940, p. 437.) Other inputs are varied and no doubt arrive from many parts of the central and southeast United States.

Knitting mills: A sizable firm engaged in the manufacture of seamless hosiery is located in Nashville and its employment largely accounts for Nashville's specialization in this industry. Sources of inputs were not determined; however it is known that Chattanooga, Tennessee, is the location of one of the three largest nylon plants in the United States. (Jones and Darkenwald, 1954, p. 531.)

Footwear, except rubber: Chief inputs include tanned leathers, textiles and miscellaneous products. Some textile products are available from the SMA itself; apparently leather inputs must arrive from considerable distances. (See map A-11, United States National Resources Committee, 1939, p. 342.)

OUTPUTS AND SERVICE AREAS OF NASHVILLE'S PROFILE INDUSTRIES

Meat products: Outputs include processed meats of all kinds. Distribution is probably to a large regional area.

Synthetic fibers: Rayon outputs from this industry are probably destined for a wide distribution. In general, more than half of the rayon output goes into broad woven cloth for the apparel industry, about one-third is utilized for tire fabrics and most of the remainder for knit goods. (Jones and Darkenwald, 1954, p. 529.)

Paints, varnishes, and related products: Specific types of outputs from this industry group were not determined. Total employment for this industry is not large, and probably a relatively small market is being served.

Miscellaneous chemicals and allied products: Miscellaneous chemicals and fertilizers are produced by these industries in Nashville. (Thomas and Crisler, 1953, p. 67.) Distribution of the fertilizers is probably mainly to the immediate hinterland, which is a rich agricultural region. (McCarty, 1940, p. 437.) Other products no doubt enjoy a regional distribution.

Knitting mills: Chief output of this industry group is seamless hosiery. (United States Department of Labor, 1957, p. 286.) Distribution is probably to a sub-national, if not national, market.

Footwear, except rubber: Several shoe manufacturers are located in Nashville. (*Ibid.,* p. 286; Thomas and Crisler, 1953, p. 67.) Distribution of these products is no doubt to a sub-national market. The city is also a home office location for a large shoe producer with national distribution.

Non-local services: McCarty (1940, p. 437) attributes Nashville's commercial prominence in part to its location in the "fertile central basin" of Tennessee and its proximity to the Tennessee "tobacco belt." The city's location on a river apparently is not of paramount importance to its economy. The port of Nashville is engaged primarily in receipt of petroleum products and sand, gravel, and crushed rock; outbound shipments are of relatively little importance. (United States Department of the Army, Corps of Engineers [1958], Part 2, p. 147.) Specialized non-local services are listed below.

Warehousing and storage: Specialization in this industry group is no doubt related to Nashville's function as an agricultural market for the Tennessee basin area. (McCarty, 1940, p. 437.)

Radio broadcasting and television: Nashville shows a relative specialization in employment in the radio and television industry group. This specialization may be in part related to the fact that Nashville has for many years claimed the title of "folk" music capital of the country. Several national network programs originate from this city.

State public administration: Nashville is the capital of Tennessee and thus the location for many state-related offices and services.

Insurance: Nashville's specialization in this industry group reflects the fact that home offices for two large insurance companies, as well as a number of smaller home offices and branches, are located in Nashville. (United States Department of Labor, 1957, p. 286.)

Hospitals: Nashville is relatively specialized in hospital employment with a large Veterans Administration hospital, Vanderbilt University Hospitals, Meharry Medical Hospital, and Madison Hospital; these provide hospital services for the hinterland area. The specific types of services available in Nashville were not determined.

Education services, private: Located in the Nashville SMA are the following private colleges and universities: Vanderbilt University, Fisk University, Ward-Belmont School for girls (now Belmont College), George Peabody College for teachers, David Lipscomb College, Trevecca Nazarene College, Madison College, and Meharry Medical College (one of the two Negro medical schools in the United States). These schools draw attendance from a fairly wide area.

SUMMARY: NASHVILLE

Some of Nashville's profile industries appear to depend upon local and hinterland resources: livestock, cotton, phosphate, tobacco. Other portions are clearly dependent upon resources gathered from distant areas. Administrative and warehousing services are performed for the immediate hinterland, but financial and educational services appear to be related to larger areas. In general, markets for Nashville manufactured products appear to be regional or sub-national.

JACKSONVILLE

SMA consists of Duval County, Florida
1950 population: central city, 204,517; SMA, 304,029
Important location feature: port on St. John's River flowing into the Atlantic Ocean
Other important feature: Federal Reserve Branch city

INPUTS AND SUPPLY AREAS FOR JACKSONVILLE'S PROFILE INDUSTRIES

Tobacco manufactures: Jacksonville's tobacco industries are engaged in the production of cigars. Various types of tobacco—filler, binder, and wrapper—are required for the manufacture of cigars. Alderfer and Michl (1957, p. 637) indicate that

> The finest grades of filler are imported from Cuba and Puerto Rico. Pennsylvania is the leading state in the production of domestic filler, with Lancaster and York counties producing most of the state's output. Wisconsin is preeminent in the production of tobacco suitable for cigar binders. Domestic wrapper tobacco is grown in the Connecticut Valley. Imported wrappers come principally from Sumatra, Java and Cuba.

In addition to these areas all three types of cigar tobacco are produced in northern Florida and southern Georgia. (See map in Jones and Darkenwald, 1954, p. 310.) The amount of tobacco grown in Florida has increased steadily since 1920; in 1950 over 22 million pounds were produced. (*1950 Census of Agriculture.*)

Table 67. Industrial Profile, Jacksonville: 1950

Category and industry	Location quotient	Per cent of employed labor force	Inputs primarily from area:	Outputs primarily to area:
(3) *First stage resource users; production for final market*				
Tobacco manufactures	9.59	1.6	B, C	C
(9) *Service industries; non-local*	1.91	24.4	*	B, C
Railroads and railway express service	2.26	(5.6)	*	B, C
Warehousing and storage	1.88	(0.3)	*	B, C
Water transportation	3.03	(1.1)	*	B, C
Air transportation	2.76	(0.5)	*	C
Services incidental to transportation	3.43	(0.2)	*	?
Telegraph (wire and radio)	2.00	(0.2)	*	B, C
Wholesale trade	1.75	(6.2)	*	B
Hotels and lodging places	1.80	(1.7)	*	C
Federal public administration	2.84	(5.1)	*	C
Total in profile industries	...	26.0	...	...

* Inputs other than labor not considered.

Cigar manufacturing in Jacksonville is almost entirely concentrated in one large plant. (See *1953 County Business Patterns* and Campbell and McLendon, 1939, p. 64.) This plant concentrates on machine-made cigars (as contrasted to the plants of Tampa which feature the hand-made types); it is the largest plant in Florida and in 1939 had the largest production of any cigar plant in the world, this being about two million cigars daily. The tobacco used is mostly domestic with some from Puerto Rico and the Philippines. In 1939 a large plant was constructed in Quincy, Florida, in the north-central area near the Georgia border, to process the West Florida tobacco inputs. (Campbell and McLendon, 1939, p. 64.) It is assumed that most of the domestic tobacco arrives from the Florida-Georgia producing area but some may arrive from the other domestic sources described above.

OUTPUTS AND SERVICE AREAS OF JACKSONVILLE'S PROFILE INDUSTRIES

Tobacco manufactures: The major cigar company located in this SMA distributes its products to a national market and in addition the company enjoys important foreign business. This company moved to Jacksonville from Newark, Ohio, in 1923, being then a small company. At this time cigar machines were just beginning to be practical and the company concentrated on the manufacture of an inexpensive cigar. (Campbell and McLendon, 1939, p. 64.)

Non-local services: "Jacksonville's location and network of rail, highway, air and water transportation facilities have made this city a leading industrial wholesale distribution center in the Southeast." (United States Department of Labor, 1957, p. 52.) A Federal Reserve Branch Bank located in this SMA has as its district the state of Florida. Non-local services in which this SMA is specialized are indicated below.

Railroads and railway express service: Jacksonville is a point of convergence for rail lines from the Northeast and the Midwest, from central Florida and from Florida's east coast. (Alexandersson, 1956, p. 93.) The importance of these rail lines in connection with Jacksonville's port is indicated below:

> Since Jacksonville is one of the principal southeastern railroad centers of the United States and the gateway to the Florida peninsula, the port is in a position to serve not only the local trade area but also much of the southeast as well. Four trunk-line railroads provide direct communication with all principal points in Florida and by means of connecting rail carriers the territory south of the Ohio and Potomac Rivers, and east of the Mississippi River. The port enjoys parity export and import rail rates with Atlantic Coast ports south of Norfolk, Virginia, to and from Central Freight Association Territory and points as far west as St. Louis, Missouri. (United States Board of Engineers for Rivers and Harbors and the United States Maritime Commission, 1948, No. 15, p. 161.)

Warehousing and storage: It is assumed that this specialization is related to Jacksonville's importance as a transportation and commercial center.

Water transportation: Jacksonville is located on the broad St. John's River 18 miles from the sea. In addition it serves as a focal point for a system of inland waterways. (McCarty, 1940, p. 469.) The traffic of Jacksonville Harbor has increased steadily since World War II, and in 1955 vessel traffic was 6,475,480 tons. The bulk of this commerce (roughly 70 per cent) was imports. Of these imports major commodities received from foreign sources included petroleum products, gypsum or plaster rock, fertilizer materials, and coffee; commodities received from domestic coastal traffic included large amounts of petroleum products, sulphur, inedible molasses and industrial chemicals; internal receipts were made up of sea shells, sand, gravel and rock, and finished steel mill products. Foreign shipments were diversified and included fruits, naval stores, lumber and wood pulp, paper products, iron and steel scrap, and fertilizer materials. Coastal shipments included chiefly paper products and fertilizer materials. Internal shipments were made up of paper products and petroleum products. (United States Department of the Army, Corps of Engineers [1956], Part 1, pp. 358-360.) In 1947 the following statements were made about the hinterland territory served by the port.

> . . . most of the commodities entering the water-borne commerce of the port either originate at or are destined to points within a radius of 150 miles of the port since the limits of the territory tributary are restricted on the north by competition from the ports of Brunswick and Savannah, Georgia, and Charleston, South Carolina; on the west by the ports of Tampa and Pensacola, Florida, and Mobile, Alabama, and on the southeast by Port Everglades and the port of Miami, Florida. (United States Board of Engineers for Rivers and Harbors and United States Maritime Commission, 1948, No. 15, p. 161.)

According to data collected in 1941, the United Kingdom was the principal market for exports from the port to foreign countries; other important foreign receivers were in order of importance: the Caribbean area, ports on the east coast of South America, ports on the west coast of Central America, Mexico, North China, and Japan. (*Ibid.*, p. 165.) Foreign imports were received chiefly from Atlantic Canada, the Caribbean area, the east and west coasts of South America, the United Kingdom, and North China. (*Ibid.*, p. 166.)

Air transportation: In 1950 Jacksonville was served by five domestic and one international airline companies. Domestic lines transported 128,125 passengers and 926 tons of cargo an average distance of 496 miles. (United States Department of Commerce, Civil Aeronautics Administration, 1951, pp. 6, 22.)

Services incidental to transportation: The specific nature of this employment was not determined.

Telegraph: It is assumed that this specialization is related to Jacksonville's importance as a transportation, commercial and financial center—a Federal Reserve System Branch Bank is located in this SMA.

Wholesale trade: McCarty (1940, p. 469) delineates Jacksonville's trade territory as including "the productive north portion of Florida as well as much of southern Georgia." In general this judgment is supported by Thomas and Crisler and Bogue in their delineation of trade areas. This hinterland is described as being abundant in forest and agricultural products.

> The areas to the north and northwest of Jacksonville include over 17 million acres of forest land which according to the United States Department of Agriculture contain over 32 billion board feet of standing saw timber, 38 million cords of pine pulpwood stock and 47 million cords of hardwood. These areas are the principal sources of raw materials for the lumber, naval stores and the large paper and pulp industries of the city.
>
> . . . To the west and south of the port are agricultural regions devoted principally to growing early season vegetables, while further south in the central part of the state are large citrus fruit growing areas. (United States Board of Engineers for Rivers and Harbors and United States Maritime Commission, 1948, No. 15, p. 162.)

The productive tobacco areas in northern Florida and southern Georgia have already been mentioned; they no doubt furnish yet another important commodity for Jacksonville's wholesale trade industry.

Hotels and lodging places: Jacksonville also enjoys considerable overnight tourist business and it is assumed that this fact accounts in large part for its specialization in hotels and lodging places. According to Thomas and Crisler (1953, p. 47), Jacksonville "serves as the gateway which more people 'pass through' than any other Florida city."

Federal public administration: A large United States Naval Air Station is located in this SMA and is engaged in the overhauling and repair of aircraft. (Thomas and Crisler, 1953, p. 47; United States Department of Labor, 1957, p. 52.)

SUMMARY: JACKSONVILLE

Only the cigar industries are large enough to show specialization as a profile manufacturing industry for the Jacksonville SMA. This industry group appears to be largely dependent on tobacco inputs gathered from the hinterland although some other domestic and some foreign tobaccos are utilized. An international market is served by this industry. Jacksonville's service industries are quite diversified and reveal this SMA to be an important transportation (rail, water, and air) center serving the Southeast United States. Commercial (wholesaling and financial) services are performed for a productive hinterland, many of the tobacco, lumber, and agricultural inputs being processed in the SMA prior to shipment. In addition Jacksonville enjoys an appreciable tourist trade and is the location for a United States Naval Air Station.

CHAPTER 14

Manufacturing Centers

This chapter brings together the descriptions of those standard metropolitan areas (SMA's) which are more notable for their manufacturing activities than for their distinctively metropolitan functions or their integration with a contiguous hinterland.

DIVERSIFIED MANUFACTURING WITH FEW METROPOLITAN FUNCTIONS

Baltimore	*Toledo*
Milwaukee	*Hartford*
Albany–Schenectady–Troy	*Syracuse*

There are six SMA's in this category. The grouping was based on the observation that these SMA's, although not highly developed in respect to metropolitan functions, do have somewhat higher levels of commercial, service, or financial activity than the "specialized manufacturing centers" (the other category treated in this chapter). Moreover, once this discrimination was made, it was noted that each of the six centers has a rather wide variety of important manufacturing activities. Hence, they are "diversified" in two senses; first, in having some nonmanufacturing specialties to complement their manufacturing industries and, second, in having some diversity of specialties within the manufacturing sector. An additional feature of similarity is that none of these SMA's bases its profile industries primarily on resource activities in its immediate hinterland. Their regional relationships are so widely scattered that the idea of a "nodal region" is not very helpful in describing their situation. Thus the reader will observe the relative infrequency of "Area B" classifications of supply and market areas. Each of these centers is within or on the margin of the manufacturing belt and maintains a complicated pattern of linkages with other centers in that belt.

BALTIMORE

SMA consists of Baltimore City, Baltimore County, and Anne Arundel County, Maryland

1950 population: central city, 949,708; SMA, 1,337,373

Important location features: port on Atlantic seaboard, Chesapeake and Delaware Canal

Other important features: Federal Reserve Branch city (Baltimore); state capital (Annapolis)

INPUTS AND SUPPLY AREAS FOR BALTIMORE'S PROFILE INDUSTRIES

Beverage industries: The inputs for the distilleries and breweries primarily involve grains. Rye and corn are assumed to be important inputs for the whiskey industry and barley for the breweries. The sources for these grains were not determined, but it is assumed that they are largely from areas beyond the city's hinterland.

Miscellaneous food preparations and kindred products: Sugar refining and spice grinding depend largely on foreign inputs. Cuba, the Philippines, Puerto Rico, and Hawaii are important sugar sources. (University of Maryland, 1951, p. 15.) Since most spices are produced in tropical areas, it is assumed that the inputs for this industry are largely from foreign sources. Although coffee is imported (*Encyclopedia Americana,* 1953, vol. 3, p. 115), the most recent indication found of roasting and grinding in Baltimore is based on 1927 data. (Maryland Development Bureau, [1931], p. 95.)

Blast furnaces, steelworks, and rolling mills: Minnesota iron ore is not used to any appreciable extent, since it is cheaper to import ore from overseas than to transport the Minnesota ore by railroad, despite the greater distance. (Nielsen, 1950, p. 618.) The relative importance

Table 68. Industrial Profile, Baltimore: 1950

Category and industry	Location quotient	Per cent of employed labor force	Inputs primarily from area:	Outputs primarily to area:
(3) *First stage resource users; production for final market*				
Beverage industries	2.33	0.8	C	C
Miscellaneous food preparations and kindred products	2.05	0.4	C	C
(4) *Second stage resource users; production for non-final market*				
Blast furnaces, steelworks, and rolling mills	4.47	5.3	C	A, C
Miscellaneous textile mill products	1.80	0.2	C?	C?
Paints, varnishes, and related products	1.90	0.2	C?	?
Miscellaneous chemicals and allied products	1.75	1.5	C	C
(6) *Resources of indirect significance; production for non-final market*				
Fabricated metal industries (incl. not specified metal)	1.65	2.5	A, C?	A, B, C?
Ship and boat building and repairing	5.11	1.4	A, C?	C
Pottery and related products	1.50	0.2	B	C?
Paperboard containers and boxes	2.00	0.4	C	A, B
(7) *Resources of indirect significance; production for final market*				
Aircraft and parts	3.26	1.5	C	C
(9) *Service industries; non-local*	1.20	15.4	*	C
Water transportation	4.08	(1.5)	*	C
Federal public administration	1.75	(3.1)	*	C
Total in profile industries	...	29.8	...	...

* Inputs other than labor not considered.

of the different foreign ore sources apparently has shifted considerably in recent years. In 1950, more than half of the imported ore was from Chile, and one-quarter was from Sweden. Brazil, Algeria, and other countries were lesser sources. (University of Maryland, 1951, p. 12.) In 1954, Venezuela was the most important source; followed by Chile, Norway-Sweden, Quebec-Labrador, Liberia, Brazil, and others. (United States Board of Engineers for Rivers and Harbors, 1956, No. 10, p. 304.) Steel mills in this area apparently use limestone from sources in eastern

Pennsylvania and coal from sources in the northern and middle Appalachians. (Jones and Darkenwald, 1954, p. 447.) Manganese and chrome ferro-alloys are imported from the Union of South Africa, India, Gold Coast, Brazil, U.S.S.R., and other countries. As in the case of iron ore, the relative importance of different countries has varied in recent years. For example, Mozambique contributed half of Baltimore's chrome imports in 1946, but only two per cent in 1950. (University of Maryland, 1951, p. 15.) Scrap is an important input and is plentiful in the industrial east. (Alexandersson, 1956, p. 41.) At least part of the scrap is shipped from Atlantic coast ports. (United States Board of Engineers for Rivers and Harbors, 1956, No. 10, p. 317.)

Miscellaneous textile mill products: The inputs were not determined in detail, although it should be noted that the port imported 31,408 long tons of textile fibers and manufactures in 1954 from foreign sources. (*Ibid.,* p. 313.) Possibly such fibers as jute and flax were imported since they are not produced in the United States.

Paints, varnishes, and related products: Linseed oil and tung oil are used in producing paints and varnishes. (Zimmermann, 1951, pp. 278, 284.) The sources were not determined, but are assumed to be based on raw materials produced outside of the hinterland.

Miscellaneous chemicals and allied products: The Baltimore port

> is one of the most important fertilizer manufacturing and shipping points in the country and is visited each year by a large number of vessels carrying full cargoes of fertilizer ingredients from various points in the United States and foreign countries. Twelve large fertilizer and chemical factories are located directly on the Baltimore waterfront, and there are a number of others at more inland points in the city. (United States Board of Engineers for Rivers and Harbors, 1956, No. 10, p. 301.)

Phosphate fertilizer materials are shipped from Gulf Coast sources, largely Tampa Harbor, Florida. (University of Maryland, 1952, p. 9.) Potash is shipped from Germany and nitrates from Chile. (McCarty, 1940, p. 634.) Sulphur, an important chemical input, is received from Texas and Louisiana sources by rail as well as by shipments from Galveston, New Orleans, and other ports. (University of Maryland, 1952, p. 10.) "Pyrites sinter, known chemically as iron disulphide, is burned in large quantities in making sulphuric acid. Baltimore receipts have their source almost exclusively at Wilmington Harbor, Delaware." (*Ibid.,* p. 11.)

Fabricated metal industries: The steel inputs are presumably from local producers. Tin inputs for the important can industry were not determined. Copper is refined in the area (Alexandersson, 1956, p. 41) and presumably is available for use in the fabricated metal industries. Other metal inputs and parts no doubt arrive from the eastern half of the manufacturing zone.

Ship and boat building and repairing: Steel products are important inputs for the building and repair of ships and presumably are supplied by local sources. The repair facilities are extensive and at least one shipyard is able to produce vessels up to 750 feet long. (United States Board of Engineers for Rivers and Harbors, 1956, No. 10, pp. 191-192.)

Pottery and related products: Ball clay, used in the production of pottery, is produced in the SMA and in other parts of Maryland. (United States Bureau of Mines, Regional Mineral Industry Divisions, 1955, p. 425.) Quartz for pottery manufacturing is also mined in Maryland. Feldspar is apparently not produced in the hinterland and is presumably obtained from Area C sources. (United States Bureau of Mines, 1953, pp. 504, 507.)

Paperboard containers and boxes: There were 142,061 short tons of wood and paper receipts from West Coast ports in 1954. Foreign sources shipped 95,334 long tons of wood and paper. (United States Board of Engineers for Rivers and Harbors, 1956, No. 10, pp. 313, 316.)

Aircraft and parts: The movement in about 1930 of a large producer of amphibious airplanes to Baltimore from Cleveland was based on "its geographical location, its proximity to the military markets in Washington, its weather conditions, its tide movement of only fourteen inches, its manufacturing facilities, its labor conditions, and its rail and water systems." (Quoted by Cunningham, 1951, p. 42, from *United States Air Services,* April, 1929, p. 46.) The SMA's activity in the aircraft industry is essentially still based on this one company engaged in the assembly of airplanes. The industrial Northeast is an important source of aircraft components in the country. (Cunningham, 1951, p. 158.)

OUTPUTS AND SERVICE AREAS OF BALTIMORE'S PROFILE INDUSTRIES

Beverage industries: Several of the whiskey distilleries located in the SMA are parts of large national companies. (Moody's Investors Service, 1950a, pp. 1393, 2737.) It is assumed that the whiskey producers have at least sub-national markets. The trade area of Baltimore's breweries was not determined.

Miscellaneous food preparations and kindred products: Spices probably are distributed nationally. It is suspected that the sugar has a sub-national distribution.

Blast furnaces, steelworks, and rolling mills: Baltimore industries such as ship building and can manufacturing offer important local markets. The industrial East is probably an important market. Baltimore is able to compete somewhat with southern steel producers by means of coastal shipping. (Chapman, 1953, pp. 303-304, 319.) In addition, iron and steel products apparently can be shipped to the West Coast by boat as cheaply as by rail from Utah steel sources. (Zimmermann, 1951, p. 664.) Although the port ships iron and steel products to a world-wide market, it should be noted that the sources include Pittsburgh, Youngstown, and Cleveland districts as well as Baltimore. (United States Board of Engineers for Rivers and Harbors, 1956, No. 10, p. 303.)

Miscellaneous textile mill products: Outputs were not determined. However, Baltimore is an important apparel producer, particularly of men's and boys' clothing. (Alderfer and Michl, 1950, p. 453.)

Paints, varnishes, and related products: The market area was not determined.

Miscellaneous chemicals and allied products: In 1954, 386,842 tons of chemicals were exported from Baltimore to foreign markets, largely in Latin America and the Far East. Most of these chemicals were produced locally. (United States Board of Engineers for Rivers and Harbors, 1956, No. 10, p. 303.) Chemicals are also an important component of Baltimore's Atlantic and Gulf Coast shipments. Sulphuric acid is shipped by barges and other vessels via Chesapeake Bay, Delaware Bay, and the Delaware River. (*Ibid.*, pp. 306, 308.) Chemicals are also shipped to Puerto Rico, the Pacific Coast, and Hawaii. (University of Maryland, 1952, p. 9.)

Fabricated metal industries: Tin cans are produced in the SMA and have an important local market because of the extensive fruit and vegetable canning activities. Bottle caps, oil burners, fabricated structural metal products, and metal stampings, coatings, and engravings are also produced in the SMA. (Thomas and Crisler, 1953, p. 36.) These products presumably have sub-national markets.

Ship and boat building and repairing: In peacetime, freighters, tankers, and ore carriers are built. (*Encyclopedia Americana,* 1953, vol. 3, p. 115.) Presumably the building and repair industries have national and international markets.

Pottery and related products: Porcelain electrical insulators are produced in the SMA. (*Ibid.*, vol. 3, p. 114.) These may enjoy markets in other cities within the manufacturing zone. However, the distribution of this and other pottery products was not determined.

Paperboard containers and boxes: It is assumed that paperboard containers and boxes have an important local and hinterland market because of the extensive canning operations. Presumably there are other important local users such as the sugar refineries.

Aircraft and parts: In January, 1950, Navy patrol and attack planes were being produced. (Cunningham, 1951, p. 156.) Distribution was to a national area.

Non-local services: "Baltimore's primary wholesale territory embraces a productive region of more than 20,000 square miles, including the State of Maryland, the District of Columbia, and parts of Pennsylvania, Virginia, and West Virginia." (United States Board of Engineers for Rivers and Harbors, 1956, No. 10, p. 299.) The Baltimore Federal Reserve Branch Bank territory includes Maryland and part of West Virginia. According to Dickinson (1947, p. 219) "metropolitan functions for a large region to the south are shared with Richmond." Baltimore is specialized in only two service industries.

Water transportation:

> Approximately 106 steamship lines provide Baltimore with regularly scheduled service. Numerous private and contract carriers and tramp vessels also participate in the port's traffic. In the foreign trades, regular sailings to the Caribbean are provided by 10 lines; East Coast South America, 11 lines; West Coast South America, 6 lines; United Kingdom and Continental Europe, 18 lines; Scandinavia and the Baltic, 7 lines; Mediterranean, 12 lines; India, Persian Gulf, and Red Sea, 7 lines; Far East, 16 lines; Australasia, 3 lines; and East, South, and West Africa, 6 lines. Baltimore is served coastwise by 4 lines and in the intercoastal trade by 6 lines. Two lines connect the port with Hawaii, and 2 serve the Baltimore – Puerto Rican trade. (United States Board of Engineers for Rivers and Harbors, 1956, No. 10, p. 319.)

The railroad freight rates between Baltimore and the interior are relevant for the port's successful competition with other Atlantic coast ports. Baltimore has had lower railroad rates to an important part of the country.

> Rates to and from this territory and the north Atlantic ports are on a compromise basis. Railroad mileage has been largely disregarded and fixed differentials have been used in the construction of the rates over or under those applicable at the port of New York. (*Ibid.*, p. 251.)

Originally, these railroad rate differentials were established to compensate for the lower shipping rates from Boston and New York. However, after 1935, all north Atlantic ports have had the same shipping rates for ocean-going commerce. "Nevertheless, the ports of Philadelphia and Baltimore and the railroads serving these ports recognize the advantages of having the differentials and continue to guard them." (*Ibid.*, p. 252.) The areas served by Baltimore's port and the nature of the port commerce are described below:

> While a large portion of the export and import commerce of the port of Baltimore originates in or is destined to plants in or closely adjacent to the metropolitan area of Baltimore, much of the traffic using the port either originates in or is consigned to the great manufacturing and agricultural centers of the inland east and the midwest. The port serves heavy manufacturing districts east of the Mississippi River and the vast agricultural regions beyond, as well as the many important centers in the Great Lakes area, the lower Ohio Valley and wide sections of the country in the central south.
>
> Baltimore's contiguous territory, that area where the port provides lower or equal freight rates than offered to other North Atlantic ports, is larger in extent than that of the ports of Philadelphia, New York, or Boston . . . the port also receives substantial freight from practically the entire area of the United States, with the exception of the southwestern states. . . .
>
> [Baltimore is] one of the principal ports of the world for the handling of bulk commodities. . . . Among the major commodities in this category handled in volume at Baltimore are metallic ores, grain, coal, chemicals, fertilizer, petroleum, gypsum rock and liquid latex. This heavy concentration of bulk commodities at Baltimore is primarily the result of two factors; the lower inland freight rates to and from Baltimore and consuming and originating points in the interior of the country; and the readiness of Baltimore port operators to speedily provide the most efficient and modern loading and unloading facilities for the movement of these freight items. . . .
>
> Baltimore is one of the principal ports of the country for the importation of bananas. More than 4,000,000 bunches of the fruit are received here annually from points in Central and South America and the West Indies. . . .
>
> Located in close proximity to some of the richest coal fields of the United States, Baltimore has long served as one of the major ports for the export of coal to points throughout the world. The trunk line railroads serving the port pass through or tap the rich bituminous coal fields of western Maryland, West Virginia, and western Pennsylvania. (United States Board of Engineers for Rivers and Harbors, 1956, No. 10, pp. 298-301.)

Federal public administration: The Bureau of Old-Age and Survivors Insurance and other federal agencies with national functions are located in the SMA. (United States Department of Labor, 1957, p. 116.)

SUMMARY: BALTIMORE

Many of Baltimore's industrial activities are based on the economical transportation of goods offered by the port. Many of the inputs are consequently from foreign sources and distant parts of the country. In turn, Baltimore can ship many of its products to foreign markets, although there are also important domestic markets. On the basis of its commercial advantages Baltimore has built up a rather diversified industry structure. The city performs some important functions for a sizable hinterland, although its metropolitan functions have not given rise to a high degree of specialization in typically metropolitan service industries.

MILWAUKEE

SMA consists of Milwaukee County, Wisconsin
1950 population: central city, 637,392; SMA 871,047
Important location feature: port on Lake Michigan
Note: The materials on Milwaukee are presented in chapter 10, pages 233-247.

ALBANY–SCHENECTADY–TROY

SMA consists of Albany, Rensselaer, and Schenectady Counties, New York
1950 population: central cities, 299,091, (Albany, 134,995; Schenectady, 91,785; Troy, 72,311); SMA, 514,490
Important location feature: Albany is a port on the Hudson River
Other important features: Albany is the capital of New York

INPUTS AND SUPPLY AREAS
FOR ALBANY–SCHENECTADY–TROY'S PROFILE INDUSTRIES

Apparel and accessories: Important inputs for this industry are textiles and miscellaneous textile products. Specific source of these inputs was not determined; however the great concentration of textile mills in the Northeast—including the New England states, New Jersey, eastern New York, and eastern Pennsylvania—would seem to indicate that supplies are readily available from close at hand. (See Alexandersson, 1956, p. 64.) The apparel industries are centered in Troy within this SMA. (Thomas and Crisler, 1953, p. 32.)

Electrical machinery, equipment, and supplies; railroad and miscellaneous transportation equipment: Important inputs for these industries are processed and fabricated metals, parts of all kinds, and fuels. Metal inputs are no doubt gathered from all parts of the manufacturing belt, particularly from the eastern half. Some steel is available from local (Troy) sources, these industries relying on ore from the Lake Superior region and from upstate New York. (See map in Zimmermann, 1951, p. 662.) Fuel inputs can only be discussed in general terms. The state of New York receives most of its inputs of coal from the producing areas of western Pennsylvania, most of these shipments arriving by rail. (See Ullman, 1957, pp. 141-142.) Natural gas is received largely from the Middle Atlantic producing region—including New Jersey, New York and Pennsylvania. (Stockton, 1952, p. 169.) Petroleum inputs arrive chiefly from the Gulf Coast producing areas by pipeline and via the port of Albany. (United States Board of Engineers for Rivers and Harbors and United States Maritime Administration, 1955, No. 6, p. 77.)

Table 69. Industrial Profile, Albany–Schenectady–Troy: 1950

Category and industry	Location quotient	Per cent of employed labor force	Inputs primarily from area:	Outputs primarily to area:
(5) *Second stage resource users; production for final market*				
Apparel and accessories	1.80	3.1	B, C?	C
(6) *Resources of indirect significance; production for non-final market*				
Electrical machinery, equipment and supplies	8.03	11.2	A, C	C
Railroad and miscellaneous transportation equipment	15.18	1.7	A, C	C
Drugs and medicines	2.09	0.2	C	C?
Miscellaneous paper and pulp products	2.14	0.5	B, C	B?
(9) *Service industries; non-local*	1.47	18.7	*	B, C
Railroads and railway express service	1.91	(4.7)	*	C
State public administration	9.77	(4.6)	*	B
Total in profile industries	...	35.4	...	...

* Inputs other than labor not considered.

Drugs and medicines: Inputs for the drug and medicine industry are chiefly chemicals of various kinds. Since chemical production in the United States is most heavily concentrated in the area from New York to Baltimore on the Atlantic Seaboard, it is probably from this area that a large number of important chemical inputs arrive. (Alexandersson, 1956, p. 73.)

Miscellaneous paper and pulp products: Inputs for miscellaneous paper and pulp products industries are derived chiefly from pulp mills. There are several mills located in the general New York and southern New England areas that produce considerable quantities of wood pulp. (Dicken, 1949, p. 71.) Also sizable quantities of wood pulp are received from the Scandinavian countries—particularly Sweden—via the port of Albany. (United States Board of Engineers for Rivers and Harbors and United States Maritime Commission, 1955, No. 6, p. 79.)

OUTPUTS AND SERVICE AREAS OF ALBANY–SCHENECTADY–TROY'S PROFILE INDUSTRIES

Apparel and accessories: Chief products of the Troy apparel industry are men's furnishings, particularly men's shirts, handkerchiefs, and other accessories. (McCarty, 1940, p. 616.) In the early 1850's Troy became the national center for a great collar and cuff industry and as late as 1940 manufactured 90 per cent of America's collars and cuffs. (*Ibid.*, p. 616; Alexandersson, 1956, p. 73.) Since Troy is the home of a company whose products receive national distribution, its market area may be said to be the entire United States. (Thomas and Crisler, 1953, p. 32.)

Electrical machinery, equipment, and supplies: Schenectady is the location of one of the largest electrical manufacturing and research companies in the country. Since this company tends to develop new products at its home plant but manufactures them elsewhere, Schenectady is not an important center for the mass production of electrical household appliances. (Alexandersson, 1956, pp. 48-49.) Instead, the concentration is on research and on the production of industrial electrical machinery including generators, turbines, and electrical control apparatus of all kinds. (United States Department of Labor, 1957, p. 192.) The markets served by this industry group may be said to be international.

Railroad and miscellaneous transportation equipment: Schenectady is also the location of a large American manufacturer of locomotives and parts. (McCarty, 1940, p. 616; Thomas and Crisler, 1953, p. 32.) Distribution of these products may be assumed to be national.

Drugs and medicines: Drugs produced in this SMA are assumed to serve a sub-national market.

Miscellaneous paper and pulp products: Specific nature of these products was not determined. It is guessed that products are supplied primarily to hinterland areas.

Non-local services: Albany as opposed to Schenectady and Troy is primarily a commercial city. McCarty (1940, p. 615) mentions as advantages enjoyed by Albany its location near the head of navigation on the Hudson River and on low-level routes to Buffalo, New York, and Montreal. Its crossroads situation early was enhanced by the building of railroads from Boston to Buffalo through Albany. Albany functions as a port of some importance. A twenty-seven foot channel is maintained from the port to the mouth of the Hudson River 143 miles to the south. (*Ibid.*, p. 615.) In the year 1953 total commerce carried on through the port of Albany equalled nearly 4 million tons, approximately 85 per cent of which were imports. Some inedible molasses, wood pulp, and fuel oil were received from foreign sources and large quantities of petroleum products and sand, gravel, and crushed rock were received from domestic ports. Exports chiefly consisted of grains and nonmetallic minerals to foreign ports. (United States Board of Engineers for Rivers and Harbors and United States Maritime Administration, 1955, No. 6, pp. 78-81.) In foreign trade, Albany exported most of its wheat and other grains to West Germany with smaller amounts going to the United Kingdom, to Yugoslavia, to Egypt, and to the Netherlands. Nonmetallic minerals were destined for Canadian ports and the ports on the Great Lakes. Important receipts included inedible molasses from Caribbean and Central American sources and woodpulp from Scandinavian sources. (*Ibid.*, pp. 76-77.) The largest single commodity in domestic trade was petroleum and its products which were received primarily from Gulf Coast ports. Also received were coal tar products from the Gulf and lumber products from West Coast ports. Receipts in internal trade were mainly grain products moving from Great Lakes ports via the Erie Canal and petroleum products originating from refineries in the New York Harbor area. Shipments were principally through the canal system, with a small percentage going down river to New York Harbor. (*Ibid.*, p. 77.)

Although it has some important commercial functions, the Albany-Schenectady-Troy SMA in many respects appears to lie within the hinterland of New York City; the SMA shows specialization in only two service industries.

Railroad and railway express service: This specialization is no doubt in part related to Albany's functions as a port city since Albany serves as a distribution point for most of the materials received and as a gathering point for the materials shipped. (United States Board of Engineers for Rivers and Harbors and United States Maritime Administration, 1955, No. 6, p. 76.) In addition a major eastern railroad maintains important yard facilities for storage and classification in Albany. (*Ibid.*, p. 59; McCarty, 1940, p. 615.)

State public administration: Specialization in this function is related to the location in Albany of the state capital of New York.

SUMMARY: ALBANY–SCHENECTADY–TROY

The Albany-Schenectady-Troy SMA receives inputs for its profile industries primarily from Area C. However some textile and wood pulp inputs may arrive from its hinterland area and some steel is available from the SMA itself. Almost all of its products are fabricated goods and are distributed to sub-national, national or international markets. Transshipment functions are performed for a fairly extensive area by Albany's rail connections and port. Political functions for the state of New York are also centered in Albany.

TOLEDO

SMA consists of Lucas County, Ohio
1950 population: central city, 303,616; SMA, 395,551
Important location feature: port on Lake Erie

INPUTS AND SUPPLY AREAS FOR TOLEDO'S PROFILE INDUSTRIES

Petroleum refining: Toledo refineries were established late in the 19th century and received their inputs from the Lima field about 45 miles south of Toledo. By the 1920's the output of petroleum in northwestern Ohio had been reduced greatly. However, the availability of petroleum from distant sources by the extension of pipe lines and the excellent location of Toledo for distributing petroleum products by land and water encouraged expansion of the refinery industry. Today the entire supply of crude petroleum reaches Toledo's four large refineries by pipe line, chiefly from the Mid-Continental and Illinois fields. (Ballert, 1947, pp. 193-194; see also figure 17, p. 102.)

Primary nonferrous industries: Principal inputs for this industry group are nonferrous metals including aluminum, lead, zinc, and fuels. Specific sources for the metal inputs were not determined. However, no near-by sources are apparent, the chief United States supplies of lead and zinc being the Ozark area in the central Midwest. (Garland, 1955, p. 214.)

Table 70. Industrial Profile, Toledo: 1950

Category and industry	Location quotient	Per cent of employed labor force	Inputs primarily from area:	Outputs primarily to area:
(2) *First stage resource users; production for non-final market*				
Petroleum refining	3.80	1.8	C	C
(6) *Resources of indirect significance; production for non-final market*				
Primary nonferrous industries	4.82	1.8	C	A, C
Fabricated metal industries	1.71	2.6	C	A, C
Machinery, except electrical	2.08	4.8	A, C	C
Electrical machinery, equipment and supplies	2.72	3.8	A, C	C
Motor vehicles and motor vehicle parts	5.89	9.1	A, C	C
Glass and glass products	16.32	4.1	B, C	C
(9) *Service industries; non-local*	1.20	15.3	*	B, C
Railroads and railway express service	1.89	(4.7)	*	C
Water transportation	2.38	(0.9)	*	C
Total in profile industries	...	43.3	...	...

* Inputs other than labor not considered.

Fabricated metal industries: Major inputs of the fabricated metal industry include such processed materials as steel plates, sheets, bars, etc., from steel works and rolling mills; boiler shop products; nuts, bolts, and screw machine products; other products of a similar nature; and fuels. Toledo relies principally upon eastern Ohio plants for its steel inputs. No steel plant or rolling mill is located in the Toledo area. (Ballert, 1947, pp. 185-186.) Other sources of inputs could not be determined but probably include many parts of the western manufacturing zone.

Machinery, except electrical: Inputs include engines, motors, boiler shop products, iron and steel castings, products of iron and steel foundries, metal stampings, and fuels. Again, steel inputs appear to arrive from eastern Ohio plants. Stampings and related materials may be obtained from the SMA itself. Other sources for inputs were not determined.

Electrical machinery, equipment and supplies: Inputs for this industry group are similar to those described above for non-electrical machinery but also include products of nonferrous foundries, copper rolling and drawing plant products and electrical control apparatus. Products of nonferrous foundries are no doubt in part supplied by the primary nonferrous industries located within the SMA. Other sources for inputs were not determined.

Motor vehicles and motor vehicle parts: Inputs include iron and steel castings, iron foundry products, tires and tubes, metal stampings, and machine shop products. Again, specific sources were not determined. Steel inputs are discussed above; the source of tires and tubes utilized in Toledo was not determined. Finally, it is assumed that many of the metal stampings and machine products are products of other industries of the SMA itself although some no doubt arrive from other parts of the manufacturing zone.

Glass and glass products: Principal inputs for the glass industry include silica sand, chemicals—particularly soda ash and lime—and fuel, the most commonly used being natural gas.

> Though sandstone from the Silica, Ohio, quarries first was used by the Toledo companies, impurities made this source unsatisfactory shortly after the turn of the century. Today, the silica sand is obtained from the Ottawa-Wedron district of Illinois. The other two major commodities—soda ash and limestone—are secured principally from nearby southeastern Michigan and northwestern Ohio respectively. (Ballert, 1947, pp. 190-191.)

Natural gas became available in northwestern Ohio in 1884 when gas wells were opened. By the end of the century, however, this supply was exhausted and the glass companies that remained in Toledo have been forced to rely on more and more distant sources for this fuel. (*Ibid.*, p. 188.) At first gas lines reached to central Ohio and later southward into West Virginia. As these supplies became depleted in the late 1930's "Toledo began supplementing this supply with gas from the Texas Panhandle. An additional line from the southwest to the Charleston area will assure further Toledo's future needs." (*Ibid.*, pp. 101-103.) One of the four large glass companies in Toledo depends chiefly upon gas produced from oil refineries in the Toledo area. (*Ibid.*, p. 189.)

Fuel inputs: Sources for natural gas and crude oil have been discussed above. Bituminous coal inputs for Toledo are received by rail largely from the Middle Appalachian fields, principally located in southern West Virginia and eastern Kentucky-Tennessee. Not all of the coal received in Toledo is utilized by industries of the SMA; as will be seen presently, Toledo is an important center for the transshipment of coal.

OUTPUTS AND SERVICE AREAS OF TOLEDO'S PROFILE INDUSTRIES

Petroleum refining: Petroleum refined in Toledo serves a broad area. Although the local and surrounding areas are served by these refineries, most of the output is destined for shipment either by water or by pipeline to more distant centers. (Ballert, 1947, pp. 86, 193-196.)

Primary nonferrous industries: A good portion of the employment in this industry group appears to be accounted for by the location in Toledo of a divisional plant of a large national lead company. Principal products are aluminum and zinc die castings. (United States Department of Labor, 1957, p. 236.) Distribution for these products was not determined; however, no doubt there is a considerable local market for these outputs as well as markets located in near-by parts of the manufacturing zone.

Fabricated metal industries:

> The fabricators of metal products provide Toledo with its principal claim to industrial diversity. Most numerous are the foundries, casting companies, pattern shops, general machine and machine tool companies, and metal stamping companies which fashion materials largely for the producer market. Nearly all of these organizations have served the automobile industry, but other fields of industry provide added stability. (Ballert, 1947, p. 186.)

Products of these industries are no doubt in part absorbed by other industries within the SMA and in part distributed to near-by sections of the manufacturing zone.

Machinery, except electrical: Non-electrical machinery produced in Toledo includes furnaces, oil well supplies and equipment, spray equipment, scales and food machines, safes, railroad brake shoes, and punch presses. (*Ibid.*, p. 186; United States Department of Labor, 1957, p. 236.) Distribution, of course, varies with the individual product; in general production for a regional and national market seems to be involved. (*Ibid.*, p. 151.)

Electrical machinery, equipment and supplies: Outputs of this industry group include floor surfacing machines and elevators. Distribution of these products is assumed to be to a primarily national market. (*Ibid.*, pp. 151, 186.)

Motor vehicles and motor vehicle parts: Toledo vehicle industries include one plant making finished motor cars and trucks and many establishments engaged in the production of parts for this local company and other vehicle companies located in or near Detroit. (*Ibid.*, p. 182.) Parts manufactured in Toledo include spark plugs, auto electrical equipment, transmissions, universal joints, carburetors, mufflers and tail pipes, and various products of auto stamping companies. (*Ibid.*, p. 182; United States Department of Labor, 1957, p. 236.) Distribution of the automobiles and trucks manufactured in Toledo is to a national and perhaps a world market; distribution of parts manufactures is to a local and regional market. Detroit is probably the most important non-local market for these manufactures. (Ballert, 1947, p. 185.)

Glass and glass products:

> Toledo's important function in the glass industry has brought it the title of "Glass Capital of America" and "Glass Center of the World." . . . In no other major American city is the relative importance of glass as great. . . . Largely responsible for Toledo maintaining her high position as a glass center has been the rapid growth and first-rank importance of laminated (safety) glass. This material is associated closely with the automotive industry and, with the exception of Ford, Toledo produces all of the laminated glass made in the Central Automobile Belt. (Ballert, 1947, p. 187.)

The other type of glass produced in Toledo is glass tableware. Both of these glass products are distributed to a national market. Although four of the country's leaders in the glass industry have their executive offices and research laboratories in Toledo, two of the group have all of their production elsewhere. (*Ibid.*, pp. 151, 187-88.)

Non-local services: Some types of non-local services are provided by Toledo for a part of northwestern Ohio and southeastern Michigan. (See map in Ballert, 1947, fig. 21, following p. 142.) However for many commercial and particularly financial functions Toledo appears to be under the dominance of Cleveland.

Railroads and railway express service: "Seventeen railroads converge on the city in a transportation net, although smaller in scale, resembling that of Chicago." (Garland, 1955, p. 134.) Toledo's importance as a rail center stems from its central location with respect to a number of manufacturing districts: Detroit to the north, Chicago to the west, St. Louis and Indianapolis to the southwest, Dayton and Cincinnati to the south and Cleveland, Akron, Youngstown, and Pittsburgh to the east. (See fig. 2 in Ballert, 1947, facing p. 1; also figs. 11 and 12 following p. 61.)

> Among the outstanding groups of traffic are six: (1) the seasonal movement of coal and ore between Toledo and areas to the south; (2) the flow, also seasonal, of wheat into Toledo from areas principally to the west and southwest; (3) the movement of sheet and coil steel from the Cleveland-Pittsburgh district to Toledo and Detroit; (4) the traffic in automobile parts and accessories through and from Toledo to Detroit; (5) the through east-west traffic with necessary interchange at Toledo by all railroads except the New York Central . . . and (6) a large proportion of the total traffic between Michigan and the states to the east and south. (*Ibid.*, p. 61.)

Water transportation: "Toledo is the world's premier coal port and America's greatest coal exporting port." (*Ibid.*, p. 90.) In addition all of the major types of commodities carried on the Lakes—ore, grain, stone products, and petroleum products—move through the port of Toledo. Movements in foreign trade to and from Toledo, the greatest volume of which was with Canada, amounted to approximately 20 per cent of the total tonnage in 1949. It was composed principally of bituminous coal, petroleum and products, and iron ore and concentrates. Lakewise traffic accounted for the remaining 80 per cent of the traffic. (United States Board of Engineers for Rivers and Harbors, 1952, No. 5, p. 85.) Iron ore and concentrates are received principally from Duluth, Superior, and Two Harbors, Michigan. (Lake Carriers' Association, 1950, p. 67.) Molding sand comes from the east shore of Lake Michigan, Portland cement entirely from Alpena, Michigan, and quartzite from the Georgian Bay area of Canada. (Ballert, 1947, p. 87.) The major points of origin for the grains received are Fort William and Port Arthur, Canada, and Duluth, Minnesota, and Superior, Wisconsin. (*Ibid.*, p. 90.) In 1950 about 25 per cent of the coal shipped from Toledo was destined for Canadian ports, 18 per cent for Lake Superior ports, 23 per cent to Lake Michigan ports, and 21 per cent to the Lower Rivers district (Detroit area). (Lake Carriers' Association, 1950, p. 80.) The chief petroleum products shipped from Toledo are crude, gasoline, and fuel oil.

> A position very similar to the East Chicago – Whiting district—at the head of one of the lower lakes with a number of refineries and pipe

> line terminals—results in Toledo ranking second as a lake shipper of petroleum products. Since 1937, shipments have exceeded receipts. The Toledo shipment of crude oil surpasses that of all other Great Lake ports, and the fuel oil shipments are a close second to those of Indiana Harbor. Crude petroleum is shipped almost in its entirety to Canada, while gasoline, fuel oil, et cetera find their major markets at Cleveland, Detroit, and Buffalo. (Ballert, 1947, pp. 86-87.)

The wheat shipped from the port of Toledo originates in the soft winter wheat producing region, roughly Ohio, Michigan, and Indiana. The city's radiating rail lines tap this area making Toledo the country's leading soft winter wheat center. (*Ibid.*, pp. 116-117.) Wheat is shipped to other Lake ports and to Canada, principally Toronto. (Lake Carriers' Association, 1950, p. 94.)

SUMMARY: TOLEDO

Toledo's manufacturing industries are dependent on fuels arriving from considerable distances (Area C) and on manufactures from its own SMA, nearby manufacturing centers such as Cleveland and Youngstown, and more distant parts of the manufacturing zone (Area C). Local raw materials play only an insignificant part in its manufacturing structure. Markets for manufactures are chiefly the SMA itself and nearby manufacturing centers, e.g., Detroit, although some products enjoy a national distribution. Some services are provided for the immediate hinterland (Area B), but Toledo's prominence as a railroad and port city would appear to be based on a broader trade area (Area C).

HARTFORD

SMA consists of part of Hartford County, Connecticut
1950 population: central city, 177,397; SMA, 358,081
Important location feature: on Connecticut River
Other important feature: capital of Connecticut

INPUTS AND SUPPLY AREAS FOR HARTFORD'S PROFILE INDUSTRIES

Fabricated metal industries: Inputs include all manner of processed and fabricated metals and parts. As McCarty (1940, p. 573) points out, most of the metal-using industries in New England must acquire their inputs from outside sources, since the region lacks ores and fuels to support ore-reduction industries. Because the distance from both input sources and markets is relatively great, the New England metal industries have specialized in lines requiring highly skilled labor and producing the more highly finished and complicated products with high value per unit weight. Hartford may be assumed to be typical of New England in these respects.

Table 71. Industrial Profile, Hartford: 1950

Category and industry	Location quotient	Per cent of employed labor force	Inputs primarily from area:	Outputs primarily to area:
(6) *Resources of indirect significance; production for non-final market*				
Fabricated metal industries	1.75	2.6	C	C
Machinery, except electrical	4.11	9.5	C	C
(7) *Resources of indirect significance; production for final market*				
Aircraft and parts	16.43	7.6	C	C
Miscellaneous manufacturing industries	1.65	1.4	C?	C
(9) *Service industries; non-local*	0.82	10.4	*	B, C
Security and commodity brokerage, and investment companies	1.62	(0.3)	*	B, C
State public administration	2.91	(1.4)	*	B
(10) *Service industries; may be local or non-local*				
Insurance	7.42	10.0	*	C
Hospitals	1.72	3.0	*	B
Total in profile industries	...	44.5	...	...

* Inputs other than labor not considered.

Machinery, except electrical: Inputs are similar to those required for the fabricated metal industries and sources are in general similar to those described in the above paragraph.

Aircraft and parts: "The aircraft industry is a consumer of semi-manufactured materials rather than of raw materials directly." (Cunningham, 1951, p. 18.) Specific sources of inputs utilized by Hartford companies were not determined but it seems clear that inputs arrive from many parts of the eastern manufacturing zone. Hartford is not far distant from New York and this is probably an important factor in its prominence as an aircraft center.

> Rather than having been influenced by the source of any one raw or processed material with respect to location, manufacturers of aircraft have tended to choose large industrial areas providing a variety of materials. Metropolitan New York with its wealth of varied materials attracted many companies and for a number of years was the leading aircraft center. (Cunningham, 1951, p. 19.)

Miscellaneous manufacturing industries: The largest employer in this residual group of industries appears to be a large firm engaged in the manufacture of brushes of all kinds. Specific sources for inputs were not determined but it seems clear that they tend to arrive from many parts of the country.

OUTPUTS AND SERVICE AREAS OF HARTFORD'S PROFILE INDUSTRIES

Fabricated metal industries: Outputs are fairly diversified with the largest employment engaged in turning out screw-machine products. Specific products include small arms, chains, and machine tools. (United States Department of Labor, 1957, p. 38.) Distribution of these products is probably to a sub-national market.

Machinery, except electrical: The largest employment group within this industry is engaged in the manufacture of metalworking machinery. Specific products of the industry group include typewriters, counting and computing devices, coffeemakers, glass-making machinery, and other precision machines. (United States Department of Labor, 1957, p. 38; Thomas and Crisler, 1953, p. 33.) Distribution of course varies with the individual product but generally a sub-national market is being served. Typewriters serve a national and even a world market. (See McCarty, 1940, p. 574.)

Aircraft and parts: Hartford is engaged in the production of engines and propellers for aircraft. (See Table XVI in Cunningham, 1951, p. 225.) Many of these parts are shipped to the West Coast for assembly. (*Ibid.,* p. 18.)

Miscellaneous manufacturing industries: Hartford is the home of one of the nation's largest brush manufacturers. (United States Department of Labor, 1957, p. 38.) Products are distributed to a national market.

Non-local services: Hartford is a commercial center of some importance, being a trading center for tobacco grown in the surrounding area. (*Encyclopedia Americana,* 1957, vol. 13, pp. 735-37.) But for many functions Hartford appears to lie within the dominance of Boston to the east and, to a somewhat lesser extent, New York to the south. Hartford's location on the Connecticut River seems to be a secondary factor in its commercial functions. In 1955 there was no traffic on the river above Hartford and a movement of some 2.5 million tons between Hartford and the river's mouth; the latter movement consisted almost wholly of receipts of coal and various forms of petroleum. (United States Department of the Army, Corps of Engineers [1956], Part 1, pp. 55, 68.) It may be surmised that the river traffic serves largely to supply fuel to Hartford's manufacturing industries. Hartford is specialized in four service industries.

Security and commodity brokerage, and investment companies: In general it would appear that this specialization is related to Hartford's prominence as an insurance center. A larger area than the hinterland only is probably being served.

State public administration: Hartford is the capital of Connecticut and thus the location for many state-related offices.

Insurance: Hartford is the "leading American life and fire insurance center, one of the largest insurance centers in the world." (Alexandersson, 1956, p. 109.) A great many large insurance companies have located their home offices in Hartford. (See Thomas and Crisler, 1953, p. 33.)

Hospitals: Hartford appears to be relatively specialized in this service; however, the particular types of hospitals contributing to its specialization were not determined. It is assumed that these services are performed for the SMA and hinterland area.

SUMMARY: HARTFORD

Sources of inputs for products manufactured in Hartford and markets for its outputs appear to lie considerable distances from the SMA, in most cases in Area C. Natural resources are only of minor significance for the profile industries, processed and fabricated materials being required for inputs. Hartford performs important specialized services for its immediate hinterland, including commercial and administrative services. Financial functions in general and insurance functions in particular are performed for a much greater area (Areas B and C).

SYRACUSE

SMA consists of Onondaga County, New York
1950 population: central city, 220,583; SMA, 341,719
Location feature: on the main channel of the New York Barge Canal

INPUTS AND SUPPLY AREAS
FOR SYRACUSE'S PROFILE INDUSTRIES

Blast furnaces, steel works, and rolling mills: The specialized steel industry in Syracuse depends on scrap inputs and does not involve the processing of ores. Coal arrives by rail from western Pennsylvania and flux probably also is brought in from Pennsylvania. (Chapman, 1953, p. 21.)

Miscellaneous chemicals and allied products: Local salt deposits provide important inputs for this industry. (McCarty, 1940, p. 613.) Other inputs were not determined but no doubt arrive from many parts of the northeastern United States.

Primary nonferrous industries: The exact nature of this industry specialization could not be determined. Apparently no nonferrous metals are mined in the near-by areas and it is assumed that inputs arrive from considerable distances for processing in Syracuse.

Machinery, except electrical: Inputs include a varied assortment of processed and fabricated metal products. Some of these inputs are no doubt available from the SMA itself, with its complement of metal industries; others probably arrive largely from the eastern parts of the manufacturing zone.

Electrical machinery, equipment and supplies: Inputs for this industry group include all manner of processed and fabricated metal products. Again, both the SMA itself and other parts of the manufacturing zone are probably the major supply areas.

Motor vehicles and motor vehicle equipment: Inputs and supply areas are probably closely similar to those described for the above two industry groups.

Pottery and related products: Inputs include coal, clays and quartz and feldspar. (Alderfer and Michl, 1950, pp. 214-215.) Specific sources could not be determined. It is likely that the coal arrives from western Pennsylvania; some clays may be locally available, but much of the finest clay is imported from England, "being brought back very cheaply by vessels which took out thousands of tons of American agricultural products and must otherwise come back well-nigh empty." (Smith and Phillips, 1946, p. 253.) Quartz and feldspar are available in the southern highlands of New York.

Drugs and medicines: Inputs for this industry group are quite varied and probably arrive from all parts of the eastern United States.

Table 72. Industrial Profile, Syracuse: 1950

Category and industry	Location quotient	Per cent of employed labor force	Inputs primarily from area:	Outputs primarily to area:
(4) *Second stage resource users; production for non-final market*				
Blast furnaces, steel works and rolling mills	1.61	1.9	C	A, C
Miscellaneous chemicals and allied products	2.73	2.4	A, C	C
(6) *Resources of indirect significance; production for non-final market*				
Primary nonferrous industries	2.37	0.9	C?	A, C
Machinery, except electrical	3.45	8.0	A, C	C
Electrical machinery, equipment and supplies	4.70	6.6	A, C	C
Motor vehicles and motor vehicle equipment	1.61	2.5	A, C	C
Pottery and related products	13.80	1.4	C	C
Drugs and medicines	3.20	0.3	C	C
(9) *Service industries; non-local*	1.02	13.0	*	B, C
Telegraph (wire and radio)	2.12	(0.2)	*	B, C
(10) *Service industries; may be local or non-local*				
Educational services, private	2.57	2.4	*	B, C
Total in profile industries	...	39.4	...	...

* Inputs other than labor not considered.

OUTPUTS AND SERVICE AREAS OF SYRACUSE'S PROFILE INDUSTRIES

Blast furnaces, steel works and rolling mills: This industry formerly produced armor plate and gun mountings, but now produces only specialized steels and steel wire. Distribution was not determined but very likely is to other industries of the Syracuse SMA and other eastern manufacturing centers.

Miscellaneous chemicals and allied products: Principal outputs of this industry group include alkalies, dyes, and miscellaneous chemicals. (United States Department of Labor, 1957, p. 202.) Soda ash, the most important alkali produced in Syracuse, "is important, not only in the chemical industry, but also in the manufacture of paper, glass, soap, and petroleum products." (Jones and Darkenwald, 1954, p. 495.) Distribution is to many parts of the United States.

Primary nonferrous industries: Distribution of primary nonferrous metal products is no doubt both to industries within the SMA and also to other near-by parts of the northeastern United States.

Machinery, except electrical: The employment in this industry group is concentrated primarily in the production of service and household machines with a considerable number being engaged in the production of metalworking machinery. Important specific products include pressing machines of various kinds and typewriters. (United States Department of Labor, 1957, p. 202.) Distribution of course varies with the individual product but most of the outputs would appear to serve at least a sub-national market. Typewriters are distributed to a national market.

Electrical machinery, equipment and supplies: Specific products of this industry group include radio and television sets, lighting equipment, air conditioning units, traffic signals, washing machines, and miscellaneous electrical equipment. (United States Department of Labor, 1957, p. 202.) Again, distribution varies with the product; however since many of these firms are subsidiaries of national corporations, distribution is very likely to a large sub-national, or in some instances even larger, market.

Motor vehicles and motor vehicle equipment: Specific outputs of the Syracuse SMA include automotive truck transmissions, bearings, and various types of automotive parts and electrical parts. (United States Department of Labor, 1957, p. 202; McCarty, 1940, p. 613.) Many of these products no doubt find their way to the Detroit area for final assembly.

Pottery and related products: A large pottery company specializing in the manufacture of china is located in Syracuse. (United States Department of Labor, 1957, p. 202.) Distribution of these products is to a national market.

Drugs and medicines: A large proportion of Syracuse's specialization of employment in this industry group is accounted for by the location in Syracuse of a large pharmaceutical laboratory producing penicillin and other drugs. (United States Department of Labor, 1957, p. 202.)

Distribution of these products is no doubt to a large sub-national market.

Non-local services: Syracuse appears to perform some non-local services for a portion of central New York state. (United States Department of Labor, 1957, p. 202.) It is an agricultural market center of some importance, and home of the New York State Fair. However, its commercial functions do not show up strongly in its profile, and for many functions it appears to be under the dominance of New York City. The location of Syracuse on the New York Barge Canal apparently is of minor commercial importance, although the canal traffic no doubt includes fuel inputs for manufacturing.

Telegraph: Syracuse does show a slight specialization in employment in telegraph services, since it is the location of one of Western Union's regional automatic, high speed message centers, with an international outlet to Canada.

Educational services, private: Syracuse is the location for a sizable private university, Syracuse University; this no doubt accounts for its specialization under this heading.

SUMMARY: SYRACUSE

Syracuse presents the picture of a rather highly diversified manufacturing center. Apparently the chemical industries are in part dependent upon natural resources available in the immediate hinterland; otherwise, industries are dependent upon inputs secured from Area C. Some of the local establishments utilize outputs of local industries, but apparently the bulk of the products of the profile industries in Syracuse is destined for sub-national or national distribution. With the exception of education, services are provided for a rather limited area.

SPECIALIZED MANUFACTURING

Providence	*Allentown–Bethlehem–Easton*
Youngstown	*Akron*
Rochester	*Springfield–Holyoke*
Dayton	*Wheeling–Steubenville*
	Charleston (West Virginia)

The nine SMA's in this group are in a class by themselves in respect to an extreme concentration on manufacturing activity combined with quite low levels of trade and service activity in relation to their size.

Moreover, in most cases their manufacturing is itself concentrated in just one or a few lines. Their lack of any noteworthy development of metropolitan functions is generally attributable to close proximity to much larger, dominant metropolitan centers. As one might surmise, conditions like these are most likely to arise within the manufacturing belt, and all of these places are, in fact, manufacturing-belt cities. Usually one is hard put to identify any extensive nodal region over which they exert greater influence than any competing centers. In general, profile industries are not based on the resource activities of such a region, although in a few instances there is significant dependence on local resource concentrations. As is true of the centers described earlier in this chapter, the most significant fact about the situation of these centers is their access to a variety of input supply centers and output market centers within the manufacturing belt, rather than their control of sources and markets within a compactly delineated "hinterland."

PROVIDENCE

SMA consists of Bristol County, parts of Kent, Providence, and Washington Counties, Rhode Island, and parts of Bristol, Norfolk and Worcester Counties, Massachusetts

1950 population: central city, 248,674; SMA, 737,203

Important location feature: port on Narragansett Bay off the Atlantic Ocean

Other important feature: capital of Rhode Island

INPUTS AND SUPPLY AREAS FOR PROVIDENCE'S PROFILE INDUSTRIES

Dyeing and finishing textiles, except knit goods: Inputs for this industry include both fabrics and raw fibers—particularly cotton and synthetic—and chemicals—especially chlorine, peroxide, silicate of soda, sulphuric acid, acetic acid, and dyestuffs. (Tanner, 1953, p. 136.) Raw cotton fibers utilized are, with the exception of some extra staple Egyptian, the product of the United States. Most of the cotton is the long staple variety coming from the territory around Memphis, Tenn., the Mississippi delta and from the El Paso section of Texas. Some short staple cotton is received from California, Arizona, and the Memphis territory. This material is shipped by rail to Rhode Island warehouses. (*Ibid.*, p. 128.) Textile inputs come from both local factories and those located in the South. Rayon is purchased directly from the large production plants of the South and is shipped by rail or truck. (*Ibid.,* pp. 128, 134.) Many of the chemical inputs arrive by truck from various producers within the state of Rhode Island. (*Ibid.,* p. 136.) However, sulphuric acid, coal tar products, and petro-chemicals originating from Gulf and East Coast ports are received via the port. Large chemical inputs also arrive by rail and truck from Delaware. (Rhode Island Development Council, 1955, pp. 12-13.)

Table 73. Industrial Profile, Providence: 1950

Category and industry	Location quotient	Per cent of employed labor force	Inputs primarily from area:	Outputs primarily to area:
(2) *First stage resource users; production for non-final market*				
Dyeing and finishing textiles, except knit goods	17.40	1.7	A, B, C	A, C
(4) *Second stage resource users; production for non-final market*				
Yarn, thread and fabric mills	9.69	15.0	A, B, C	A, C
Miscellaneous textile mill products	9.65	1.0	A, B, C	C
(6) *Resources of indirect significance; production for non-final market*				
Machinery, except electrical	1.72	4.0	C	A, C
Professional equipment and supplies	2.76	0.6	C	C
Paperboard containers and boxes	2.10	0.4	C?	B, C
Rubber products	4.95	2.1	A, C	C
(7) *Resources of indirect significance; production for final market*				
Watches, clocks and clockwork-operated devices	2.65	0.2	A, B, C	B, C
Miscellaneous manufacturing industries	11.65	9.6	A, B, C	C
(9) *Service industries; non-local*	0.72	9.2	*	B
Total in profile industries	...	43.8	...	...

* Inputs other than labor not considered.

Yarn, thread and fabric mills; Miscellaneous textile mill products: There is considerable diversification within the textile industries located in Providence. Major inputs for these industries are fabrics and processed fibers (although some raw goods are utilized by the yarn, thread, and fabric mills) and chemicals. Sources for cotton and rayon textiles and raw fiber inputs are discussed above. Woolen industries comprise the most important employers of the category. The principal source of wool used by these industries is Australia, although considerable amounts are also obtained from Uruguay, South Africa, Argentina, and the Western United States. Most of this wool is received through the port of Boston, "the wool capital of the United States," and is shipped by truck to Providence. Chemicals used in the processing—scouring and finishing—of wool are soaps and detergents, soda ash, dyes, penetrates and other chemicals. These are obtained in Rhode Island through chemical concerns some of which are local, some national but maintaining Providence warehouses. They are shipped by truck to the woolen plants. (Tanner, 1953, p. 132.) Sources of chemicals utilized by other types of textile producers are described above. Inputs for the lace industry are largely cottons whose sources are described above. In addition, some fine cotton yarn is imported from England, and small amounts of silk are imported from Japan and Italy.

Machinery, except electrical: Machinery inputs are largely processed materials, metals, and fuels. Indications are that these are imported almost entirely from the eastern end of the manufacturing zone. (McCarty, 1940, p. 573.) Primary nonferrous metals and some fabricated metal, however, may be obtained within the SMA as there is indication of some concentration of these industries within the area.

Fuel inputs for Providence industries may be discussed only in general terms. Large quantities of petroleum originating from the Gulf states—chiefly Texas, to a lesser degree Louisiana—and minor quantities from Venezuela and Trinidad in the Caribbean and the Philadelphia–Baltimore and New York–Bayonne areas are received through the port. (Rhode Island Development Council, 1955, p. 5.) Bituminous coal is brought to the port of Providence via Hampton Roads from mines in the West Virginia–Kentucky area.

Professional equipment and supplies: Material inputs for professional equipment industries are a relatively minor matter. According to Alexandersson (1956, p. 62), transportation costs play a rather insignificant role in the localization of these industries. No information is available to us on the source of the various material inputs; however, it is assumed that almost all of them are from various sections of the manufacturing zone.

Paperboard containers and boxes: Paperboard factories require chiefly paper and pulp inputs. Historically, the New England states have been the central producers in this industry and although they now compete with Southern, North Central, and Northwestern producers, many are still important contributors. (Alexandersson, 1956, pp. 76-77.) Wood pulp mills located in New York, New Hampshire, Massachusetts, and Maine utilize the spruce and poplar forests of these areas. (U. S. National Resources Planning Board, 1943, p. 138; also see Dicken, 1949, pp. 71-73.) Canadian forests are also important suppliers of wood for these mills. As little or no pulp or paper enters the port (Rhode Island Development Council, 1955, p. 15), it is assumed that rail and truck lines are used to bring the materials to Providence.

Rubber products: Important inputs for the rubber industries are rubber, both crude and synthetic, the products of textile mills, and chemicals. Crude rubber used in Providence is produced chiefly on plantations in the East Indies and Malaya, considerable amounts coming from Ceylon and Liberia. This crude rubber is shipped mostly to New York from where it is sent to Providence by truck if in sheet form or by rail if in a liquid state. Sources of synthetic rubber are plants located in Texas, Louisiana, West Virginia and Connecticut and shipments arrive by both truck and rail. Important chemicals utilized by the rubber industry include sulphur, zinc oxide, carbon black, titanium oxide, and clay. Most of these chemicals are domestic in origin and are obtained through major American chemical companies. Textile needs are supplied by local companies or are produced by the rubber plants themselves. (Tanner, 1953, pp. 166-167.)

Watches, clocks, and clockwork-operated devices: Watch making industries, like professional equipment concerns, have high labor and low material input costs. (Alexandersson, 1956, pp. 62-63.) The nature and sources of specific inputs are unknown but it is assumed that various fabricated parts arrive from the SMA itself and from nearby New England cities since many of them have a heavy concentration of diversified light metal industries (Dicken, 1949, p. 408), while the less specialized inputs presumably arrive from the eastern end of the manufacturing zone.

Miscellaneous manufacturing industries: A large share of Providence's specialization in miscellaneous manufacturing industries is a result of a large employment in jewelry and silverware production. Alexandersson (1956, p. 63) refers to Providence as the "leading Anglo-American center for jewelry production," and indicates that the industry has a long history in this city. Principal inputs for the jewelry industry include metals of all kinds—particularly brass (80 per cent), with smaller quantities of nickel, stainless steel, aluminum, and gold being used—and stones, imitation and synthetic. Most of the metals used are of domestic origin, with brass very likely arriving from Connecticut where Waterbury is known as the American brass center. (Alexandersson, 1956, p. 63.) Specific sources of the other metal inputs could not be determined. However, considerable gold deposits are found in nearby Ontario, Canada. (Renner, 1951, p. 463.) It is known that most of the gold filled and gold rolled plate utilized by the jewelry firms is manufactured by Providence firms. Stone inputs include imitation varieties largely from Czechoslovakia, Austria, and Germany, and synthetic varieties chiefly from Germany. Precious stones are rarely used by Providence firms. (Tanner, 1953, p. 158.) Specific sources of silver used in the silver- and plated-ware industries were not determined. However, it is known that Mexico is the world's largest producer contributing about 40 per cent of the world's output. The United States follows in second place with Idaho, Utah, and Montana producing considerable amounts. (Renner, 1951, p. 464.) It is assumed that Providence industries draw on these sources.

OUTPUTS AND SERVICE AREAS OF PROVIDENCE'S PROFILE INDUSTRIES

Textile industries: Outputs of the textile industry include chiefly woolen and worsted products and the finer grades of cotton textiles. (McCarty, 1940, pp. 567-569.) Distribution of these products is undoubtedly nation- and even world-wide; however the apparel industries located in Providence itself take up part of the output and large quantities of goods go to New York City, the center of the American apparel industry. Other nearby apparel centers specializing in men's clothing are Philadelphia, Boston, Baltimore, and Rochester. (Alexandersson, 1956, pp. 70-73.)

Machinery, except electrical: Major outputs of the machinery industries are textile machinery and machine tools. (Renner, 1951, pp. 532-533, 536.) Much of the textile machinery is probably utilized in Providence itself but some of it and most of the machine tool output no doubt go to the eastern part of the manufacturing zone.

Professional equipment and supplies: Output of the professional equipment industries appears to be chiefly ophthalmic goods which undoubtedly enjoy a nation-wide market.

Paperboard containers and boxes: Boxes and miscellaneous paper products of the paperboard industries probably serve a market limited to surrounding New England states since heavy competition is offered from Southern, North Central, and Northwestern producers.

Rubber products: Rubber products include rubber footwear, wire and cables, and miscellaneous rubber goods and enjoy a national and international market. (Tanner, 1953, p. 168.)

Watches, clocks and clockwork-operated devices: A branch of a large watch manufacturing company is located in Providence and specializes in the manufacture of watch cases. (United States Department of Labor, 1957, p. 270.) Distribution of these products is no doubt to nearby manufacturing centers.

Miscellaneous manufacturing industries: Important outputs here include all types of jewelry, ranging from trinkets to the finest silverware. Specific products include costume and men's jewelry, expansion bracelets, school rings, insignia, and silverware–hollow-ware. (United States Department of Labor, 1957, p. 270.) Distribution varies with the specific product but in many cases a national and even international market is being served. (Tanner, 1953, p. 168.)

Non-local services: Providence's non-local service structure is relatively quite under-developed, being completely dwarfed by nearby Boston in financial, commercial, and wholesale functions. (McCarty, 1940, pp. 575-577.) Providence is the capital of Rhode Island and so does perform important administrative services for the state. Fairly large naval installations are also located there. (United States Department of Labor, 1957, p. 270.) Some port commodities, particularly oil, are distributed to the surrounding hinterland. In fact, at Providence, coal and petroleum represent 98 per cent of the port's total tonnage. (Rhode Island Development Council, 1955, p. 4.) Origins of the coal and petroleum shipments are discussed above. The distribution of petroleum received is principally by truck to consumers in Rhode Island and neighboring areas of Connecticut and Massachusetts and by pipeline to Worcester and Springfield, Mass. and Hartford, Conn. As in the case of oil, the service area of coal received at the port is largely limited to Rhode Island and nearby parts of Connecticut and Massachusetts. (Rhode Island Development Council, 1955, pp. 5-6, 8.) For the most part, commodities received via the port are limited in their distribution to the immediate localities of the port and to a restricted adjoining hinterland. (United States Board of Engineers for Rivers and Harbors and United States Maritime Commission, 1954, No. 4, p. 68.) With regard to outward shipments, the situation of Providence resembles that of several ports in southern New England:

> Although the densely populated southern New England area contains one of the heaviest and most diversified concentrations of industry in the United States, very little of its production moves

> through these local ports. All but a negligible part of the high grade manufactured products shipped out of the territory in foreign or domestic trade moves by rail or truck, the great preponderance of the export tonnage being routed through New York. (*Idem.*)

Thus, in terms of tonnage, receipts are vastly more important than outbound shipments of the Port of Providence. (U. S. Department of the Army, Corps of Engineers [1956], Part 5, p. 17.)

SUMMARY: PROVIDENCE

Providence is almost completely dependent on distant, outside sources for its raw material inputs. Many processed and fabricated inputs arrive from nearby manufacturing centers. However, there appears to be considerable linkage between the Providence industries, since several stages of textile manufacturing are carried on and textile machinery is manufactured within the SMA. Except for this linkage, Providence appears to be producing largely for non-local markets. Service industries are not highly developed, although administrative functions are performed for the state of Rhode Island and transshipment functions are performed in connection with the port commerce.

YOUNGSTOWN

SMA consists of Mahoning and Trumbull Counties, Ohio, and Mercer County, Pennsylvania

1950 population: central city, 168,330; SMA, 528,498

INPUTS AND SUPPLY AREAS FOR YOUNGSTOWN'S PROFILE INDUSTRIES

Blast furnaces, steel works, and rolling mills: Important inputs for the blast furnaces are coke, iron ore and limestone, and dolomite (flux). Coking coal arrives by rail from Ohio, Pennsylvania, and Kentucky, the primary source being western Pennsylvania. (Rodgers, 1952, p. 338.) Most of the coal is shipped an average distance of 100 miles by rail. (Chapman, 1953, p. 21.) Iron ore arrives from the Lake Superior region (northern Wisconsin and Michigan and northeastern Minnesota). The ore moves by rail to one of several shipping ports (Two Harbors and Duluth, Minnesota; Superior and Ashland, Wisconsin; and Marquette, Michigan) from where it travels some 850 miles by boat to be received at numerous Ohio ports. From this point it is shipped by rail to Youngstown furnaces. The total rail distance traveled is approximately 100 miles. (See map, Zimmermann, 1951, p. 662; Chapman, 1953, p. 21.) How long Youngstown may continue to depend on Lake Superior iron ore inputs is an important question. Rodgers (1952, p. 335) comments on some of the steps being taken by the steel companies to assure a continued supply:

> All of the local mills are faced with the major problems of imminent depletion of the Lake Superior iron ore deposits. To cope with this problem these firms are spending millions of dollars on facilities for the concentration of low grade taconite in the Mesabi Range, and for the development of iron ore supplies in foreign areas, notably Labrador and Venezuela.

Most of the limestone and dolomite used in Youngstown comes from western Pennsylvania although smaller inputs arrive from western Ohio and from West Virginia. This material is shipped by rail approximately 50 miles. (*Ibid.*, p. 340; Chapman, 1953, p. 21.)

Table 74. Industrial Profile, Youngstown: 1950

Category and industry	Location quotient	Per cent of employed labor force	Inputs primarily from area:	Outputs primarily to area:
(4) *Second stage resource users; production for non-final market*				
Blast furnaces, steel works, and rolling mills	21.24	25.1	C	A, C
Other primary iron and steel industries	3.00	1.5	A, C	C
(6) *Resources of indirect significance; production for non-final market*				
Fabricated metal industries	3.26	4.9	A, C	C
Electrical machinery, equipment and supplies	4.09	5.7	A, C	C
Railroad and miscellaneous transportation equipment	5.13	0.6	A, C	C
Pottery and related products	7.22	0.7	B	C?
Leather: tanned, curried and finished	3.16	0.7	C	C?
(9) *Service industries; non-local*	0.71	9.0	*	A
Total in profile industries	...	48.2	...	...

* Inputs other than labor not considered.

Other primary iron and steel industries: These industries receive their important inputs from the blast furnaces. It may be assumed that the majority of the inputs arrive from furnaces located within the SMA. Sources for fuel inputs (coal) are described above.

Fabricated metal industries; electrical machinery, equipment and supplies; railroad and miscellaneous transportation equipment: Inputs for these industries include all manner of processed and fabricated metals and parts. Primary metals no doubt arrive from the blast furnaces located within the SMA. Other inputs probably arrive from all parts of the manufacturing zone. (See map in Ullman, 1957, p. 123.) Fuels utilized include coal, natural gas and petroleum. General sources of coal utilized in Ohio include (in order of importance) West Virginia, Ohio itself, eastern Kentucky, Pennsylvania, and Virginia. (Haynes, 1955, p. 15.) Ohio receives most of its natural gas by pipeline from the Gulf states; smaller amounts are received from the Mid-Continent and from Kentucky and Mississippi and some is available within Ohio. (Stockton, 1952, pp. 169-170.) Oil and oil products are likewise received from the Gulf states and from the Mid-Continent producing fields. (Zimmermann, 1951, p. 529.)

Pottery and related products: The heaviest concentration of pottery manufacturers in the country is found in eastern Ohio. Two factors favor their location here. First the local area furnishes sufficient quantities of natural gas for this industry (Garland, 1955, p. 178) and secondly the best pottery clays in the United States are available in this area. (McCarty, 1940, p. 540; Federal Reserve Bank of Cleveland, 1957b.)

Leather: tanned, curried, and finished: Hides and chemicals are the important inputs for the leather industry. Ullman shows that most of the animals and animal products utilized in Ohio arrive from the north central states, particularly Illinois and Iowa. (Ullman, 1957, p. 120.) The large numbers of German-born citizens in Youngstown's population are said to be an important factor in its specialization as a center for the curing of leather. (Alexandersson, 1956, p. 81.)

OUTPUTS AND SERVICE AREAS OF YOUNGSTOWN'S PROFILE INDUSTRIES

Blast furnaces, steel works, and rolling mills: Rodgers (1952, p. 336) estimates that no more than one-tenth of the steel produced in Youngstown is consumed by other industries within the local (Mahoning) valley. He indicates that normally about two-thirds of the output of this region is sold in three states: Ohio, Pennsylvania, and Michigan, with the remaining third being widely distributed throughout the rest of the nation. The flat rolled steel output of Youngstown is utilized largely by the automobile industry in Michigan.

Other primary iron and steel industries: Specific products include angle bars and plates, rods, bars, and pipes. (United States Department of Labor, 1957, p. 238.) These products are largely distributed to other parts of the manufacturing zone; the pipe and tube production is largely utilized by the gas and oil industry of the Southwest and the construction industry, largely located in the industrial East. (Rodgers, 1952, p. 336.)

Fabricated metal industries: The largest employment in this industry group is engaged in the production of structural metal products. Specific products include steel kitchen sinks, wire, auto cable, metal doors, sash, frames and moulding and steel auto bumpers. (United States Department of Labor, 1957, p. 238.) Distribution is no doubt to all parts of the country, but particularly to other cities of the manufacturing zone.

Electrical machinery, equipment and supplies: Specific products include power and distribution transformers and electric lamps. (United States Department of Labor, 1957, p. 238.) Distribution is no doubt principally to other parts of the manufacturing zone.

Railroad and miscellaneous transportation equipment: The specific nature of these products was not determined. It is guessed that products flow to other parts of the manufacturing zone.

Pottery and related products: It was not determined what type of pottery product was produced in Youngstown. Ohio is a national center for the manufacture of pottery and it is guessed that these products enjoy at least a sub-national distribution.

Leather: tanned, curried and finished: Since there is only a small employment in leather-using industries, it is assumed that leather outputs are utilized by other manufacturing centers.

Non-local services: It appears that Youngstown is dependent upon other areas for many commercial and wholesaling services. Indications are that these services are performed for Youngstown and its surrounding area by the Cleveland and Pittsburgh SMA's. (See McCarty, 1940, pp. 548-551.)

SUMMARY: YOUNGSTOWN

Youngstown is a heavily industrialized city, concentrated largely on the production and processing of steel. Important raw materials—coal and iron ore—are procured from rather distant areas (Area C). Fabricating industries located in Youngstown are in part dependent on material produced within the SMA by these primary iron and steel industries. Youngstown does not perform important central-place functions for the surrounding trade area and indeed is itself dependent in part on Cleveland and Pittsburgh for these services.

ROCHESTER

SMA consists of Monroe County, New York
1950 population: central city, 332,488; SMA, 487,632
Location feature: on Lake Ontario and New York State Barge Canal

INPUTS AND SUPPLY AREAS FOR ROCHESTER'S PROFILE INDUSTRIES

Canning and preserving fruits, vegetables, and sea foods: Rochester is centrally located within a fertile agricultural region which produces various vegetables and fruits, and livestock, dairy, and poultry products. (*Encyclopedia Americana,* 1953, vol. 23, p. 591.) Perhaps of particular importance is the location in its hinterland of "one of the nation's top-ranking fruit-producing areas." (Federal Reserve Bank of New York, 1953, p. 12.) Inputs no doubt are also obtained from Area C sources. For example, mustard seeds are probably obtained from western or foreign growers. (See Nielsen, 1950, p. 257.) A major can producer has a plant in the SMA. (Moody's Investors Service, 1950a, p. 2623.)

Beverage industries: The major output of this industry is malt liquors and the inputs are presumably obtained from midwestern and other Area C sources.

Miscellaneous food preparations and kindred products: Inputs were not determined.

Apparel and accessories: Rochester is an important center in the production of men's clothing. Woolen, cotton, and other textile inputs are no doubt obtained from diverse sources, with New England, Mid-Atlantic, and Southern manufacturers probably the most important. This industry became important in the SMA, it is said, after the arrival of "immigrants skilled in the needle trades." (*Encyclopedia Americana,* 1953, vol. 23, p. 591.) A substantial amount of woolen cloth is imported, primarily from Great Britain.

Machinery, except electrical; electrical machinery, equipment, and supplies; railroad and miscellaneous transportation equipment: Inputs for these industries involve various metals, fabricated parts, and components. No doubt the manufacturing belt is the major source for such inputs. Rochester is near the heavy-industry Buffalo SMA and perhaps draws steel inputs from this important eastern producer.

Table 75. Industrial Profile, Rochester: 1950

Category and industry	Location quotient	Per cent of employed labor force	Inputs primarily from area:	Outputs primarily to area:
(3) *First stage resource users; production for final market*				
Canning and preserving fruits, vegetables, and sea foods	2.00	0.5	B, C	C
Beverage industries	1.67	0.6	C	B?
Miscellaneous food preparations and kindred products	1.65	0.3	?	C
Not specified food industries	5.29	0.4	...	...
(5) *Second stage resource users; production for final market*				
Apparel and accessories	2.82	4.9	C	C
(6) *Resources of indirect significance; production for non-final market*				
Machinery, except electrical	1.54	3.6	C	C
Electrical machinery, equipment, and supplies	2.31	3.2	C	C
Railroad and miscellaneous transportation equipment	4.73	0.5	C	C
Professional equipment and supplies	21.90	4.6	B?, C	C
Photographic equipment and supplies	162.00	13.0	B?, C	C
Paperboard containers and boxes	2.65	0.5	A, B	A?
(7) *Resources of indirect significance; production for final market*				
Miscellaneous manufacturing industries	1.67	1.4	C?	C
Footwear, except rubber	1.83	0.9	C	C
Leather products, except footwear	1.50	0.1	C?	?
(9) *Service industries; non-local*	0.69	8.8	*	B
Total in profile industries	...	43.3	...	...

* Inputs other than labor not considered.

Professional equipment and supplies; photographic equipment and supplies: The importance of skilled labor and the relative insignificance of raw material costs in these industries are emphasized by Alexandersson (1956, p. 62). The SMA's significant position in these industries is said to be related to its being the residence of George Eastman.

> The photographic equipment industry became concentrated in Rochester, New York, because George Eastman happened to live here. His firm grew from six employees in the early 1880's to about 40,000. Eastman was an amateur photographer with inventive talents and a business genius. He started his firm in 1880 making dry plates. The great expansion came with the introduction of the first practicable roll film in 1884 and the first compact handheld camera . . . in 1888. (*Ibid.,* p. 63.)

Although material inputs are probably less important in these industries, it is essential that they be of high quality. For example, optical glass cannot be made from the same sand which is generally used in making ordinary glass. Similarly, "optical instruments require crystals of special quality and purity." (Zimmermann, 1951, p. 774.) No doubt such factors tend to further increase the use of Area C sources for inputs. Optical fluorite, an important mineral for highly specialized optical use, is produced in southern Illinois. Optical calcite apparently also must be obtained from various domestic and foreign sources. Its properties are exploited in petrographic microscopes, polariscopes, colorimeters, photometers, dischroscopes, and saccharimeters. Perhaps indicative of the relative insignificance of transportation costs in the total manufacturing costs of such products is the fact that Iceland spar, an optical input, cost between $10 and $25 a pound before the Second World War. Metals used in the production of cases for instruments and cameras, and chemicals, such as silver salts used for the production of photographic supplies, are no doubt obtained primarily from Area C sources. For example, gelatine inputs are probably largely obtained from Peabody, Mass. (See Moody's Investors Service, 1950a, p. 1919.) The hinterland may contribute some inputs since, according to Dicken (1949, p. 410), soda found in the Albany-Buffalo subregion is used in glass making.

Paperboard containers and boxes: Paperboard is probably supplied by mills in the SMA and hinterland.

Miscellaneous manufacturing industries: Inputs for the variety of products included in this category were not determined. However Area C sources are probably important.

Footwear, except rubber: The settlement of German immigrants in Rochester (Hoover, 1937, p. 224) and the introduction of new shoe machinery (*Encyclopedia Americana,* 1953, vol. 23, p. 591) were factors in the growth of the shoe industry in the SMA. Apparently very little leather tanning takes place in Rochester (Hoover, 1937, p. 262) and it is assumed that leather inputs come primarily from Area C tanneries in the East.

Leather products, except footwear: It is speculated that the leather inputs are obtained from Area C sources.

OUTPUTS AND SERVICE AREAS OF ROCHESTER'S PROFILE INDUSTRIES

Canning and preserving fruits, vegetables, and sea foods: Distribution of these products is probably to national and sub-national markets. Several national food processors have plants in the SMA. (Moody's Investors Service, 1950a, p. 2441; Thomas and Crisler, 1953, p. 58.) Mustard is distributed nationally.

Beverage industries: Distribution of beer was not determined. It is however assumed that at least hinterland markets are served.

Miscellaneous food preparations: The flavorings, macaroni and spaghetti, and other food preparations of the SMA are probably distributed sub-nationally.

Apparel and accessories: Rochester is one of the leading cities in the manufacture of men's and boys' clothing. In 1954, the sales of eight Rochester concerns amounted to 3.4 per cent of the national total for men's and boys' tailored clothing. (Alderfer and Michl, 1957, p. 440.) The SMA is "noted as a center for the production of high-grade clothing." (*Ibid.,* p. 441.) Distribution is to national and broad sub-national markets. A company which maintained retail stores in more than 20 states in 1950 has one of its plants in Rochester. (Moody's Investors Service, 1950a, p. 1370.) Of interest is the fact that the SMA is more important in the manufacture of clothing for men than for women. Apparently fashion is a more important factor in women's garments and thus a larger proportion of the nation's production of such clothing is located at the style center, New York City. (Alderfer and Michl, 1957, p. 445.) Products include men's suits, overcoats, topcoats, sport coats, and slacks. (Moody's Investors Service, 1950a, p. 199.) In addition some women's clothing is manufactured in the SMA. (United States Department of Labor, 1957, p. 200.)

Machinery, except electrical: Products include gear cutting machines; a wide variety of machine tools such as boring and turning mills, drilling machines, lathes, milling machines and others; commercial laundry machines; and other products. (United States Department of Labor, 1957, p. 200; Moody's Investors Service, 1950a, pp. 1746, 2694.) Distribution of these products is primarily to broad sub-national and national markets. In many cases distribution is probably limited more by the location of industrial users than by transportation and other distribution costs.

Electrical machinery, equipment, and supplies: Products of one of the major producers in the SMA include electronics and communication equipment—switchboards, telephones, radio and television sets, sound systems and electrical accessories. (Moody's Investors Service, 1950a, p. 1265.) Distribution is to national markets.

Railroad and miscellaneous transportation equipment: Railroad cars are built and repaired in the SMA. (Moody's Investors Service, 1950b, p. 991.) Locomotive frames are also produced in the SMA.

Professional equipment and supplies: The SMA is a major center for the production of optical goods, precision instruments, and scientific equipment. (Federal Reserve Bank of New York, 1953, p. 12.) Several optical companies are located in Rochester (Thomas and Crisler, 1953, p. 58) and the instruments and lenses are no doubt distributed nationally. A similar nation-wide market is probably found for the medical and dental equipment (Moody's Investors Service, 1950a, p. 1260) and the industrial and scientific instruments (United States Department of Labor, 1957, p. 200) which are produced. Dicken (1949, p. 410) notes that the production of cameras and optical devices in Rochester increased upon the decline of the German industry following World War II.

Photographic equipment and supplies: A producer of cameras and photographic equipment and supplies is "the largest single industrial concern in Rochester. . . . This company has been a dominant influence in Rochester life for many years, but its continued growth has provided strength to the Rochester economy, instead of the vulnerability often associated with community dependence upon a single concern." (Federal Reserve Bank of New York, 1953, p. 12.) The SMA is the largest center in the nation for the production of photographic products (United States Department of Labor, 1957, p. 200) and there are a number of additional companies in Rochester in this industry. (See for example, Moody's Investors Service, 1950a, pp. 789, 1714.) The still and motion cameras, projectors, photographic apparatus, photocopying machinery, photographic paper, and other materials produced in the SMA (*ibid.*, pp. 789, 1714, 1919) are distributed nationally.

Paperboard containers and boxes: Presumably the SMA's industries provide a major market for the box board, solid fiber, and corrugated shipping containers produced in Rochester. (Moody's Investors Service, 1950a, p. 1168.)

Miscellaneous manufacturing industries: By definition, a variety of products are produced in this category. One company in the SMA apparently manufactures pianos and player rolls and they are distributed to national and international markets. (*Ibid.*, p. 396.) Buttons are manufactured in Rochester. (*Ibid.*, p. 168.) Although the company has two smaller plants further west, its distribution of sales offices suggests that national or broad sub-national markets are served. Other products are carbon paper and inked ribbons, toys and sporting goods, and signs and advertising displays. Distribution of these products is assumed to be primarily sub-national or national.

Footwear, except rubber: This industry has declined in importance in Rochester. (Federal Reserve Bank of New York, 1953, p. 12.) Distribution is presumably to a sub-national market.

Leather products, except footwear: Products of this industry were not determined.

Non-local services: Eight New York State counties around Rochester are apparently integrated with the SMA (Federal Reserve Bank of New York, 1953, p. 14), which is described as the "economic center for much of the Finger Lakes district." (McCarty, 1940, p. 612.) Its harbor on Lake Ontario is apparently of limited significance, with bituminous coal and salt comprising the major commodities moved. (United States Department of the Army, Corps of Engineers [1956], Part 3, p. 122.) Some port development is anticipated on the basis of the St. Lawrence Seaway project. The current importance of its location by the New York State Barge Canal was not determined. Rochester is served by five railroads. There are no non-local service profile industries.

SUMMARY: ROCHESTER

Although there are exceptions, such as the food processing industry, Rochester's industrial activities apparently bear little relationship to its hinterland, either as a source of raw materials or as a special market for its output. The most important manufacturing activities—the photographic, optical, and instrument industries—are probably less affected by competitive transportation costs and more by technological skills and innovations. Its labor force has an unusually large percentage of skilled workers. "In 1950, the proportion of professional, technical and skilled workers (30 per cent) was among the highest in the Nation."

(United States Department of Labor, 1957, p. 200.) Alexandersson (1956, p. 63) likens the situation in Rochester to that of New England in regard to the significance of skilled labor in the industry structure. Rochester also performs non-local services for a limited area in upstate New York.

DAYTON

SMA consists of Greene and Montgomery Counties, Ohio
1950 population: central city, 243,872; SMA, 457,333

INPUTS AND SUPPLY AREAS FOR DAYTON'S PROFILE INDUSTRIES

Machinery, except electrical: Specific inputs and their sources were not determined; however processed and fabricated metals and parts of many kinds constitute the important inputs for this industry. It is assumed that these inputs arrive from many parts of the manufacturing zone. No doubt iron and steel arrive from both the Chicago-Gary and the Pittsburgh and Cleveland areas. Gray iron and nonferrous castings are available from industries within the SMA. (Federal Reserve Bank of Cleveland, 1957c, p. 8.) Fuels are discussed in general terms below.

Electrical machinery, equipment and supplies: Again inputs include processed and fabricated metals and parts of various kinds; sources were not determined. Probably the manufacturing zone is again the major source for the inputs.

Motor vehicles and motor vehicle equipment: Inputs and supply areas are similar to those described above for machinery products.

Professional equipment and supplies: Ophthalmic lenses are manufactured in the SMA. The chief input here is glass pressings moulded into the desired form. (Moody's Investors Service, 1950a, p. 1132.) This glass is purchased from other companies probably within Ohio since this is an important state in the manufacture of glass products.

Printing, publishing, and allied industries: The most important input for this industry is paper of various types. Paper is manufactured within the SMA and in western Ohio generally. In fact, "Ohio's position in the paper and paper products industry is third, behind New York and Pennsylvania." (Ohio Development and Publicity Commission, 1950, p. 39.) It is assumed that hinterland sources are utilized chiefly. The nearby cities of Hamilton and Middletown, Ohio, are important producers of paper. (McCarty, 1940, p. 433.) It is also assumed that printing inks are available within the state since in 1947 Ohio ranked fifth in printing ink production among the states. (Ohio Development and Publicity Commission, 1950, p. 43.)

Table 76. Industrial Profile, Dayton: 1950

Category and industry	Location quotient	Per cent of employed labor force	Inputs primarily from area:	Outputs primarily to area:
(6) *Resources of indirect significance; production for non-final market*				
Machinery, except electrical	7.41	17.1	C	C
Electrical machinery, equipment and supplies	3.51	4.9	C	C
Motor vehicles and motor vehicle equipment	2.31	3.6	C	C
Professional equipment and supplies	2.48	0.5	C	C
Printing, publishing, and allied industries	2.03	3.1	A, B	A, C
Miscellaneous paper and pulp products	4.27	0.9	A, B, C?	?
Rubber products	2.90	1.2	C	C
(9) *Service industries; non-local*	1.17	14.9	*	C
Federal public administration	4.61	(8.3)	*	C
Total in profile industries	...	46.2	...	...

* Inputs other than labor not considered.

Miscellaneous paper and pulp products: These industries utilize, as their most important inputs, purchased paper and paperboard. It is assumed that local and hinterland sources are of greatest importance for these inputs but some paper and paperboard may arrive from outside this area.

Rubber products: Inputs for rubber products industries include rubber—both crude and synthetic—products of textile mills, and chemicals. Sources of crude rubber utilized in the United States industries are chiefly the countries of Malaya, Indonesia, Thailand, and Ceylon. In 1950 about 65 per cent of this crude rubber entered the United States through the port of New York. Synthetic rubber plants are located in Texas, Louisiana, California, Ohio, Pennsylvania, West

Virginia, Connecticut, and Kentucky. The plants closest to Dayton are located in Akron, Ohio, and Louisville, Ky. A third source of raw materials for rubber production is reclaimed rubber; however its importance has been declining with the increasing use of synthetic rubber. (United States Department of Commerce, National Production Authority, 1952, pp. VI-2-4.) Sources of chemical and textile inputs for this industry were not determined, but it appears that Area C sources are involved.

Fuels: A general discussion of fuel sources would seem to be in order for this SMA since manufacturing industries constitute an important part of the profile. General sources of coal utilized in Ohio include (in order of importance) West Virginia, Ohio itself (in the southeast part of the state—see map in Ohio Development and Publicity Commission, 1950, pp. 66-67), eastern Kentucky, Pennsylvania, and Virginia. (Haynes, 1955, p. 15.) Natural gas is available within Ohio (for map of fields and pipelines see Ohio Development and Publicity Commission, 1950, p. 73), but large amounts also arrive by pipeline from the Mid-Continent field and from Kentucky and Mississippi. (Stockton, 1952, pp. 169-170.) Some oil is also available in Ohio, chiefly in the northern and eastern sections (see map in Ohio Development and Publicity Commission, 1953, pp. 70-71), and oil arrives in Dayton by pipeline from Allen County in the northern part of the state. (*Ibid.*, p. 71.) In addition, however, oil and oil products are received from the Gulf states and from the Mid-Continent producing fields. (Zimmermann, 1951, p. 529.)

OUTPUTS AND SERVICE AREAS OF DAYTON'S PROFILE INDUSTRIES

Machinery, except electrical: This industry,

> which includes the production of household appliances, accounts for about 40 per cent of the manufacturing employment and value added by manufacture in the Dayton area. Included in this group is the area's largest plant (in terms of employment) with a workforce of about 20,000, as well as several other establishments employing more than 1,000 persons. The following product lines are represented: refrigerators, office machinery and forms, air conditioners, condensers, machine tools, printing machinery, pumps, air compressors, valves, machine tool accessories, scales and balances. (Federal Reserve Bank of Cleveland, 1957c, pp. 7-8.)

The large plant referred to above is the world's leading manufacturer of cash registers and allied products including accounting machines of all kinds. Distribution is to a world market as the company maintains sales branches and agencies in most of the important cities of the world. (Moody's Investors Service, 1950a, p. 1538.) Alexandersson (1956, p. 48) suggests that since so large a part of the output of this company is exported, the Dayton location may not be an optimum one. Other industries in this industry group no doubt are serving national or broad sub-national markets.

Electrical machinery, equipment and supplies:

> The production of electrical industrial apparatus is the second largest manufacturing industry in the Dayton area, accounting for about 13 per cent of manufacturing employment and value added. The industry includes one very large plant with a workforce of several thousand, and several others with more than 1,000 employees. The following are some of the group's products: electric motors, alternators and generators, rotary solenoids and switches, relays, transformers, and regulators, electrical instruments. (Federal Reserve Bank of Cleveland, 1957c, p. 8.)

Distribution of these products is no doubt to sub-national and national markets.

Motor vehicles and motor vehicle equipment: Within the SMA are two large plants of the major auto manufacturers engaged in the production of automobile parts of various kinds. (*Ibid.*, p. 8.) It is assumed that these products are shipped for assembly to Detroit and other major assembly points in the country.

Professional equipment and supplies: This specialization appears to be largely the result of the location in Dayton of a manufacturer of ophthalmic lenses used in the optical trade for eyeglasses. The products of this firm are sold as semi-finished and rough blanks to wholesalers for finishing to meet prescription requirements. In addition, plastic lenses for safety goggles used in industry are manufactured. This firm maintains office and storage space in both New York City and San Francisco and thus it is assumed that their products are distributed to a national market. (Moody's Investors Service, 1950a, pp. 1132-1133.)

Printing, publishing, and allied industries: "In addition to local newspapers and printing establishments, catering to local needs, magazines and business forms are produced for a national market." (Federal Reserve Bank of Cleveland, 1957c, p. 8.) At least two nationally distributed magazines are published in this SMA. (Thomas and Crisler, 1953, p. 65.)

Miscellaneous paper and pulp products: Specific products of this industry group were not determined but it appears that envelopes (stationery manufacturers are located in this SMA) and paper containers and bags are among the products. Market areas were not determined.

Rubber products:

> The production of rubber goods accounts for about 8 per cent of manufacturing employment and value added. Tires and inner tubes are turned out by the largest plant in this group. A smaller plant manufactures rubber ring seals. (Federal Reserve Bank of Cleveland, 1957c, p. 8.)

Non-local services: Dayton does not appear to be specialized in the performance of non-local services for a hinterland area. In fact Thomas and Crisler (1953, p. 65) include Dayton in the trade area served by Cincinnati. This may be the case for some types of service, particularly since Cincinnati is the location for a branch of the Federal Reserve System. However for some other types of non-local service this designation may not be too accurate. McCarty (1940, p. 433) insists that Dayton has "rapidly growing wholesaling and banking interests." He goes on to point out that neither Dayton nor Springfield shows a strong economic relation to Cincinnati.

> As stations on the National Road, they had little historical intercourse with Cincinnati, more with Columbus and Indianapolis. Their industries are not of the heavy type, but turn out the more highly fabricated products. Dayton, especially, has its own highly developed trading and financial interests and is in every sense a "complete" city. Dayton and Springfield are included in the Cincinnati area for geographic rather than economic reasons. (*Ibid.*, p. 434.)

Be that as it may, in non-local services as of 1950 Dayton showed only one specialization.

Federal public administration: "The Federal Government employs an estimated 18 per cent of the total workforce in the Dayton metropolitan area, most of it at the Wright-Patterson airfield and other military installations." (Federal Reserve Bank of Cleveland, 1957c, p. 8.) This Air Force base was in 1957 specialized in the procuring of air materiel. (United States Department of Labor, 1957, p. 230.)

SUMMARY: DAYTON

The Dayton SMA profile manufacturing industries are highly concentrated in the fabrication of various types of products. Thus raw materials play only a secondary role in the economy of this area and its position in the manufacturing zone is of great importance for the obtaining of its inputs. Finished products are distributed to a national and international market, and parts are sent to other cities of the manufacturing zone for assembly. A large air force base is located in the SMA. Hinterland services (wholesaling) doubtless are performed but these services are relatively unimportant from the standpoint of the industrial profile of the SMA.

ALLENTOWN-BETHLEHEM-EASTON

SMA consists of Lehigh and Northampton Counties, Pennsylvania, and Warren County, New Jersey

1950 population: central cities, 208,728 (Allentown, 106,756; Bethlehem, 66,340; Easton, 35,632); SMA, 437,824

INPUTS AND SUPPLY AREAS FOR ALLENTOWN-BETHLEHEM-EASTON'S PROFILE INDUSTRIES

Cement, and concrete, gypsum and plaster products: The major activity within this industry group is the production of hydraulic cement. Important inputs for the cement industry are limestone (75 per cent), clay or shale (20 per cent), and small quantities of gypsum. The raw materials may be blast furnace slag, shells, rocks, or mixtures. (Zimmermann, 1951, p. 772.) The important raw materials are available in the immediate area, the Lehigh Valley.

> There are several reasons for the supremacy of the Lehigh cement district in the United States and in Pennsylvania. Probably most important of all is the excellent location with respect to market, close to New York City and to the populous northeastern seaboard country in general. A second important factor is the presence of the "cement rock." Nowhere else has a large belt of such perfectly designed cement material been found, and the occurrence together of the two raw materials, clay and limestone, markedly reduces quarrying costs. Finally, a third point must be considered. The Lehigh district had an early start and has established a wide reputation. (Murphy and Murphy, 1937, pp. 287-288.)

Blast furnaces, steel works and rolling mills: Central inputs for blast furnaces and steel work industries are coke, iron ore, limestone and alloying materials. Iron ore is available in some quantities from deposits near Lebanon, Pa., about 60 miles southwest of Bethlehem. This ore bank is the only iron mine now operating in the state; the others have all been found either too low-grade or too limited in quantity to operate profitably in competition with the Lake Superior deposits.

Table 77. Industrial Profile, Allentown-Bethlehem-Easton:1950

Category and industry	Location quotient	Per cent of employed labor force	Inputs primarily from area:	Outputs primarily to area:
(4) *Second stage resource users; production for non-final market*				
Cement, and concrete, gypsum and plaster products	14.79	2.8	B	C
Blast furnaces, steel works and rolling mills	8.87	10.5	B, C	A, C
Other primary iron and steel industries	2.55	1.3	A, C	C
Yarn, thread and fabric mills	2.81	4.4	C	A, C?
Miscellaneous textile mill products	2.80	0.3	C	C?
Paints, varnishes and related products	3.30	0.3	C?	C
(5) *Second stage resource users; production for final market*				
Knitting mills	5.50	1.9	A, C	C
Apparel and accessories	5.06	8.8	A, C	C
Miscellaneous fabricated textile products	2.93	0.4	A, C	C
(6) *Resources of indirect significance; production for non-final market*				
Miscellaneous paper and pulp products	4.59	1.0	C?	C
(9) *Service industries; non-local*	0.65	8.3	*	B
Total in profile industries	...	40.0	...	...

* Inputs other than labor not considered.

(*Ibid.*, p. 274.) Chapman (1953, p. 21) indicates that the principal supply of iron ore utilized in eastern Pennsylvania blast furnaces arrives from New York, from the Lake traffic, and from foreign sources. Cheap market scrap iron is also an important source of iron. (Alexandersson, 1956, p. 41.) Coking coals arrive from western Pennsylvania, chiefly by rail. Limestone and other flux materials are available in the hinterland area. (Chapman, 1953, Table 6, p. 21.) Sources for alloys were not determined.

Other primary iron and steel industries: Inputs for primary iron and steel industries include the products of blast furnaces, coke and products, and some waste products of iron and steel. Apparently the iron and steel utilized by these industries comes largely from the local blast furnaces although this could not be definitely determined. Sources for coking coal are described above.

Yarn, thread, and fabric mills; miscellaneous textile mill products: Cotton and rayon broad- and narrow-woven fabrics are the principal products of this industry group. Inputs include cotton fibers and materials, fuels, cellulose, chemicals (sulfuric acid, caustic soda and acetic anhydride), and a good water supply. (Zimmermann, 1951, p. 370.) Exact sources of cotton inputs were not determined but it is certain that they arrive from considerable distances. Likewise other sources for material inputs for this industry were not determined. It seems clear that inputs (except for water and labor) arrive from considerable distances; chief location determinants appear to be an abundant supply of soft water (Alderfer and Michl, 1950, p. 421) and an adequate supply of cheap female labor (Alexandersson, 1956, p. 68).

Paints, varnishes and related products: Inputs include vegetable oils (particularly linseed and tung oils), lead, petroleum products and inorganic chemicals. Sources of inputs can only be discussed in the most general terms. Linseed oil derived from flaxseed is produced in this country chiefly in Minnesota and North Dakota. External sources include Argentina and Uruguay. (Zimmermann, 1951, pp. 277-278.) Tung oil is produced in this country along the Gulf of Mexico from Florida to eastern Texas; Mississippi is now the most important producer. However, domestic industries furnish only a small part of our needs and large quantities of the oil are imported from abroad. (*Ibid.,* pp. 284-285.) Lead is mined in this country in the central and western states, particularly Missouri, Idaho, Kansas, and Oklahoma. (*Ibid.,* p. 736.) Sources of petroleum products and inorganic chemicals utilized by this industry were not determined.

Knitting mills: Inputs include yarns and threads of varying kinds. These inputs no doubt are furnished in part by other industries within the SMA and in part by other manufacturing centers in the general area.

Apparel and accessories; miscellaneous fabricated textile products: Inputs include products of spinning, weaving, and dyeing mills, and minor inputs such as furs, leather, etc. Inputs no doubt arrive from other industries within the SMA and from other textile centers of the eastern United States.

Miscellaneous paper and pulp products: Inputs include chiefly products of paper and board mills. Inputs are probably chiefly from New England mills but a larger supply area may be involved.

OUTPUTS AND SERVICE AREAS
OF ALLENTOWN-BETHLEHEM-EASTON'S PROFILE INDUSTRIES

Cement, and concrete, gypsum, and plaster products: Portland cement from plants of the Lehigh Valley does not dominate cement production to the same extent that was once the case. For example, in 1900 these plants accounted for about 70 per cent of the nation's production. Nevertheless, the Valley remains the leading cement-producing region of the United States, with about one-fifth of the national output. (Alexandersson, 1956, p. 59.)

Blast furnaces, steel works and rolling mills: Products of this industry group include steel ingots as well as sheet steel and forged steel products. A local steel company is the largest steel concern operating in eastern Pennsylvania and it may be assumed that its products enjoy a large sub-national distribution (Murphy and Murphy, 1937, p. 293) in addition to feeding local industries.

Other primary iron and steel industries: Major products of this grouping are structural shapes of steel utilizing inputs from the blast furnaces of the area. (*Ibid.*, p. 293; United States Department of Labor, 1957, p. 246.) Distribution is assumed to be to a large sub-national area.

Yarn, thread and fabric mills: Outputs include yarns, threads and fabrics, particularly silk and rayon products. (McCarty, 1940, p. 636.) Undoubtedly a large part of this output is utilized by local textile mills and apparel industries although a larger region may be served by these establishments.

Miscellaneous textile mill products: The nature of these products was not determined. It is assumed however that textile mills in general serve a larger area than the SMA and its hinterland.

Paints, varnishes and related products: Products include paints and varnishes of various kinds. Distribution is no doubt to a regional market.

Knitting mills: Important products of this industry group include, roughly in order of importance, full-fashioned hosiery, knit underwear, and other knitted fabrics. It is assumed that these products serve a sub-national market.

Apparel and accessories: These industries show considerable diversity in the kinds of apparel produced. The largest employment is engaged in turning out men's and boys' furnishings, chiefly dress shirts, nightwear, and trousers. Employment in the manufacture of women's and children's undergarments constitutes the next largest group. Finally a sizable number are employed in the manufacture of women's and misses' outerwear, chiefly blouses and dresses. Distribution of these products is assumed to be to a national market.

Miscellaneous fabricated textile products: The specific nature of these outputs was not determined; however these products too probably are serving a market larger than the SMA and hinterland region.

Miscellaneous paper and pulp products: Employment in this industry group is largely accounted for by the location in Easton of a large establishment engaged in the manufacture of individual paper drinking cups. (Murphy and Murphy, 1937, p. 295; United States Department of Labor, 1957, p. 246.) Distribution of these products is assumed to be to a sub-national market.

Non-local services: It appears that the Allentown-Bethlehem-Easton SMA performs services only for a very small surrounding area, probably not much larger than the SMA itself. Allentown is the largest of the central cities and probably serves as the retail-trade center. (Murphy and Murphy, 1937, p. 289.) For many functions this SMA would appear to be under the financial and commercial dominance of Philadelphia to the southeast.

SUMMARY: ALLENTOWN-BETHLEHEM-EASTON

This SMA's importance as a manufacturing center would appear to rest largely on its general location at the eastern end of the manufacturing belt and within the textile region of New England. However local deposits of accessible limestone serve as the foundation of the important cement industry and have some importance for the iron and steel industry. Services are performed only for a limited area, inasmuch as the SMA appears to lie well within the sphere of dominance of Philadelphia.

AKRON

SMA consists of Summit County, Ohio

1950 population: central city, 274,605; SMA, 410,032

INPUTS AND SUPPLY AREAS FOR AKRON'S PROFILE INDUSTRIES

Fabricated metal industries: Steel and other metal inputs are probably obtained from relatively nearby Area C sources. The Canton, Ohio, SMA, which is adjacent to Summit County, has integrated steel works and rolling mills and is an important center for the production of stainless and alloy steels. In addition there are important foundries in Canton. (Federal Reserve Bank of Cleveland, 1957a, p. 11.) Further, the SMA is close to the primary metal centers of Cleveland and Youngstown.

Table 78. Industrial Profile, Akron: 1950

Category and industry	Location quotient	Per cent of employed labor force	Inputs primarily from area:	Outputs primarily to area:
(6) *Resources of indirect significance; production for non-final market*				
Fabricated metal industries	2.30	3.4	C	C
Pottery and related products	4.40	0.4	A, C	C
Rubber products	74.33	31.2	C	C
(7) *Resources of indirect significance; production for final market*				
Aircraft and parts	3.20	1.5	C	C
Miscellaneous manufacturing industries	1.70	1.4	C	C
(9) *Service industries; non-local*	0.66	8.5	*	B, C
Trucking service	1.89	(2.0)	*	C
Total in profile industries	...	46.4	...	...

* Inputs other than labor not considered.

Pottery and related products: The early prosperity of Akron was based in large part on its native clay deposits, and the clay products industry which grew up is still of large proportions. (*Encyclopedia Americana,* 1953, vol. 1, p. 296.) It is assumed that part of the inputs are obtained from local sources since clays are mined in the SMA. (United States Bureau of Mines, Regional Mineral Industry Divisions, 1955, p. 734.) The pottery fabrication industry has high labor costs and the raw material is apparently an insignificant location factor. (Alexandersson, 1956, p. 60.) Consequently clays are probably also obtained from various Area C sources. (Ohio Development and Publicity Commission, 1950, p. 76.) Natural gas is supplied to the SMA by pipeline (see map in *ibid.,* p. 73) and coal is available from nearby Area C sources.

Rubber products: Rubber products is Akron's major industry and, in turn, the SMA "is well known as the Nation's leading center for the production of automotive tires and tubes." (United States Department of Labor, 1957, p. 220.) Since there seem to be no "special location factors or other qualities in Akron which favor rubber manufacturing" (Dicken, 1949, p. 413) over many other cities in the region, an examination of the significance of the early history of the rubber industry for the present location pattern is of interest. Alexandersson (1956, pp. 79-80) indicates that New England was the site of small establishments manufacturing rubber boots and shoes in the early days following the discovery of vulcanization by Goodyear. The relocation of the Goodrich plant from Hastings, N. Y., to Akron in 1870 is said to have been due to the financial encouragement of a friend of Goodrich. The success of this first small plant attracted other companies to the city, which became a center for making pneumatic tires for the carriage industry of the Middle West. Akron's convenient location to supply the automobile factories of Detroit enabled it to capitalize on its early start as the automobile boom got under way after 1910.

Inputs are primarily from Area C sources. Akron uses about one-half of all the rubber imported into the country. (*Encyclopedia Americana,* 1953, vol. 1, p. 296.) Malaya, Indonesia, Thailand, Ceylon, Liberia, and Indochina were the United States' major sources of natural rubber in 1950. (See United States Department of Commerce, National Production Authority, 1952, p. VI-3.) New York City is the major port of entry for this input. The supply and price of natural rubber are complicated by a number of international factors. (See Zimmermann, 1951, pp. 392-397.) Prices have been controlled in the past; this led several American companies to establish their own foreign plantations. (United States Department of Commerce, National Production Authority, 1952, p. V-3.) Three American companies produce about five per cent of the world production of natural rubber. (*Ibid.,* p. V-1.) Cotton fabrics, an important material for the production of tires, are probably obtained from Area C sources such as Barnesville and Silvertown, Ga. (Moody's Investors Service, 1950a, pp. 1850; 1880), and New Bedford, Mass., and Goodyear, Conn. (Roterus, 1931, p. 87.) "The fabric is such an important element of the tire that all of the large companies own their own textile mills, and some even have their own cotton plantations." (*Idem.*) A number of chemicals are also used. A standard sized tire requires several pounds of carbon black whether it is made of synthetic or natural rubber. (Zimmermann, 1951, pp. 565-566.) Texas is the major source of this product since nearly 70 per cent of the nation's production in 1950 was in this state (United States Bureau of Mines,

1953, p. 194) and rubber companies used 93 per cent of total domestic production. (*Ibid.*, p. 199.) The rubber industry used 75 thousand long tons of native sulphur in 1950 (*ibid.*, p. 1181, Table 9) and Texas and Louisiana were the major domestic sources. (*Ibid.*, p. 1177.) Other chemical inputs for natural rubber were not examined in detail, but it is assumed that the chemicals used are predominantly from Area C sources.

Although the manufacturing of synthetic rubber is primarily a chemical process, the rapid increase in its use makes this an important input. Research on the production of synthetic rubber was stimulated by the control of natural rubber prices by the British during the 'twenties. (Zimmermann, 1951, p. 392.) However only Germany and the U.S.S.R. had developed a synthetic rubber industry before World War II. During the Second World War the United States, as well as other belligerents, developed a huge synthetic rubber industry very quickly—one which came to rival the natural rubber industry in volume of output. While the German industry was based on benzene, in the United States the raw materials for the new product were petroleum and natural gas. There are several types of rubber and "the tendency has been to use the lowest-priced material that would result in the production of goods of adequate quality." (U. S. Department of Commerce, National Production Authority, 1952, p. IX-2.) No doubt Akron uses large quantities of synthetic rubber. There is a synthetic rubber plant located in Akron (Steelman, 1950, p. 96, Table C-1) and probably synthetic rubber is also obtained from many of the plants located outside the hinterland. Reclaimed rubber is made from worn-out and discarded rubber products (United States Department of Commerce, National Production Authority, 1952, p. I-4) and presumably is obtained primarily from Area C sources.

The SMA is well situated for obtaining coal for fuel. In 1952, Ohio was the fifth ranking producer of coal in the nation. Most of the major coal producing counties are near the SMA and there is also some coal mined in the hinterland counties. (United States Bureau of Mines, Regional Mineral Industry Divisions, 1955, p. 711.) Probably the coal fields of western Pennsylvania and other states are sources. Also petroleum and natural gas are obtained in the state, in the C area.

Aircraft and parts: Sources for the aircraft parts produced in the SMA were not determined. It is assumed that metal inputs come primarily from nearby Area C sources.

Miscellaneous manufacturing industries: Inputs for the production of matches and fishing tackle are assumed to be primarily from Area C sources.

OUTPUTS AND SERVICE AREAS
OF AKRON'S PROFILE INDUSTRIES

Fabricated metal industries: Structural metal products and metal stampings and coatings are two of the important products. Industrial boilers and valves are produced in the SMA (Federal Reserve Bank of Cleveland, 1957a, p. 10) and the products of this industry are probably distributed to sub-national markets.

Pottery and related products: Porcelain electrical supplies (*idem*) and chemical stoneware (*Encyclopaedia Britannica,* 1955, vol. 1, p. 485) are two of the products of this industry. Distribution is assumed to be primarily subnational.

Rubber products: Although distribution probably varies by product and company, the SMA clearly serves an Area C market. In addition to tires and tubes, "a large variety of fabricated rubber goods" are produced in the SMA. (Federal Reserve Bank of Cleveland, 1957a, p. 10.) Tires and tubes no doubt have an important market in midwest and eastern automobile assemblers and in the replacement market. However, "as the assembly of automobiles shifted to Los Angeles, so did the tire industry." (Zierer, 1956, p. 292.) Alexandersson (1956, p. 80) indicates that this movement was undertaken to secure economies in distribution. The large rubber companies have established plants in several states—particularly in California, where the saving of freight costs over the East is greatest. Secondary tire centers are also located in Detroit and in Gadsden, Ala. The Akron tire industry is thus limited in distribution westward by the second largest center, Los Angeles, which "supplies not only the California assembly plants but the larger part of the retail replacement trade of the eleven Western states, Alaska, Hawaii, and other countries of the Pacific." (Zierer, 1956, p. 292.) The decentralization of the rubber industry and its increased mechanization are partly responsible for declines between 1947 and 1954 in employment in Akron's rubber industry. (Federal Reserve Bank of Cleveland, 1957a, p. 10.) The general offices of a number of the rubber companies are located in the SMA. (See, for example, Moody's Investors Service, 1950a, pp. 698, 711, 1880, 2381.)

Aircraft and parts: Aircraft parts are produced in the SMA (Federal Reserve Bank of Cleveland, 1957a, p. 10) and are probably distributed to assembly plants located in Area C.

Miscellaneous manufacturing industries: Matches produced in the SMA are undoubtedly distributed to sub-national or national markets. In addition, fishing tackle (*Encyclopaedia Britannica,* 1955, vol. 1, p. 485) is distributed to national markets.

Non-local services: The Akron SMA appears to be primarily a manufacturing city with, in general, little emphasis in the service industries. It is located close to Cleveland and presumably receives many services from this larger SMA. Akron has not been recognized as metropolitan in any of the delimitations of metropolitan regions discussed in Chapter 4. The single profile service industry is discussed below.

Trucking service: The SMA's position as a big trucking center (Thomas and Crisler, 1953, p. 61) is probably at least partially due to the use of motor transportation for distributing tires to markets. (See Roterus, 1931, p. 90.)

SUMMARY: AKRON

Akron is "one of the most specialized industrial cities in the country." (Federal Reserve Bank of Cleveland, 1957a, p. 10.) Inputs for the rubber industry are primarily from Area C sources and the output is distributed to Area C users. Other profile industries in the SMA appear to be also dependent on Area C sources and markets, although perhaps somewhat closer to Akron since the SMA is well located in the northern industrial belt of the nation. Although the SMA had regional advantages for the location of the rubber industry (see Roterus, 1931, p. 52), Akron had no peculiar features which made it more desirable than many other cities located in the area. In the rapid development of the automobile industry, the already established rubber industry of the SMA was suitably located to meet the requirements of this great new market for rubber products. With the exception of trucking, the SMA performs very limited non-local services.

SPRINGFIELD-HOLYOKE

SMA consists of parts of Hamden and Hampshire Counties, Massachusetts and part of Hartford County, Connecticut

1950 population: central cities, 217,060 (Springfield, 162,399; Holyoke, 54,661); SMA, 407,255

Important location feature: on Connecticut River

INPUTS AND SUPPLY AREAS FOR SPRINGFIELD-HOLYOKE'S PROFILE INDUSTRIES

Other primary iron and steel industries: Important inputs for this industry group are iron and steel products and fuels, particularly coke.

Iron and steel inputs apparently arrive from outside the immediate vicinity or hinterland areas. The nearest major centers of iron and steel production appear to be located in Buffalo, N. Y., and Bethlehem, Pa. (See map 4 in Chapman, 1953, following p. 22.) However in 1951 a center was under construction near Trenton, N. J., and a second was projected near Camden. (United States Council of Economic Advisers, Committee on the New England Economy, 1951, p. 95.) As to fuels,

> All coal, petroleum products, and natural gas consumed in New England are brought in from outside. Their continued flow is vital to the operation of almost all phases of the region's life. (National Planning Association, Committee of New England, 1954, p. 138.)

For specific sources of these fuels see the discussion below.

Yarn, thread, and fabric mills: Location of these industries in this SMA appears to result from historical factors, Massachusetts being an early leader in the textile field because of the availability of water power. (Alexandersson, 1956, p. 64.) The development of the Connecticut River for power purposes was an important factor in the economy of this SMA. (United States Department of Labor, 1957, p. 132.) In the early development of the textile industry in New England the power of small streams and rivers was directly harnessed. Now most of the New England textile mills are electrified (Jones and Darkenwald, 1954, p. 508), but the bulk of this electrical power is developed by steam generators fed by out-of-state coal. (See National Planning Association, Committee of New England, 1954, p. 171.) Inputs other than fuel include both cotton and wool raw materials. In the early days of the industry "Wool was produced from sheep on New England farms or was brought in by traders; cotton came from the West Indies and from the Southern United States." (*Ibid.,* p. 505.) It is assumed today that the inputs for cotton are similar to those described for Providence textile industries. Domestic inputs of long staple cotton arrive from the territory around Memphis, Tenn., the Mississippi delta and from the El Paso section of Texas. Some short staple cotton is received from California, Arizona, and the Memphis territory. This material is shipped by rail. (Tanner, 1953, p. 128.) Wool arrives chiefly from Australia although considerable amounts are also obtained from Uruguay, South Africa, Argentina, and the western United States. Some of this wool is received through the port of Boston. Jones and Darkenwald (1954, p. 520) indicate that about 60 per cent of the wool from the western states is shipped by rail, the remainder arriving by water.

Today New England textile companies are competing with produc-

Table 79. Industrial Profile, Springfield-Holyoke: 1950

Category and industry	Location quotient	Per cent of employed labor force	Inputs primarily from area:	Outputs primarily to area:
(4) *Second stage resource users; production for non-final market*				
Other primary iron and steel industries	1.96	1.0	C	A, C?
Yarn, thread, and fabric mills	2.25	3.5	C	A, C
Miscellaneous textile mill products	4.00	0.4	A	?
Miscellaneous chemicals and allied products	2.18	1.9	C	C
Pulp, paper and paperboard mills	6.39	2.6	B, C	A, C
(5) *Second stage resource users; production for final market*				
Carpets, rugs and other floor coverings	16.17	1.9	A, C	C
(6) *Resources of indirect significance; production for non-final market*				
Fabricated metal industries	2.56	3.8	C	C
Machinery, except electrical	2.20	5.1	C	C
Electrical machinery, equipment and supplies	3.64	5.1	C	C
Railroad and miscellaneous transportation equipment	3.82	0.4	C	C
Printing, publishing, and allied industries	1.75	2.7	A	A, C
Paperboard containers and boxes	2.55	0.5	A, B?	A, C
Miscellaneous paper and pulp products	6.32	1.4	A, B?	C
Rubber products	4.88	2.0	A, C	C
(7) *Resources of indirect significance; production for final market*				
Miscellaneous manufacturing industries	3.94	3.2	C	C
Leather products, except footwear	2.83	0.3	A, C	C
(9) *Service industries; non-local*	0.77	9.9	*	B
(10) *Service industries; may be local or non-local*				
Insurance	1.57	2.1	*	C
Educational services, private	2.22	2.1	*	B, C
Total in profile industries	...	49.9	...	...

* Inputs other than labor not considered.

ers in the Southern Appalachians and are forced to capitalize on their advantages, which include skilled labor, entrepreneurial experience, proximity to major distribution centers (Boston and New York), and access to the region in which textile machinery is manufactured. (Jones and Darkenwald, 1954, p. 508.) The New England companies tend to specialize in high-grade textiles and fabrics requiring highly skilled labor and high quality fiber inputs.

Miscellaneous textile mill products: It is assumed that this industry group utilizes, at least in part, inputs available in the SMA itself, from the yarn, thread and fabric mills.

Miscellaneous chemicals and allied products: New England chemical industries in general and this SMA's industries in particular appear to be concentrated in the production of chemicals which have a high value added by manufacture.

> The absence of basic chemical raw materials, the problem of transportation and relatively high costs of fuel and power have fostered a process of natural selection in the development of New England's chemical industry. . . .
>
> Proximity to markets has been the major orienting factor in developing the chemical industry in New England. Availability of qualified labor, plentiful and high-grade water, and port locations have been auxiliary aids in this development. (Federal Reserve Bank of Boston, 1952, No. 4, p. 2.)

Inputs no doubt arrive chiefly from outside the immediate or hinterland area. Also fuels are not available in the region.

Pulp, paper, and paperboard mills: The pulp and paperboard mills of this SMA lie at the southern end of the forest areas of New England in the central hardwoods region. (See map in National Resources Planning Board, Region One, 1942, facing p. 22.) More than three-fourths of the land area of New England is forested. (National Planning Association, Committee of New England, 1954, p. 25.) Wood cut for pulpwood in New England in recent years totalled two million cords of which 1.6 million were cut in Maine. (*Ibid.*, p. 34.) Massachusetts itself, around 1940, contained 3.3 million acres of wood (2.6 being of the hardwood types) of the 29.8 million acres in New England. (National Resources Planning Board, Region One, 1942, Appendix, p. 6.)

> While most of the present pulpwood supply comes from New England forests, eastern Canada has been shipping in about one-third of the pulpwood or its pulp equivalent which New England mills consume. On the other hand, New England exports some pulpwood to New York state and wood pulp to other points.
>
> The supply from Canada is not a certainty. The expanding Cana-

> dian paper industry is requiring steadily larger quantities of pulpwood, and it could eventually absorb the output of the eastern Canadian forests. (National Planning Association, Committee of New England, 1954, p. 26.)

In recent years hardwoods have been utilized in the manufacture of pulp and in 1953 it was estimated that 367,000 tons, equivalent to 22 per cent of New England's total pulp production, was based on this process. (Federal Reserve Bank of Boston, 1954, p. 2.) This may be particularly important for the pulp mills of Massachusetts since, as we have seen, the forests in this area are predominantly of the hardwood type. No specific information was found on the sources of wood utilized by the pulp mills of this SMA but it is assumed that hinterland hardwood sources are utilized as well as wood received from northern New England and Canada.

In addition to the pulp and paperboard mills located in this SMA, Holyoke is an important center for the production of fine writing paper. (Thomas and Crisler, 1953, p. 28.) Necessary inputs are as follows:

> Soft, rosin-free coniferous woods, such as spruce and hemlock, are preferred for the manufacture of paper. Aspen, yellow poplar, and other woods are also used, however. . . .
>
> Book paper is generally made by the sulphite process, that is, by boiling wood chips (primarily spruce, hemlock, or fir) in a solution of calcium bisulphite. Rags are added to increase quality. Most writing papers are sized or loaded with kaolin, rosin, alum, animal sizing, or talc, to fill up the pores and prevent blurring. (Nielsen, 1950, p. 297.)

Spruce and fir forests occur in New England predominantly in northern Maine, but this type of forest also is found farther south extending into the western portion of Massachusetts. (See map in National Resources Planning Board, Region One, 1942, facing p. 22.) Of the other materials required for the production of fine paper, only talc appears to be available in large quantities in New England. As of 1949, the region's production of talc was concentrated almost entirely in Vermont; a large proportion of this talc went into the production of paper products. (National Planning Association, Committee of New England, 1954, p. 156.) It is assumed that other materials are gathered from outside the region.

Carpets, rugs and other floor coverings: Important inputs for this industry group are wool and cotton raw materials as well as yarns, threads, and fabrics. Sources for the wool and cotton raw materials are considered to be similar to those described above for the fabric mills except that the coarse, short fiber wool used for carpets and rugs is received chiefly from Asia. (Jones and Darkenwald, 1954, p. 520.) This wool no doubt arrives by truck chiefly from Boston. It is assumed that thread and fabric inputs arrive from other industries within the SMA or from nearby textile producing centers in New England.

Fabricated metal industries; machinery, except electrical; electrical machinery, equipment and supplies; railroad and miscellaneous transportation equipment: Inputs for these manufacturing industries are generally similar in nature and thus may be considered as a group. The general problem of access to inputs for the Springfield-Holyoke SMA is undoubtedly similar to that of all New England. Writers on the economy of the region never fail to point out its lack of mineral resources and consequent dependence on transportation connections with the rest of the country for fuel and metal inputs. (National Planning Association, Committee of New England, 1954, p. 137.) Better than half of New England's requirements for bituminous coal are met by shipments from Virginia and southern West Virginia, with the central Pennsylvania fields also being an important source of supply. Fuel oil moves by ocean vessels from Texas Gulf Coast ports and from Louisiana, Mississippi, and Venezuela; most of it is refined before reaching New England. Natural gas pipelines have recently been constructed to serve New England. Although the region has developed its potential hydroelectric power, this source can meet only a small fraction of requirements; the remainder must be met by steam generators using imported fuel. (*Ibid.*, pp. 171, 187-88.)

Printing, publishing, and allied industries: Employment in this industry group shows considerable diversity, with commercial printing dominating other types of employment. Important inputs include inks and paper. Ink supply sources were not determined; it is assumed that a large part of the paper utilized is available from SMA paper manufacturers.

Paperboard containers and boxes: It is assumed that the pulp and paperboard inputs necessary for this industry group are available from the pulp and paper mills located within the SMA and surrounding hinterland.

Miscellaneous paper and pulp products: It is assumed that inputs for this industry group arrive chiefly from the paper mills of the SMA.

Rubber products: Specialization in this industry group appears to be the result of the location in this SMA of a subsidiary of a large United States company engaged in the production of automobile and truck tires. (United States Department of Labor, 1957, p. 132.) Important inputs are rubber, sulphur, and textile products. It is assumed that much of the rubber arrives via the port of Boston. In 1955, 69,001 tons were received at that port, chiefly from Malaya (57 per cent), Indonesia (22 per cent), Thailand (8 per cent), and Viet-Nam, Laos, and Cambodia (8 per cent). (United States Board of Engineers for Rivers and Harbors and the Maritime Administration, 1957, No. 3, p. 245.) It is assumed that textile inputs arrive from industries within the SMA. Sulphur is imported into the New England states chiefly by water, although considerable quantities arrive by rail. (National Planning Association, Committee of New England, 1954, p. 142.)

Miscellaneous manufacturing industries: It may be supposed that these industries, like the other manufacturing industries discussed above, are dependent upon extra-regional sources for the majority of their material and fuel inputs.

Leather products, except footwear: Inputs for this industry include tanned light leather products of various kinds and miscellaneous textile inputs. Little tanning of leather is performed within the SMA, and it is assumed that tanned leather products arrive chiefly from Boston, which in 1929 was by far the leading city in the country in sales of wholesalers of leather and leather goods. (Hoover, 1937, p. 148.) According to the *1948 Census of Business* 23 agents or brokers in Boston sold over 52 million dollars worth of hides, skins, and raw furs. Data on other types of wholesalers who were presumably dealing in hides were too highly aggregated to be of use. It is assumed that textile inputs are available from industries within the SMA itself.

OUTPUTS AND SERVICE AREAS OF SPRINGFIELD-HOLYOKE'S PROFILE INDUSTRIES

Other primary iron and steel industries: Products of this industry group include iron and steel forgings. (United States Department of Labor, 1957, p. 132.) It is assumed that these products are utilized by other manufacturing industries within the SMA but may also find markets in nearby SMA's.

Yarn, thread, and fabric mills: Outputs of this industry group include both woolen and cotton threads and fabrics. It is assumed that distribution is both to local industries (miscellaneous textile products, carpets, rubber and leather products) and to other SMA's specializing in the production of apparel.

Miscellaneous textile mill products: Nature of the outputs of this industry group was not determined.

Miscellaneous chemicals and allied products: Apparently the most important outputs of this industry group are plastics of various kinds. (United States Department of Labor, 1957, p. 132; Thomas and Crisler, 1953, p. 28.) It is assumed that distribution of these products is to a sub-national market.

Pulp, paper, and paperboard mills: Holyoke is internationally famous for its production of fine paper. It is assumed that distribution of paper is to an international market. Since the SMA contains important paperboard container manufacturing industries, it is assumed that the bulk of the paperboard output is utilized by local industries.

Carpets, rugs and other floor coverings: It is assumed that the products of this industry group enjoy at least sub-national markets.

Fabricated metal industries: This industry group contains a rather diverse assortment of establishments producing a variety of products. Of great importance in this employment group is the location in Springfield of an armory engaged in the production of rifles and machine gun parts. This manufacturing activity has deep historical roots:

> This area received an early start as a manufacturing center when the Nation's first arsenal was established here by the Continental Congress in 1778 on the recommendation of General George Washington. Skills developed at the Springfield Armory were responsible for the growth of the firearms industry in southern New England and also brought about the establishment of sizable numbers of metalworking firms in the area. (United States Department of Labor, 1957, p. 132.)

Other products of the fabricated metals industry group within this SMA include machine parts, iron, steel, and brass valves, and miscellaneous fabricated metals and parts. (*Idem.*) It is assumed that the ordnance outputs are distributed to a national market; probably the other outputs of this industry group serve sub-national markets.

Machinery, except electrical: Again the industries making up this group are quite diverse as are their products; however the greatest concentration of employment is in the production of service and household machines. Distribution of these products is assumed to be to a sub-national area.

Electrical machinery, equipment and supplies: A subsidiary establishment of one of the country's largest electrical firms is located in this SMA in addition to several other companies engaged in the production of electrical equipment. Specific products of the industry group include air-conditioning equipment, water coolers, radio, and television components and various sorts of electrical appliances.

(United States Department of Labor, 1957, p. 132.) It is assumed that distribution of these products is to a national market.

Railroad and miscellaneous transportation equipment: The specific nature of these products was not determined. It is assumed that because of their nature they are marketed in a sub-national area.

Printing, publishing, and allied industries: Although services are performed for the local SMA, the bulk of this industry is concentrated in commercial printing which presumably serves a larger area. In general, Massachusetts is an important state in the publishing business. (Federal Reserve Bank of Boston, 1953b, pp. 2-3.) Specifically, a company which publishes a nationally distributed dictionary is located in Springfield. (Thomas and Crisler, 1953, p. 28.)

Paperboard containers and boxes: It is assumed that the products of this industry group are utilized both by local firms for the packaging of products and are distributed to other SMA's of the region.

Miscellaneous paper and pulp products: Envelopes are the most important product of this industry group. As this industry group is probably related to the manufacture of fine paper products in this SMA, it is assumed that these products enjoy a national distribution or larger.

Rubber products: A subsidiary establishment of a large national rubber company is located in this SMA and produces automobile and truck tires. (United States Department of Labor, 1957, p. 132.) It is assumed that these products enjoy a sub-national distribution.

Miscellaneous manufacturing industries: Probably the most important industries included within this group are those engaged in the production of sporting equipment. A large United States sporting goods manufacturer has an establishment within the SMA. (United States Department of Labor, 1957, p. 132.) It is assumed that products are distributed to at least a sub-national market.

Leather products, except footwear: A major firm engaged in the manufacture of leather wallets is located within the SMA (Thomas and Crisler, 1953, p. 28), no doubt distributing its products to a national market.

Non-local services: The non-local service structure of this SMA is comparatively underdeveloped for a SMA but Springfield appears to perform some important non-local services. Thomas and Crisler (1953, p. 28) refer to it as "a leading trade center in the Connecticut Valley." Tobacco is a leading crop within this Valley. Bogue assigns to Springfield the western third of Massachusetts as a hinterland and probably some services are provided for roughly this area. However, for many non-local services, it appears that this SMA falls under the dominance of Boston. There are two service industries in which this SMA is specialized.

Insurance: Springfield is the home of a large New England insurance company. It is assumed that this firm and the others of the SMA serve chiefly a sub-national area.

Educational services, private: Private colleges in Springfield include Springfield College and American International College and in Holyoke, Mt. Holyoke College. These colleges presumably serve in addition to the local SMA, a hinterland, and to some extent a national area.

SUMMARY: SPRINGFIELD-HOLYOKE

This SMA contains an unusually large and diverse industry profile for its size. With the exception of some forest inputs available in its hinterland for its pulp and paper industries there does not seem to be any important natural resource basis for these industries. Rather, historical factors including the early development of the water potential in the area account for the location of industries in the area. There is considerable linkage between the industries within the SMA with both processing and fabricating industries being found in the areas of paper and textile production. Except for those cases where outputs from one industry become inputs for another, it appears that the industries in this SMA are in general serving a national or a sub-national market in most cases. Service industries are relatively undeveloped. Some insurance and educational functions are performed for a sub-national area but in respect to many services this SMA appears to be subordinate to Boston.

WHEELING-STEUBENVILLE

SMA consists of Brooke, Hancock, Marshall and Ohio Counties, West Virginia, and Belmont and Jefferson Counties, Ohio

1950 population: central cities, 94,763 (Wheeling, 58,891; Steubenville, 35,872); SMA, 354,092

INPUTS AND SUPPLY AREAS FOR WHEELING-STEUBENVILLE'S PROFILE INDUSTRIES

Coal mining: Wheeling and Steubenville lie near the center of the northern half of the Appalachian coal field, the largest and most important bituminous coal area in the United States. (Chapman, *et al.*, 1953, p. 16.) In 1952 those counties comprising the SMA located in West Virginia produced approximately 3.4 million tons of bituminous coal. This accounted for only a very small part of the total coal production of the state which in the same year produced 141.7 million tons. This state is the ranking bituminous coal producing state in the nation. (United States Bureau of Mines, Regional Mineral Industry Divisions, 1955, p. 970.) On the other hand the two counties comprising the Ohio portion of the SMA produced in 1952 approximately 12.5 million tons, a quantity accounting for nearly one-third of Ohio's total bituminous coal production. (*Ibid.*, p. 712.)

Table 80. Industrial Profile, Wheeling-Steubenville: 1950

Category and industry	Location quotient	Per cent of employed labor force	Inputs primarily from area:	Outputs primarily to area:
(1) (*Primary resource extractors; production for non-final market*)				
Coal mining	9.77	8.9	A	A, C
(4) *Second stage resource users; production for non-final market*				
Blast furnaces, steel works and rolling mills	17.36	20.5	A, B, C	A, C
Other primary iron and steel industries	2.55	1.3	A	A, C
Miscellaneous petroleum and coal products	3.20	0.2	A	A, C
(6) (*Resources of indirect significance; production for non-final market*)				
Glass and glass products	8.48	2.1	B, C	C
Pottery and related products	21.00	2.1	B, C	C
(9) *Service industries; non-local*	0.68	8.6	*	B
Total in profile industries	...	43.7	...	...

* Inputs other than labor not considered.

Because specialization in employment in an extractive industry is somewhat unusual for an SMA we may note where the miners tend to reside within the SMA. According to the *1950 Census of Population,* approximately 2,500 of the 11,500 miners within the SMA reside within the Wheeling urbanized area and less than 1,000 within the city limits of Wheeling. Only about 150 miners reside within the city limits of Steubenville. By far the largest group of miners (5,300) reside in Belmont County which is situated to the west of Wheeling, across the Ohio River. The second largest concentration (3,000) is to be found in Jefferson County which includes Steubenville and territory to the west.

Blast furnaces, steel works, and rolling mills: The early development of this industry in Wheeling and Steubenville was due to "ready access to coal deposits"; the coal was obtained from "drift mines driven horizontally into exposed coal seams along the sides of valleys." (Garland, 1955, p. 182.) There are still abundant coal deposits in the local area and coking coal is available from the SMA and hinterland areas. Iron ore arrives via lake shipment and rail from the deposits in the Lake Superior region. Ore arrives from the Lake Erie ports of Huron, Lorain, Cleveland, Fairport, and from the inland city of Pittsburgh. (Zimmermann, 1951, p. 662.) Limestone and dolomite inputs are available in the local and hinterland area. (See McCarty, 1940, p. 555.)

Other primary iron and steel industries: This industry group is largely made up of foundries receiving inputs from iron and steel furnaces. (See Zimmermann, 1951, p. 649.) It is assumed that iron, steel, and coke inputs all arrive largely from industries in the SMA.

Miscellaneous petroleum and coal products: Probably specialization in this industry group is due to employment resulting from the utilization of by-products from coke ovens located in the SMA.

Glass and glass products: Inputs for this industry are sand, soda ash, lime and fuel. In 1951-52, 695,000 tons of glass sand were produced in West Virginia, the principal producing counties being Morgan, Monongalia, and Fayette Counties. (Monongalia County is quite close to the SMA.) (United States Bureau of Mines, Regional Mineral Industry Divisions, 1955, p. 972.) In Ohio, glass sand was obtained in 1952 from Perry, Knox, Geauga, and Scioto Counties. (*Ibid.*, p. 717.) (Perry and Knox are relatively near the SMA.) Lime and limestone inputs are available from local and hinterland areas. One of the major limestone producing areas in West Virginia in 1952 was Jefferson County, a part of this SMA. (*Ibid.*, p. 974.) Fuel is of great importance in the glass industries. At first charcoal was used, later coal and finally natural gas. Alexandersson (1956, pp. 61-62) says that glass manufacturing is "one of the few industries still significantly influenced by geographic differences in fuel costs," and that this factor leads to a concentration of the industry in the Appalachian Plateau section of Pennsylvania, Ohio, and West Virginia. The same writer indicates that when the industry turned to natural gas it expanded rapidly in Ohio and West Virginia, where this resource is available. The district where glass manufacturing is concentrated has now been linked to the Midcontinent Field by pipeline.

Pottery and related products: Important inputs include clays (common ball clay and china clay), flint, which gives rigidity to the body, feldspar, which acts as a flux to bind the materials as they fuse, glazes of numerous kinds and fuels. (See Alderfer and Michl, 1957, p. 204.) Pottery clays are widely available in the United States but are found chiefly in the Appalachian district.

> Flint clays were first utilized by Reese Thomas in Scioto County for the manufacture of fire brick. From this small start, the clay industry of Ohio has increased until today the State leads the Nation as a producer. In 1952 output was reported from 124 clay pits, including 18 underground mines, operating in 42 counties. Fire clay, which comprised 52 per cent of tonnage and 80 per cent of value, was the more important type of clay produced in 1952. . . . Approximately 63 per cent of the total clay output was utilized in manufacturing heavy clay products. (United States Bureau of Mines, Regional Mineral Industry Divisions, 1955, p. 714.)
>
> Despite West Virginia's prominent position in the china-ware and clay-products industry, the State has a relatively minor output of raw material for these items. (*Ibid.*, p. 972.)

Thus it would appear that although some of the clay inputs for pottery may be available from the immediate hinterland, the better grades of clay must be brought in from elsewhere. Alderfer and Michl (1957, p. 204) indicate that

> . . . the American pottery industry has long depended upon foreign sources, primarily England, for a large part of its supplies, especially for the manufacture of high-grade table and sanitary ware. Recent developments have made possible the greater use of domestic clays, to which most manufacturers of sanitary ware and hotel china shifted. Georgia is the source of some of the best clay used in the manufacture of high-grade chinaware.

Sources for flint and feldspar utilized by these industries were not determined. Both coal and natural gas are utilized for fuel. (Alexandersson, 1956, p. 60.) Coal is available in great quantities in the local area and the sources of natural gas are described above in connection with the glass industries.

OUTPUTS AND SERVICE AREAS
OF WHEELING-STEUBENVILLE'S PROFILE INDUSTRIES

Coal mining: Coal mined in the SMA and surrounding hinterland is utilized by local industries, chiefly the blast furnaces, steel works, iron and steel foundries, coke ovens, and the glass and pottery manufacturers. However, the production of coal is quite large and no doubt large quantities of coal (and coke) are shipped to other manufacturing areas within and outside the states of Ohio and West Virginia.

Blast furnaces, steel works and rolling mills: Iron and steel products feed local foundries and machinery companies as well as manufacturing centers located outside the hinterland.

Other primary iron and steel industries: Foundry products no doubt serve both local and non-local manufacturing firms.

Miscellaneous petroleum and coal products: The specific nature of the products of this industry group was not determined. Probably the best guess is that they include the by-products of coke ovens (tars and oils). Distribution of these products is probably to local chemical companies as well as to chemical companies located in the Ohio Valley.

Glass and glass products: Two large companies making fine glass tableware are located in this SMA. (United States Department of Labor, 1957, p. 328.) Their products are no doubt distributed to a national market. In addition many smaller glass firms are located in the SMA and no doubt serve regional markets.

Pottery and related products: Two large companies making china tableware are located in this SMA. (United States Department of Labor, 1957, p. 328.) Their products no doubt enjoy at least a subnational market.

Non-local services: Only a relatively small proportion of this SMA's labor force is engaged in non-local services, and the industrial profile does not show specialization in any specific non-local service. Thomas and Crisler (1953) place the SMA well within the trade area served by Pittsburgh.

SUMMARY: WHEELING-STEUBENVILLE

Most of the profile industries within the Wheeling-Steubenville SMA are related in some way to the availability of large supplies of bituminous coal within the immediate and hinterland areas. The mining of this coal constitutes a significant employment group within the SMA and the availability of coal was no doubt a primary reason for the location of primary iron and steel industries and the glass and pottery industries in this area. Local supplies of natural gas were also an important item for the continuing development of the latter two industries. Important inputs for the profile industries also arrive from Area C. Iron ore and the better types of pottery clay are among these. Some of the outputs of the local iron and steel industries are no doubt utilized by other industries within the SMA but it appears that the preponderance of these are utilized in industries located in other SMA's. Glass and pottery products enjoy a national market. The non-local service structure of this SMA appears to be relatively undeveloped and apparently nearby Pittsburgh pre-empts the hinterland market for many of these services.

CHARLESTON (WEST VIRGINIA)

SMA consists of Fayette and Kanawha Counties, West Virginia
1950 population: central city, 73,501; SMA, 322,072
Important feature: capital of West Virginia

INPUTS AND SUPPLY AREAS FOR CHARLESTON'S PROFILE INDUSTRIES

Coal mining: Charleston lies at roughly the center of the great Appalachian coal field, which stretches southwestward along the Appalachian Highlands from northwestern Pennsylvania to central Alabama. This field is considered one of the most important in the United States. (Nielsen, 1950, p. 486.) Lumber inputs in the form of mine timbers were for many years cut in the local area. However, in the recent past more and more non-local timber sources are called upon. (Davis, 1946, pp. 255, 258.) A word about labor supply might be appropriate since coal mining is an unusual specialization for an SMA. According to the *1950 Census of Population* only a very small part of the large mining employment of this SMA resides in the central city, or in any city of any size within the SMA. Fayette county contains well over half of the miners and over three-fourths of this county's residents are classified as rural-nonfarm.

Paints, varnishes, and related products: Inputs include vegetable oils, particularly linseed and tung oils, lead, petroleum products and inorganic chemicals. Sources of inputs can only be discussed in general terms. Linseed oil derived from flaxseed is produced in this country chiefly in Minnesota and North Dakota. External sources include Argentina and Uruguay. (Zimmermann, 1951, pp. 277-278.) Tung oil is produced in this country along the Gulf of Mexico from Florida to eastern Texas; Mississippi is now the most important producer. However, domestic sources furnish only a small part of our needs and large quantities of the oil are imported from abroad. (*Ibid.*, pp. 284-285.) Lead is mined in this country in the Central and Western states, particularly Missouri, Idaho, Kansas and Oklahoma. (*Ibid.*, p. 736.) Inorganic chemicals are probably received from chemical firms within the SMA. Sources of petroleum products were not determined.

Table 81. Industrial Profile, Charleston, West Virginia: 1950

Category and industry	Location quotient	Per cent of employed labor force	Inputs primarily from area:	Outputs primarily to area:
(1) *Primary resource extractors; production for non-final market*				
Coal mining	21.25	19.3	B	B, C
(4) *Second stage resource users; production for non-final market*				
Paints, varnishes, and related products	2.90	0.3	C	B?
Miscellaneous chemicals and allied products	13.20	11.8	B, C	C
(6) (*Resources of indirect significance; production for non-final market*)				
Glass and glass products	9.72	2.4	B	C
(9) *Service industries; non-local*	0.85	10.9	*	B
State public administration	3.36	(1.6)	*	B
Total in profile industries	...	44.7	...	...

* Inputs other than labor not considered.

Miscellaneous chemicals and allied products: The chemical industries of this area depend in large part on local supplies of fuel: both natural gas and coal. In addition coal is used as a raw material. Salt brines are available in the local area and constitute an important input for many of the chemical industries. However, many of the inputs are non-local, barytes arriving from Tennessee, rock salt from New York and Michigan, etc. (Davis, 1946, pp. 265-267.) Although inputs may arrive today from many parts of the eastern United States, the original natural resources of the valley were important determinants in bringing these chemical industries to Charleston. (See Garland, 1955, p. 178.) According to Davis (1946, pp. 255, 265-266), who discusses the growth of chemical manufacturing in this area,

> The development has been determined by use of mineral resources of the valley, since local brines, bituminous coal deposits, oil pools, and natural gas pockets, influence directly or indirectly economic pursuits of the region. . . .
>
> Close relationship between fuels, brines, adequate transportation and local chemical development cannot be overstated. Nearby deposits of high grade bituminous coal and cheap natural gas and oil served to bring a number of chemical plants to the valley. . . . Brine pumping is a sustained activity at both Malden and north of Point Pleasant . . . and supplies a basic material for certain chemical plants.

Glass and glass products: Local inputs have also played an important role in this industry group. Sand, limestone, and fuels are the important inputs for this industry. All three are available in the local area. (Garland, 1955, p. 182.) "Company-owned gas wells are drawn upon and nearby gasoline plants are utilized in supplying fuel needs." (Davis, 1946, p. 266.)

OUTPUTS AND SERVICE AREAS OF CHARLESTON'S PROFILE INDUSTRIES

Coal mining: According to the *1954 Census of Mineral Industries,* West Virginia ranked third among the states in number employed in mining and sixth in value of shipments. In 1949, West Virginia production of coal amounted to 123 million tons, of which 10 million tons were produced in Fayette County and 7 million in Kanawha County. (United States Bureau of Mines, 1953, p. 321.) This coal enjoys a wide distribution. Industrial firms located in the local Kanawha valley depend almost entirely upon coal mined in the local area while large amounts are shipped north for use by industries of the greater Ohio valley. "Most of West Virginia's coal moves by rail or by the Ohio and its tributaries, and much is shipped to the eastern seaboard and the Great Lakes." (Garland, 1955, p. 180.) Almost all of the coal mined in Fayette and Kanawha counties was shipped by rail or water. (United States Bureau of Mines, 1953, p. 321.)

Paints, varnishes, and related products: The specific nature of these products could not be determined. No doubt a relatively small area is being served as the employment in this industry group is not large.

Miscellaneous chemicals and allied products: Important outputs include ammonia, the raw materials of nylon and polyethylene plastics, chlorine, carbon bisulphide (used for rayon and cellophane), antifreeze, and many other items. (United States Department of Labor, 1957, p. 324.) Distribution depends on the individual product but many items no doubt enjoy a national market.

Glass and glass products: Glass produced in Charleston includes both sheet plate glass and machine-blown bottles. Distribution of these products is probably to a sub-national area. (Davis, 1946, p. 266.)

Non-local services: Charleston does not appear to have a very highly developed non-local service structure. It does serve as the leading wholesale center of West Virginia (see McCarty, 1940, p. 237) but indications are that its trade area is relatively small. For many services it appears to be dependent upon Richmond, Va., to the east.

State public administration: Charleston is the capital of West Virginia and thus the location for many state-related offices.

SUMMARY: CHARLESTON

The profile industries of Charleston SMA are closely tied in with local natural resources: coal, natural gas, salt, sand, limestone, etc. Industries utilizing these materials are in general serving a national or sub-national market. Charleston is the capital of West Virginia but does not otherwise appear to perform extensive services for its hinterland.

CHAPTER 15

Special Cases

Washington	*Norfolk–Portsmouth*
San Diego	*Wilkes-Barre – Hazleton*
San Antonio	*Tampa – St. Petersburg*
Miami	*Knoxville*
	Phoenix

Nine standard metropolitan areas (SMA's) do not fit the major categories of our classification. The reasons are varied, having to do in part with inadequacies of statistical units and of our methods of analysis, and in part with unusual if not unique features of the SMA's themselves.

Washington, the nation's capital, belongs in a class by itself for obvious reasons. Flamboyant Miami has no peer among the larger SMA's as a resort center. Much of its activity is connected with its own rapid growth and is not readily analyzed in terms of our categories. Three centers owe much of their size and national importance to military installations—San Diego, San Antonio, and Norfolk-Portsmouth. Under some points of view there might be reason to group these with centers where aircraft production is a major, seemingly "exogenous" industry. Such a category of "defense centers" would gain other important representatives among SMA's smaller than those we have studied in detail.

Extractive industries are unusually important in the four remaining SMA's falling in the category of "special cases." Wilkes-Barre – Hazleton is specialized in coal mining, while Tampa-St. Petersburg, Knoxville, and Phoenix have unusually large proportions of agricultural workers. To some extent, the prominence of extractive activities in these instances may be due to the way in which SMA boundaries are drawn. Phoenix in particular is a special case of an "oasis city."

Since our analytical methods were specifically adapted to the study of centers of the types described in earlier chapters and not to take care of the variety of "special cases," the reader must be prepared for a somewhat skimpy and none too informative treatment of the latter in this chapter.

WASHINGTON

SMA consists of District of Columbia; Montgomery and Prince Georges Counties, Maryland; Alexandria city, Falls Church city, Arlington and Fairfax Counties, Virginia
1950 population: central city, 802,178; SMA, 1,464,089
Important location feature: on Potomac River
Other important feature: capital of United States

INPUTS AND SUPPLY AREAS FOR WASHINGTON'S PROFILE INDUSTRIES

Printing, publishing, and allied industries: Nearly half of the persons employed in this category are government workers. Since the latter category is probably predominantly federal, the rather high activity in this industry group is due to the federal government's extensive array of publications and documents. The paper sources were not determined and it is assumed that they are from relatively distant areas.

OUTPUTS AND SERVICE AREAS OF WASHINGTON'S PROFILE INDUSTRIES

Printing, publishing, and allied industries: The importance of the federal government in the SMA's only outstanding manufacturing industry is suggested by the reputation of the Government Printing Office as the "largest single printing and publishing establishment in the world." (Alexandersson, 1956, p. 86.) Government publications are distributed throughout the world.

Non-local services: Services, like manufacturing, reflect largely the impact of the federal government on the local economy. Alexandersson (1956, p. 117) emphasizes Washington's relatively small commercial activity as suggested by its low employment in wholesale trade. The Alexandria, Va., part of the SMA is, however, a commercial center for northern Virginia. (*Encyclopaedia Britannica,* 1955, vol. 1, p. 580.) When Washington was selected as the capital of the nation, its prospects as a port were considered favorable. (Alexandersson, 1956, p. 117.) However, the Potomac River is apparently a minor factor in the local economy, although in terms of tonnage the water traffic at Washington is comparable with that of, say, Richmond. Direct rail and truck service is available from Baltimore harbor, 40 miles distant. In 1955, Washington harbor receipts were primarily sand, gravel, crushed rock, and petroleum products. The most important receipts of Alexandria, Va., were petroleum products, newsprint paper, and sand, gravel, and crushed rock. (United States Department of the Army, Corps of Engineers [1956], Part 1, pp. 272-290.)

Table 82. Industrial Profile, Washington: 1950

Category and industry	Location quotient	Per cent of employed labor force	Inputs primarily from area:	Outputs primarily to area:
(6) (*Resources of indirect significance; production for non-final market*)				
Printing, publishing, and allied industries	2.42	3.7	C	C
(9) *Service industries; non-local*	2.83	36.1	*	C
Air transportation	2.88	(0.5)	*	C
Telegraph (wire and radio)	1.62	(0.1)	*	C
Hotels and lodging places	1.54	(1.4)	*	C
Miscellaneous professional and related services	3.00	(0.4)	*	C
Federal public administration	15.21	(27.4)	*	C
Total in profile industries	...	39.8	...	...

* Inputs other than labor not considered.

Air transportation: Twelve airlines serve the SMA. The location of the federal government in the SMA leads to a considerable flow of tourists and business visitors between the SMA and other parts of the nation. In 1950, 811,625 passengers and 5,320 tons of cargo were carried an average distance of 490 miles by domestic lines. (United States Department of Commerce, Civil Aeronautics Administration, 1951, p. 6.)

Telegraph (wire and radio): This specialization possibly reflects the activity of several hundred newspapers, news agencies, and wire services in the national capital. No doubt federal agencies likewise make extensive use of telegraph facilities.

Hotels and lodging places: The large number of tourists and visitors for business purposes no doubt is an important factor in this industry.

Miscellaneous professional and related services: Because of the legislative and administrative activities, various national organizations locate their offices or representatives in the SMA. (McCarty, 1940, p. 441.)

Federal public administration: The SMA is the center for the executive, legislative, and judicial branches of the federal government. Agencies such as the Atomic Energy Commission, Bureau of Engraving and Printing, National Archives, Federal Trade Commission, Departments of Agriculture, Justice, Commerce, Defense, State, and Labor all have their administrative centers in the SMA. It is perhaps well to point out, however, that only about one worker in nine in federal public administration in the entire country is employed in the Washington area. Two branches in particular—defense and postal—are geographically dispersed.

SUMMARY: WASHINGTON

As is well known, the location of Washington had little to do with prospective economic advantages of the site, but was decided by legislative fiat on the basis of political considerations. The economy of the Washington SMA remains to this day overwhelmingly influenced by the presence and activities of federal offices and has relatively little to do with the regional situation of the city. Within a sample afforded by the cities of a single nation, therefore, Washington is quite unique.

SAN DIEGO

SMA consists of San Diego County, California
1950 population: central city, 334,387; SMA, 556,808
Important location feature: port on Pacific Ocean

INPUTS AND SUPPLY AREAS FOR SAN DIEGO'S PROFILE INDUSTRIES

Canning and preserving fruits, vegetables, and sea foods: Fish canneries are the important employers in this industry group, particularly the canners of tuna. (California State Chamber of Commerce, 1954, p. 802.) San Diego leads the country in this industry; in the early 1940's over 50 per cent of the tuna catch of the United States was canned in San Diego. (Coons and Miller, 1941, p. 330.) Important inputs are tuna fish and tin cans. Tuna is gathered from the waters off southern California and Lower California by large fleets operating out of San Diego. (McCarty, 1940, p. 75.) The small employment in metal fabricating industries located in San Diego SMA indicates that most if not all of the tins used in canning must be imported from other areas. Inasmuch as California leads the country in the manufacture of tin cans, it is assumed that much of San Diego's supply arrives from such centers as Los Angeles and San Francisco. (Zierer, 1956, p. 307.)

Table 83. Industrial Profile, San Diego: 1950

Category and industry	Location quotient	Per cent of employed labor force	Inputs primarily from area:	Outputs primarily to area:
(3) *First stage resource users; production for final market*				
Canning and preserving fruits, vegetables, and sea foods	5.15	1.3	B, C	C
(7) *Resources of indirect significance; production for final market*				
Aircraft and parts	14.41	6.6	C	C
(9) *Service industries; non-local*	1.38	17.7	*	C
Hotels and lodging places	1.84	(1.7)	*	C
Federal public administration	4.62	(8.3)	*	C
(10) *Service industries; may be local or non-local*				
Miscellaneous entertainment and recreation services	2.42	0.9	*	A, C
Total in profile industries	...	26.5	...	...

* Inputs other than labor not considered.

Aircraft and parts: Employment in the aircraft industry in San Diego is concentrated in airframe production and hence in final assembly. (*Ibid.*, p. 293.) Inputs are almost entirely processed and fabricated materials. These include alloy steels, copper, aluminum sheet and tubing, aluminum castings and similar materials. Manufactured parts include chiefly airplane engines and propellers. (Cunningham, 1951, p. 18.) The manufacturing process is described as follows:

> Presenting some contrast to the local automobile plants, where most parts are received finished and ready to be routed on the assembly line, the aircraft assembly plant is the scene of much fabrication. The airframe is usually completely manufactured from raw stock—aluminum sheets, tubing, extrusions, forgings, and castings—and all the necessary shaping and precision machining takes place in the plant. The many preliminary operations, plus the final assembly, require huge plants and great numbers of laborers. Consequently, southern California airframe plants are the largest manufacturing units west of the Mississippi and among the largest in the country. (Zierer, 1956, p. 293.)

Sources for these inputs can be discussed only in general terms. Within recent years important iron and steel supply centers have grown up in the Pacific Southwest, and according to Zierer (1956, p. 298), amounts produced within the region now are sufficient to meet most of its own needs. Plants closest to San Diego include the Fontana mill west of Los Angeles, the Torrance mill south of Los Angeles and several mills within Los Angeles. (*Ibid.,* pp. 298-300.) As far as could be determined the nearest aluminum plants are to be found in the Pacific Northwest, chiefly Washington, and in the South, chiefly Texas, Louisiana, and Arkansas. (Alderfer and Michl, 1957, p. 111.) Copper is available from California. (Zierer, 1956, pp. 224-225.) Cromite is received from Turkey, Southern Rhodesia and New Caledonia. Manganese is now obtained from India rather than from Russia, and tungsten comes from Portugal, Spain, Japan, Thailand, Korea, Australia, and Bolivia. (*Ibid.,* p. 304.) Many processed inputs no doubt arrive from the manufacturing zone.

Engines and propellers are not produced in the Pacific Southwest. (Zierer, 1956, p. 293.) Important centers for the production of airplane engines are, in order of importance, Hartford, Indianapolis, New York, and Boston, while New York, Hartford, and Dayton are propeller manufacturing centers. (Cunningham, 1951, pp. 225-226.) "The large transports and bombers from Pacific coast plants are equipped almost exclusively with engines, propellers and instruments from the New York and New England areas." (*Ibid.,* p. 18.) It was not determined which centers supply most of San Diego's needs. Power and fuel requirements for this industry are minimal. (*Ibid.,* p. 19.)

The general question might be raised here as to why San Diego has become a national center for the production of aircraft in view of the distant sources of many of the major inputs. Some answers are provided by the following statement:

> The location of aircraft manufacturing while conditioned in recent developments, of course, by the influence of already invested capital and other economic ties, was initially determined neither by the presence of a special natural resource to be incorporated in its finished goods nor by the necessities of close market contacts with the consumers of its products. . . . Its location in San Diego was conditioned by the favorability of climate, the availability of open ground and water for testing purposes, both natural factors of no mean importance, and by the early establishment of San Diego as a naval base and as a base for naval aeronautical activity. (Coons and Miller, 1941, p. 344.)

OUTPUTS AND SERVICE AREAS OF SAN DIEGO'S PROFILE INDUSTRIES

Canning and preserving fruits, vegetables, and sea foods: San Diego is "the most important tuna fishing and canning center in the country." (Thomas and Crisler, 1953, p. 138.) Distribution of this product is to a national and international market. Port statistics indicate that canned fish accounted for 80 per cent (in terms of tonnage) of San Diego's foreign exports between 1936 and 1945. (United States Board of Engineers for Rivers and Harbors and United States Maritime Commission, 1947, No. 27, p. 84.)

Aircraft and parts: Airplanes produced by San Diego aircraft plants undoubtedly enjoy a similar national and world market. The difficulty in identifying precise markets for aircraft manufacturers is that the

> market for commercial and military planes is never centralized, is almost impossible to localize, and presents advantage to no single manufacturing region. The airplane, a highly mobile commodity, is, of course, remarkably independent of market cities. Delivery time to any point on earth is but a matter of hours, and delivery cost is but a fraction of the total cost of the larger and more expensive planes. (Zierer, 1956, p. 295.)

Non-local services: San Diego performs some central-place functions for a small surrounding hinterland. Commodities such as citrus fruit, avocados, vegetables, flowers and livestock are gathered from surrounding areas. (Thomas and Crisler, 1953, p. 138.) However, San Diego is nationally important as a military center and as a tourist center and these functions are discussed below.

San Diego also has some importance as a Pacific port which in 1955 handled almost two million tons of freight traffic. (United States Department of the Army, Corps of Engineers, [1956], Part 4, p. 138.) In that year over 80 per cent of the traffic was made up of coastwise receipts. The bulk of these receipts were petroleum products largely from Los Angeles. (Zierer, 1956, p. 216.) Lumber, shingles, and newsprint paper arrive from the Pacific Northwest while pipes and fittings are from both Atlantic and Gulf ports. (Day and Zimmerman, Inc. [1945], book 4, vol. 7, p. 23.) Foreign imports consist of fish from offshore Mexican water, newsprint from British Columbia and Sweden, and nitrogenous fertilizer material. (*Idem.*) Foreign exports include animal feeds, unmanufactured cotton, and iron and steel scrap. (United States Department of the Army, Corps of Engineers, [1956], Part 4, pp. 138-139.) The scrap is destined largely for Japan. (Day and Zimmerman, Inc. [1945], book 4, vol. 7, p. 24.) Zierer (1956, p. 327) discusses the cotton exports:

> More than 100,000 bales of cotton moved through the port of San Diego during the 1953-1954 shipping season. For more than twenty years no cotton had moved across San Diego docks. In 1953, the San Diego and Arizona Eastern Railroad reduced its rate on Mexican cotton, and a flood of bales swamped the San Diego waterfront. Nearly all of the cotton was shipped to Japan. Expansion of cotton warehouse space is being provided by the San Diego Harbor Commission to accommodate future shipments. Cottonseed meal from Mexico and Arizona has also begun to move through San Diego harbor to foreign markets.

Almost no shipments moved from the port of San Diego to other United States coastal ports in 1955. (United States Department of the Army, Corps of Engineers [1956], Part 4, pp. 138-139.) It is estimated that the area served by the San Diego port includes the southern counties of California, part of Yuma County in Arizona, and northern Mexico. (United States Board of Engineers for Rivers and Harbors and United States Maritime Commission, 1947, No. 27, p. 159.)

The non-local services in which San Diego specializes reflect its tourist trade and military functions.

Hotels and lodging places: It is assumed that this industry group shows specialization because of San Diego's importance as a tourist center. The dry climate, cool summer, mild winter and proximity to Mexico are regarded as tourist attractions. Some of the specific attractions to be found in San Diego include "the nearby Del Mar race track, bullfights at nearby Tijuana, fishing, boating, swimming, Balboa Park zoo, and nearby Mt. Palomar (telescope)." (Thomas and Crisler, 1953, p. 138.)

Federal public administration: With an excellent natural harbor, the first United States port north of the Panama Canal, San Diego "has long been important as a base for the United States Navy." (Zierer, 1956, p. 337.) Much commercial and service activity centers on the military installations, which include the headquarters for the Eleventh Naval District, a naval air station, the United States Naval Repair Facility, and Camp Pendleton. (Thomas and Crisler, 1953, p. 138; United States Department of Labor, 1957, p. 24.)

Miscellaneous entertainment and recreation services: Specialization in these services is no doubt related to San Diego's extensive tourist trade as well as the military installations located in the area.

SUMMARY: SAN DIEGO

"The economy of San Diego County since 1940 has been based primarily on aircraft production and military installations, which together account for about 30 per cent of the area's wage and salary employment." (United States Department of Labor, 1957, p. 24.) These two activities plus the commerce functions of the port are services relating San Diego to the national economy. Inputs for the tuna industry arrive from nearby fishing areas but products are marketed chiefly in Area C. Some local services are performed but it would appear that San Diego lies within the shadow of Los Angeles for many commercial and financial services. The extensive tourist business and the large military installations would appear to account for San Diego's specialization in hotel and entertainment functions. Presumably these services are performed for a national area.

SAN ANTONIO

SMA consists of Bexar County, Texas
1950 population: central city, 408,442; SMA, 500,460
Important feature: Federal Reserve System Branch city

INPUTS AND SUPPLY AREAS FOR SAN ANTONIO'S PROFILE INDUSTRIES

Meat products: Major input for the meat products industry is livestock. San Antonio in 1950 ranked fifth in the nation as a calf market (205,000 calves being received); considerable numbers of cattle (310,000), hogs (78,000) and sheep, lambs and goats (236,000) were also received. (United States Department of Agriculture, Production and Marketing Administration, 1951, pp. 7-8.) Indications are that most of the livestock received originates in the nearby hinterland, particularly from the Edwards Plateau District in south-central Texas, an area the size of Pennsylvania which is devoted almost exclusively to the raising of cattle, sheep and Angora goats. Although by no means all of the livestock raised in this area are marketed in San Antonio, San Antonio remains the center for this industry. (McCarty, 1940, pp. 223-24, 387.) It is significant that a very large proportion of the livestock received in San Antonio is trucked in (93 per cent of the cattle, 88 per cent of the calves, 99 per cent of the hogs, and 88 per cent of the sheep and goats), indicating that great distances are probably not involved. (United States Department of Agriculture, Production and Marketing Administration, 1951, p. 10.)

Table 84. Industrial Profile, San Antonio: 1950

Category and industry	Location quotient	Per cent of employed labor force	Inputs primarily from area:	Outputs primarily to area:
(3) *First stage resource users; production for final market*				
Meat products	2.06	1.0	B	C
Miscellaneous food preparations and kindred products	2.28	0.5	C	C?
(9) *Service industries; non-local*	1.92	24.5	*	B, C
Air transportation	1.55	(0.3)	*	C
Wholesale trade	1.50	(5.3)	*	B
Federal public administration	6.24	(11.2)	*	C
(10) *Service industries; may be local or non-local*				
Miscellaneous entertainment and recreation services	1.65	0.6	*	A, C
Total in profile industries	...	26.6	...	...

* Inputs other than labor not considered.

Miscellaneous food preparations and kindred products: San Antonio's specialization in miscellaneous food products is no doubt in great part due to its extensive pecan industry. San Antonio has been the center of the United States pecan shelling industry for more than 50 years. About half of the nation's seedling pecans were shelled there each year, between the years of 1930 and 1940. (Billings, 1946, p. 226.)

Sources for pecans are quite widespread geographically. Pecans grow naturally in the southern parts of the United States bordering the Gulf of Mexico, extend north along the Mississippi valley to southwest Wisconsin, branch west into Kansas, Oklahoma, and Texas, and east into Alabama. Improved varieties are found from Mississippi to Virginia, extending along the eastern Gulf and southern Atlantic coastal plains. (*Ibid.*, pp. 220-221.) The specific parts of this broad area which serve San Antonio are unknown.

OUTPUTS AND SERVICE AREAS OF SAN ANTONIO'S PROFILE INDUSTRIES

Meat products: Nothing specific is known about the markets served by the meat products industry of the San Antonio SMA. Indications are, however, because of the location of competing centers to the northeast and northwest, that San Antonio's market is limited mostly to the areas of the southwest United States.

Miscellaneous food preparations and kindred products: Outputs of the pecan industry no doubt find their way to a national market since San Antonio controls such a large share of the production in this country.

Non-local services: "The San Antonio area is the economic, social, trade, and educational center for a large predominantly agricultural, section of southwest Texas." (United States Department of Labor, 1957, p. 302.) As well as serving its agricultural hinterland, considerable quantities of petroleum from the local area are refined in San Antonio. (Chambers, 1940, p. 294.) Services in which San Antonio shows a specialization in employment are described below.

Air transportation: San Antonio with seven airlines is one of the larger Texas air centers. In 1950, 86,529 passengers and 2,396 tons of cargo were carried an average distance of 701 miles. (United States Department of Commerce, Civil Aeronautics Administration, 1951, p. 19.)

Wholesale trade: San Antonio is generally considered to dominate a large portion of central and southern Texas as a wholesale center. In addition, San Antonio has important trade connections with Mexico. "Since several important railroads and highways radiate from this city into Mexico, much of the trade with that country passes through or originates there." (Chambers, 1940, p. 294.) However, Vance and Smith (1954, pp. 128-29) point out that whatever the trading functions performed by San Antonio, these are performed under the shadow of Dallas.

Federal public administration: San Antonio is an important Army and Air Force center, seven important military installations being located here. (United States Department of Labor, 1957, p. 302.) Among the more important are the Headquarters for the Fourth Army, Lackland Air Force Base, Randolph Air Force Base, and Brooke Army Medical Center.

Miscellaneous entertainment and recreation services: The high employment in this service is no doubt related to the location of a large military base in the area. However, in addition, San Antonio is an important tourist center, both for its own sake (site of the historic Alamo) and as a gateway into Mexico. (McCarty, 1940, p. 387.)

SUMMARY: SAN ANTONIO

San Antonio is dependent on nearby areas (Areas A and B) for its livestock supply and fuels, but reaches far out into Area C to gather inputs for its miscellaneous foods industry. Central place functions are performed for a sizable but sparsely populated section of central and southern Texas; however, it would appear that San Antonio's size is in large part a result of its military installations—a function presumably performed for the whole country.

MIAMI

SMA consists of Dade County, Florida
1950 population: central city, 249,276; SMA, 495,084
Important location feature: port on Atlantic Ocean

OUTPUTS AND SERVICE AREAS OF MIAMI'S PROFILE INDUSTRIES

Non-local services: All of Miami's profile industries seem to be linked in one way or another with its functions as a major resort. McCarty (1940, p. 468) recounts how Miami rose from an "Indian trading post" in the 1890's to a "major southern city," experiencing a fantastic boom which collapsed in the middle of the 1920's, at which time the city also underwent a destructive hurricane. The city was rebuilt, and has experienced extraordinary, rapid growth—between 1940 and 1950 the SMA population increased by 85 per cent. Apparently in recent years Miami has begun to develop a more diversified economy.

One of the youngest and fastest growing metropolitan areas of its size in the nation, the Miami area now has 703,777 residents, almost

> three times the 1940 population. . . . The presence of this tremendous consumer market has greatly stimulated manufacturing and trade and invited the influx of market oriented industries. Due to this immigration Miami, predominantly a resort area long dependent on tourism, is developing a more diversified economy. The tourist-dominated trade and service industries, which in 1940 accounted for 63.7 per cent of total employment, has dropped to less than 50 per cent by the end of 1955. These factors have combined to reduce the seasonal variation between summer and winter employment levels from 25 per cent in 1947 to 10 per cent in 1955. . . . Manufacturing . . . exemplifies the sound development of the area. Although limited to light manufacturing it has almost doubled in the past five years without creating any one dominant manufacturing industry. (United States Department of Labor, 1957, p. 54.)

However apparently none of these developments has been large enough or occurred early enough to be reflected in Miami's 1950 industry profile.

Table 85. Industrial Profile, Miami: 1950

Category and industry	Location quotient	Per cent of employed labor force	Inputs primarily from area:	Outputs primarily to area:
(9) *Service industries; non-local*	1.57	20.0	*	C
Air transportation	25.88	(4.4)	*	C
Hotels and lodging places	5.18	(4.8)	*	C
Radio broadcasting and television	1.73	(0.2)	*	C
(10) *Service industries; may be local or non-local*				
Miscellaneous entertainment and recreation services	4.13	1.6	*	C
Total in profile industries	...	21.6	...	...

* Inputs other than labor not considered.

With regard to commercial activity, Thomas and Crisler (1953, p. 48) report that Miami is a commercial center and shipping point for avocados and other fruits and vegetables. As of 1955, according to the First Research Corporation (1955, p. 19) Miami served as a wholesale trade center for a large portion of southern Florida.

Although not showing specialization in water transportation, Miami harbor shows a steadily increasing volume of port traffic. In 1955, 2,-881,301 tons of cargo and 583,146 passengers were transported via the port. Of this total freight traffic, 300,000 tons were foreign imports (chiefly building cement, newsprint paper, finished steel mill products, lumber, fuel oil, and bananas); 80,000 tons were foreign exports (chiefly lumber and metal manufactures); 900,000 tons were coastwise receipts (including canned fruits and vegetables, petroleum products, cement and finished steel mill products); and only 20,000 tons coastwise shipments (largely fuel oil). Internal receipts totalled 430,000 tons and consisted mostly of petroleum products, limestone, sand, gravel, and crushed rock; internal shipments totalled 460,000 tons and were made up almost entirely of fuel oil and some limestone. (United States Department of the Army, Corps of Engineers [1956], Part 1, pp. 373-375.)

Air transportation: No doubt this industry is closely related to Miami's functions as a tourist center. In addition Miami is an important air terminal for Latin American trade. (Thomas and Crisler, 1953, p. 48.)

> An important factor contributing to Miami's growth is its geographical position at the crossroads of two continents. Miami is now one day's flight from any part of the western hemisphere in North or South America. By virtue of this ideal location the huge Miami International Airport is one of the Nation's busiest airports, ranking among the leaders in total air tonnage, number of passengers handled and volume of air traffic. Through these excellent air transportation facilities the Miami market now services consumers in the currently expanding Caribbean area as well as southern Florida. (United States Department of Labor, 1957, p. 54.)

The following figures indicate the size and importance of air transportation for Miami:

> In and around the vast Miami International Airport flows a vital stream of cargo and passenger traffic, supplemented by an airplane maintenance and airlines working force of nearly 20,000 people. In 1954, for example, some 2,537,000 passengers arrived and departed at the Miami International Airport, making it one of the busiest airports in the United States, ranking just behind Idlewild [in New York]. Total cargo handled at the Miami International Airport in 1954, was 128,516,000 pounds, which means that the airport handles more air cargo tonnage, than any airport in the United States. . . .
>
> In 1954, 75% of the cargo carried was to and from points outside the United States, indicating the international nature of Miami as a business center. (First Research Corporation, 1955, pp. 13-14.)

Hotels and lodging places: This service industry is of course related to the Miami SMA's functions as a tourist center. In 1954 Miami and Miami Beach combined had 42,967 hotel rooms and 7,729 motor court rooms. (First Research Corporation, 1955, p. 15.) According to this research group,

> . . . it is . . . a mistaken theory to assume that the tourist industry is a highly cyclical business, moving sharply up and down on some national economic whim. Basically, an analysis of the past twenty-five years indicates that by and large, the tourist industry has a much smaller cyclical trend than does industry and trade as a whole. By and large, tourism has become a year-round business, made so by increased use of leisure time, higher standards of living and greater ease of travel. (*Idem.*)

Radio broadcasting and television: It is assumed that these facilities are also related to the SMA's importance as a resort and entertainment area.

Miscellaneous entertainment and recreation services: Thomas and Crisler (1953, p. 48) indicate that Miami is "famous for salt water fishing, yachting, and horseracing at Hialeah, Gulfstream, and Tropical Parks. It is near Everglades National Park; Parrot Jungle, Monkey Jungle, and Musa Isle Indian (Seminole) Village are among the other tourist attractions around Miami."

SUMMARY: MIAMI

All of Miami's profile industries appear to be related to its functions as a major United States tourist center. In addition its airport facilities and location make it an important center for air services between the two Americas. Miami harbor is engaged chiefly in the transshipment of lumber, petroleum and some manufactured products.

NORFOLK-PORTSMOUTH

SMA consists of Norfolk city, Portsmouth city, South Norfolk city, and Norfolk and Princess Anne Counties, Virginia

1950 population: central cities, 293,552 (Norfolk, 213,513; Portsmouth, 80,039); SMA, 446,200

Important location feature: port on the Atlantic Ocean

INPUTS AND SUPPLY AREAS
FOR NORFOLK-PORTSMOUTH'S PROFILE INDUSTRIES

Ship and boat building: Norfolk-Portsmouth is the site of the Norfolk Navy Yard, one of the largest shipbuilding yards in the world. (Alexandersson, 1956, p. 55.) Important inputs for this industry include products from steel works and rolling mills and structural metal products. Specific sources of inputs could not be determined; however the iron center at Sparrows Point and those of southern Pennsylvania are not far distant. (See map 4 in Chapman, 1953, following p. 22.) Other structural metal products are no doubt furnished by many parts of the eastern half of the manufacturing zone.

Table 86. Industrial Profile, Norfolk-Portsmouth: 1950

Category and industry	Location quotient	Per cent of employed labor force	Inputs primarily from area:	Outputs primarily to area:
(6) (*Resources of indirect significance; production for non-final market*)				
Ship and boat building and repairing	24.89	7.0	C	C
(9) *Service industries; non-local*	2.02	25.8	*	C
Water transportation	6.03	(2.2)	*	C
Federal public administration	6.65	(12.0)	*	C
Total in profile industries	...	32.8	...	...

* Inputs other than labor not considered.

OUTPUTS AND SERVICE AREAS
OF NORFOLK-PORTSMOUTH'S PROFILE INDUSTRIES

Ship and boat building: In addition to the naval shipyard, some of the largest oil tankers in the world are built at the plant in Norfolk. Also there are smaller yards used chiefly for constructing or repairing towboats, barges, and other small boats. (United States Board of Engineers for Rivers and Harbors and United States Maritime Commission, 1949, No. 11, p. 31.) It would seem to be safe to conclude that ships built in the Norfolk-Portsmouth area are in use in many parts of this country and of the world.

Water transportation: For many years Norfolk has been a leading coal transshipping port. (*Ibid.*, p. 186.) The Hampton Roads area is the gateway for vast quantities of fine steam coal from the Pocahontas and New River fields, and two of the three major coal-carrying railroads in the area have provided piers at Norfolk for transshipping coal to foreign and domestic markets. (*Idem.;* see also Zimmermann, 1951, p. 461). In terms of total tonnage, Norfolk Harbor ranked as seventh leading port in the United States in 1955. (United States Department of the Army, Corps of Engineers [1956], Part 5, pp. 17-18.) About one-third of this traffic was accounted for by exports of coal to foreign countries and about one-sixth by domestic coal shipments. However, the port also handled foreign and domestic traffic in every major commodity classification.

Federal public administration: Specialization in this industry group is largely due to the location in Portsmouth of the Norfolk Naval Shipyard and the location in Norfolk of the headquarters of the Fifth Naval District. (United States Department of Labor, 1957, p. 312.)

Other non-local services: Norfolk-Portsmouth SMA appears to perform some important wholesale functions for surrounding areas. (Vance and Smith, 1954, pp. 128-29.) McCarty (1940, p. 472) describes the wholesale area as extending southwest almost to Raleigh and reaching down the coast nearly to Wilmington. However, for many financial and commercial services Norfolk appears to lie within the shadow of Richmond. Vance and Smith class Norfolk-Portsmouth as a "subdominant with metropolitan characteristics."

SUMMARY: NORFOLK-PORTSMOUTH

While Norfolk-Portsmouth may be said to perform some services for the immediate hinterland, all of its profile industries appear to be oriented to serving more extensive areas. The port functions dominate with the naval installations, the shipbuilding industries, and the transshipment of commodities all serving a national area.

WILKES-BARRE – HAZLETON

SMA consists of Luzerne County, Pennsylvania

1950 population: central cities, 112,317; Wilkes-Barre, 76,826; Hazleton, 35,491); SMA, 392,241

INPUTS AND SUPPLY AREAS
FOR WILKES-BARRE – HAZLETON'S PROFILE INDUSTRIES

Coal mining: Wilkes-Barre is located at the southern end of the Northern Anthracite Field, Hazleton in the center of the Eastern Middle Anthracite Field. Coal is prepared for market by being treated in breakers which separate the coal from the slate and other impurities. These breakers are operated primarily by electricity. (Murphy and Murphy, 1937, pp. 325, 330-332.) We may briefly consider labor inputs for this industry as it is somewhat unusual for an SMA to specialize in an extractive industry. Of the more than 31,000 employed in the coal mines in this SMA only about 4,000 reside in Wilkes-Barre and about 2,000 in Hazleton. However, within the Wilkes-Barre urbanized area 22,000 miners are found. Other smaller cities in Luzerne County (the county is 83 per cent urban) contain large numbers of miners.

Table 87. Industrial Profile, Wilkes-Barre – Hazleton: 1950

Category and industry	Location quotient	Per cent of employed labor force	Inputs primarily from area:	Outputs primarily to area:
(1) *Primary resource extractors; production for non-final market*				
Coal mining	24.76	22.5	A, B	C
(3) *First stage resource users; production for final market*				
Tobacco manufactures	13.06	2.2	B, C	C
(4) *Second stage resource users; production for non-final market*				
Other primary iron and steel industries	1.76	0.9	A, C	C?
Yarn, thread, and fabric mills	2.83	4.4	C	A, C
Miscellaneous textile mill products	6.50	0.6	C	C
(5) *Second stage resource users; production for final market*				
Bakery products	2.59	1.3	C?	A
Apparel and accessories	5.41	9.4	A, C	C
(9) *Service industries; non-local*	0.72	9.2	*	B
Total in profile industries	...	50.5	...	...

* Inputs other than labor not considered.

Tobacco manufactures: Tobacco for the production of cigars is grown in the southern portion of the state. (*Ibid.*, p. 224.) In fact, Pennsylvania is the leading state in the production of domestic filler tobacco, with Lancaster and York counties producing most of the state's output. (Alderfer and Michl, 1950, p. 638.) Sources for other tobaccos utilized were not determined but the near-by Connecticut Valley is an important domestic producer of cigar wrappers while Wisconsin is pre-eminent in the production of tobacco suitable for cigar binders. In recent years the manufacture of the cheaper machine-made cigars has localized in the larger urban centers. (Murphy and Murphy, 1937, p. 242.)

Other primary iron and steel industries: Inputs may be discussed only in general terms. Some coking coal no doubt arrives from western Pennsylvania; but anthracite coal available locally may be utilized for this purpose. (Chapman, 1953, p. 18.) Products of blast furnaces may arrive from the Bethlehem mills to the south of Wilkes-Barre and from other SMA's of the northeastern United States.

Yarn, thread, and fabric mills; Miscellaneous textile mill products: A large supply of female labor, rather than any natural resources, has attracted many silk, rayon, and cotton mills to this area along with firms manufacturing miscellaneous textile mill products. (McCarty, 1940, pp. 639-640.) Specific sources of material inputs for these mills and manufacturing companies were not determined. However, many of the inputs for cotton and rayon fabrics no doubt arrive from both New England mills and from the Southern Piedmont region.

Bakery products: Specific sources for the inputs for bakeries were not determined.

Apparel and accessories: Again, female labor supply is decisive in bringing these industries to this SMA. Inputs no doubt arrive from other industries of the SMA itself as well as from more distant textile centers.

OUTPUTS AND SERVICE AREAS OF WILKES-BARRE – HAZLETON'S PROFILE INDUSTRIES

Coal mining: Production of Pennsylvania anthracite in 1950 totalled 44 million net tons, of which 16 million tons were produced in Luzerne County making it the highest anthracite coal producing county in the state. Of the Luzerne coal about 14 million tons were shipped outside the producing region, 2 million were sold to local trade and one-half million were utilized as colliery fuel. The majority of Pennsylvania coal was consumed in the Middle Atlantic States—New Jersey, New York and Pennsylvania—with the New England states coming second. (United States Bureau of Mines, 1953, pp. 346, 365, 377.) "The Middle Atlantic States . . . are the home of anthracite and here about three-fourths of it is consumed." (Murphy and Murphy, 1937, p. 358; see also map in Ullman, 1957, p. 142.) Anthracite coal is used almost entirely for domestic heating and for heating hotels, apartment houses, office buildings, and the like. (Murphy and Murphy, 1937, p. 332.)

Tobacco manufactures: Several large firms engaged in the manufacture of cigars are located in this SMA. (United States Department of Labor, 1957, p. 266.) Distribution of these products is no doubt to at least a sub-national market.

Other primary iron and steel industries: The exact nature of these products was not determined. Distribution is assumed to be chiefly to other near-by manufacturing centers.

Yarn, thread, and fabric mills: Yarns and fabrics produced in this SMA are no doubt distributed to other firms within the SMA and to firms located in near-by textile cities.

Miscellaneous textile mill products: The exact nature of these products was not determined. Distribution is probably to a regional market.

Bakery products: No doubt the market involved is not much larger than the SMA itself.

Apparel and accessories: There is considerable diversity in the products of these industries, men's, women's, and children's garments being manufactured. Specific products include shirts, girdles and brassieres, and children's and infants' dresses. (United States Department of Labor, 1957, p. 266.) Distribution is probably to a sub-national market.

Non-local services: The proximity of Wilkes-Barre – Hazleton to New York to the northeast, Philadelphia to the southeast and Pittsburgh to the west no doubt accounts for this SMA's deficiency as a commercial, wholesale and financial center. Retail and some wholesale services are no doubt performed for the immediate hinterland.

SUMMARY: WILKES-BARRE – HAZLETON

An important segment of Wilkes-Barre – Hazleton SMA's profile industries is related to the extraction of a local natural resource: anthracite coal. Some tobacco inputs are gathered from near-by areas for processing in the SMA. The textile industries appear to receive inputs from considerable distances, although there is some industry linkage, outputs from one set of industries being utilized by others in the SMA. For the most part outputs are destined for markets in Area C. This SMA's service industries are not highly developed and no doubt serve only a relatively small surrounding area.

TAMPA – ST. PETERSBURG

SMA consists of Hillsborough and Pinellas Counties, Florida

1950 population: central cities, 221,419 (Tampa, 124,981; St. Petersburg, 96,738); SMA, 409,143

Important location feature: port on Gulf of Mexico

INPUTS AND SUPPLY AREAS FOR TAMPA – ST. PETERSBURG'S PROFILE INDUSTRIES

Canning and preserving fruits, vegetables, and sea foods: The canning industries of this SMA are primarily engaged in the canning of citrus fruits. West central Florida is the most important of the fruit growing areas in Florida. According to the *1950 Census of Agriculture,* this area contained 345,000 acres of land in bearing and non-bearing fruit orchards, groves, vineyards and planted nut trees out of the 500,000 acres of such land in the state. (This area includes the Tampa-St. Petersburg SMA and nonmetropolitan state economic area five.) The most important commercial fruits include oranges, grapefruit, tangerines and mandarins, limes and lemons. Some vegetables are also grown in this same area and are packed for shipment in St. Petersburg. (See *1950 Census of Agriculture* and Thomas and Crisler, 1953, p. 47.) Commercial vegetables raised in Florida include green beans, tomatoes, watermelon, cabbage, and sweet corn. Tin cans are available locally; the two largest companies in the United States operate plants in this SMA. (Alderfer and Michl, 1957, p. 577; United States Department of Labor, 1957, p. 58.)

Tobacco manufactures: "Tampa . . . manufactures more Havana cigars . . . than any other city." (Thomas and Crisler, 1953, p. 47.) Campbell and McLendon (1939, p. 43) discuss the history of the cigar industries in Florida, where production of cigars began in Key West as early as 1831:

> Others were engaged in cigar manufacturing in the period prior to 1868, but that year, marked by rebellion in Cuba against Spanish rule, saw the Key West industry begin more than two decades of growth. Development of cigar manufacture in Key West required the presence of skilled Cuban cigarmakers. Many such persons were

among those forced to flee the Island of Cuba because of political views or activities. . . .

For twenty-five years preceding 1894, Key West held the title of "Clear Havana Cigar Center of the United States."

Alexandersson (1956, p. 79) suggests that another major reason for the movement of the cigar industry from Cuba to Florida was an American duty imposed on cigars from Havana. This made it profitable to manufacture "Havana Cigars" in Florida with imported tobacco. In the late 1880's some cigar firms were induced to move from Key West to Tampa because of its climatic and transportation advantages and because of the offer of cheap factory land. The location of these industries in Tampa is said to have been a decisive factor in this city's early growth. (Campbell and McLendon, 1939, pp. 43, 55.)

Table 88. Industrial Profile, Tampa – St. Petersburg: 1950

Category and industry	Location quotient	Per cent of employed labor force	Inputs primarily from area:	Outputs primarily to area:
(3) *First stage resource users; production for final market*				
Canning and preserving fruits, vegetables, and sea foods	5.00	1.3	A, B	C
Tobacco manufactures	24.53	4.2	A, C	C
(9) *Service industries; non-local*	1.18	15.1	*	B, C
Water transportation	2.46	(0.9)	*	B, C
Wholesale trade	1.55	(5.4)	*	B
Hotels and lodging places	2.59	(2.4)	*	C
Total in profile industries	...	20.6	...	...

* Inputs other than labor not considered.

Turning to inputs, various types of tobacco are required for the manufacture of cigars. Alderfer and Michl (1957, p. 637) indicate that the best grades of filler tobaccos are imported from Cuba and Puerto Rico, while Pennsylvania is the leading domestic producer. Wisconsin leads in the production of the type of tobacco needed for cigar binders. The Connecticut Valley is a domestic source of wrapper tobacco, while imports come from Sumatra, Java and Cuba. The Tampa cigar industry relies on several of these sources. Many types of cigars are manufactured in Tampa. The most expensive is the "clear Havana" type; here both the wrapper and the filler tobaccos are imported from Cuba. (Campbell and McLendon, 1939, p. 14.) Other machine manufacturers combine Cuban filler with domestic wrappers. The best type of domestic wrapper is grown in Connecticut and an inferior type produced in West Florida and South Georgia. The highest type of domestic binders come from Wisconsin; others utilized in Tampa arrive from Connecticut, Pennsylvania and the Middle Western states. Most of the domestic filler arrives from Pennsylvania but some is also grown in Ohio and other Mid-western states and in the West Florida-South Georgia district. (*Ibid.*, p. 16.)

Cuban tobacco is usually shipped from Havana to Port Tampa, Florida via steamship. (Campbell and McLendon, 1939, p. 15.) In 1937 over 13 million pounds of Cuban tobacco were imported by the United States, 3.9 million pounds of which entered through the port of Tampa. The tobacco received in Tampa was of the following types: 46 per cent unstemmed filler, 27 per cent stemmed filler, 22 per cent scrap filler, 3 per cent wrapper and 1 per cent full wrapper. (*Ibid.*, pp. 130-131.) In 1941 tobacco received via the port from Cuba had been reduced to 2.6 million pounds (United States Board of Engineers for Rivers and Harbors and United States Maritime Commission, 1948, No. 17, p. 138) and in 1955 to 1.6 million pounds. (United States Department of the Army, Corps of Engineers [1956], Part 2, p. 7.) The amount of tobacco grown in Florida has increased steadily since 1920; in 1950 over 22 million pounds were produced. (*1950 Census of Agriculture.*) Amounts of tobacco received in Tampa from sources other than Cuba were not determined. Cigar boxes are manufactured in the SMA. (Thomas and Crisler, 1953, p. 47.)

OUTPUTS AND SERVICE AREAS OF TAMPA – ST. PETERSBURG'S PROFILE INDUSTRIES

Canning and preserving fruits, vegetables, and sea foods: Distribution of canned fruits and juices is assumed to serve a national and to some extent international market. Jones and Darkenwald (1954, p. 249) offer some comparisons on the amount of production of citrus fruits in the various centers in the United States which have some implications for their distribution. According to these authors, in recent years Florida has been the leading producer of citrus fruits, with 58 per cent of the total production (71 per cent of the grapefruit, 58 per cent of the oranges, and a large part of the tangerines), as compared with 33 per cent for California, 5 per cent for Texas, and 3 per cent for Arizona. Bengtson and Van Royen (1950, p. 172) indicate that American oranges are sold primarily in domestic markets and in Canada. Although the larger crops of recent years have stimulated sizable shipments to Europe, particularly the United Kingdom, this export trade is meeting growing competition from Mediterranean countries and South Africa. Canning and preserving companies in this SMA vary greatly in size. In 1953, two establishments employed over 500 workers, one establishment between 250 and 499, four establishments between 100 and 249, and several fewer than 50. (*County Business Patterns, 1953.*) In recent years the canning of citrus juice has become a major industry. Alexandersson (1956, p. 90) calls attention to the rapid growth in popularity of frozen orange juice since World War II; he indicates that quick freezing is primarily a Florida specialty and that over half of the orange crop in Florida is processed into this form. Vegetables packed in this SMA likewise enjoy virtually a national distribution.

Tobacco manufactures: Distribution of cigars produced in Tampa is assumed to be to a national market. Tampa is considered one of the two dominating cigar manufacturing centers in the United States, the other being Philadelphia. The entire industry has been transformed as a result of mechanization and competition from cigarettes following World War I. (Alexandersson, 1956, p. 79.) Campbell and McLendon (1939, p. 10) describe the problems thus created for the Tampa manufacturers:

> The plants of Tampa were started and developed for the production of quality cigars. They were equipped to produce high-price cigars made with the finest Havana tobacco, and expert hand labor. . . .
>
> When the market demand for quality cigars declined, the Tampa plants were left with an antiquated system of hand manufacture. . . . They have been striving to produce these low-price cigars with their old methods, in competition with companies making them by machine. . . .

How far mechanization has proceeded in the Tampa cigar industry was not determined. However it appears that the largest American cigar companies are located outside Tampa. (Compare Alderfer and Michl, 1957, pp. 639-640 with Thomas and Crisler, 1953, p. 47.) According to the *County Business Patterns 1953,* the SMA contains 48 establishments of greatly varying sizes, engaged in the production of cigars. Three of these establishments employed over 500 persons.

Non-local services: According to McCarty (1940, p. 468), Tampa and

St. Petersburg "effectively dominate the west coast of Florida." This general statement appears to hold for some functions but not for others. It does appear to be the case for the citrus fruits and vegetables grown in west central Florida, many of which are processed and packed in the SMA. It also appears to be the case for certain items which enter into the port commerce. It is estimated that this port hinterland includes in whole or in part

> approximately 23 counties located in the central section of the State. This hinterland area which embraces a total of 19,978 square miles, or 36 per cent of the total area of the State of Florida, is one of the most productive in the State. (United States Board of Engineers for Rivers and Harbors and United States Maritime Commission, 1948, No. 17, p. 131.)

In particular the gathering and shipment of phosphate rock from Tampa's hinterland is a major industry.

> The State of Florida ranks first in the United States as a producer of phosphate rock. The principal commercial deposits of this natural resource are found within 60 miles of Tampa in an area of roughly circular outline, mainly in the southwestern part of Polk County and the eastern part of Hillsborough County but extending over into northwestern Hardee and northeastern Manatee Counties. (*Ibid.,* p. 132.)
>
> [This area] is the source of much of the world's production of phosphate pebble, immense tonnages of which leave Tampa and are shipped over all the world for use in the production of fertilizer. (*Ibid.,* p. 69.)

However for certain other functions this SMA appears to lie within the dominance of Jacksonville, "Florida's major industrial, financial, and wholesaling center." (Thomas and Crisler, 1953, p. 47.) Tampa-St. Petersburg specializes in three specific non-local services.

Water transportation: Tampa is Florida's leading seaport. (Thomas and Crisler, 1953, p. 47.) According to 1955 statistics a total of over 10.5 million tons of freight traffic was moved through Tampa Harbor. The breakdown of traffic was as follows: foreign imports, 700,000 tons, of which the major items (in terms of tonnage) were petroleum products, building cement, bananas, and nitrogenous fertilizer material; foreign exports, 2,200,000 tons, made up of largely phosphate fertilizer material but also including iron and steel scrap and canned fruit juices; coastwise receipts, 4,600,000 tons, largely consisting of petroleum products but also including sulphur, industrial chemicals and finished steel mill products; coastwise exports, 1,500,000 tons, again largely made up of phosphate fertilizer material and including residual fuel oil and canned fruits and vegetables; internal receipts, only 100,000 tons, largely sulphur, fertilizer, and petroleum products; and internal shipments, 400,000 tons, consisting of fuel oil, fertilizer material, and sea shells. The commerce of the port of Tampa has been steadily rising since the war; in 1946 only 3,700,000 tons of commerce were moved through the port. St. Petersburg also is a port but at present only a small amount of traffic is moved through this harbor. In 1955, 200,000 tons were involved, almost the entire quantity consisting of petroleum products received via internal traffic. (United States Department of the Army, Corps of Engineers [1956], Part 2, pp. 6-8.)

Wholesale trade: This is one of six SMA's in the size group 300,000 to 500,000 which was above the national average for all SMA's in per capita wholesale sales of assemblers of farm products, according to calculations based on data in the *1948 Census of Business*. The importance of Tampa as a fruit and vegetable packing center has already been considered above and it was pointed out that these products are gathered from a rich productive hinterland. McCarty (1940, p. 408) suggests that the SMA's trade territory includes a large portion of the west coast of Florida and ranks second only to Jacksonville among Florida's wholesale centers.

Hotels and lodging places: This specialization is due to Tampa's and St. Petersburg's function as a major United States tourist center. St. Petersburg, according to Thomas and Crisler (1953, p. 47), is the

> major resort center on Florida's west coast with its economy based almost entirely on tourism. Shuffleboard, horseshoes, swimming, fishing, yachting, and greyhound racing are among the leading sports. . . . The Sunken Gardens and Florida Wild Animal Ranch are two of the local tourist attractions.

Tampa is a leading winter resort center and serves as the spring training ground for several major league baseball teams.

SUMMARY: TAMPA – ST. PETERSBURG

Tampa and St. Petersburg gather fruits and vegetables from their productive hinterland and phosphate from nearby mines and ship these products (after processing the fruits and vegetables) to a national market. Tobacco inputs appear to arrive chiefly from Area C. Tampa appears to perform some central-place functions for its hinterland, as reflected by some aspects of its port activity and its wholesale trade specialization. Other aspects of its port activity and this SMA's specialization as a major tourist center involve services performed for the nation.

KNOXVILLE

SMA consists of Anderson, Blount, and Knox Counties, Tennessee
1950 population: central city, 124,769; SMA, 337,105
Location feature: port on the Tennessee River

INPUTS AND SUPPLY AREAS FOR KNOXVILLE'S PROFILE INDUSTRIES

Cement, and concrete, gypsum, and plaster products: Important inputs for Knoxville's cement industry are limestone (75 per cent), clay or shale (20 per cent) and small quantities of gypsum. One of the state's six large cement plants is located in Knoxville. The chief locational influences on these Tennessee mills, aside from accessibility to population centers, included proximity to abundant coal deposits of the Cumberland Plateau and to limestone, clay, and shale. In addition to the cement industry, three limekilns are located within the SMA in Knox county. Limestone inputs for these industries are likewise available from Knoxville's hinterland. (United States Bureau of Mines, Regional Mineral Industry Divisions, 1955, pp. 845-47.)

Yarn, thread, and fabric mills: It appears that the production of cotton textiles is of chief importance in this industry group. Inputs can be discussed only in general terms. It appears that cotton inputs do not come from the immediate hinterland area to any great extent.

> The distribution of the textile industry . . . bears only a secondary relationship to the location of resources. Only a scattering of cotton textile plants is to be found in the vicinity of the centers of cotton production. Although the piedmont mills are near to an old cotton raising area, the location of the cotton textile industry primarily reflects the historical development of the industry in New England and its migration to the southern piedmont in quest of a cheap labor supply. (U. S. National Resources Committee, 1939, p. 44.)

Today southern mills get the bulk of their cotton from the western part of the cotton belt. (Jones and Darkenwald, 1954, pp. 508-509, 192-193.) However some cotton is hauled by wagon and truck from local gins to the southern mills. (*Ibid.*, p. 509.) An important feature is the availability of cheap electrical power in the SMA from the Tennessee Valley Authority.

Table 89. Industrial Profile, Knoxville: 1950

Category and industry	Location quotient	Per cent of employed labor force	Inputs primarily from area:	Outputs primarily to area:
(4) *Second stage resource users; production for non-final market*				
Cement, and concrete, gypsum and plaster products	2.26	0.4	B	A, B, C
Yarn, thread and fabric mills	1.90	2.9	B, C	A, C
Miscellaneous chemicals and allied products	6.84	6.0	B, C?	C
(5) *Second stage resource users; production for final market*				
Knitting mills	5.56	1.9	A, B, C	C
(6) (*Resources of indirect significance; production for non-final market*)				
Primary nonferrous industries	14.79	5.6	B, C	C
(9) *Service industries; non-local*	0.97	12.4	*	B, C
(10) *Service industries; may be local or non-local*				
Educational services, government	1.60	4.4	*	B, C?
Total in profile industries	...	33.6	...	...

* Inputs other than labor not considered.

Miscellaneous chemicals and allied products: Knoxville fits into a "conspicuous string of chemical plants" (Alexandersson, 1956, p. 74) which runs from northern Virginia into Tennessee. The location of the largest of the chemical plants in this SMA is due to the fact that the Knoxville SMA includes a large portion of Oak Ridge, the site of the Atomic Energy Commission installation. Other than this power, specific inputs were not determined for this plant. The other large chemical firm in this SMA may be classified as a "fine chemical" firm which, in contrast with heavy chemical firms, turns out "more intricate compounds made to grade and specification for specialized uses at a high unit price but in relatively small volume." (Alderfer and Michl, 1957, p. 243.) Principal input for this firm appears to be acrylic acid (Jones and Darkenwald, 1954, p. 500), but its source could not be determined.

Undoubtedly both firms receive power inputs (electrical) from the TVA and other inputs from many parts of the eastern United States.

Knitting mills: Important inputs here are threads and yarn. These inputs no doubt arrive both from the mills of the SMA and from mills located in the southern piedmont textile area. (See map in McCarty, 1940, p. 375.) Again, electrical power is important.

Primary nonferrous industries: Knoxville shows specialization in this industry group but not in category (6) of which this industry group is a part. Specialization in this industry group appears to be chiefly a result of the location in Alcoa, Tenn., a part of the Knoxville SMA, of two companies engaged in the production of aluminum. The major input is alumina (processed bauxite) which arrives almost entirely from a plant located in Mobile, Ala. Since large quantities of electrical power are required to transform the alumina to aluminum, Knoxville with its TVA electricity supply would appear to be advantageously situated. (Zimmermann, 1951, pp. 721-724.)

Fuels: As Knoxville carries on various manufacturing activities, a discussion of fuel sources would seem to be in order. In general fuel sources are discussed for the state of Tennessee as a whole. Coal is available from the state itself in considerable quantities. Output in 1952 totalled 5,265,000 short tons (about one per cent of the United States output) and came largely from the Cumberland Plateau Region located just to the west of Knoxville. (United States Bureau of Mines, Regional Mineral Industry Divisions, 1955, p. 852; see also map in Thomas and Crisler, 1953, p. 66 showing location of Cumberland Plateau Region relative to Knoxville.) Other important sources of coal for Tennessee in 1952 in order of importance were west Kentucky, east Kentucky, Virginia, and Alabama. (Haynes, 1955, p. 16.) The TVA has become a major consumer of coal in recent years moving from a consumption of less than one million tons in 1943 to a high of over seven million tons in 1954 (the last year for which figures were available in the source used). (*Ibid.*, p. 58.) This reflects the growing demand for TVA power consequent upon industrialization and the installation of Atomic Energy Commission facilities; hydro production could not keep up with this demand, which had to be met by steam electricity production. Only minor quantities of natural gas are available within the state itself (U. S. Bureau of Mines, Regional Mineral Industry Divisions, 1955, p. 852), and Tennessee receives its major inputs from the West South Central producing fields, particularly Texas, Louisiana, Oklahoma, and Arkansas. In 1950 over 70 billion cubic feet of gas were received in Tennessee. (Stockton, 1952, pp. 168, 170-171.) Petroleum products no doubt arrive from the same areas as natural gas as well as from refining centers of the Central and Eastern states. The location of the TVA power generating plants in the vicinity of Knoxville assures it of a large and continuing supply of electric power. (For a diagram of the TVA water control system and statistics of capacity of electrical generating plants, see Zimmermann, 1951, pp. 585-586.)

OUTPUTS AND SERVICE AREAS
OF KNOXVILLE'S PROFILE INDUSTRIES

Cement, and concrete, gypsum, and plaster products: Shipments of cement products will be discussed for Tennessee as a whole since no specific information on Knoxville's cement industries was located. Production and shipments of portland cement in Tennessee in 1952 totalled 7,439,900 and 7,428,600 barrels, respectively.

> Shipments of portland cement largely have gone to Tennessee and to States south and east, particularly Florida, Georgia, Mississippi, North Carolina, and South Carolina. Some shipments, however, have gone to Virginia, West Virginia, and Kentucky and small shipments to 1 or 2 other Northern States. (United States Bureau of Mines, Regional Mineral Industry Divisions, 1955, p. 845.)

Production of lime in Tennessee in 1951 and 1952 was confined to three companies within the Knoxville SMA.

> Both quick and hydrated limes, including chemical lime, are produced in Tennessee. Output in 1952 totaled 100,200 short tons valued at $1,005,200. . . . Of the 1952 output, 80 per cent was quicklime and 95 per cent (including both quick and hydrated material) chemical lime. (*Ibid.*, p. 847.)

Distribution of these products was not determined but it is assumed that at least some of the output is utilized by local chemical firms.

Yarn, thread and fabric mills: Products include yarns, threads and fabrics, particularly of the broad-woven kind. (United States Department of Labor, 1957, p. 282.) Some of these products no doubt are utilized by knitting mills and apparel industries within the SMA itself. Probably in addition some products are distributed to other knitting and apparel centers of the southeast United States.

Miscellaneous chemicals and allied products: Products of these firms include various "atomic energy products" and plexi-glass. (United States Department of Labor, 1957, p. 282.) Both types no doubt enjoy a national or sub-national distribution. The acrylics—a group of optically clear plastics of which plexi-glass is one example—were invented in 1931 and were first used as glass adhesives and textile coatings. During World War II transparent bomber noses were the chief use; since that time they have been utilized in many ways including as material for display cases and transparent globes. (Jones and Darkenwald, 1954, p. 500.)

Knitting mills: Chief products of these mills are men's knit underwear. (United States Department of Labor, 1957, p. 282.) Several large establishments are located within the SMA (see *County Business Patterns, 1953*) and it is assumed that a sub-national market is being served.

Primary nonferrous industries: Outputs of this industry group are sheet, tubular, and foil aluminum products. (United States Department of Labor, 1957, p. 282.) As there are only a few aluminum producing plants in this country (see Zimmermann, 1951, p. 724), it is assumed that products from the Knoxville plants serve at least a sub-national market.

Non-local services: There are indications that Knoxville performs central-place functions for a small hinterland. Thomas and Crisler (1953, p. 67) assign to Knoxville the northeastern portion of Tennessee and the southeastern corner of Kentucky; they describe Knoxville as the "commercial center of the Upper Tennessee Valley," where tobacco, apples, peaches, corn, small grains, livestock, and poultry are produced. Knoxville serves as the headquarters of the Tennessee Valley Authority and the government atomic energy development is located within the SMA at Oak Ridge. (United States Department of Labor, 1957, p. 282.) Knoxville is also a port on the Tennessee River. This river is formed at Knoxville by the confluence of the Clinch, the Holston, and the French Broad Rivers. One of the purposes of the TVA was the creation of a nine foot navigation channel between Knoxville and the mouth of the Tennessee River. (Zimmermann, 1951, pp. 584, 587.) Freight traffic in 1955 consisted almost entirely of imports, a total of 968,000 tons of cargo being received in that year. Chief commodities represented in this traffic were petroleum products, wheat and inedible molasses. (United States Department of the Army, Corps of Engineers [1956], Part 2, pp. 147-148.) Knoxville is classified by Vance and Smith (1954, pp. 128, 133) as a "subdominant" on the basis of their metropolitan function scale, and their diagram suggests that Knoxville is dependent on Atlanta to the south and Cincinnati to the north for the performance of some metropolitan services.

The only non-local service industry in Knoxville which showed specialization relative to the United States by our criteria was government educational services. Knoxville is the location of the state university of Tennessee (United States Department of Labor, 1957, p. 282) and thus serves as an important educational center for the state and to a lesser degree for surrounding areas.

SUMMARY: KNOXVILLE

The Knoxville SMA receives important inputs from its immediate area and hinterland (Areas A and B) including supplies of limestone and related products, some cotton, coal, and electricity. The abundant supplies of electrical power available to the SMA through the TVA is probably the most important reason for the location in Knoxville of the aluminum and chemical industries. From Area C, Knoxville receives cotton inputs, varied inputs for the chemical industries, alumina and important fuels including coal, petroleum, and natural gas. Some services are performed for the surrounding area and educational services are performed for the state, but in regard to some important commercial services Knoxville appears to be subordinate to nearby SMA's.

PHOENIX

SMA consists of Maricopa County, Arizona
1950 population: central city, 106,818; SMA, 331,770
Important feature: capital of Arizona

OUTPUTS AND SERVICE AREAS FOR PHOENIX'S PROFILE INDUSTRIES

Non-local services: Phoenix is a relatively new city dating from 1871 and receiving its early impetus to growth in 1911 with the completion of the Salt River Irrigation Project, one of the federal government's first reclamation ventures. "Today, the city is the trading center for an extensive area of irrigated land, as well as being the political capital and economic center for the entire state." (Zierer, 1956, p. 332.) All the industries in which Phoenix shows specialization are classified as services.

Other and not specified utilities: It is assumed that specialization in this category is largely due to the importance in Phoenix of irrigation employment. The history and importance of irrigation for Arizona's Salt River Valley is described by McCarty (1940, p. 156):

Here the federal government in 1910 built the Roosevelt Dam some seventy-five miles above Phoenix on the Salt River, a tributary of the Gila. And here emerged an oasis which is now responsible for growing nearly the entire American crop of long-staple Egyptian cotton (but less than 1 per cent of the national production of cotton of all types). Winter vegetables are likewise of prime importance. The Salt River Valley regularly grows about one-seventh of the nation's commercial crop of lettuce and a similar fraction of the nation's cantaloupes. Local farms also grow much alfalfa for the pasturing of sheep and cattle. In general, however, the agriculture of the district is devoted to specialties such as winter vegetables, subtropical fruits, and long-staple cotton.

Table 90. Industrial Profile, Phoenix: 1950

Category and industry	Location quotient	Per cent of employed labor force	Inputs primarily from area:	Outputs primarily to area:
(9) *Service industries; non-local*	1.36	17.4	*	B, C
Other and not specified utilities	14.67	(0.9)	*	B
Wholesale trade	1.66	(5.8)	*	B
Hotels and lodging places	2.39	(2.2)	*	C
State public administration	2.02	(1.0)	*	B
(10) *Service industries; may be local or non-local*				
Miscellaneous entertainment and recreation services	1.79	0.7	*	C
Total in profile industries	...	18.1	...	...

* Inputs other than labor not considered.

As might be guessed, agricultural employment for Phoenix is high for an SMA; but the SMA does not show specialization in extractive industries relative to the United States as a whole. A major factor accounting for the high employment in agriculture for this SMA is the large size of Maricopa County (all of which by definition is included in the SMA) and the relatively small size of the central city, Phoenix. In 1950, 1.9 million acres of the Phoenix SMA were under irrigation as farm land; this constituted 92.3 per cent of all farmland in this area. The county to the east (Pinal) and the county to the west (Yuma) of Phoenix also have quite extensive acreage under irrigation. (United

States Bureau of the Census, *United States Census of Agriculture: 1950, Irrigation of Agricultural Lands,* 1952, pp. 1-3, 1-12; for a map showing irrigated lands of the Pacific Southwest as of 1950 and a discussion of these systems, see Zierer, 1956, pp. 135-145.)

Wholesale trade: Phoenix is one of six SMA's in the size class 300 to 500 thousand, showing a larger than average per capita amount of wholesale sales for assemblers of farm products, according to calculations based on data from the *1948 Census of Business.* McCarty (1940, p. 174) indicates that, "Phoenix collects, ships, and finances the growing of Salt River Valley cotton and winter vegetables." Vegetable crops grown in the Salt River Valley include the following: broccoli, cabbage, celery, carrot, cauliflower, lettuce, muskmelon, onion, sweet potato, white potato, asparagus, and watermelon. These products are distributed to national markets. Arizona field crops include barley, alfalfa, cotton (both the upland and American-Egyptian types), and hay. (Zierer, 1956, pp. 160-164, 167.) Probably only the cotton products are involved in national trade. The trade area served by Phoenix appears to include only the southern and eastern portions of the state. It appears that Los Angeles serves western Arizona.

Hotels and lodging places; Miscellaneous entertainment and recreation services: Phoenix has gained national importance as a winter resort and recreation area as well as a beneficial area for persons suffering from respiratory disorders. It is also a stop-over area for tourists on their way to California and Mexico. (See McCarty, 1940, p. 174; Thomas and Crisler, 1953, p. 116.)

State public administration: Phoenix is the capital of Arizona and many state-related offices are located in this SMA.

SUMMARY: PHOENIX

Phoenix SMA performs important central place functions for the surrounding richly productive Salt River Valley. Employment in Phoenix helps maintain and develop the irrigation systems making this oasis possible, while Phoenix's wholesalers gather these products and distribute many of them to a national market. Administrative services are performed for the state while tourist and entertainment functions are performed for the entire United States.

APPENDIX

Sources and Adjustments of Data

The following notes supplement the text and do not repeat all information given there. We do not give detailed citations to standard tables in the censuses of population, business, and manufactures, because the kinds of census data used here are readily located therein. Sources of data on the individual metropolitan areas treated in Part IV are given in text references to the Bibliography. The items covered in this Appendix are the following (chapters for which the notes are relevant are indicated in parentheses):

- Population potential (chapters 2, 5, 7, and 8)
- Distance (chapters 5, 6, 7, and 8)
- Per capita wholesale sales, business services receipts, and value added by manufacture (chapters 5 and 11)
- Bank deposits (chapters 5 and 11)
- Interdistrict Settlement Fund clearings (chapter 6)
- Sample of state economic areas (chapters 7 and 8)
- Index of local urbanization (chapters 7 and 8)
- Coal reserves and production (chapter 8)
- Soil quality (chapter 8)
- Agricultural statistics (chapter 8).

Population potential. Although we speak of the population potential of an areal unit, such as a city or a state economic area, this measure is literally defined only at a point, and varies from point to point over space. In characterizing an areal unit by a single population potential figure, therefore, we have in mind a rough average of the potential values over the area or the potential at a more or less representative point within the area. According to its strict definition, the potential of population at a point, L, is obtained by ascertaining the distance from that point of each individual in the population inhabiting the universe of territory under study, computing the reciprocal of each distance, and summing the reciprocals. In practice, one proceeds by subdividing the universe of territory into a manageable number of areal units, ascertaining the population of each unit, assuming that this population is concentrated at a single (central) point within the areal unit, and measuring distances to L from each such point. Population potential at L is then the sum of P_i/D_i, where P_i is the population of the ith areal unit and D_i is the distance of its central point from L, and the summation is over all areal units. When potential has been computed for a number of points within the territory in the fashion described for point L, it is possible to estimate the potential at other points by interpolation. In particular, a map of isopotential lines is obtained by finding the loci of points with equal potentials by such interpolation.

The map which shows isopotential lines for the United States in 1950 (figure 1) was taken from O. D. Duncan (1957a, Figure 2). This map was prepared in the following manner. An unpublished work map of the United States, showing boundaries of state economic areas, was obtained from the Bureau of the Census. The scale of this map was such that 1-3/8 inches represented approximately 150 miles. For computational purposes, the United States was divided into, or the state economic areas grouped into, 154 sub-areas; 116 of these sub-areas contained one or more metropolitan state economic areas. For the 116 sub-areas with metropolitan state economic areas, it was assumed that the entire population of the sub-area was concentrated at the center of the most populous metropolitan area. For the 38 sub-areas which included no metropolitan area, a point of concentration was selected after examining a map showing the distribution of population over the sub-area. The delineation of the 154 sub-areas and the selection of concentration points involved, of course, arbitrary decisions. The sub-area populations ranged from 9,556,000 for the area centered on New York City to 203,000 for the area centered on York County, Pa.

An acetate overlay, with a series of concentric zones each 1-3/8 inches (150 miles) in width, was prepared. The center of the set of concentric zones was placed on the point for which potential was to be calculated, and the population falling in each of the concentric zones was aggregated. In this manner, a distribution of the United States population by distance zone from the point for which potential was to be calculated was obtained. The aggregate population in each distance zone was divided by the mid-point of the distance interval; the sum of the quotients over all zones represented the population potential for the given point.

The operation described in the preceding paragraph was carried out for 241 points outside metropolitan state economic areas, including the center of each of the 100 sample nonmetropolitan state economic areas. Potential values for the 241 points ranged from 595,000 in the northern part of Schuylkill County, Pa., to 110,000 in the northern part of Curry County, Ore.

As indicated in the foregoing description, population potentials were ascertained directly for each of the 100 sample state economic areas studied in chapters 7 and 8. However, this map was not designed to give highly precise potential values in the immediate neighborhood of metropolitan centers. Consequently, as is explained in chapter 5, potentials assigned to standard metropolitan areas are merely rough approximations to the actual potentials in the vicinity of these areas, rather than values that would be obtained on a direct calculation of potentials at their centers.

Readers interested in further discussion of the rationale and significance of population potential as a measure of population distribution may consult publications by J. Q. Stewart and William Warntz, listed in the Bibliography. In this volume we have not emphasized the physical science analogues of population potential to which the inventor of the concept (Stewart) refers. Instead, we have taken a cue from the discussion by Harris (1954) of "market potential," a closely related concept, and have simply thought of population potential as a convenient indicator of generalized accessibility.

Distance. In chapter 5 we employ the variable, distance of each SMA (standard metropolitan area) to nearest larger SMA. These distances were taken from the table of inter-city railroad mileages given in *Rand McNally Standard World Atlas* (Chicago, 1957); distances not shown in this table were ascertained from the accompanying railroad map on pp. 240-241. In chapter 6 we deal with the distances separating zones in the Federal Reserve System, and in chapter 5 with distances between Federal Reserve Districts. These are railroad distances, ascertained from the indicated source, between the Bank or Branch cities of the respective zones or districts. In chapters 7 and 8, we employ the distance of each nonmetropolitan state economic area, measured from its approximate center, to the nearest metropolitan center, or SMA. This distance was taken as airline distance and approximated by measurements on a small-scale map. Distances were transformed to logarithms, since this appeared to improve the approximation of the regressions to a linear form. Such a transformation was not required in the earlier chapters, because the measure of relationship was rank correlation, which is invariant under monotonic transformation.

Per capita wholesale sales, business services receipts, and value added by manufacture. Dollar values were obtained from the *Census of Business* and *Census of Manufactures.* In the quite small number of instances where data were withheld to avoid disclosure it was possible to make reasonable estimates from information given on number of establishments or employment; in all these cases data were given for the bulk of establishments and it was necessary, in effect, to estimate for only a small proportion of the total volume of sales, receipts, or value added. Per capita figures were calculated on the basis of estimated 1948 population, as given by Cuzzort (1955, Appendix Table A-2); for the few SMA's not covered in Cuzzort's table, 1948 populations were estimated by linear interpolation between the 1940 and 1950 census figures.

Bank deposits. The available data (given in the *County and City Data Book, 1952*) include the total and time deposits of individuals, partnerships, and corporations in all banks (commercial, mutual savings, and other types combined) in continental United States as of December 30, 1950. Deposits in branches located outside of the county of the head office have been included with figures for the counties in which the branches are located, rather than with those for the county of the head office. Our figure, "demand deposits," was obtained by subtracting time deposits from total deposits and was reduced to a per capita basis by dividing by the population of the standard metropolitan area as reported in the 1950 census.

Interdistrict Settlement Fund clearings. These data, described in some detail in chapter 6, are incomplete in that no information is given for the flow between the Detroit and Chicago zones or for intradistrict flows within the Twelfth (San Francisco) District. No basis was found for making a close estimate of the flow between Detroit and Chicago. We arbitrarily set the gross flow total for the four-week period at $3.5 billion, which is approximately equal to the gross flow between the Detroit and New York zones. This figure may well be double the actual flow, or it may be an underestimate. There is no clear norm of comparison to establish its plausibility, but we may note that the flow between the New York and Los Angeles zones was $2.0 billion, as compared with about $1.2 billion between the San Francisco and Los Angeles zones (the second figure here also is an estimate).

For the intra-district flows in the Twelfth District, a somewhat more reasonable basis of estimation was available. Daane *et al.* (1955, Table E-5) give a table of intra-district clearings in the Twelfth District for the entire year 1953. The same source shows clearings of each of the five zones in the Twelfth District with each other zone in the Federal Reserve System for the year 1953. We compared these interdistrict flows for the five Twelfth District zones in 1953 with the corresponding figures from our four-week sample of 1957, and found that the relative magnitude of the 1957 sample flows varied from about 1/11 of the 1953 interdistrict flows of the Salt Lake City zone to about 1/8 of the 1953 interdistrict flows of the Los Angeles zone. For the entire district the sample 1957 gross flow with other districts was 11.31 per cent of the 1953 gross flow. Disregarding the fairly small variation among zones, we used the latter factor to make the 1953 figures comparable to our 1957 figures; e.g., Daane *et al.* indicate that the 1953 gross flow between San Francisco and Los Angeles zones was $10.9 billion, and we computed an estimated 1957 sample figure of (.1131) ($10.9) = $1.2 billion. This estimate, of course, rests on the assumption that relative sizes of intra- and interdistrict flows for the Twelfth District were about the same in 1957 as in 1953; this seems like a reasonable assumption, but it is one for which we have no direct evidence.

In working with the modified gravity model of flows, the requisite population figures were taken from the *1950 Census of Population;* they were compiled by zones using the list of counties in each zone given in the Appendix of the *Fortieth Annual Report of the Board of Governors of the Federal Reserve System, 1953,* which takes note of the boundary change for the Detroit branch territory made in 1954.

Sample of state economic areas. The universe from which the sample was drawn comprises the 351 nonmetropolitan SEA's defined in Table C of *State Economic Areas* (United States Bureau of the Census, 1951). The sampling unit was the nonmetropolitan SEA. A systematic sample of 100 units, or 2 of every 7 units in the universe, was selected from the list of 351 nonmetropolitan SEA's. The sampling frame consisted of this list, which is ordered alphabetically by states and in increasing numerical order within states. The initial sample unit included in the sample was determined at random. Thereafter, alternating intervals of 4 and 3 units were used to select the sample, which, therefore, consists of units appearing in fourth, eighth, eleventh, fifteenth, eighteenth, etc., place in the list.

Index of local urbanization. This index was computed from 1950 census data giving the size-of-place distribution of population in each state economic area by the following categories: (a) part of an urbanized area; (b) urban place of 50,000 or more; (c) urban place of 25,000 to 50,000; (d) urban place of 10,000 to 25,000; (e) urban place of 2,500 to 10,000; (f) rural nonfarm; and (g) rural farm. These seven categories were assigned arbitrary scores ranging from 1 for (g) to 7 for (a), and the weighted average score was computed with proportions in each category as weights. We are indebted to Donald J. Bogue for access to his unpublished tables giving rural-farm and rural-nonfarm population in each state economic area. The figures for the urban size groups were compiled from published census tables.

Coal reserves and production. The estimates of recoverable coal reserves for state economic areas were compiled from published estimates for states and counties. These estimates appear in a variety of sources, pertain to varying dates, are given in greater or lesser areal detail, and appear to be subject to widely differing errors of estimation. For a summary of available information at the state level, see Paul Averitt, Louise R. Berryhill, and Dorothy A. Taylor, *Coal Resources of the United States,* United States Geological Survey Circular 293 (1953). Estimates based on fairly complete and up-to-date information are available for 16 of the 35 states underlain by coal-bearing rock; these 16 states account for an estimated 65 per cent of the remaining national reserves. For the other 19 states, which contain an estimated 35 per cent of the national reserves, reliance must be placed on estimates prepared prior to 1928, supplemented in some cases by more recent surveys for parts of these states. County data, which are readily aggregated to form state economic area data, are available in various sources for the first group of states, and only minor adjustments are necessary to reconcile them with figures published by the United States Geological Survey. For the second group only partial and/or qualitative indications of intra-state distributions of reserves are available. In dealing with these it was necessary to select an arbitrary basis for allocating state reserves to state economic areas. The list of basic sources and the description of details of the estimating procedures are too lengthy to include here. It can only be said that the work was carried out in a rather meticulous fashion, but that in the nature of the case only rough approximations, at best, are possible. No doubt the statistics give an adequate general picture of the distribution of reserves over the country, insofar as this is now known. An unpublished tabular summary of the estimates and a more detailed statement of the estimating procedures are on file at the Population Research and Training Center, University of Chicago.

Statistics on net tonnage of coal produced in 1949 on a county basis were taken from United States Bureau of Mines, *Minerals Yearbook, 1950* (Washington: Government Printing Office, 1953) and aggregated to form production figures for state economic areas. In cases where county data were withheld or where counties were grouped, allocations to SEA's were made on the basis of data from the *1939 Census of Mineral Industries.* Reported production of "bituminous" coal was allocated into the two categories, "bituminous" and "sub-bituminous" on the basis of the distribution of estimated reserves by rank. Given the production figures by rank, an aggregate production estimate standardized for rank was obtained by converting tonnage produced to equivalent in British thermal units, using the following conversion factors: 26.0 million Btu's per ton of bituminous, 25.4 per ton of anthracite, 19.0 ton of subbituminous coal and 13.4 million Btu's per ton of lignite. (This is the same procedure followed in aggregating estimated reserves.) The production/reserve ratio represents the Btu equivalent of tonnage produced in 1949 per 1,000,000 Btu equivalent of 1953 remaining recoverable reserves. In the regression analysis, the calculations were carried out in terms of the logarithm of this ratio.

Soil quality. As noted in chapter 8, a rough indicator of soil quality was constructed from estimates of ground conductivity. The latter are based on a map, "Ground Conductivity in the United States and Canada," prepared by the Federal Communications Commission in 1938 and kindly supplied by that agency in correspondence. From the limited information available about the preparation of this map, it appears that reliance was placed on supposed correlations of ground conductivity with soil type based on a comparatively small number of actual measurements. The Federal Communications Commission in its more recent work on measurement of ground conductivity does not make use of such correlations. But it remains true that the 1938 map was based on systematic consideration of information about soils, and therefore may be of value as an indication of soil characteristics. The FCC map shows ground conductivity values of areas as 1, 1.5, 2, 3, 4, 5, 6, 7, 8, 10, 15, 20, or 30 E.M.U. $\times 10^{14}$. A state economic area map was superimposed on this map, and the proportion of the area of each SEA falling within each of these intervals was estimated. After expressing the units of ground conductivity in logarithms, the weighted average for each SEA was calculated, using as weights the respective proportions of land area. The result is the "ground conductivity index," or "index of soil quality" referred to in the text.

Agricultural statistics. The proportion of land in farms is obtained by dividing total land in farms reported in the *1950 Census of Agricul-*

ture by the total land area. In the agriculture census, land in farms includes land under cultivation, land used for pasture or grazing, and other land held by farm operators, unless it is specifically for nonagricultural purposes. Acreage of land in farms along with approximate acreage of total land area is published in Economic Area Table 1 of Vol. I of the census, these data being shown for each SEA (state economic area) which was recognized as an areal unit for agricultural tabulations.

The system of SEA's used for the census tabulations is not altogether comparable with the system employed in this volume. Among the 100 nonmetropolitan SEA's in our sample, 71 were identical with those used in the 1950 agriculture tabulations. In 28 cases the SEA as defined for the agriculture census included one of our sample SEA's together with one or more metropolitan SEA's; in one instance the census SEA was made up of one of our sample nonmetropolitan SEA's and another nonmetropolitan SEA not included in our sample. In these 29 cases of noncomparability, an adjustment was made by subtracting from the total for the census SEA that part contributed by counties excluded from the SEA in the system of SEA's we used. In all instances county agricultural statistics comparable as to definition with the SEA statistics could be obtained from the County Tables of Vol. I, *1950 Census of Agriculture*. The adjustments appear satisfactory despite the fact that all published SEA statistics were based on samples of farms while some of the county statistics were based on the complete count of farms.

The proportion of farmland in cropland is obtained by dividing total cropland by total land in farms. In the *1950 Census of Agriculture* cropland includes cropland harvested, cropland used only for pasture, and cropland not harvested and not pastured. The published SEA figures on acres of total cropland are found in Economic Area Table 8, Vol. I of the census. Per-acre value of farm products sold was obtained by dividing the reported value of products sold (Table 9, Vol. I) by the acreage of land in farms. In the 1950 agriculture census, value of farm products sold approximates the gross cash income of farms; because inter-farm sales are included, gross sales as reported for farms overstate the gross income to all agriculture. The mean value of land and buildings per acre for each SEA in the census tabulation system is given in Economic Area Table 5 of Vol. I. The value of farm land and buildings represents the respondent's estimate of the approximate amount for which the land and the buildings on it would sell. Each of the variables mentioned in this paragraph was adjusted to the SEA system used in this study by the method indicated above.

In this volume, rural-farm population density represents the rural-farm population as reported in the *1950 Census of Population* per 1,000 acres of land in farms as reported in the *1950 Census of Agriculture.* Unpublished tabulations of the number of rural-farm inhabitants of each SEA were available from the manuscript of the forthcoming monograph by Donald J. Bogue and Calvin L. Beale. Only minor changes were required to adjust these figures to the SEA system used in our study.

The proportion of part-time and residential farms is the number of farms so classified divided by all farms; the data are published in Economic Area Table 8, Vol. I., *1950 Census of Agriculture.* In this census, part-time farms were defined as those for which the value of sales from farm products was $250 to $1,199 and the farm operator reported either 100 or more days of off-farm work in 1949 or a family income from nonfarm sources exceeding the value of farm products sold. Residential farms included all farms, except so-called abnormal farms, with a total value of sales of farm products below $250. These data were adjusted to our SEA system, as previously described.

Bibliography

[Numbers in square brackets following each entry are the pages on which the item is cited]

Albrecht, William A. 1956. "Physical, Chemical, and Biochemical Changes in the Soil Community," in *Man's Role in Changing the Face of the Earth,* ed. by William L. Thomas, Jr. Chicago: University of Chicago Press. [187]

———. 1957. "Soil Fertility and Biotic Geography," *Geographical Review,* 47: 86-105. [187]

Alderfer, E. B., and Michl, H. E. 1950, 1957. *Economics of American Industry.* 1st and 3rd eds. New York: McGraw-Hill Book Co. [282-84, 286, 292, 294-95, 297, 305, 322-24, 337, 346, 377, 394, 404, 424-25, 434, 437, 448, 465, 482, 492, 511, 522, 535, 537-38, 540, 544]

Alexander, John W. 1954. "The Basic-Nonbasic Concept of Urban Economic Functions," *Economic Geography,* 30: 246-61. [32-33, 38, 42]

Alexandersson, Gunnar. 1956. *The Industrial Structure of American Cities.* Lincoln: University of Nebraska Press. [32, 34, 35, 75, 242, 280, 284, 286, 295-96, 298-99, 301-02, 304, 306, 308-09, 312, 314, 317, 324, 330, 332, 338, 346, 348-49, 356, 368, 372-74, 378, 388, 400-01, 404, 416, 420-21, 426, 430, 439, 446-47, 451, 453, 464, 471-73, 477, 481, 485, 488, 491-93, 495-96, 498, 500, 510-11, 518-19, 532, 538, 540, 544]

Allen, G. R. 1954. "The 'Courbe des Populations': A Further Analysis," *Bulletin of the Oxford University Institute of Statistics,* 16: 179-89. [54]

Anderson, Theodore R. 1955a. "Intermetropolitan Migration: A Comparison of the Hypotheses of Zipf and Stouffer," *American Sociological Review,* 20: 287-91. [139]

———. 1955b. "Reply to Iklé," *American Sociological Review,* 20: 714-15. [137-38]

———, and Collier, Jane. 1956. "Metropolitan Dominance and the Rural Hinterland," *Rural Sociology,* 21: 152-57. [185]

Andrews, Richard B. 1953-56. "Mechanics of the Urban Economic Base" (a series of twelve articles with various subtitles), *Land Economics,* vols. 29-32. [32, 229]

Angell, Robert C. 1947. "The Social Integration of American Cities of More than 100,000 Population," *American Sociological Review,* 12: 335-42. [46]

Ballert, Albert George. 1947. *The Primary Functions of Toledo, Ohio.* Chicago: Department of Geography, University of Chicago. [455-61]

———. 1953. "The Great Lakes Coal Trade: Present and Future," *Economic Geography,* 29: 48-59. [242]

Beckmann, Martin J. 1958. "City Hierarchies and the Distribution of City Size," *Economic Development and Cultural Change,* 6: 243-48. [54]

Bengtson, Nels A., and Van Royen, William. 1950. *Fundamentals of Economic Geography.* 3rd ed. New York: Prentice-Hall. [313, 320, 324, 429-30, 540]

Berry, Brian J. L., and Garrison, William L. 1958a. "Alternate Explanations of Urban Rank-Size Relationships," *Annals of the Association of American Geographers,* 48: 83-91. [55]

———, and Garrison, William L. 1958b. "The Functional Basis of the Central Place Hierarchy," *Economic Geography,* 34: 145-54. [50]

———, and Garrison, William L. 1958c. "A Note on Central Place Theory and the Range of a Good," *Economic Geography,* 34: 304-11. [51, 79]

Billings, Isabel K. 1946. "Pecan Industry in the United States," *Economic Geography,* 22: 220-27. [421, 526-27]

Blumenfeld, Hans. 1955. "The Economic Base of the Metropolis," *Journal of the American Institute of Planners,* 21: 114-32. [229]

Bogue, Donald J. 1949. *The Structure of the Metropolitan Community.* Ann Arbor: University of Michigan Press. [8, 12, 44, 85-86, 90, 100, 102, 123-24, 128, 159-60, 194, 249]

———. 1954. "An Outline of the Complete System of Economic Areas," *American Journal of Sociology,* 60: 136-39. [184]

———. 1955. "Nodal Versus Homogeneous Regions, and Statistical Techniques for Measuring the Influence of Each," paper presented at the meetings of the International Statistical Institute, Rio de Janeiro, June, 1955. [100, 102, 246, 249, 401, 441]

———. 1959. "Population Distribution," Chapter 17 in P. M. Hauser and O. D. Duncan, editors, *The Study of Population: An Inventory and Appraisal.* Chicago: University of Chicago Press. [49, 277]

Boulding, K. E. 1956. "Toward a General Theory of Growth," in J. J. Spengler and O. D. Duncan, editors, *Population Theory and Policy.* Glencoe, Ill.: Free Press. [30]

Bowsher, Norman N., Daane, J. Dewey, and Einzig, Robert. 1957. "The Flows of Funds between Regions of the United States," *Papers and Proceedings of the Regional Science Association,* 3: 139-59. [134-35]

Brush, J. E. 1953a. "The Hierarchy of Central Places in Southwestern Wisconsin," *Geographical Review,* 43: 380-402. [51]

Brush, J. E. 1953b. "The Urban Hierarchy in Europe," *Geographical Review,* 43: 414-16. [51]

California State Chamber of Commerce. 1954. *Economic Survey of California and Its Counties* (reprinted from *California Blue Book*). Sacramento: California State Printing Office. [521]

Campbell, A. Stuart, and McLendon, W. Porter. 1939. *The Cigar Industry of Tampa, Florida.* Gainesville: Bureau of Economic and Business Research, University of Florida. [438-39, 537-40]

Carlson, Lucile. 1950. "Duwamish River: Its Place in the Seattle Industrial Plan," *Economic Geography,* 26: 144-54. [361]

Carrothers, Gerald A. P. 1956. "An Historical Review of the Gravity and Potential Concepts of Human Interaction," *Journal of the American Institute of Planners,* 22: 94-102. [136]

Chambers, William T. 1940. "San Antonio, Texas," *Economic Geography,* 16: 291-98. [527]

Chapman, H. H. (with the collaboration of W. M. Adamson, H. D. Bonham, H. D. Pallister, and E. C. Wright). 1953. *The Iron and Steel Industries of the South.* Bureau of Business Research, School of Commerce and Business Administration, Printed Series Number 17. University, Ala.: University of Alabama Press. [294, 388, 398-401, 403, 448, 465, 475-76, 491, 500, 509, 532, 535]

City Planning Commission of Cincinnati. 1946. *Industrial Land Use: Present and Future.* Cincinnati: City Planning Commission. [329-32]

Colby, Charles C., and Foster, Alice. 1947. *Economic Geography: Industries and Resources of the Commercial World.* Boston: Ginn & Co. [322]

Cooley, Charles Horton, 1894. "The Theory of Transportation," reprinted in *Sociological Theory and Social Research.* New York: Henry Holt & Co., 1930. [23, 25]

Coons, Arthur G., and Miller, Arjay R. 1941. *An Economic and Industrial Survey of the Los Angeles and San Diego Areas.* Sacramento: California State Planning Board. [521, 523]

Cumberland, John H. 1956. "Interindustry Analysis, New Tool in Economics," *Scientific Monthly,* 83: 189-97. [201]

Cunningham, William Glenn. 1951. *The Aircraft Industry: A Study in Industrial Location.* Los Angeles: Lorrin L. Morrison. [325, 359, 372, 404, 422, 447, 449, 462-63, 522]

Cuzzort, Ray P. 1955. *Suburbanization of Service Industries within Standard Metropolitan Areas.* Oxford, Ohio: Scripps Foundation. [554]

Daane, J. Dewey, Einzig, Robert, and Bowsher, Norman N. 1955. "Task Force Report on Interregional Flows of Funds and District Member Bank Reserves," in *Record of the Federal Reserve System Conference on the Interregional Flow of Funds.* Washington: Board of Governors of the Federal Reserve System. [555]

Davis, Leslie Martz. 1946. "Economic Development of the Great Kanawha Valley," *Economic Geography,* 22: 255-67. [513-16]

Day and Zimmerman, Inc. [1945]. *Day and Zimmerman Report.* San Diego: Chamber of Commerce. [524]

Denver Planning Office. 1953. *Working Denver: An Economic Analysis by the Denver Planning Office.* Denver: Planning Commission. [375, 377-80]

Dicken, Samuel Newton. 1949. *A Regional Economic Geography.* Boston: D. C. Heath and Co. [302, 320, 382, 384, 387, 394, 424, 453, 472, 481, 483, 496]

Dickinson, Robert E. 1934. "Metropolitan Regions of the United States," *Geographical Review,* 24: 278-86. [98]

———. 1947. *City Region and Regionalism: A Geographical Contribution to Human Ecology.* London: Kegan Paul, Trench, Trubner & Co. [5, 25, 38, 42, 98, 250, 345, 449]

Duddy, Edward A., and Revzan, David A. 1931. *The Supply Area of the Chicago Livestock Market.* University of Chicago Studies in Business Administration, Vol. II, No. I. Chicago: University of Chicago Press. [302]

Duncan, Beverly. 1957. "Population Distribution and Economic Activity: The Nonmetropolitan United States in 1950," unpublished Ph.D. dissertation, Department of Sociology, University of Chicago. [viii]

Duncan, Otis Dudley. 1951. "Optimum Size of Cities," in P. K. Hatt and A. J. Reiss, Jr., editors, *Reader in Urban Sociology*. Glencoe, Ill.: Free Press. [55]

———. 1952. "Urbanization and Retail Specialization," *Social Forces,* 30: 267-71. [74, 123]

———. 1956a. "Research on Metropolitan Population: Evaluation of Data," *Journal of the American Statistical Association,* 51: 591-96. [92, 273]

———. 1956b. "Gradients of Urban Influence on the Rural Population," *Midwest Sociologist,* 18: 27-30. [185, 196]

———. 1956c. "Note on Farm Tenancy and Urbanization," *Journal of Farm Economics,* 38: 1043-47. [185, 196]

———. 1957a. "The Measurement of Population Distribution," *Population Studies,* 11: 27-45. [50, 552]

———. 1957b. "Population Distribution and Community Structure," *Cold Spring Harbor Symposia on Quantitative Biology,* 22: 357-71. [42, 55]

———. 1959a. "Human Ecology and Population Studies," in P. M. Hauser and O. D. Duncan, editors, *The Study of Population: An Inventory and Appraisal.* Chicago: University of Chicago Press. [3, 54]

———. 1959b. "Services Industries and the Urban Hierarchy," *Papers and Proceedings of the Regional Science Association,* 5: 105-20. [50, 55, 66, 74, 78]

———. Cuzzort, Ray P., and Duncan, Beverly. 1960. *Statistical Geography: Problems in Analyzing Areal Data.* Glencoe, Ill.: Free Press. [39, 103]

———, and Reiss, Albert J., Jr. 1956. *Social Characteristics of Urban and Rural Communities, 1950.* New York: John Wiley & Sons. [vii, 32, 34-35, 55, 59, 273]

———, and Schnore, Leo F. 1959. "Cultural, Behavioral, and Ecological Perspectives in the Study of Social Organization," *American Journal of Sociology,* 65: 132-46. [3]

Eckert, James B. 1956. "Business Loans of Member Banks," *Federal Reserve Bulletin,* 42: 327-40. [106-7]

Encyclopedia Americana. 1953, 1957. New York: Americana Corporation. [239, 286, 292, 295, 300, 312, 324-25, 327, 333, 339, 342-44, 347, 349-50, 366, 370-71, 388, 391, 393, 396, 413, 417, 431-32, 444, 448-49, 464, 479, 482, 495-96]

Encyclopaedia Britannica. 1955, 1957. Chicago: Encyclopaedia Britannica, Inc. [301, 317, 335, 347-49, 380, 392, 432-33, 498, 519]

Federal Reserve Bank of Boston. 1952. "The New England Chemical Industry," *Monthly Review,* Vol. 34, No. 4, pp. 1-4. [502]

———. 1953a. "Industrial Opportunities in New England: Instruments," *Monthly Review,* Vol. 35, No. 3, pp. 7-8. [282, 284, 287]

———. 1953b. "Printing and Publishing in New England: A Small Industry with Wide Influence," *Monthly Review,* Vol. 35, No. 5, pp. 1-3. [282, 286, 507]

———. 1953c. "A Survey of New England's Electronics Industry," *Monthly Review,* Vol. 35, No. 10, pp. 1-6. [285]

———. 1953d. "New England Shoe Industry Improves Position in Changing Market," *Monthly Review,* Vol. 35, No. 11, pp. 1-3. [287]

———. 1954. "Hardwood Pulp," *Monthly Review,* Vol. 36, No. 1, pp. 1-3. [503]

———. 1956a. "New England Institutional Investors Show Postwar Expansion in Assets and Employment," *Monthly Review,* Vol. 38, No. 2, pp. 1-4. [290]

———. 1956b. "Outlook Bright for Electronics Industry," *New England Business Review,* April 1956, pp. 1-4. [280-85]

Federal Reserve Bank of Chicago. 1956. "Big, Thriving Economies: Indianapolis, Milwaukee," *Annual Report 1956.* [405-6]

———. 1957. "Location of Business Borrowers," *Business Conditions,* April 1957, pp. 11-14. [129]

Federal Reserve Bank of Cleveland. 1957a. "Cross Sections of the Fourth Federal Reserve District, II: Cleveland and Eastern Lake Erie," *Monthly Business Review,* March 1957, pp. 2-24. [314, 495, 498-99]

———. 1957b. "Cross Sections of the Fourth Federal Reserve District, III: Pittsburgh, Youngstown and the Upper Ohio Valley," *Monthly Business Review,* May 1957, pp. 2-6. [292, 295, 297-98, 300-301, 477]

———. 1957c. "Cross Sections of the Fourth Federal Reserve District, IV: Central and Southwestern Ohio," *Monthly Business Review,* July 1957, pp. 3-23. [485, 487-89]

———. 1958. "Business Borrowers at Fourth District Banks," *Monthly Business Review,* July 1958, pp. 7-13. [106, 112]

Federal Reserve Bank of New York. 1952. "Department Store Sales in Buffalo, 1925-52," *Monthly Review,* 34: 135-37. [322]

———. 1953. "Department Store Sales in Rochester, 1925-52," *Monthly Review,* 35: 12-14. [479, 483-84]

———. 1957. *Commercial Loans Outstanding at Second Federal Reserve District Banks in 1955.* (Published by the Federal Reserve Bank of New York.) [107, 109-11]

Federal Reserve Bank of San Francisco. 1949. "Fruit and Vegetable Canning, Twelfth District—Review and Outlook," *Monthly Review,* pp. 68-71. [338]

———. 1951. "The Sugar Beet Industry in the Twelfth Federal Reserve District," *Monthly Review,* supplement, April 1951. [337, 339]

———. 1953. "Coffee and the Twelfth District Economy," *Monthly Review,* pp. 123-27. [337-38]

Fiduciary Publishers, Inc. 1954. *Directory of Institutional Investors of the United States and Canada.* New York: Fiduciary Publishers, Inc. [290, 351]

First Research Corporation. 1955. *Miami Economic Report.* Miami: Industrial Development and Research Division, City of Miami. [529-31]

Florence, P. Sargant. 1955. "Economic Efficiency in the Metropolis," in *The Metropolis in Modern Life,* ed. by R. M. Fisher. Garden City, N. Y.: Doubleday & Co. [86-88]

Freeman, Otis W. 1945. "Indianapolis: Hoosier Metropolis," *Journal of Geography,* 44: 91-98. [402]

———, and Martin, Howard H. (eds.). 1954. *The Pacific Northwest.* New York: John Wiley & Sons. [358-60, 362-63, 365-67]

Freutel, Guy. 1951. "The Shoe Industry and Eighth District Development," *Monthly Review* (Federal Reserve Bank of St. Louis), 33: 153-62. [306-7, 309]

Friedmann, John R. P. 1956. "Locational Aspects of Economic Development," *Land Economics,* 32: 213-27. [88, 90]

Garland, John H. (ed.). 1955. *The North American Midwest.* New York: John Wiley & Sons. [238, 241, 295, 302, 310, 312-13, 320, 324, 326-27, 329-30, 333, 348, 355, 394-97, 403-4, 407, 418-20, 456, 460, 477, 510, 515]

Glaser, Ezra. 1951. "Interindustry Economics Research," *American Statistician,* 5 (April-May 1951): 9-11. [201]

Gras, N. S. B. 1922a. *An Introduction to Economic History*. New York: Harper & Bros. [7-9, 21, 83-84, 105, 132, 159]

———. 1922b. "The Development of Metropolitan Economy in Europe and America," *American Historical Review*, 27: 695-708. [7, 83]

———. 1926. "The Rise of the Metropolitan Community," in *The Urban Community*, ed. by E. W. Burgess. Chicago: University of Chicago Press. [83]

Gray, James. 1954. *Business without Boundary: The Story of General Mills*. Minneapolis: University of Minnesota Press. [323]

Green, F. H. W. 1958. "Community of Interest Areas: Notes on the Hierarchy of Central Places and Their Hinterlands," *Economic Geography*, 34: 210-26. [51]

Green, Howard L. 1955. "Hinterland Boundaries of New York City and Boston in Southern New England," *Economic Geography*, 31: 283-300. [287, 289]

Green, L. P. 1957. "Johannesburg," in *Great Cities of the World*, 2nd edition, ed. by William A. Robson. New York: Macmillan. [91-92]

Hammer, Carl, and Iklé, Fred Charles. 1957. "Intercity Telephone and Airline Traffic Related to Distance and the 'Propensity to Interact,' " *Sociometry*, 20: 306-16. [137]

Hamming, Edward. 1952. *The Port of Milwaukee*. Research Paper No. 26. Chicago: Department of Geography, University of Chicago. [239, 246]

Harris, Chauncy D. 1954. "The Market as a Factor in the Localization of Industry in the United States," *Annals of the Association of American Geographers*, 44: 315-48. [12, 35, 41-42, 162, 166, 197, 553]

———, and Ullman, Edward L. 1945. "The Nature of Cities," *Annals of the American Academy of Political and Social Science*, 242: 7-17; reprinted in Paul K. Hatt and Albert J. Reiss, Jr., editors, *Cities and Society*. Glencoe, Ill.: Free Press, 1957. [5, 26]

Hartsough, Mildred L. 1925. *The Twin Cities as a Metropolitan Market*. Studies in the Social Sciences, No. 18. Minneapolis: University of Minnesota. [351]

Hawley, Amos H. 1941. "An Ecological Study of Urban Service Institutions," *American Sociological Review*, 6: 629-39. [123]

———. 1950. *Human Ecology: A Theory of Community Structure*. New York: Ronald Press. [3, 40, 91, 102-3, 188]

Haynes, William W. 1955. *Present and Prospective Markets for West Kentucky Coal*. Bureau of Business Research, College of Commerce, Bulletin Number 30. Lexington: University of Kentucky. [329, 395, 403, 477, 487, 545]

Heberle, Rudolf. 1954. "The Mainsprings of Southern Urbanization," in Rupert B. Vance and Nicholas J. Demerath, editors, *The Urban South*. Chapel Hill: University of North Carolina Press. [26]

Henderson, David A. 1954. " 'Corn Belt' Cattle Feeding in Eastern Colorado's Irrigated Valleys," *Economic Geography*, 30: 364-72. [375]

Henning, Albert Lee. 1953. "Metal Industries of the Milwaukee Metropolitan Area," unpublished thesis, Department of Geography, University of Chicago. [239-43]

Highsmith, Richard M. Jr. (ed.). [1953]. *Atlas of the Pacific Northwest: Resources and Development*. Corvallis: Oregon State College. [357-59, 362-63, 365, 367]

Hildebrand, G. H., and Mace, Arthur. 1950. "The Employment Multiplier in an Expanding Industrial Market: Los Angeles County, 1940-47," *Review of Economics and Statistics*, 32: 241-49. [33, 209]

Hoover, Calvin B., and Ratchford, B. U. 1951. *Economic Resources and Policies of the South*. New York: Macmillan Co. [368-69]

Hoover, Edgar M. 1937. *Location Theory and the Shoe and Leather Industries.* Harvard Economic Studies, Vol. LV. Cambridge, Mass.: Harvard University Press. [283, 482, 505]

———. 1948. *The Location of Economic Activity.* New York: McGraw-Hill. [24, 337]

———. 1955. "The Concept of a System of Cities," *Economic Development and Cultural Change,* 3: 196-98. [47, 54, 74]

Houston Chamber of Commerce. 1940. *Houston, Centennial Edition, 1840-1940.* Houston: Chamber of Commerce. [382, 384]

———, Research Committee. [1958.] *Statistical Abstract of Industry and Trade for Harris County and Other Texas Gulf Counties.* Houston: Chamber of Commerce. [383]

Hunker, Henry L. 1958. *Industrial Evolution of Columbus, Ohio.* Monograph No. 93. Columbus: Bureau of Business Research, College of Commerce and Administration, Ohio State University. [407-13]

Iklé, Fred Charles. 1954. "Sociological Relationship of Traffic to Population and Distance," *Traffic Quarterly,* 8: 123-36. [137]

———. 1955. "Comment on Theodore R. Anderson's 'Intermetropolitan Migration: A Comparison of the Hypotheses of Zipf and Stouffer,'" *American Sociological Review,* 20: 713-14. [137]

Isard, Walter. 1948. "Some Locational Factors in the Iron and Steel Industry since the Early Nineteenth Century," *Journal of Political Economy,* 56: 203-17. [294]

———. 1951. "Interregional and Regional Input-Output Analysis: A Model of a Space-Economy," *Review of Economics and Statistics,* 33: 318-28. [5, 44, 200]

———. 1956. *Location and Space-Economy.* New York: John Wiley & Sons. [30-31, 39]

———, and Capron, William M. 1949. "The Future Locational Pattern of Iron and Steel Production in the United States," *Journal of Political Economy,* 57: 118-33. [294, 297-98]

———, and Kavesh, Robert. 1954. "Economic Structural Interrelations of Metropolitan Regions," *American Journal of Sociology,* 60: 152-62. [44]

———, and Whitney, Vincent. 1949. "Metropolitan Site Selection," *Social Forces,* 27: 263-69. [123]

James, Preston E., and Jones, Clarence F., editors. 1954. *American Geography: Inventory and Prospect.* Syracuse: Syracuse University Press. [40]

Jones, Clarence Fielden, and Darkenwald, Gordon Gerald. 1954. *Economic Geography.* Revised edition. New York: Macmillan Co. [282, 286, 302, 322, 325, 404, 424-25, 429-30, 434-36, 438, 446, 467, 500, 502, 504, 539, 543-44, 547]

Jones, Victor. 1953. "Economic Classification of Cities and Metropolitan Areas," *The Municipal Year Book 1953.* Chicago: International City Managers' Association. [28, 34]

Kansas City, City Plan Commission. 1945. *Agriculture: Greater Kansas City.* Kansas City: City Plan Commission. [353-56]

Kendall, M. G. 1939. "The Geographical Distribution of Crop Productivity in England," *Journal of the Royal Statistical Society,* 102: 21-62. [185]

Lake Carriers' Association. 1950. *Annual Report of the Lake Carriers' Association 1950.* [245, 320, 460-61]

Leven, Charles L. 1956. "Measuring the Economic Base," *Papers and Proceedings of the Regional Science Association,* 2: 250-58. [32, 34, 209]

Lewis, Edwin H. 1952a. *Wholesaling in the Twin Cities.* University of Minnesota

Studies in Economics and Business, No. 15, Parts I and II. Minneapolis: University of Minnesota. [349-50]

———. 1952b. *Minnesota's Interstate Trade.* University of Minnesota Studies in Economics and Business, No. 16. Minneapolis: University of Minnesota. [344, 347-48]

Lösch, August. 1954. *The Economics of Location,* translated by William H. Woglom with the assistance of Wolfgang F. Stolper. New Haven: Yale University Press. [5, 25-27, 31, 39-40, 48-50, 54, 79, 106, 188]

Lotka, Alfred J. 1925. *Elements of Physical Biology.* Baltimore: Williams & Wilkins. [54]

Louisiana Legislative Council. 1955. *Louisiana: Its History, People, Government, and Economy.* Research Study No. 7. Baton Rouge: Louisiana Legislative Council. [387]

Madden, Carl H. 1956. "On Some Indications of Stability in the Growth of Cities in the United States," *Economic Development and Cultural Change,* 4: 236-52. [54]

Maryland Development Bureau. [1931]. *Brief Analysis of Basic Factors in the Economic Structure of Maryland.* Baltimore: Baltimore Association of Commerce. [444]

Mather, Eugene. 1950. "The Production and Marketing of Wyoming Beef Cattle," *Economic Geography,* 26: 81-93. [375, 418]

Mattila, John M., and Thompson, Wilbur R. 1955. "The Measurement of the Economic Base of the Metropolitan Area," *Land Economics,* 31: 215-28. [92, 209-10]

McCarty, Harold Hull. 1940. *The Geographic Basis of American Economic Life.* New York: Harper & Bros. [244, 283, 286-89, 300, 310, 319, 322-23, 326, 332-33, 343, 345, 348, 359-62, 368, 370, 374, 376-77, 379, 383, 388, 392-93, 396-97, 399-402, 406, 412, 416-17, 420-23, 426, 432, 434-36, 440-41, 446, 453-55, 461, 463, 465, 467, 473-74, 477-78, 484, 489, 493, 510, 516, 520-21, 526, 528, 533, 535, 540, 542, 545, 548, 550]

McKenzie, R. D. 1933. *The Metropolitan Community.* New York: McGraw-Hill. [8, 84-86, 90, 92, 95, 159, 232, 259, 367]

McKnight, Tom Lee. 1956. *Manufacturing in Dallas: A Study of Effects.* Texas Industry Series No. 5. Austin: Bureau of Business Research, University of Texas. [372-73]

McLaughlin, Glenn E. 1938. *Growth of American Manufacturing Areas: A Comparative Analysis with Special Emphasis on Trends in the Pittsburgh District.* University of Pittsburgh, Bureau of Business Research Monographs, No. 7. Pittsburgh: University of Pittsburgh. [293, 299-301]

Melamid, Alexander. 1955. "Some Applications of Thuenen's Model in Regional Analysis of Economic Growth," *Papers and Proceedings of the Regional Science Association,* 1: L1-L5. [85, 185]

Miller, E. Willard. 1943. "The Industrial Development of the Allegheny Valley of Western Pennsylvania," *Economic Geography,* 19: 388-401. [295-96, 299]

Moody's Investors Service. 1950a. *Moody's Manual of Investments, American and Foreign: Industrial Securities.* New York: Moody's Investors Service. [283-84, 286, 296, 298-99, 305, 308-09, 313-14, 316, 323, 325, 330, 335, 340, 346, 347, 447, 479, 481-85, 488, 496, 498]

———. 1950b. *Moody's Manual of Investments, American and Foreign: Railroad Securities.* New York: Moody's Investors Service. [309, 483]

———. 1950c. *Moody's Manual of Investments, American and Foreign: Banks, In-*

METROPOLIS AND REGION

Erratum

In the preface (p. xvii) and bibliography (p. 569) reference is made to *Regional Economic Growth in the United States,* by Harvey S. Perloff, Edgar S. Dunn, Jr., Eric E. Lampard, and Richard F. Muth. The title of this book was changed to REGIONS, RESOURCES, AND ECONOMIC GROWTH after *Metropolis and Region* went to press.

surance Companies, Investment Trusts, Real Estate, Finance and Credit Companies. New York: Moody's Investors Service. [291, 343, 352]

———. 1954. *Moody's Industrial Manual, American and Foreign.* New York: Moody's Investors Service. [308, 347]

Morrissett, Irving. 1958. "The Economic Structure of American Cities," *Papers and Proceedings of the Regional Science Association,* 4: 239-56. [28-29]

Murphy, Raymond E., and Murphy, Marion. 1937. *Pennsylvania: A Regional Geography.* Harrisburg: The Pennsylvania Book Service. [294-95, 298, 490-91, 493-94, 534-36]

National Planning Association, Committee of New England. 1954. *The Economic State of New England.* New Haven: Yale University Press. [282, 288-91, 500, 502-5]

National Resources Planning Board, Region One. 1942. *Forestry in New England.* Publication No. 70 (December 1942). Boston: National Resources Planning Board. [502-3]

Neff, Philip, and Williams, Robert M. 1954. *The Industrial Development of Kansas City.* Kansas City: Federal Reserve Bank of Kansas City. [354-56]

Nelson, Howard J. 1955. "A Service Classification of American Cities," *Economic Geography,* 31: 189-210. [32, 34]

Nielsen, A. M. 1950. *Economic and Industrial Geography.* New York: Pitman Publishing Corp. [238, 320, 327, 377, 444, 479, 503, 513]

Nisco Basic Survey. 1935. *Nisco Basic Survey of South Texas and Important South Texas Cities.* [383]

Ogburn, William F. 1937. *Social Characteristics of Cities.* Chicago: International City Managers' Association. [55]

Ohio Development and Publicity Commission. 1950. *Ohio: An Empire within an Empire.* Columbus: F. J. Heer Printing Co. [486-87, 495]

Oklahoma Planning and Resources Board. 1945. *Your Oklahoma.* Stillwater, Okla.: Crossman's. [429-32]

Pappenfort, Donnell M. 1959. "The Ecological Field and the Metropolitan Community: Manufacturing and Management," *American Journal of Sociology,* 64: 380-85. [11, 86, 160-61]

Park, R. E., and Newcomb, Charles. 1933. "Newspaper Circulation and Metropolitan Regions," chapter viii in McKenzie (1933). [95, 249, 362, 371, 397, 401, 426]

Perloff, Harvey S., Dunn, Edgar S., Jr., Lampard, Eric E., and Muth, Richard F. 1960. *Regional Economic Growth in the United States.* Baltimore: Johns Hopkins Press. [viii, 5, 45, 56, 177, 202]

Peterson, Elmore. 1936. *A Market Analysis of the Denver Wholesale Trade Territory.* Boulder: University of Colorado. [379]

Pfanner, John Adams, Jr. 1940. *A Statistical Study of the Drawing Power of Cities for Retail Trade* ("Studies in Business Administration," *The Journal of Business of the University of Chicago,* Vol. X, No. 3). Chicago: University of Chicago Press. [123]

Pfouts, R. W. 1957. "An Empirical Testing of the Economic Base Theory," *Journal of the American Institute of Planners,* 23: 64-69. [229]

———, and Curtis, Erle T. 1958. "Limitations of the Economic Base Analysis," *Social Forces,* 36: 303-10. [229]

Pickett, Victor G., and Vaile, Roland S. 1933. *The Decline of Northwestern Flour*

Milling. University of Minnesota Studies in Economics and Business, No. 5. Minneapolis: University of Minnesota. [350]

Reiss, Albert J., Jr. 1957. "Functional Specialization of Cities," *The Municipal Year Book 1957.* Chicago: International City Managers' Association. [28]

Reith, John W. 1949. "Coal Supply of the City of Milwaukee," *Journal of Geography,* 48: 71-77. [242]

Renner, George T., *et al.* 1951. *World Economic Geography: An Introduction to Geonomics.* New York: Thomas Y. Crowell Co. [360, 473]

Rhode Island Development Council. 1955. *Port of Providence: An Economic Survey.* Prepared for the City of Providence and the Town of East Providence. [470-72, 474]

Robertson, Ross M. 1954. "St. Louis: Central Reserve City, 1887-1922," *Monthly Review* (Federal Reserve Bank of St. Louis), 36: 85-92. [310-11]

Rodgers, Allen. 1952. "The Iron and Steel Industry of the Mahoning and Shenango Valleys," *Economic Geography,* 28: 331-41. [475-78]

Roterus, Victor. 1931. "The Distributive Aspects of the United States Tire Industry." Unpublished thesis, Department of Geography, University of Chicago. [414, 496, 499]

Schettler, Clarence. 1943. "Relation of City-Size to Economic Services," *American Sociological Review,* 8: 60-62. [55]

Schnore, Leo F. 1957. "The Growth of Metropolitan Suburbs," *American Sociological Review,* 22: 165-73. [3, 35]

———, and Varley, David W. 1955. "Some Concomitants of Metropolitan Size," *American Sociological Review,* 20: 408-14. [24, 28, 55]

Seeman, Albert L. 1935. "Seattle as a Port City," *Economic Geography,* 11: 20-32. [358, 362, 367]

Shryock, Henry S., Jr. 1957. "The Natural History of Standard Metropolitan Areas," *American Journal of Sociology,* 63: 163-170. [4, 92]

Simon, Herbert A. 1957. *Models of Man.* New York: John Wiley & Sons. [54]

Smailes, Arthur E. 1944. "The Urban Hierarchy in England and Wales," *Geography,* 29: 41-51. [52-53, 55]

Smith, J. Russell, and Phillips, M. Ogden. 1946. *Industrial and Commercial Geography.* New York: Henry Holt & Co. [346, 466]

Spelt, Jacob. 1958. "Towns and Umlands: A Review Article," *Economic Geography,* 34: 362-69. [51]

Standard Advertising Register. 1955. *The Agency List* (No. 115, May 1955). New York: National Register Publishing Co. [343]

Steelman, John R. 1950. "A Report to the President on the Maintenance of the Synthetic Rubber Industry . . . ," in *Synthetic Rubber: Recommendations of the President Transmitted to the Congress, January 1950.* Washington: United States Government Printing Office. [497]

Stewart, Charles T., Jr. 1958. "The Size and Spacing of Cities," *Geographical Review,* 48: 222-45. [50, 54]

Stewart, John Q. 1947a. "An Inverse Distance Variation for Certain Social Influences," *Science* (n.s.), 93: 89-90 [257]

———. 1947b. "Empirical Mathematical Rules Concerning the Distribution and Equilibrium of Population," *Geographical Review,* 37: 461-85; reprinted in J. J. Spengler and O. D. Duncan, editors, *Demographic Analysis.* Glencoe, Ill.: Free Press, 1956. [42, 553]

———. 1950. "Potential of Population and Its Relationship to Marketing," in *Theory in Marketing,* ed. by Reavis Cox and Wroe Alderson. Chicago: Richard D. Irwin. [106, 553]

———, and Warntz, William. 1958a. "Macrogeography and Social Science," *Geographical Review,* 48: 167-84. [139, 553]

———, and Warntz, William. 1958b. "Physics of Population Distribution," *Journal of Regional Science,* 1: 99-123. [553]

Stockton, John R. 1952. *Economics of Natural Gas in Texas.* Bureau of Business Research, College of Business Administration, Research Monograph Number 15. Austin: University of Texas. [330, 377, 386, 395, 404, 452, 477, 487, 545]

Taaffe, Edward James. 1952. *The Air Passenger Hinterland of Chicago.* Research Paper No. 24, Department of Geography, University of Chicago. [259]

Talbert, Robert H. 1956. *Cowtown—Metropolis: Case Study of a City's Growth and Structure.* Fort Worth: Leo Potishman Foundation, Texas Christian University. [421-22]

Tanner, Earl C., *et al.* 1953. *An Introduction to the Economy of Rhode Island.* Providence: Rhode Island Development Council. [469-74, 500]

Thomas, Lewis F. 1927. *The Localization of Business Activities in Metropolitan St. Louis.* Washington University Studies, Social and Philosophical Sciences (new series), No. 1. St. Louis: Washington University. [302, 306-7]

———, and Crisler, Robert M. 1953. *A Manual of the Economic Geography of the United States Based on Trade Areas and Geographic Regions.* St. Louis: Educational Publishers. [98, 100, 330-32, 335, 337, 344, 362, 365-67, 371, 379-80, 389, 392, 396, 412, 414, 416, 425, 432, 436, 441, 448, 451, 453-54, 463-64, 482-83, 488-89, 499, 503, 506-07, 512, 523-25, 529-31, 537, 539-42, 547, 550]

Thorndike, E. L. 1939. *Your City.* New York: Harcourt, Brace & Co., 1939. [46]

Tiebout, Charles M. 1956. "The Urban Economic Base Reconsidered," *Land Economics,* 32: 95-99. [229]

———. 1957a. "The Community Income Multiplier: A Case Study" (abstract), *Econometrica,* vol 25. [33]

———. 1957b. "Location Theory, Empirical Evidence, and Economic Evolution," *Papers and Proceedings of the Regional Science Association,* 3: 74-86. [31]

Tower, J. Allen. 1958. "Industrial Development in Alabama: Growth and Distribution," *Bulletin of Birmingham—Southern College,* vol. 51 (suppl. to No. 3). [400]

Ullman, Edward. 1941. "A Theory of Location for Cities," *American Journal of Sociology,* 46: 853-64; reprinted in Paul K. Hatt and Albert J. Reiss, Jr., editors, *Cities and Society.* Glencoe, Ill.: Free Press, 1957. [25, 49]

———. 1957. *American Commodity Flow.* Seattle: University of Washington Press. [359-60, 365, 385, 393, 395, 415, 429-30, 452, 477, 536]

United States Board of Engineers for Rivers and Harbors. *Lake Series.* Washington: United States Government Printing Office.

No. 1. 1952. The Ports of Buffalo, N. Y., and Erie, Pa. (1951). [320, 322-26]

No. 2. 1951. The Ports of Conneaut, Ashtabula, and Fairport, Ohio (1950). [293, 318]

No. 3. 1951. The Port of Cleveland, Ohio (1950). [313, 316, 318]

No. 5. 1952. The Port of Toledo, Ohio (1950). [460]

No. 8. 1953. The Ports of Milwaukee, Manitowoc, and Green Bay, Wis., and Escanaba, Mich. (1951). [244-45]

United States Board of Engineers for Rivers and Harbors and United States Maritime Commission. *Port Series*. Washington: United States Government Printing Office.

No. 3. 1957. The Port of Boston, Massachusetts (revised 1956). [280, 283, 287-88, 505]

No. 4. 1954. The Ports of Southern New England (1952). [474-75]

No. 6. 1955. The Port of Albany, New York (1954). [452-55]

No. 10. 1956. The Port of Baltimore, Maryland (1955). [445-50]

No. 11. 1949. The Port of Hampton Roads, Virginia (1948). [532-33]

No. 15. 1948. The Port of Jacksonville, Florida (1947). [439-41]

No. 17. 1948. The Port of Tampa, Florida (1947). [539, 541]

No. 20. 1947. The Port of New Orleans, Louisiana (1947). [388, 390-91]

No. 24. 1949. The Port of Houston, Texas (1948). [385]

No. 27. 1947. The Port of San Diego, California (1946). [523-24]

No. 30. 1952. The Ports of San Francisco and Redwood City, California (1951). [335, 339-42]

No. 31. 1953. The Ports of Oakland, Alameda, and Richmond and Ports on San Pablo Bay, Carquinez Strait, and Mare Island Strait, California (1951). [339-40, 342]

No. 34. 1954. The Port of Portland, Oregon (1952). [363, 366]

No. 36. 1953. The Port of Seattle, Washington (1952). [360-61]

United States Board of Governors of the Federal Reserve System. 1954. *The Federal Reserve System: Purposes and Functions*. Washington: The Board. [97, 134]

United States Brewers Foundation. 1958. *The Brewing Industry in the United States* (Brewers Almanac 1958). New York: United States Brewers Foundation, Inc. [327, 388]

United States Bureau of Mines. 1953. *Minerals Yearbook 1950*. Washington: Government Printing Office. [304-06, 308, 319, 323, 383-84, 398-99, 428, 430, 447, 496-97, 515, 536, 557]

United States Bureau of Mines, Regional Mineral Industry Divisions. 1955. *Minerals Yearbook*, Vol. III: *Area Reports 1952*. Washington: Government Printing Office. [294, 302, 305, 316, 322, 324, 388, 427-28, 447, 495, 497, 509-11, 543, 545-46]

United States Bureau of the Census. 1950. *United States Census of Manufactures: 1947*, Vol. III: *Statistics by States*. Washington: Government Printing Office. [131, 199, 201-02, 229, 236-37, 284, 298, 309, 317, 332, 335, 554]

———. 1951. *State Economic Areas*, by Donald J. Bogue. Washington: Government Printing Office. [555]

———. 1951. *United States Census of Business: 1948*, Vol. V: *Wholesale Trade—Area Statistics*. Washington: Government Printing Office. [366, 379, 406, 431, 505, 542, 550, 554]

———. 1951. *United States Census of Business: 1948*, Vol. VII: *Service Trade—Area Statistics*. Washington: Government Printing Office. [554]

———. 1952. *United States Census of Agriculture: 1950*, Vol. I: *Counties and State Economic Areas*. Washington: Government Printing Office. [192, 438, 537, 539, 557-59]

———. 1952. *United States Census of Agriculture: 1950*, Vol. III: *Irrigation of Agricultural Lands*. Washington: Government Printing Office. [378-79, 431, 550]

———. 1952. *United States Census of Agriculture: 1950,* Vol. V, Part 4, *Land Utilization—A Graphic Summary.* Washington: Government Printing Office. [191]

———. 1952. *United States Census of Population: 1950,* Vol. II: *Characteristics of the Population,* Parts 1-50. Washington: Government Printing Office. [53, 56, 60, 199, 201, 205, 210, 229-30, 382, 398, 509, 513, 555, 559]

———. 1953. *County and City Data Book, 1952.* Washington: Government Printing Office. [554]

———. 1956. *United States Census of Business: 1954,* Vol. VI: *Selected Service Trades—Area Statistics,* Parts 1 and 2. Washington: Government Printing Office. [77-78, 124, 131]

———. 1957. *County and City Data Book, 1956.* Washington: Government Printing Office. [16]

———. 1957. *United States Census of Manufactures: 1954,* Vol. III: *Area Statistics.* Washington: Government Printing Office. [230, 331]

———. 1957. *United States Census of Mineral Industries: 1954.* Washington: Government Printing Office. [397, 515]

———, and United States Bureau of Old-Age and Survivors Insurance. 1955. *County Business Patterns, First Quarter 1953,* Parts 1-10. Washington: Government Printing Office. [201, 362, 371, 410, 413, 432, 438, 540, 547]

———, and United States Bureau of Old-Age and Survivors Insurance. 1958. *County Business Patterns, First Quarter 1956,* Parts 1-10. Washington: Government Printing Office. [201]

United States Council of Economic Advisers, Committee on the New England Economy. 1951. *The New England Economy.* Washington: Government Printing Office. [287, 500]

United States Department of Agriculture, Production and Marketing Administration. 1951. "Livestock Market News Statistics and Related Data 1950," *Market News, Livestock Branch.* Statistical Bulletin No. 104. [238, 302, 352-53, 375-76, 402, 407, 418, 421, 429, 433, 525-26]

United States Bureau of Agricultural Economics and Bureau of the Census. 1952. *Agriculture 1950: A Graphic Summary (1950 Census of Agriculture,* Special Reports, Vol. V, Part 6). Washington: Government Printing Office. [388]

United States Department of Commerce, Civil Aeronautics Administration. 1951. "Enplaned Airline Traffic by Community: Calendar Year 1950." Washington: Government Printing Office. [326, 334, 342, 349, 355, 361, 370, 374, 378, 386, 391, 416, 423, 431, 441, 519-20, 527]

United States Department of Commerce, National Production Authority. 1952. "Materials Survey: Rubber" (compiled for the National Security Resources Board). Washington: Government Printing Office. [404, 487, 496-97]

United States Department of Labor. 1957. *Area Manpower Guidebook: 174 Metropolitan Labor Market Areas* (Bureau of Employment Security Pub. No. R-174). Washington: Government Printing Office. [16, 290-91, 309, 314, 316, 323, 341, 344, 347, 357, 360, 368-70, 373, 375, 380, 389, 396, 406, 413, 415-18, 420, 422, 425-27, 430, 432, 434-37, 439, 441, 450, 453, 458-59, 463, 467-68, 474, 478, 482-83, 485, 489, 493-94, 496, 500, 504-07, 512, 516, 525, 527-30, 533, 536-37, 546-48]

United States Department of the Army, Corps of Engineers. [1956]. *Waterborne Commerce of the United States, Calendar Year 1955.* (Published by the Corps of Engineers in 5 parts.) [300, 304-05, 308, 312, 329, 331, 333, 390, 397, 426, 440, 464, 475, 484, 519, 523-24, 530, 533, 539, 542, 547]

———. [1958]. *Waterborne Commerce of the United States, Calendar Year 1957.* (Published by the Corps of Engineers in 5 parts.) [436]

United States National Recovery Administration, Division of Research and Planning. 1935. *A Study of Natural Areas of Trade in the United States.* Washington: National Recovery Administration, February, 1935. [98, 374]

United States National Resources Board. 1934. *Report on National Planning and Public Works.* Washington: Government Printing Office. [172, 186]

United States National Resources Committee. 1935. *Regional Factors in National Planning.* Washington: Government Printing Office. [90, 103, 434-35]

———. 1939. *The Structure of the American Economy.* Part 1: *Basic Characteristics.* Washington: Government Printing Office. [543]

United States National Resources Planning Board. 1943. *Industrial Location and Natural Resources.* Washington: Government Printing Office. [166, 186, 368, 376-77, 404, 472]

United States Office of the National Recovery Administration, Division of Review. 1936. *An Explanatory Report on the Study of Natural Areas of Trade in the United States and a Guide to the Methodology Used in Its Preparation,* by Robert A. Dier ("Work Materials No. 42, Industry Studies Section"). Washington: National Recovery Administration, February, 1936. [96]

United States Senate. 1914. *Location of Reserve Districts in the United States,* Document No. 485, Senate Documents, Vol. 16, 63rd Congress, 2nd Session. Washington: Government Printing Office. [96]

University of Maryland, Bureau of Business and Economic Research. 1951. "Baltimore in Import Competition," *Studies in Business and Economics,* Vol. 5, No. 3. [444-46]

———. 1952. "Baltimore in Coastwise Trade," *Studies in Business and Economics,* Vol. 6, No. 2. [446, 448]

———. 1954. "A Regional Interindustry Study of Maryland," *Studies in Business and Economics,* Vol. 8, No. 2. [201]

Vaile, Roland S., and Nordstrom, Alvin L. 1932. *Public Merchandise Warehousing in the Twin Cities.* University of Minnesota Studies in Economics and Business, No. 3. Minneapolis: University of Minnesota. [349, 351]

Van Cleef, Eugene. 1937. *Trade Centers and Trade Routes.* New York: D. Appleton-Century Co. [44]

Vance, Rupert B. 1935. *Human Geography of the South.* Chapel Hill: University of North Carolina Press. [388-89]

———, and Smith, Sara. 1954. "Metropolitan Dominance and Integration," in *The Urban South,* ed. by Rupert B. Vance and Nicholas J. Demerath. Chapel Hill: University of North Carolina Press. [8, 88-90, 124, 128, 154, 256, 351, 370-71, 374-75, 386, 389, 400, 416, 422, 426, 527, 533, 547]

Vining, Rutledge. 1952a. "Reflections upon Reading Mr. Ezra Glaser's Description of Interindustry Economics Research," *American Statistician,* 6 (April-May 1952): 23-26. [135]

———. 1952b. "A Discussion of the Spatial Aspects of the Structure and Functioning of an Economic System," *Econometrica,* 20: 478-79. [135]

———. 1953. "Delimitation of Economic Areas: Statistical Conceptions in the Study of the Spatial Structure of an Economic System," *Journal of the American Statistical Association,* 48: 44-64. [135, 159]

———. 1955. "A Description of Certain Spatial Aspects of an Economic System," *Economic Development and Cultural Change*, 3: 147-95. [25, 48, 51, 159]

Warntz, William. 1957. "Geography of Prices and Spatial Interaction," *Papers and Proceedings of the Regional Science Association*, 3: 118-29. [137]

Whitbeck, R. H., and Finch, V. C. 1941. *Economic Geography*. New York: McGraw-Hill. [241, 329, 368, 388, 396, 416]

Winsborough, Hal H. 1959a. "Variation in Occupational and Industrial Composition by City Size," unpublished M.A. thesis, Department of Sociology, University of Chicago. [viii, 59]

———. 1959b. "Variations in Industrial Composition with City Size," *Papers and Proceedings of the Regional Science Association*, 5: 121-31. [74]

Wooldridge, S. W., and East, W. Gordon. 1951. *The Spirit and Purpose of Geography*. London: Hutchinson's University Library. [157]

Zierer, Clifford M. (ed.). 1956. *California and the Southwest*. New York: John Wiley & Sons. [335, 337, 339, 341, 498, 521-25, 548, 550]

Zimmermann, Erich W. 1951. *World Resources and Industries*. Rev. ed. New York: Harper & Bros. [292, 294, 296, 304, 314, 316, 320, 328, 372, 382, 384, 395, 399, 435, 446, 448, 452, 476-77, 481, 487, 490, 492, 496-97, 510, 514, 533, 545-47]

Index

[For author entries see Bibliography]